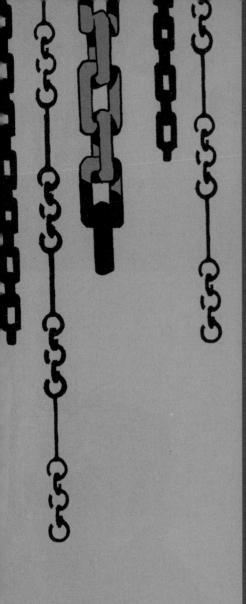

JOHN CONSTANTINE, HELLBLAZER: H I G H W A T E R

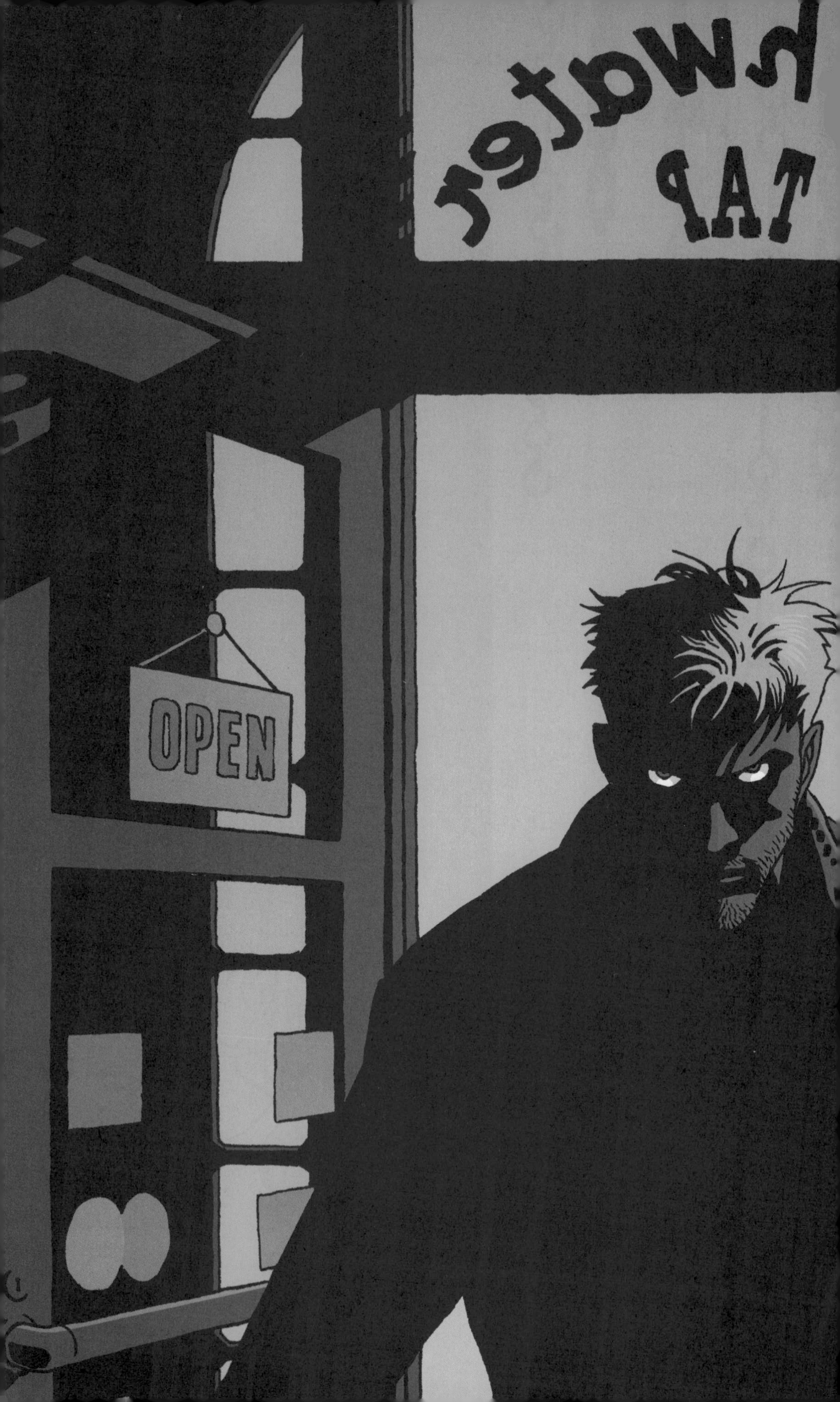
OPEN

JOHN CONSTANTINE, HELLBLAZER:
HIGHWATER

Brian Azzarello
Writer

Marcelo Frusin
Giuseppe Camuncoli
Cameron Stewart
Artists

Lee Loughridge
James Sinclair
Colorists

Clem Robins
Letterer

Tim Bradstreet
Original Series Covers

Karen Berger	VP-Executive Editor
Will Dennis, Tony Bedard	Editors-original series
Zachary Rau, Tammy Beatty	Assistant Editors-original series
Scott Nybakken	Editor-collected edition
Robbin Brosterman	Senior Art Director
Paul Levitz	President & Publisher
Georg Brewer	VP-Design & Retail Product Development
Richard Bruning	Senior VP-Creative Director
Patrick Caldon	Senior VP-Finance & Operations
Chris Caramalis	VP-Finance
Terri Cunningham	VP-Managing Editor
Stephanie Fierman	Senior VP-Sales & Marketing
Alison Gill	VP-Manufacturing
Rich Johnson	VP-Book Trade Sales
Hank Kanalz	VP-General Manager-WildStorm
Lillian Laserson	Senior VP & General Counsel
Jim Lee	Editorial Director-WildStorm
Paula Lowitt	Senior VP-Business & Legal Affairs
David McKillips	VP-Advertising & Custom Publishing
John Nee	VP-Business Development
Gregory Noveck	Senior VP-Creative Affairs
Cheryl Rubin	Senior VP-Brand Management
Bob Wayne	VP-Sales

JOHN CONSTANTINE, HELLBLAZER: HIGHWATER

Published by DC Comics. Cover and compilation copyright © 2004
DC Comics. All Rights Reserved.

Originally published in single magazine form as HELLBLAZER
164-174. Copyright © 2001, 2002 DC Comics. All Rights Reserved.
All characters, their distinctive likenesses and related elements
featured in this publication are trademarks of DC Comics. The stories,
characters and incidents featured in this publication are entirely
fictional. DC Comics does not read or accept unsolicited submissions
of ideas, stories or artwork.

DC Comics, 1700 Broadway, New York, NY 10019
A Warner Bros. Entertainment Company
Printed in Canada. Second Printing.

ISBN: 1-4012-0223-3

Cover illustration by Tim Bradstreet.

Publication design by Peter Hamboussi.

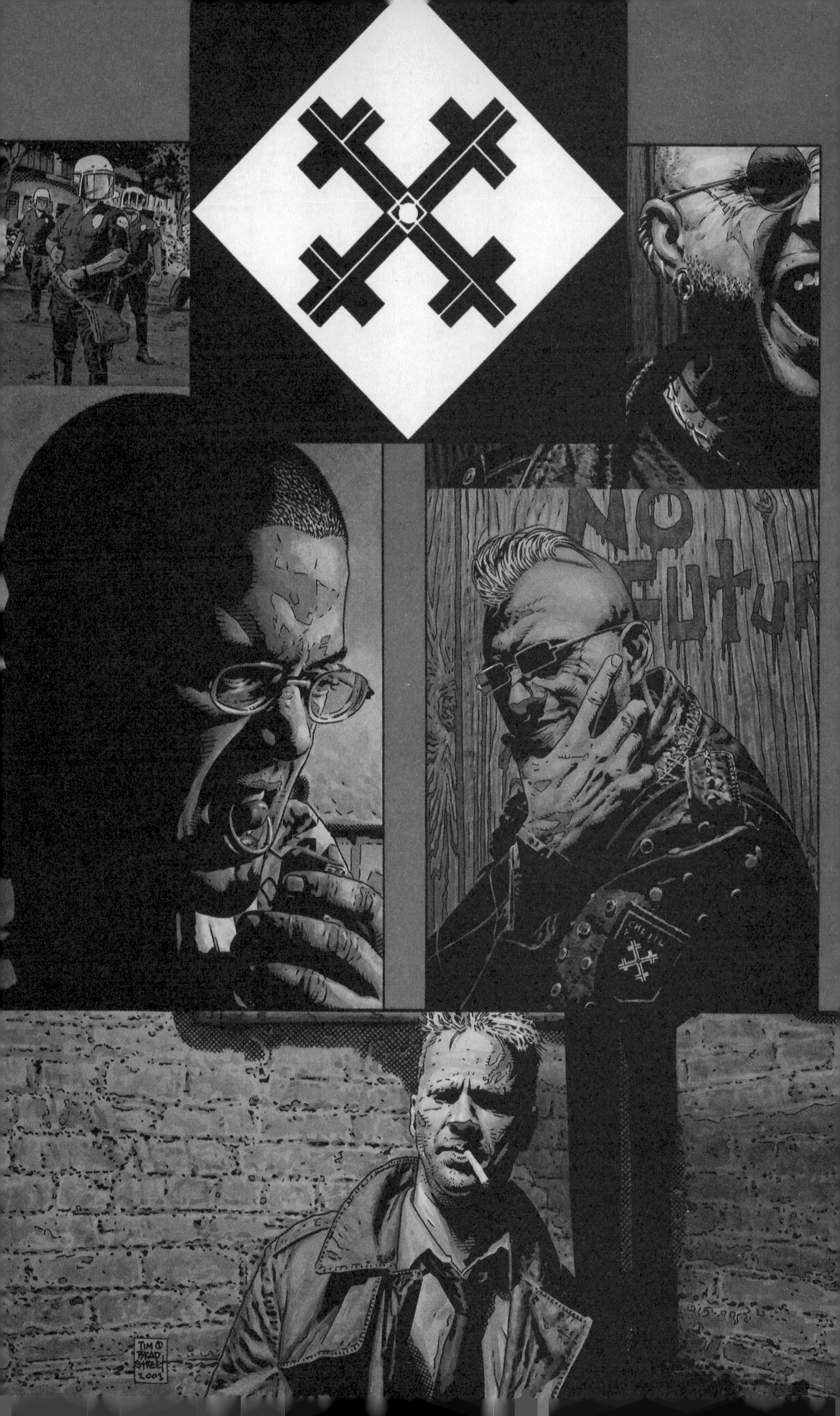
NO
FUTUR
TIM BRAD STREET 2001

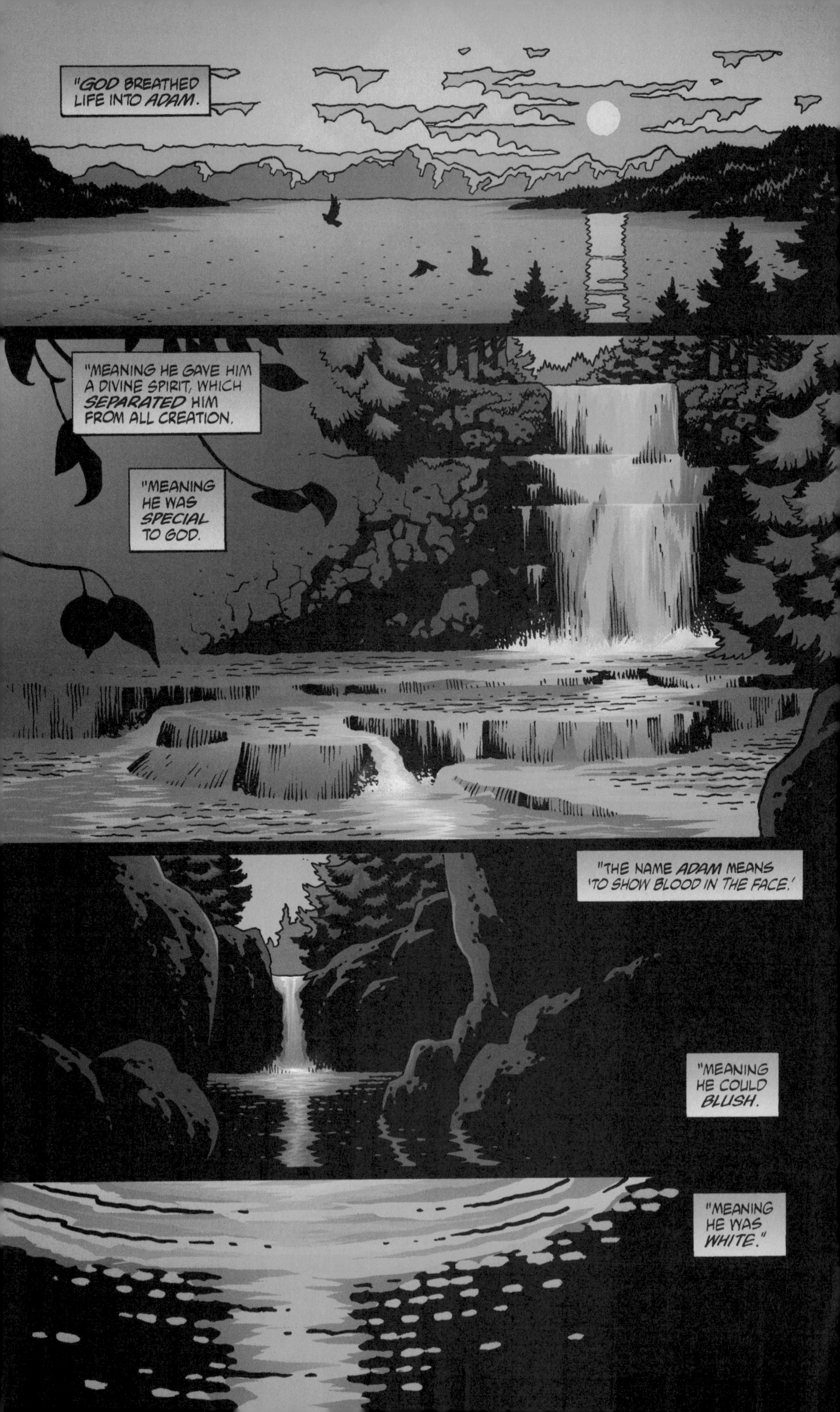

"GOD BREATHED LIFE INTO ADAM.
"MEANING HE GAVE HIM A DIVINE SPIRIT, WHICH SEPARATED HIM FROM ALL CREATION.
"MEANING HE WAS SPECIAL TO GOD.
"THE NAME ADAM MEANS 'TO SHOW BLOOD IN THE FACE.'
"MEANING HE COULD BLUSH.
"MEANING HE WAS WHITE."

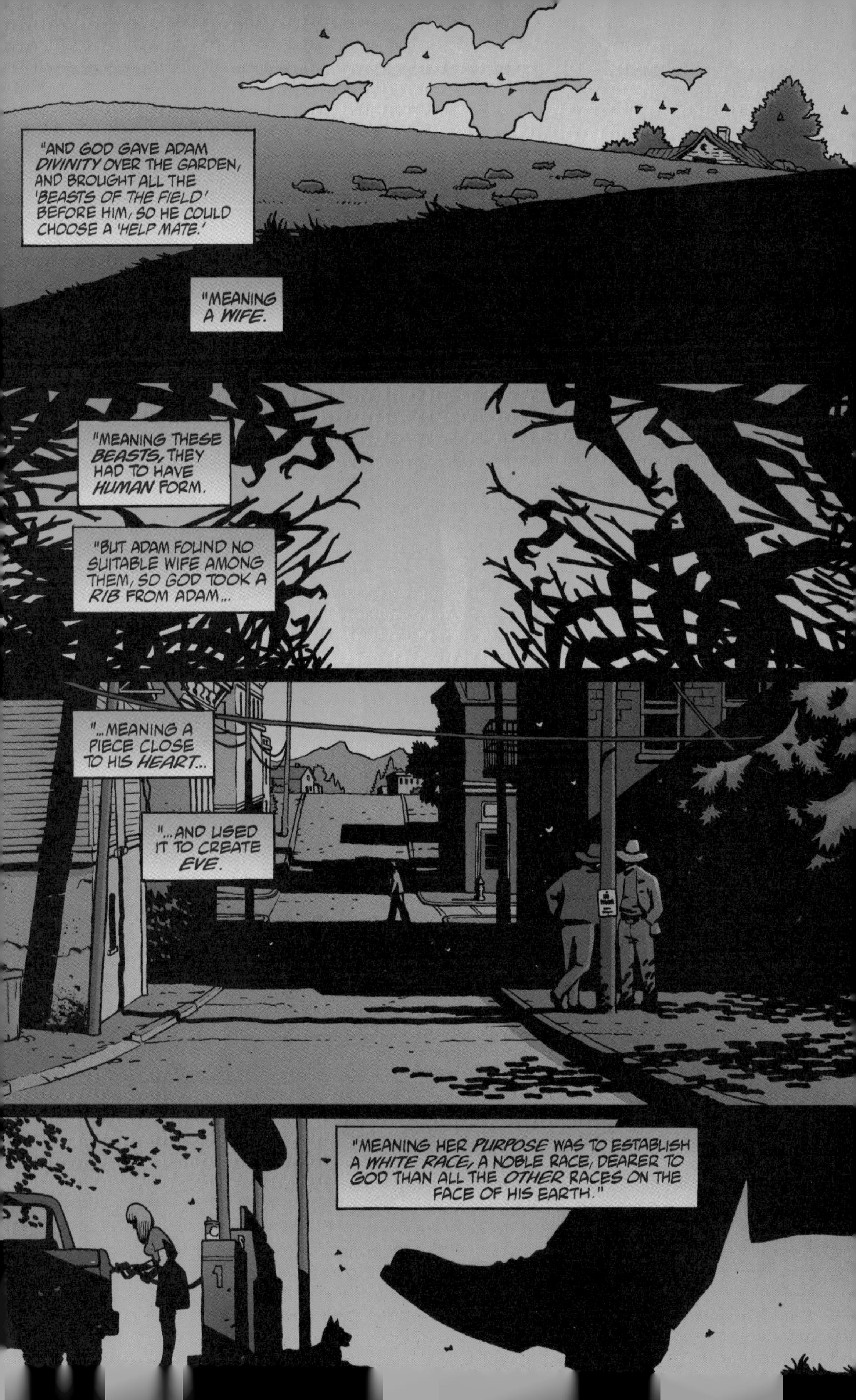
"AND GOD GAVE ADAM DIVINITY OVER THE GARDEN, AND BROUGHT ALL THE 'BEASTS OF THE FIELD' BEFORE HIM, SO HE COULD CHOOSE A 'HELP MATE.'
"MEANING A WIFE.
"MEANING THESE BEASTS, THEY HAD TO HAVE HUMAN FORM.
"BUT ADAM FOUND NO SUITABLE WIFE AMONG THEM, SO GOD TOOK A RIB FROM ADAM...
"...MEANING A PIECE CLOSE TO HIS HEART...
"...AND USED IT TO CREATE EVE.
"MEANING HER PURPOSE WAS TO ESTABLISH A WHITE RACE, A NOBLE RACE, DEARER TO GOD THAN ALL THE OTHER RACES ON THE FACE OF HIS EARTH."

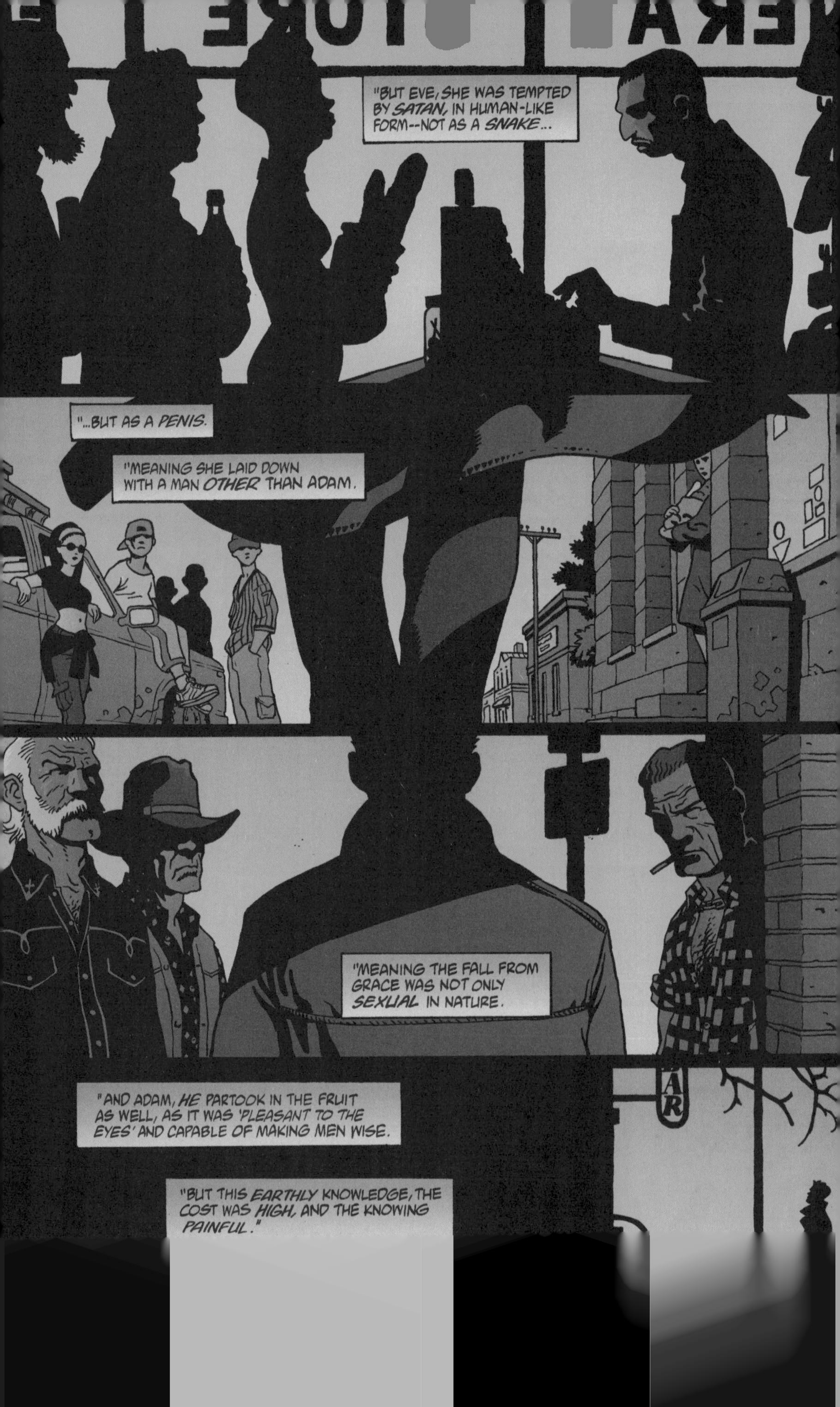
"BUT EVE, SHE WAS TEMPTED BY SATAN, IN HUMAN-LIKE FORM--NOT AS A SNAKE...
"...BUT AS A PENIS.
"MEANING SHE LAID DOWN WITH A MAN OTHER THAN ADAM.
"MEANING THE FALL FROM GRACE WAS NOT ONLY SEXUAL IN NATURE.
"AND ADAM, HE PARTOOK IN THE FRUIT AS WELL, AS IT WAS 'PLEASANT TO THE EYES' AND CAPABLE OF MAKING MEN WISE.
"BUT THIS EARTHLY KNOWLEDGE, THE COST WAS HIGH, AND THE KNOWING PAINFUL."

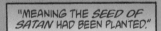

"MEANING THE *SEED OF SATAN* HAD BEEN PLANTED."

HIGHWATER
PART ONE OF FOUR

BRIAN   MARCELO   CLEM   JAMES   LEE   TIM   TAMMY   TONY
AZZARELLO FRUSIN   ROBINS   SINCLAIR   LOUGHRIDGE BRADSTREET   BEATTY   BEDARD

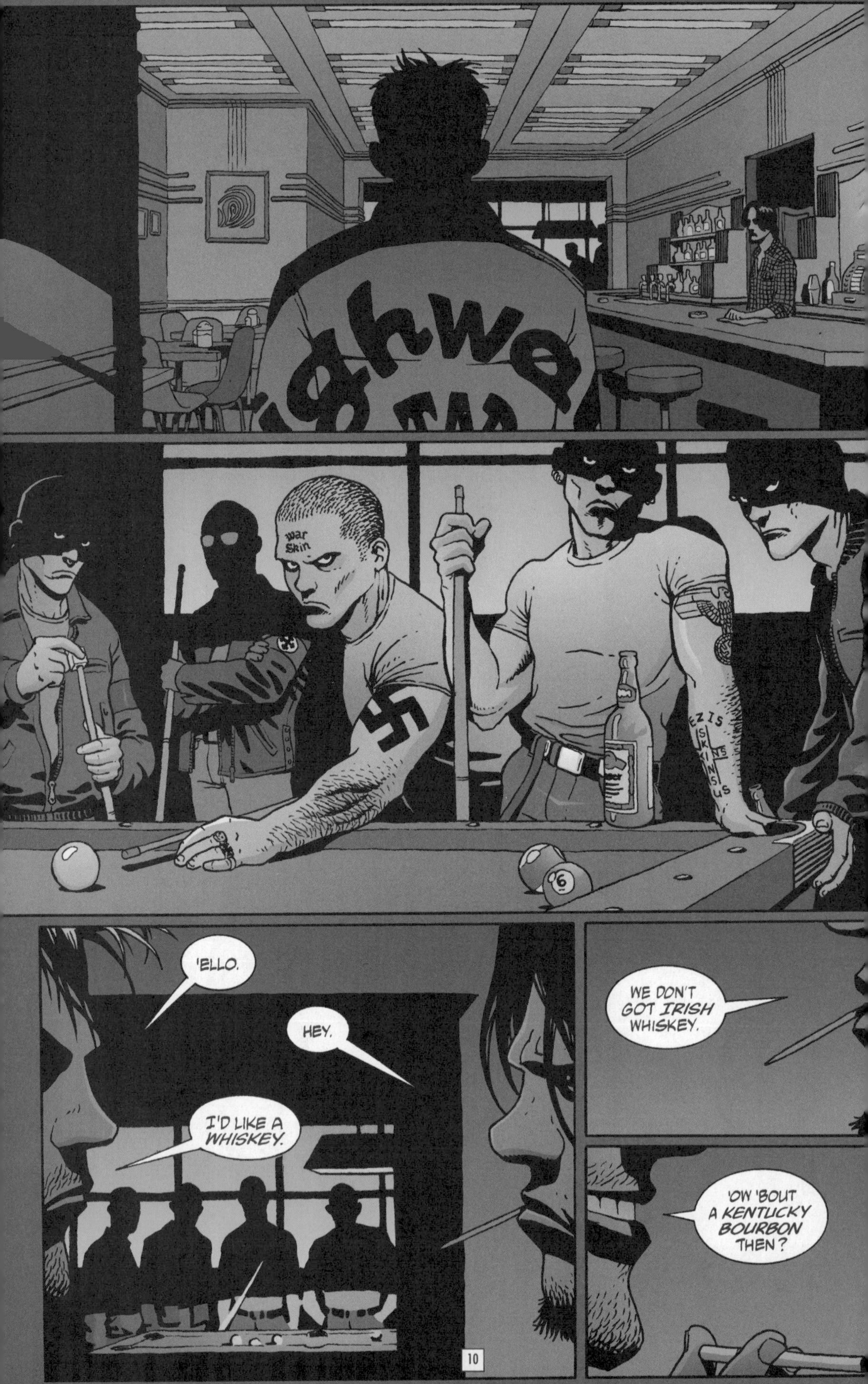
'ELLO.
HEY.
I'D LIKE A *WHISKEY*.
WE DON'T GOT *IRISH* WHISKEY.
'OW 'BOUT A *KENTUCKY BOURBON* THEN?

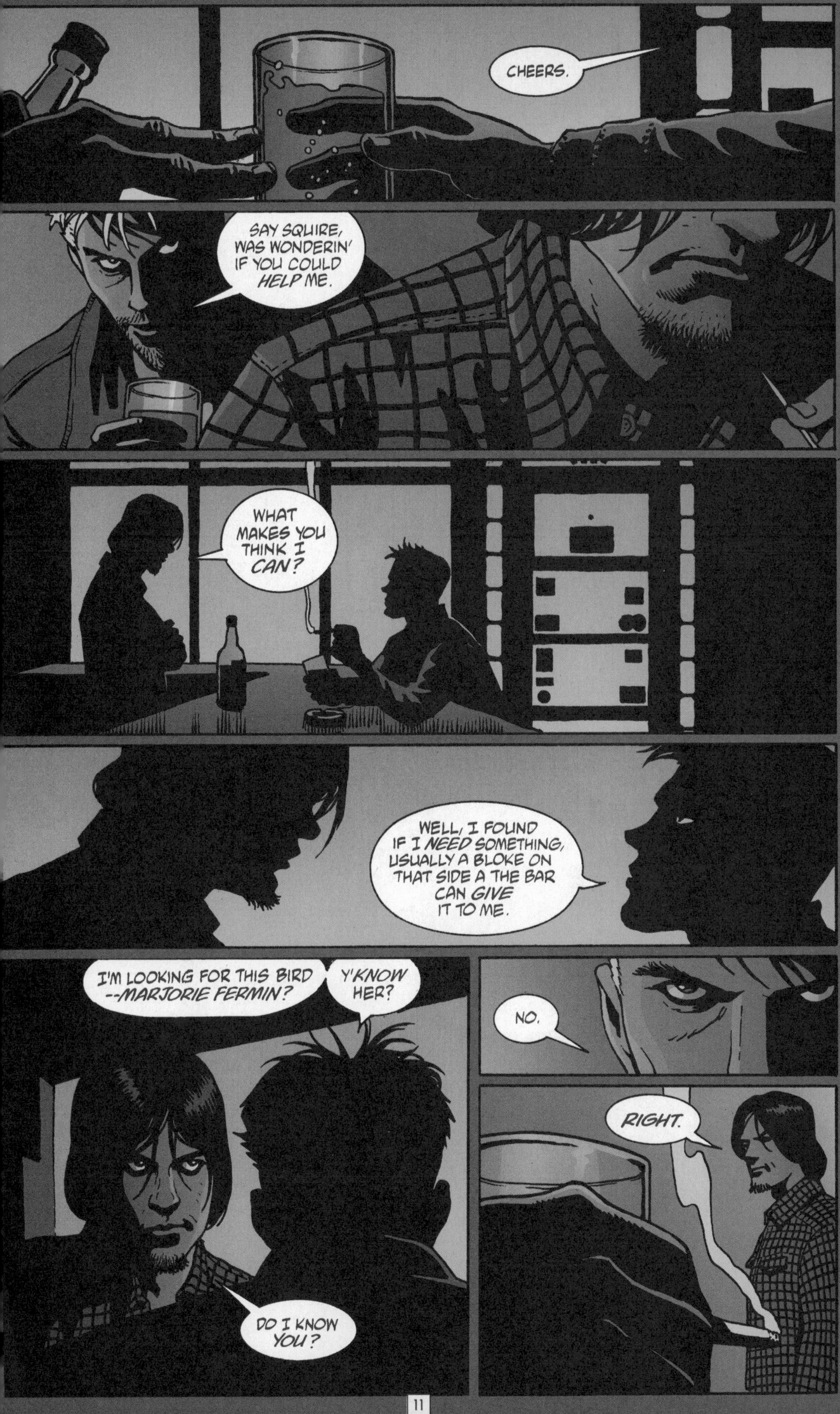
CHEERS.
SAY SQUIRE, WAS WONDERIN' IF YOU COULD *HELP* ME.
WHAT MAKES YOU THINK I *CAN*?
WELL, I FOUND IF I *NEED* SOMETHING, USUALLY A BLOKE ON THAT SIDE A THE BAR CAN *GIVE* IT TO ME.
I'M LOOKING FOR THIS BIRD --*MARJORIE FERMIN*?
Y'*KNOW* HER?
DO I KNOW *YOU*?
NO.
RIGHT.

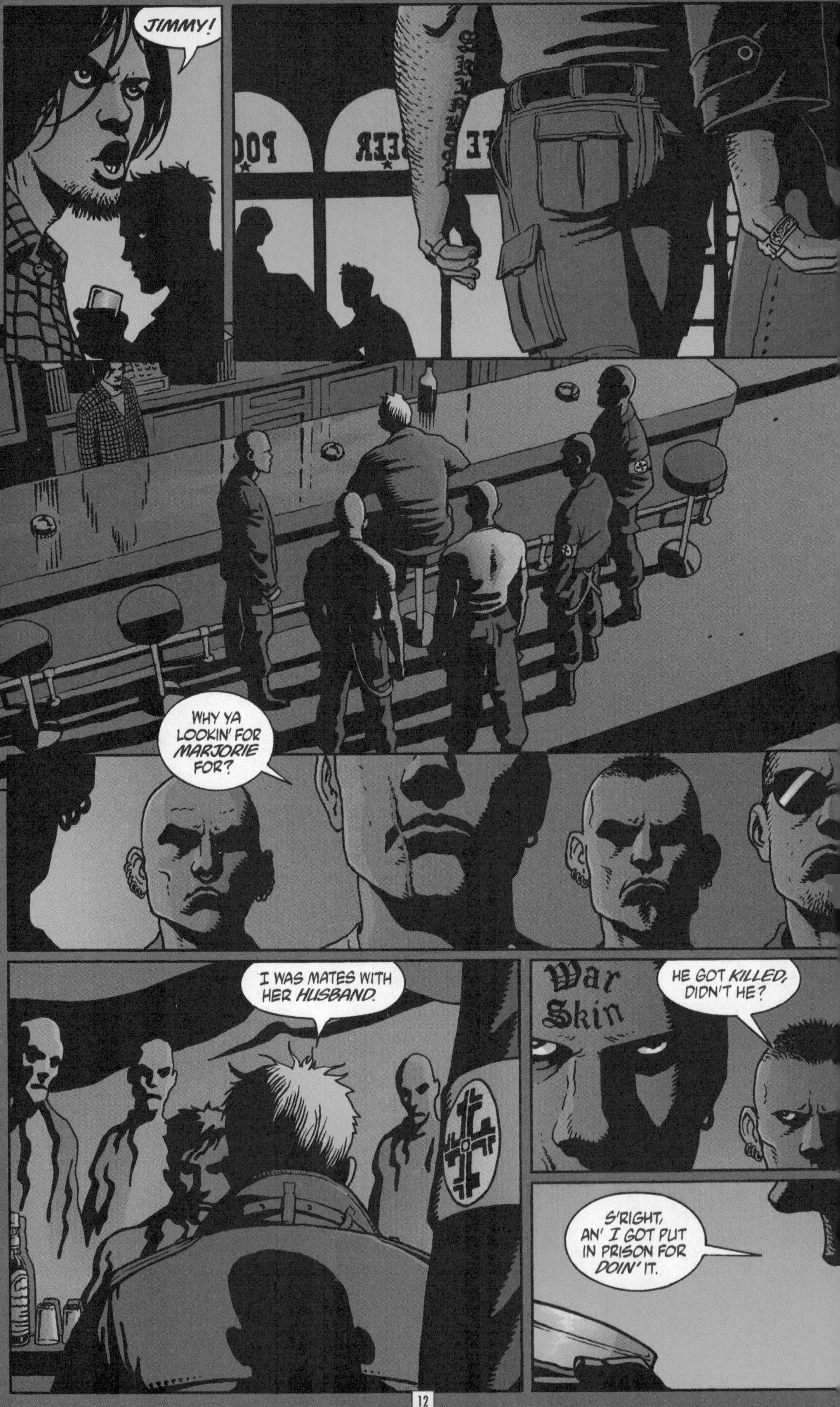
JIMMY!
WHY YA LOOKIN' FOR MARJORIE FOR?
I WAS MATES WITH HER HUSBAND.
War Skin
HE GOT KILLED, DIDN'T HE?
S'RIGHT, AN' I GOT PUT IN PRISON FOR DOIN' IT.

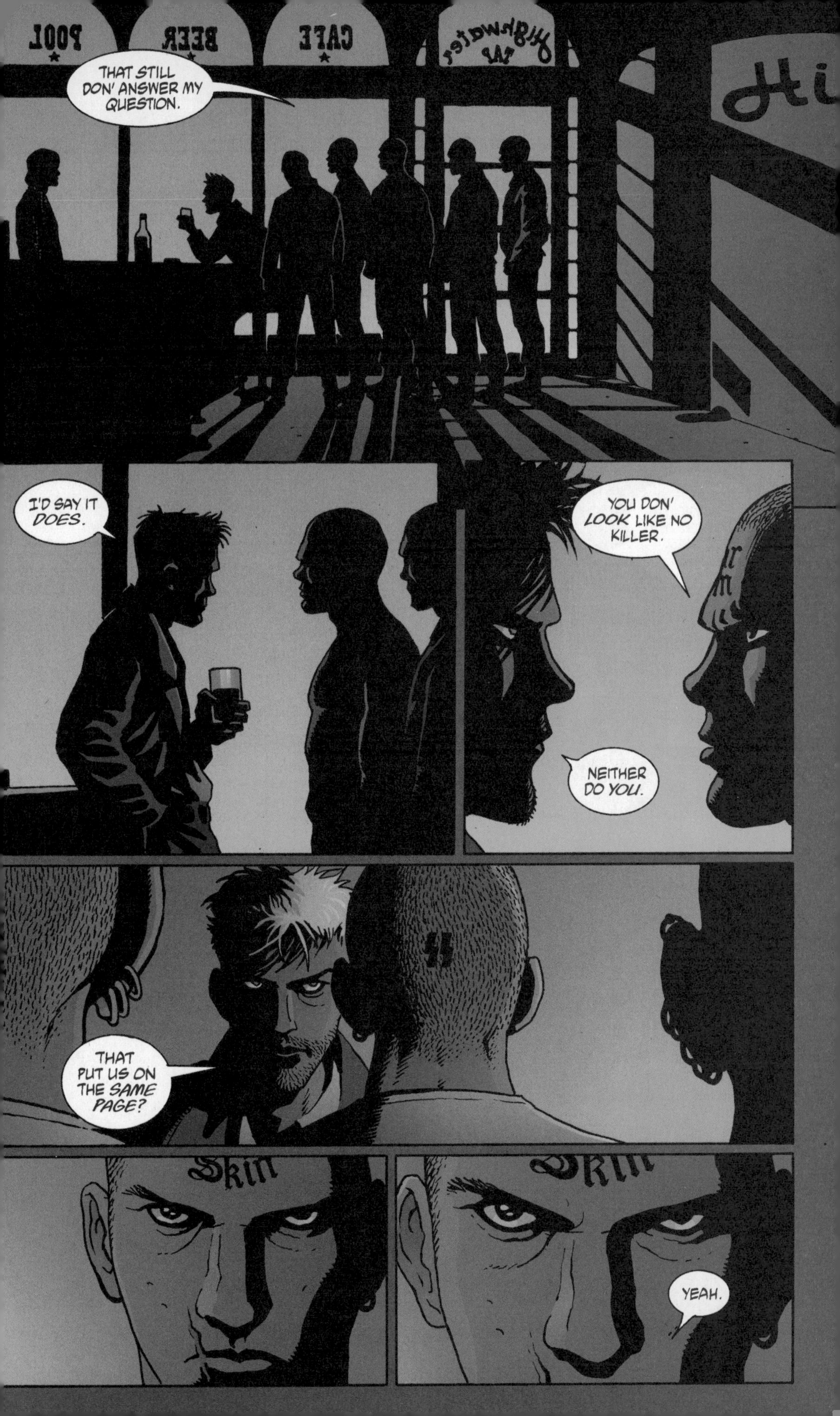
POOL
BEER
CAFE
Highwater TAP
THAT STILL DON' ANSWER MY QUESTION.
I'D SAY IT *DOES*.
YOU DON' *LOOK* LIKE NO KILLER.
NEITHER DO *YOU*.
THAT PUT US ON THE *SAME PAGE*?
Skin
Skin
YEAH.

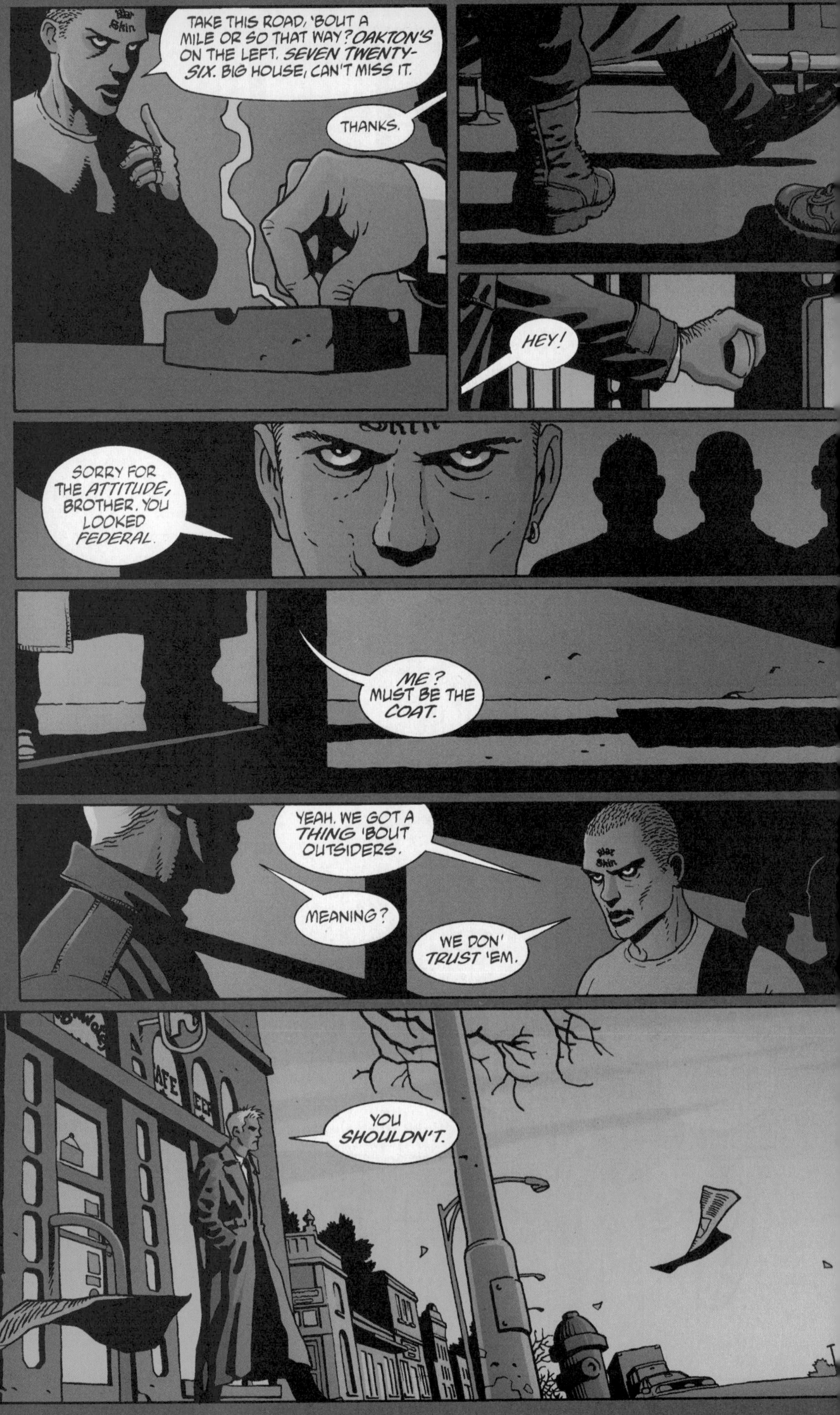
TAKE THIS ROAD, 'BOUT A MILE OR SO THAT WAY? OAKTON'S ON THE LEFT. SEVEN TWENTY-SIX. BIG HOUSE, CAN'T MISS IT.
THANKS.
HEY!
SORRY FOR THE ATTITUDE, BROTHER. YOU LOOKED FEDERAL.
ME? MUST BE THE COAT.
YEAH. WE GOT A THING 'BOUT OUTSIDERS.
MEANING?
WE DON' TRUST 'EM.
YOU SHOULDN'T.

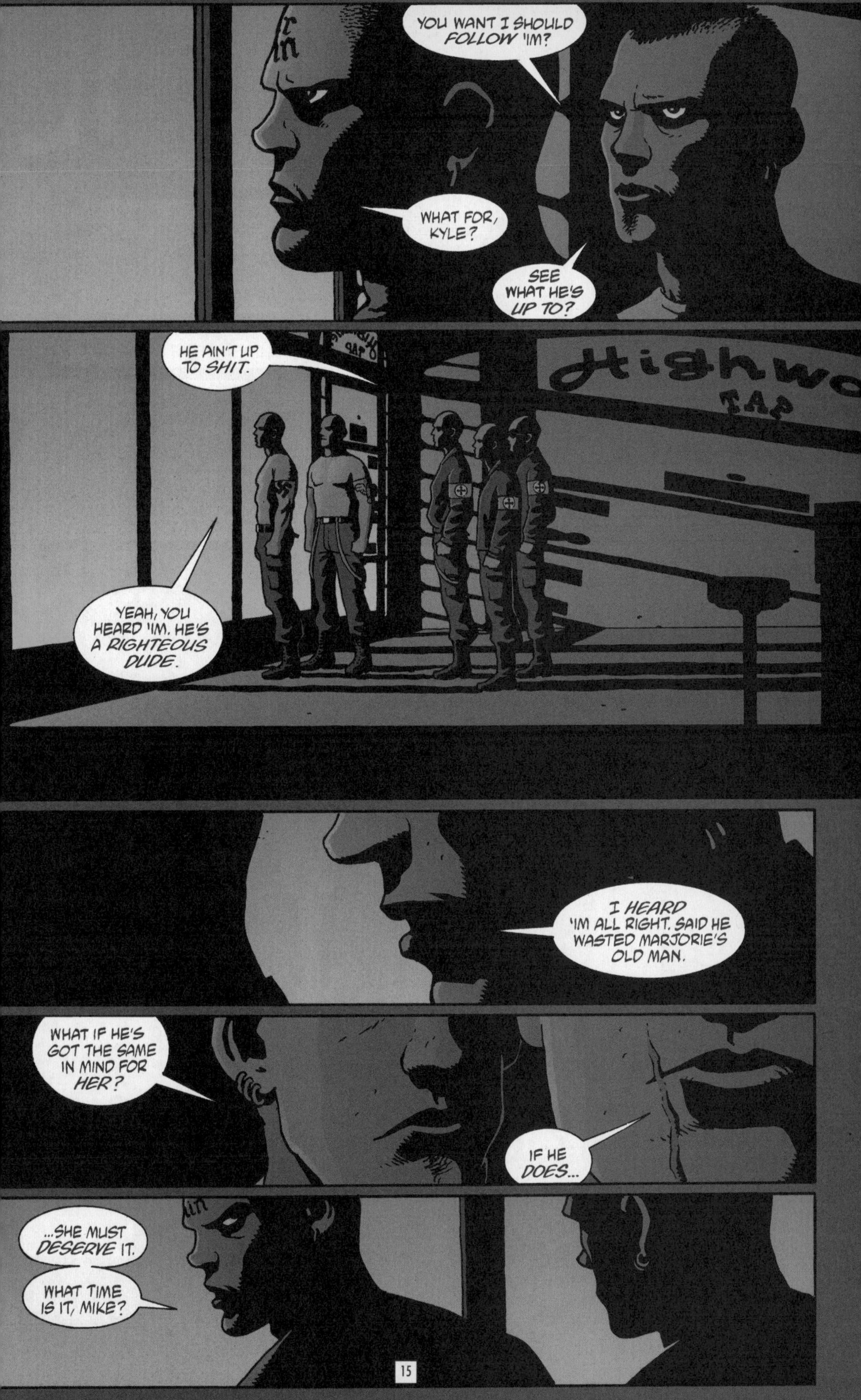
YOU WANT I SHOULD FOLLOW 'IM?
WHAT FOR, KYLE?
SEE WHAT HE'S UP TO?
HE AIN'T UP TO SHIT.
Highw
TAP
YEAH, YOU HEARD 'IM. HE'S A RIGHTEOUS DUDE.
I HEARD 'IM ALL RIGHT. SAID HE WASTED MARJORIE'S OLD MAN.
WHAT IF HE'S GOT THE SAME IN MIND FOR HER?
IF HE DOES...
...SHE MUST DESERVE IT.
WHAT TIME IS IT, MIKE?

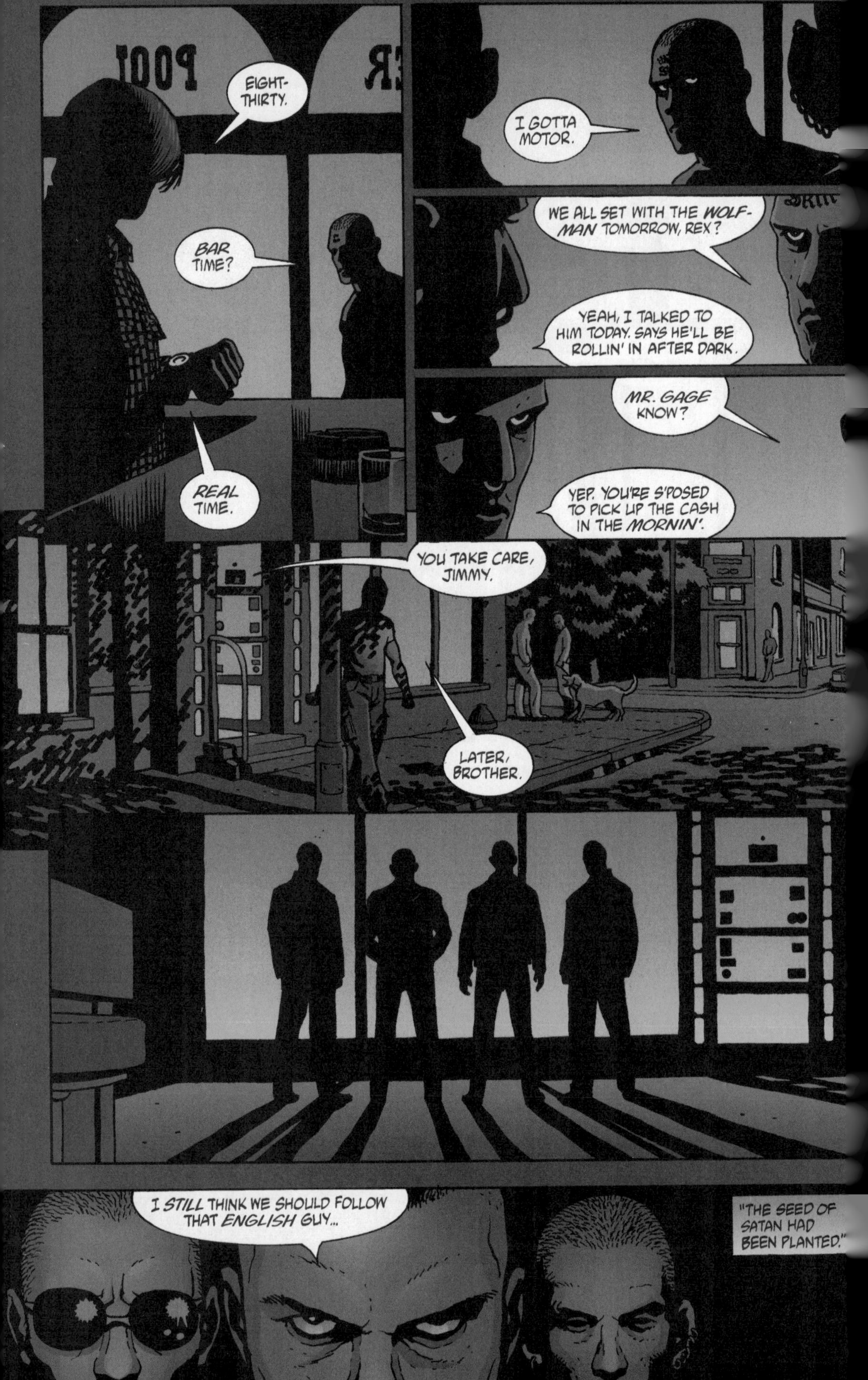
EIGHT-THIRTY.
BAR TIME?
REAL TIME.
I GOTTA MOTOR.
WE ALL SET WITH THE WOLF-MAN TOMORROW, REX?
YEAH, I TALKED TO HIM TODAY. SAYS HE'LL BE ROLLIN' IN AFTER DARK.
MR. GAGE KNOW?
YEP. YOU'RE S'POSED TO PICK UP THE CASH IN THE MORNIN'.
YOU TAKE CARE, JIMMY.
LATER, BROTHER.
I STILL THINK WE SHOULD FOLLOW THAT ENGLISH GUY...
"THE SEED OF SATAN HAD BEEN PLANTED."

"MEANING THAT IN THE ACT OF ORIGINAL SIN, THE *SATANIC RACE* WAS BORN.

"MEANING THAT EVE HAD CONCEIVED A CHILD OF *SATAN* AS WELL AS *ADAM*. CAIN AND ABEL--TWIN SONS OF DIFFERENT FATHERS.

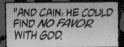

"MEANING ONLY *ABEL* CARRIED ADAM'S BLOODLINE, WHICH WAS RIGHTEOUS AND PURE.

"AND CAIN, HE COULD FIND *NO FAVOR* WITH GOD.

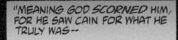

"MEANING GOD *SCORNED* HIM, FOR HE SAW CAIN FOR WHAT HE TRULY WAS--

"--A *MONGREL*."

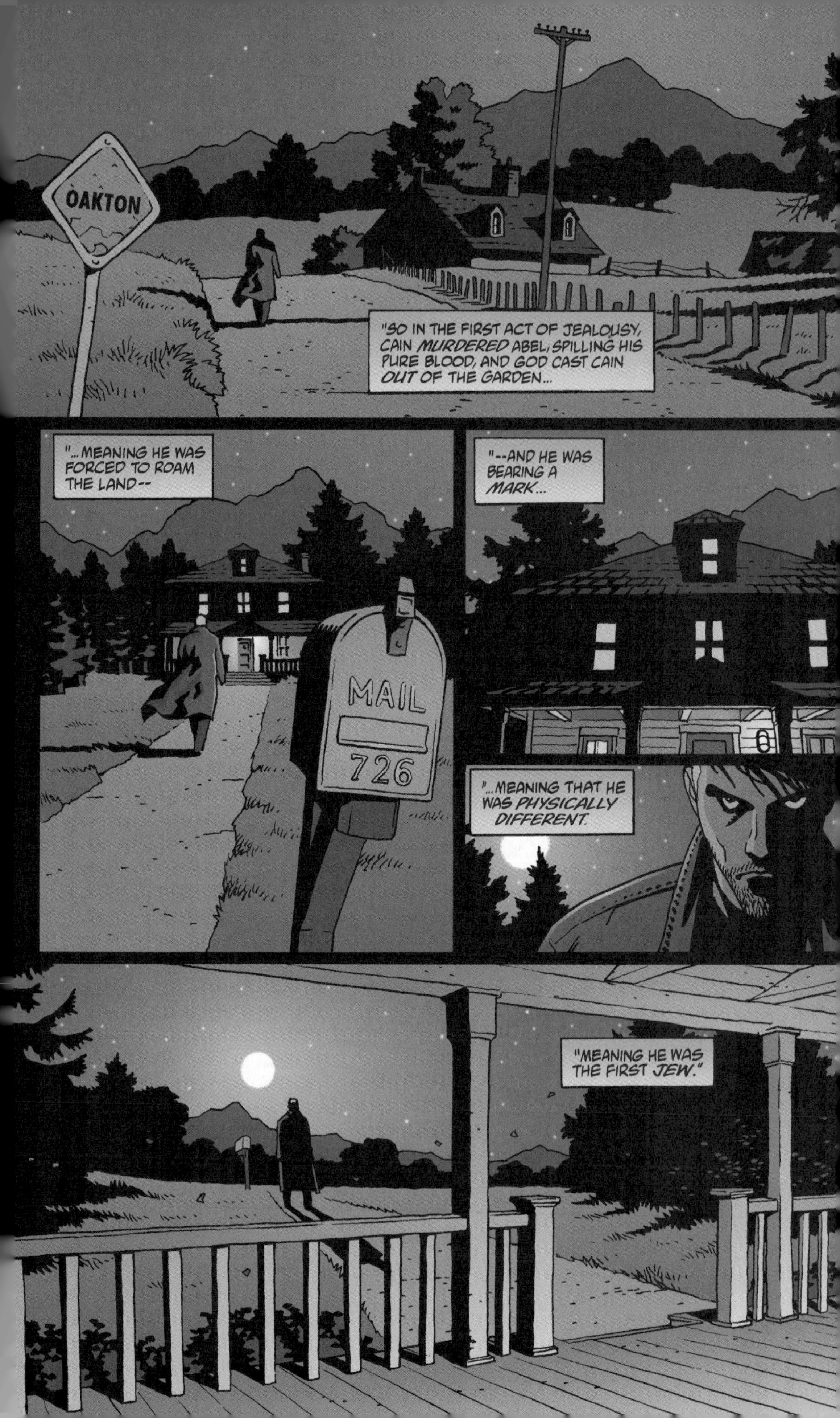
OAKTON
"SO IN THE FIRST ACT OF JEALOUSY, CAIN *MURDERED* ABEL, SPILLING HIS PURE BLOOD, AND GOD CAST CAIN *OUT* OF THE GARDEN...
"...MEANING HE WAS FORCED TO ROAM THE LAND--
MAIL
726
"--AND HE WAS BEARING A *MARK*...
"...MEANING THAT HE WAS *PHYSICALLY DIFFERENT.*
"MEANING HE WAS THE FIRST *JEW.*"

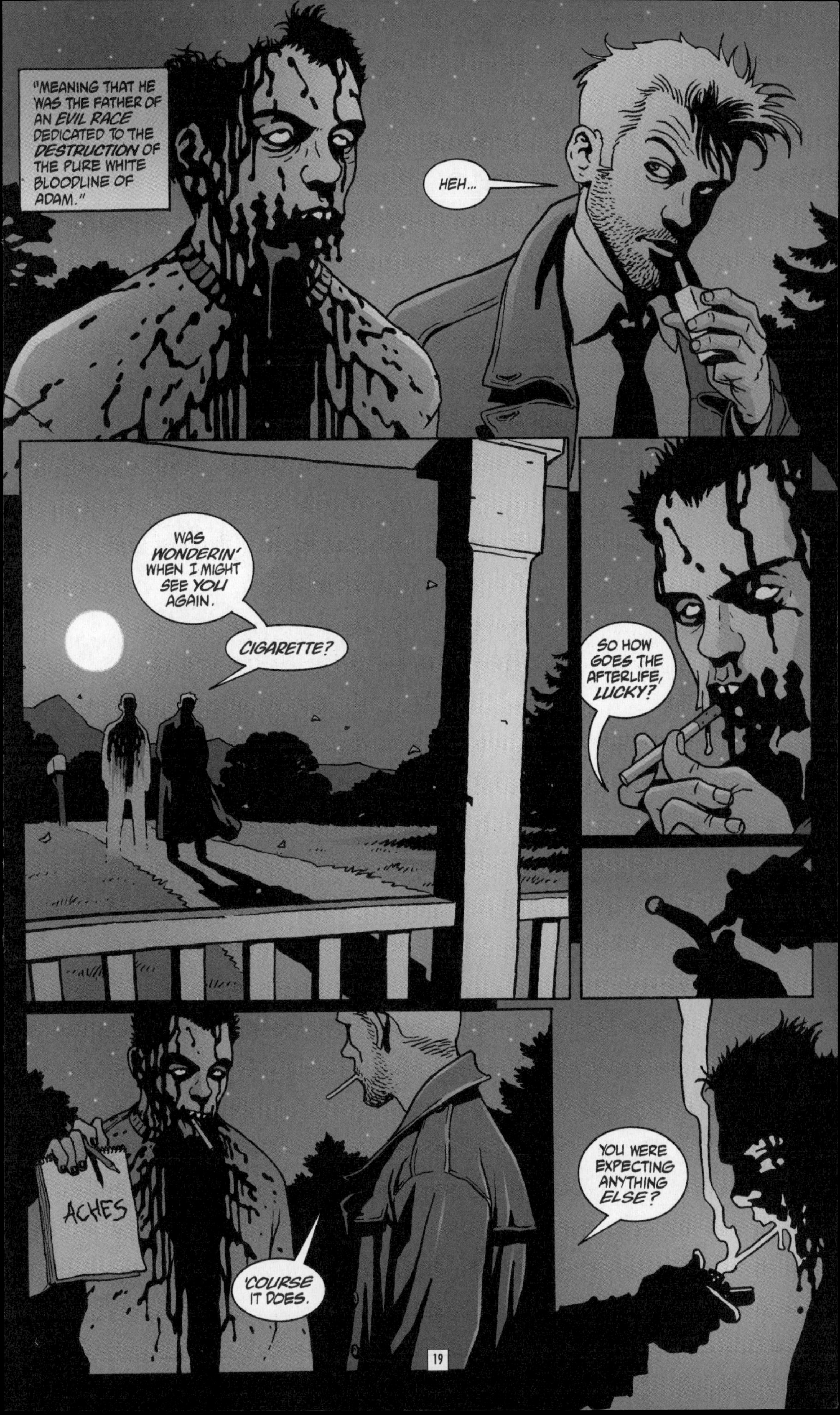
"MEANING THAT HE WAS THE FATHER OF AN *EVIL RACE* DEDICATED TO THE ***DESTRUCTION*** OF THE PURE WHITE BLOODLINE OF ADAM."
HEH...
WAS ***WONDERIN'*** WHEN I MIGHT SEE ***YOU*** AGAIN.
CIGARETTE?
SO HOW GOES THE AFTERLIFE, ***LUCKY?***
ACHES
'COURSE IT DOES.
YOU WERE EXPECTING ANYTHING ***ELSE?***

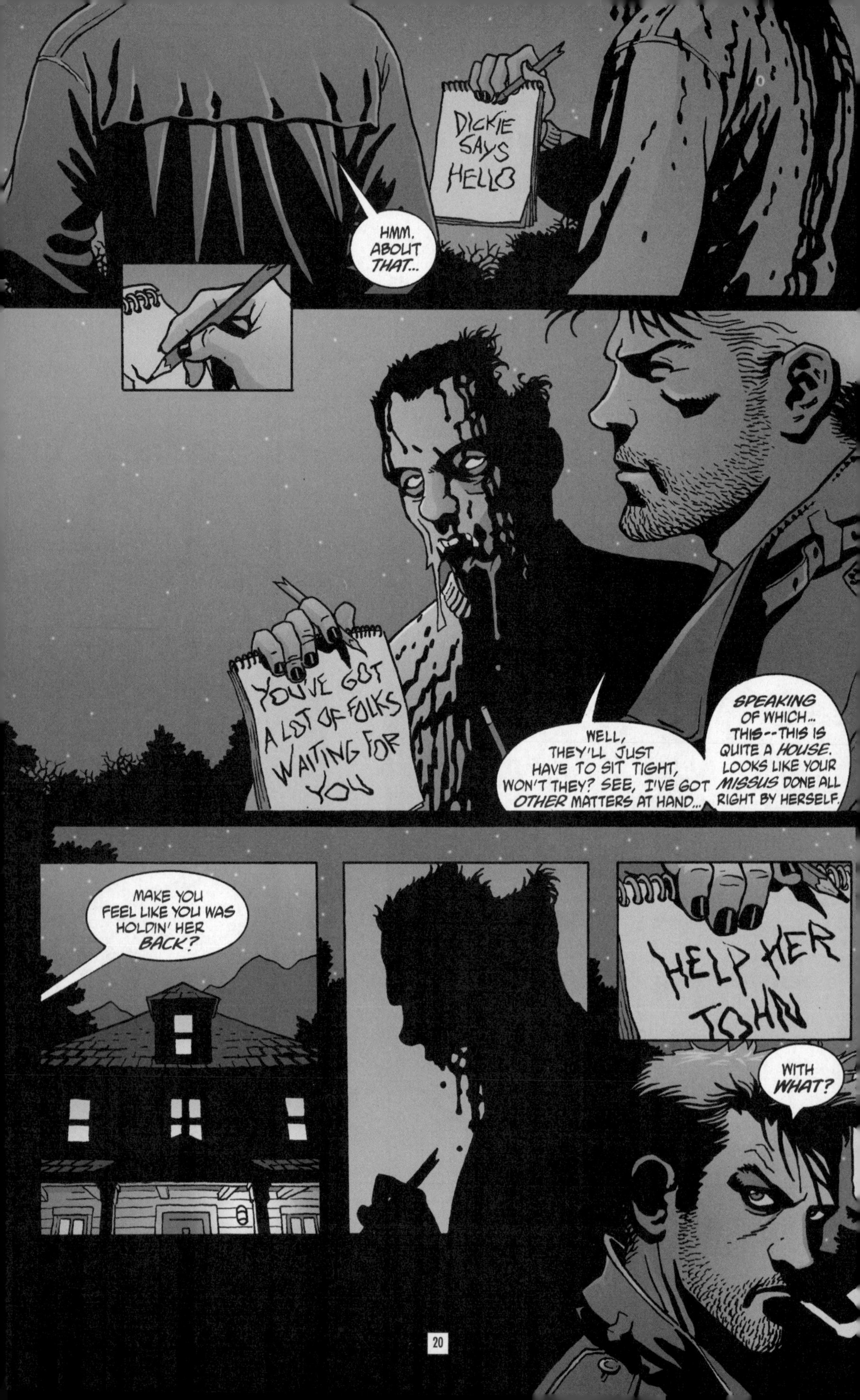
DICKIE SAYS HELLO
HMM. ABOUT THAT...
YOU'VE GOT A LOT OF FOLKS WAITING FOR YOU
WELL, THEY'LL JUST HAVE TO SIT TIGHT, WON'T THEY? SEE, I'VE GOT OTHER MATTERS AT HAND...
SPEAKING OF WHICH... THIS--THIS IS QUITE A HOUSE. LOOKS LIKE YOUR MISSUS DONE ALL RIGHT BY HERSELF.
MAKE YOU FEEL LIKE YOU WAS HOLDIN' HER BACK?
HELP HER JOHN
WITH WHAT?

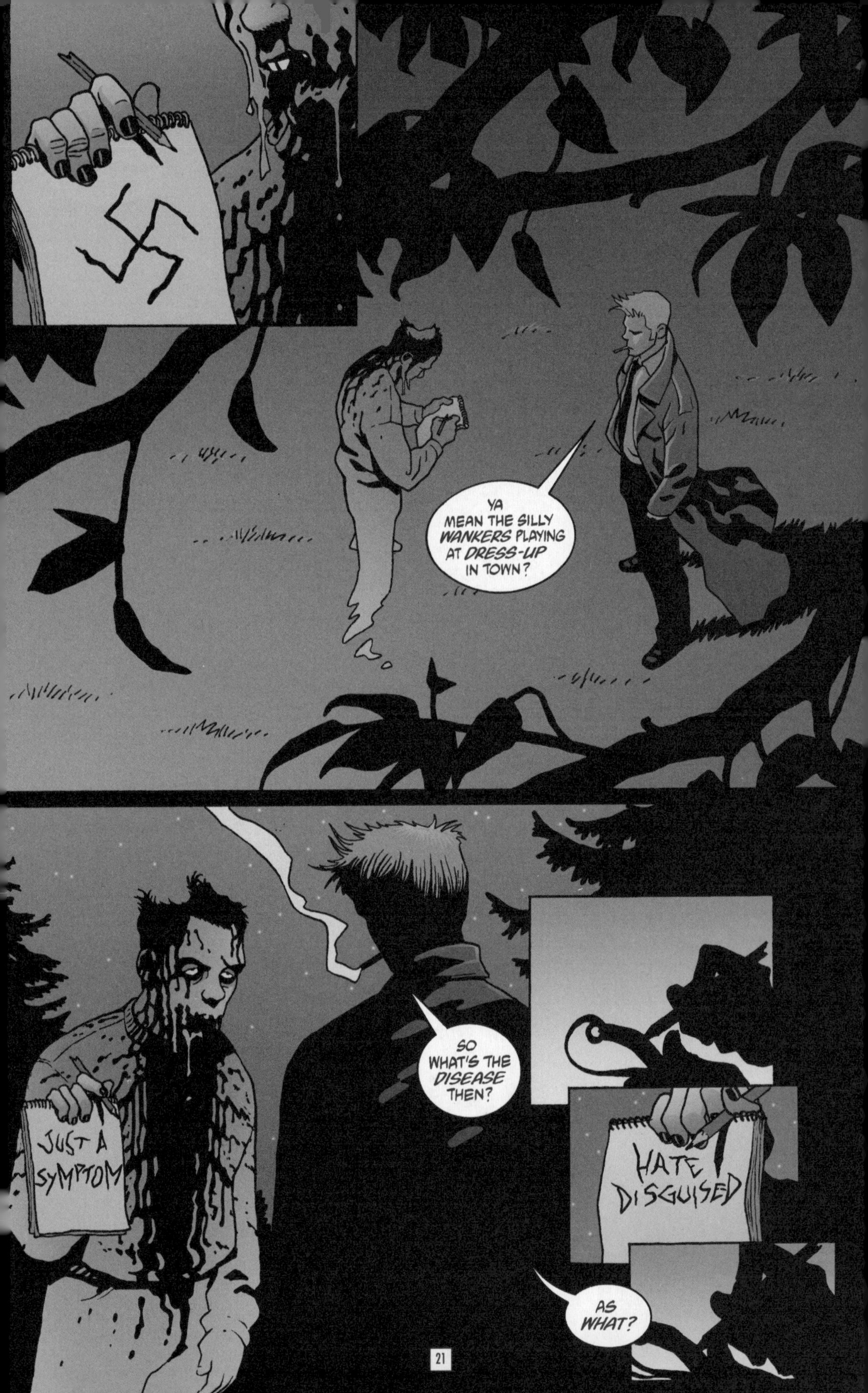
YA MEAN THE SILLY WANKERS PLAYING AT DRESS-UP IN TOWN?
JUST A SYMPTOM
SO WHAT'S THE DISEASE THEN?
HATE DISGUISED
AS WHAT?

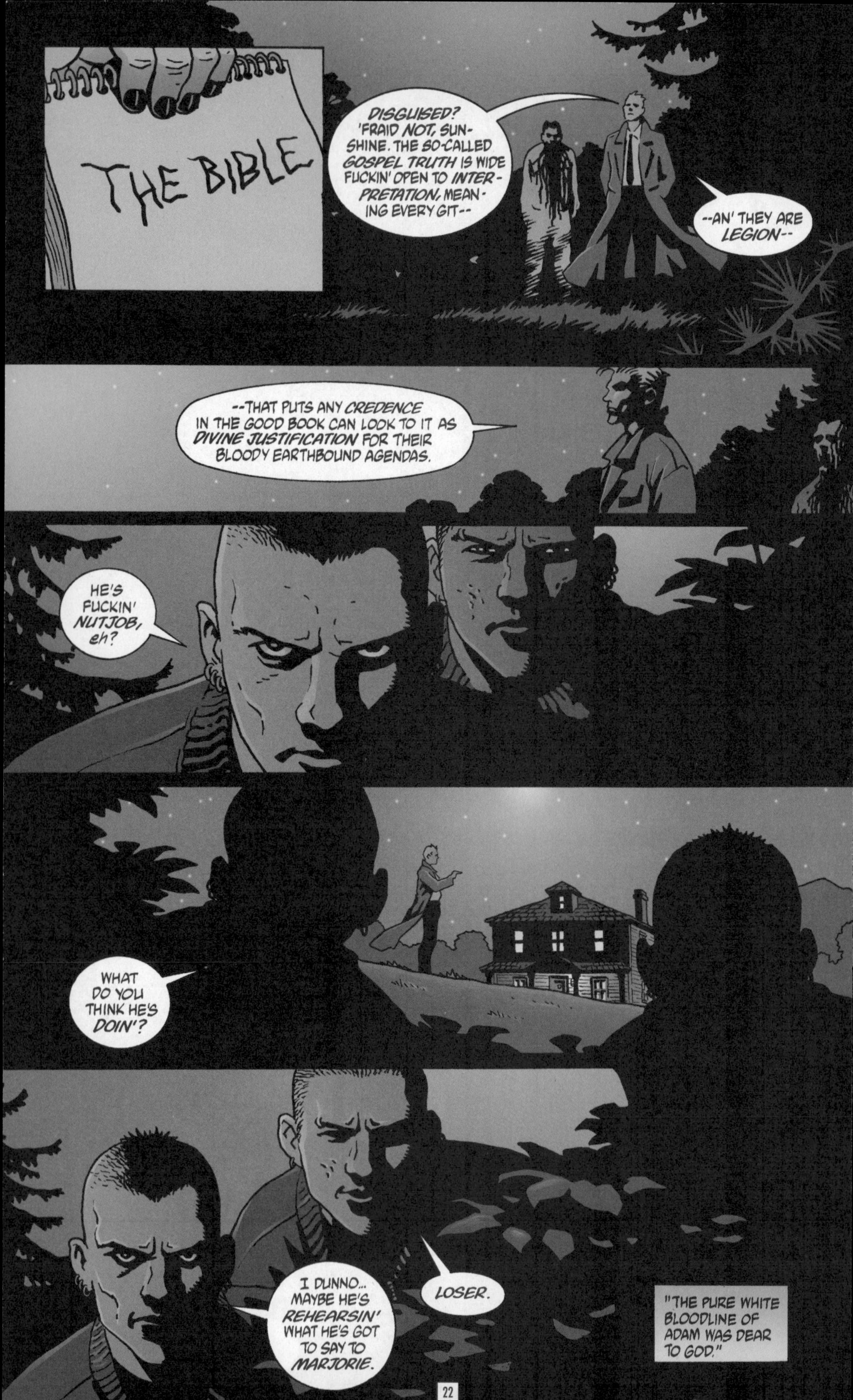
THE BIBLE
DISGUISED? 'FRAID NOT, SUNSHINE. THE SO-CALLED GOSPEL TRUTH IS WIDE FUCKIN' OPEN TO INTERPRETATION, MEANING EVERY GIT--
--AN' THEY ARE LEGION--
--THAT PUTS ANY CREDENCE IN THE GOOD BOOK CAN LOOK TO IT AS DIVINE JUSTIFICATION FOR THEIR BLOODY EARTHBOUND AGENDAS.
HE'S FUCKIN' NUTJOB, eh?
WHAT DO YOU THINK HE'S DOIN'?
I DUNNO... MAYBE HE'S REHEARSIN' WHAT HE'S GOT TO SAY TO MARJORIE.
LOSER.
"THE PURE WHITE BLOODLINE OF ADAM WAS DEAR TO GOD."

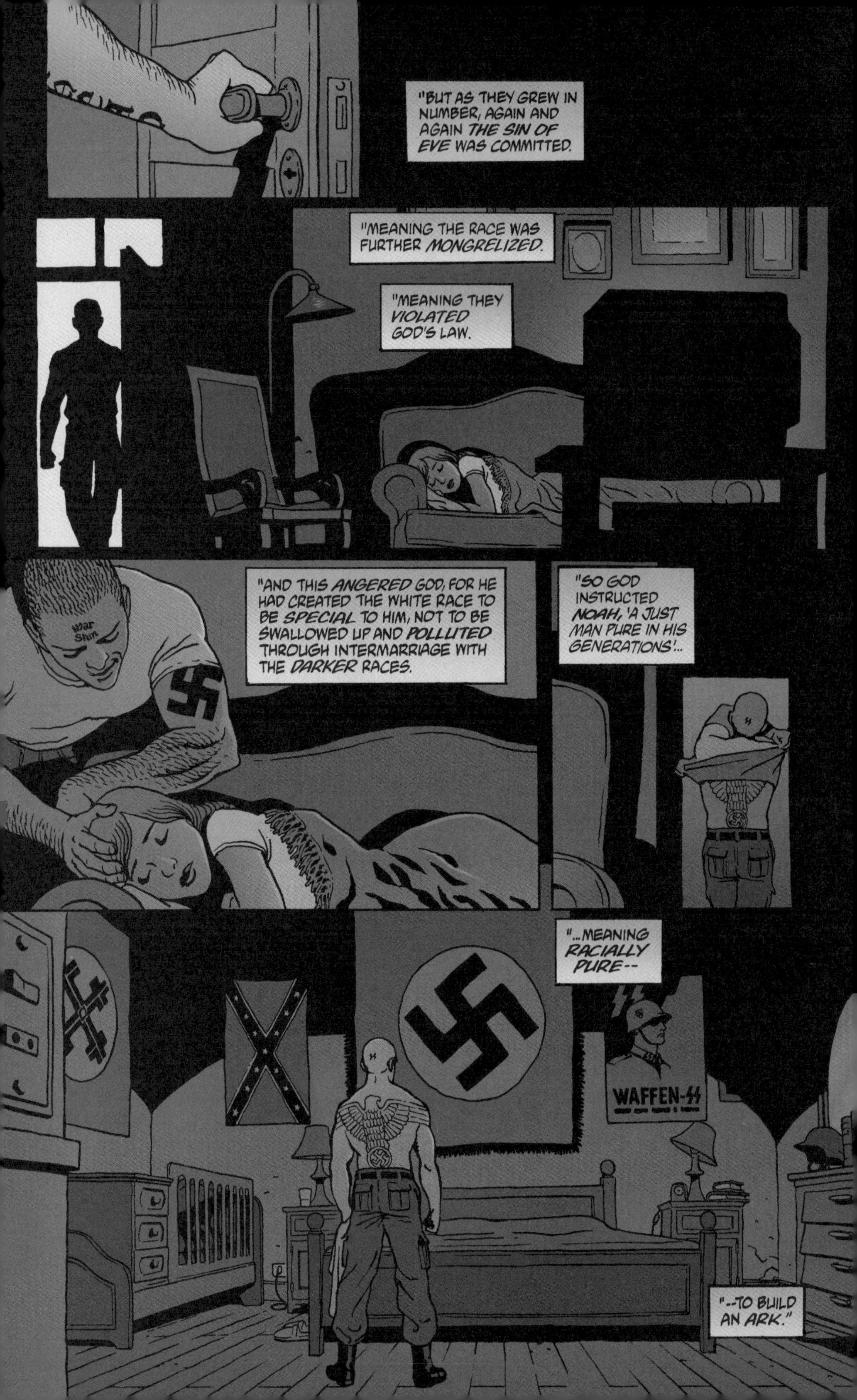
"BUT AS THEY GREW IN NUMBER, AGAIN AND AGAIN *THE SIN OF EVE* WAS COMMITTED.
"MEANING THE RACE WAS FURTHER *MONGRELIZED*.
"MEANING THEY *VIOLATED* GOD'S LAW.
"AND THIS *ANGERED* GOD, FOR HE HAD CREATED THE WHITE RACE TO BE *SPECIAL* TO HIM, NOT TO BE SWALLOWED UP AND *POLLUTED* THROUGH INTERMARRIAGE WITH THE *DARKER* RACES.
"SO GOD INSTRUCTED *NOAH*, 'A JUST MAN PURE IN HIS GENERATIONS'...
"...MEANING *RACIALLY PURE*--
WAFFEN-SS
"--TO BUILD AN *ARK*."

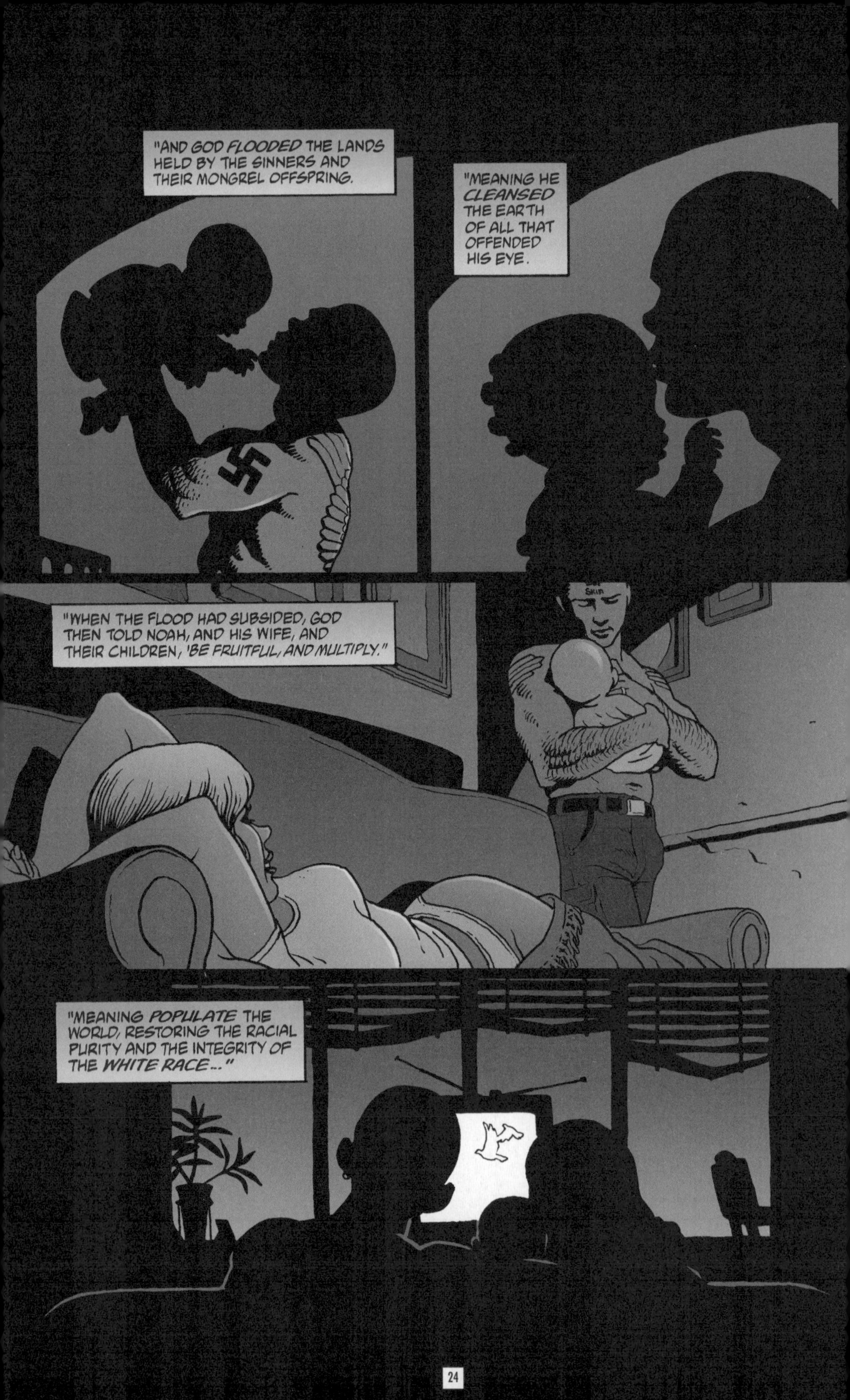
"AND GOD *FLOODED* THE LANDS HELD BY THE SINNERS AND THEIR MONGREL OFFSPRING.
"MEANING HE *CLEANSED* THE EARTH OF ALL THAT OFFENDED HIS EYE.
"WHEN THE FLOOD HAD SUBSIDED, GOD THEN TOLD NOAH, AND HIS WIFE, AND THEIR CHILDREN, 'BE FRUITFUL, AND MULTIPLY.'
"MEANING *POPULATE* THE WORLD, RESTORING THE RACIAL PURITY AND THE INTEGRITY OF THE *WHITE RACE*..."

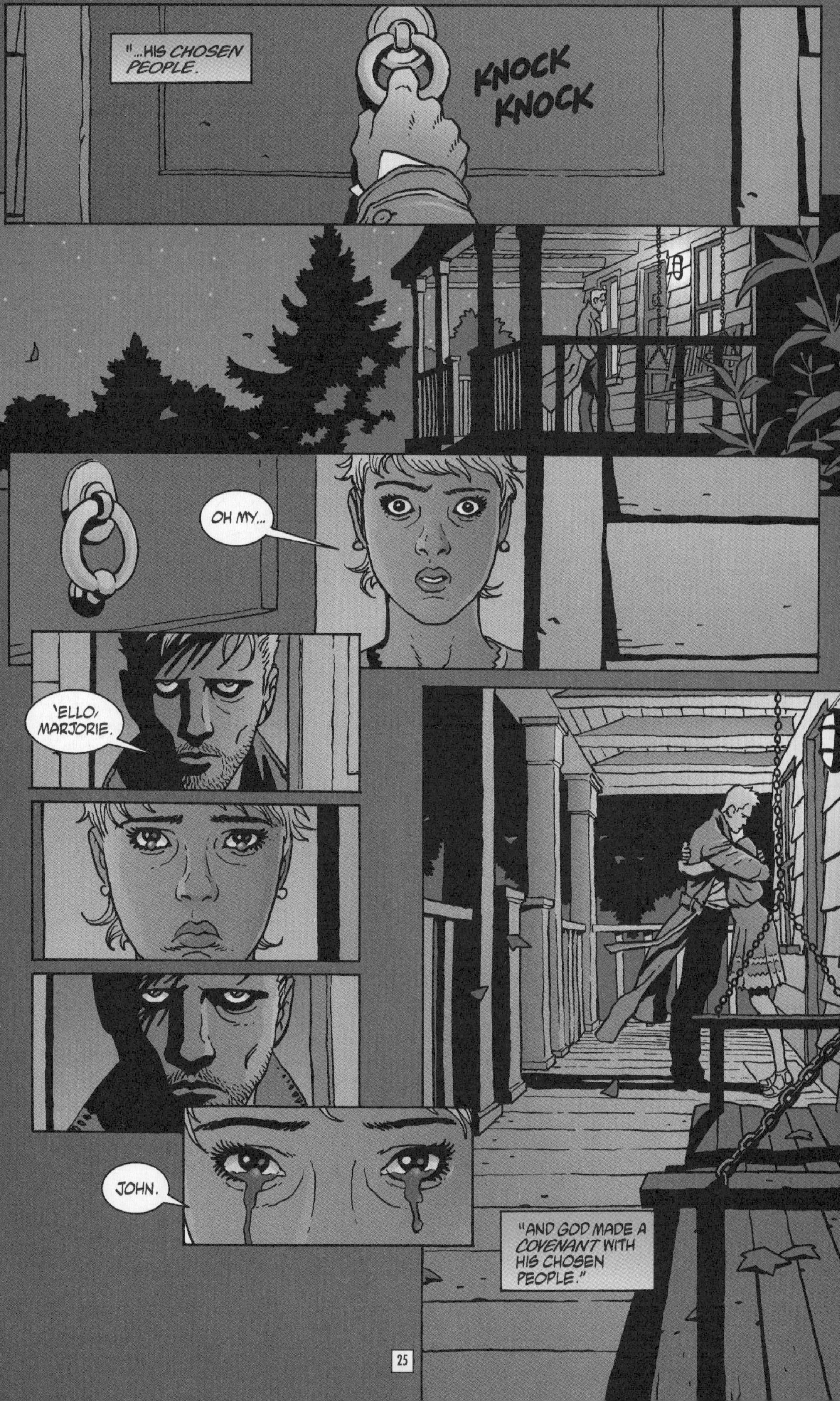
"...HIS CHOSEN PEOPLE.
KNOCK KNOCK
OH MY...
'ELLO, MARJORIE.
JOHN.
"AND GOD MADE A COVENANT WITH HIS CHOSEN PEOPLE."

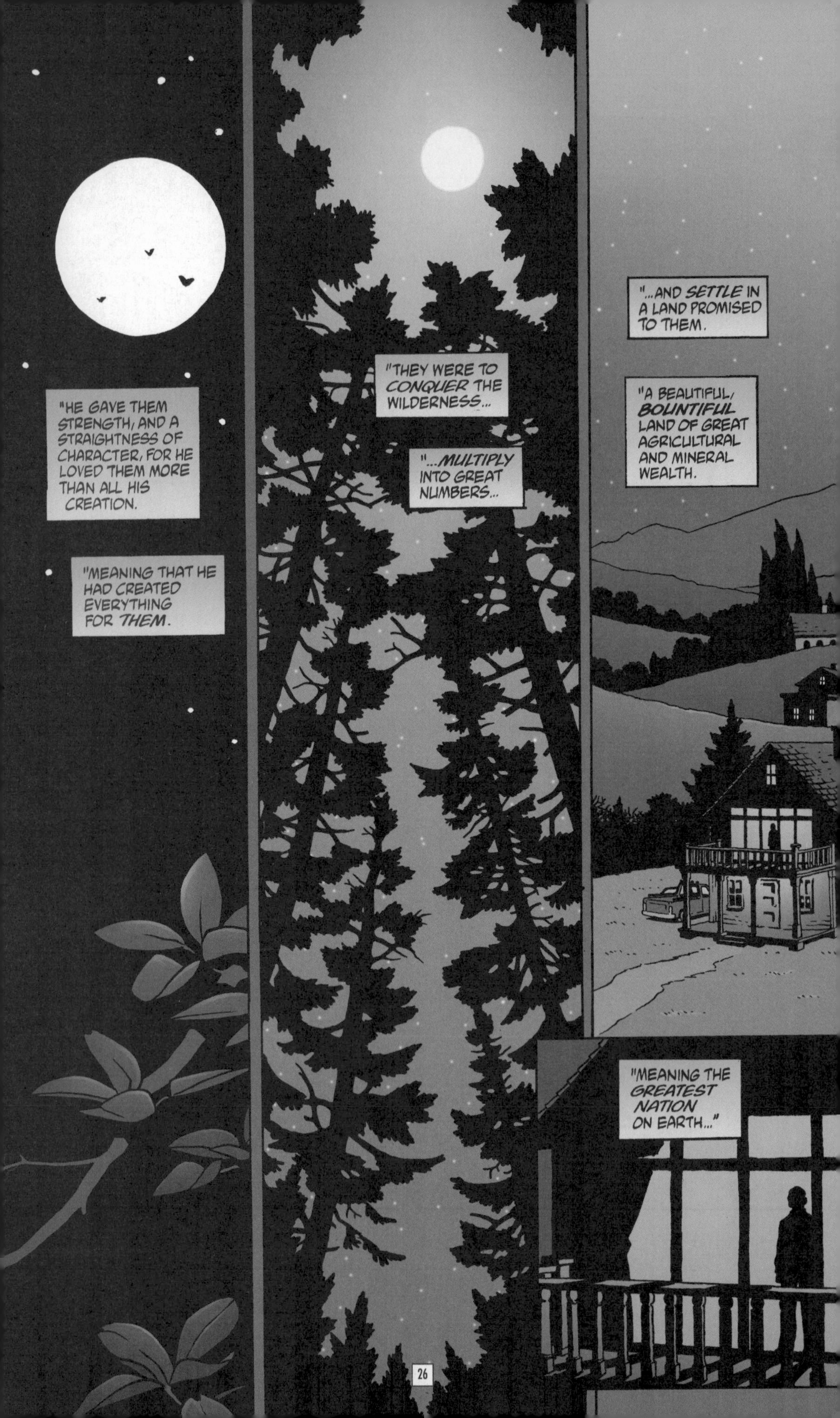
"HE GAVE THEM STRENGTH, AND A STRAIGHTNESS OF CHARACTER, FOR HE LOVED THEM MORE THAN ALL HIS CREATION.
"MEANING THAT HE HAD CREATED EVERYTHING FOR THEM.
"THEY WERE TO CONQUER THE WILDERNESS...
"...MULTIPLY INTO GREAT NUMBERS...
"...AND SETTLE IN A LAND PROMISED TO THEM.
"A BEAUTIFUL, BOUNTIFUL LAND OF GREAT AGRICULTURAL AND MINERAL WEALTH.
"MEANING THE GREATEST NATION ON EARTH..."

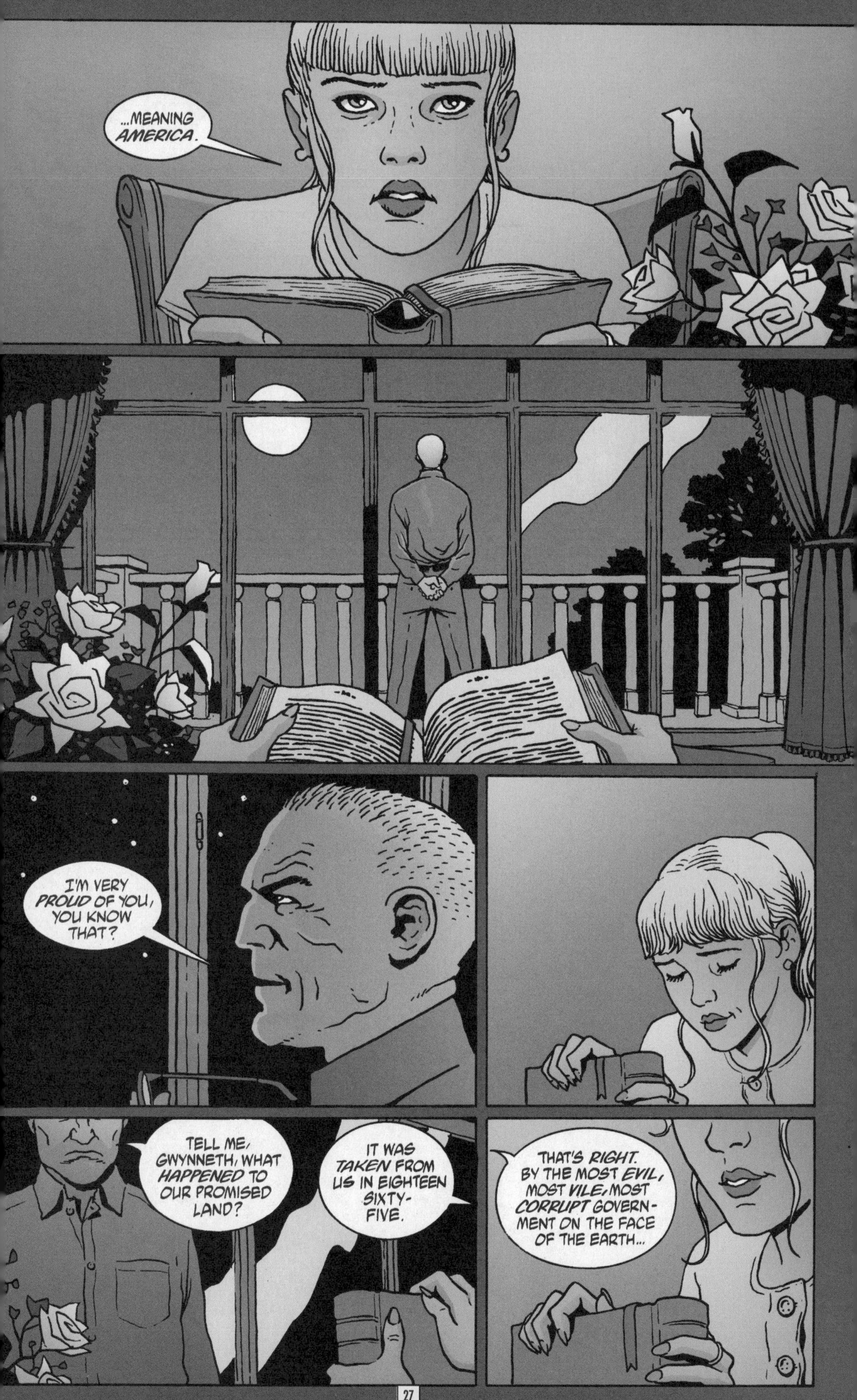
...MEANING AMERICA.
I'M VERY PROUD OF YOU, YOU KNOW THAT?
TELL ME, GWYNNETH, WHAT HAPPENED TO OUR PROMISED LAND?
IT WAS TAKEN FROM US IN EIGHTEEN SIXTY-FIVE.
THAT'S RIGHT. BY THE MOST EVIL, MOST VILE, MOST CORRUPT GOVERNMENT ON THE FACE OF THE EARTH...

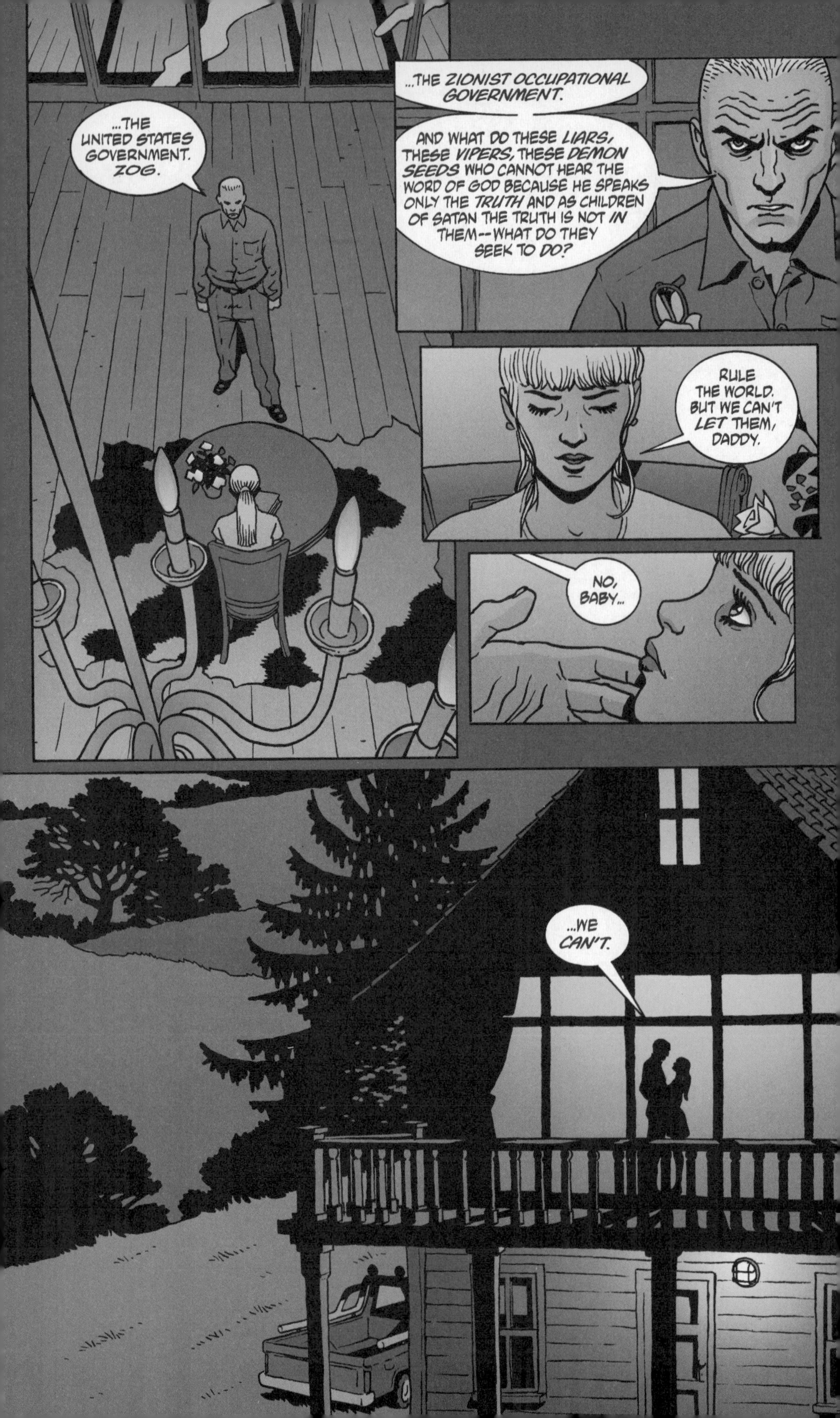
...THE UNITED STATES GOVERNMENT. ZOG.
...THE ZIONIST OCCUPATIONAL GOVERNMENT.
AND WHAT DO THESE LIARS, THESE VIPERS, THESE DEMON SEEDS WHO CANNOT HEAR THE WORD OF GOD BECAUSE HE SPEAKS ONLY THE TRUTH AND AS CHILDREN OF SATAN THE TRUTH IS NOT IN THEM--WHAT DO THEY SEEK TO DO?
RULE THE WORLD. BUT WE CAN'T LET THEM, DADDY.
NO, BABY...
...WE CAN'T.

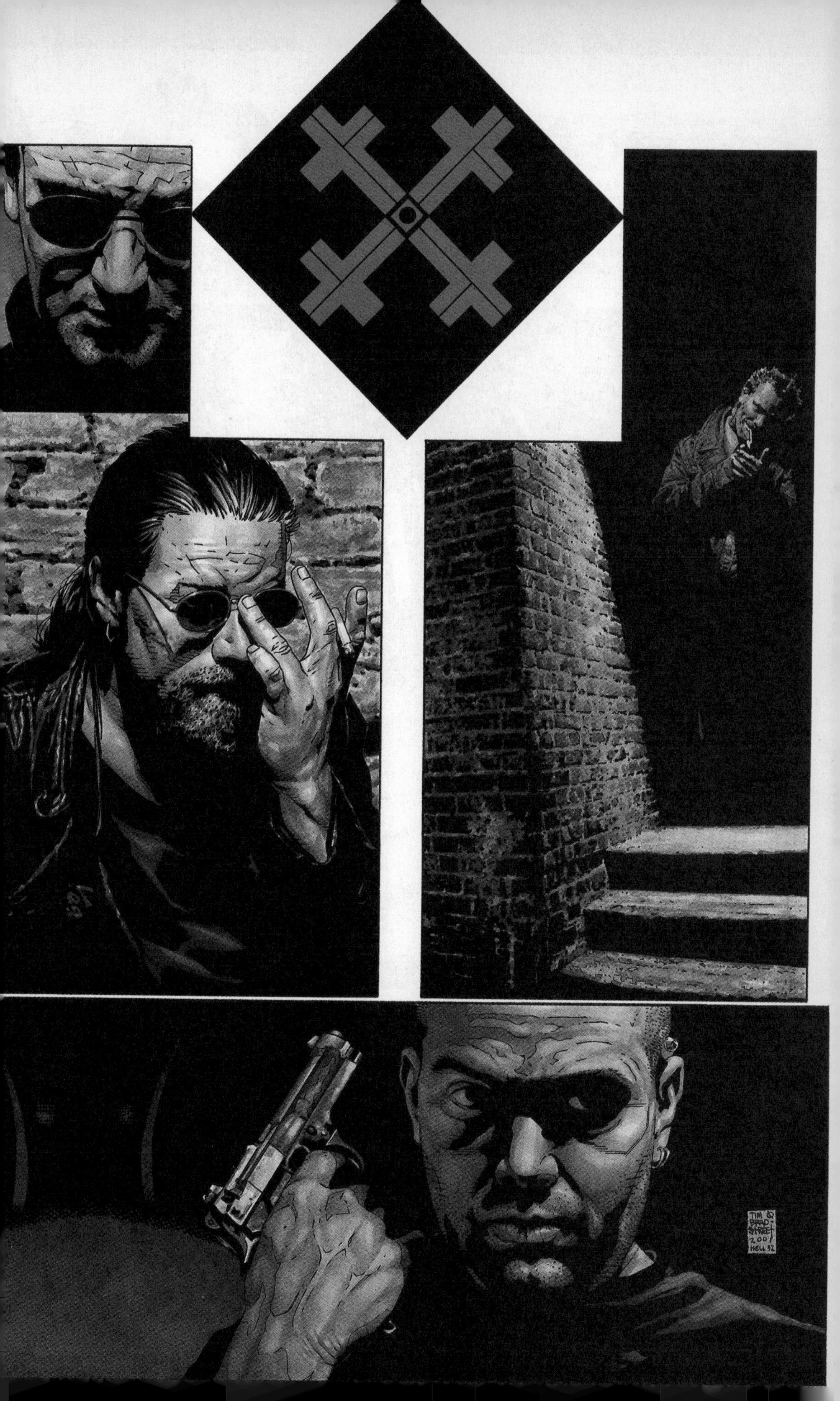
TIM & BRAD-STREET 2001 HELL 32

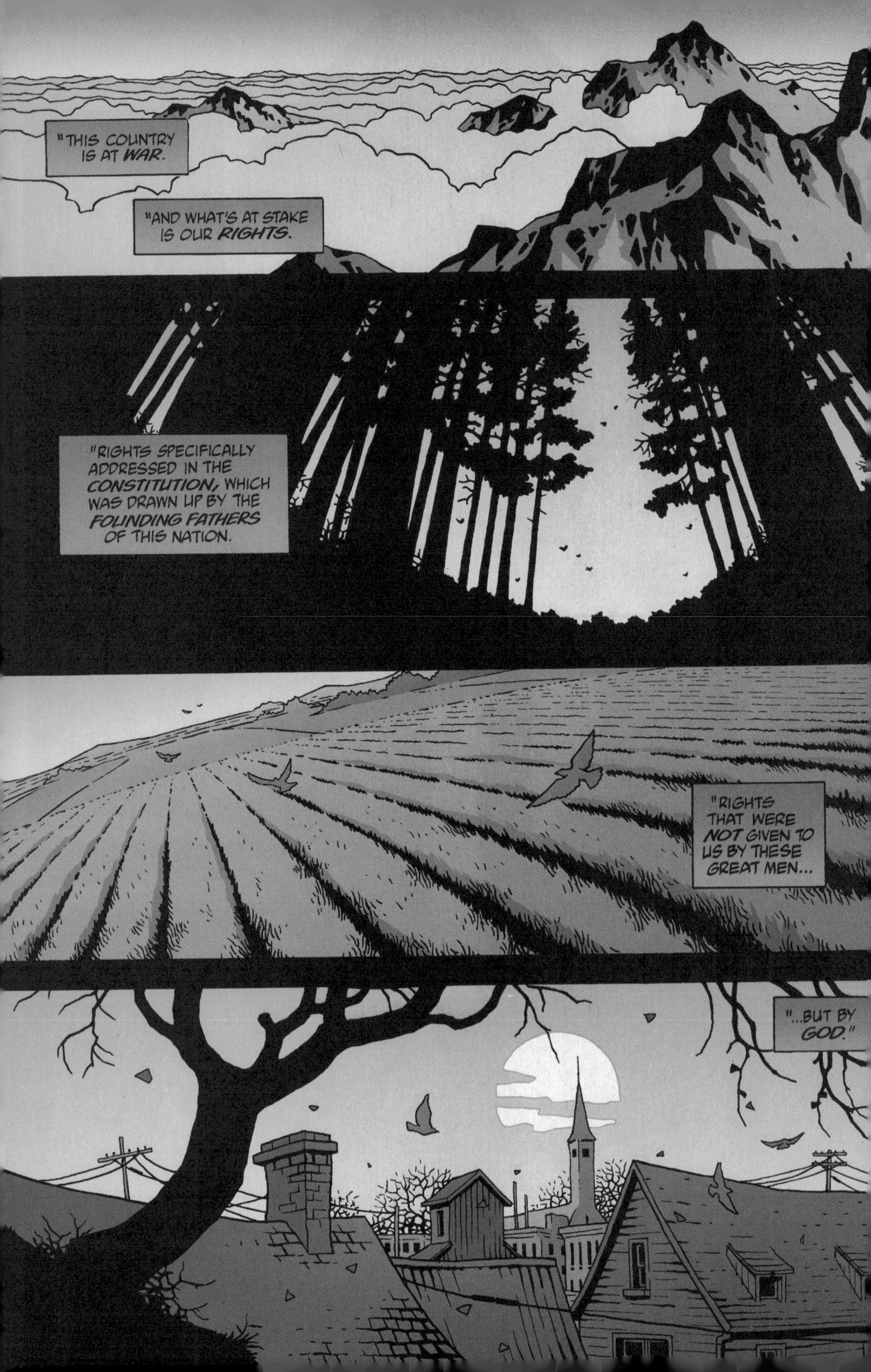
"THIS COUNTRY IS AT WAR.
"AND WHAT'S AT STAKE IS OUR RIGHTS.
"RIGHTS SPECIFICALLY ADDRESSED IN THE CONSTITUTION, WHICH WAS DRAWN UP BY THE FOUNDING FATHERS OF THIS NATION.
"RIGHTS THAT WERE NOT GIVEN TO US BY THESE GREAT MEN...
"...BUT BY GOD."

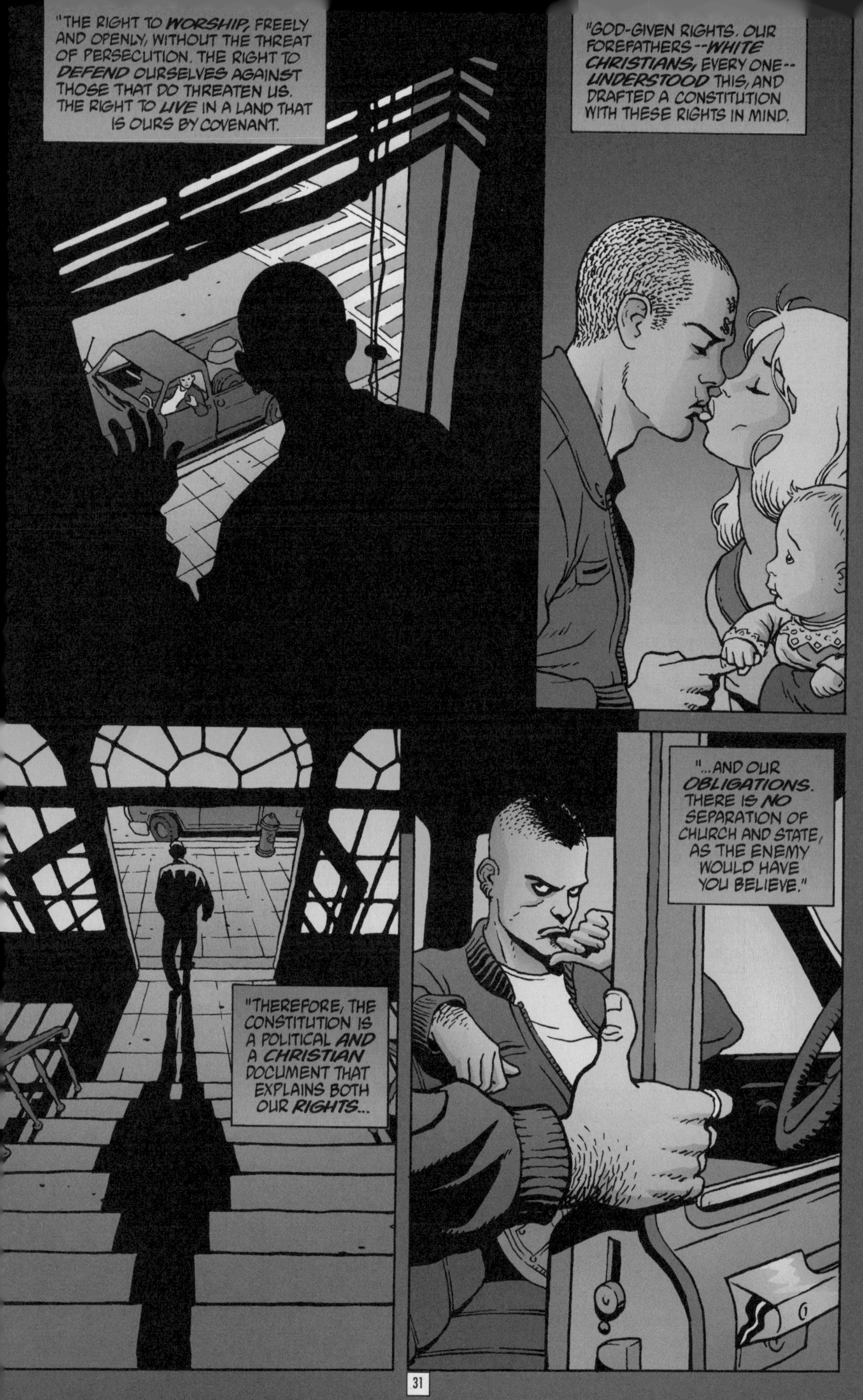
"THE RIGHT TO WORSHIP, FREELY AND OPENLY, WITHOUT THE THREAT OF PERSECUTION. THE RIGHT TO DEFEND OURSELVES AGAINST THOSE THAT DO THREATEN US. THE RIGHT TO LIVE IN A LAND THAT IS OURS BY COVENANT.
"GOD-GIVEN RIGHTS. OUR FOREFATHERS--WHITE CHRISTIANS, EVERY ONE--UNDERSTOOD THIS, AND DRAFTED A CONSTITUTION WITH THESE RIGHTS IN MIND.
"THEREFORE, THE CONSTITUTION IS A POLITICAL AND A CHRISTIAN DOCUMENT THAT EXPLAINS BOTH OUR RIGHTS...
"...AND OUR OBLIGATIONS. THERE IS NO SEPARATION OF CHURCH AND STATE, AS THE ENEMY WOULD HAVE YOU BELIEVE."

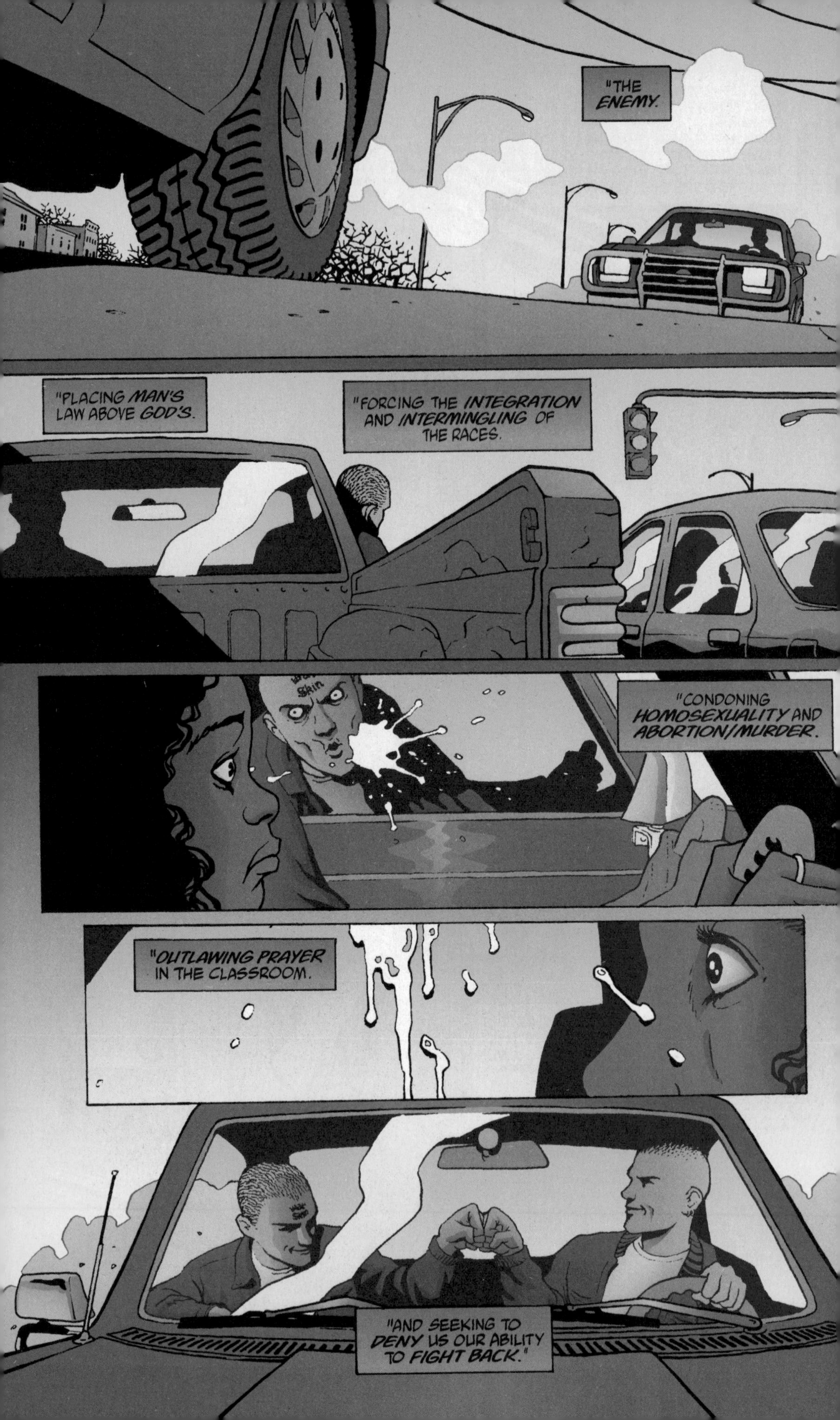
"THE ENEMY.
"PLACING MAN'S LAW ABOVE GOD'S.
"FORCING THE INTEGRATION AND INTERMINGLING OF THE RACES.
"CONDONING HOMOSEXUALITY AND ABORTION/MURDER.
"OUTLAWING PRAYER IN THE CLASSROOM.
"AND SEEKING TO DENY US OUR ABILITY TO FIGHT BACK."

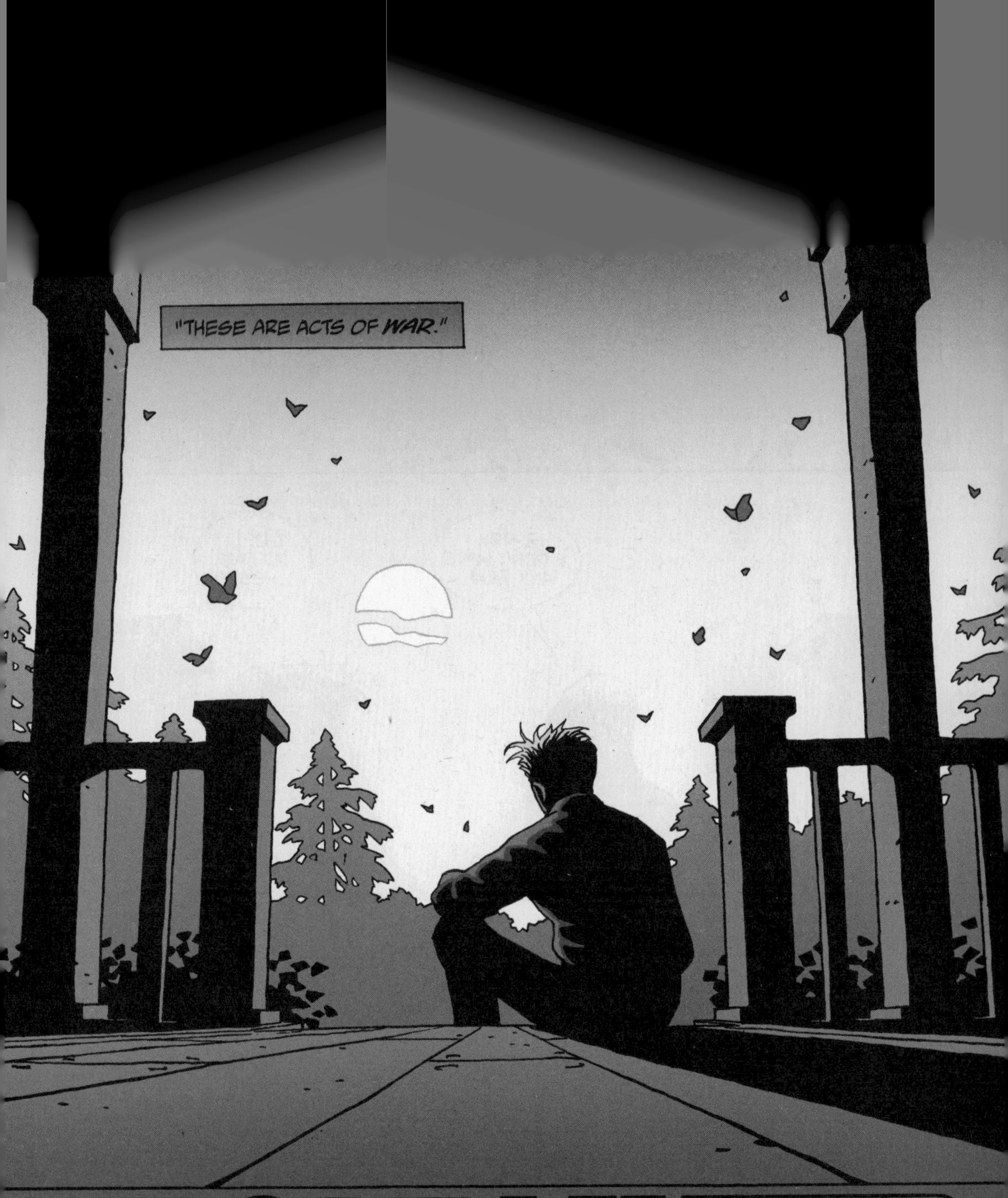
"THESE ARE ACTS OF WAR."

HIGHWATER

PART TWO OF FOUR

BRIAN **AZZARELLO** writer
MARCELO **FRUSIN** artist
CLEM **ROBINS** letterer
JAMES **SINCLAIR** colorist
ZYLONOL separator
TIM **BRADSTREET** cover
TAMMY **BEATTY** asst. editor
TONY **BEDARD** editor

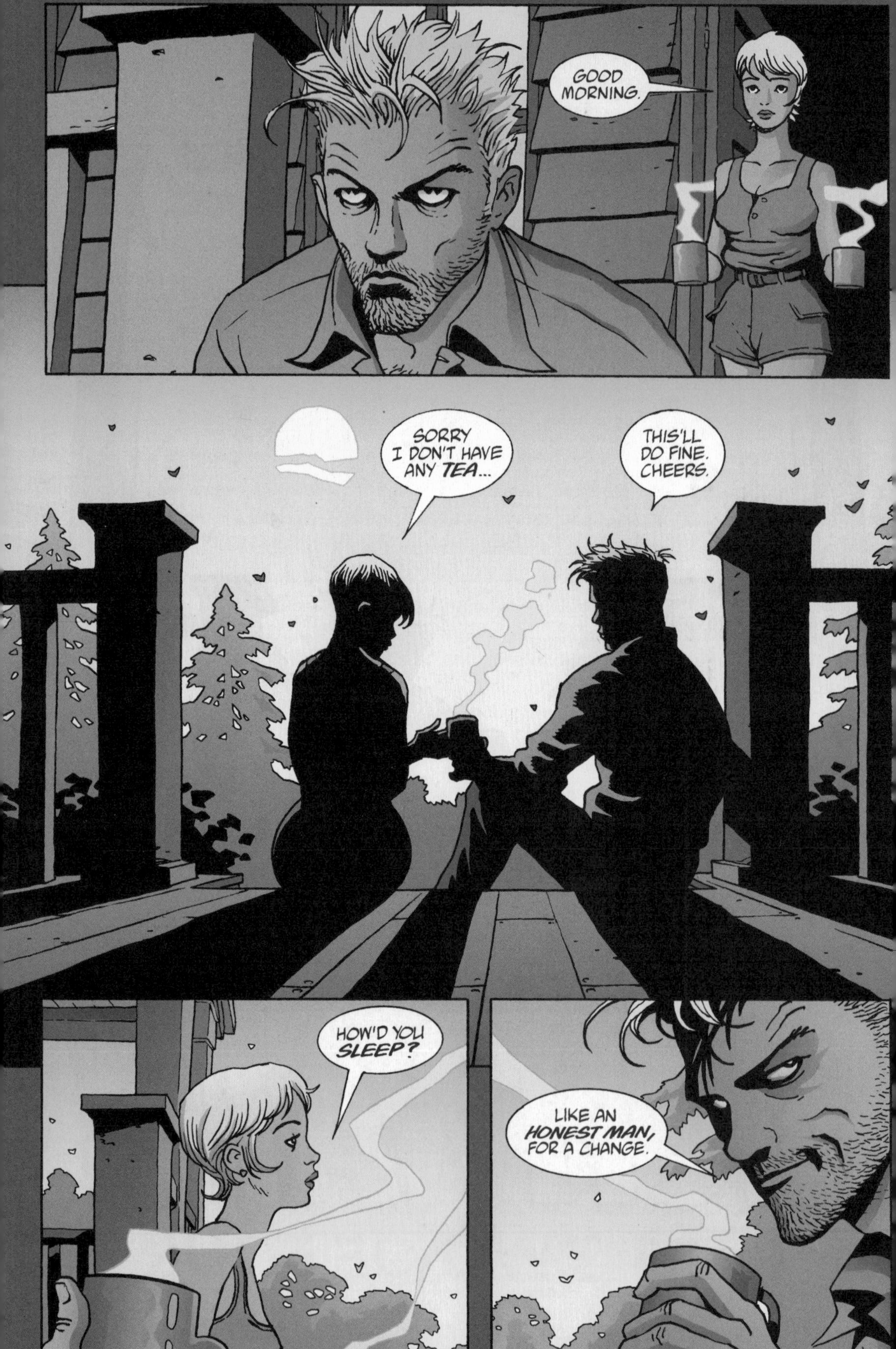
GOOD MORNING.
SORRY I DON'T HAVE ANY TEA...
THIS'LL DO FINE. CHEERS.
HOW'D YOU SLEEP?
LIKE AN HONEST MAN, FOR A CHANGE.

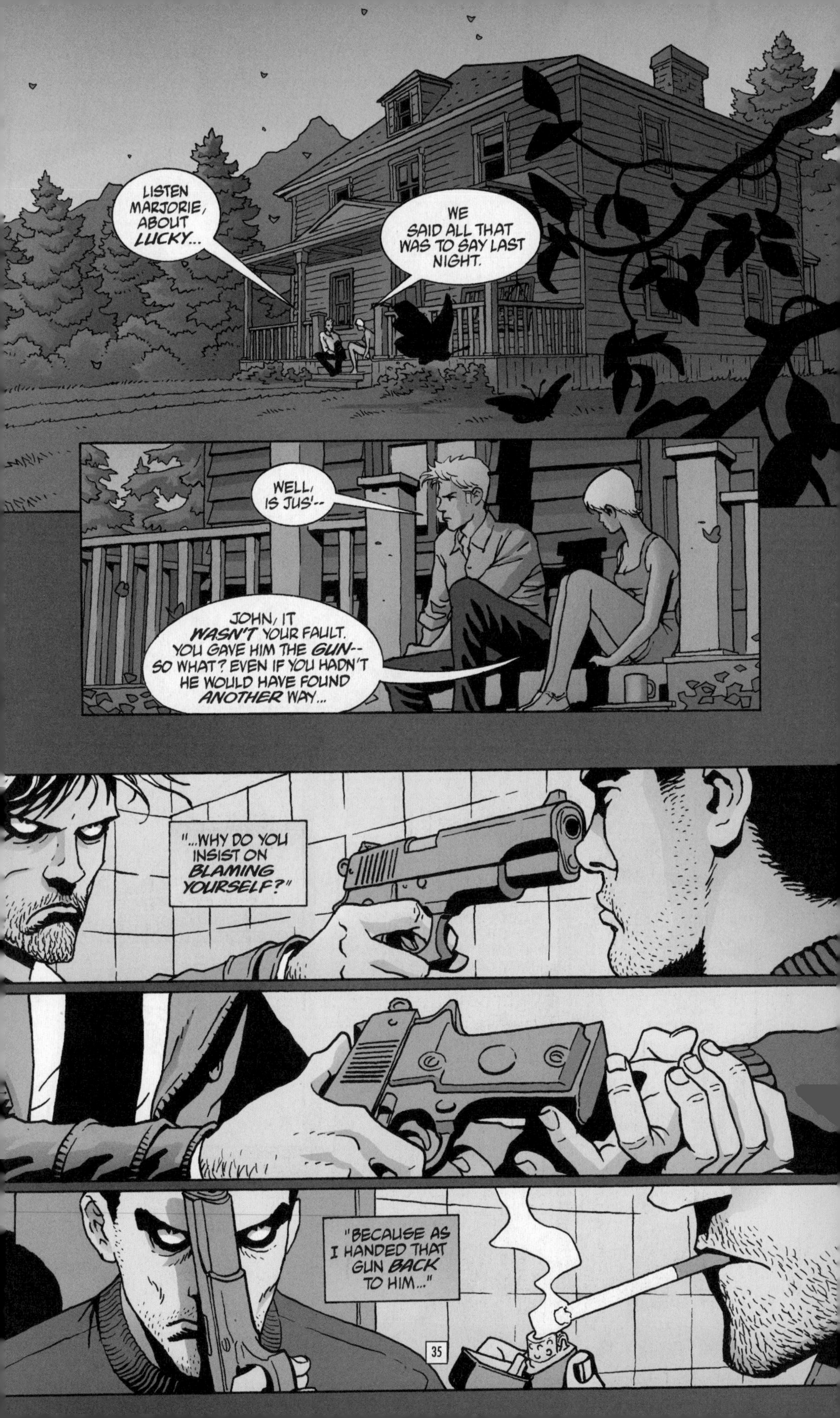

LISTEN MARJORIE, ABOUT LUCKY...
WE SAID ALL THAT WAS TO SAY LAST NIGHT.
WELL, IS JUS'--
JOHN, IT WASN'T YOUR FAULT. YOU GAVE HIM THE GUN-- SO WHAT? EVEN IF YOU HADN'T HE WOULD HAVE FOUND ANOTHER WAY...
"...WHY DO YOU INSIST ON BLAMING YOURSELF?"
"BECAUSE AS I HANDED THAT GUN BACK TO HIM..."

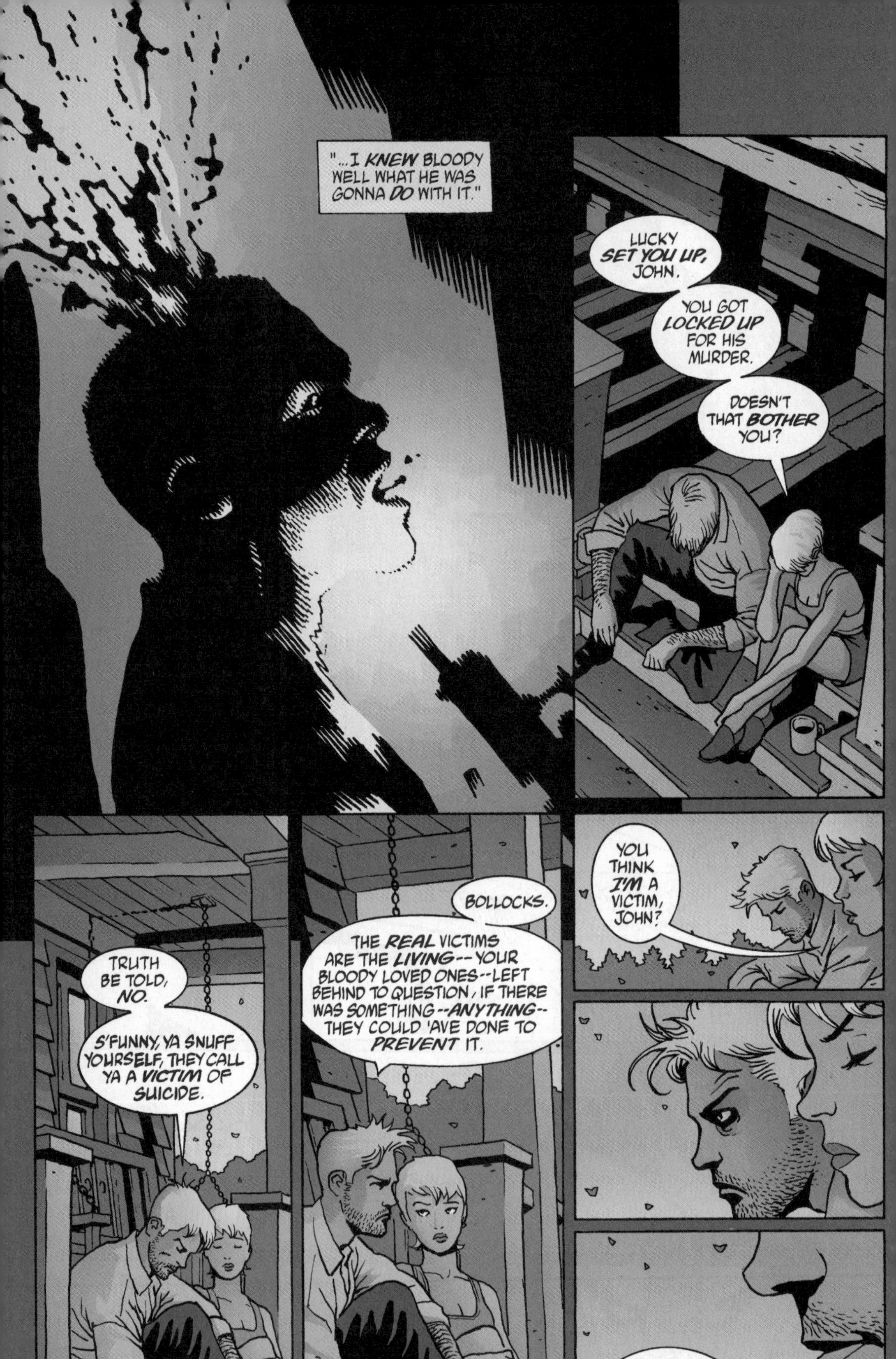
"...I KNEW BLOODY WELL WHAT HE WAS GONNA DO WITH IT."
LUCKY SET YOU UP, JOHN.
YOU GOT LOCKED UP FOR HIS MURDER.
DOESN'T THAT BOTHER YOU?
TRUTH BE TOLD, NO.
S'FUNNY, YA SNUFF YOURSELF, THEY CALL YA A VICTIM OF SUICIDE.
BOLLOCKS.
THE REAL VICTIMS ARE THE LIVING-- YOUR BLOODY LOVED ONES--LEFT BEHIND TO QUESTION, IF THERE WAS SOMETHING --ANYTHING-- THEY COULD 'AVE DONE TO PREVENT IT.
YOU THINK I'M A VICTIM, JOHN?
I WENT TO PRISON SO YOU WOULDN'T THINK YOU WERE.

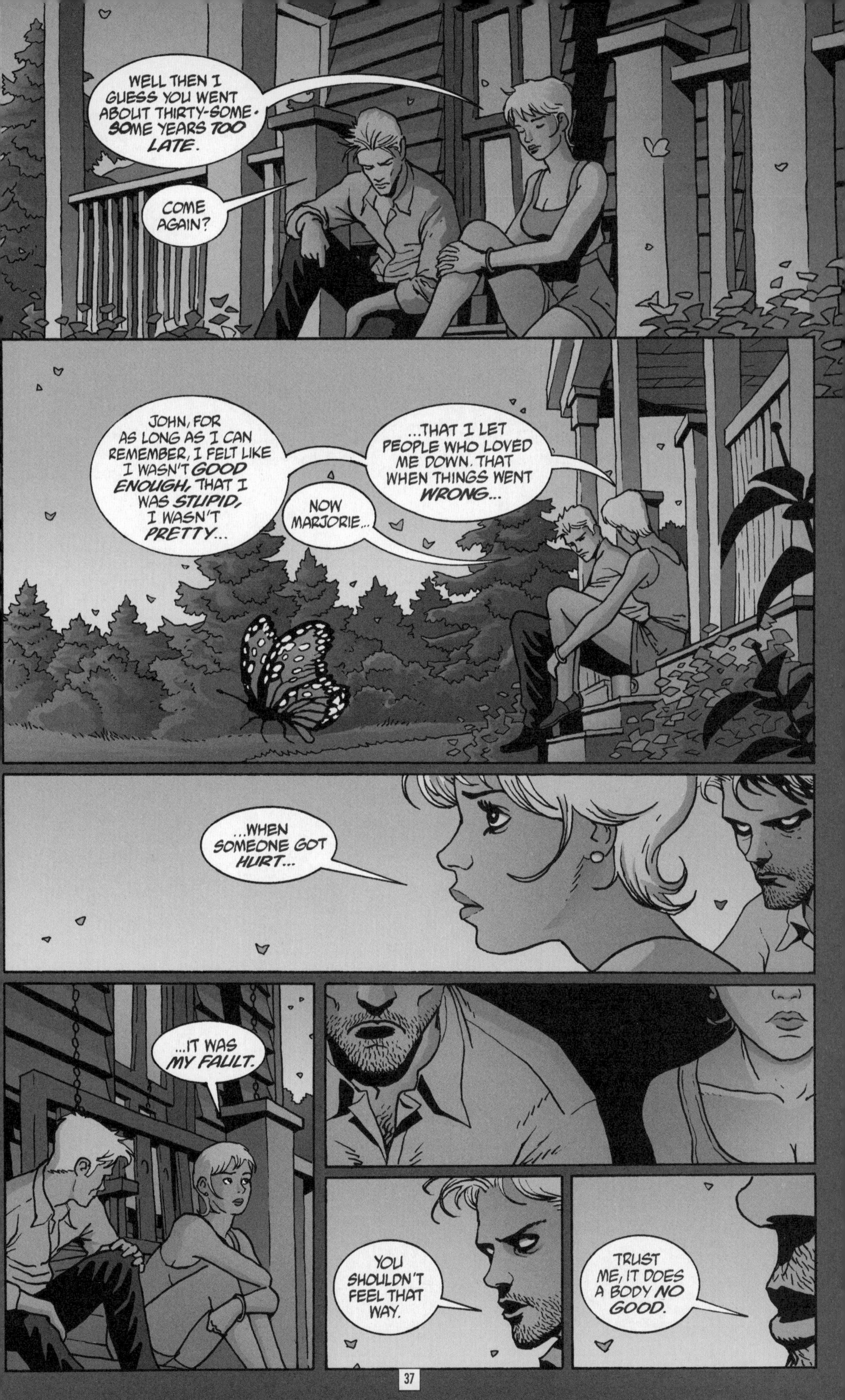
WELL THEN I GUESS YOU WENT ABOUT THIRTY-SOME-SOME YEARS TOO LATE.
COME AGAIN?
JOHN, FOR AS LONG AS I CAN REMEMBER, I FELT LIKE I WASN'T GOOD ENOUGH, THAT I WAS STUPID, I WASN'T PRETTY...
NOW MARJORIE...
...THAT I LET PEOPLE WHO LOVED ME DOWN. THAT WHEN THINGS WENT WRONG...
...WHEN SOMEONE GOT HURT...
...IT WAS MY FAULT.
YOU SHOULDN'T FEEL THAT WAY.
TRUST ME, IT DOES A BODY NO GOOD.

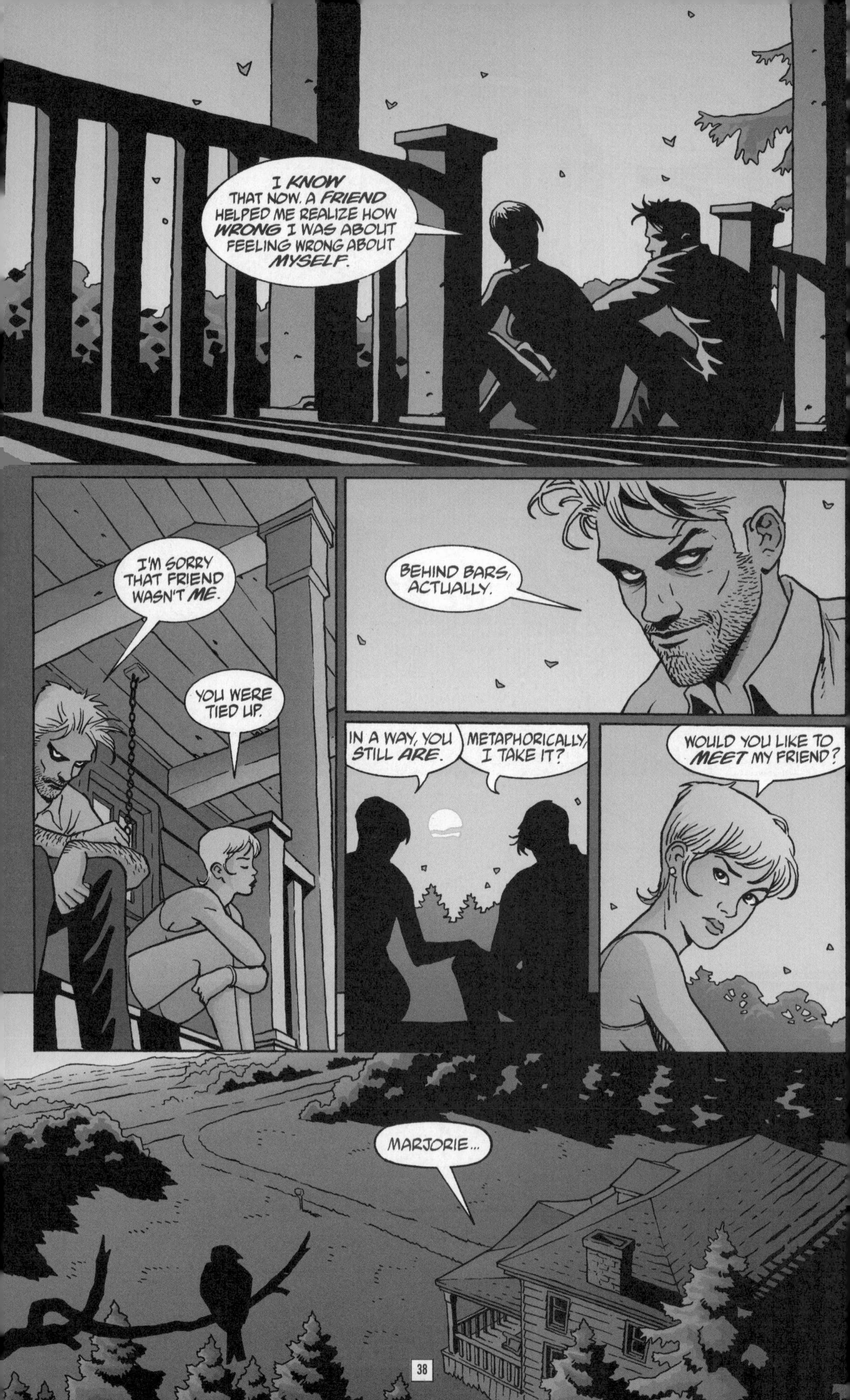
I KNOW THAT NOW. A FRIEND HELPED ME REALIZE HOW WRONG I WAS ABOUT FEELING WRONG ABOUT MYSELF.
I'M SORRY THAT FRIEND WASN'T ME.
YOU WERE TIED UP.
BEHIND BARS, ACTUALLY.
IN A WAY, YOU STILL ARE.
METAPHORICALLY, I TAKE IT?
WOULD YOU LIKE TO MEET MY FRIEND?
MARJORIE...

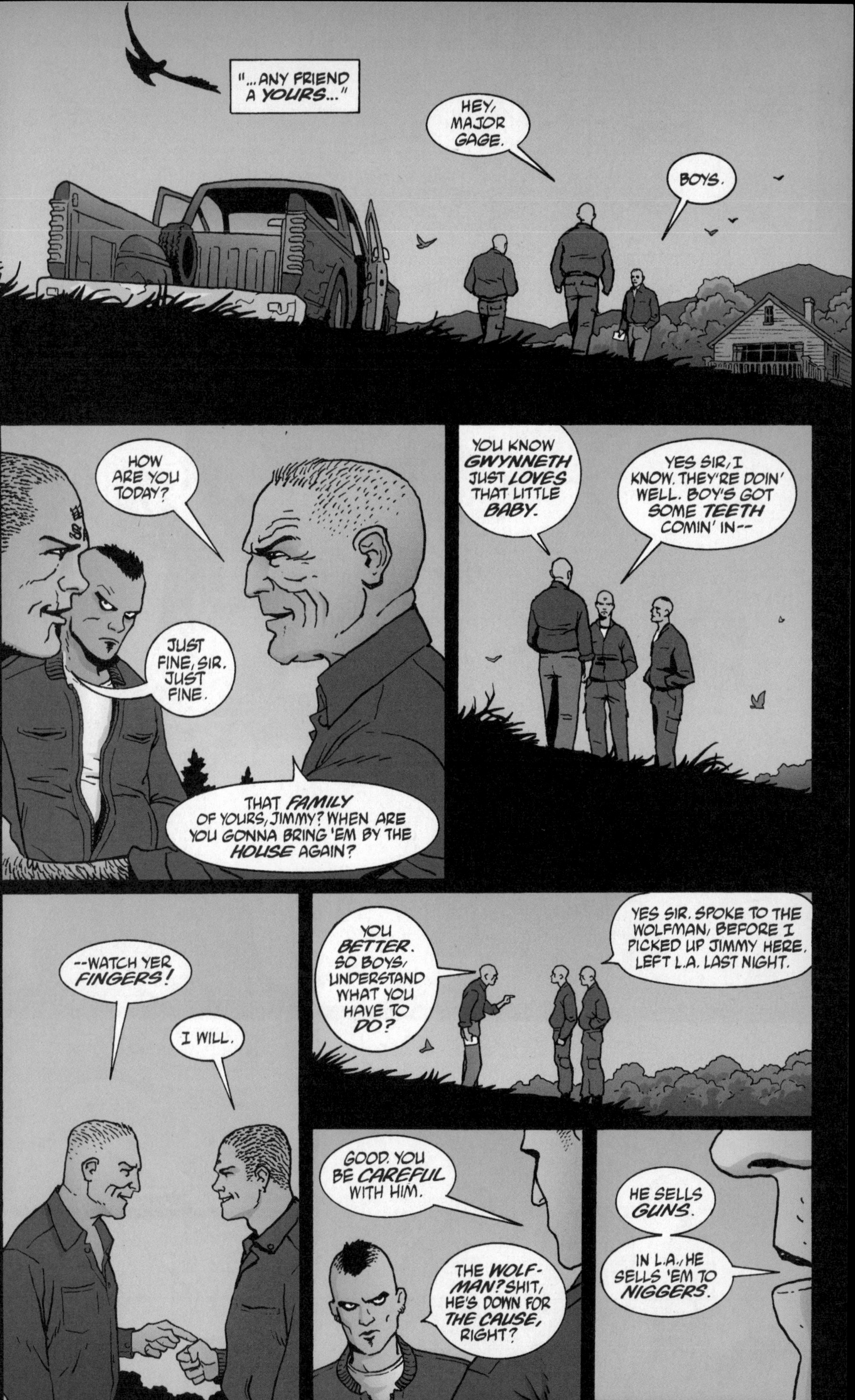
"...ANY FRIEND A YOURS..."
HEY, MAJOR GAGE.
BOYS.
HOW ARE YOU TODAY?
JUST FINE, SIR. JUST FINE.
THAT FAMILY OF YOURS, JIMMY? WHEN ARE YOU GONNA BRING 'EM BY THE HOUSE AGAIN?
YOU KNOW GWYNNETH JUST LOVES THAT LITTLE BABY.
YES SIR, I KNOW. THEY'RE DOIN' WELL. BOY'S GOT SOME TEETH COMIN' IN--
--WATCH YER FINGERS!
I WILL.
YOU BETTER. SO BOYS, UNDERSTAND WHAT YOU HAVE TO DO?
YES SIR. SPOKE TO THE WOLFMAN, BEFORE I PICKED UP JIMMY HERE. LEFT L.A. LAST NIGHT.
GOOD. YOU BE CAREFUL WITH HIM.
THE WOLF-MAN? SHIT, HE'S DOWN FOR THE CAUSE, RIGHT?
HE SELLS GUNS.
IN L.A., HE SELLS 'EM TO NIGGERS.

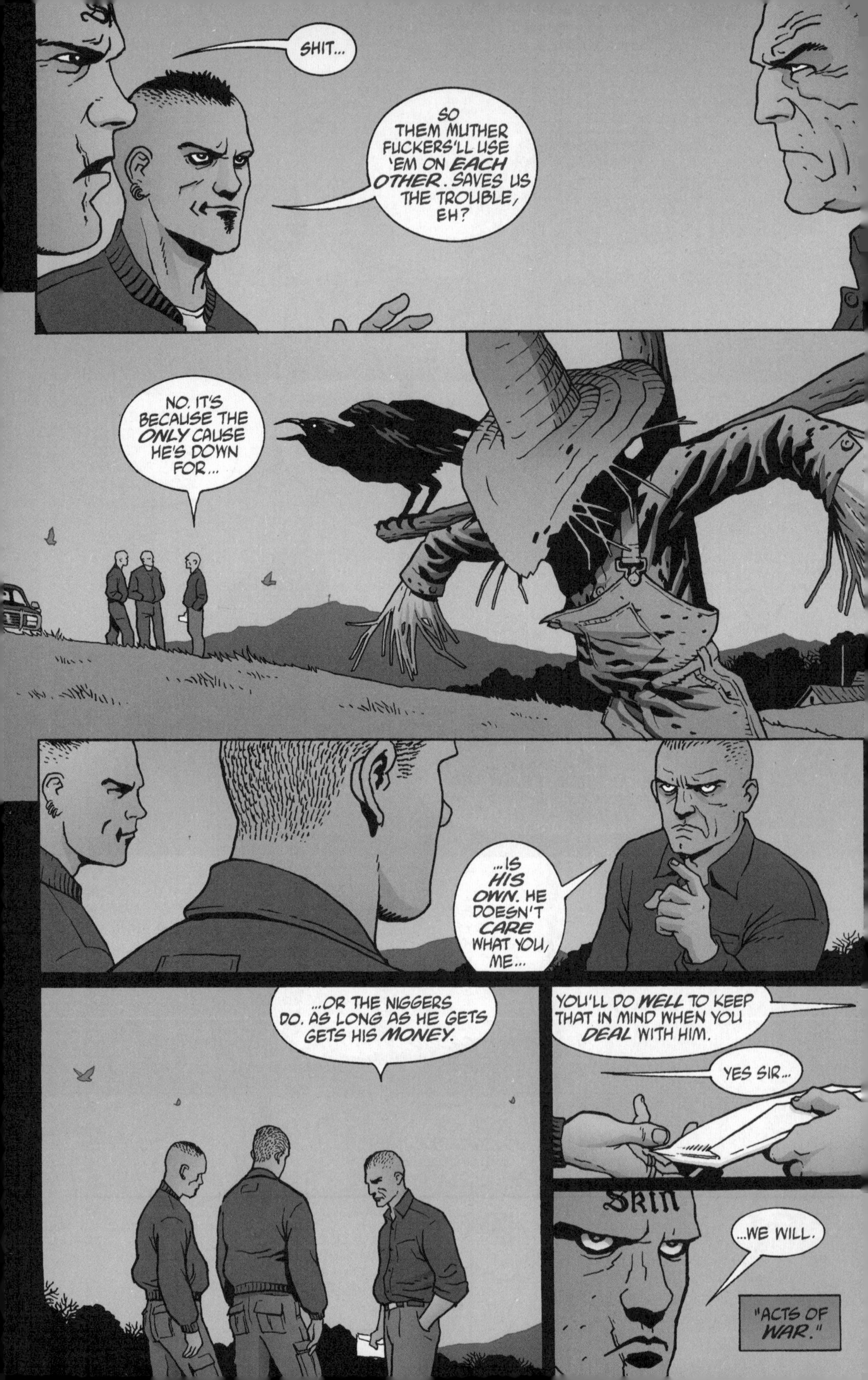
SHIT...
SO THEM MUTHER FUCKERS'LL USE 'EM ON EACH OTHER. SAVES US THE TROUBLE, EH?
NO. IT'S BECAUSE THE ONLY CAUSE HE'S DOWN FOR...
...IS HIS OWN. HE DOESN'T CARE WHAT YOU, ME...
...OR THE NIGGERS DO. AS LONG AS HE GETS GETS HIS MONEY.
YOU'LL DO WELL TO KEEP THAT IN MIND WHEN YOU DEAL WITH HIM.
YES SIR...
Skin
...WE WILL.
"ACTS OF WAR."

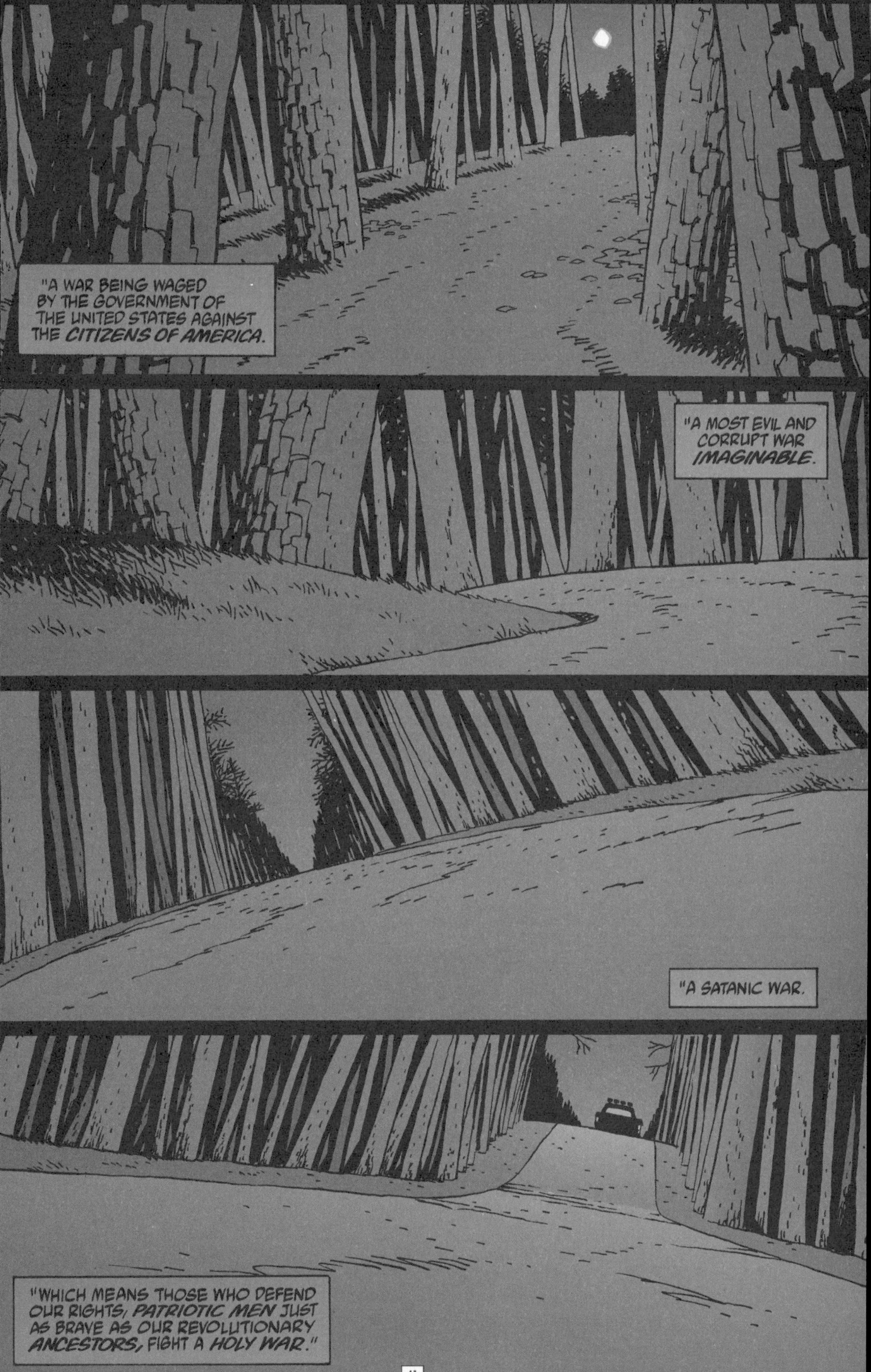
"A WAR BEING WAGED BY THE GOVERNMENT OF THE UNITED STATES AGAINST THE CITIZENS OF AMERICA.
"A MOST EVIL AND CORRUPT WAR IMAGINABLE.
"A SATANIC WAR.
"WHICH MEANS THOSE WHO DEFEND OUR RIGHTS, PATRIOTIC MEN JUST AS BRAVE AS OUR REVOLUTIONARY ANCESTORS, FIGHT A HOLY WAR."

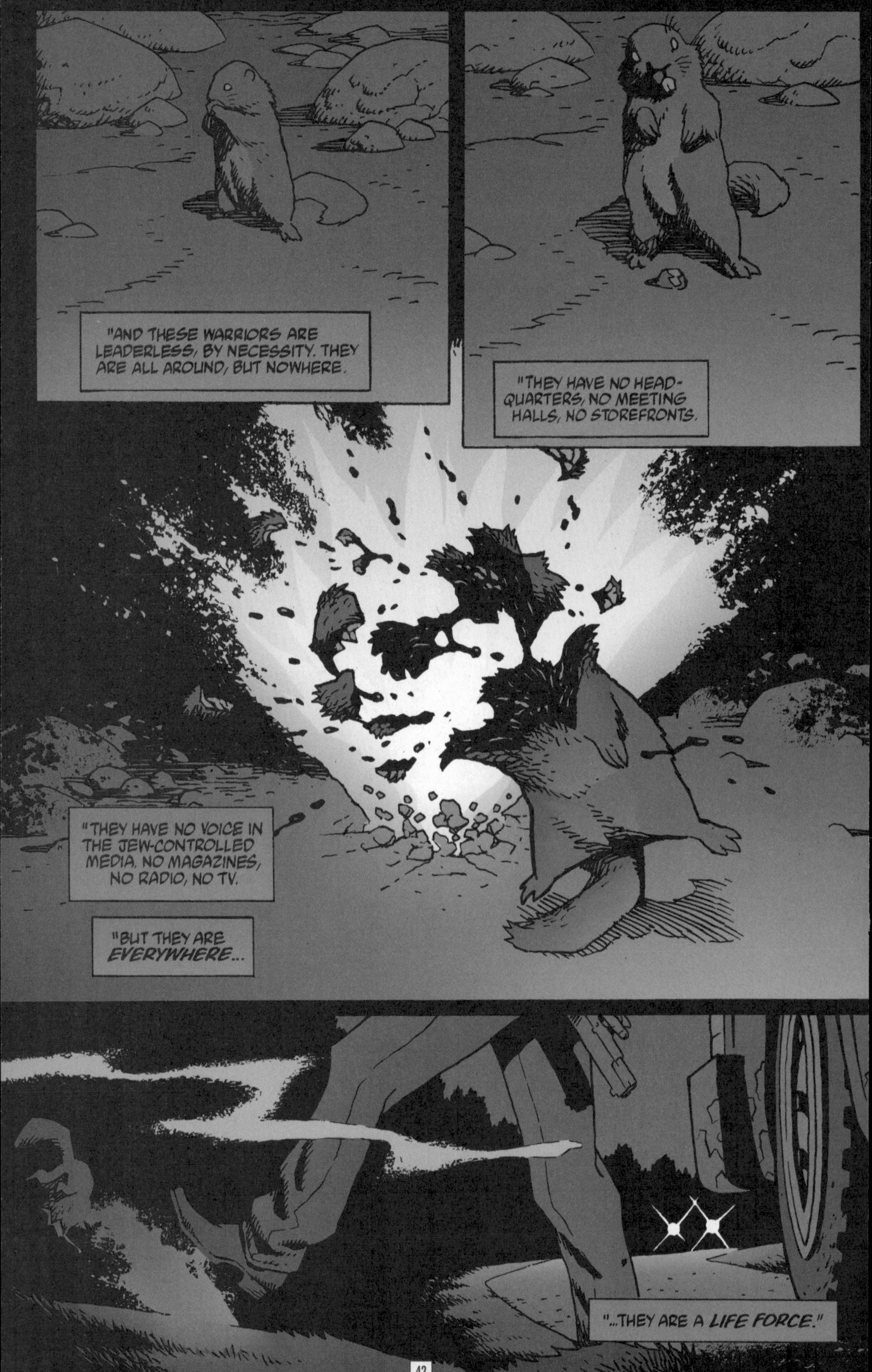
"AND THESE WARRIORS ARE LEADERLESS, BY NECESSITY. THEY ARE ALL AROUND, BUT NOWHERE.
"THEY HAVE NO HEAD-QUARTERS, NO MEETING HALLS, NO STOREFRONTS.
"THEY HAVE NO VOICE IN THE JEW-CONTROLLED MEDIA, NO MAGAZINES, NO RADIO, NO TV.
"BUT THEY ARE *EVERYWHERE*...
"...THEY ARE A *LIFE FORCE*."

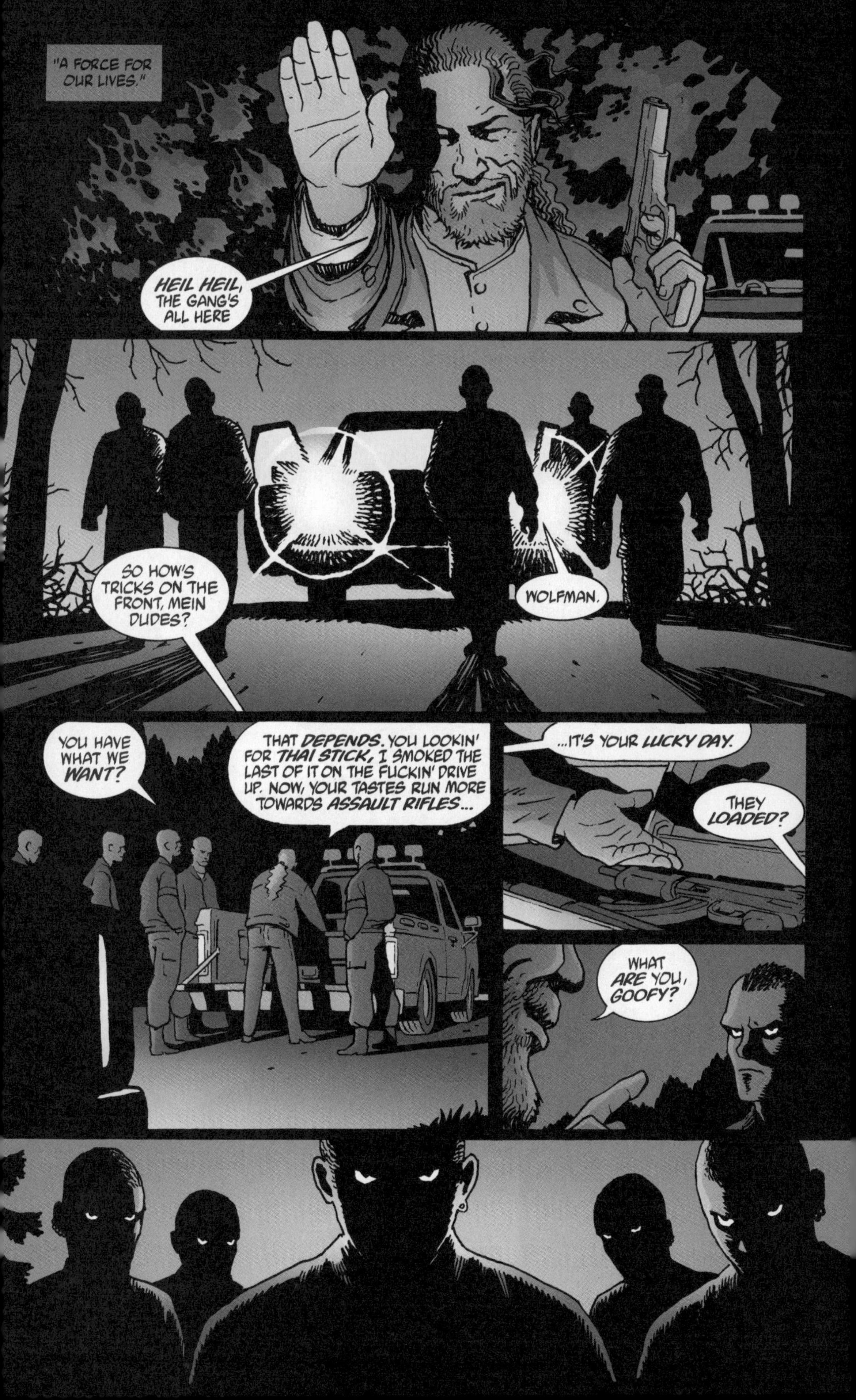
"A FORCE FOR OUR LIVES."
HEIL HEIL, THE GANG'S ALL HERE
SO HOW'S TRICKS ON THE FRONT, MEIN DUDES?
WOLFMAN.
YOU HAVE WHAT WE WANT?
THAT DEPENDS. YOU LOOKIN' FOR THAI STICK, I SMOKED THE LAST OF IT ON THE FUCKIN' DRIVE UP. NOW, YOUR TASTES RUN MORE TOWARDS ASSAULT RIFLES...
...IT'S YOUR LUCKY DAY.
THEY LOADED?
WHAT ARE YOU, GOOFY?

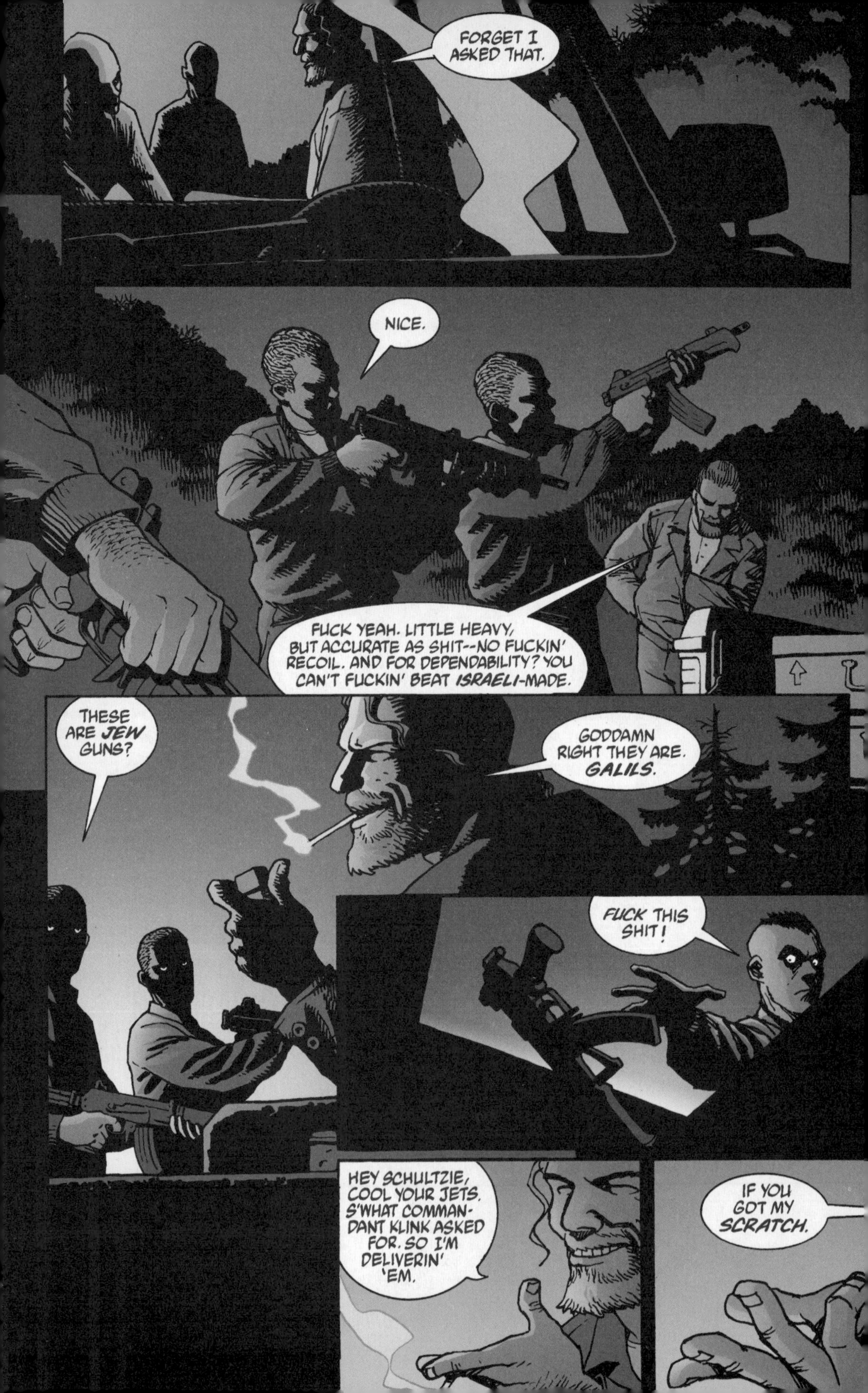
FORGET I ASKED THAT.
NICE.
FUCK YEAH. LITTLE HEAVY, BUT ACCURATE AS SHIT--NO FUCKIN' RECOIL. AND FOR DEPENDABILITY? YOU CAN'T FUCKIN' BEAT ISRAELI-MADE.
THESE ARE JEW GUNS?
GODDAMN RIGHT THEY ARE. GALILS.
FUCK THIS SHIT!
HEY SCHULTZIE, COOL YOUR JETS. S'WHAT COMMAN-DANT KLINK ASKED FOR. SO I'M DELIVERIN' 'EM.
IF YOU GOT MY SCRATCH.

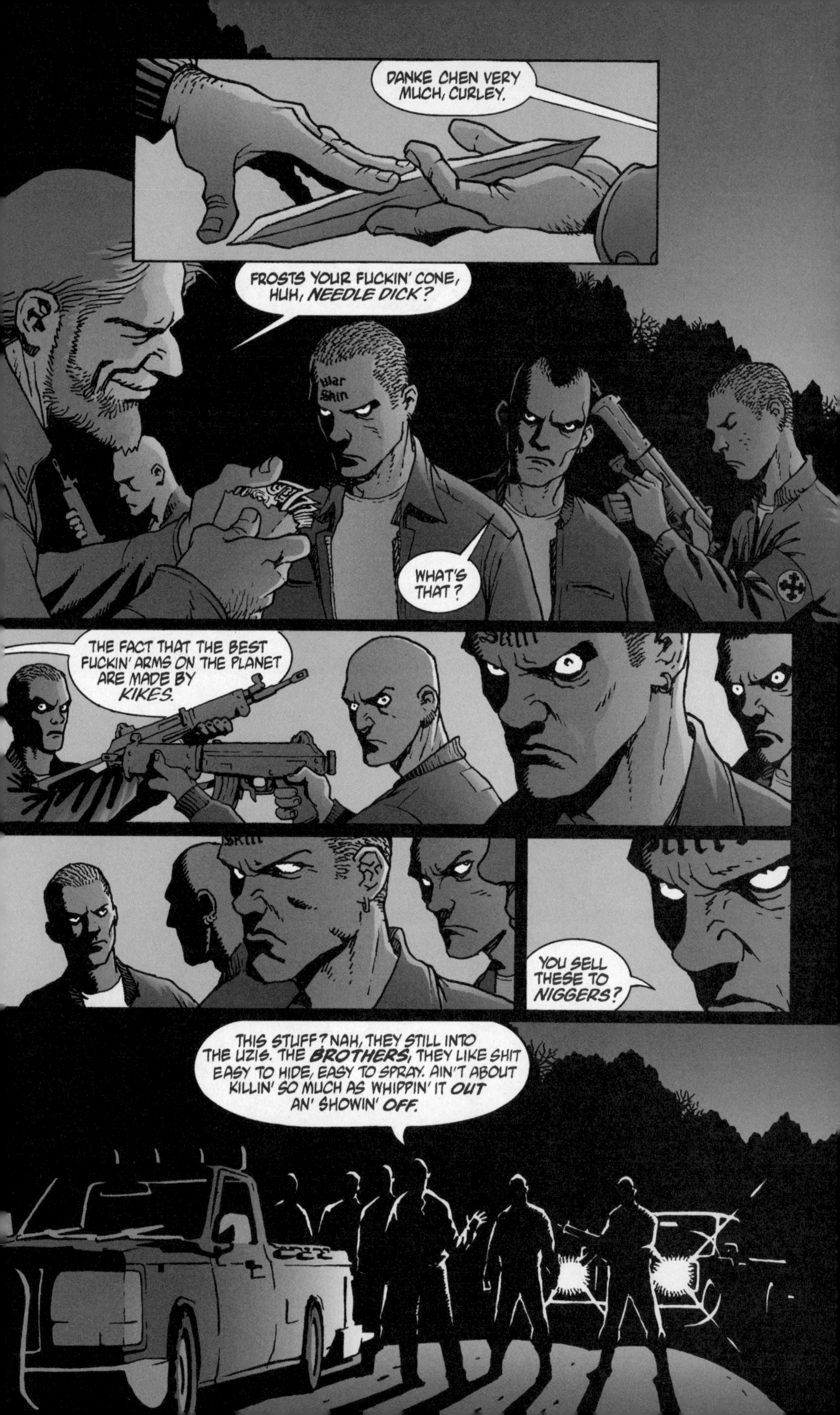
DANKE CHEN VERY MUCH, CURLEY.
FROSTS YOUR FUCKIN' CONE, HUH, NEEDLE DICK?
WHAT'S THAT?
THE FACT THAT THE BEST FUCKIN' ARMS ON THE PLANET ARE MADE BY KIKES.
YOU SELL THESE TO NIGGERS?
THIS STUFF? NAH, THEY STILL INTO THE UZIS. THE BROTHERS, THEY LIKE SHIT EASY TO HIDE, EASY TO SPRAY. AIN'T ABOUT KILLIN' SO MUCH AS WHIPPIN' IT OUT AN' SHOWIN' OFF.

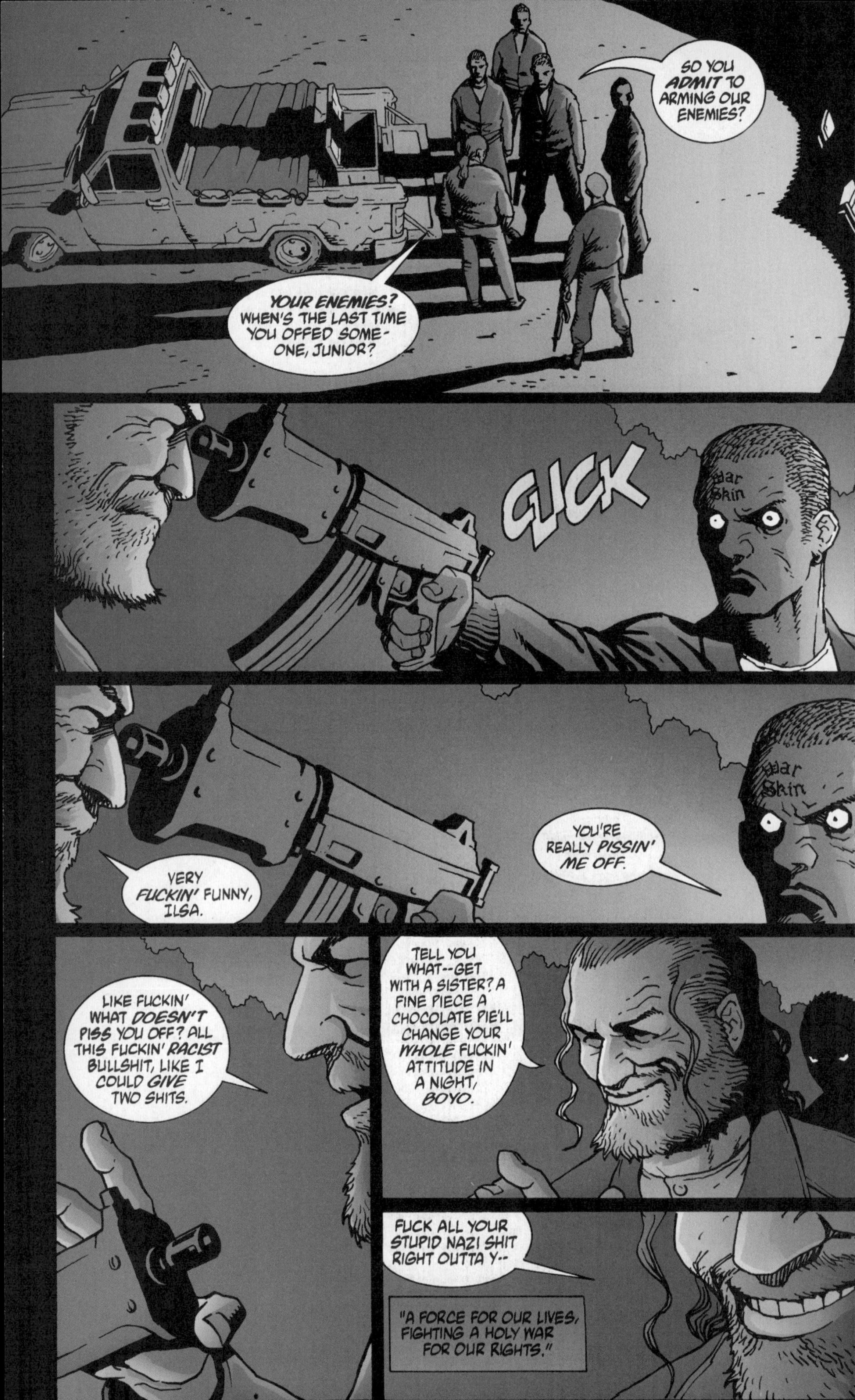
SO YOU ADMIT TO ARMING OUR ENEMIES?
YOUR ENEMIES? WHEN'S THE LAST TIME YOU OFFED SOME-ONE, JUNIOR?
CLICK
War Skin
War Skin
VERY FUCKIN' FUNNY, ILSA.
YOU'RE REALLY PISSIN' ME OFF.
LIKE FUCKIN' WHAT DOESN'T PISS YOU OFF? ALL THIS FUCKIN' RACIST BULLSHIT, LIKE I COULD GIVE TWO SHITS.
TELL YOU WHAT--GET WITH A SISTER? A FINE PIECE A CHOCOLATE PIE'LL CHANGE YOUR WHOLE FUCKIN' ATTITUDE IN A NIGHT, BOYO.
FUCK ALL YOUR STUPID NAZI SHIT RIGHT OUTTA Y--
"A FORCE FOR OUR LIVES, FIGHTING A HOLY WAR FOR OUR RIGHTS."

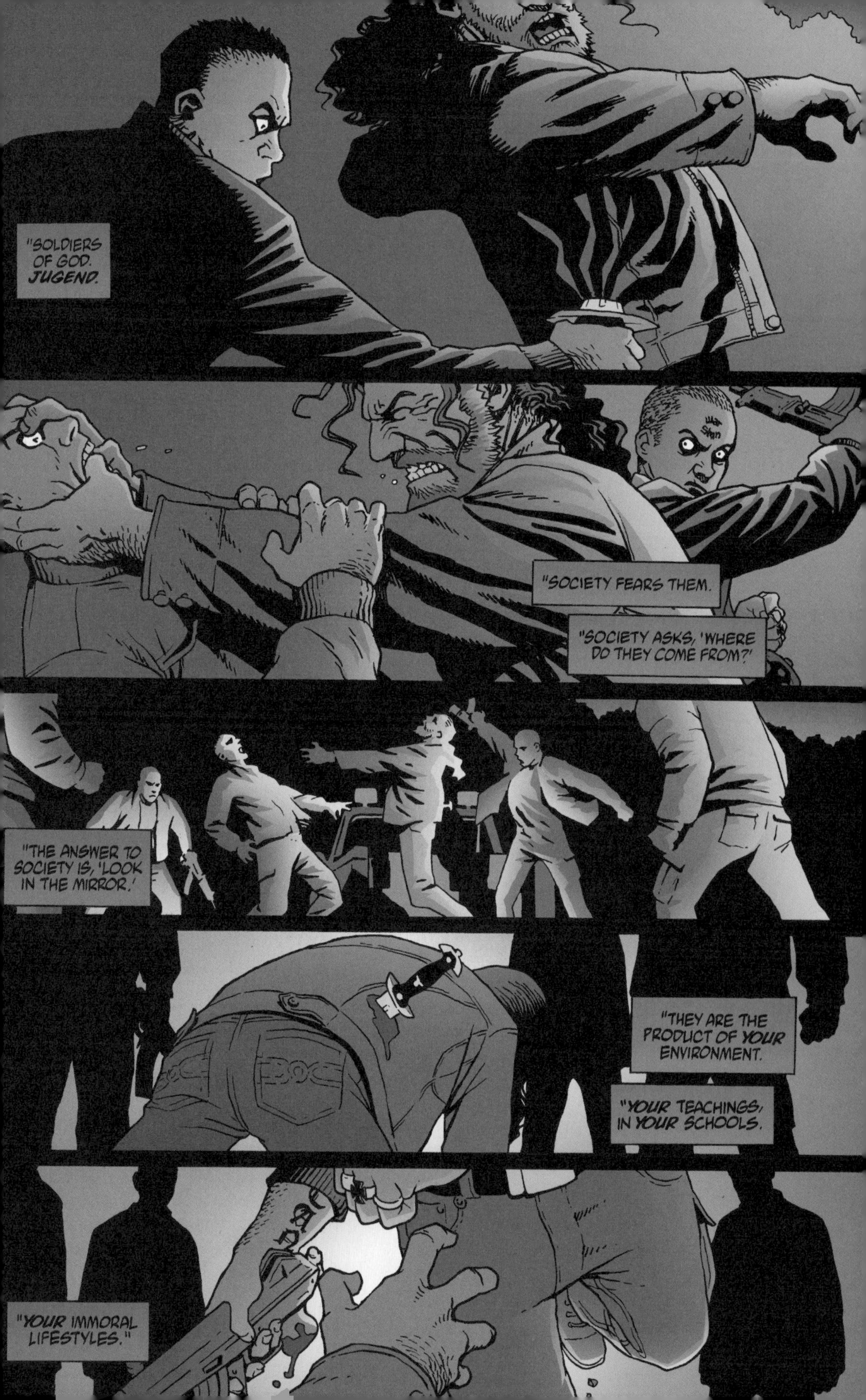
"SOLDIERS OF GOD. JUGEND.
"SOCIETY FEARS THEM.
"SOCIETY ASKS, 'WHERE DO THEY COME FROM?'
"THE ANSWER TO SOCIETY IS, 'LOOK IN THE MIRROR.'
"THEY ARE THE PRODUCT OF YOUR ENVIRONMENT.
"YOUR TEACHINGS, IN YOUR SCHOOLS.
"YOUR IMMORAL LIFESTYLES."

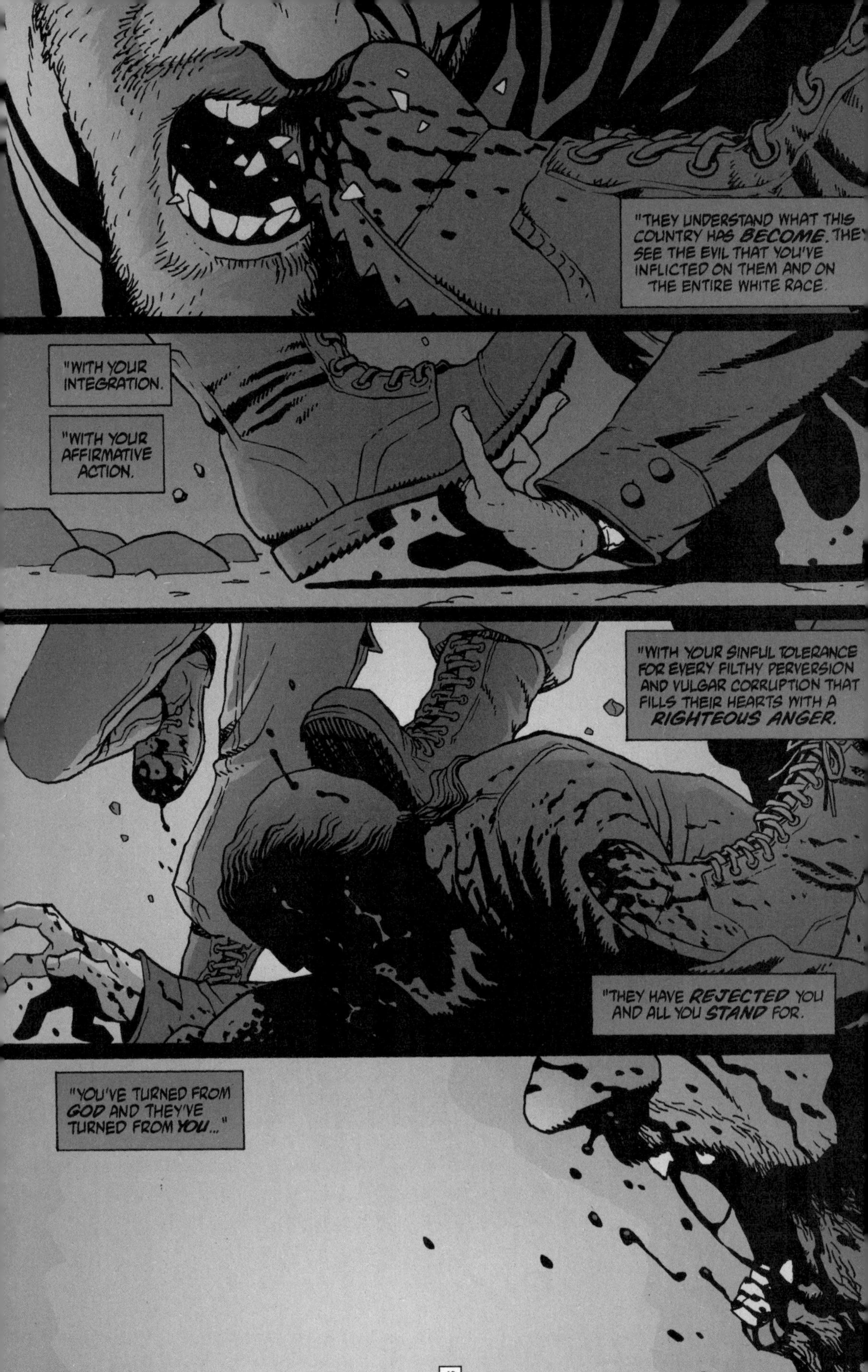
"THEY UNDERSTAND WHAT THIS COUNTRY HAS BECOME. THEY SEE THE EVIL THAT YOU'VE INFLICTED ON THEM AND ON THE ENTIRE WHITE RACE.
"WITH YOUR INTEGRATION.
"WITH YOUR AFFIRMATIVE ACTION.
"WITH YOUR SINFUL TOLERANCE FOR EVERY FILTHY PERVERSION AND VULGAR CORRUPTION THAT FILLS THEIR HEARTS WITH A RIGHTEOUS ANGER.
"THEY HAVE REJECTED YOU AND ALL YOU STAND FOR.
"YOU'VE TURNED FROM GOD AND THEY'VE TURNED FROM YOU..."

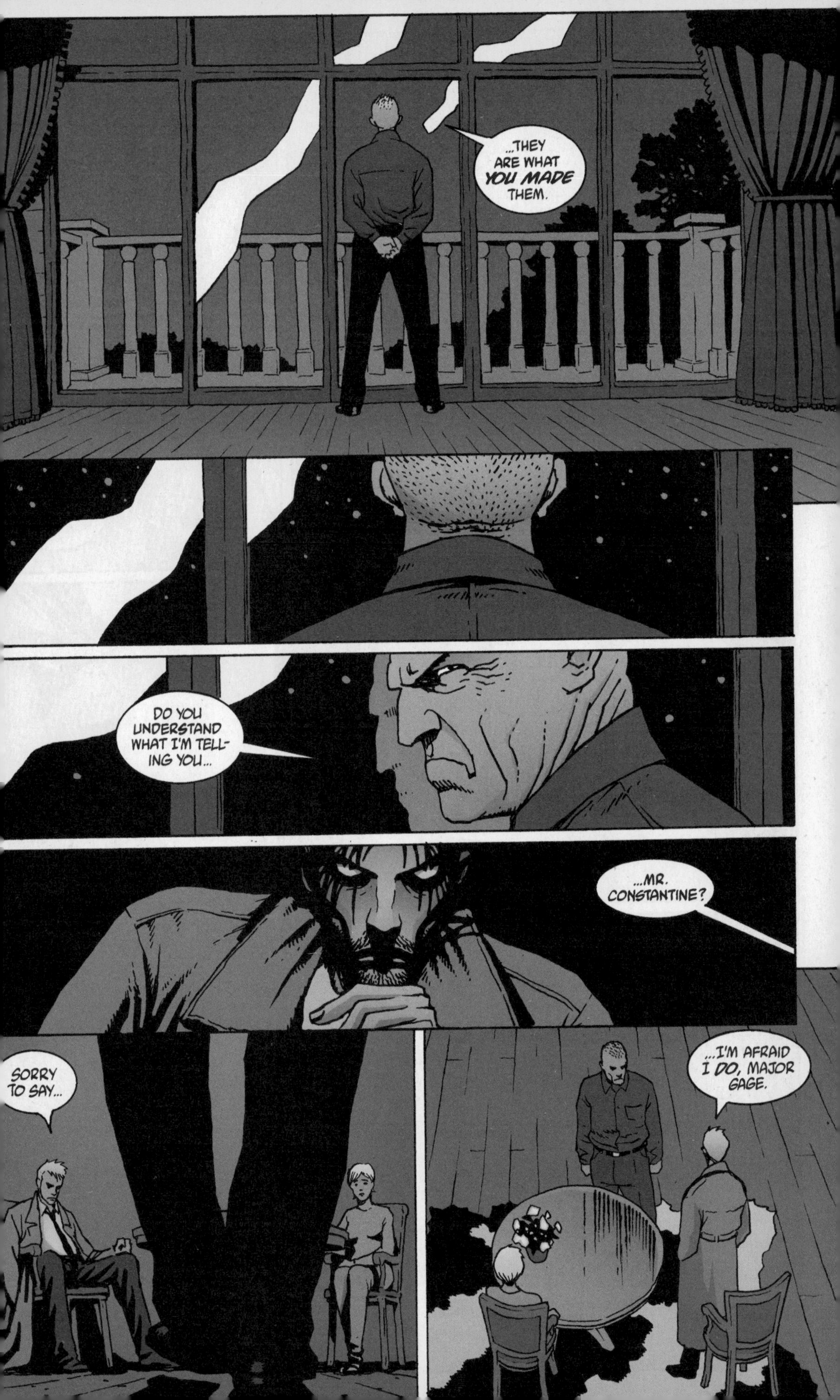
...THEY ARE WHAT YOU MADE THEM.
DO YOU UNDERSTAND WHAT I'M TELL-ING YOU...
...MR. CONSTANTINE?
SORRY TO SAY...
...I'M AFRAID I DO, MAJOR GAGE.

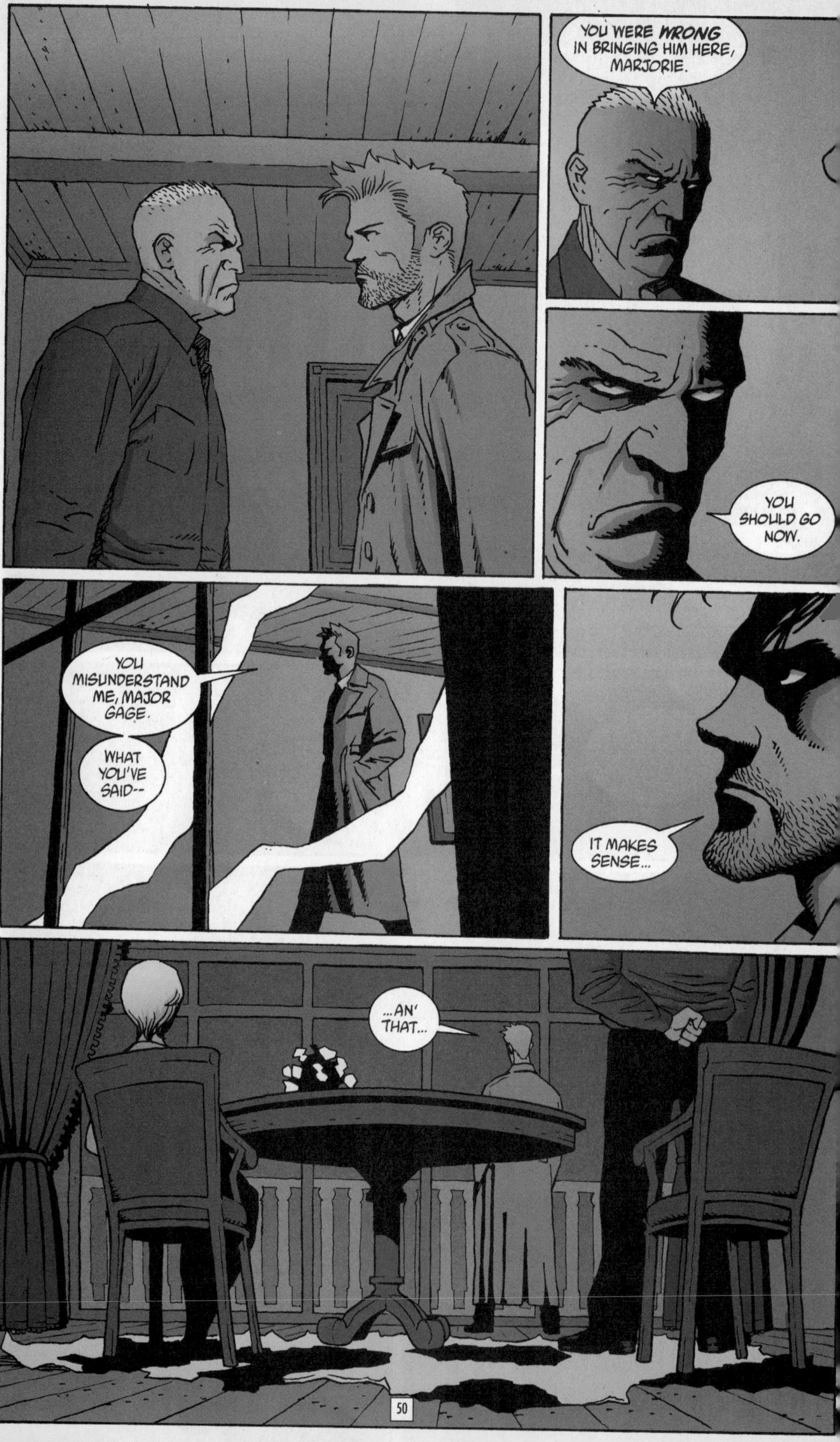
YOU WERE WRONG IN BRINGING HIM HERE, MARJORIE.
YOU SHOULD GO NOW.
YOU MISUNDERSTAND ME, MAJOR GAGE.
WHAT YOU'VE SAID--
IT MAKES SENSE...
...AN' THAT...

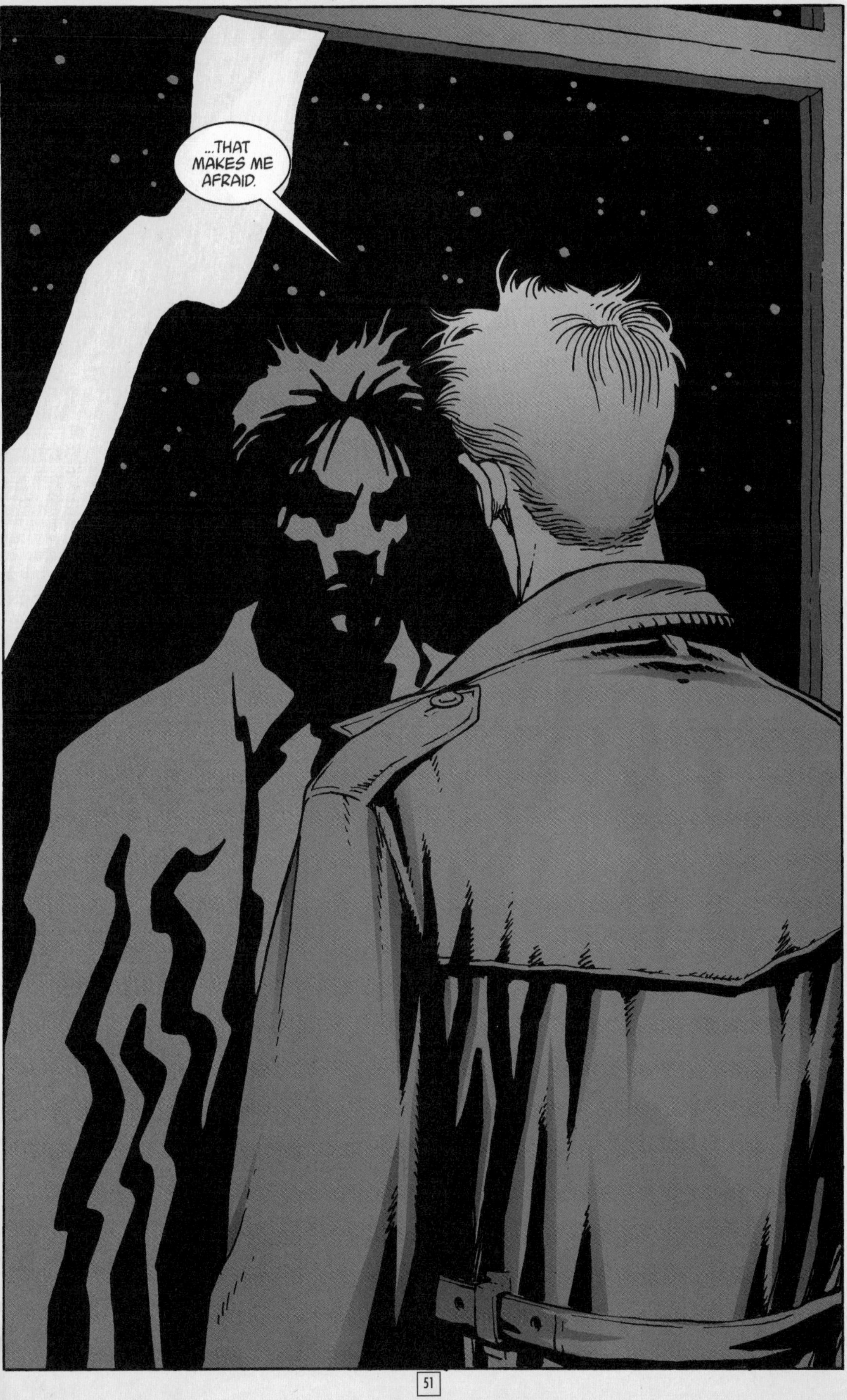
...THAT MAKES ME AFRAID.

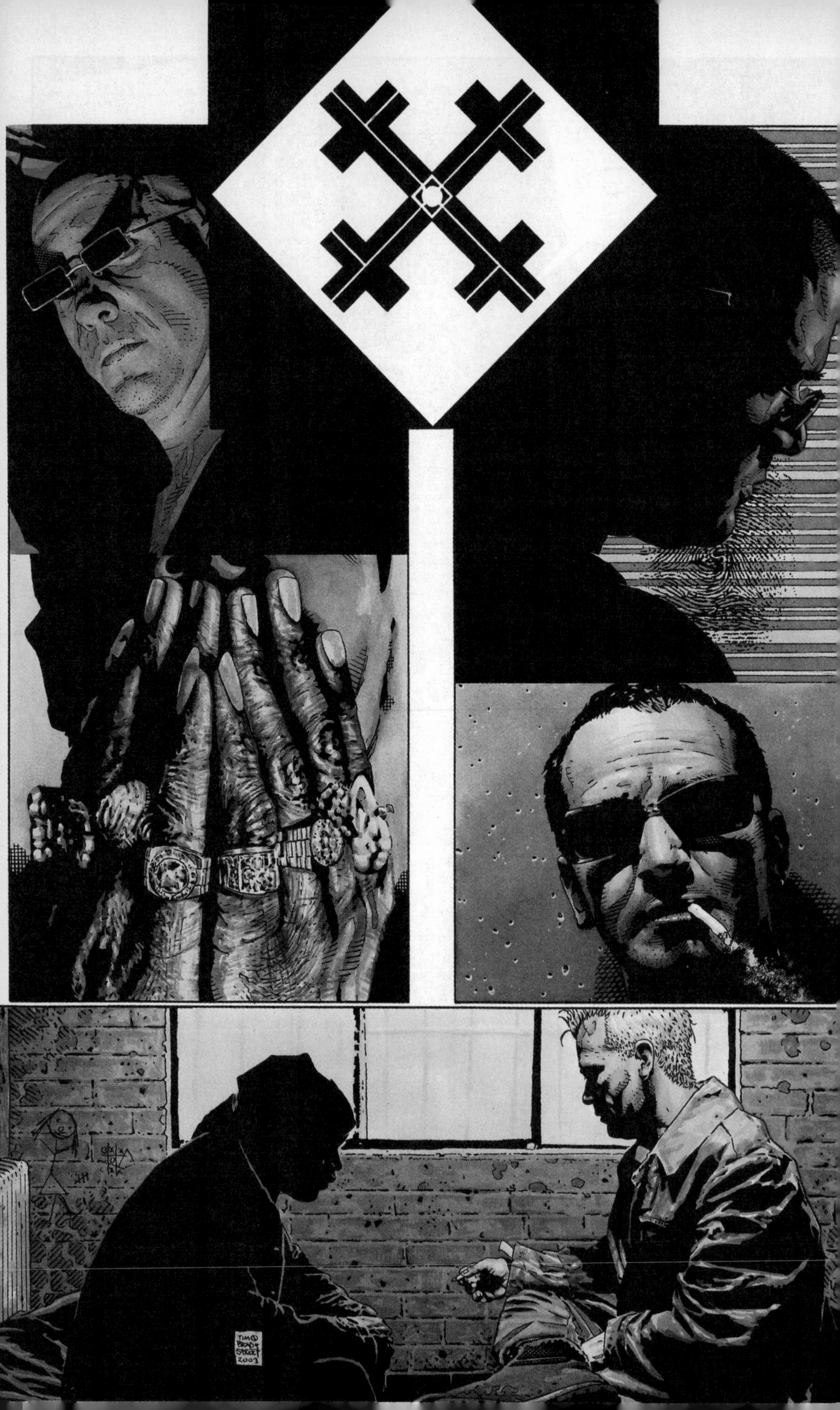
TIM © BRAD STREET 2003

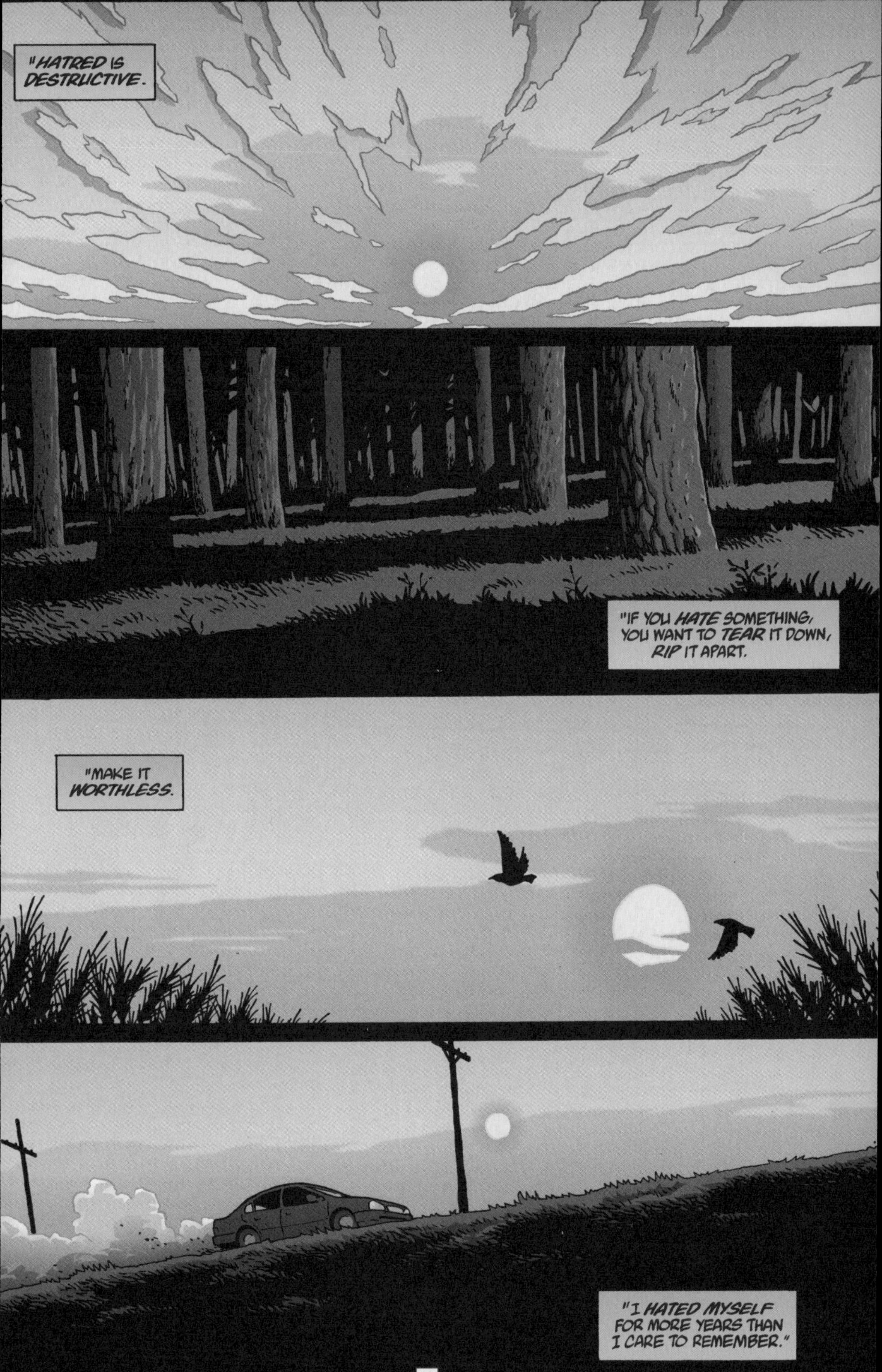
"HATRED IS DESTRUCTIVE.
"IF YOU HATE SOMETHING, YOU WANT TO TEAR IT DOWN, RIP IT APART.
"MAKE IT WORTHLESS.
"I HATED MYSELF FOR MORE YEARS THAN I CARE TO REMEMBER."

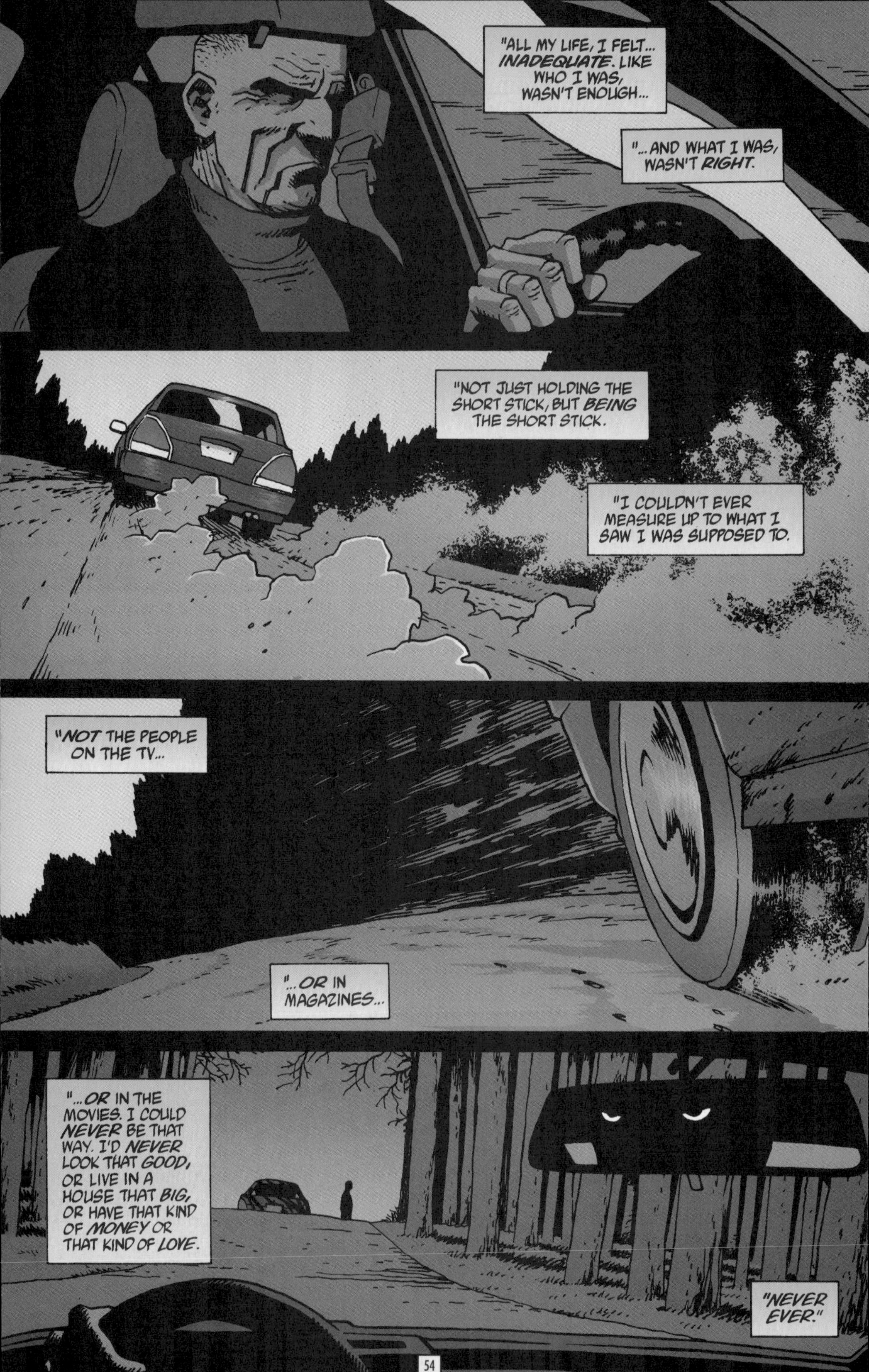
"ALL MY LIFE, I FELT... INADEQUATE. LIKE WHO I WAS, WASN'T ENOUGH...
"...AND WHAT I WAS, WASN'T RIGHT.
"NOT JUST HOLDING THE SHORT STICK, BUT BEING THE SHORT STICK.
"I COULDN'T EVER MEASURE UP TO WHAT I SAW I WAS SUPPOSED TO.
"NOT THE PEOPLE ON THE TV...
"...OR IN MAGAZINES...
"...OR IN THE MOVIES. I COULD NEVER BE THAT WAY. I'D NEVER LOOK THAT GOOD, OR LIVE IN A HOUSE THAT BIG, OR HAVE THAT KIND OF MONEY OR THAT KIND OF LOVE.
"NEVER EVER."

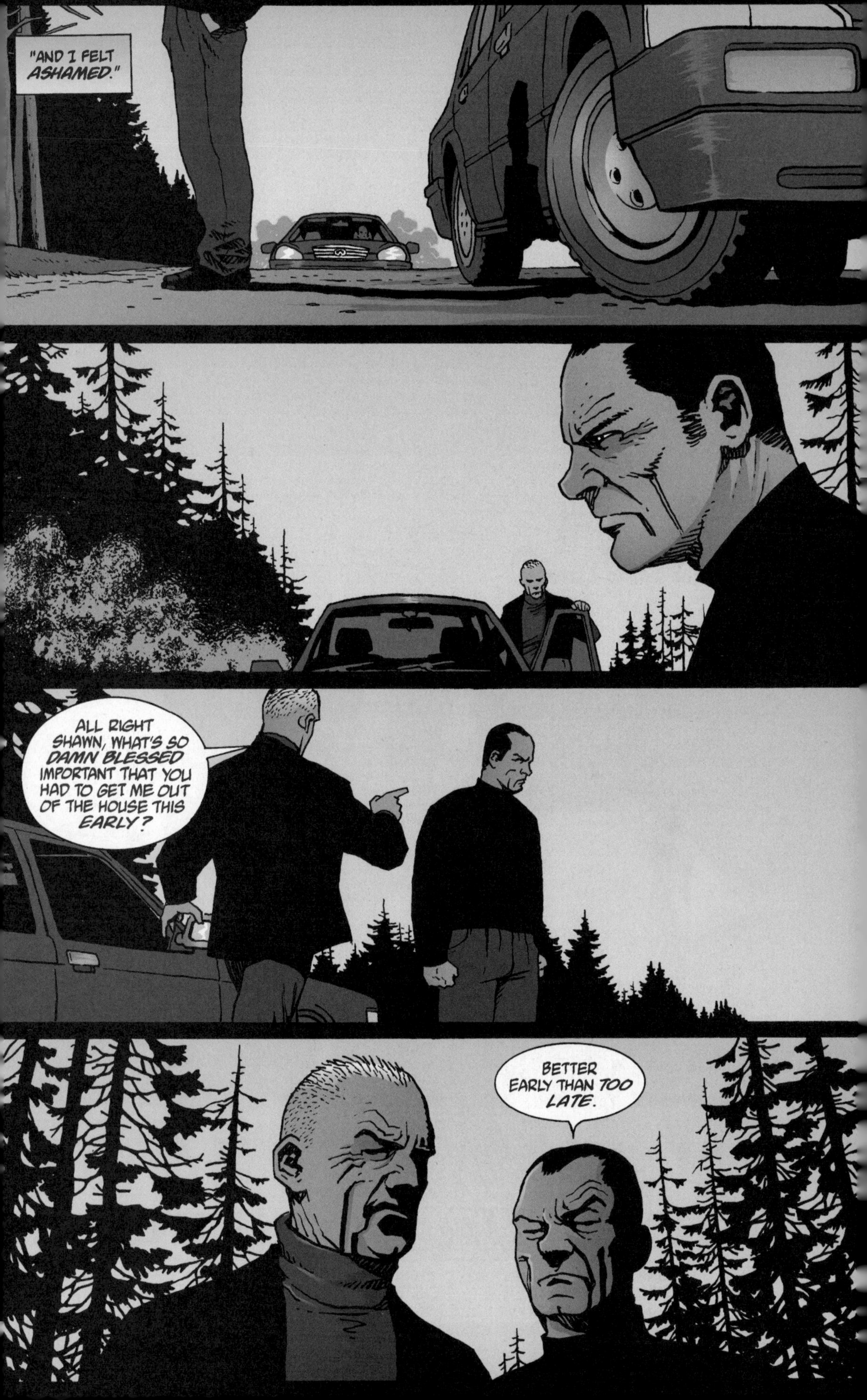
"AND I FELT ASHAMED."
ALL RIGHT SHAWN, WHAT'S SO DAMN BLESSED IMPORTANT THAT YOU HAD TO GET ME OUT OF THE HOUSE THIS EARLY?
BETTER EARLY THAN TOO LATE.

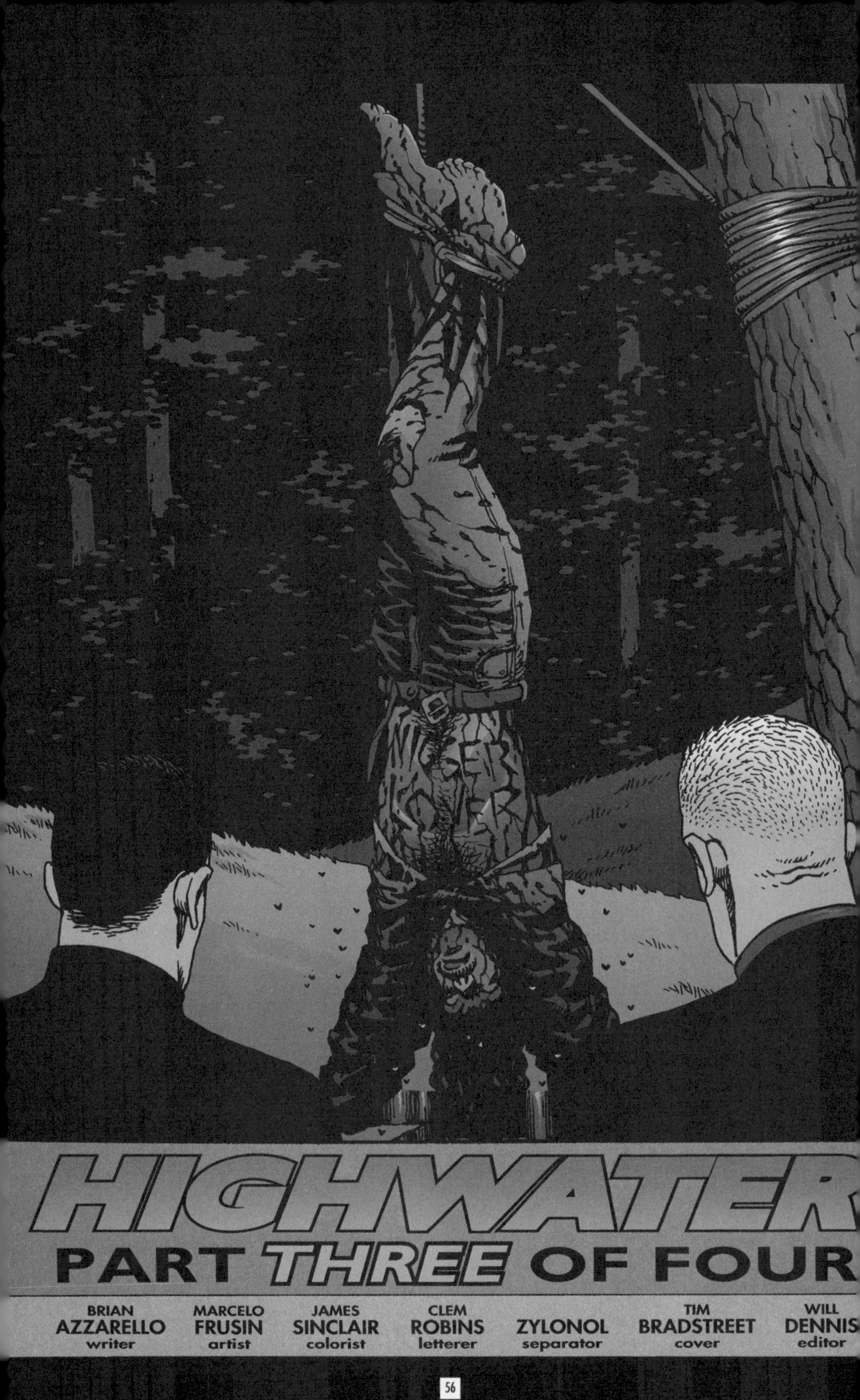

HIGHWATER
PART THREE OF FOUR
BRIAN AZZARELLO writer
MARCELO FRUSIN artist
JAMES SINCLAIR colorist
CLEM ROBINS letterer
ZYLONOL separator
TIM BRADSTREET cover
WILL DENNIS editor

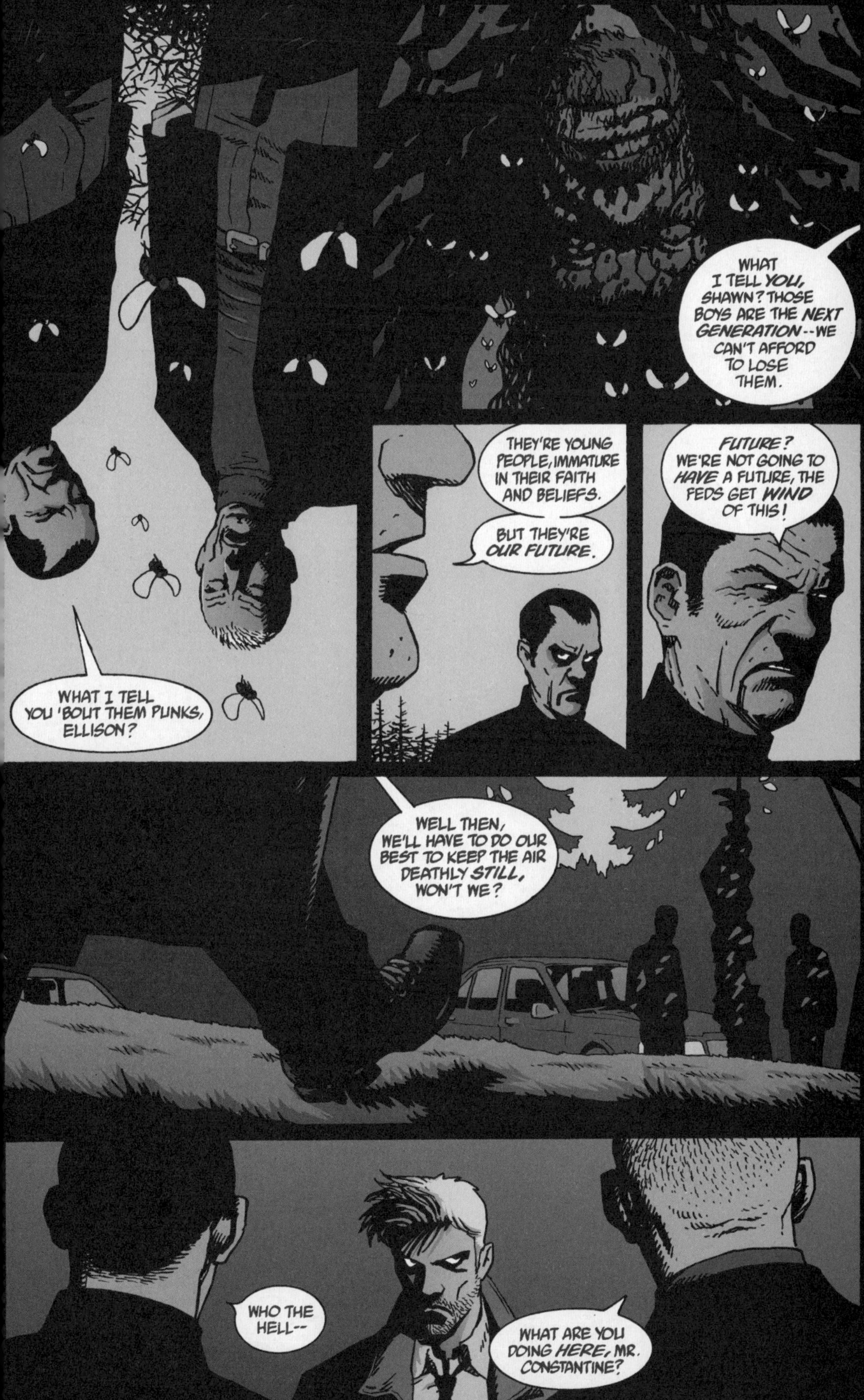

WHAT I TELL YOU, SHAWN? THOSE BOYS ARE THE NEXT GENERATION--WE CAN'T AFFORD TO LOSE THEM.
WHAT I TELL YOU 'BOUT THEM PUNKS, ELLISON?
THEY'RE YOUNG PEOPLE, IMMATURE IN THEIR FAITH AND BELIEFS.
BUT THEY'RE OUR FUTURE.
FUTURE? WE'RE NOT GOING TO HAVE A FUTURE, THE FEDS GET WIND OF THIS!
WELL THEN, WE'LL HAVE TO DO OUR BEST TO KEEP THE AIR DEATHLY STILL, WON'T WE?
WHO THE HELL--
WHAT ARE YOU DOING HERE, MR. CONSTANTINE?

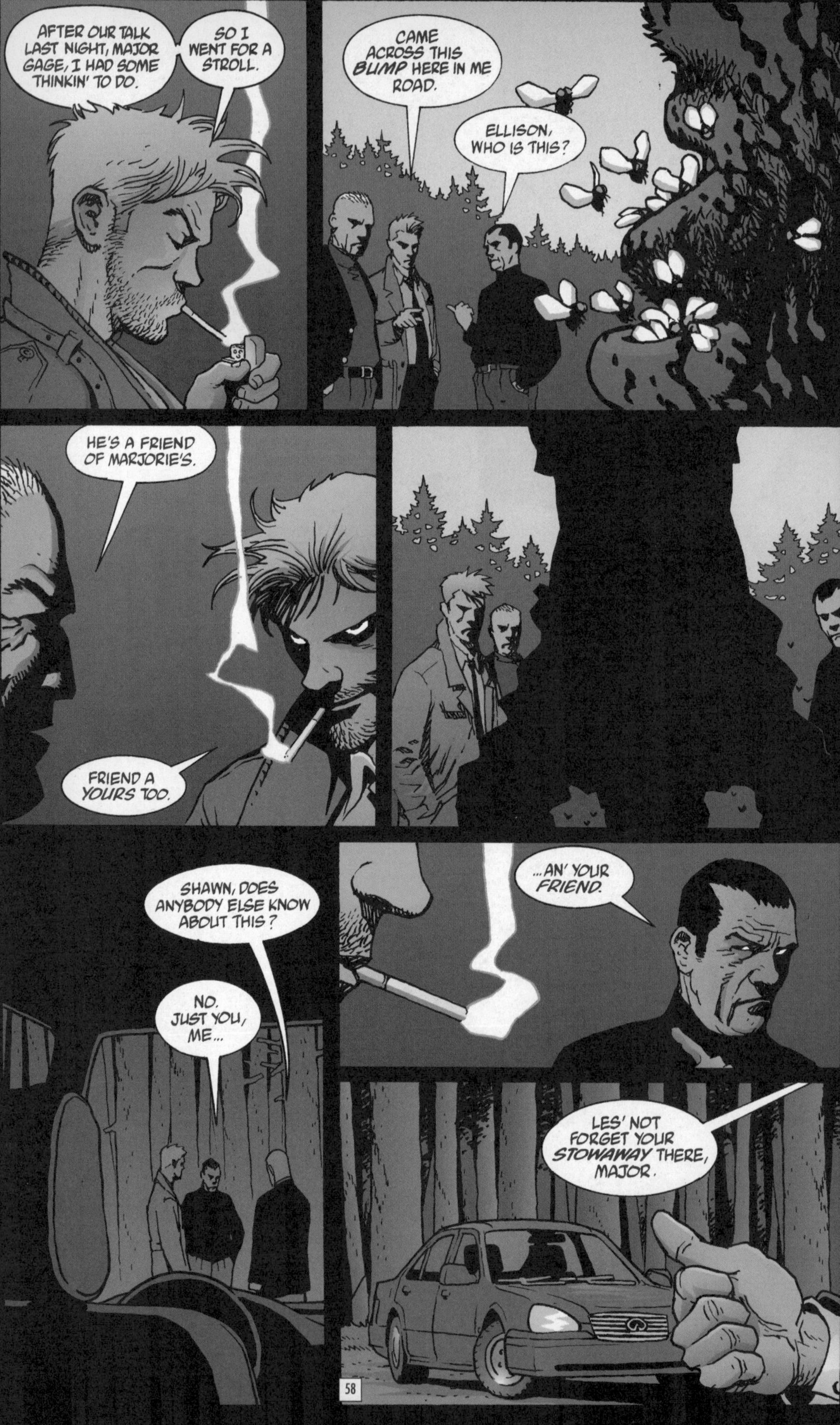
AFTER OUR TALK LAST NIGHT, MAJOR GAGE, I HAD SOME THINKIN' TO DO.
SO I WENT FOR A STROLL.
CAME ACROSS THIS BUMP HERE IN ME ROAD.
ELLISON, WHO IS THIS?
HE'S A FRIEND OF MARJORIE'S.
FRIEND A YOURS TOO.
SHAWN, DOES ANYBODY ELSE KNOW ABOUT THIS?
NO. JUST YOU, ME...
...AN' YOUR FRIEND.
LES' NOT FORGET YOUR STOWAWAY THERE, MAJOR.

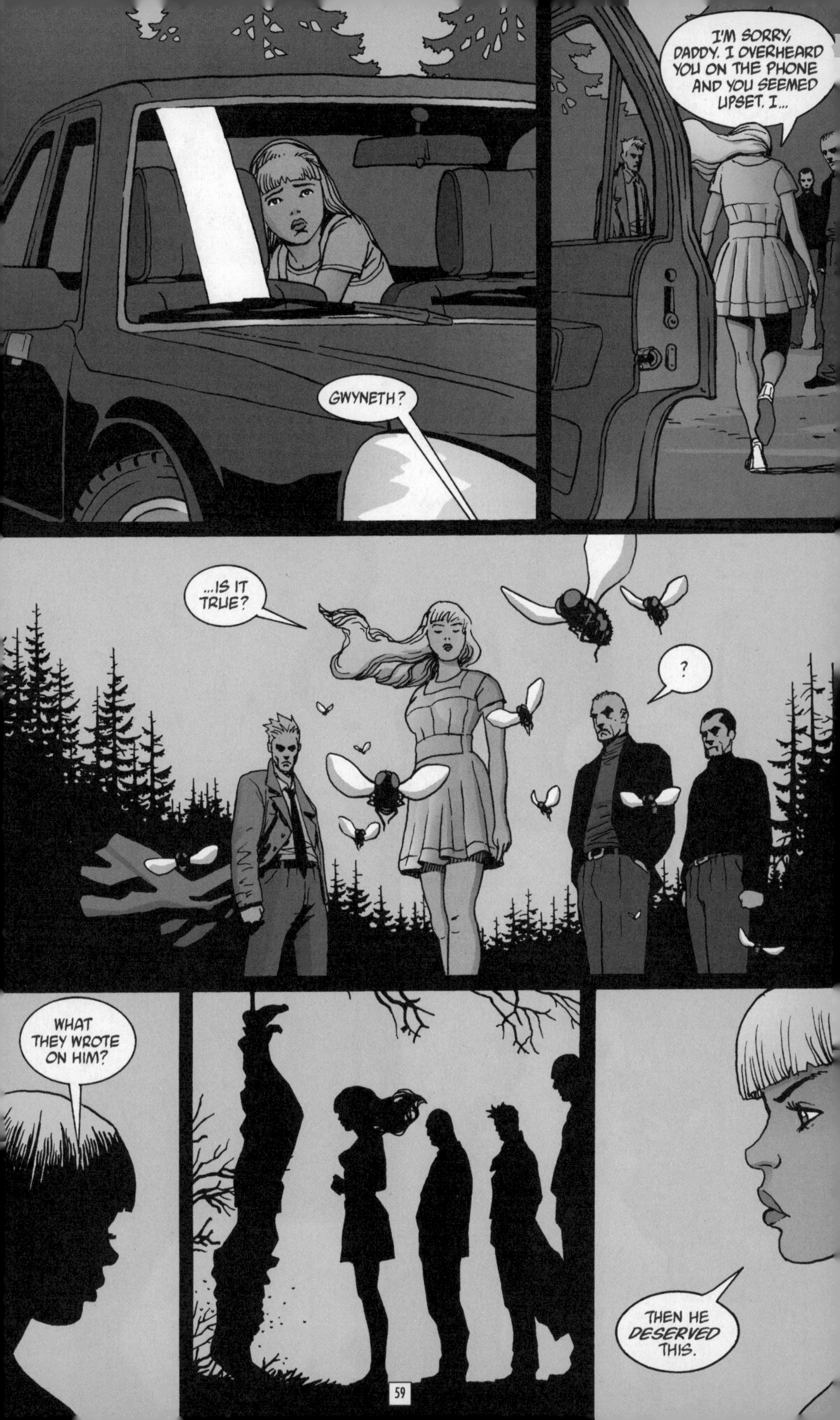
GWYNETH?
I'M SORRY, DADDY. I OVERHEARD YOU ON THE PHONE AND YOU SEEMED UPSET. I...
...IS IT TRUE?
?
WHAT THEY WROTE ON HIM?
THEN HE DESERVED THIS.

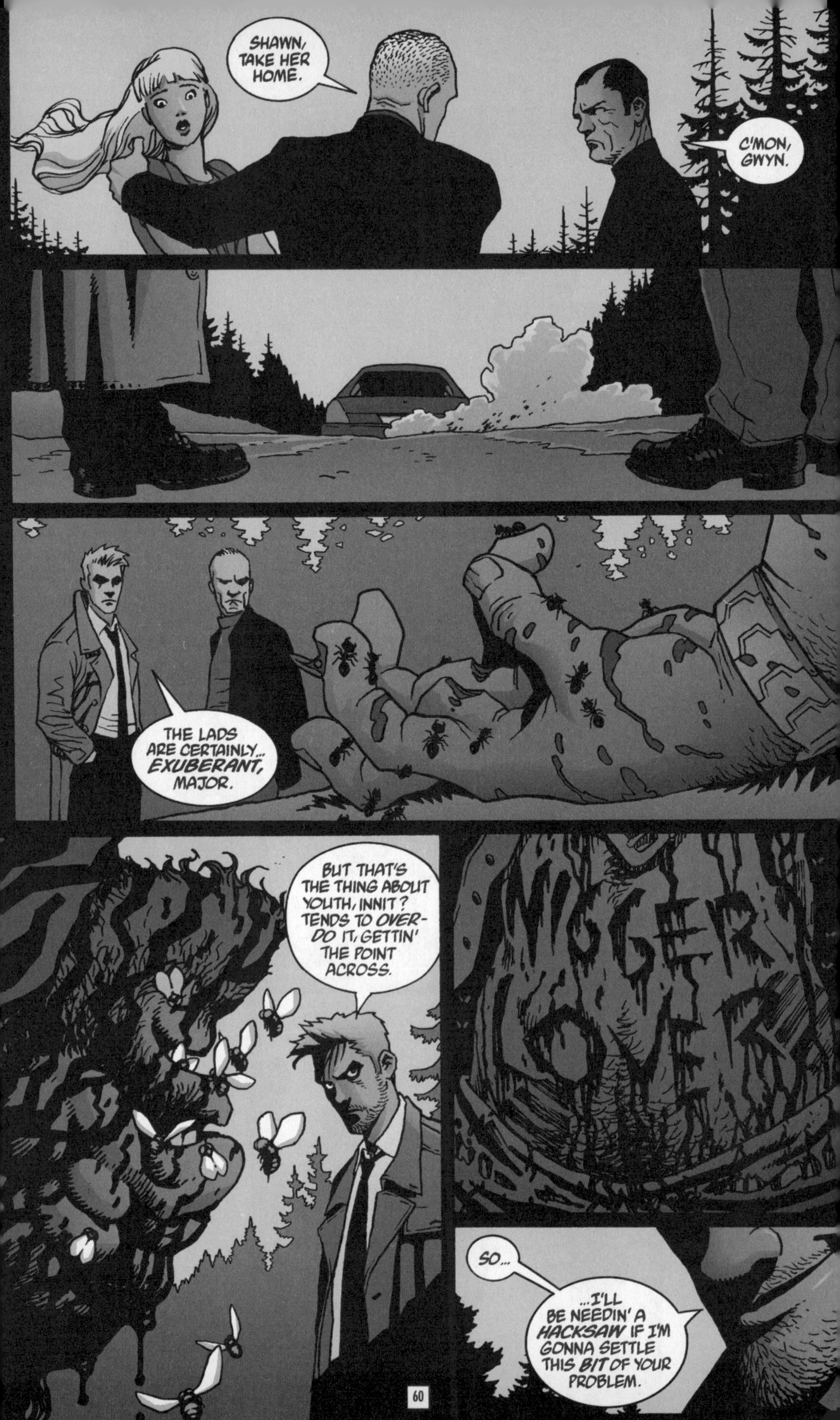
SHAWN, TAKE HER HOME.
C'MON, GWYN.
THE LADS ARE CERTAINLY... EXUBERANT, MAJOR.
BUT THAT'S THE THING ABOUT YOUTH, INNIT? TENDS TO OVER-DO IT, GETTIN' THE POINT ACROSS.
NIGGER LOVER
SO...
...I'LL BE NEEDIN' A HACKSAW IF I'M GONNA SETTLE THIS BIT OF YOUR PROBLEM.

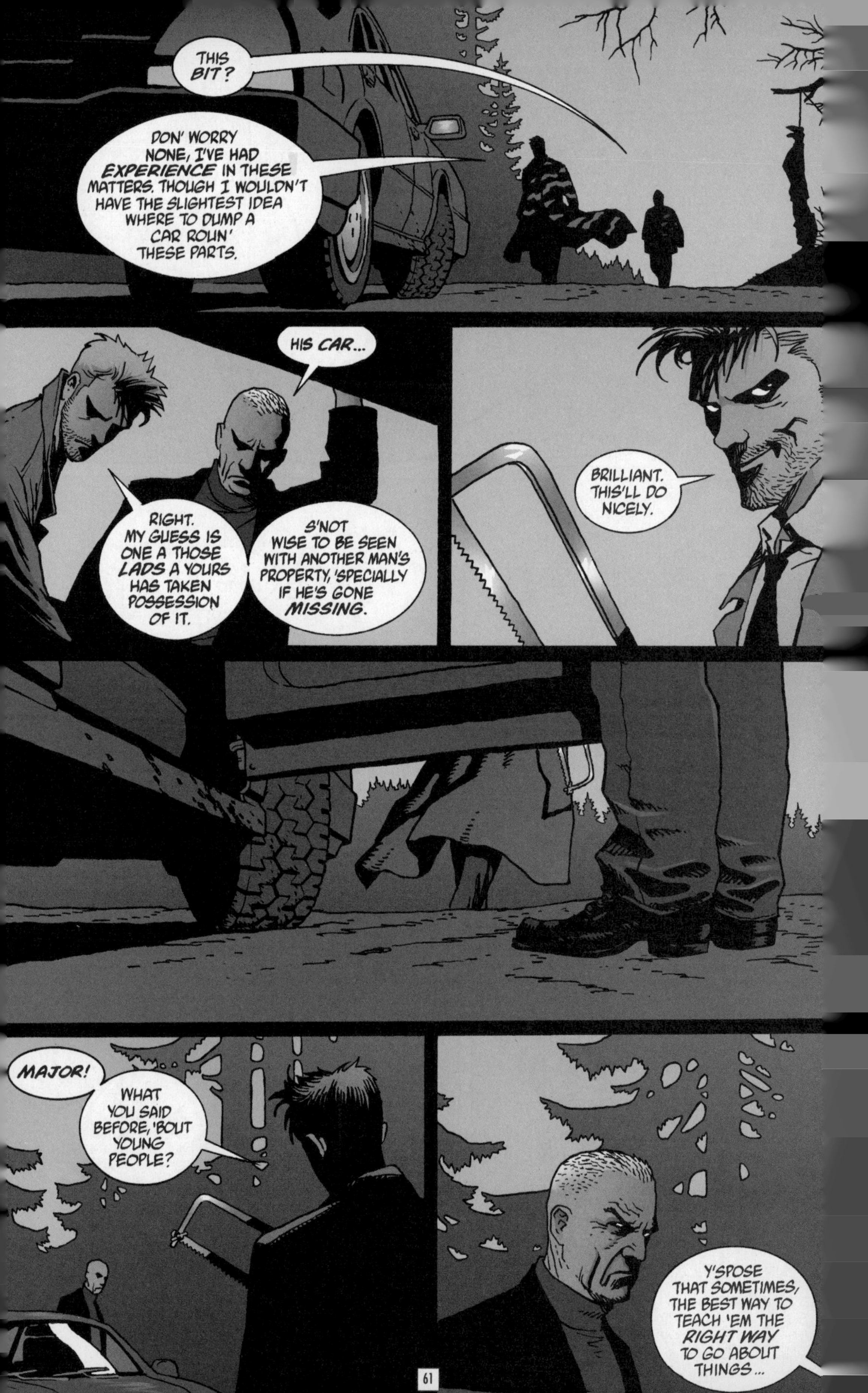
THIS BIT?
DON' WORRY NONE, I'VE HAD EXPERIENCE IN THESE MATTERS. THOUGH I WOULDN'T HAVE THE SLIGHTEST IDEA WHERE TO DUMP A CAR ROUN' THESE PARTS.
HIS CAR...
RIGHT. MY GUESS IS ONE A THOSE LADS A YOURS HAS TAKEN POSSESSION OF IT.
S'NOT WISE TO BE SEEN WITH ANOTHER MAN'S PROPERTY, 'SPECIALLY IF HE'S GONE MISSING.
BRILLIANT. THIS'LL DO NICELY.
MAJOR!
WHAT YOU SAID BEFORE, 'BOUT YOUNG PEOPLE?
Y'SPOSE THAT SOMETIMES, THE BEST WAY TO TEACH 'EM THE RIGHT WAY TO GO ABOUT THINGS...

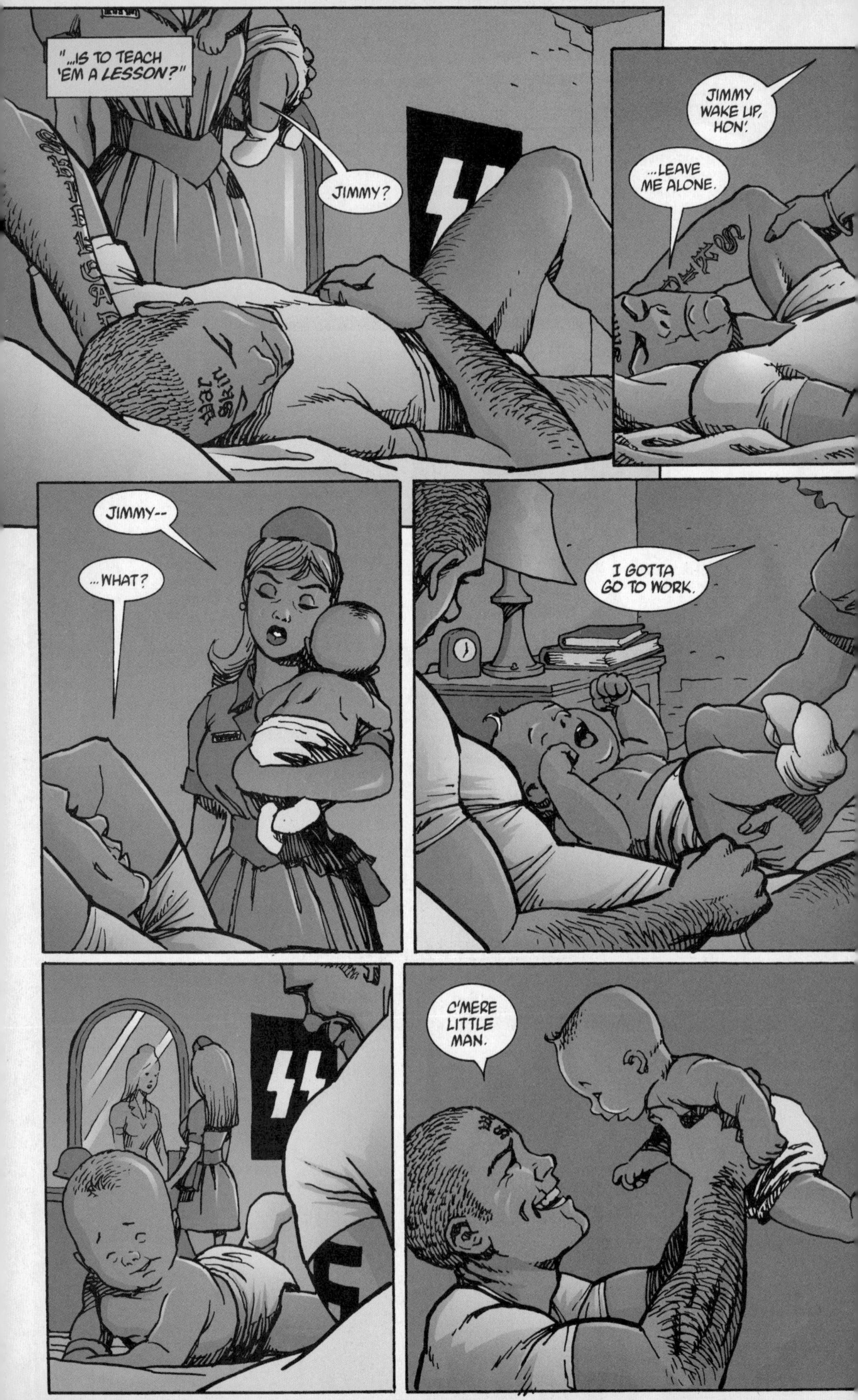
"...IS TO TEACH 'EM A *LESSON*?"
JIMMY?
JIMMY WAKE UP, HON'.
...LEAVE ME ALONE.
JIMMY--
...WHAT?
I GOTTA GO TO WORK.
C'MERE LITTLE MAN.

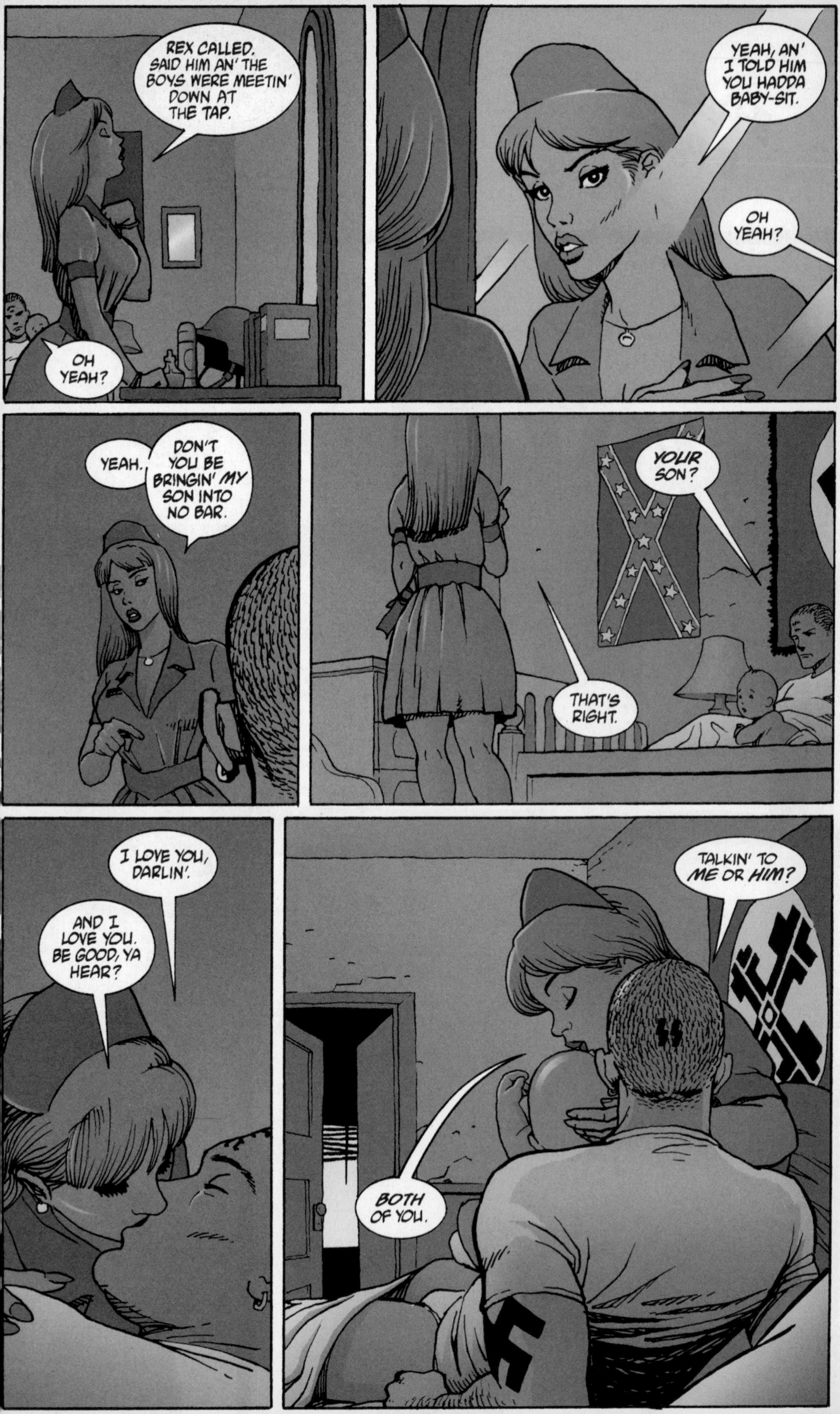
REX CALLED. SAID HIM AN' THE BOYS WERE MEETIN' DOWN AT THE TAP.
OH YEAH?
YEAH, AN' I TOLD HIM YOU HADDA BABY-SIT.
OH YEAH?
YEAH.
DON'T YOU BE BRINGIN' MY SON INTO NO BAR.
YOUR SON?
THAT'S RIGHT.
I LOVE YOU, DARLIN'.
AND I LOVE YOU. BE GOOD, YA HEAR?
TALKIN' TO ME OR HIM?
BOTH OF YOU.

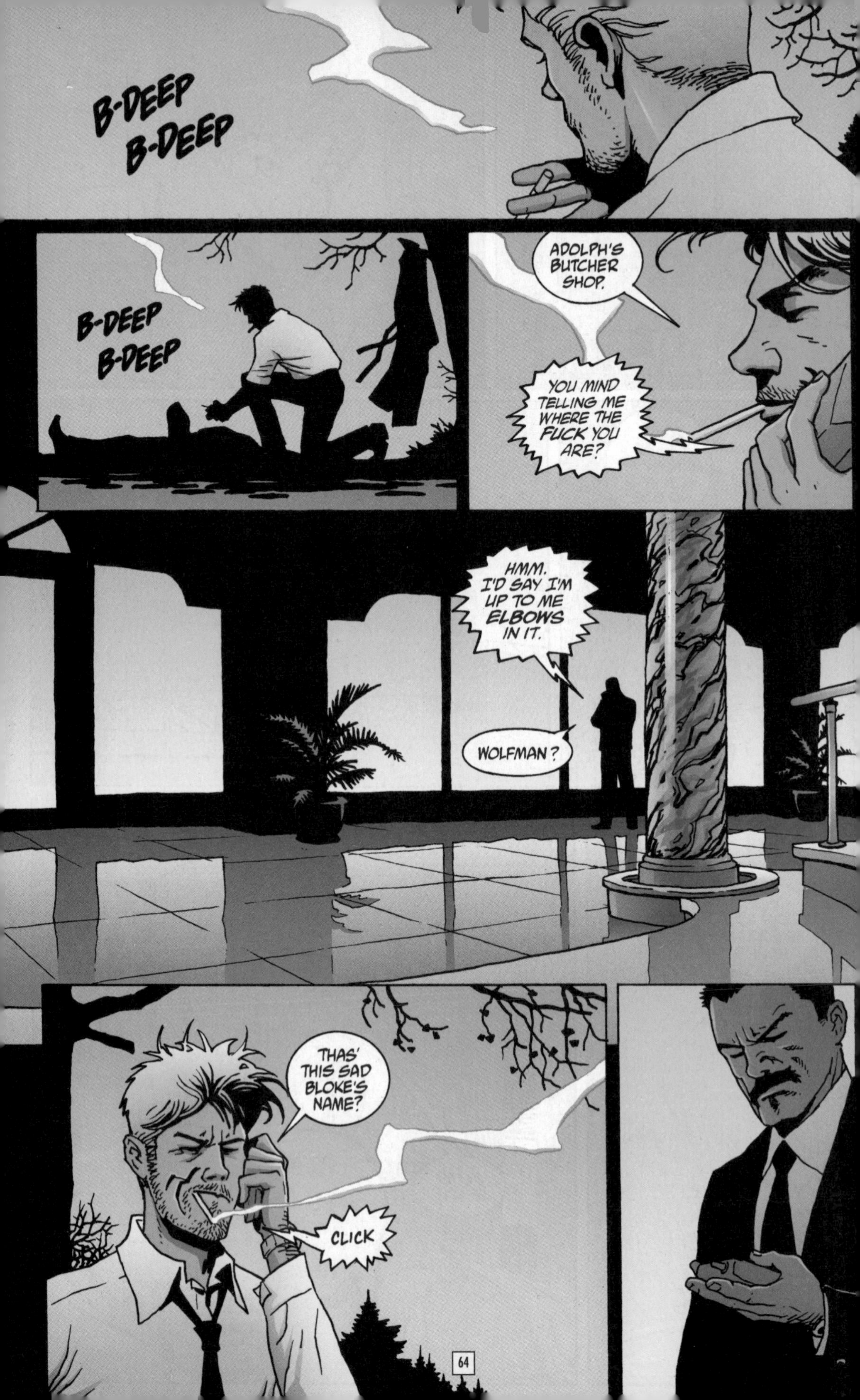

B-DEEP
B-DEEP
B-DEEP
B-DEEP
ADOLPH'S BUTCHER SHOP.
YOU MIND TELLING ME WHERE THE FUCK YOU ARE?
HMM. I'D SAY I'M UP TO ME ELBOWS IN IT.
WOLFMAN?
THAS' THIS SAD BLOKE'S NAME?
CLICK

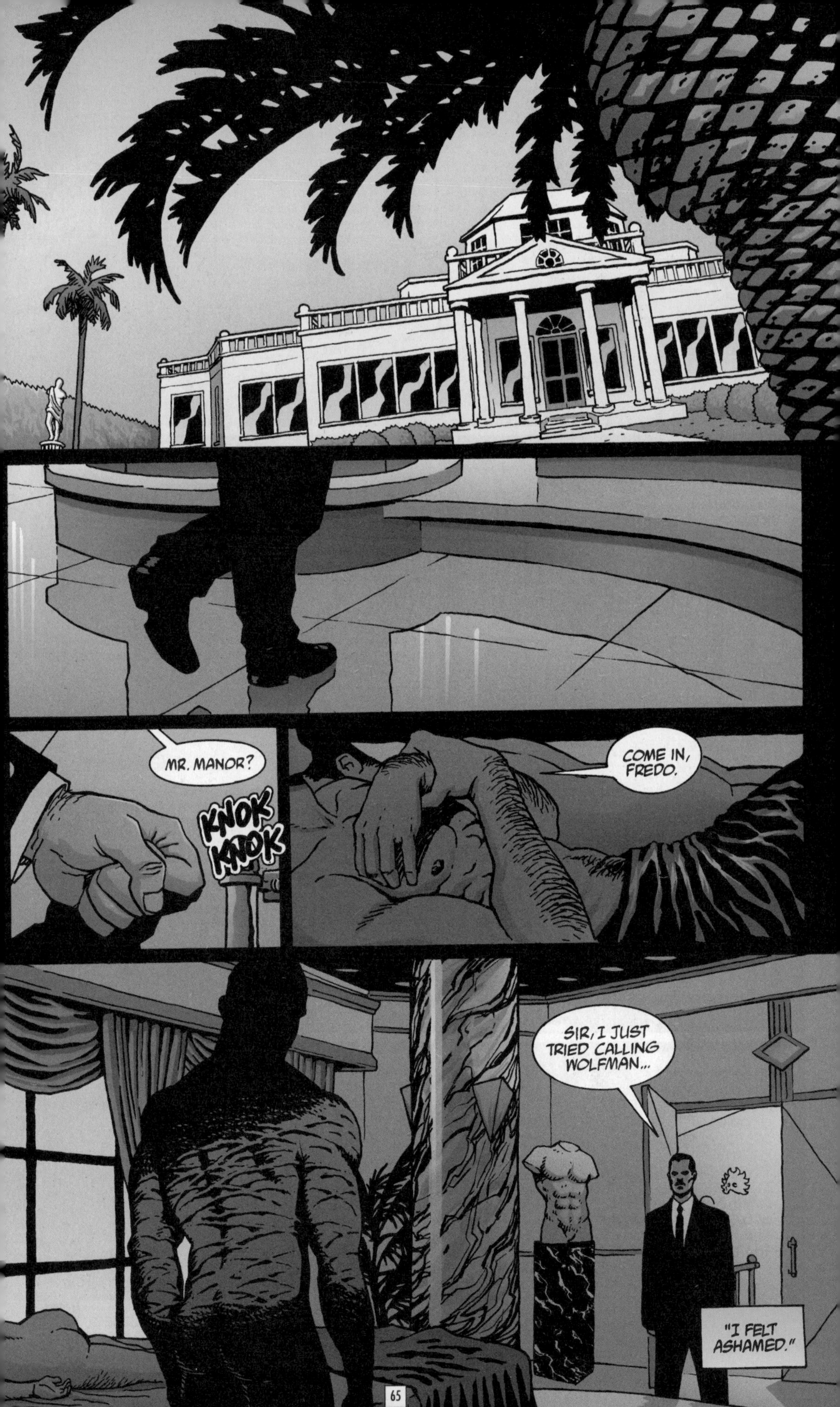

MR. MANOR?
KNOK KNOK
COME IN, FREDO.
SIR, I JUST TRIED CALLING WOLFMAN...
"I FELT ASHAMED."

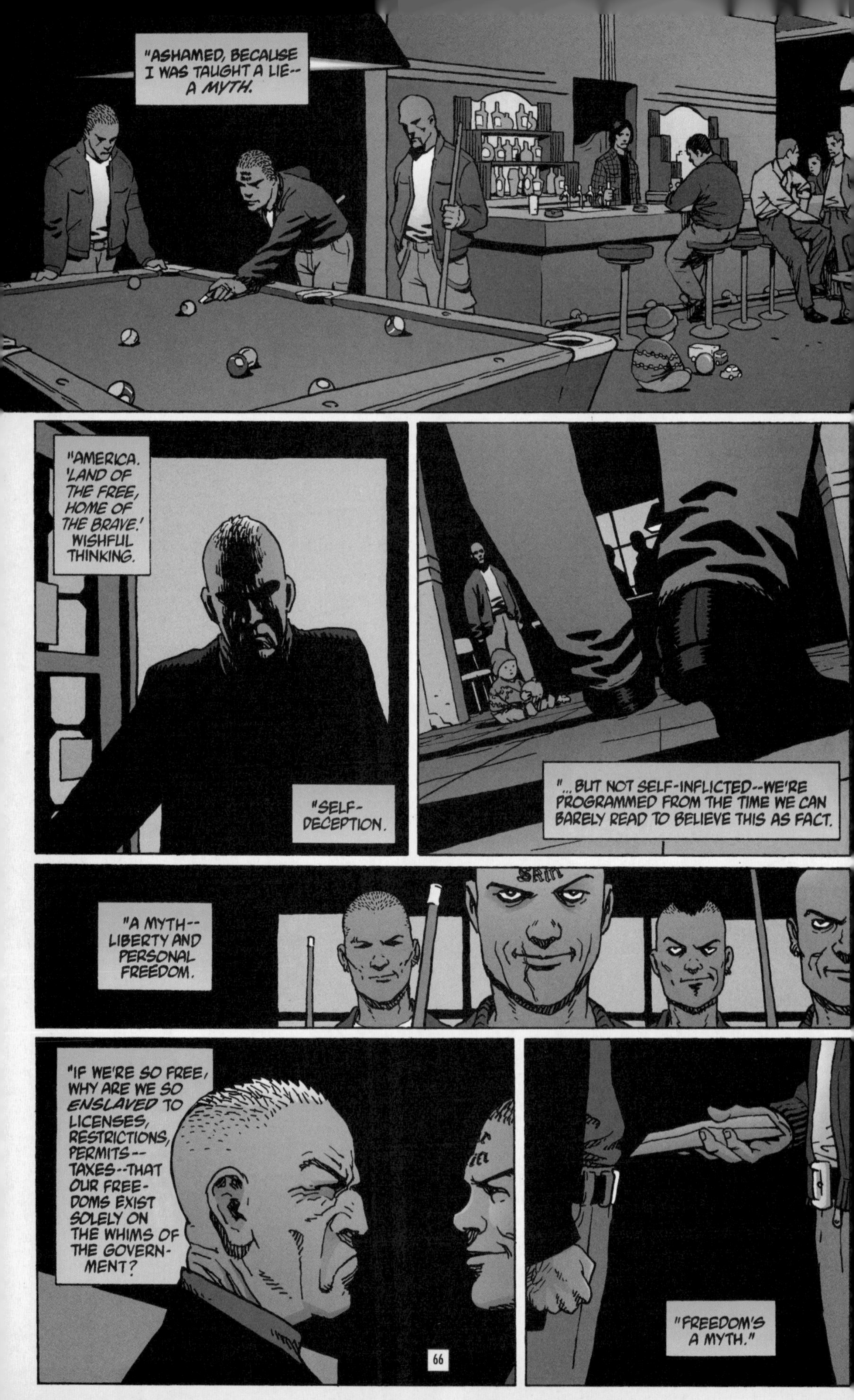
"ASHAMED, BECAUSE I WAS TAUGHT A LIE-- A *MYTH*.
"AMERICA. 'LAND OF THE FREE, HOME OF THE BRAVE.' WISHFUL THINKING.
"SELF-DECEPTION.
"... BUT NOT SELF-INFLICTED--WE'RE PROGRAMMED FROM THE TIME WE CAN BARELY READ TO BELIEVE THIS AS FACT.
SKIN
"A MYTH-- LIBERTY AND PERSONAL FREEDOM.
"IF WE'RE SO FREE, WHY ARE WE SO *ENSLAVED* TO LICENSES, RESTRICTIONS, PERMITS-- TAXES--THAT OUR FREEDOMS EXIST SOLELY ON THE WHIMS OF THE GOVERNMENT?
"FREEDOM'S A MYTH."

" 'ALL MEN ARE CREATED EQUAL.' WE'RE TAUGHT THIS *MYTH* TOO, WHEN IT'S SUCH AN OBVIOUS FACT TO BOTH WHITES *AND* BLACKS...

"...THAT IT'S JUST *NOT* TRUE.

"IF WE'RE SO *EQUAL*, WHY DO WE NEED *REVERSE DISCRIMINATION?* AFFIRMATIVE ACTION, QUOTA SYSTEMS --WELFARE?

"IT DOESN'T EVEN SEEM LIKE THE LIBERALS THAT *CAME UP WITH* THESE POLICIES *BELIEVE* BLACKS ARE EQUAL.

"AND THEY *DON'T.* THE TRUTH IS--THIS COUNTRY'S GONE TO THE *DEVIL.*

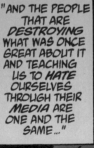

"AND THE PEOPLE THAT ARE *DESTROYING* WHAT WAS ONCE GREAT ABOUT IT AND TEACHING US TO *HATE* OURSELVES THROUGH THEIR *MEDIA* ARE ONE AND THE SAME..."

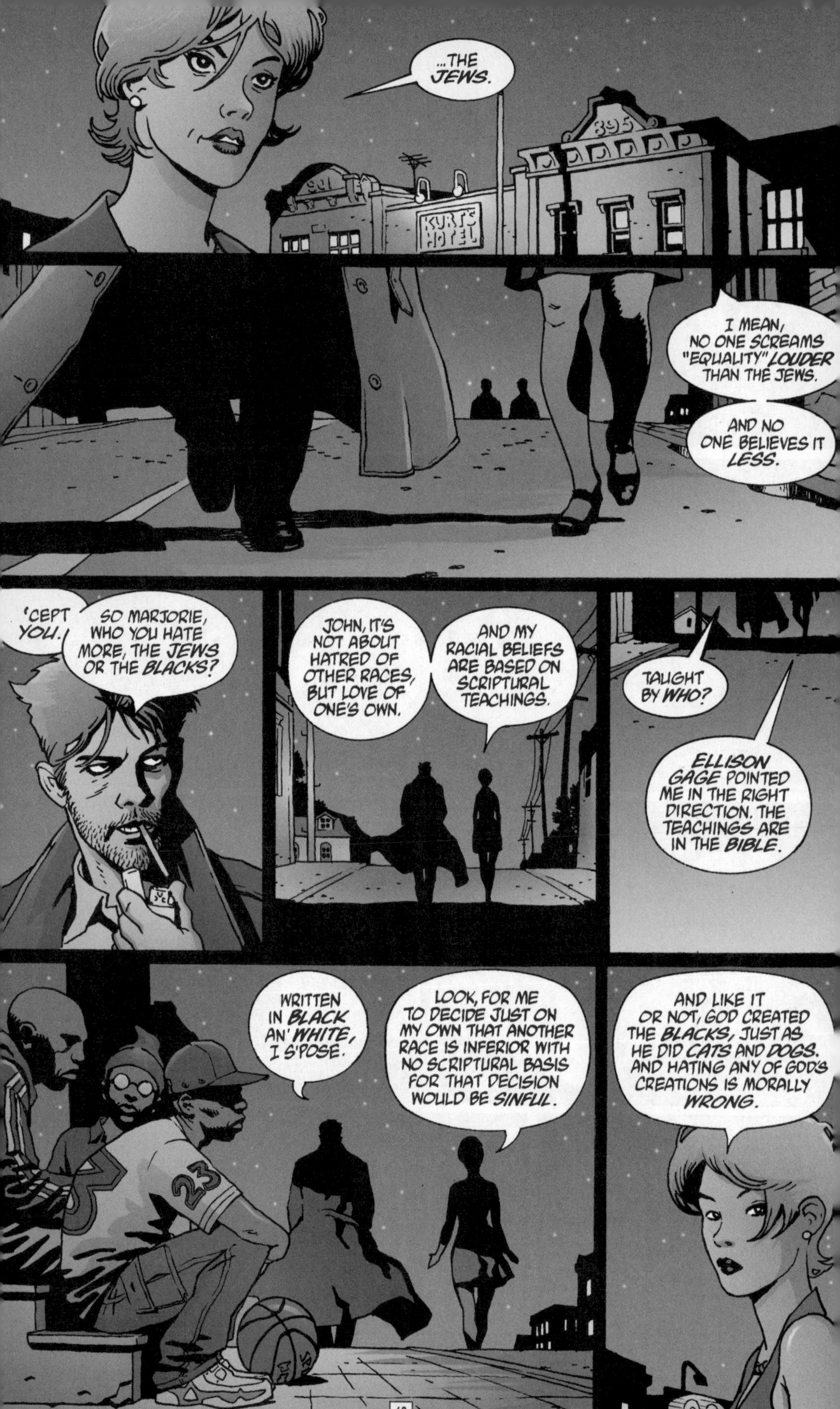
...THE JEWS.
I MEAN, NO ONE SCREAMS "EQUALITY" LOUDER THAN THE JEWS.
AND NO ONE BELIEVES IT LESS.
'CEPT YOU.
SO MARJORIE, WHO YOU HATE MORE, THE JEWS OR THE BLACKS?
JOHN, IT'S NOT ABOUT HATRED OF OTHER RACES, BUT LOVE OF ONE'S OWN.
AND MY RACIAL BELIEFS ARE BASED ON SCRIPTURAL TEACHINGS.
TAUGHT BY WHO?
ELLISON GAGE POINTED ME IN THE RIGHT DIRECTION. THE TEACHINGS ARE IN THE BIBLE.
WRITTEN IN BLACK AN' WHITE, I S'POSE.
LOOK, FOR ME TO DECIDE JUST ON MY OWN THAT ANOTHER RACE IS INFERIOR WITH NO SCRIPTURAL BASIS FOR THAT DECISION WOULD BE SINFUL.
AND LIKE IT OR NOT, GOD CREATED THE BLACKS, JUST AS HE DID CATS AND DOGS. AND HATING ANY OF GOD'S CREATIONS IS MORALLY WRONG.

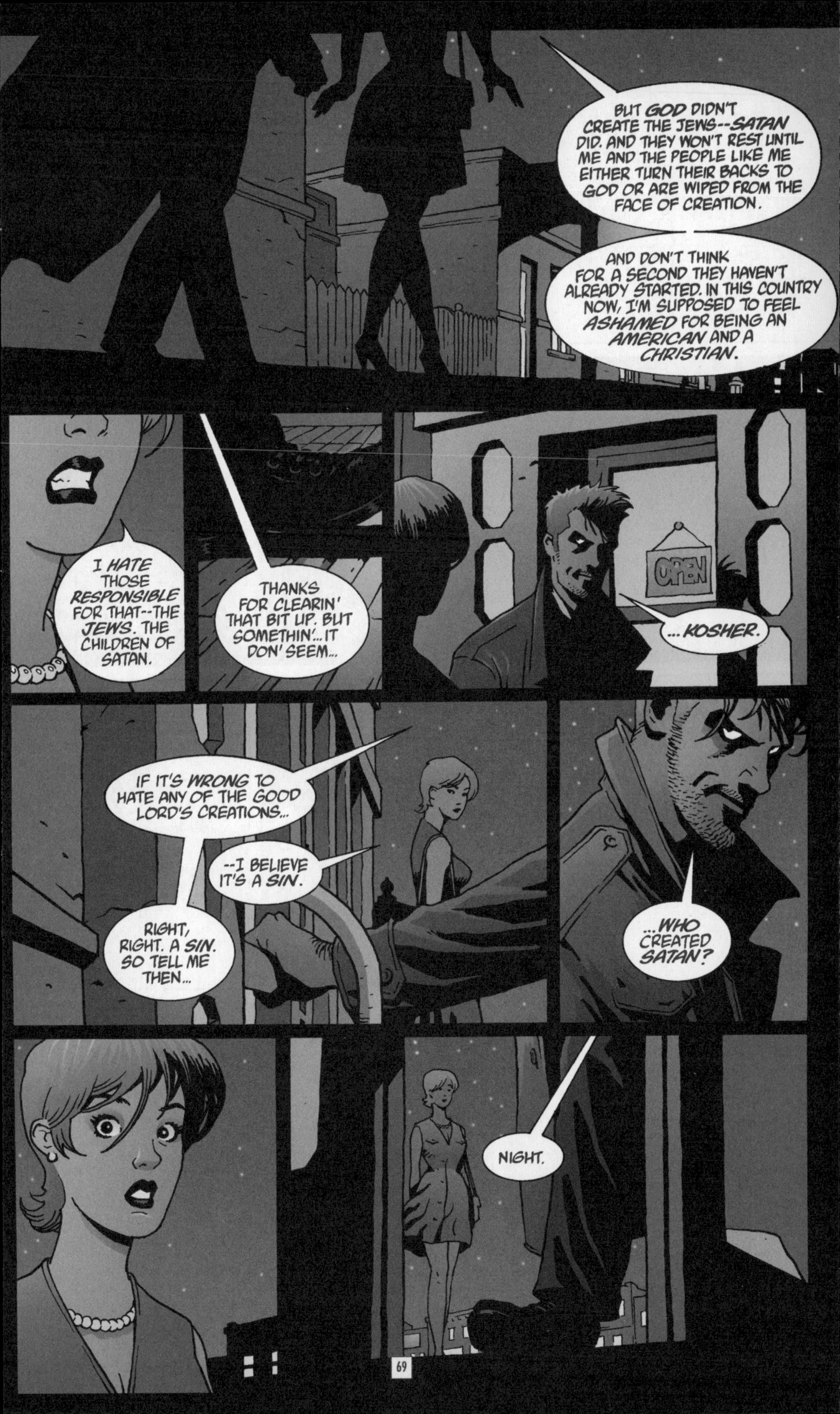
BUT GOD DIDN'T CREATE THE JEWS--SATAN DID. AND THEY WON'T REST UNTIL ME AND THE PEOPLE LIKE ME EITHER TURN THEIR BACKS TO GOD OR ARE WIPED FROM THE FACE OF CREATION.
AND DON'T THINK FOR A SECOND THEY HAVEN'T ALREADY STARTED. IN THIS COUNTRY NOW, I'M SUPPOSED TO FEEL ASHAMED FOR BEING AN AMERICAN AND A CHRISTIAN.
I HATE THOSE RESPONSIBLE FOR THAT--THE JEWS. THE CHILDREN OF SATAN.
THANKS FOR CLEARIN' THAT BIT UP. BUT SOMETHIN'... IT DON' SEEM...
OPEN
...KOSHER.
IF IT'S WRONG TO HATE ANY OF THE GOOD LORD'S CREATIONS...
--I BELIEVE IT'S A SIN.
RIGHT, RIGHT. A SIN. SO TELL ME THEN...
...WHO CREATED SATAN?
NIGHT.

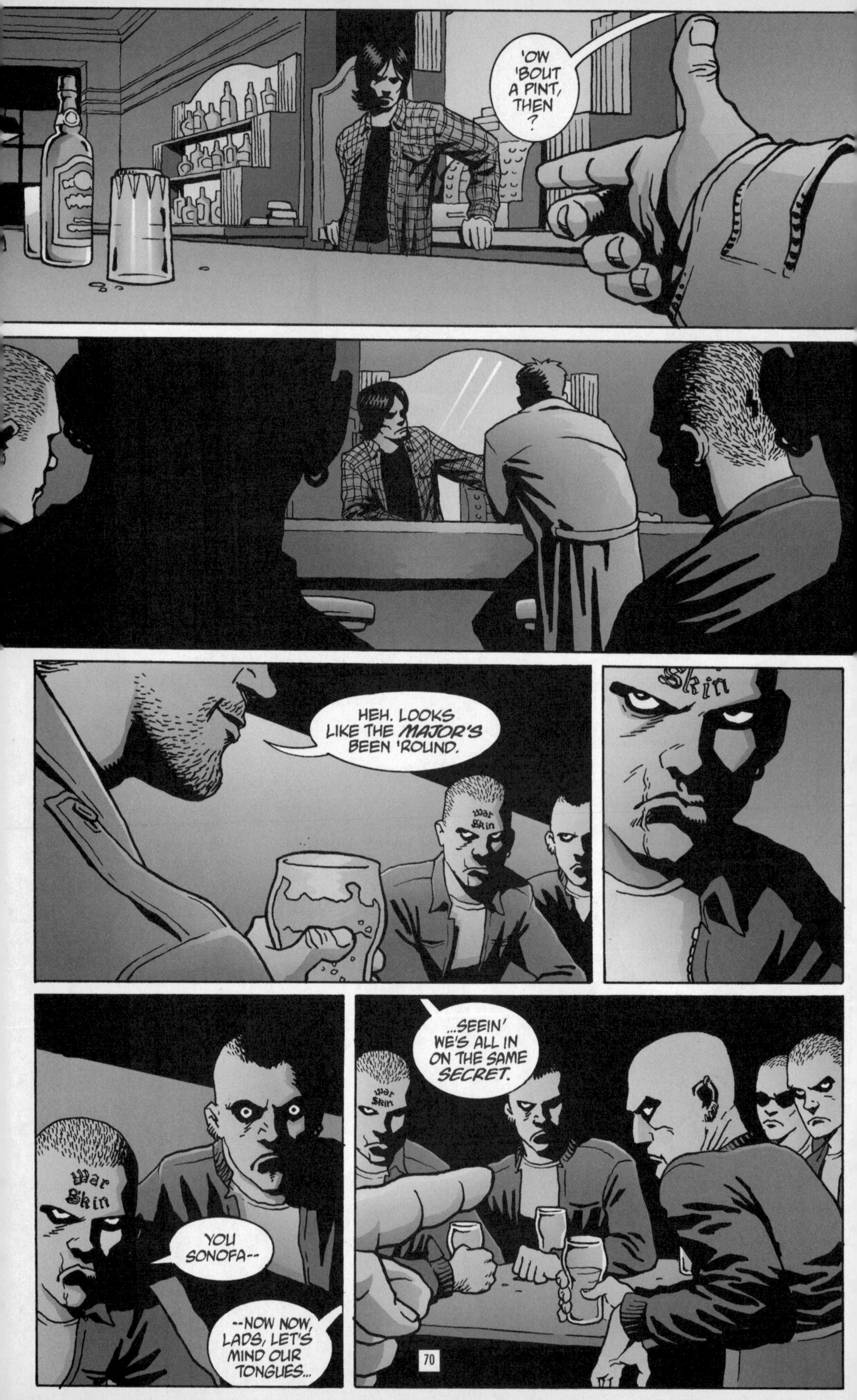

'OW 'BOUT A PINT, THEN?
HEH. LOOKS LIKE THE MAJOR'S BEEN 'ROUND.
Skin
War Skin
War Skin
YOU SONOFA--
--NOW NOW, LADS, LET'S MIND OUR TONGUES...
...SEEIN' WE'S ALL IN ON THE SAME SECRET.
War Skin

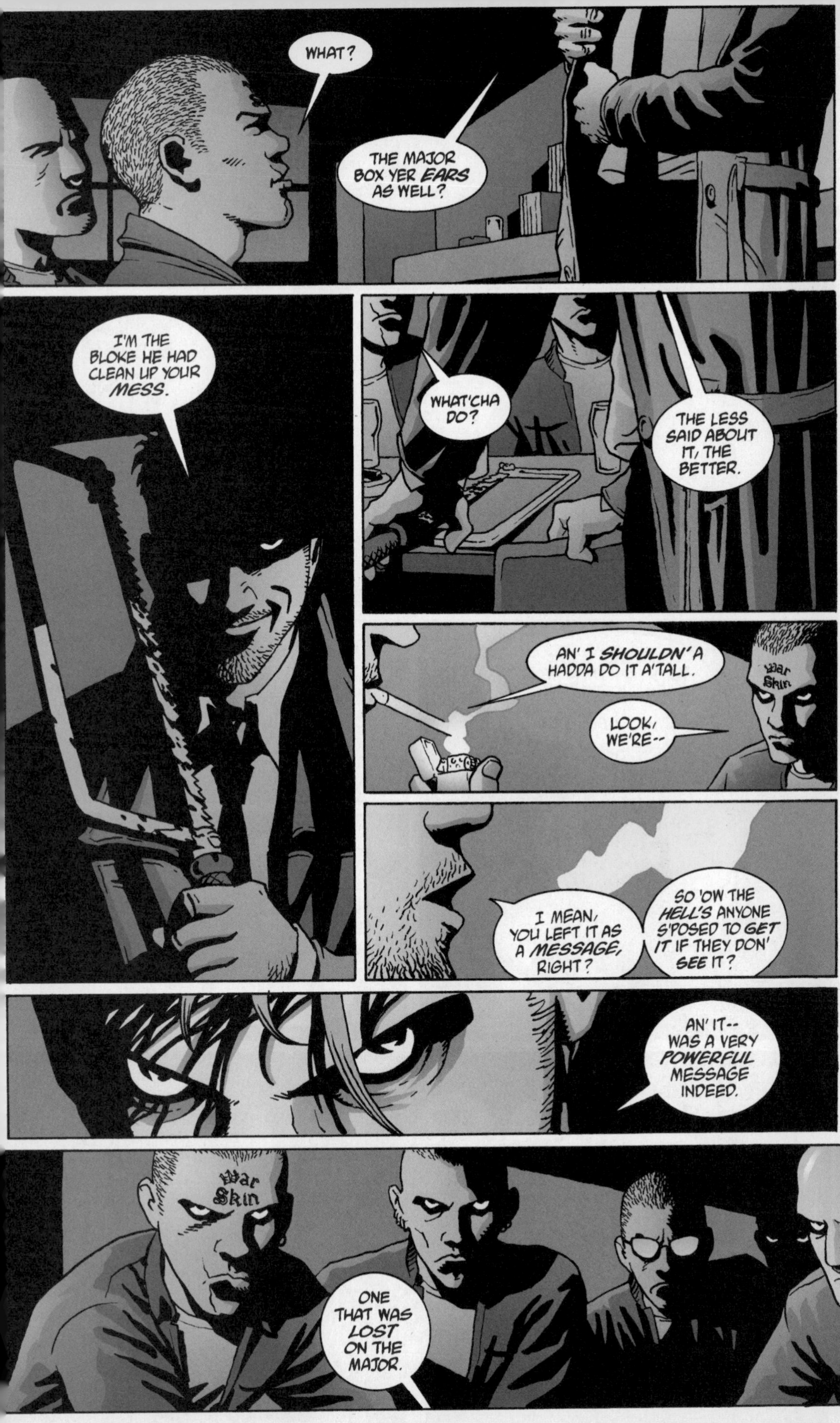
WHAT?
THE MAJOR BOX YER EARS AS WELL?
I'M THE BLOKE HE HAD CLEAN UP YOUR MESS.
WHAT'CHA DO?
THE LESS SAID ABOUT IT, THE BETTER.
AN' I SHOULDN' A HADDA DO IT A'TALL.
War Skin
LOOK, WE'RE--
I MEAN, YOU LEFT IT AS A MESSAGE, RIGHT?
SO 'OW THE HELL'S ANYONE S'POSED TO GET IT IF THEY DON' SEE IT?
AN' IT-- WAS A VERY POWERFUL MESSAGE INDEED.
War Skin
ONE THAT WAS LOST ON THE MAJOR.

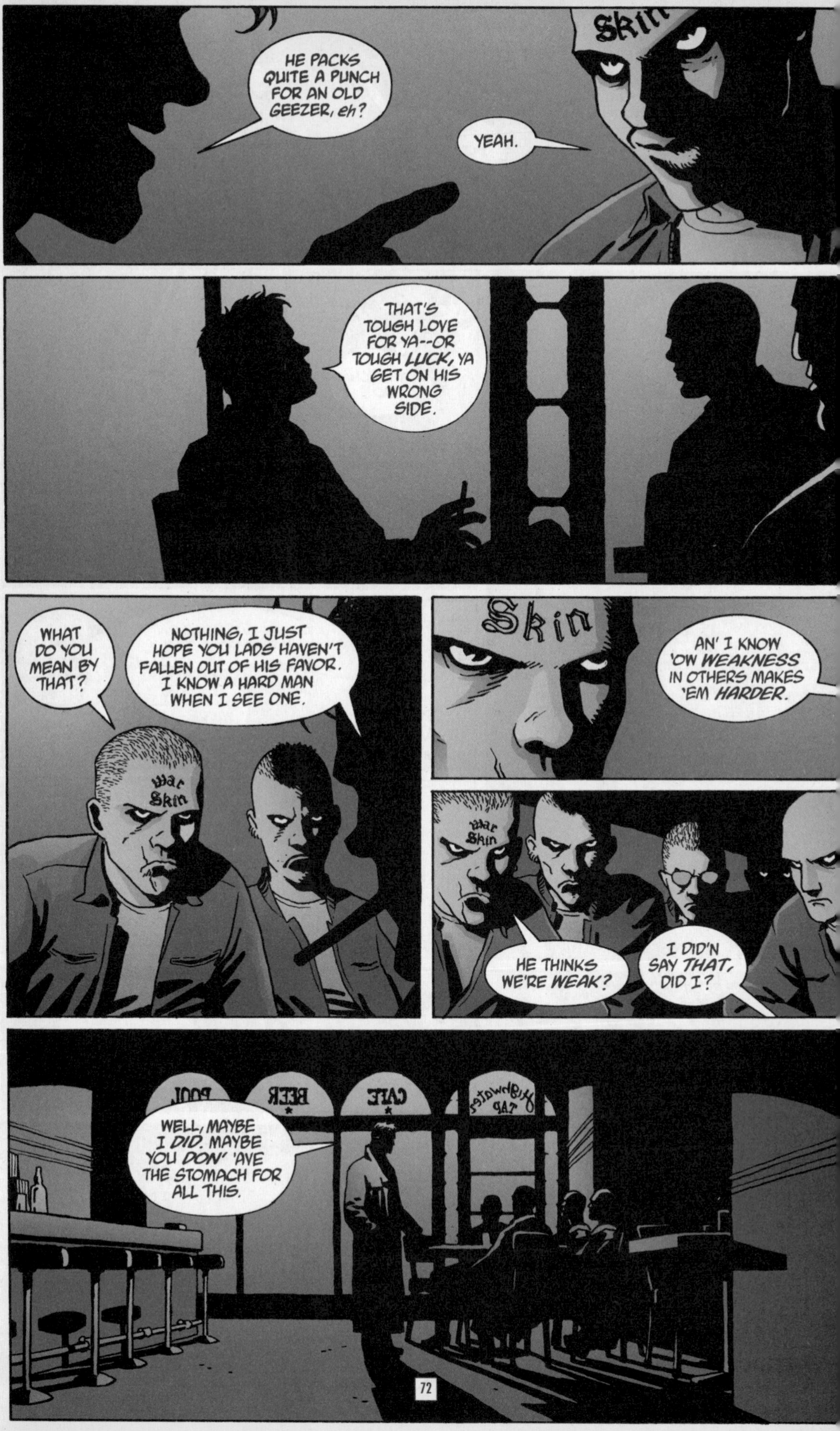
HE PACKS QUITE A PUNCH FOR AN OLD GEEZER, eh?
YEAH.
THAT'S TOUGH LOVE FOR YA--OR TOUGH *LUCK*, YA GET ON HIS WRONG SIDE.
WHAT DO YOU MEAN BY THAT?
NOTHING, I JUST HOPE YOU LADS HAVEN'T FALLEN OUT OF HIS FAVOR. I KNOW A HARD MAN WHEN I SEE ONE.
AN' I KNOW 'OW *WEAKNESS* IN OTHERS MAKES 'EM *HARDER*.
HE THINKS WE'RE *WEAK*?
I DID'N SAY *THAT*, DID I?
WELL, MAYBE I *DID*. MAYBE YOU *DON'* 'AVE THE STOMACH FOR ALL THIS.

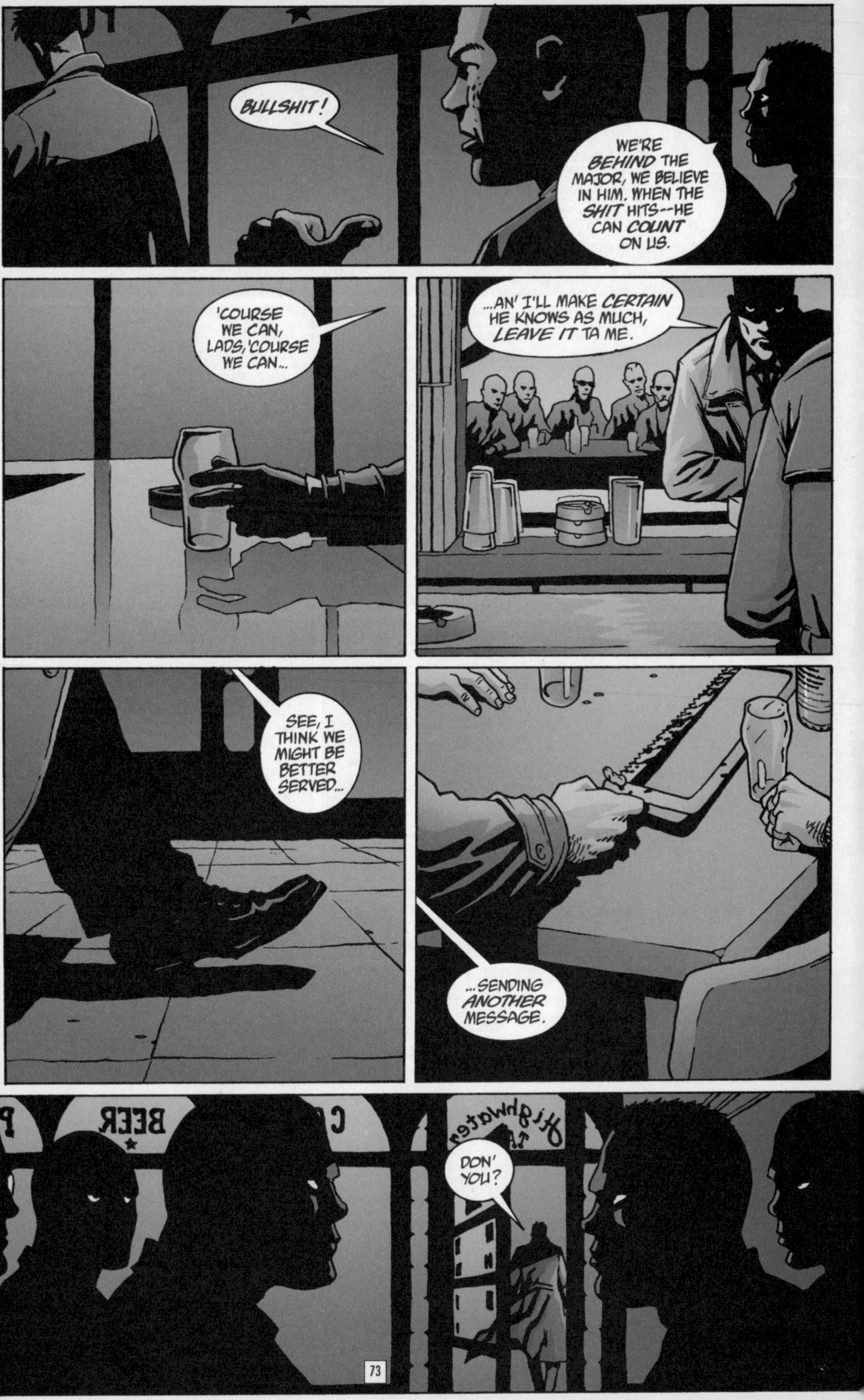
BULLSHIT!
WE'RE BEHIND THE MAJOR, WE BELIEVE IN HIM. WHEN THE SHIT HITS--HE CAN COUNT ON US.
'COURSE WE CAN, LADS, 'COURSE WE CAN...
...AN' I'LL MAKE CERTAIN HE KNOWS AS MUCH, LEAVE IT TA ME.
SEE, I THINK WE MIGHT BE BETTER SERVED...
...SENDING ANOTHER MESSAGE.
BEER
DON' YOU?

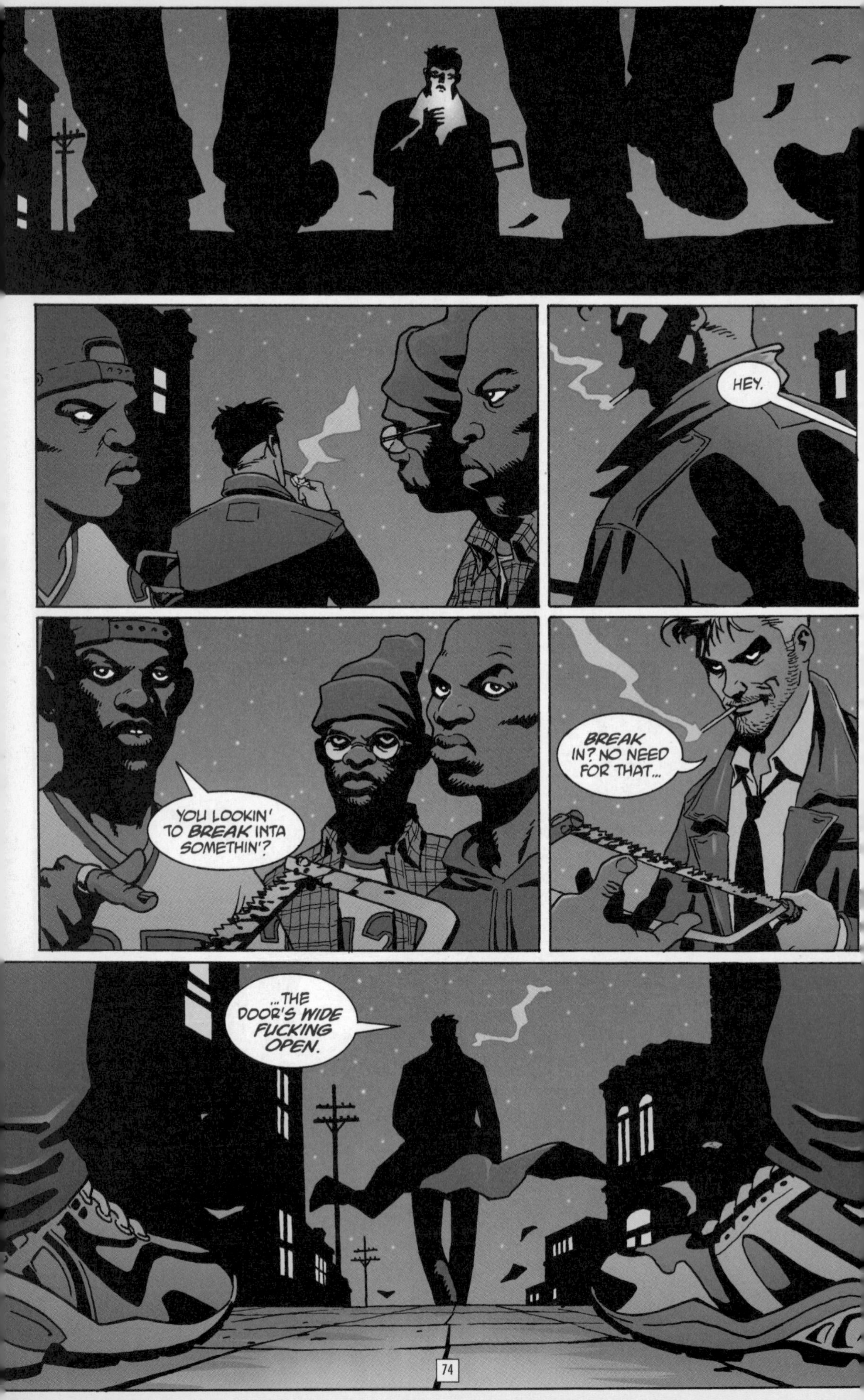
HEY.
YOU LOOKIN' TO BREAK INTA SOMETHIN'?
BREAK IN? NO NEED FOR THAT...
...THE DOOR'S WIDE FUCKING OPEN.

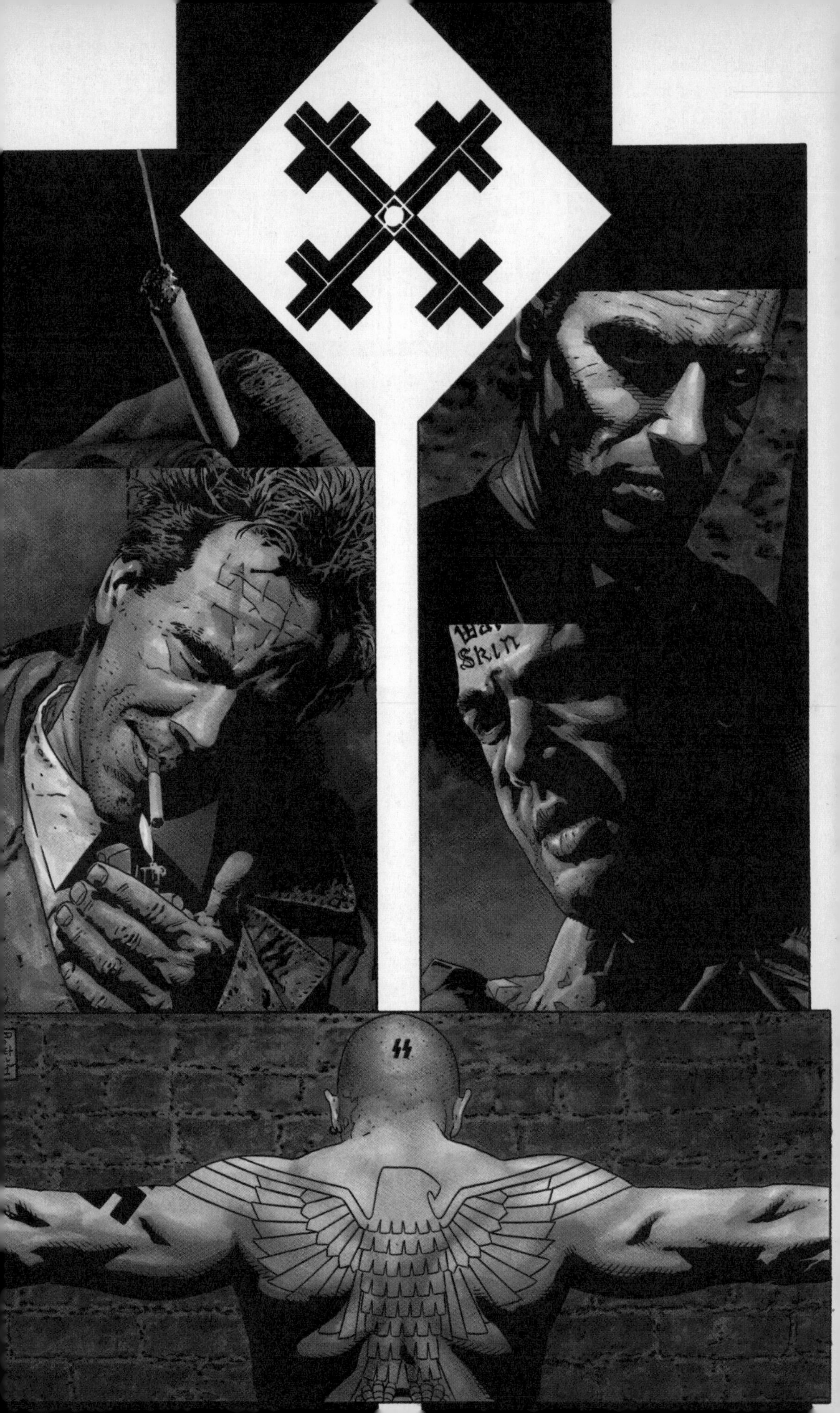
Skin

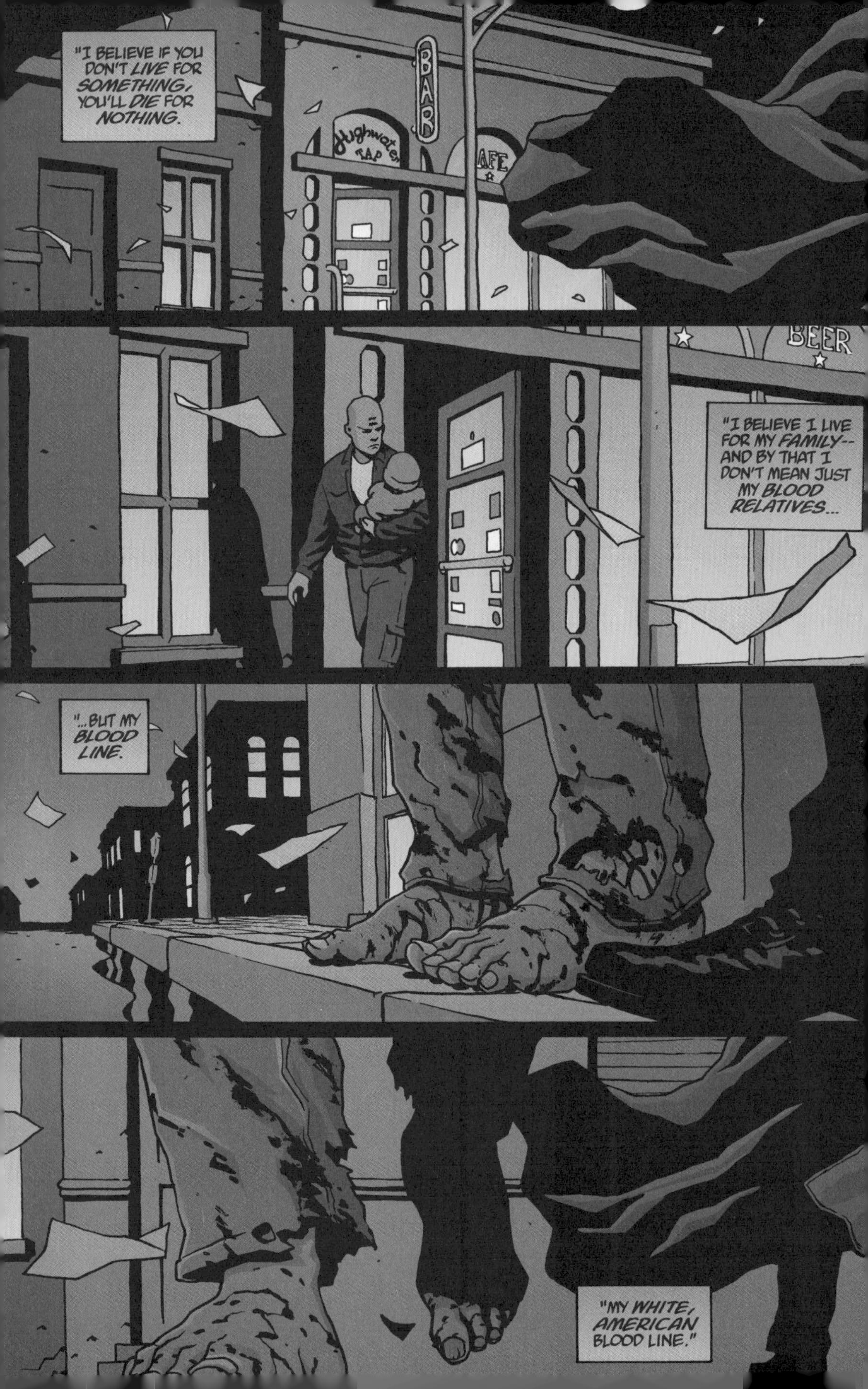
"I BELIEVE IF YOU DON'T *LIVE* FOR *SOMETHING*, YOU'LL *DIE* FOR *NOTHING*.
BAR
CAFE
BEER
"I BELIEVE I LIVE FOR MY *FAMILY*-- AND BY THAT I DON'T MEAN JUST MY *BLOOD RELATIVES*...
"...BUT MY *BLOOD LINE*.
"MY *WHITE, AMERICAN* BLOOD LINE."

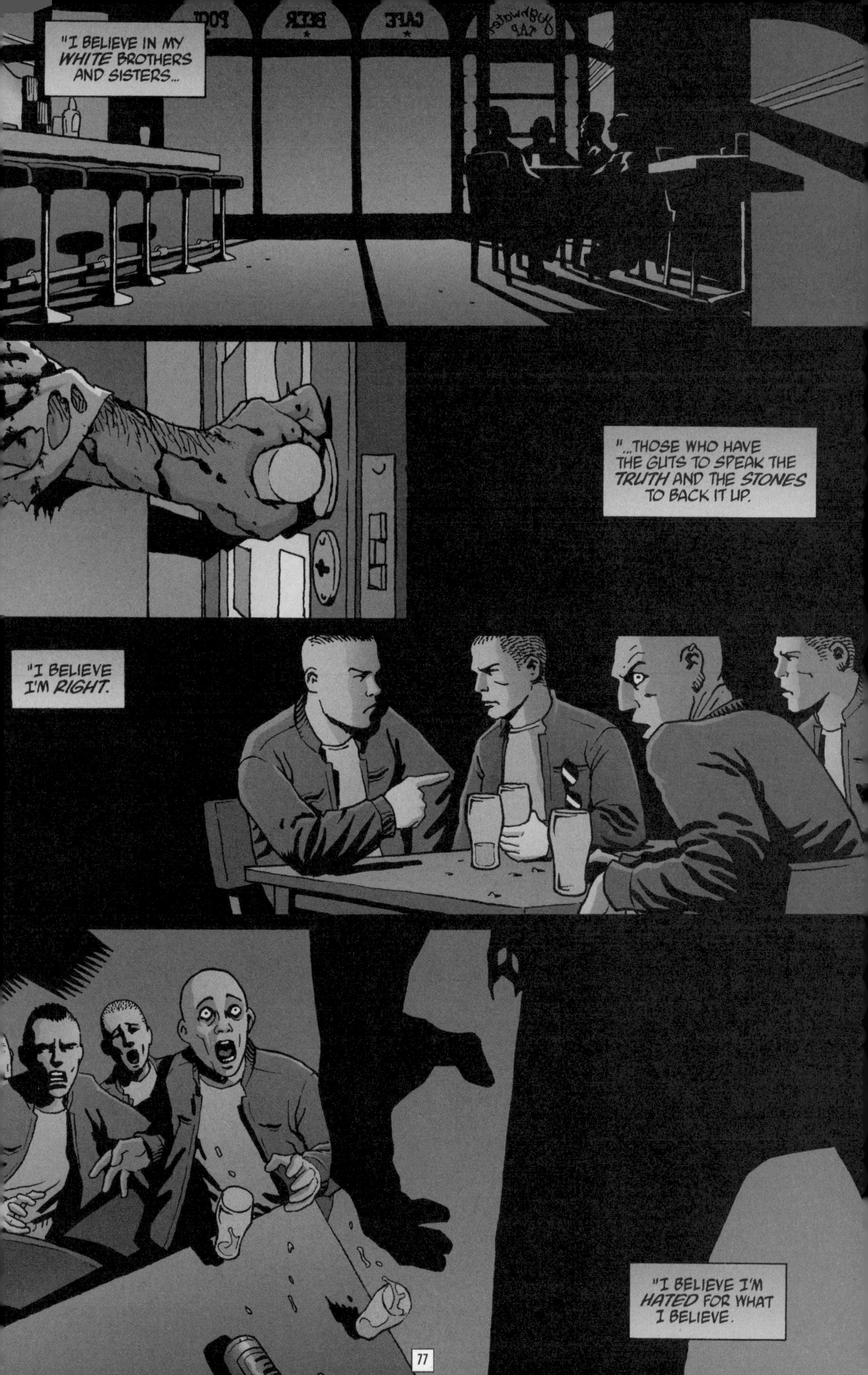
"I BELIEVE IN MY *WHITE* BROTHERS AND SISTERS...
"...THOSE WHO HAVE THE GUTS TO SPEAK THE *TRUTH* AND THE *STONES* TO BACK IT UP.
"I BELIEVE I'M *RIGHT*.
"I BELIEVE I'M *HATED* FOR WHAT I BELIEVE.

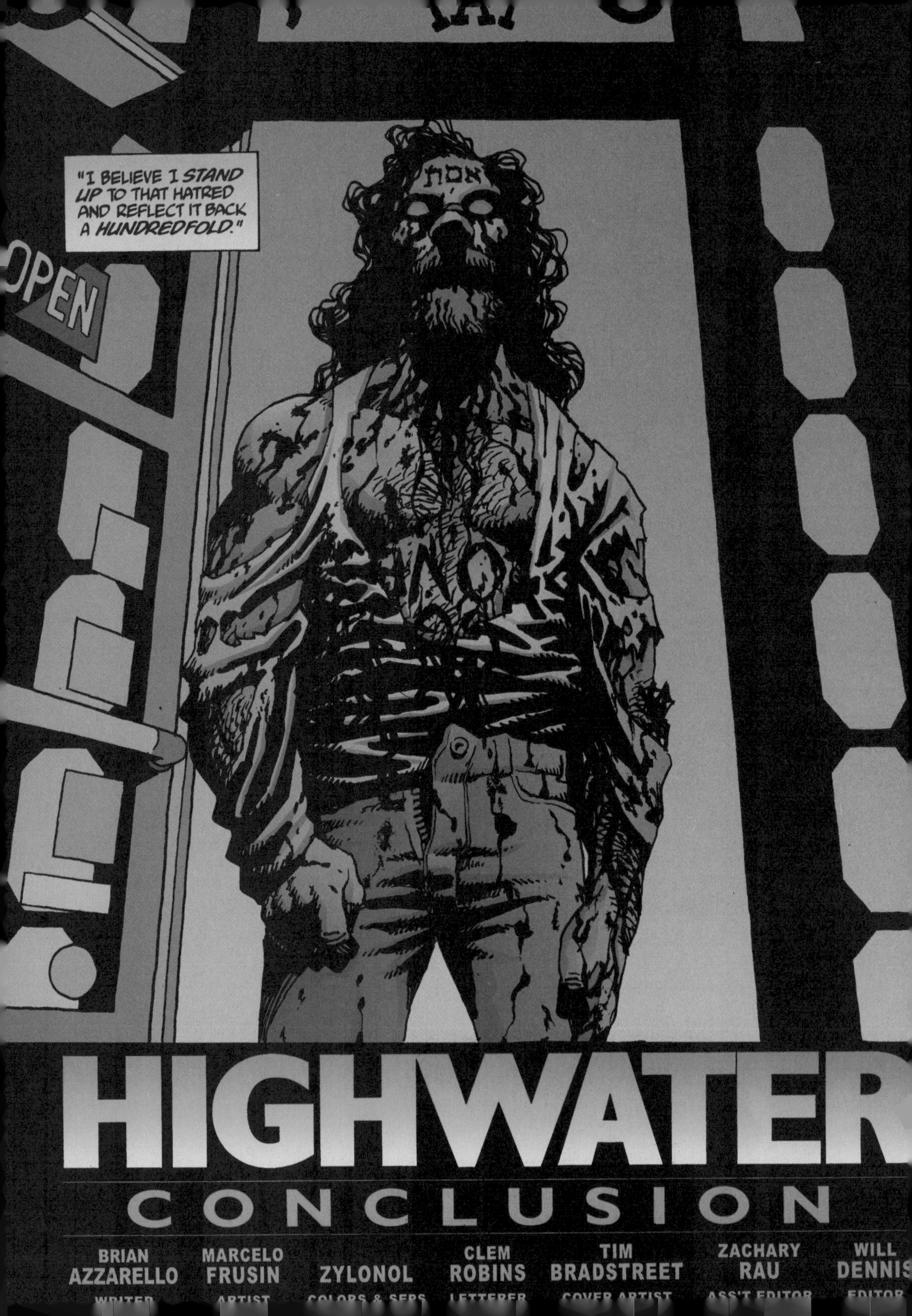
"I BELIEVE I STAND UP TO THAT HATRED AND REFLECT IT BACK A HUNDREDFOLD."
OPEN
HIGHWATER
CONCLUSION
BRIAN AZZARELLO WRITER
MARCELO FRUSIN ARTIST
ZYLONOL COLORS & SEPS
CLEM ROBINS LETTERER
TIM BRADSTREET COVER ARTIST
ZACHARY RAU ASS'T EDITOR
WILL DENNIS EDITOR

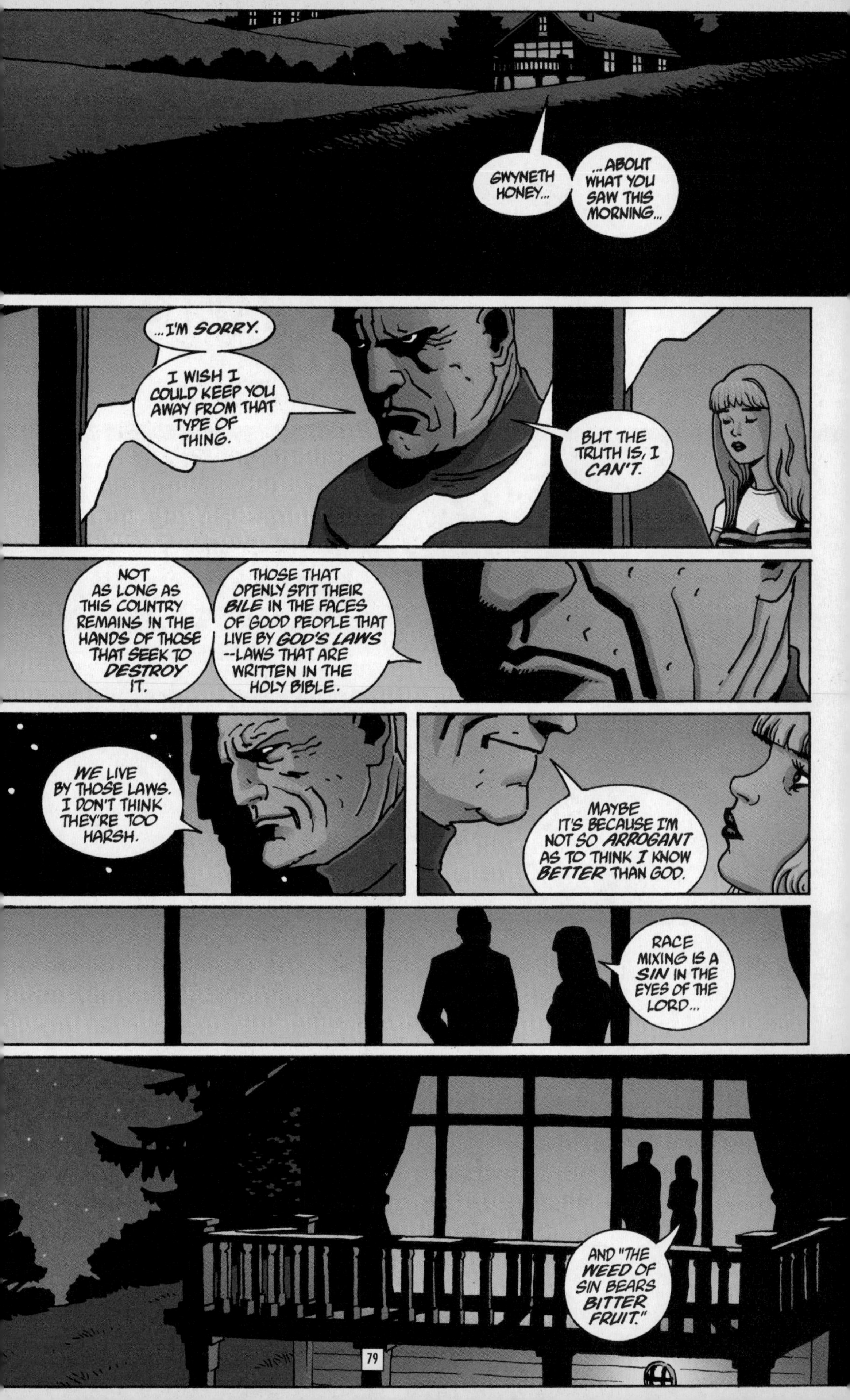
GWYNETH HONEY...
...ABOUT WHAT YOU SAW THIS MORNING...
...I'M SORRY.
I WISH I COULD KEEP YOU AWAY FROM THAT TYPE OF THING.
BUT THE TRUTH IS, I CAN'T.
NOT AS LONG AS THIS COUNTRY REMAINS IN THE HANDS OF THOSE THAT SEEK TO DESTROY IT.
THOSE THAT OPENLY SPIT THEIR BILE IN THE FACES OF GOOD PEOPLE THAT LIVE BY GOD'S LAWS --LAWS THAT ARE WRITTEN IN THE HOLY BIBLE.
WE LIVE BY THOSE LAWS. I DON'T THINK THEY'RE TOO HARSH.
MAYBE IT'S BECAUSE I'M NOT SO ARROGANT AS TO THINK I KNOW BETTER THAN GOD.
RACE MIXING IS A SIN IN THE EYES OF THE LORD...
AND "THE WEED OF SIN BEARS BITTER FRUIT."

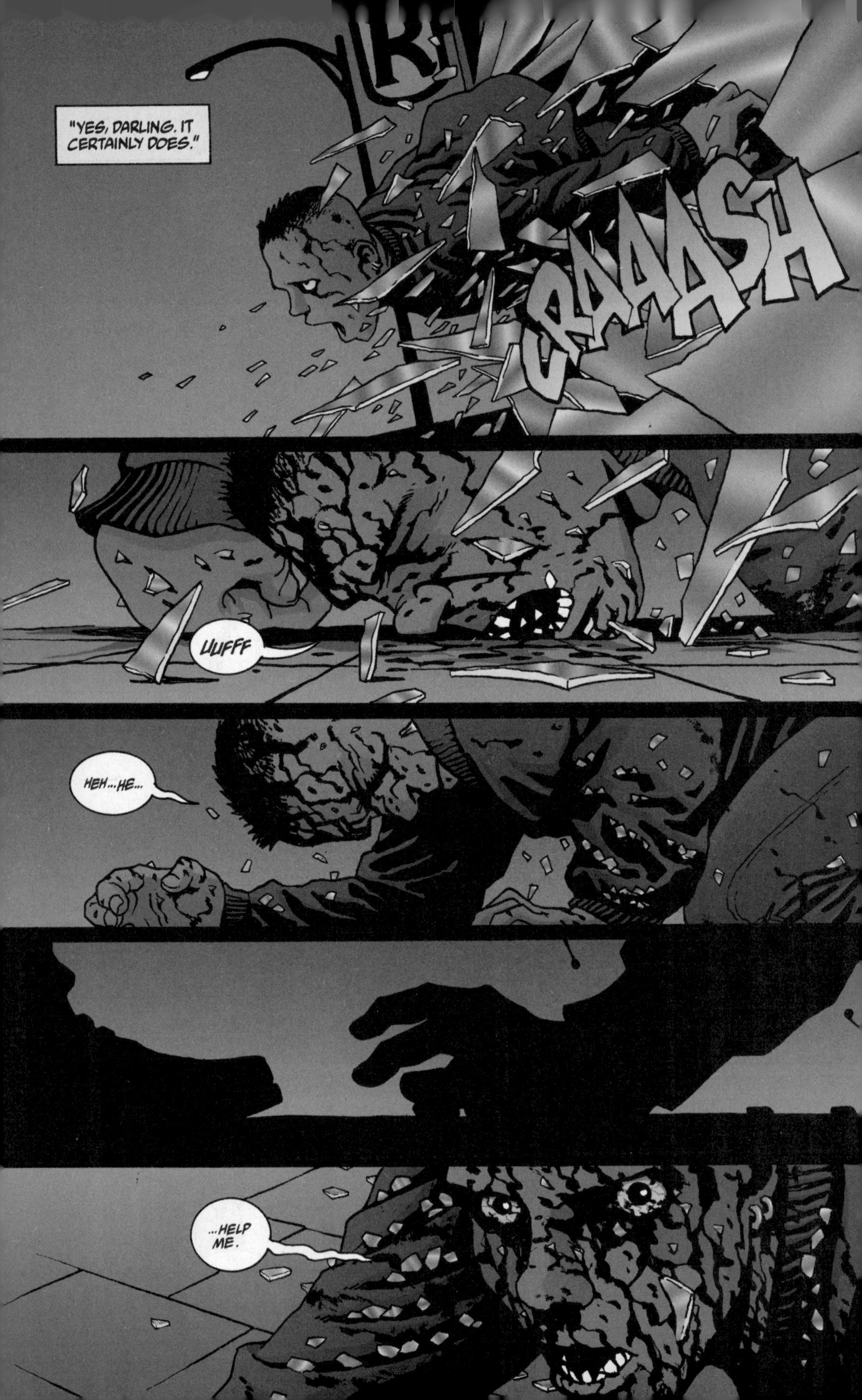
"YES, DARLING. IT CERTAINLY DOES."
CRAAAASH
UUFFF
HEH...HE...
...HELP ME.

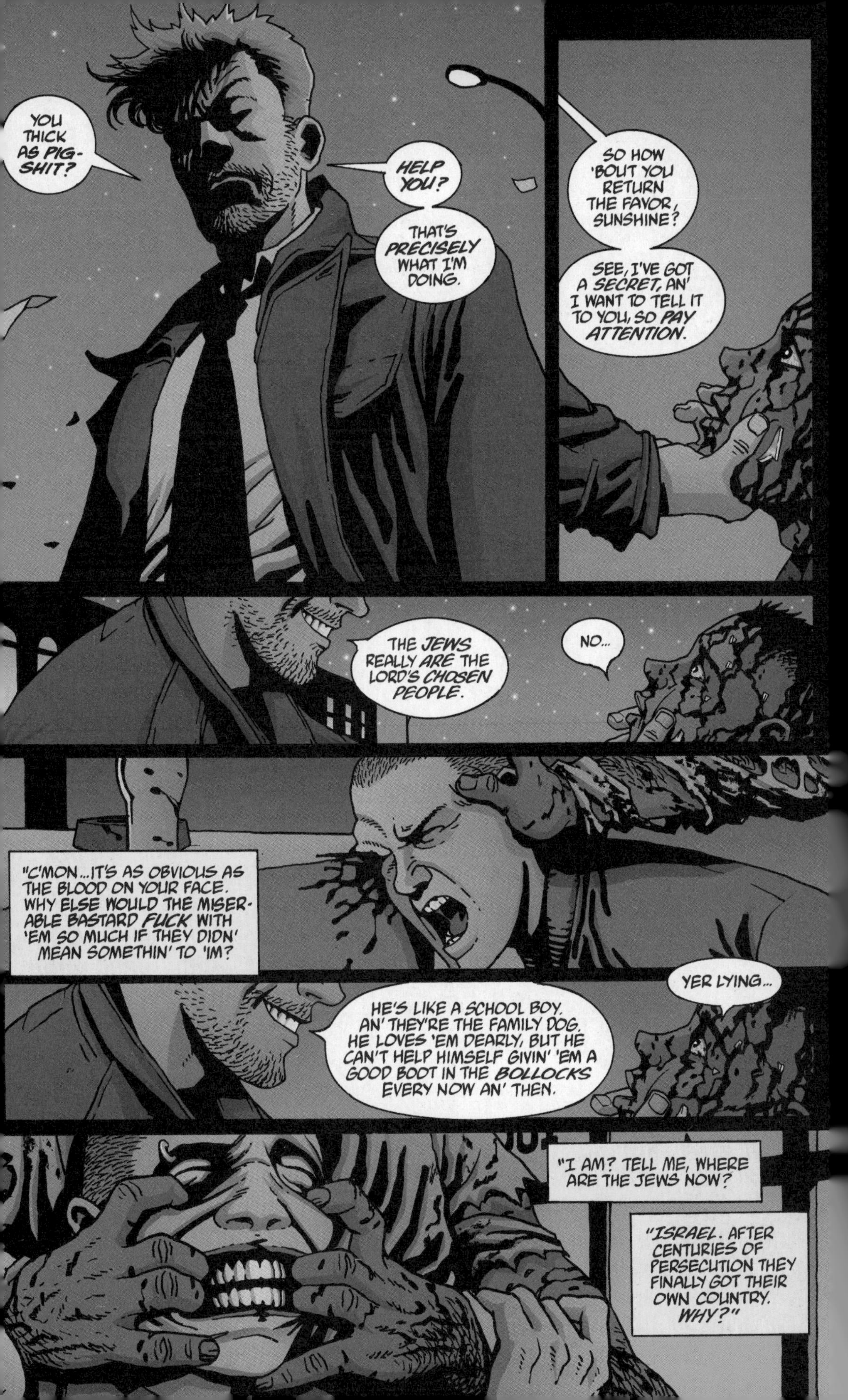
YOU THICK AS PIG-SHIT?
HELP YOU?
THAT'S PRECISELY WHAT I'M DOING.
SO HOW 'BOUT YOU RETURN THE FAVOR, SUNSHINE?
SEE, I'VE GOT A SECRET, AN' I WANT TO TELL IT TO YOU, SO PAY ATTENTION.
THE JEWS REALLY ARE THE LORD'S CHOSEN PEOPLE.
NO...
"C'MON...IT'S AS OBVIOUS AS THE BLOOD ON YOUR FACE. WHY ELSE WOULD THE MISER-ABLE BASTARD FUCK WITH 'EM SO MUCH IF THEY DIDN' MEAN SOMETHIN' TO 'IM?
YER LYING...
HE'S LIKE A SCHOOL BOY. AN' THEY'RE THE FAMILY DOG. HE LOVES 'EM DEARLY, BUT HE CAN'T HELP HIMSELF GIVIN' 'EM A GOOD BOOT IN THE BOLLOCKS EVERY NOW AN' THEN.
"I AM? TELL ME, WHERE ARE THE JEWS NOW?
"ISRAEL. AFTER CENTURIES OF PERSECUTION THEY FINALLY GOT THEIR OWN COUNTRY. WHY?"

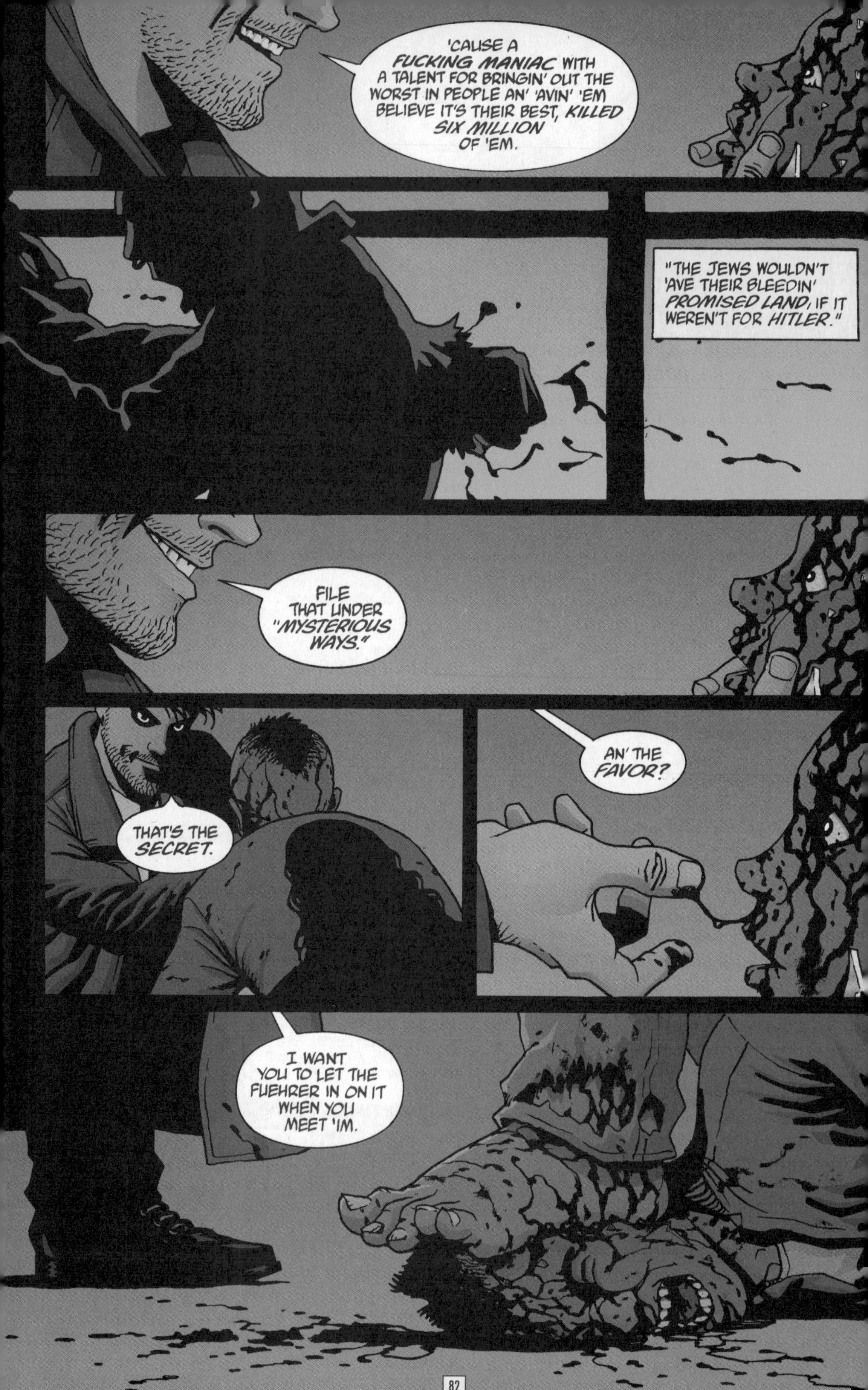
'CAUSE A FUCKING MANIAC WITH A TALENT FOR BRINGIN' OUT THE WORST IN PEOPLE AN' 'AVIN' 'EM BELIEVE IT'S THEIR BEST, KILLED SIX MILLION OF 'EM.
"THE JEWS WOULDN'T 'AVE THEIR BLEEDIN' PROMISED LAND, IF IT WEREN'T FOR HITLER."
FILE THAT UNDER "MYSTERIOUS WAYS."
THAT'S THE SECRET.
AN' THE FAVOR?
I WANT YOU TO LET THE FUEHRER IN ON IT WHEN YOU MEET 'IM.

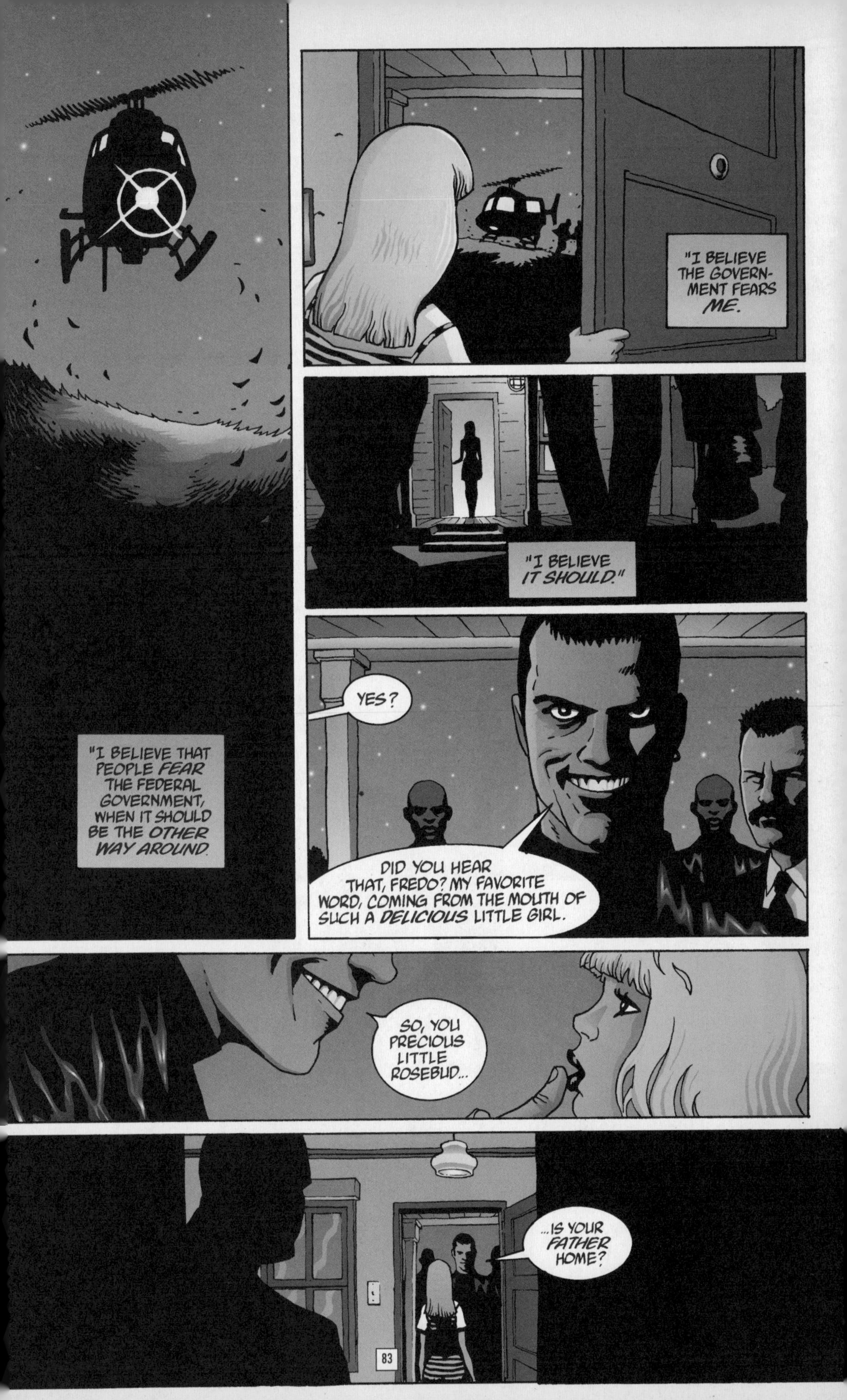
"I BELIEVE THE GOVERN-MENT FEARS *ME*.
"I BELIEVE *IT SHOULD*."
"I BELIEVE THAT PEOPLE *FEAR* THE FEDERAL GOVERNMENT, WHEN IT SHOULD BE THE *OTHER WAY AROUND*.
YES?
DID YOU HEAR THAT, FREDO? MY FAVORITE WORD, COMING FROM THE MOUTH OF SUCH A *DELICIOUS* LITTLE GIRL.
SO, YOU PRECIOUS LITTLE ROSEBUD...
...IS YOUR *FATHER* HOME?

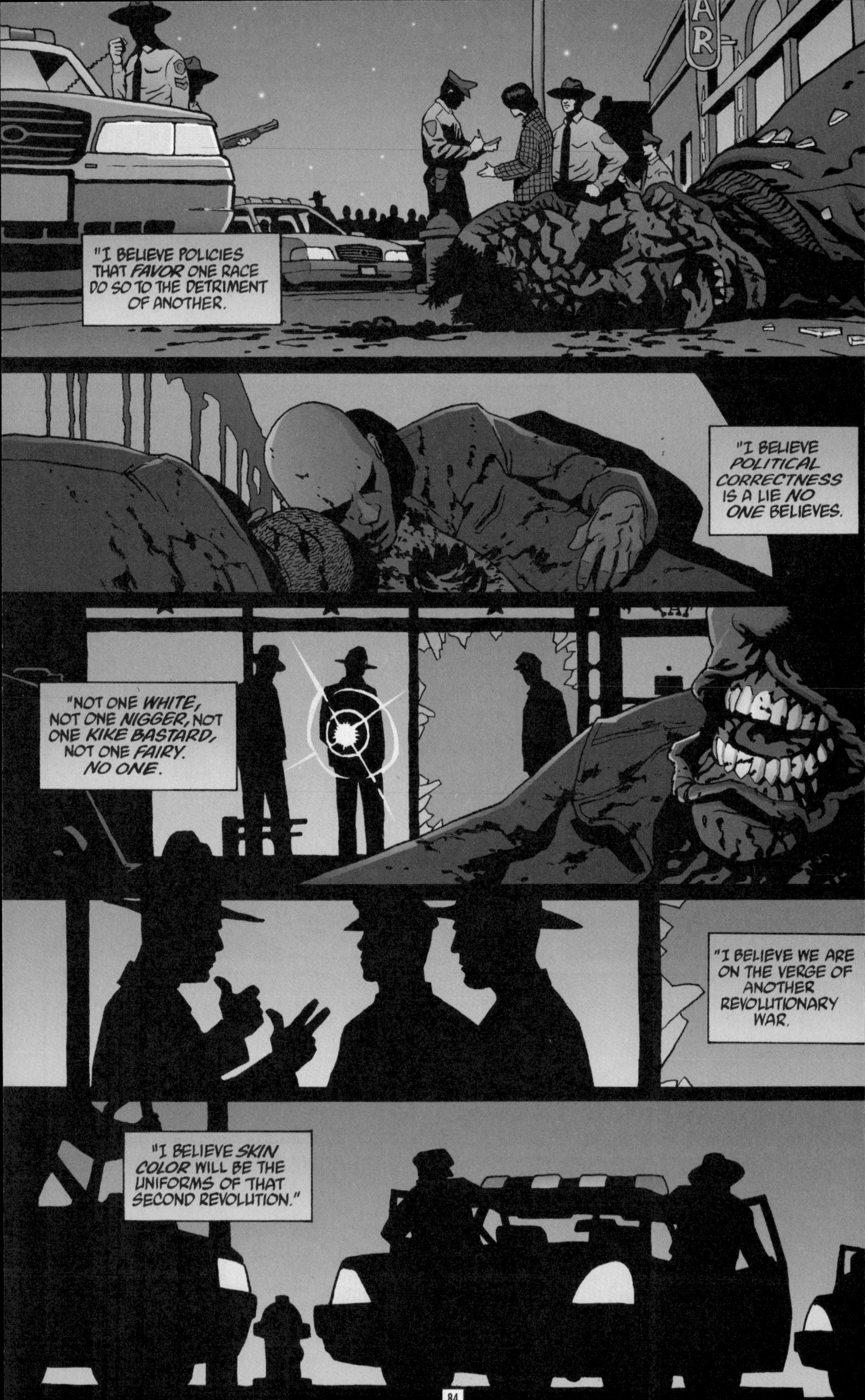
"I BELIEVE POLICIES THAT FAVOR ONE RACE DO SO TO THE DETRIMENT OF ANOTHER.
"I BELIEVE POLITICAL CORRECTNESS IS A LIE NO ONE BELIEVES.
"NOT ONE WHITE, NOT ONE NIGGER, NOT ONE KIKE BASTARD, NOT ONE FAIRY. NO ONE.
"I BELIEVE WE ARE ON THE VERGE OF ANOTHER REVOLUTIONARY WAR.
"I BELIEVE SKIN COLOR WILL BE THE UNIFORMS OF THAT SECOND REVOLUTION."

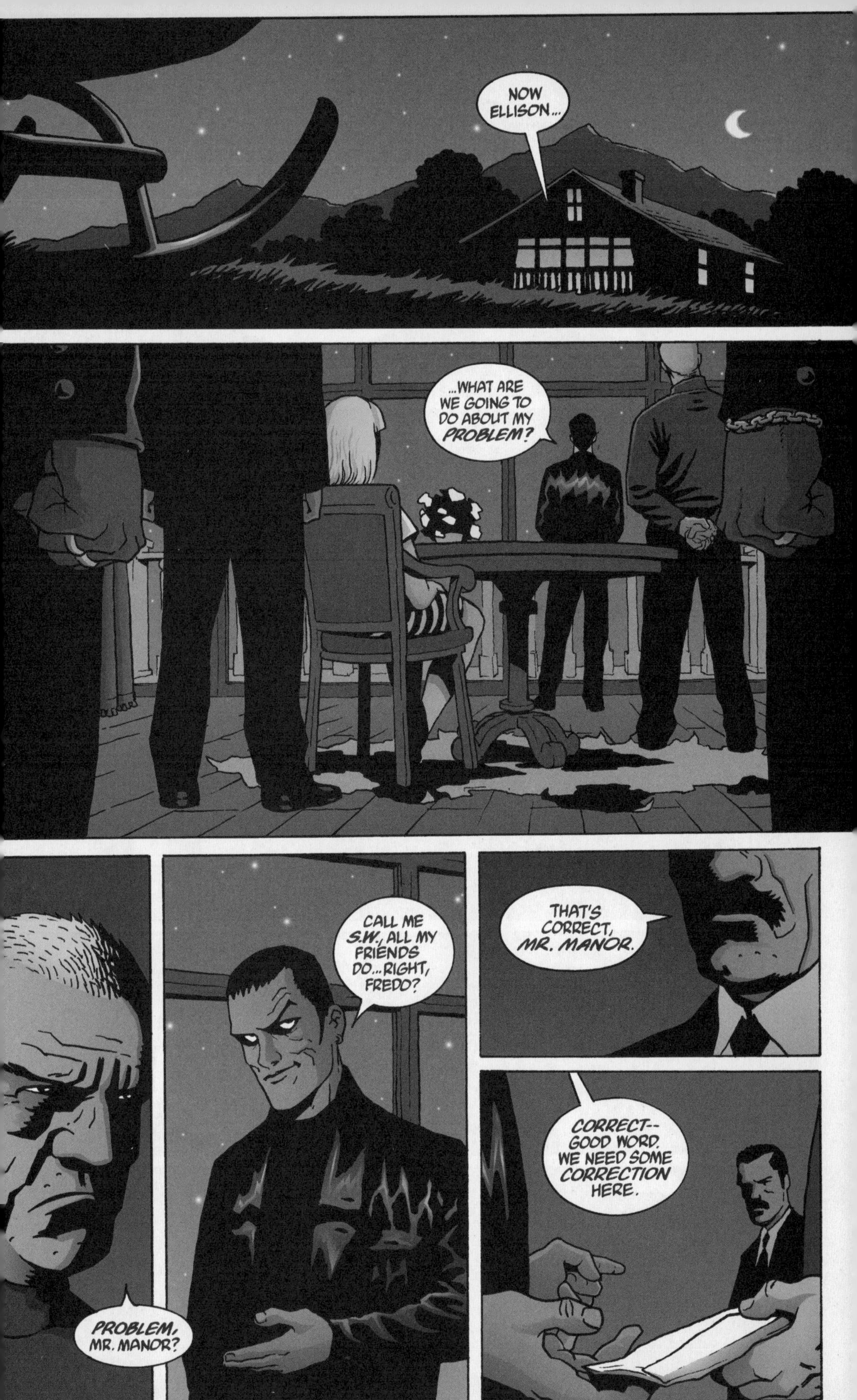
NOW ELLISON...
...WHAT ARE WE GOING TO DO ABOUT MY PROBLEM?
PROBLEM, MR. MANOR?
CALL ME S.W., ALL MY FRIENDS DO...RIGHT, FREDO?
THAT'S CORRECT, MR. MANOR.
CORRECT-- GOOD WORD. WE NEED SOME CORRECTION HERE.

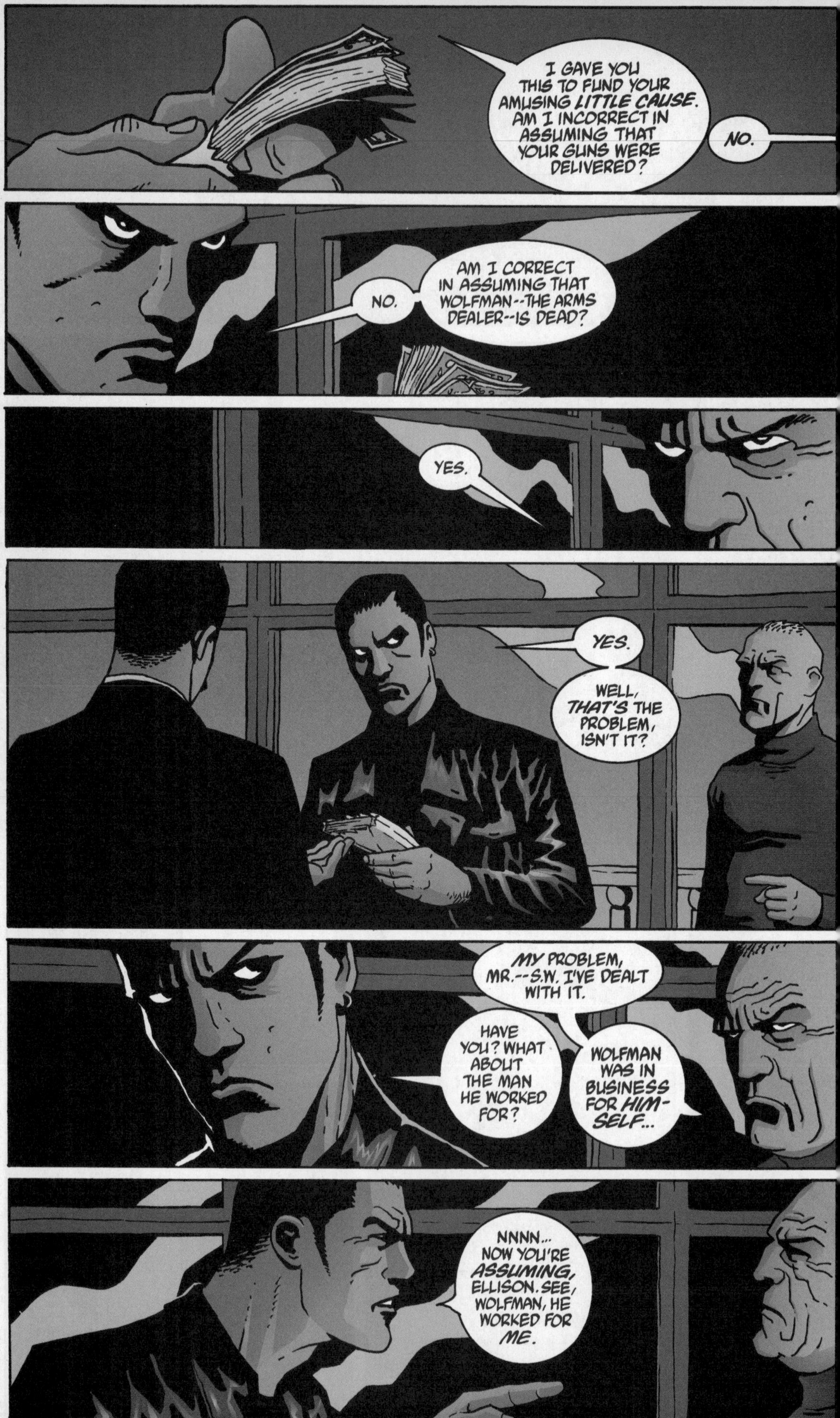
I GAVE YOU THIS TO FUND YOUR AMUSING LITTLE CAUSE. AM I INCORRECT IN ASSUMING THAT YOUR GUNS WERE DELIVERED?
NO.
AM I CORRECT IN ASSUMING THAT WOLFMAN--THE ARMS DEALER--IS DEAD?
NO.
YES.
YES.
WELL, THAT'S THE PROBLEM, ISN'T IT?
MY PROBLEM, MR.--S.W. I'VE DEALT WITH IT.
WOLFMAN WAS IN BUSINESS FOR HIM-SELF...
HAVE YOU? WHAT ABOUT THE MAN HE WORKED FOR?
NNNN... NOW YOU'RE ASSUMING, ELLISON. SEE, WOLFMAN, HE WORKED FOR ME.

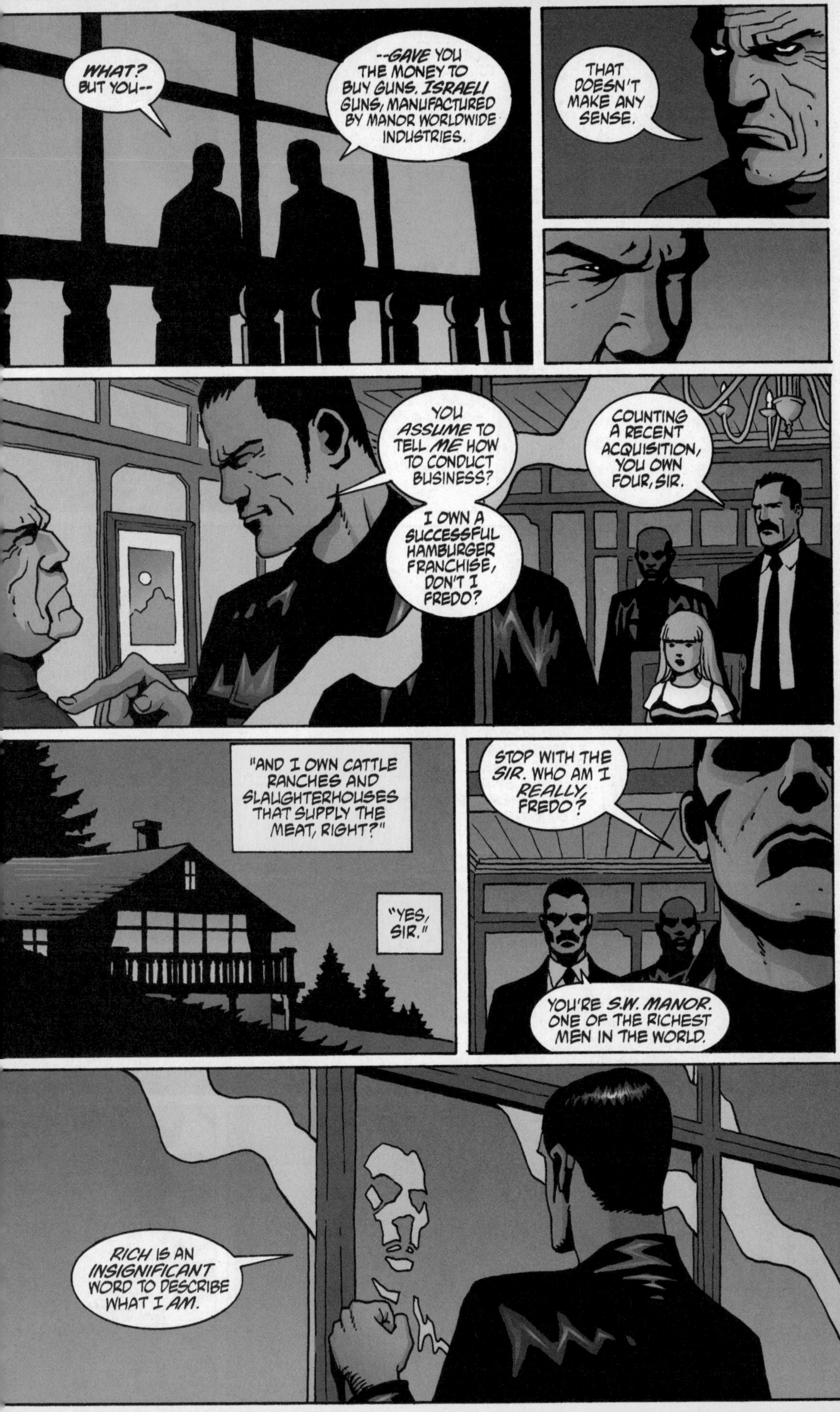
WHAT? BUT YOU--
--GAVE YOU THE MONEY TO BUY GUNS. ISRAELI GUNS, MANUFACTURED BY MANOR WORLDWIDE INDUSTRIES.
THAT DOESN'T MAKE ANY SENSE.
YOU ASSUME TO TELL ME HOW TO CONDUCT BUSINESS?
I OWN A SUCCESSFUL HAMBURGER FRANCHISE, DON'T I FREDO?
COUNTING A RECENT ACQUISITION, YOU OWN FOUR, SIR.
"AND I OWN CATTLE RANCHES AND SLAUGHTERHOUSES THAT SUPPLY THE MEAT, RIGHT?"
"YES, SIR."
STOP WITH THE SIR. WHO AM I REALLY, FREDO?
YOU'RE S.W. MANOR. ONE OF THE RICHEST MEN IN THE WORLD.
RICH IS AN INSIGNIFICANT WORD TO DESCRIBE WHAT I AM.

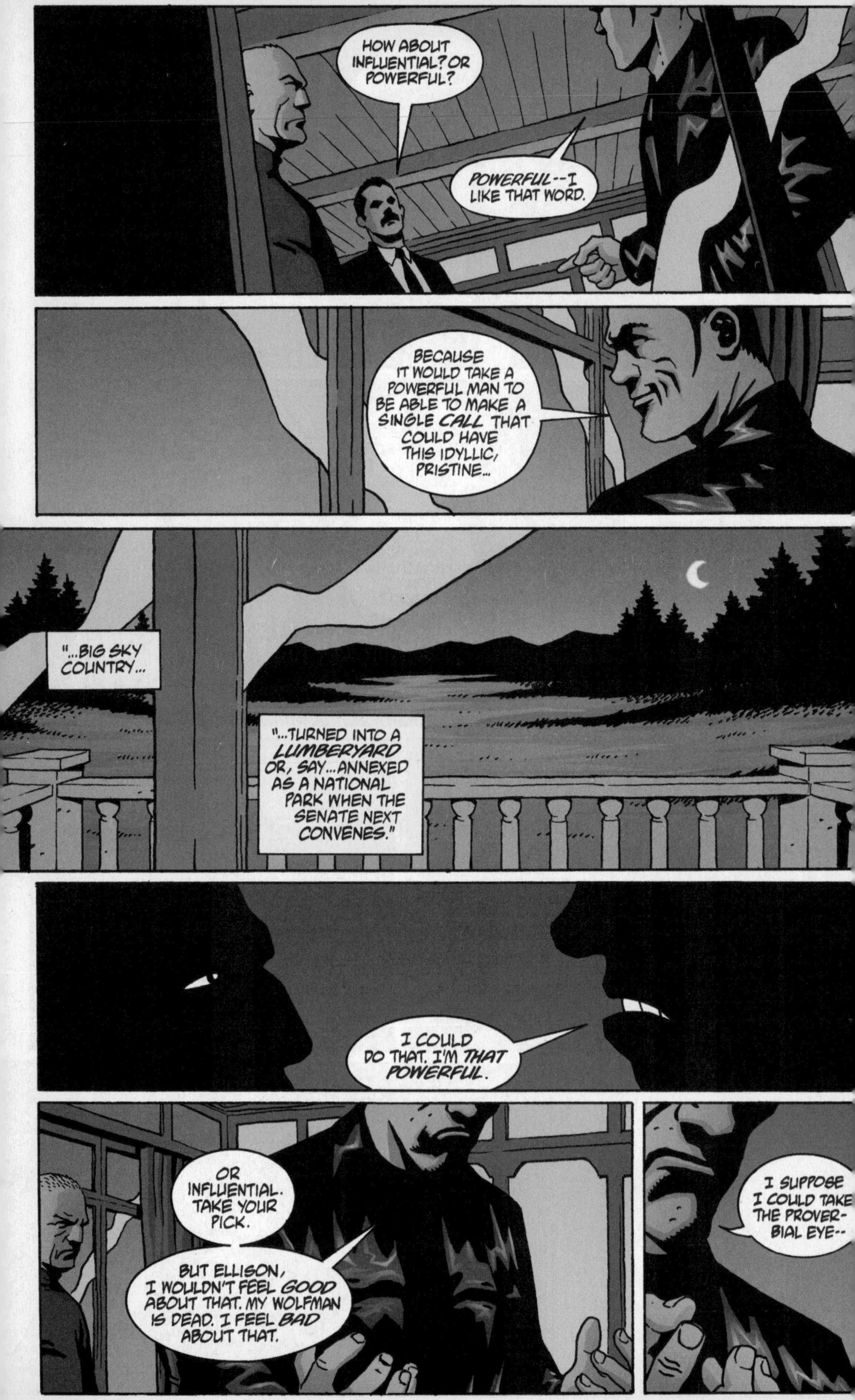
HOW ABOUT INFLUENTIAL? OR POWERFUL?
POWERFUL--I LIKE THAT WORD.
BECAUSE IT WOULD TAKE A POWERFUL MAN TO BE ABLE TO MAKE A SINGLE CALL THAT COULD HAVE THIS IDYLLIC, PRISTINE...
"...BIG SKY COUNTRY...
"...TURNED INTO A LUMBERYARD OR, SAY...ANNEXED AS A NATIONAL PARK WHEN THE SENATE NEXT CONVENES."
I COULD DO THAT. I'M THAT POWERFUL.
OR INFLUENTIAL. TAKE YOUR PICK.
BUT ELLISON, I WOULDN'T FEEL GOOD ABOUT THAT. MY WOLFMAN IS DEAD. I FEEL BAD ABOUT THAT.
I SUPPOSE I COULD TAKE THE PROVERBIAL EYE--

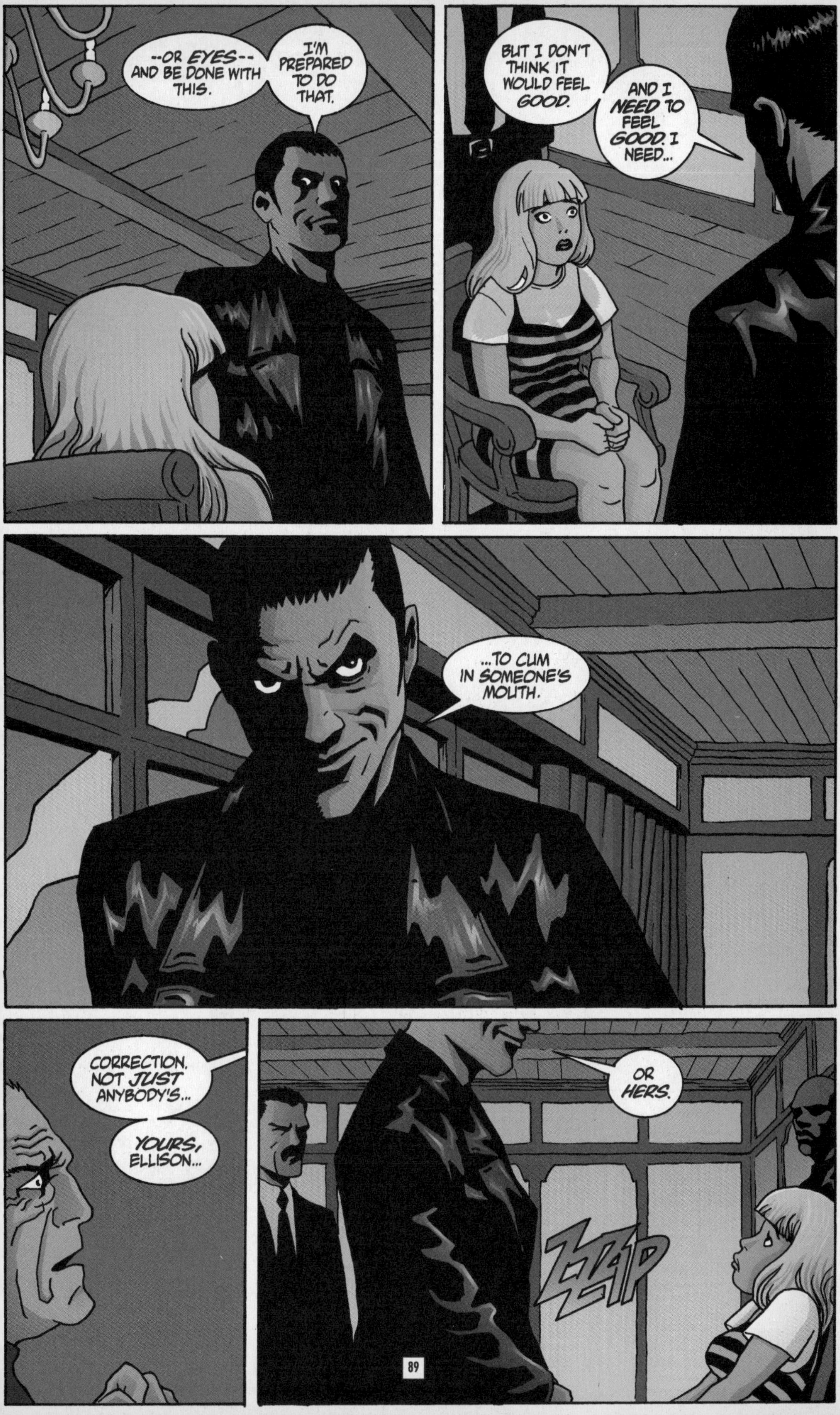

--OR EYES-- AND BE DONE WITH THIS.
I'M PREPARED TO DO THAT.
BUT I DON'T THINK IT WOULD FEEL GOOD.
AND I NEED TO FEEL GOOD. I NEED...
...TO CUM IN SOMEONE'S MOUTH.
CORRECTION. NOT JUST ANYBODY'S...
YOURS, ELLISON...
OR HERS.
ZZZIP

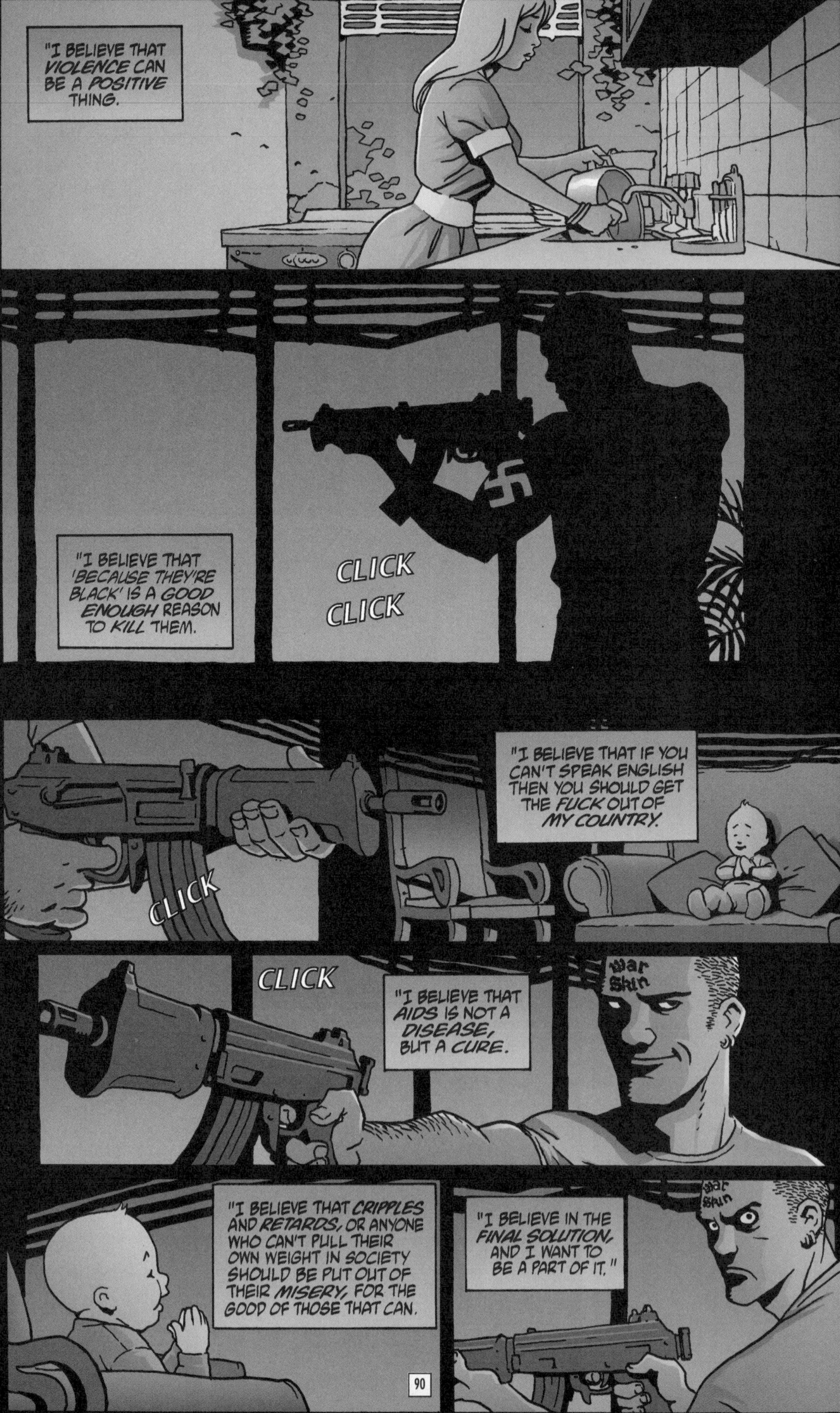
"I BELIEVE THAT *VIOLENCE* CAN BE A *POSITIVE* THING.
"I BELIEVE THAT *'BECAUSE THEY'RE BLACK'* IS A *GOOD ENOUGH* REASON TO *KILL* THEM.
CLICK
CLICK
"I BELIEVE THAT IF YOU CAN'T SPEAK ENGLISH THEN YOU SHOULD GET THE *FUCK* OUT OF *MY COUNTRY.*
CLICK
CLICK
"I BELIEVE THAT *AIDS* IS NOT A *DISEASE,* BUT A *CURE.*
"I BELIEVE THAT *CRIPPLES* AND *RETARDS,* OR ANYONE WHO CAN'T PULL THEIR OWN WEIGHT IN SOCIETY SHOULD BE PUT OUT OF THEIR *MISERY,* FOR THE GOOD OF THOSE THAT CAN.
"I BELIEVE IN THE *FINAL SOLUTION,* AND I WANT TO BE A PART OF IT."

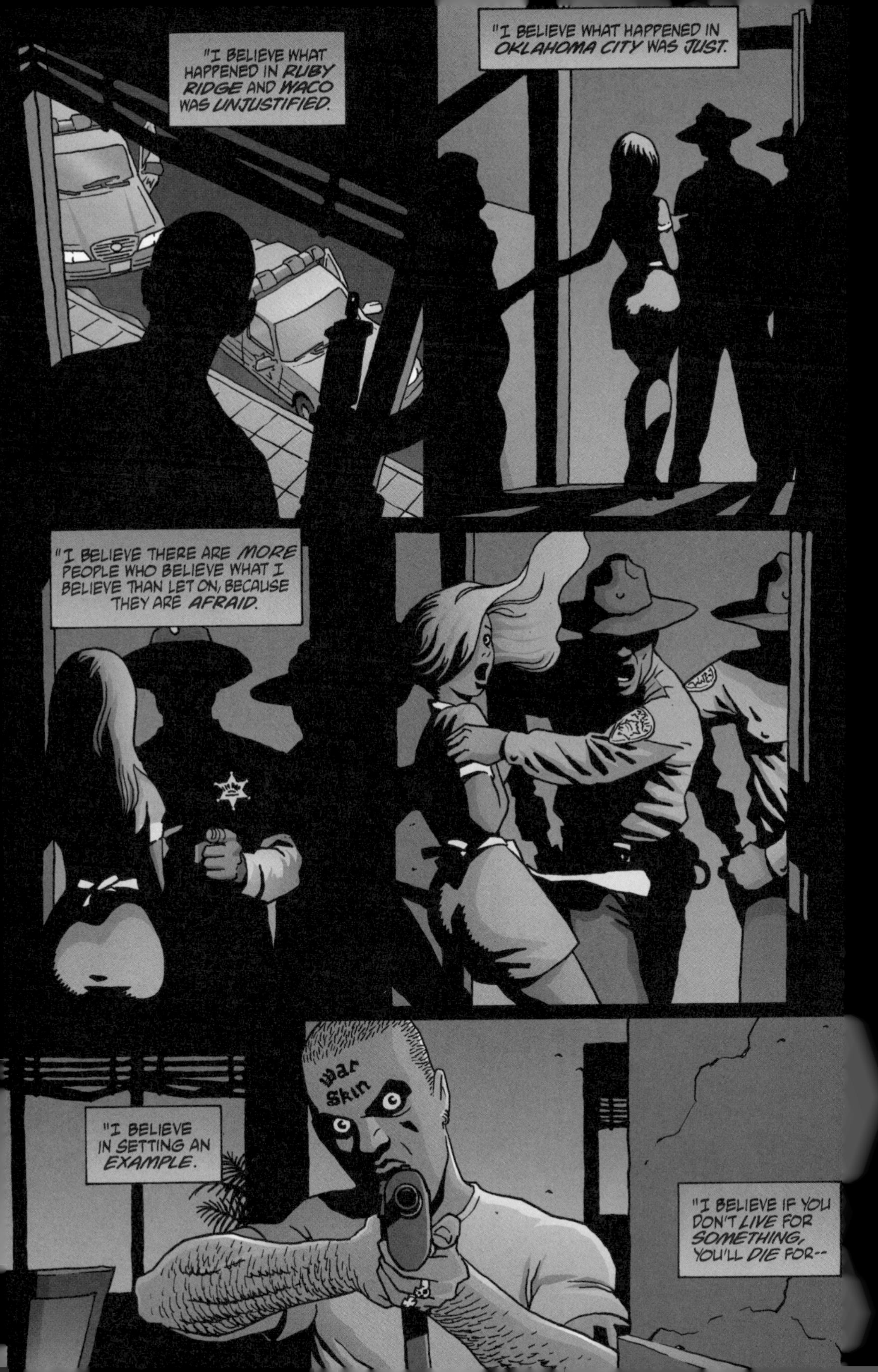
"I BELIEVE WHAT HAPPENED IN RUBY RIDGE AND WACO WAS UNJUSTIFIED.
"I BELIEVE WHAT HAPPENED IN OKLAHOMA CITY WAS JUST.
"I BELIEVE THERE ARE MORE PEOPLE WHO BELIEVE WHAT I BELIEVE THAN LET ON, BECAUSE THEY ARE AFRAID.
"I BELIEVE IN SETTING AN EXAMPLE.
War Skin
"I BELIEVE IF YOU DON'T LIVE FOR SOMETHING, YOU'LL DIE FOR--

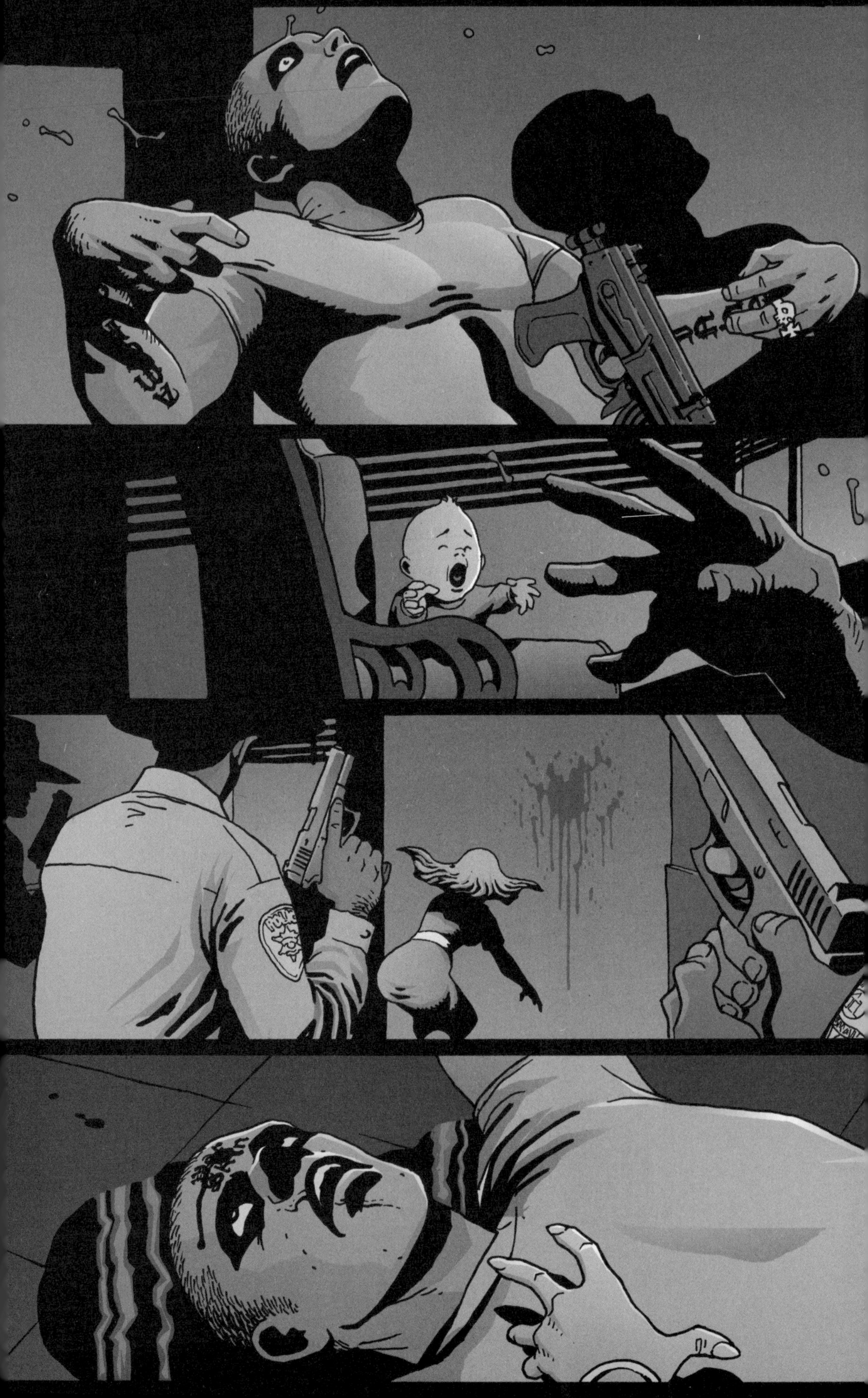

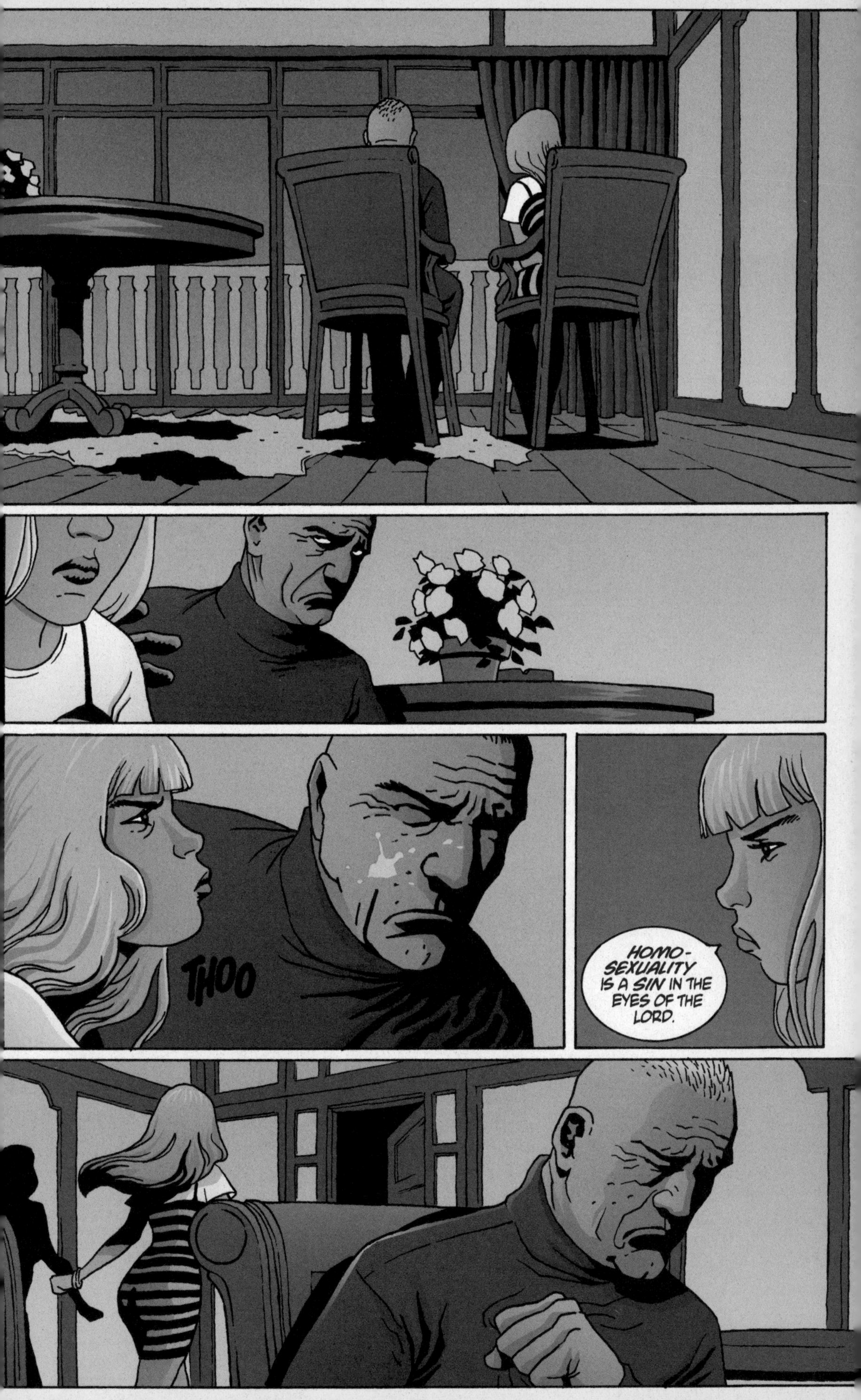
THOO
HOMO-SEXUALITY IS A SIN IN THE EYES OF THE LORD.

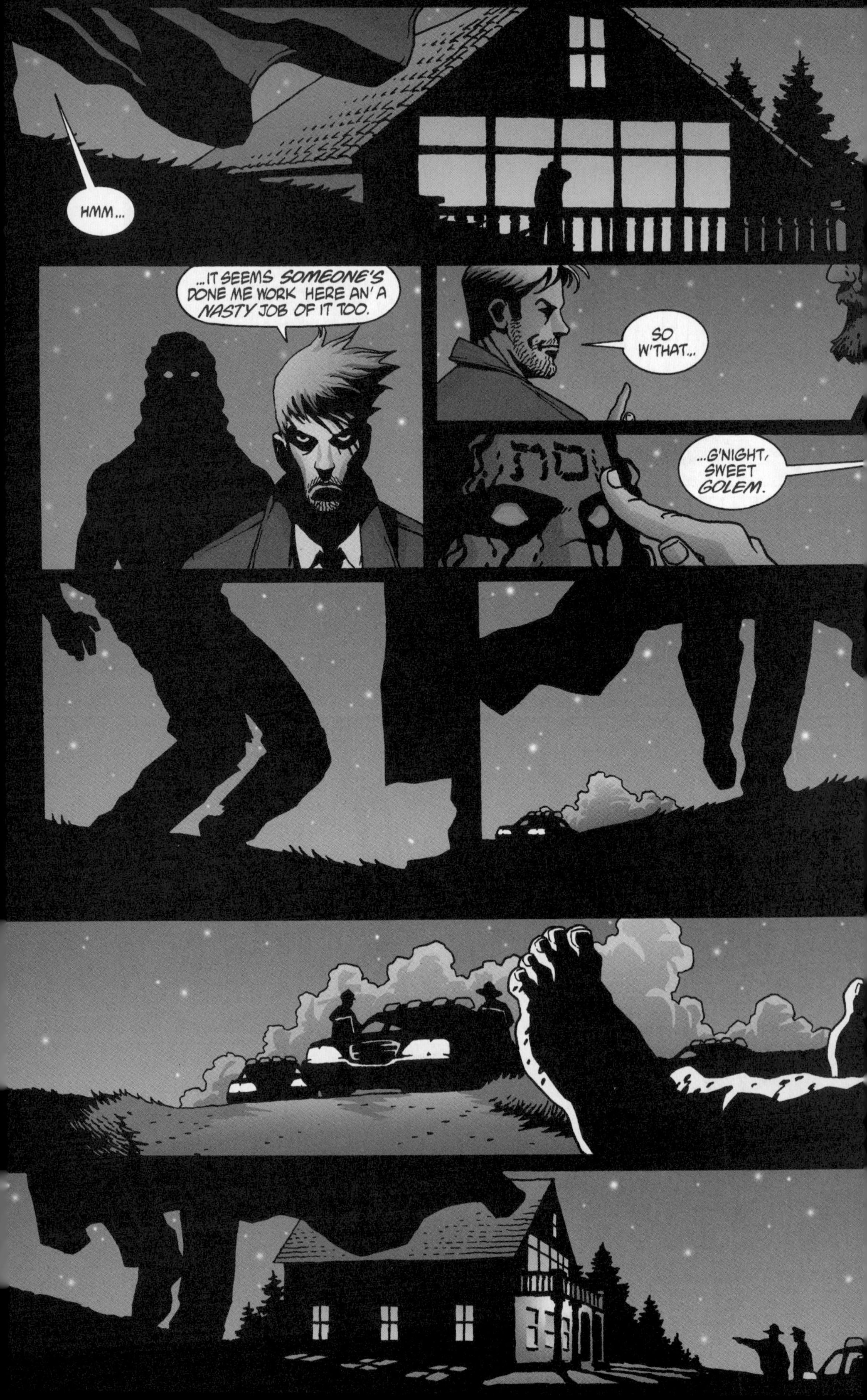
HMM...
...IT SEEMS SOMEONE'S DONE ME WORK HERE AN' A NASTY JOB OF IT TOO.
SO W'THAT...
...G'NIGHT, SWEET GOLEM.

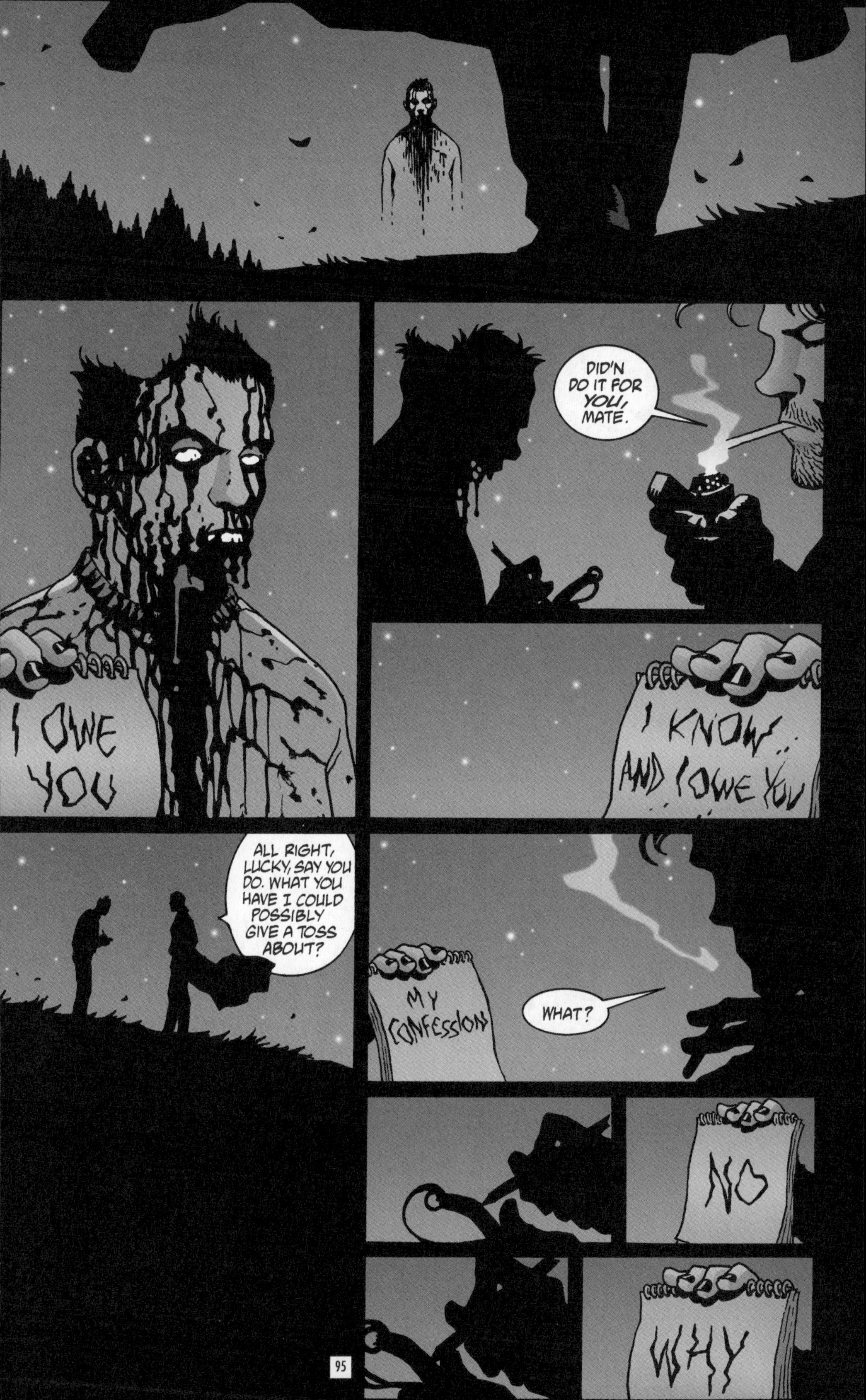

I OWE YOU
DID'N DO IT FOR YOU, MATE.
I KNOW.. AND I OWE YOU
ALL RIGHT, LUCKY, SAY YOU DO. WHAT YOU HAVE I COULD POSSIBLY GIVE A TOSS ABOUT?
MY CONFESSION
WHAT?
NO
WHY

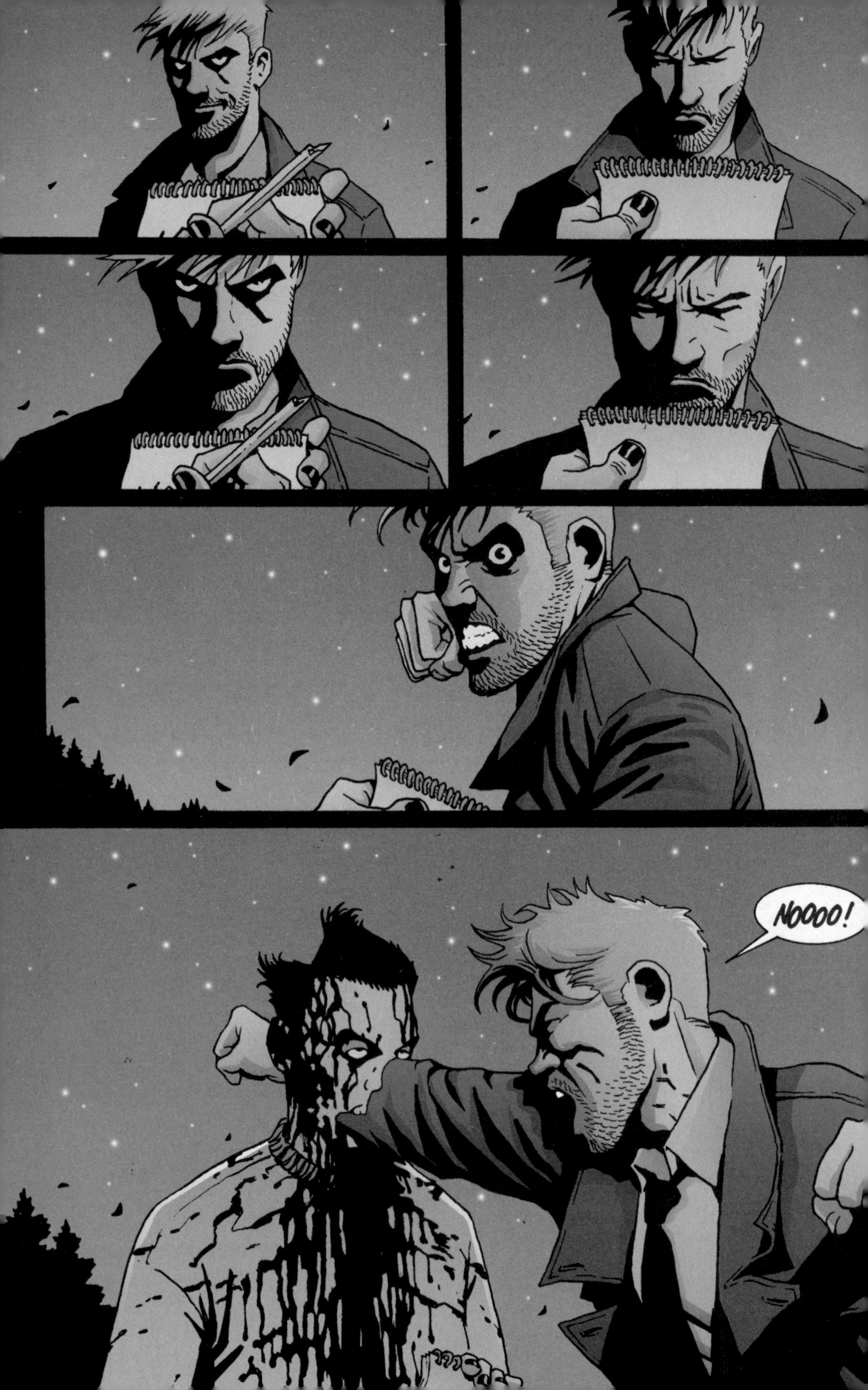
NOOOO!

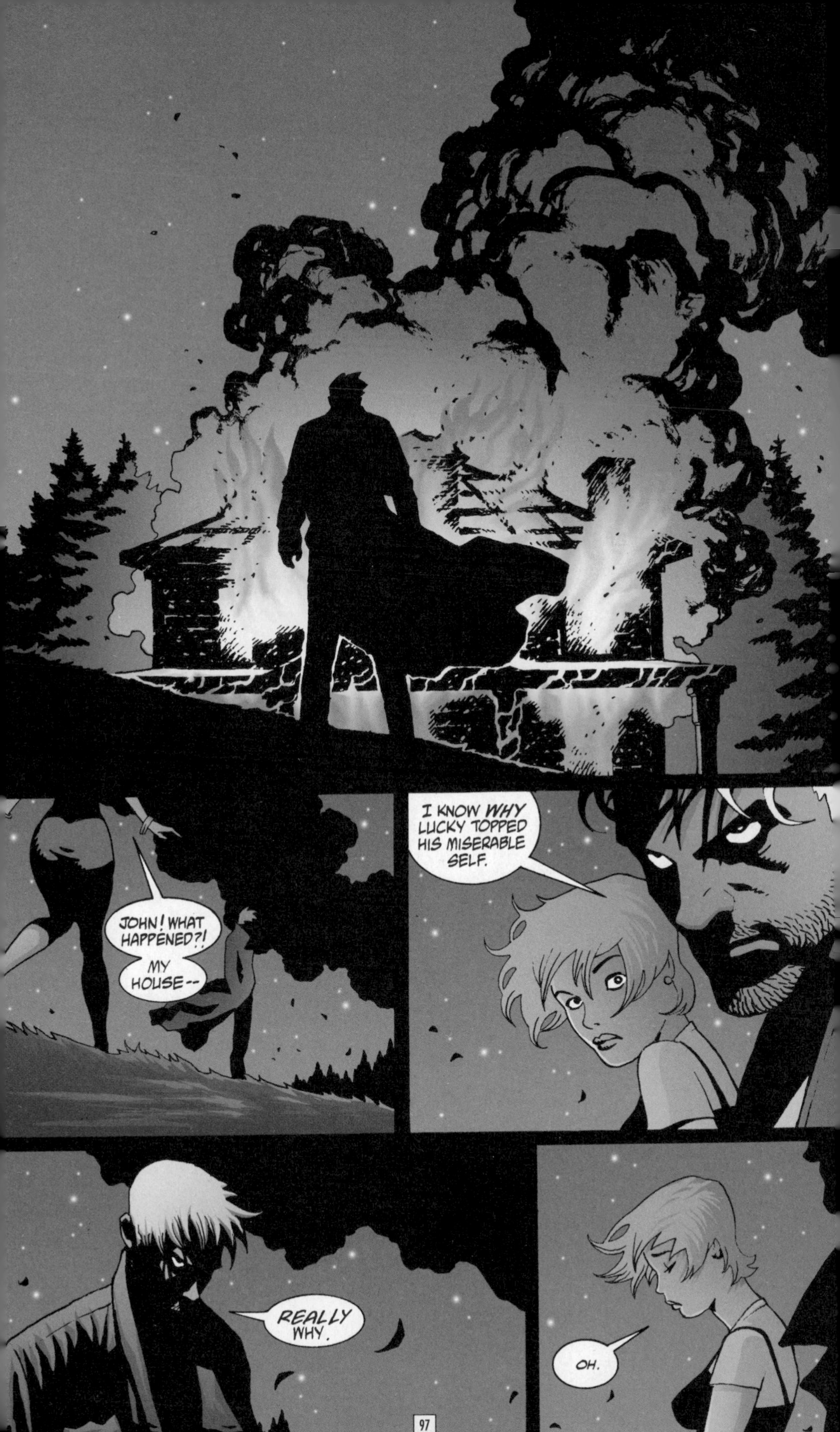
JOHN! WHAT HAPPENED?!
MY HOUSE--
I KNOW WHY LUCKY TOPPED HIS MISERABLE SELF.
REALLY WHY.
OH.

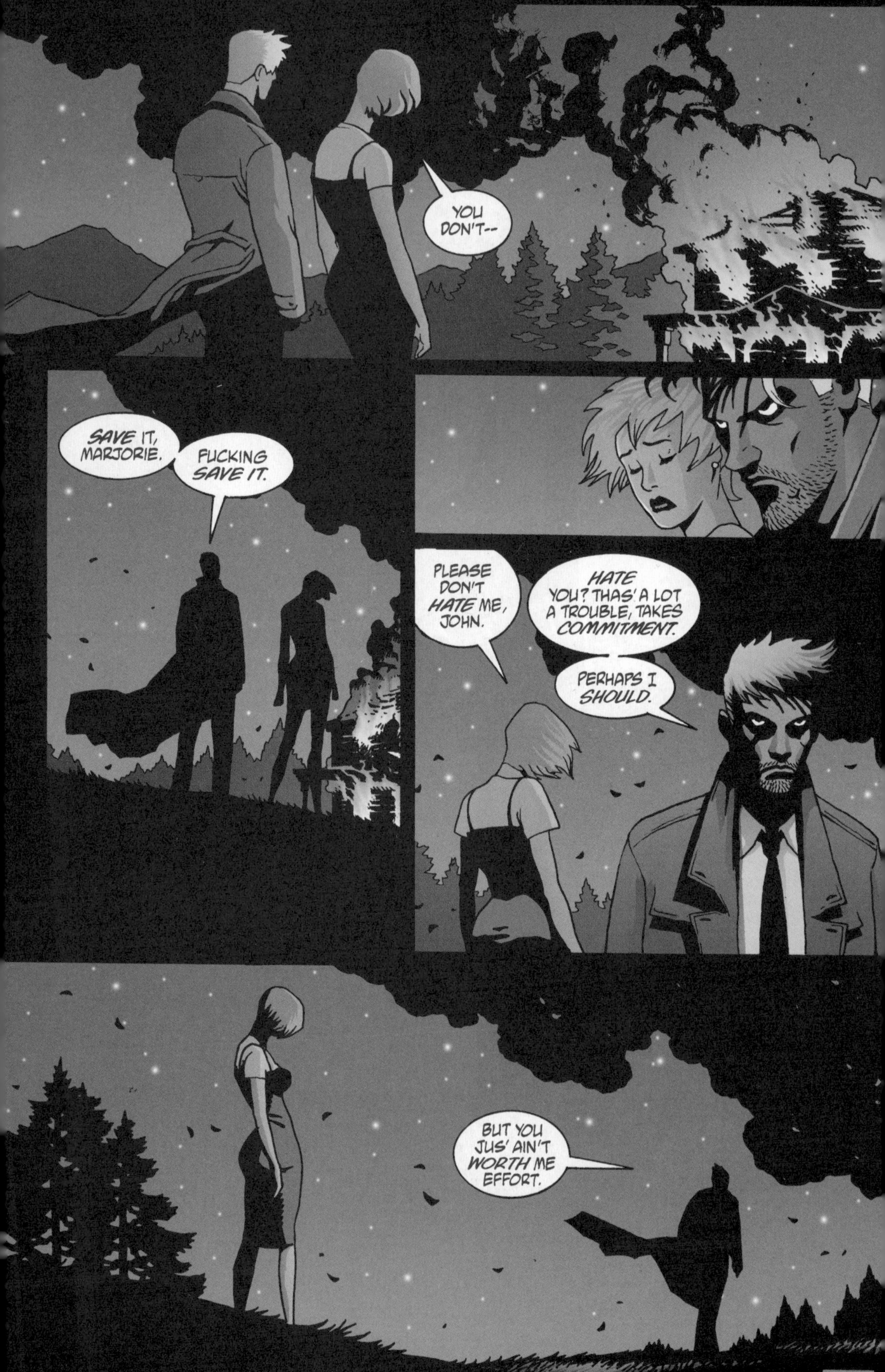
YOU DON'T--
SAVE IT, MARJORIE.
FUCKING SAVE IT.
PLEASE DON'T HATE ME, JOHN.
HATE YOU? THAS' A LOT A TROUBLE, TAKES COMMITMENT.
PERHAPS I SHOULD.
BUT YOU JUS' AIN'T WORTH ME EFFORT.
end

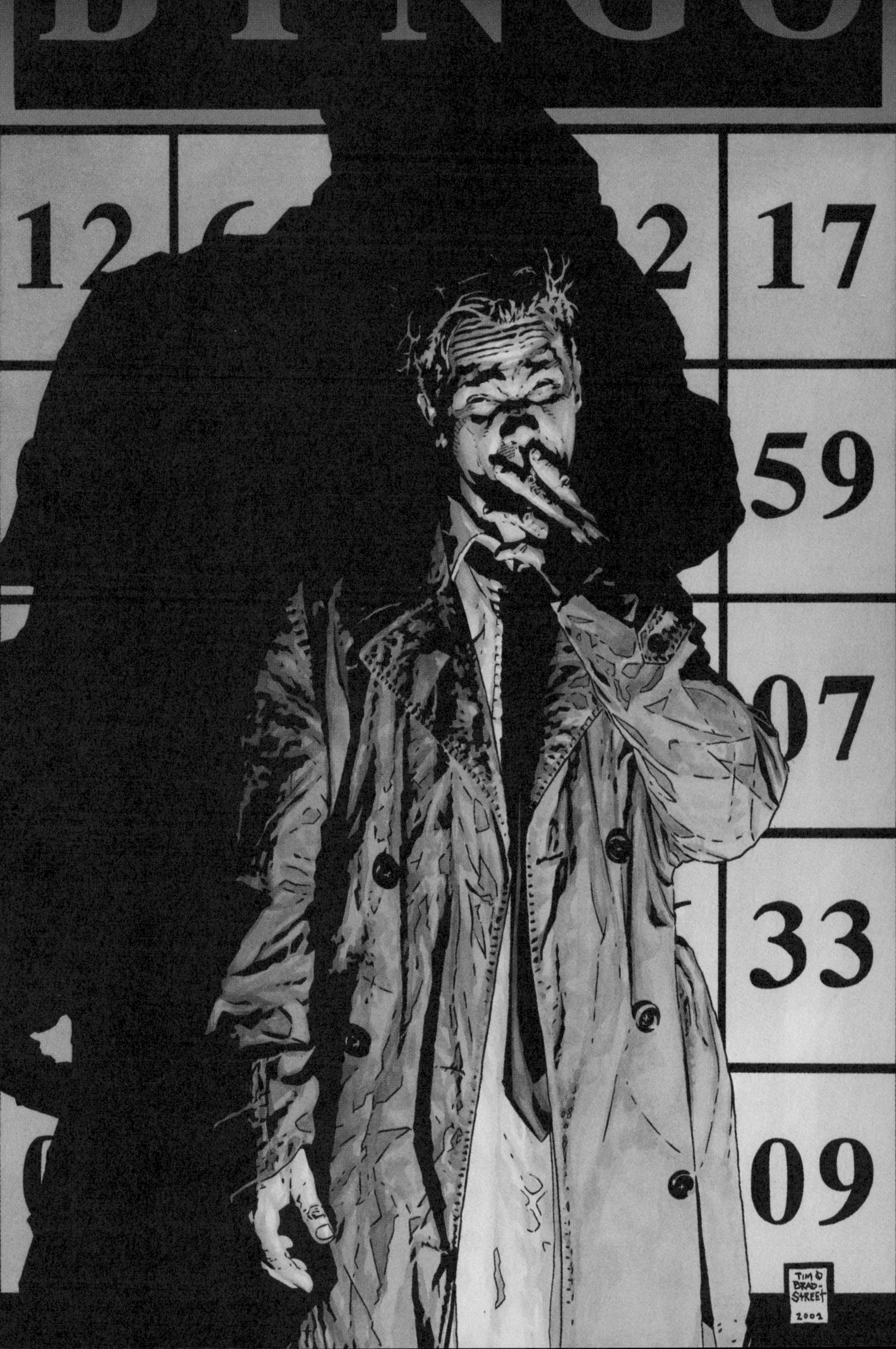

12
2
17
59
07
33
09
TIM BRAD-STREET
2002

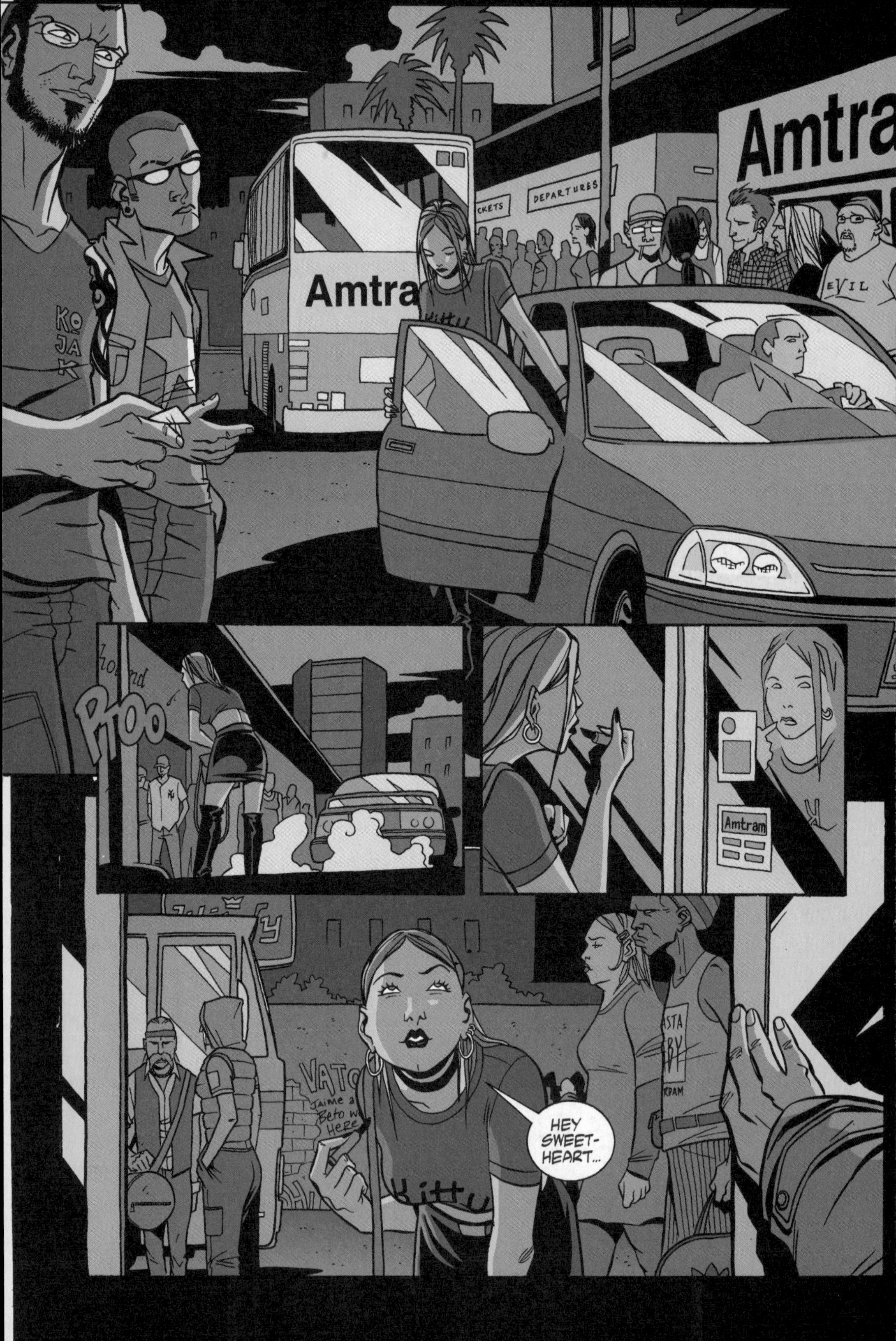
Amtra
DEPARTURES
CKETS
Amtra
KOJAK
EVIL
PTOO
Amtram
VATO
Jaime a
Beto w
Here
HEY SWEET-HEART...

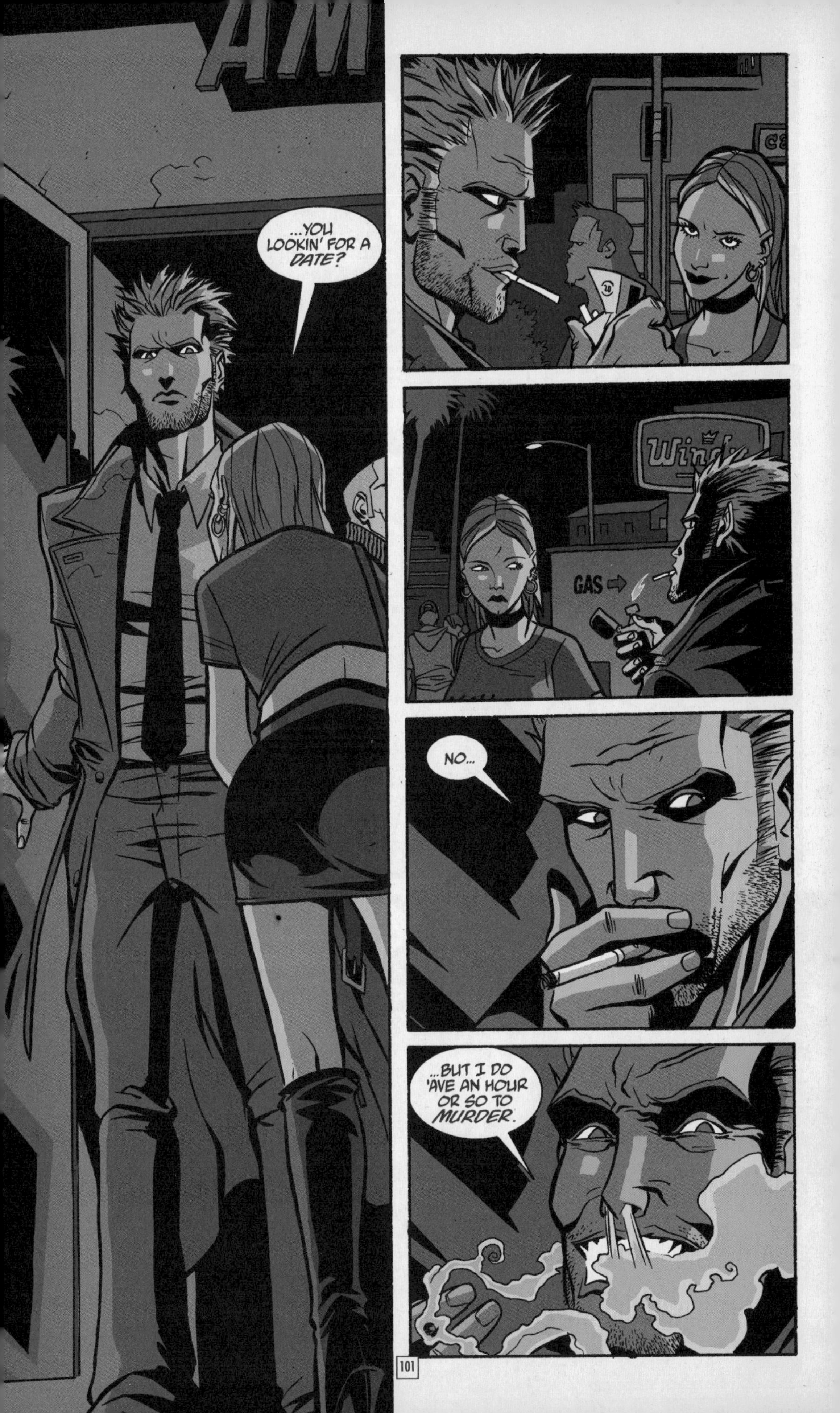
...YOU LOOKIN' FOR A DATE?
Wind
GAS
NO...
...BUT I DO 'AVE AN HOUR OR SO TO MURDER.

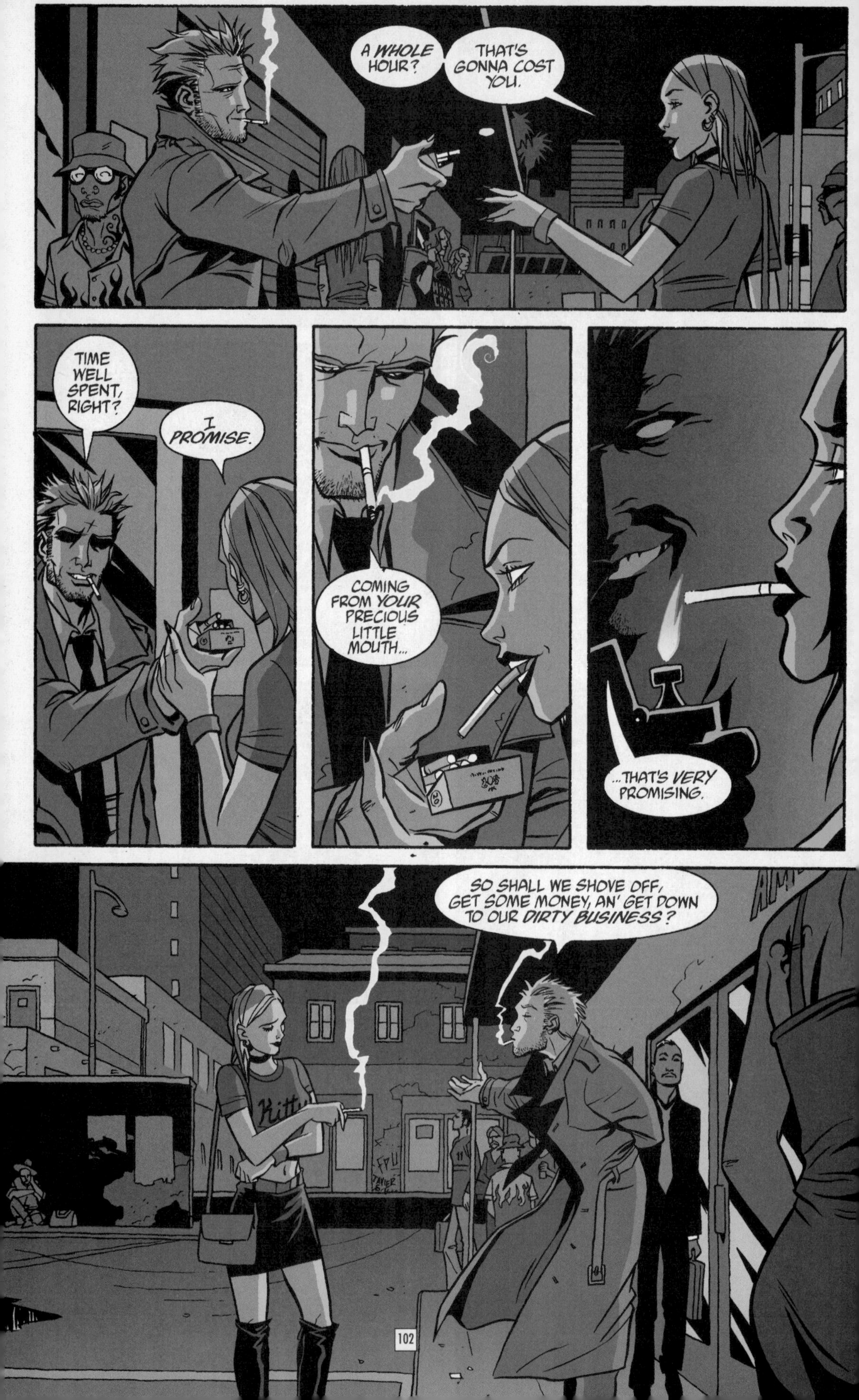
A WHOLE HOUR?
THAT'S GONNA COST YOU.
TIME WELL SPENT, RIGHT?
I PROMISE.
COMING FROM YOUR PRECIOUS LITTLE MOUTH...
...THAT'S VERY PROMISING.
SO SHALL WE SHOVE OFF, GET SOME MONEY, AN' GET DOWN TO OUR DIRTY BUSINESS?

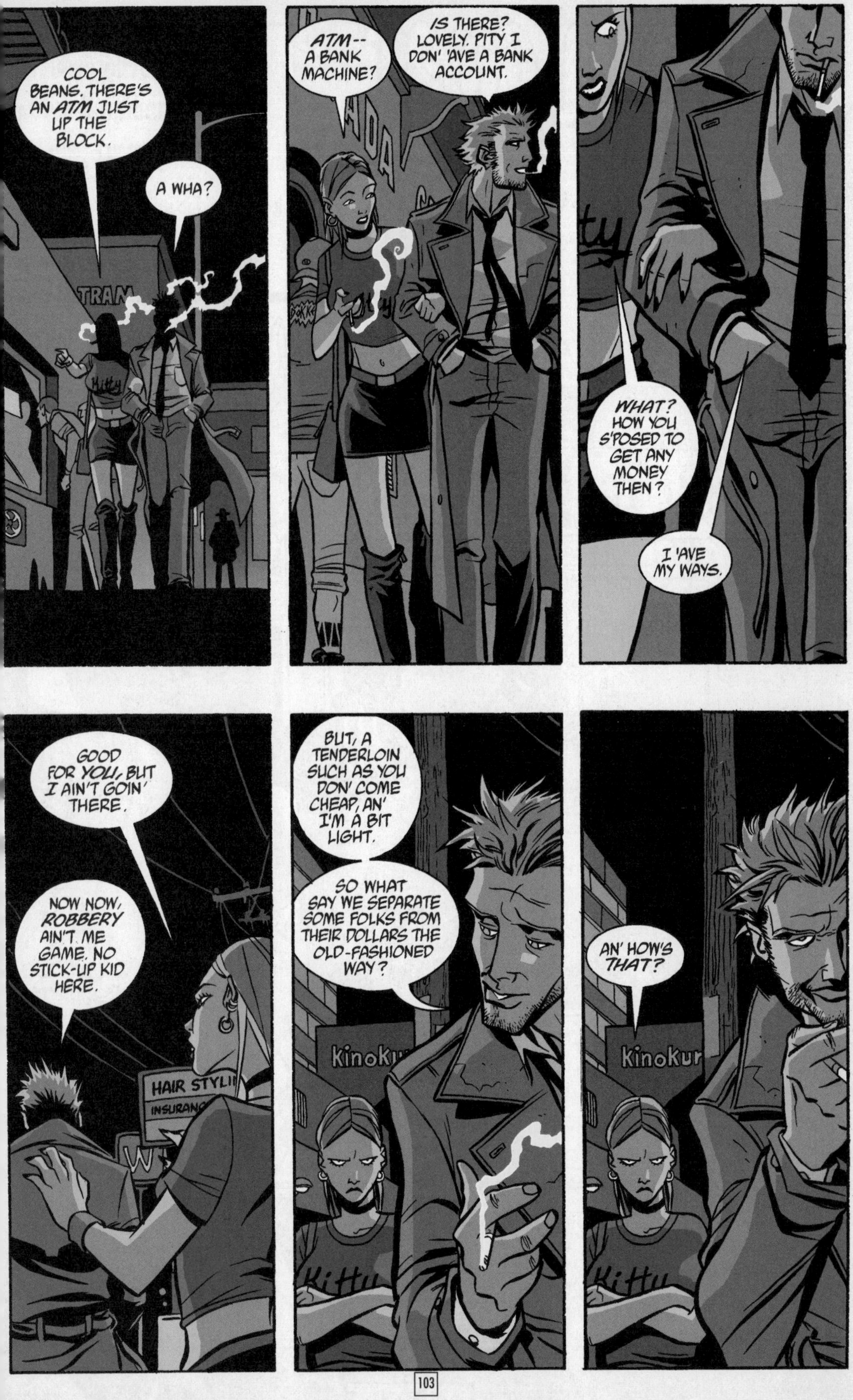

COOL BEANS. THERE'S AN *ATM* JUST UP THE BLOCK.
A WHA?
TRAM
ATM -- A BANK MACHINE?
IS THERE? LOVELY. PITY I DON' 'AVE A BANK ACCOUNT.
WHAT? HOW YOU S'POSED TO GET ANY MONEY THEN?
I 'AVE MY WAYS.
GOOD FOR *YOU*, BUT *I* AIN'T GOIN' THERE.
NOW NOW, *ROBBERY* AIN'T ME GAME. NO STICK-UP KID HERE.
HAIR STYLI
BUT, A TENDERLOIN SUCH AS YOU DON' COME CHEAP, AN' I'M A BIT LIGHT.
SO WHAT SAY WE SEPARATE SOME FOLKS FROM THEIR DOLLARS THE OLD-FASHIONED WAY?
KinoKur
AN' HOW'S *THAT*?
KinoKur

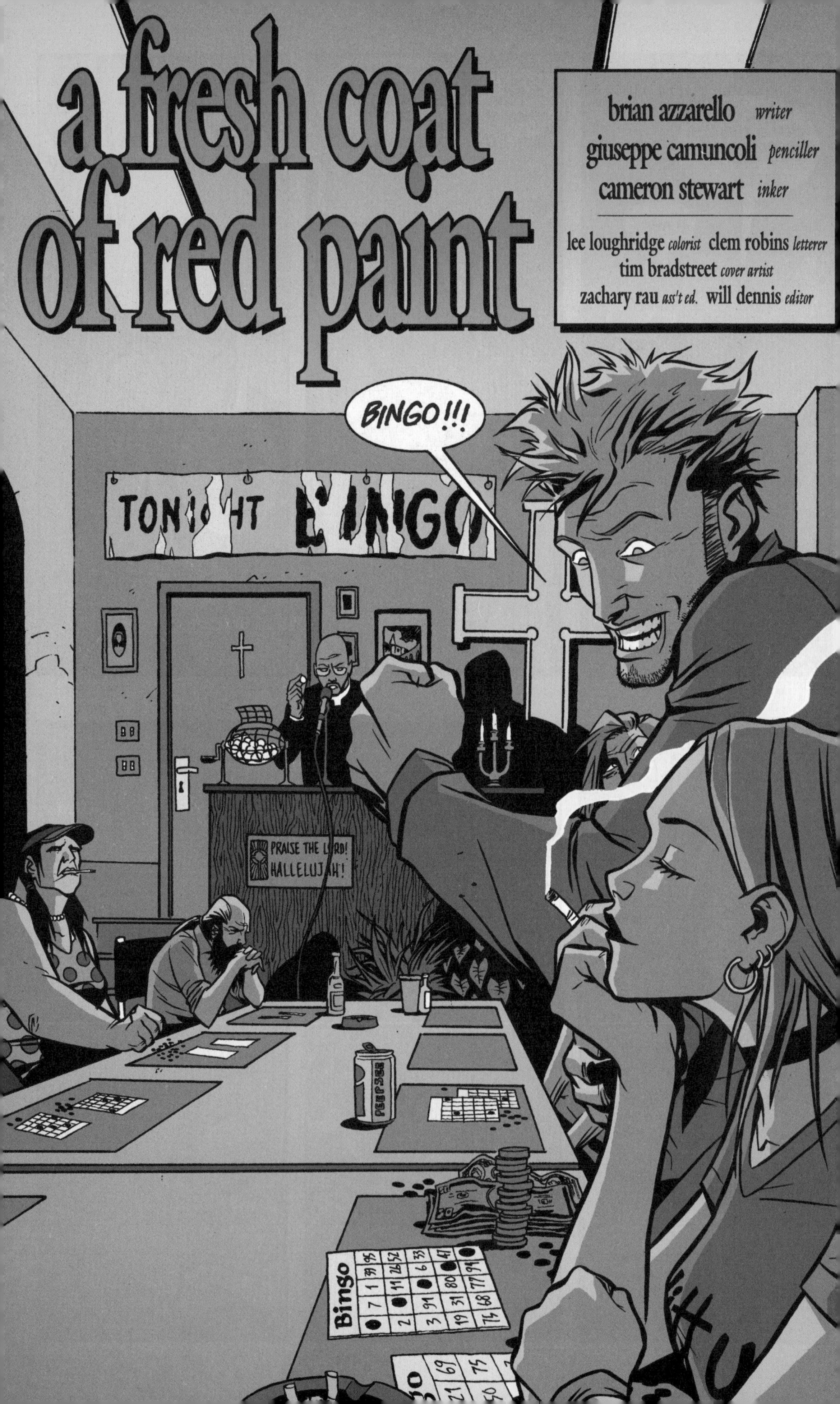

a fresh coat of red paint
brian azzarello writer
giuseppe camuncoli penciller
cameron stewart inker
lee loughridge colorist clem robins letterer
tim bradstreet cover artist
zachary rau ass't ed. will dennis editor
BINGO!!!
PRAISE THE LORD! HALLELUJAH!
Bingo

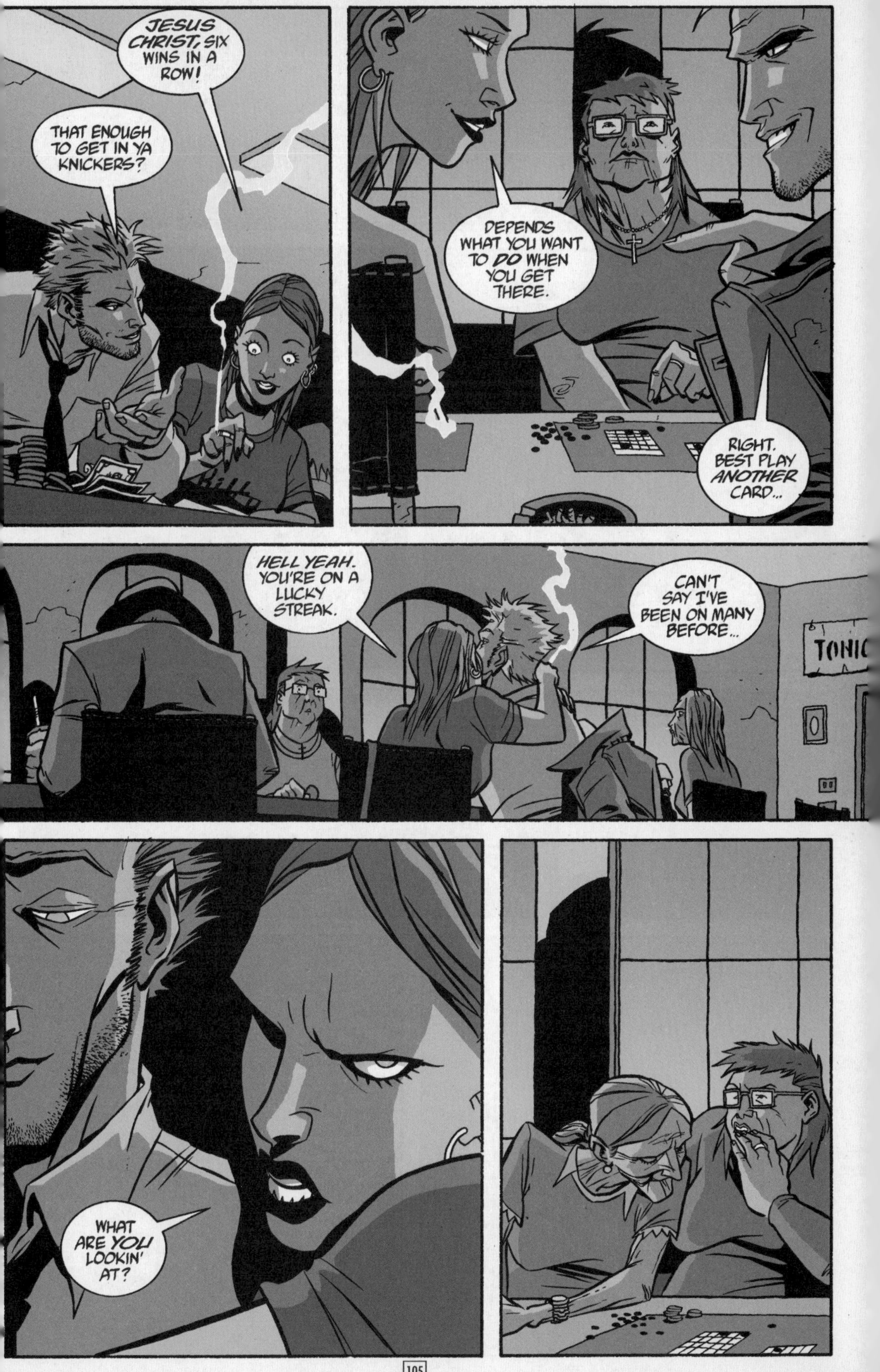

JESUS CHRIST, SIX WINS IN A ROW!
THAT ENOUGH TO GET IN YA KNICKERS?
DEPENDS WHAT YOU WANT TO DO WHEN YOU GET THERE.
RIGHT. BEST PLAY ANOTHER CARD...
HELL YEAH. YOU'RE ON A LUCKY STREAK.
CAN'T SAY I'VE BEEN ON MANY BEFORE...
TONIC
WHAT ARE YOU LOOKIN' AT?

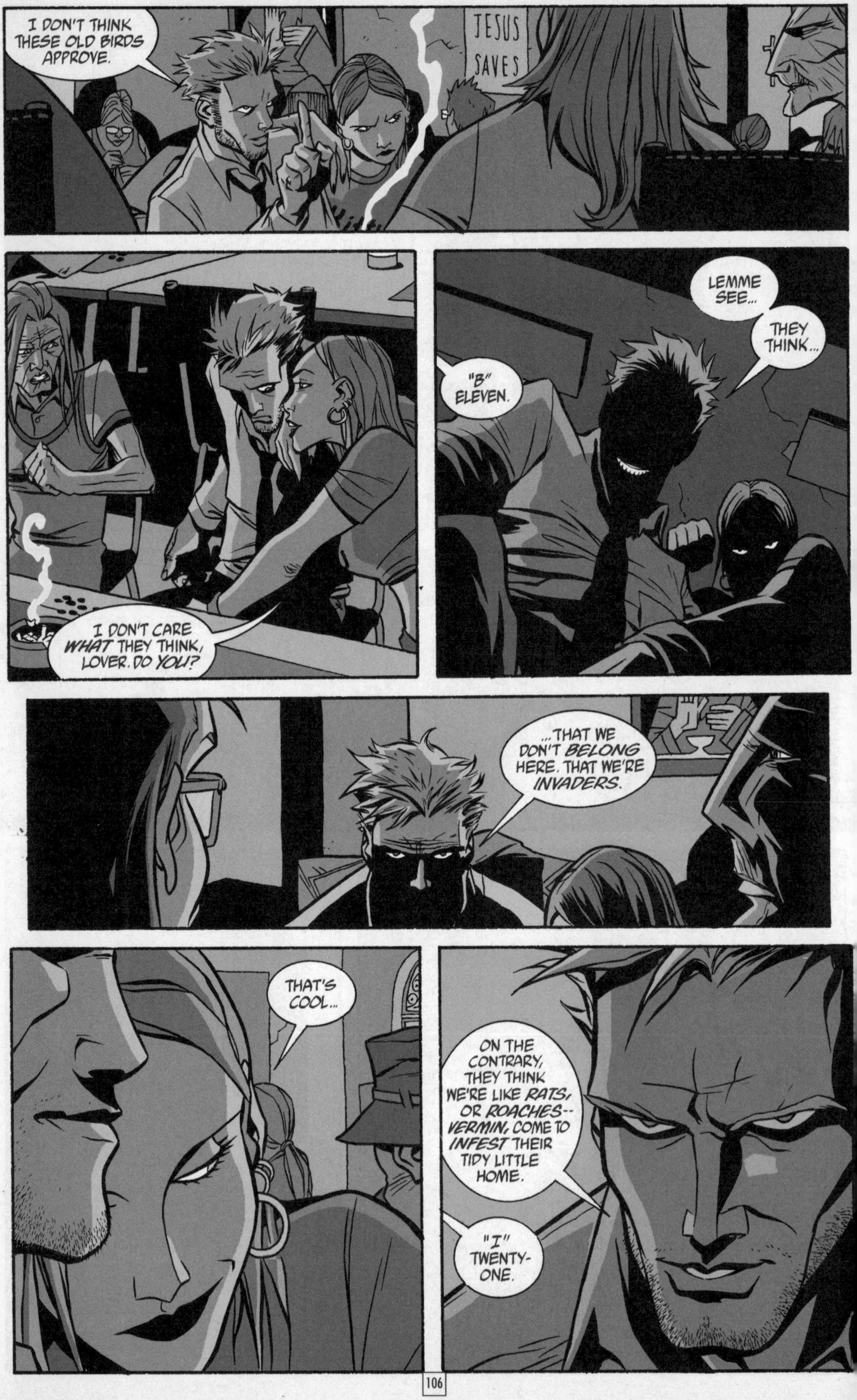
I DON'T THINK THESE OLD BIRDS APPROVE.
JESUS SAVES
I DON'T CARE *WHAT* THEY THINK, LOVER. DO *YOU*?
LEMME SEE...
THEY THINK...
"B" ELEVEN.
...THAT WE DON'T *BELONG* HERE. THAT WE'RE *INVADERS*.
THAT'S COOL...
ON THE CONTRARY, THEY THINK WE'RE LIKE *RATS*, OR *ROACHES*-- *VERMIN*, COME TO *INFEST* THEIR TIDY LITTLE HOME.
"I" TWENTY-ONE.

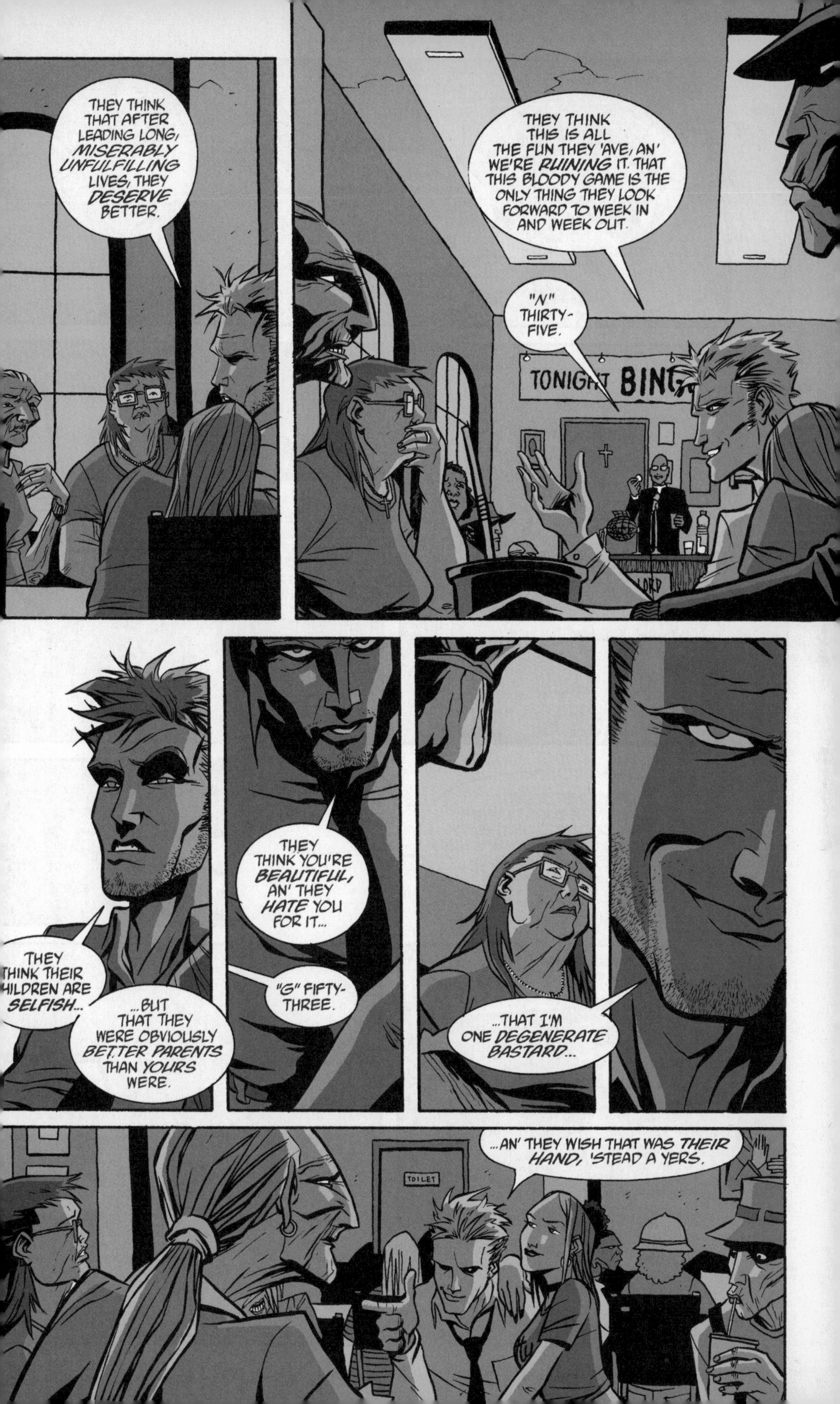
THEY THINK THAT AFTER LEADING LONG, MISERABLY UNFULFILLING LIVES, THEY DESERVE BETTER.
THEY THINK THIS IS ALL THE FUN THEY 'AVE, AN' WE'RE RUINING IT. THAT THIS BLOODY GAME IS THE ONLY THING THEY LOOK FORWARD TO WEEK IN AND WEEK OUT.
"N" THIRTY-FIVE.
TONIGHT BING
LORD
THEY THINK YOU'RE BEAUTIFUL, AN' THEY HATE YOU FOR IT...
THEY THINK THEIR HILDREN ARE SELFISH...
...BUT THAT THEY WERE OBVIOUSLY BETTER PARENTS THAN YOURS WERE.
"G" FIFTY-THREE.
...THAT I'M ONE DEGENERATE BASTARD...
...AN' THEY WISH THAT WAS THEIR HAND, 'STEAD A YERS.
TOILET

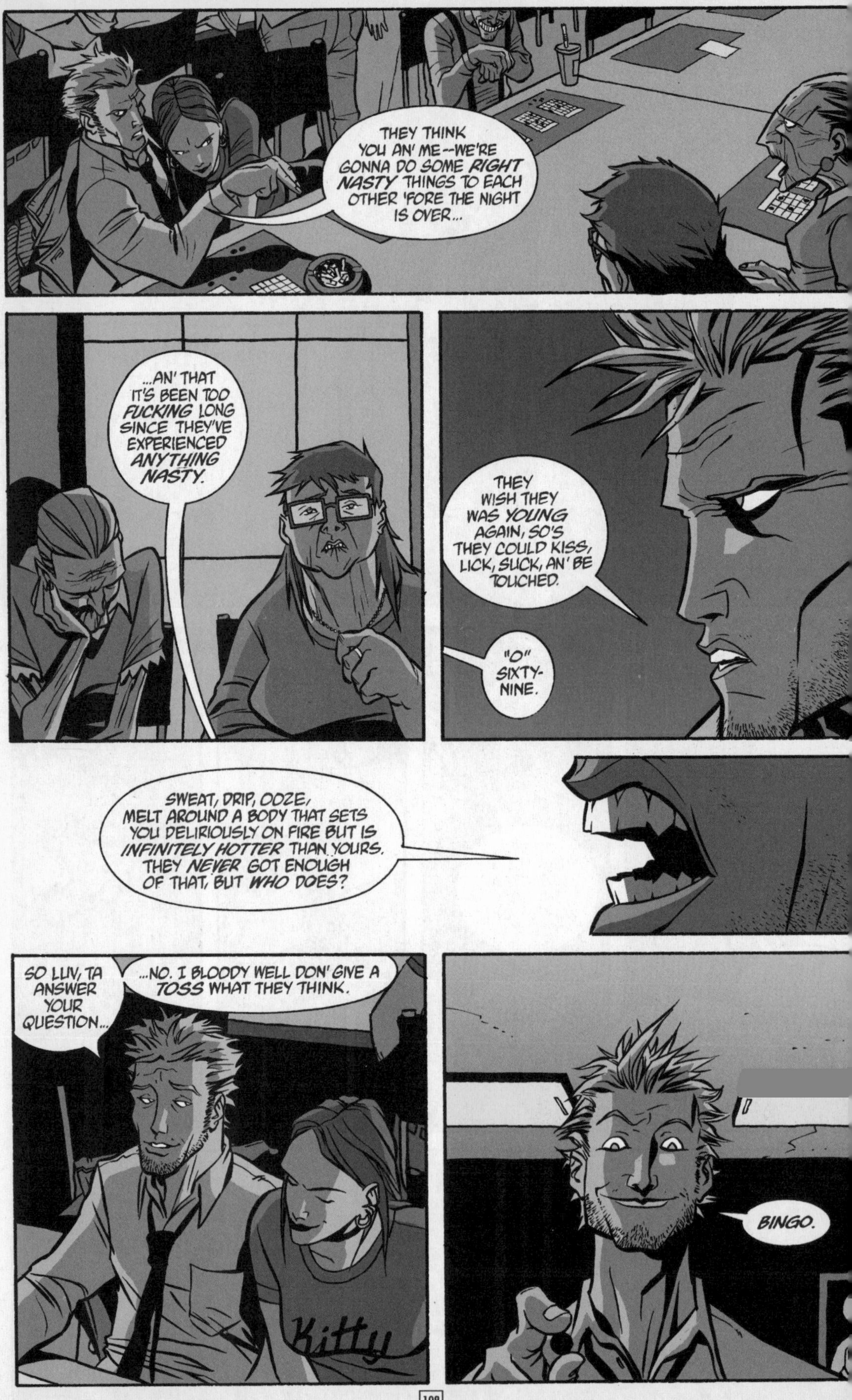

THEY THINK YOU AN' ME--WE'RE GONNA DO SOME *RIGHT NASTY* THINGS TO EACH OTHER 'FORE THE NIGHT IS OVER...
...AN' THAT IT'S BEEN TOO *FUCKING* LONG SINCE THEY'VE EXPERIENCED *ANYTHING NASTY*.
THEY WISH THEY WAS *YOUNG* AGAIN, SO'S THEY COULD KISS, LICK, SUCK, AN' BE TOUCHED.
"O" SIXTY-NINE.
SWEAT, DRIP, OOZE, MELT AROUND A BODY THAT SETS YOU DELIRIOUSLY ON FIRE BUT IS *INFINITELY HOTTER* THAN YOURS. THEY *NEVER* GOT ENOUGH OF THAT, BUT *WHO DOES?*
SO LUV, TA ANSWER YOUR QUESTION...
...NO. I BLOODY WELL DON' GIVE A *TOSS* WHAT THEY THINK.
Kitty
BINGO.

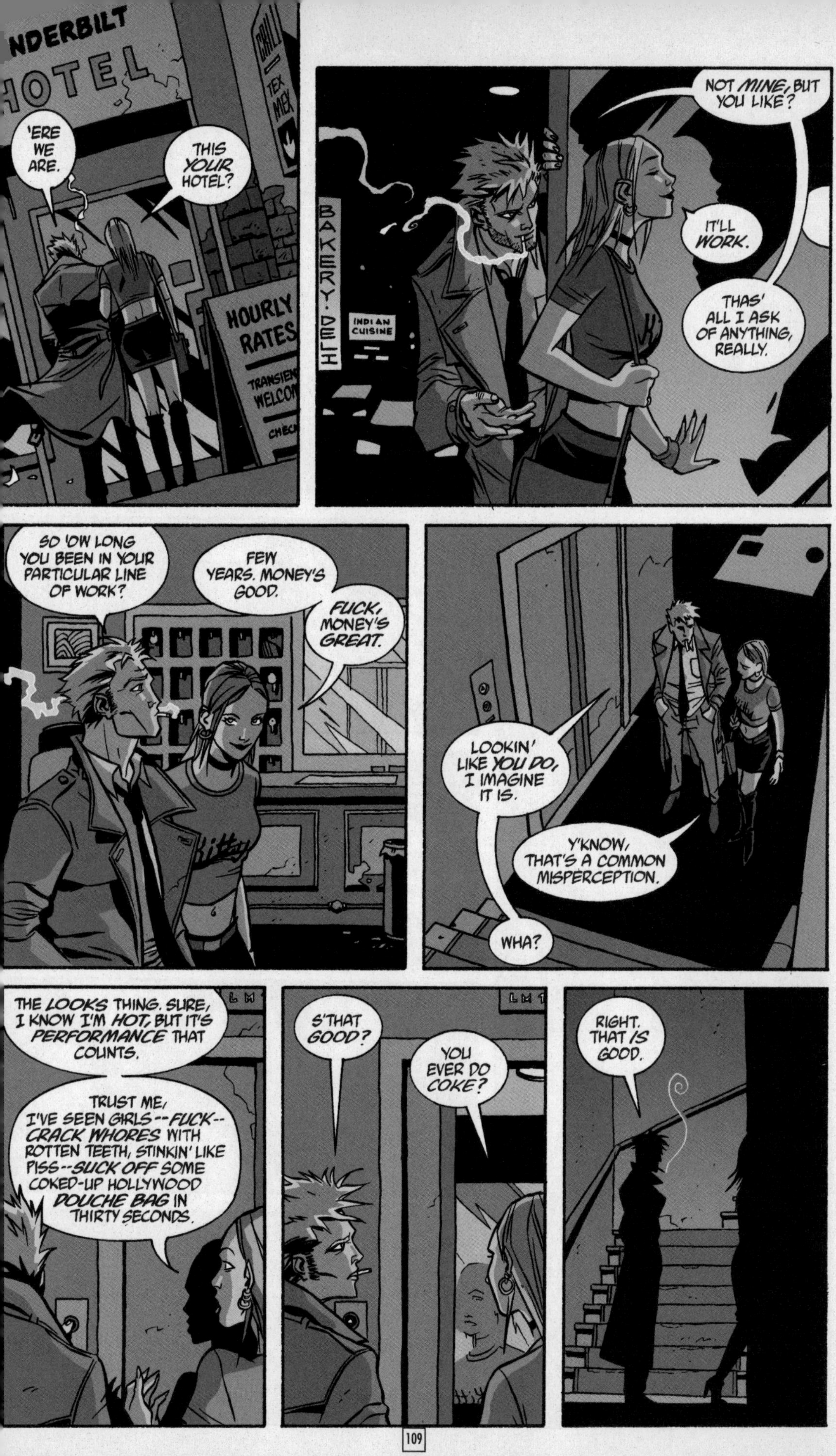
NDERBILT HOTEL
CHILI TEX MEX
'ERE WE ARE.
THIS YOUR HOTEL?
HOURLY RATES
TRANSIENTS WELCOME
BAKERY DELI
INDIAN CUISINE
NOT MINE, BUT YOU LIKE?
IT'LL WORK.
THAS' ALL I ASK OF ANYTHING, REALLY.
SO 'OW LONG YOU BEEN IN YOUR PARTICULAR LINE OF WORK?
FEW YEARS. MONEY'S GOOD.
FUCK, MONEY'S GREAT.
LOOKIN' LIKE YOU DO, I IMAGINE IT IS.
Y'KNOW, THAT'S A COMMON MISPERCEPTION.
WHA?
THE LOOKS THING. SURE, I KNOW I'M HOT, BUT IT'S PERFORMANCE THAT COUNTS.
TRUST ME, I'VE SEEN GIRLS--FUCK--CRACK WHORES WITH ROTTEN TEETH, STINKIN' LIKE PISS--SUCK OFF SOME COKED-UP HOLLYWOOD DOUCHE BAG IN THIRTY SECONDS.
S'THAT GOOD?
YOU EVER DO COKE?
RIGHT. THAT IS GOOD.

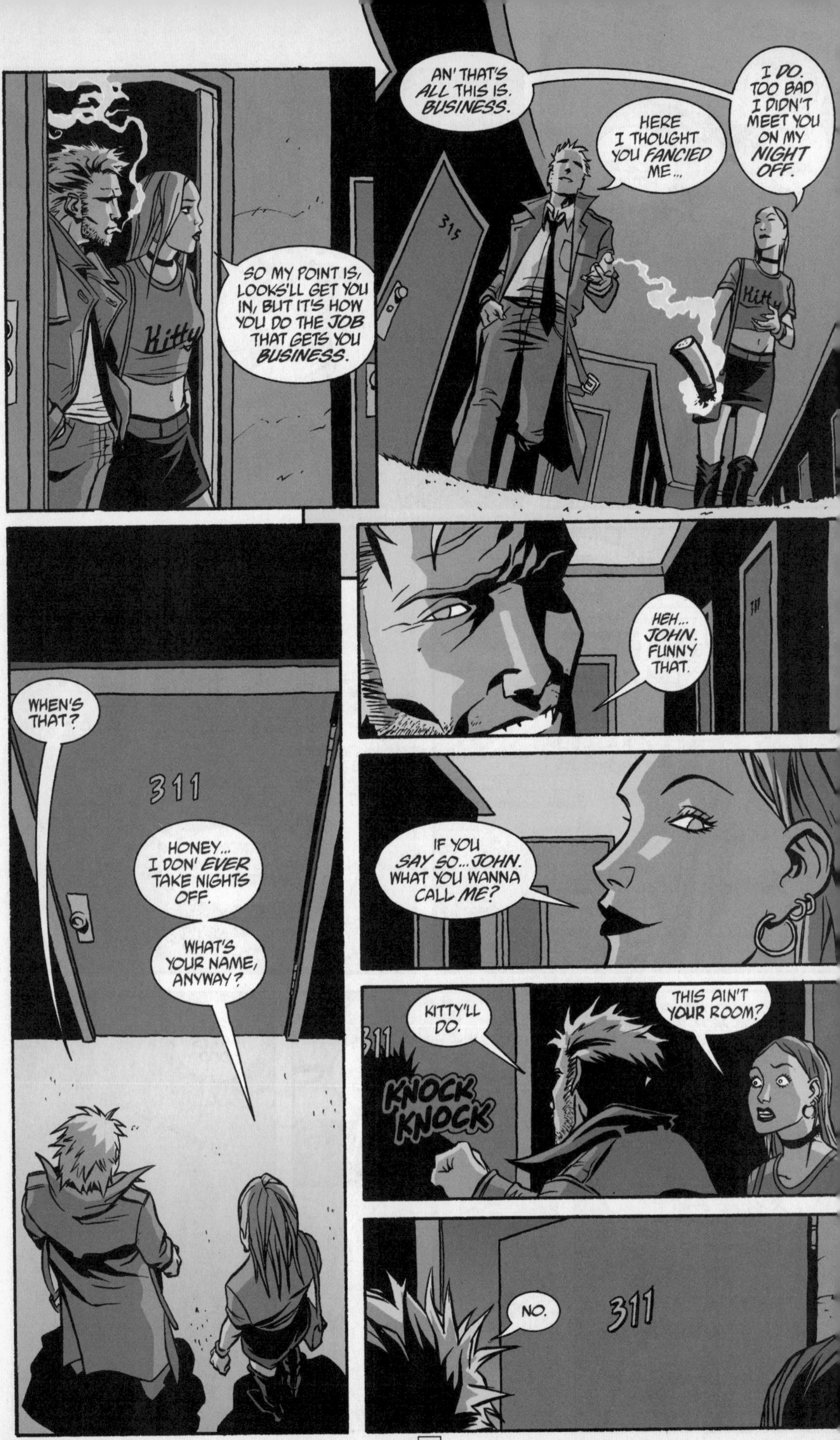
SO MY POINT IS, LOOKS'LL GET YOU IN, BUT IT'S HOW YOU DO THE JOB THAT GETS YOU BUSINESS.
AN' THAT'S ALL THIS IS. BUSINESS.
HERE I THOUGHT YOU FANCIED ME...
I DO. TOO BAD I DIDN'T MEET YOU ON MY NIGHT OFF.
WHEN'S THAT?
HONEY... I DON' EVER TAKE NIGHTS OFF.
WHAT'S YOUR NAME, ANYWAY?
HEH... JOHN. FUNNY THAT.
IF YOU SAY SO... JOHN. WHAT YOU WANNA CALL ME?
KITTY'LL DO.
KNOCK KNOCK
THIS AIN'T YOUR ROOM?
NO.

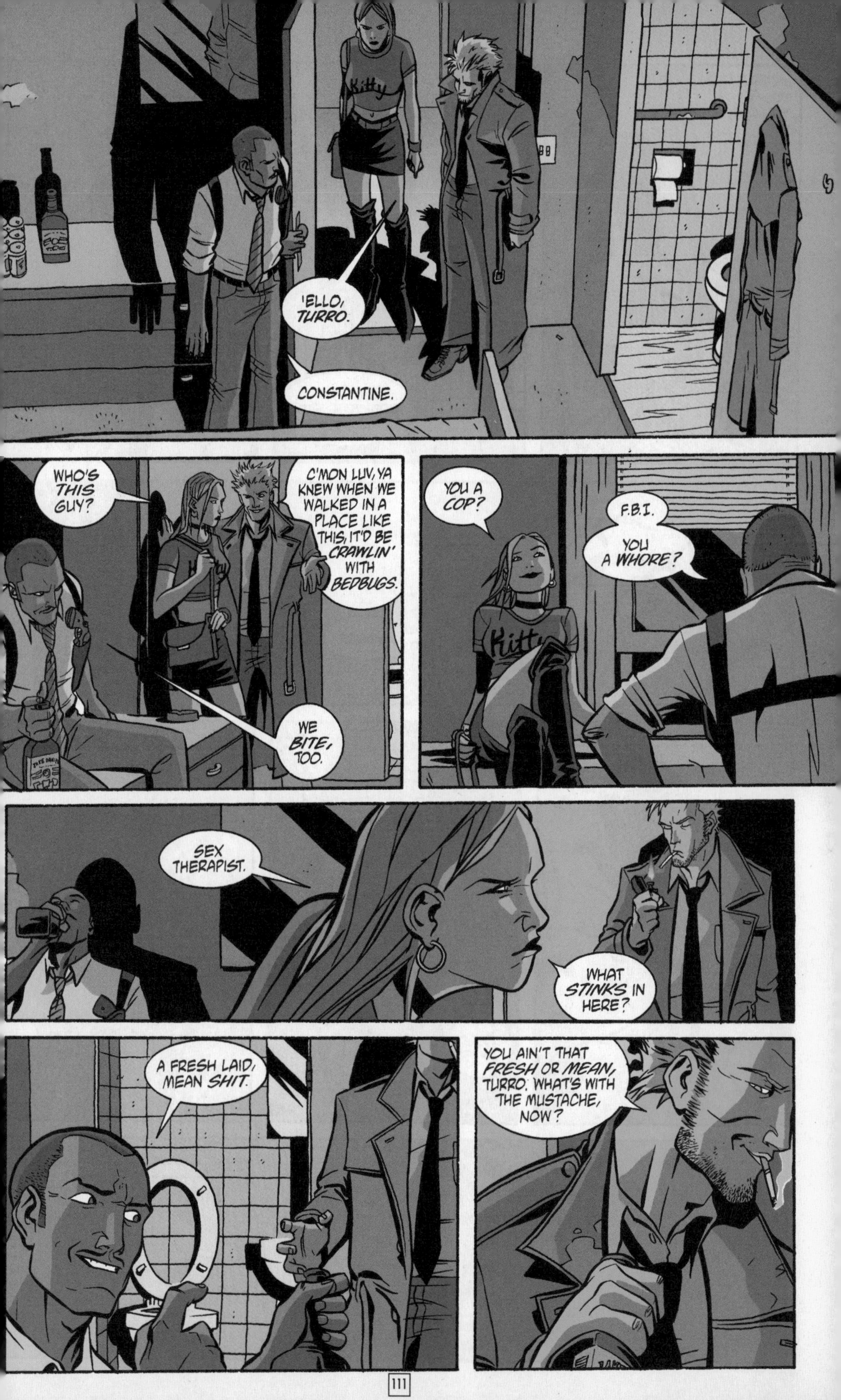
'ELLO, TURRO.
CONSTANTINE.
WHO'S THIS GUY?
C'MON LUV, YA KNEW WHEN WE WALKED IN A PLACE LIKE THIS, IT'D BE CRAWLIN' WITH BEDBUGS.
WE BITE, TOO.
YOU A COP?
F.B.I.
YOU A WHORE?
SEX THERAPIST.
WHAT STINKS IN HERE?
A FRESH LAID, MEAN SHIT.
YOU AIN'T THAT FRESH OR MEAN, TURRO. WHAT'S WITH THE MUSTACHE, NOW?

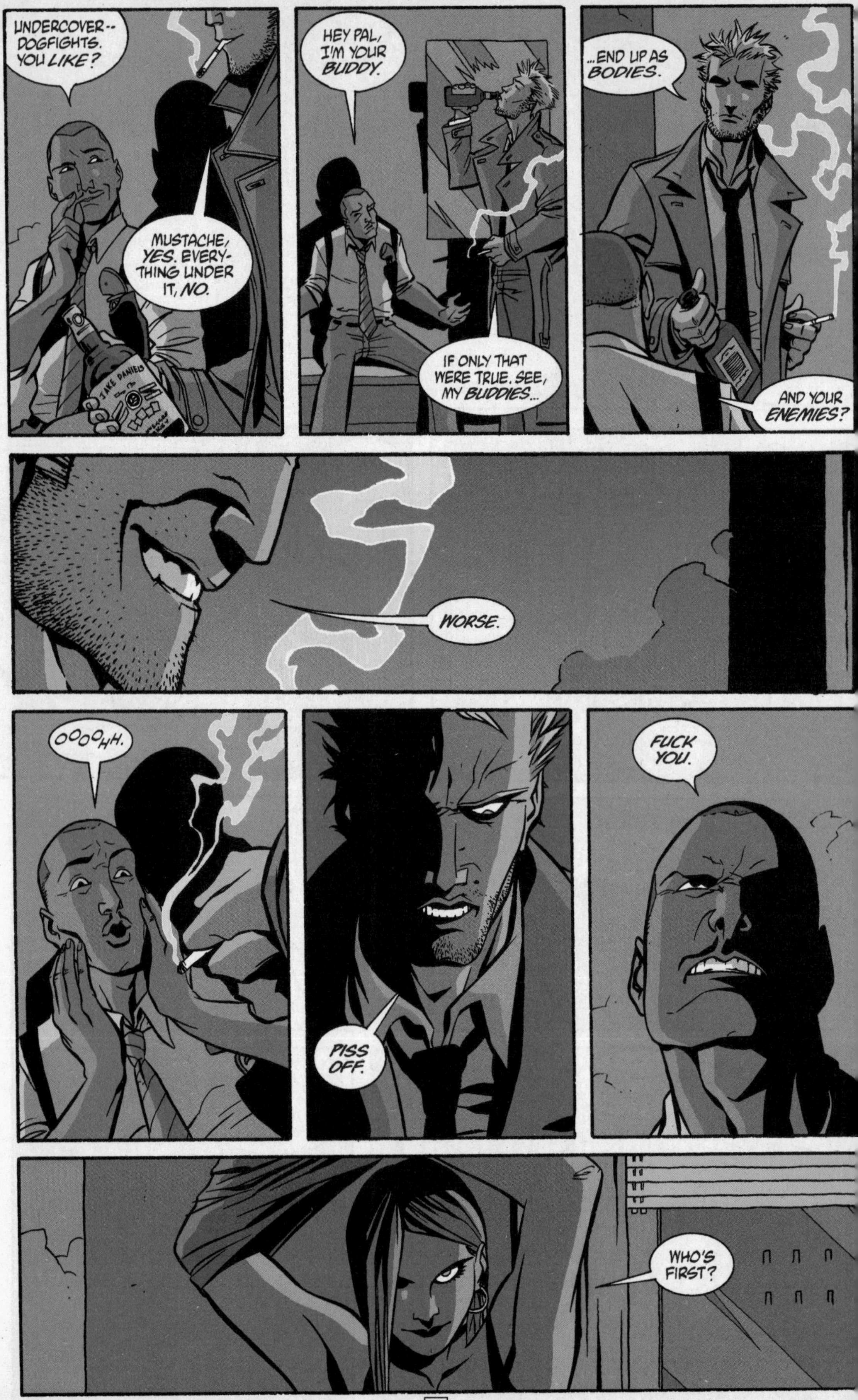
UNDERCOVER-- DOGFIGHTS. YOU LIKE?
MUSTACHE, YES. EVERYTHING UNDER IT, NO.
HEY PAL, I'M YOUR BUDDY.
IF ONLY THAT WERE TRUE. SEE, MY BUDDIES...
...END UP AS BODIES.
AND YOUR ENEMIES?
WORSE.
OOOOHH.
PISS OFF.
FUCK YOU.
WHO'S FIRST?

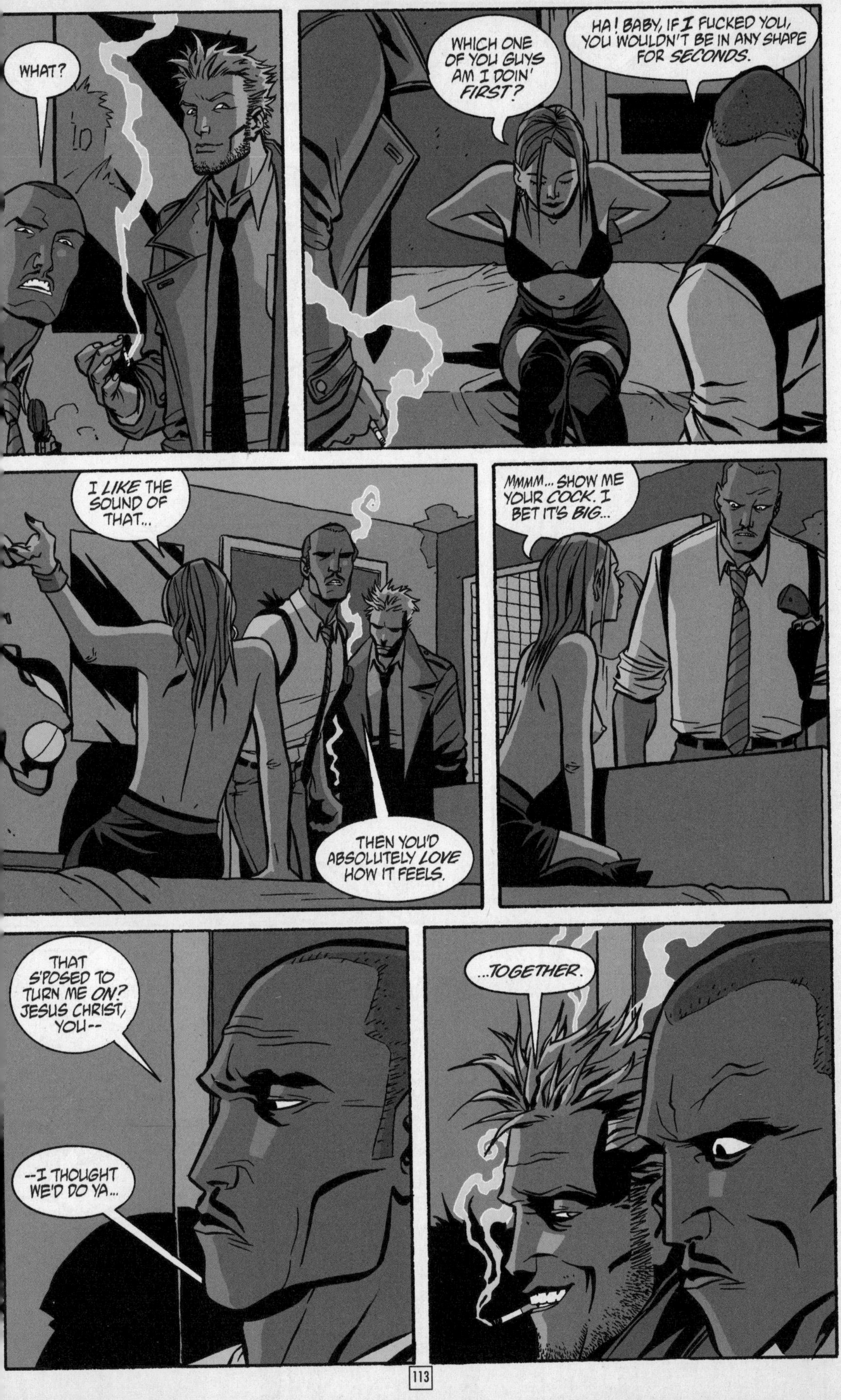
WHAT?
WHICH ONE OF YOU GUYS AM I DOIN' FIRST?
HA! BABY, IF I FUCKED YOU, YOU WOULDN'T BE IN ANY SHAPE FOR SECONDS.
I LIKE THE SOUND OF THAT...
THEN YOU'D ABSOLUTELY LOVE HOW IT FEELS.
MMMM... SHOW ME YOUR COCK. I BET IT'S BIG...
THAT S'POSED TO TURN ME ON? JESUS CHRIST, YOU--
--I THOUGHT WE'D DO YA...
...TOGETHER.

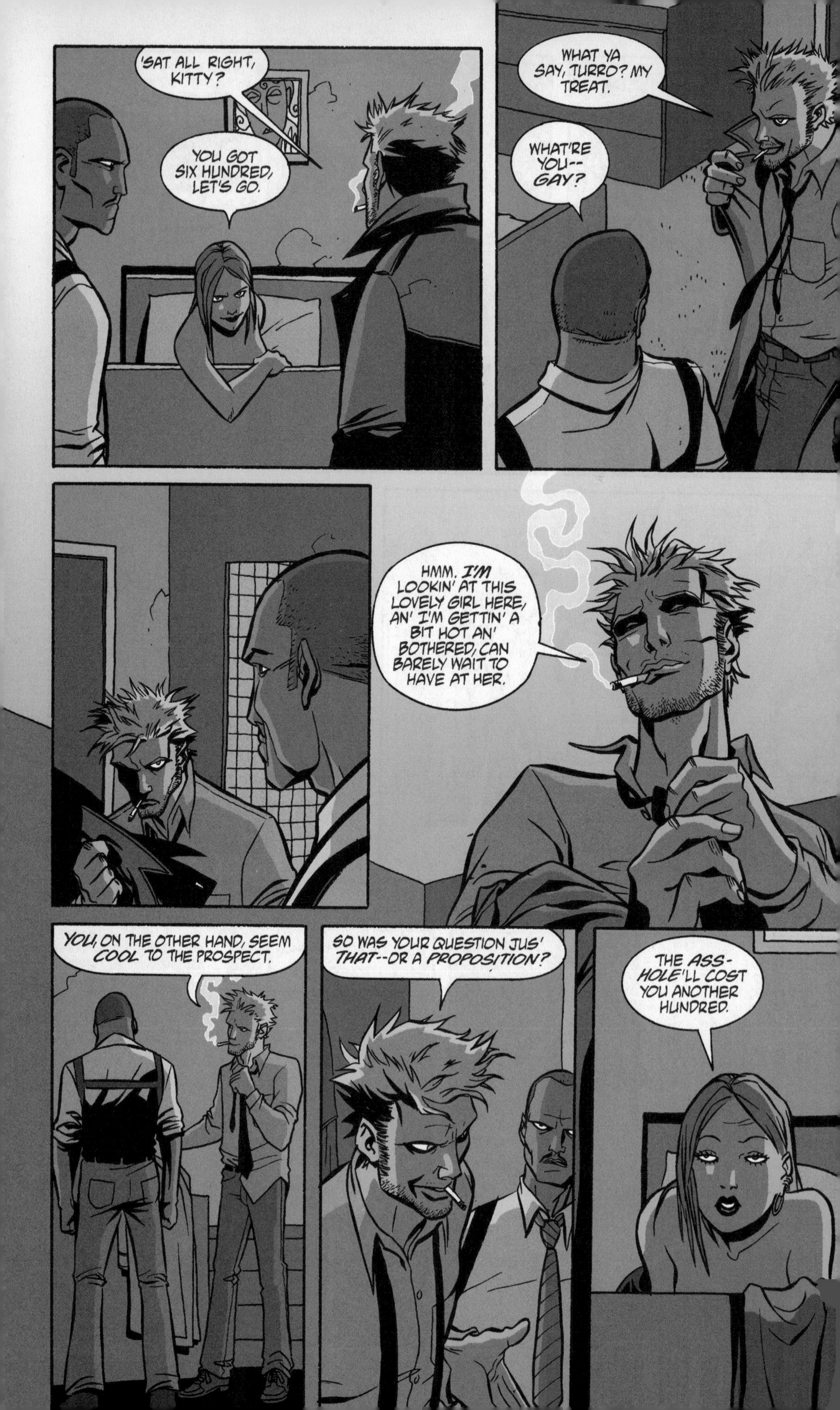

'SAT ALL RIGHT, KITTY?
YOU GOT SIX HUNDRED, LET'S GO.
WHAT YA SAY, TURRO? MY TREAT.
WHAT'RE YOU-- GAY?
HMM. I'M LOOKIN' AT THIS LOVELY GIRL HERE, AN' I'M GETTIN' A BIT HOT AN' BOTHERED, CAN BARELY WAIT TO HAVE AT HER.
YOU, ON THE OTHER HAND, SEEM COOL TO THE PROSPECT.
SO WAS YOUR QUESTION JUS' THAT--OR A PROPOSITION?
THE ASS-HOLE'LL COST YOU ANOTHER HUNDRED.

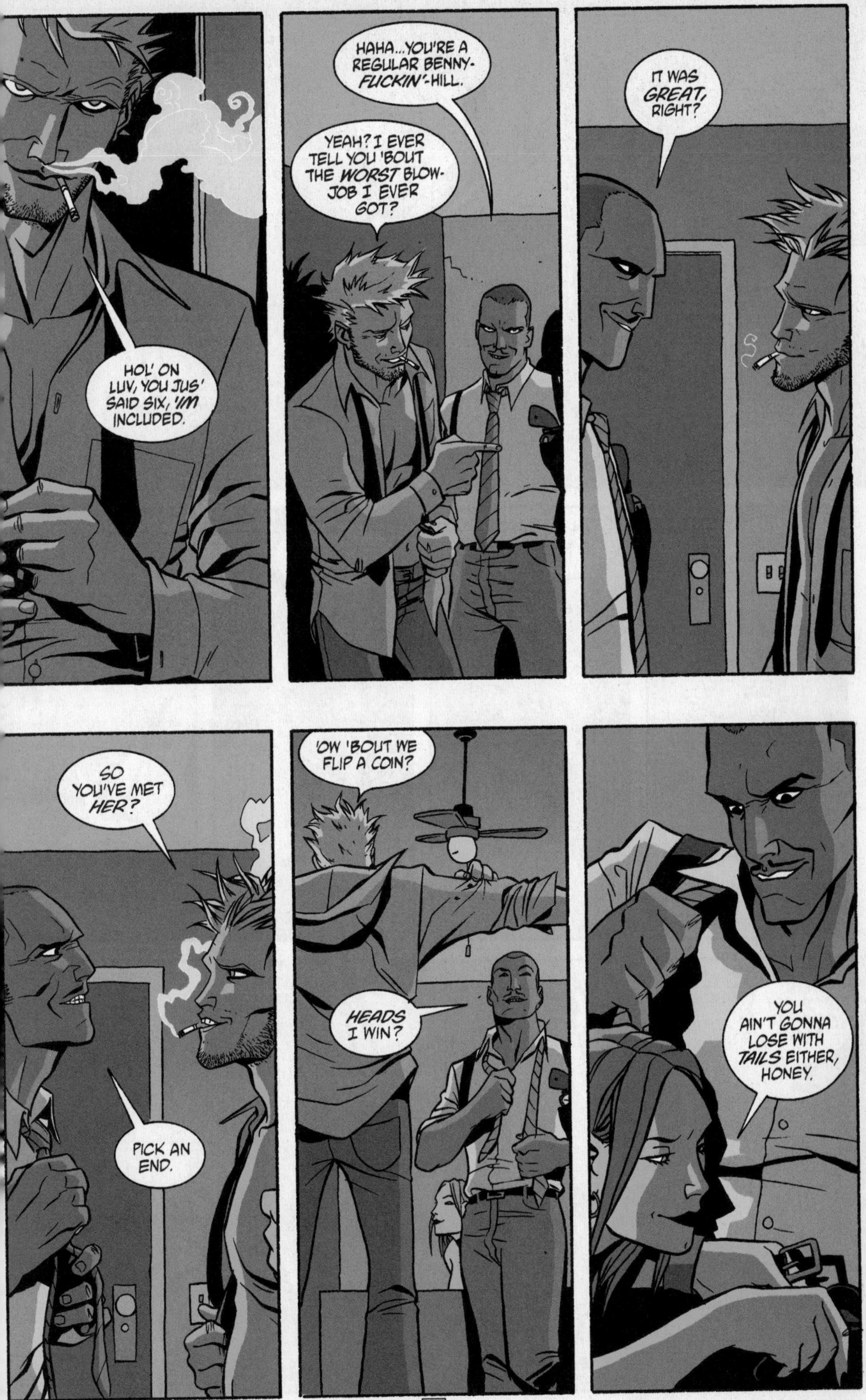
HOL' ON LUV, YOU JUS' SAID SIX, 'I'M INCLUDED.
HAHA...YOU'RE A REGULAR BENNY-FUCKIN'-HILL.
YEAH? I EVER TELL YOU 'BOUT THE WORST BLOW-JOB I EVER GOT?
IT WAS GREAT, RIGHT?
SO YOU'VE MET HER?
PICK AN END.
'OW 'BOUT WE FLIP A COIN?
HEADS I WIN?
YOU AIN'T GONNA LOSE WITH TAILS EITHER, HONEY.

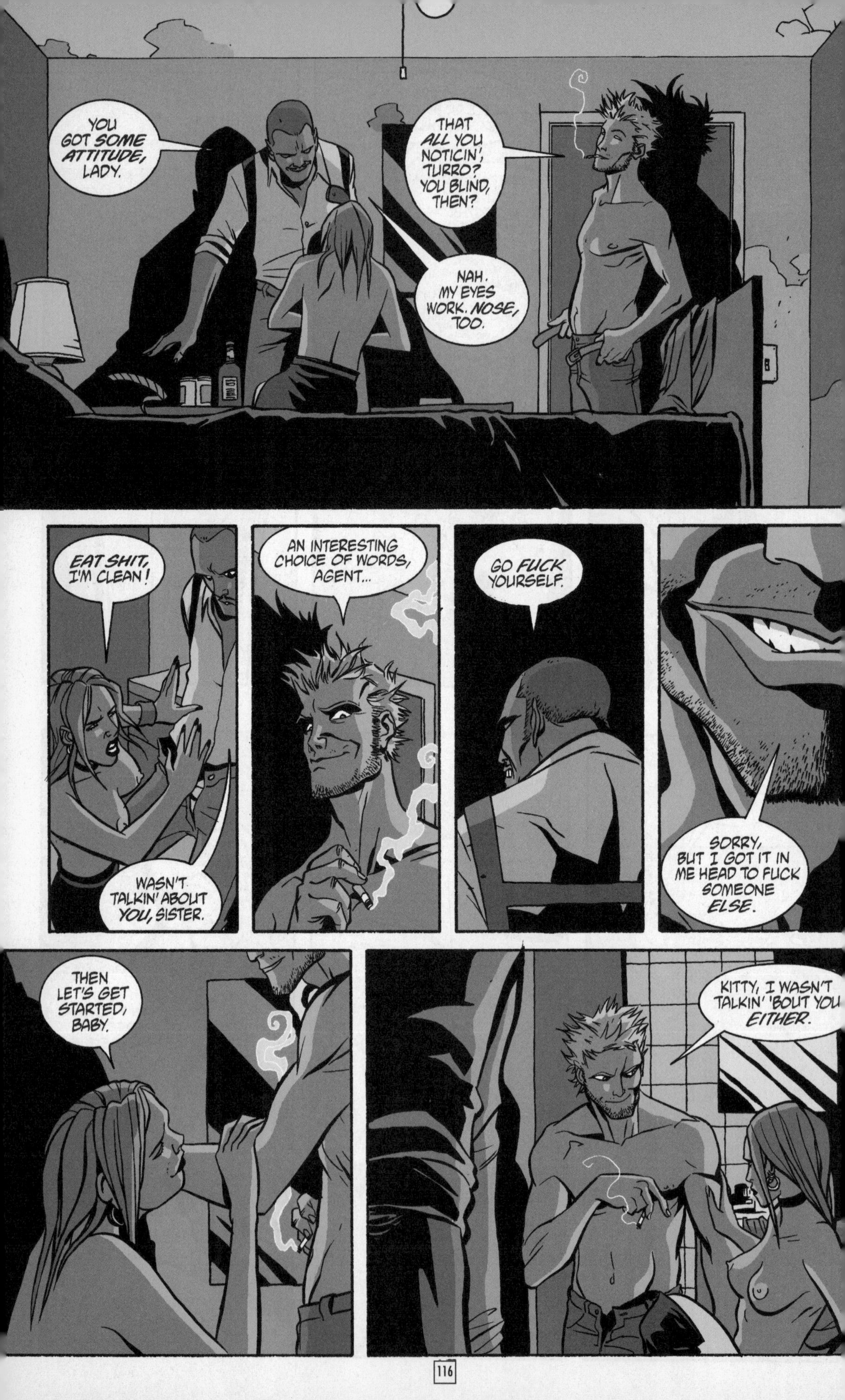

YOU GOT SOME ATTITUDE, LADY.
THAT ALL YOU NOTICIN', TURRO? YOU BLIND, THEN?
NAH. MY EYES WORK. NOSE, TOO.
EAT SHIT, I'M CLEAN!
WASN'T TALKIN' ABOUT YOU, SISTER.
AN INTERESTING CHOICE OF WORDS, AGENT...
GO FUCK YOURSELF.
SORRY, BUT I GOT IT IN ME HEAD TO FUCK SOMEONE ELSE.
THEN LET'S GET STARTED, BABY.
KITTY, I WASN'T TALKIN' 'BOUT YOU EITHER.

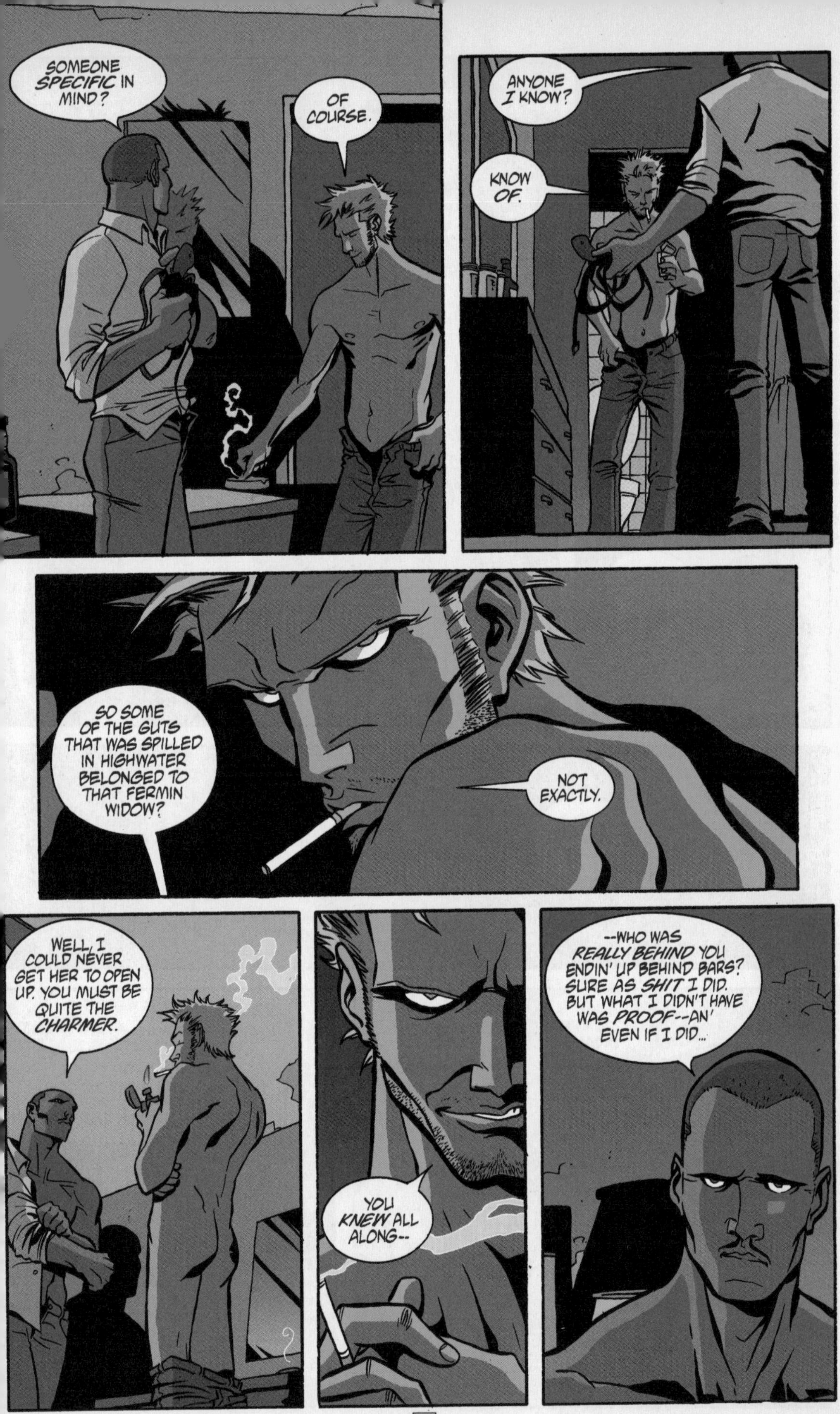
SOMEONE SPECIFIC IN MIND?
OF COURSE.
ANYONE I KNOW?
KNOW OF.
SO SOME OF THE GUTS THAT WAS SPILLED IN HIGHWATER BELONGED TO THAT FERMIN WIDOW?
NOT EXACTLY.
WELL, I COULD NEVER GET HER TO OPEN UP. YOU MUST BE QUITE THE CHARMER.
YOU KNEW ALL ALONG--
--WHO WAS REALLY BEHIND YOU ENDIN' UP BEHIND BARS? SURE AS SHIT I DID. BUT WHAT I DIDN'T HAVE WAS PROOF--AN' EVEN IF I DID...

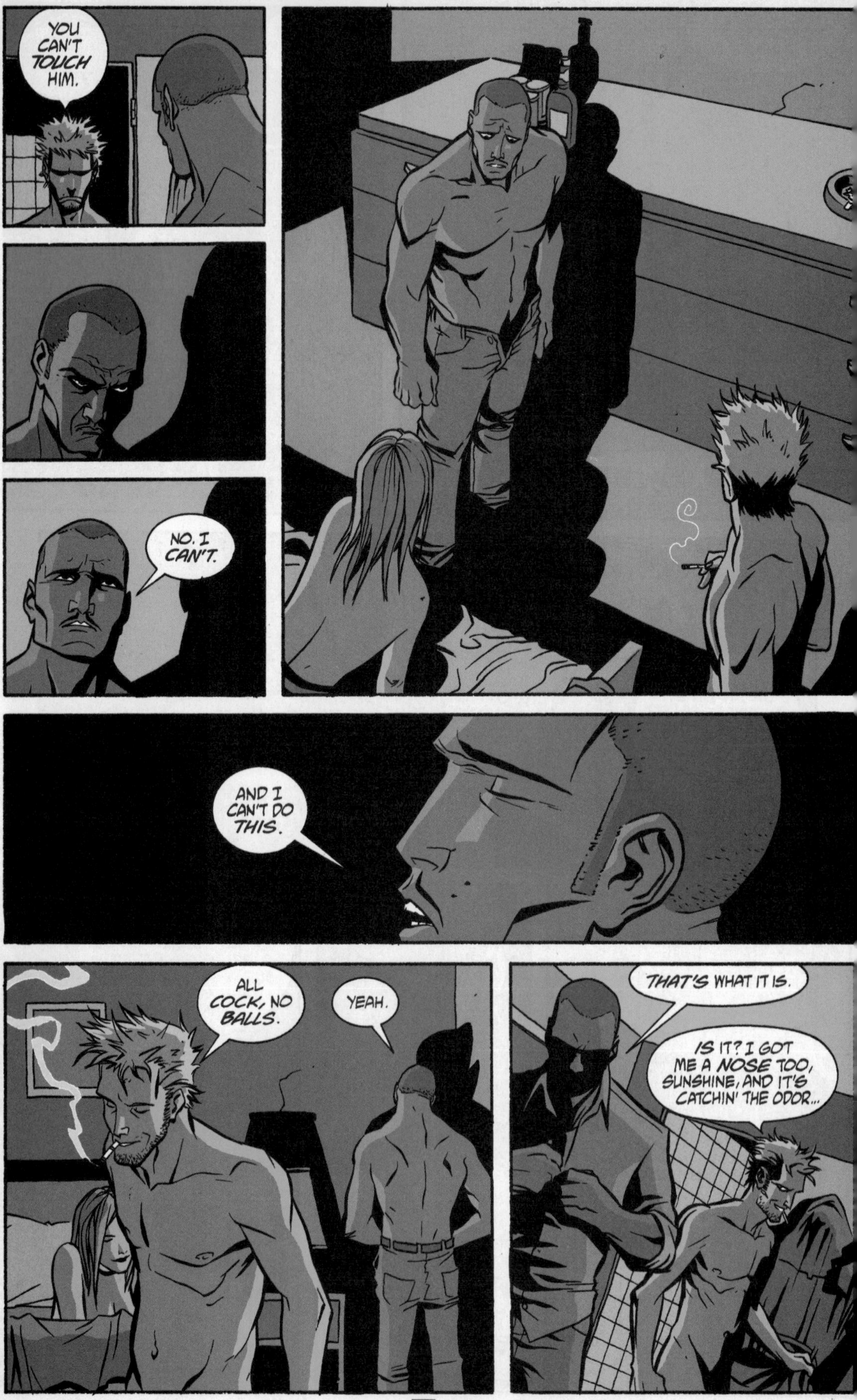
YOU CAN'T TOUCH HIM.
NO. I CAN'T.
AND I CAN'T DO THIS.
ALL COCK, NO BALLS.
YEAH.
THAT'S WHAT IT IS.
IS IT? I GOT ME A NOSE TOO, SUNSHINE, AND IT'S CATCHIN' THE ODOR...

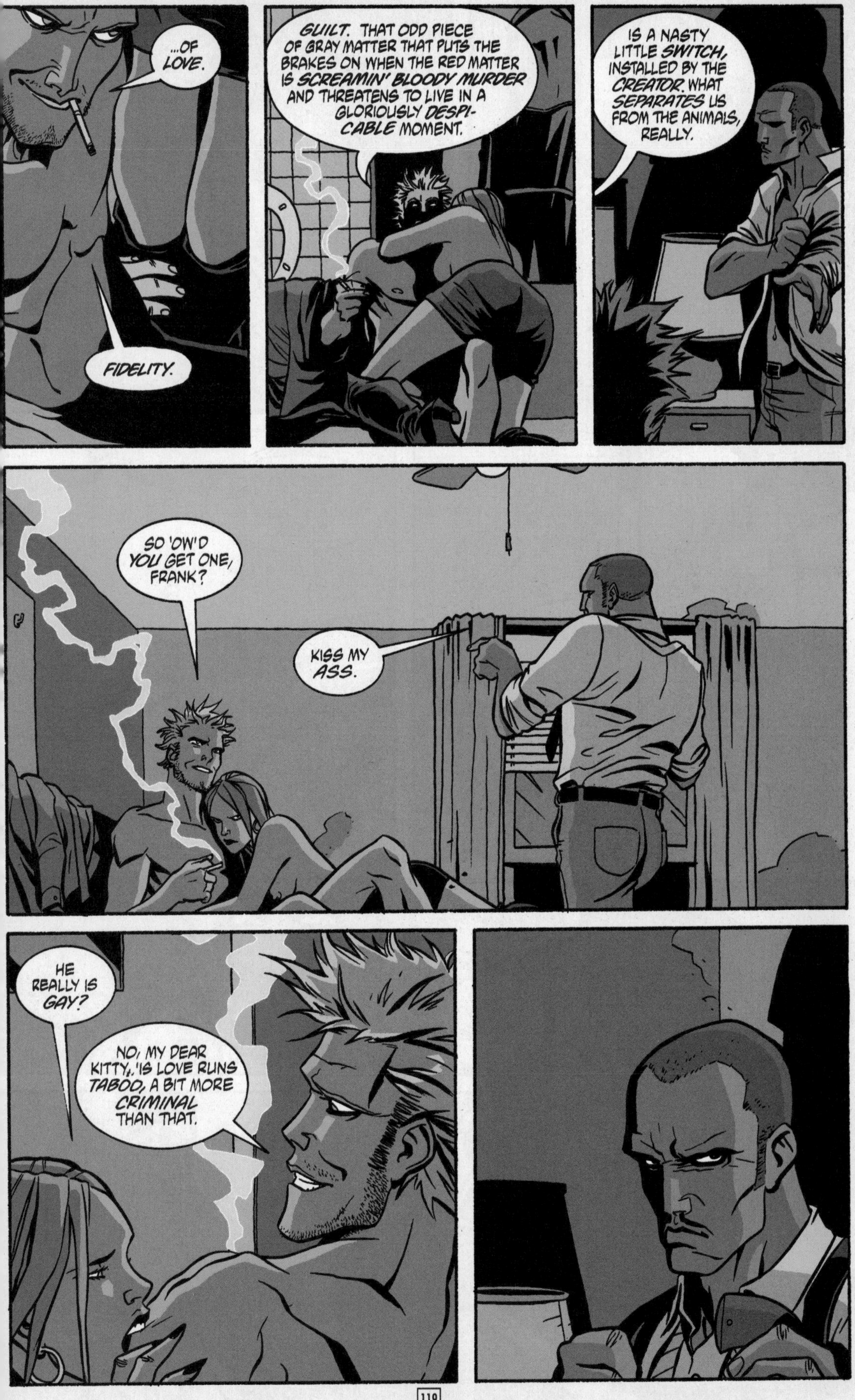

...OF LOVE.
FIDELITY.
GUILT. THAT ODD PIECE OF GRAY MATTER THAT PUTS THE BRAKES ON WHEN THE RED MATTER IS SCREAMIN' BLOODY MURDER AND THREATENS TO LIVE IN A GLORIOUSLY DESPI-CABLE MOMENT.
IS A NASTY LITTLE SWITCH, INSTALLED BY THE CREATOR. WHAT SEPARATES US FROM THE ANIMALS, REALLY.
SO 'OW'D YOU GET ONE, FRANK?
KISS MY ASS.
HE REALLY IS GAY?
NO, MY DEAR KITTY, 'IS LOVE RUNS TABOO, A BIT MORE CRIMINAL THAN THAT.

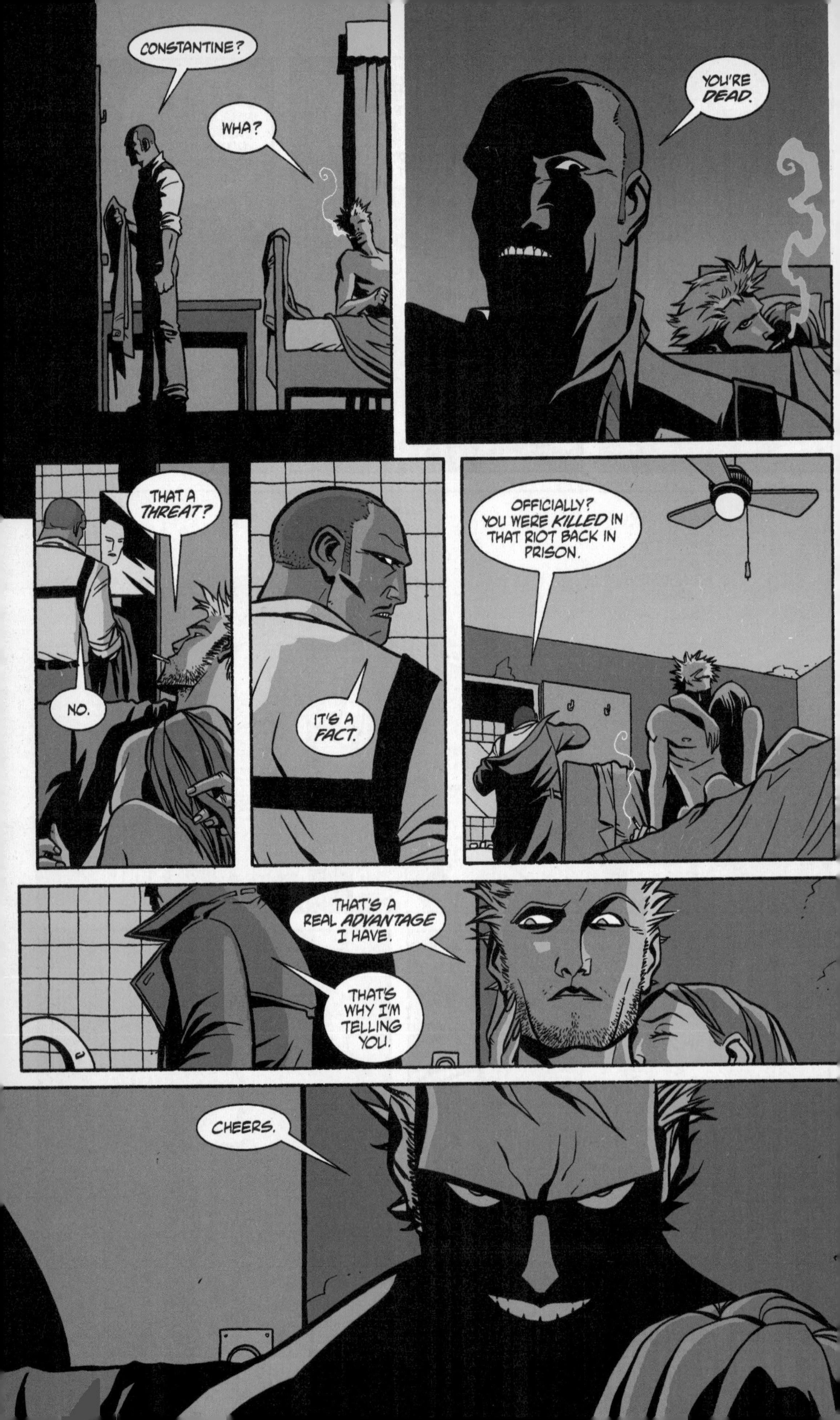
CONSTANTINE?
WHA?
YOU'RE DEAD.
THAT A THREAT?
NO.
IT'S A FACT.
OFFICIALLY? YOU WERE KILLED IN THAT RIOT BACK IN PRISON.
THAT'S A REAL ADVANTAGE I HAVE.
THAT'S WHY I'M TELLING YOU.
CHEERS.

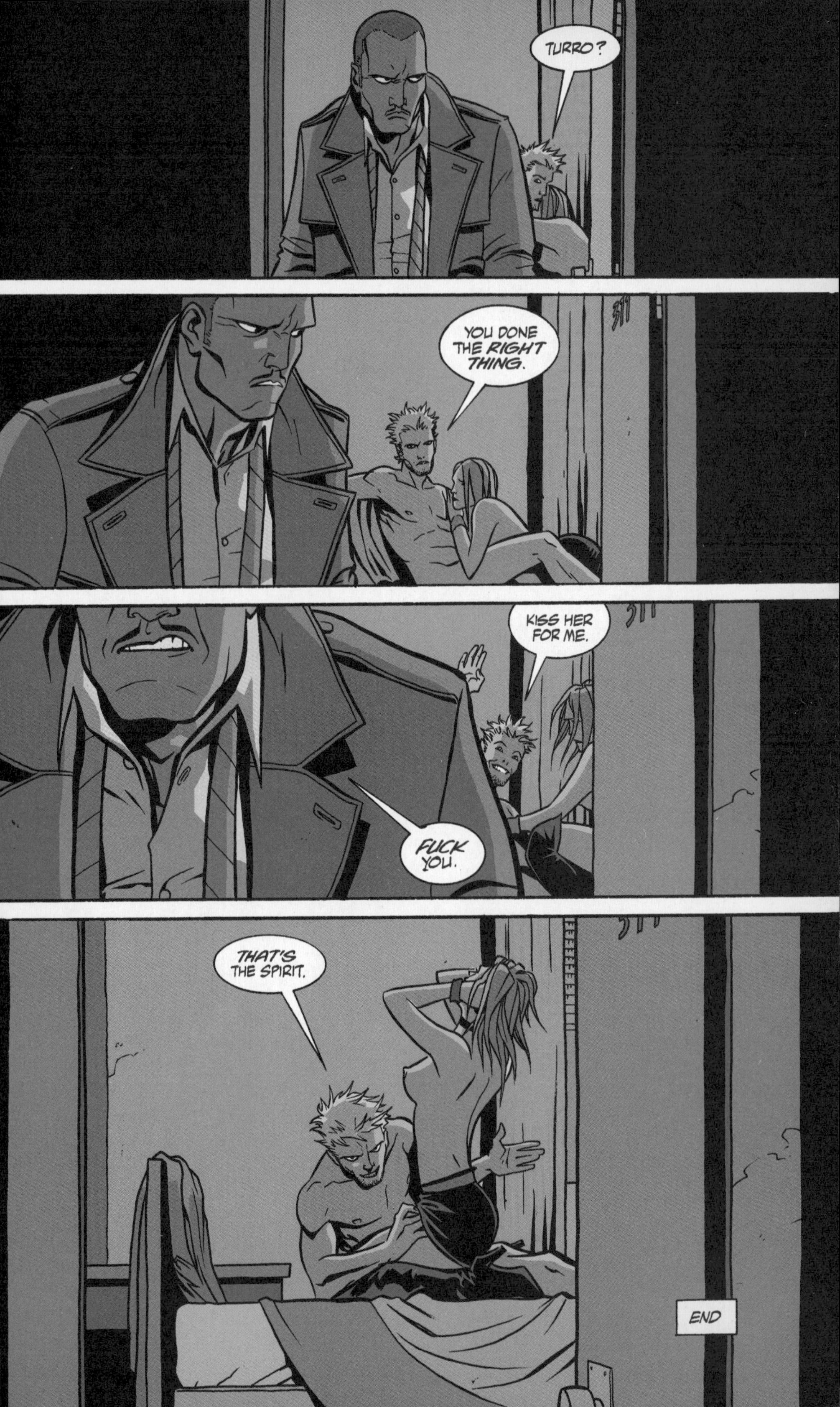
TURRO?
YOU DONE THE RIGHT THING.
KISS HER FOR ME.
FUCK YOU.
THAT'S THE SPIRIT.
END

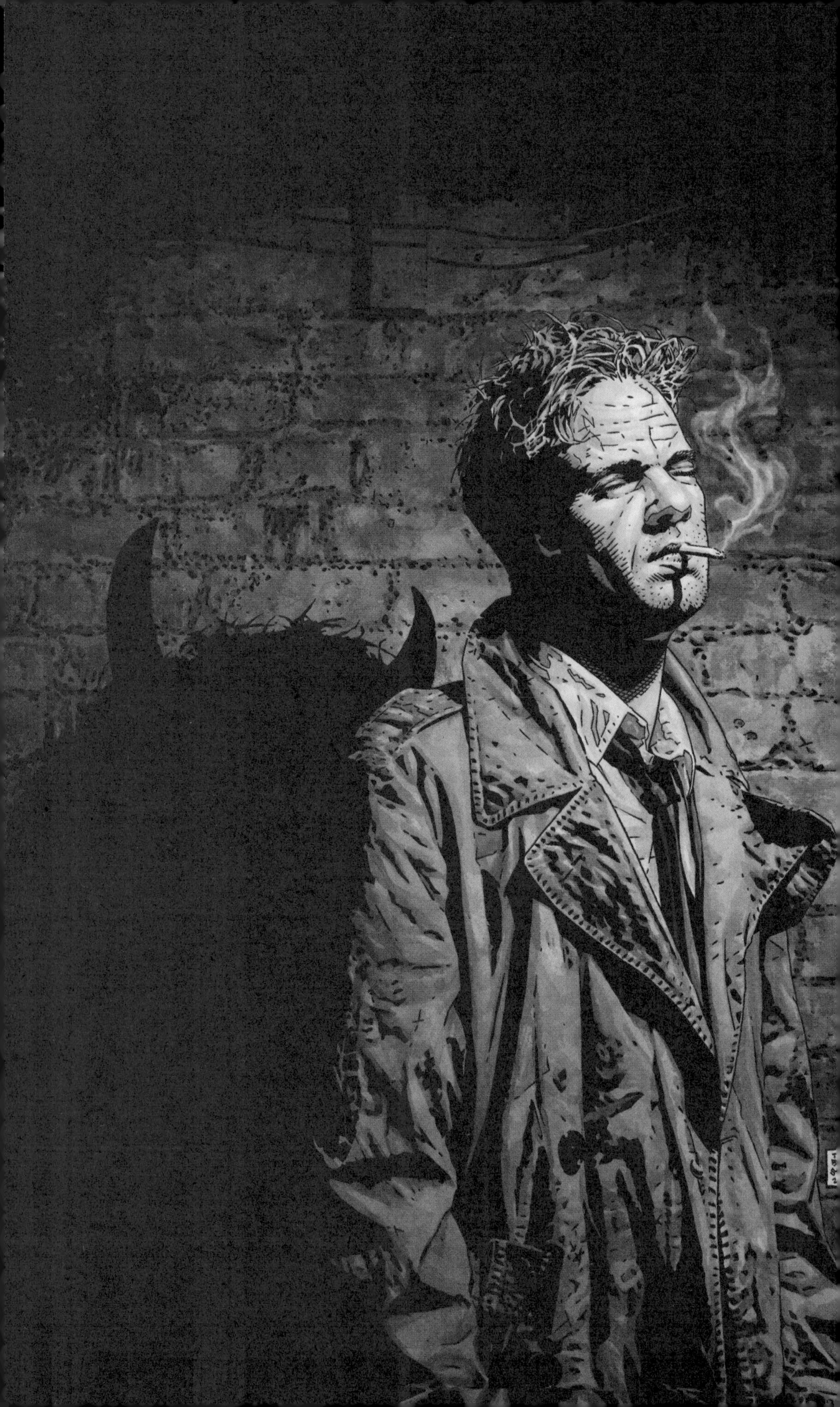

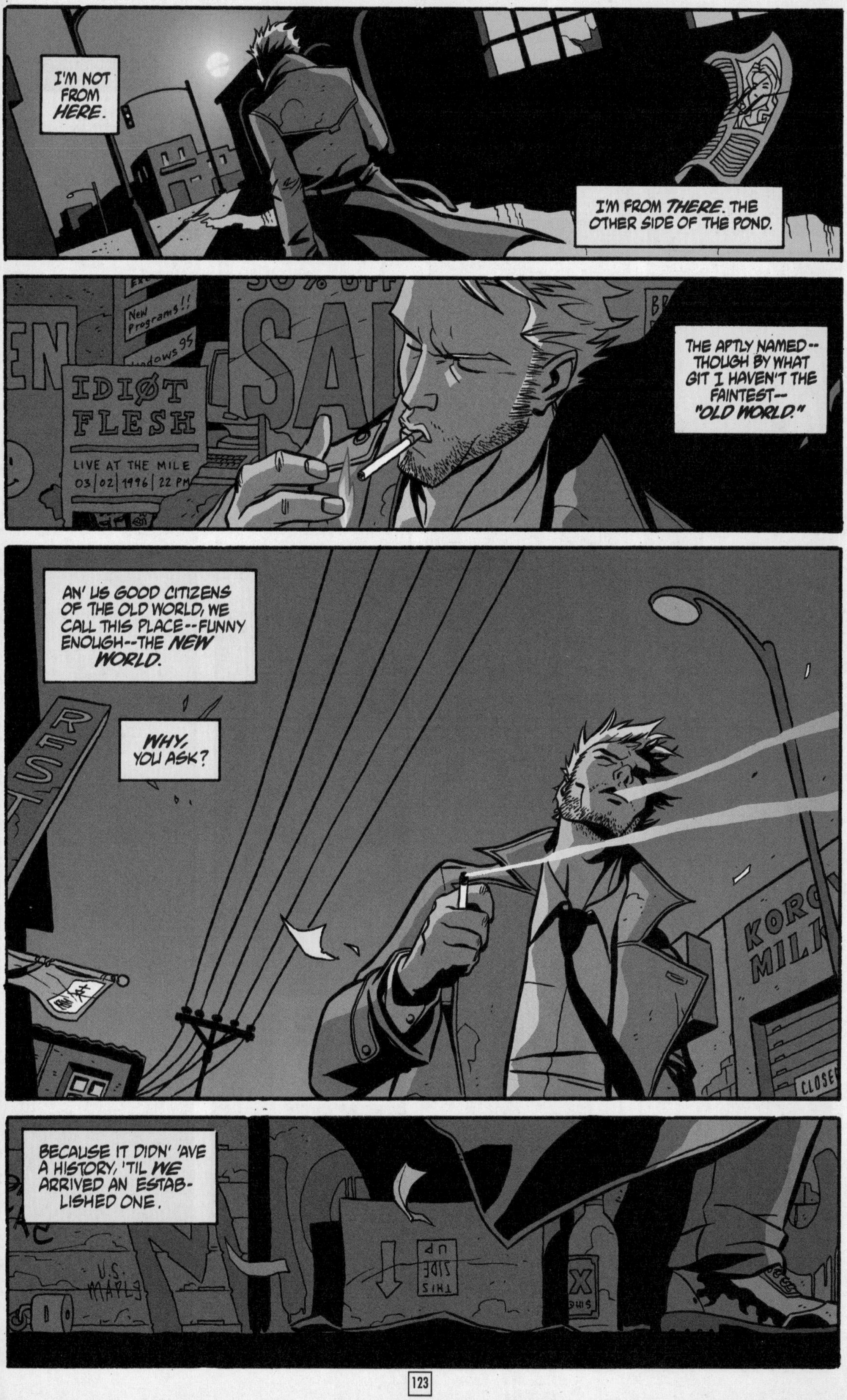

I'M NOT FROM HERE.
I'M FROM THERE. THE OTHER SIDE OF THE POND.
IDIØT FLESH
LIVE AT THE MILE
03|02|1996|22 PM
New Programs!!
THE APTLY NAMED-- THOUGH BY WHAT GIT I HAVEN'T THE FAINTEST-- "OLD WORLD."
AN' US GOOD CITIZENS OF THE OLD WORLD, WE CALL THIS PLACE--FUNNY ENOUGH--THE NEW WORLD.
WHY, YOU ASK?
KORO MILK
CLOSE
BECAUSE IT DIDN' 'AVE A HISTORY, 'TIL WE ARRIVED AN ESTAB-LISHED ONE.
THIS SIDE UP

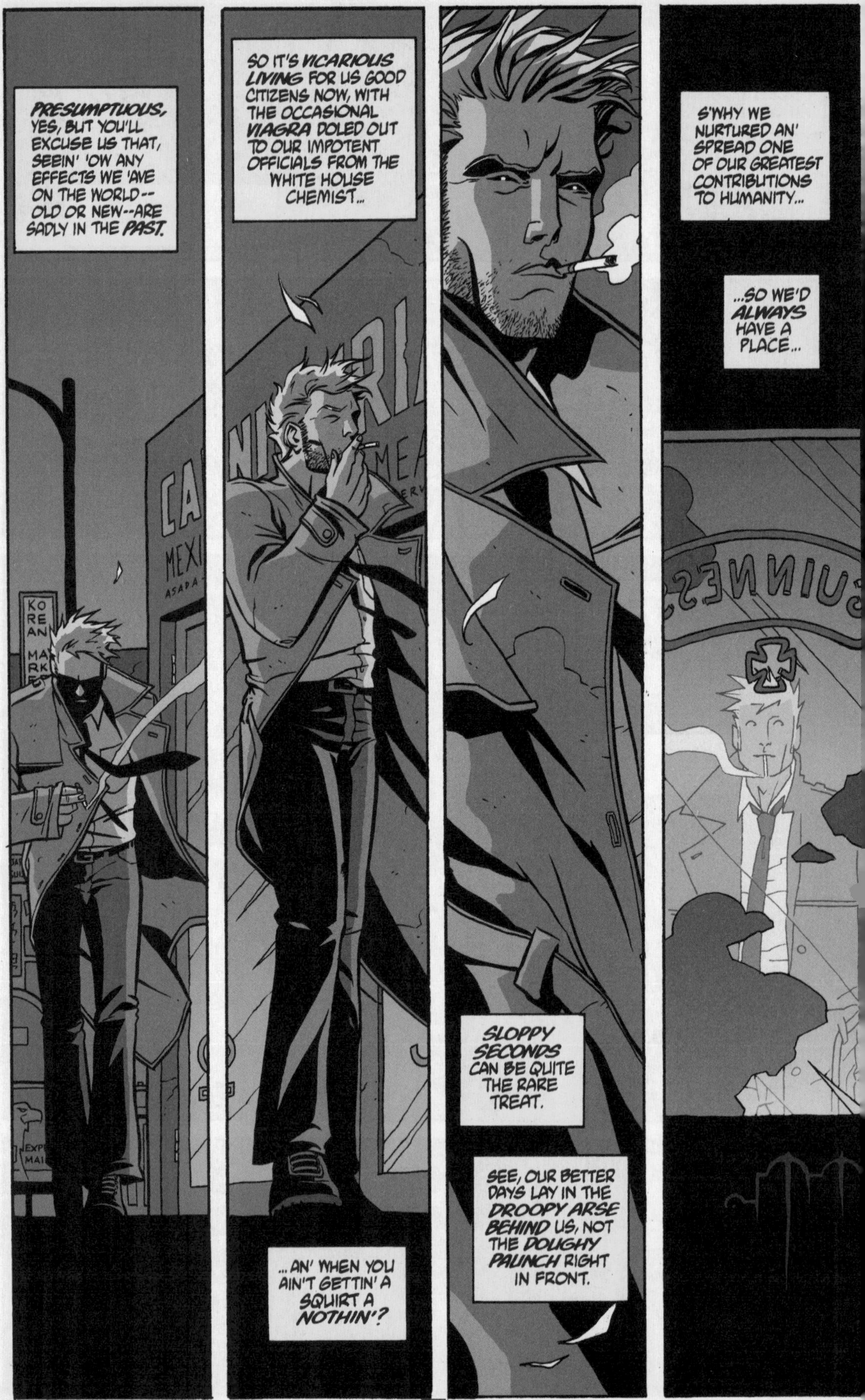
PRESUMPTUOUS, YES, BUT YOU'LL EXCUSE US THAT, SEEIN' 'OW ANY EFFECTS WE 'AVE ON THE WORLD--OLD OR NEW--ARE SADLY IN THE PAST.
SO IT'S VICARIOUS LIVING FOR US GOOD CITIZENS NOW, WITH THE OCCASIONAL VIAGRA DOLED OUT TO OUR IMPOTENT OFFICIALS FROM THE WHITE HOUSE CHEMIST...
...AN' WHEN YOU AIN'T GETTIN' A SQUIRT A NOTHIN'?
SLOPPY SECONDS CAN BE QUITE THE RARE TREAT.
SEE, OUR BETTER DAYS LAY IN THE DROOPY ARSE BEHIND US, NOT THE DOUGHY PAUNCH RIGHT IN FRONT.
S'WHY WE NURTURED AN' SPREAD ONE OF OUR GREATEST CONTRIBUTIONS TO HUMANITY...
...SO WE'D ALWAYS HAVE A PLACE...

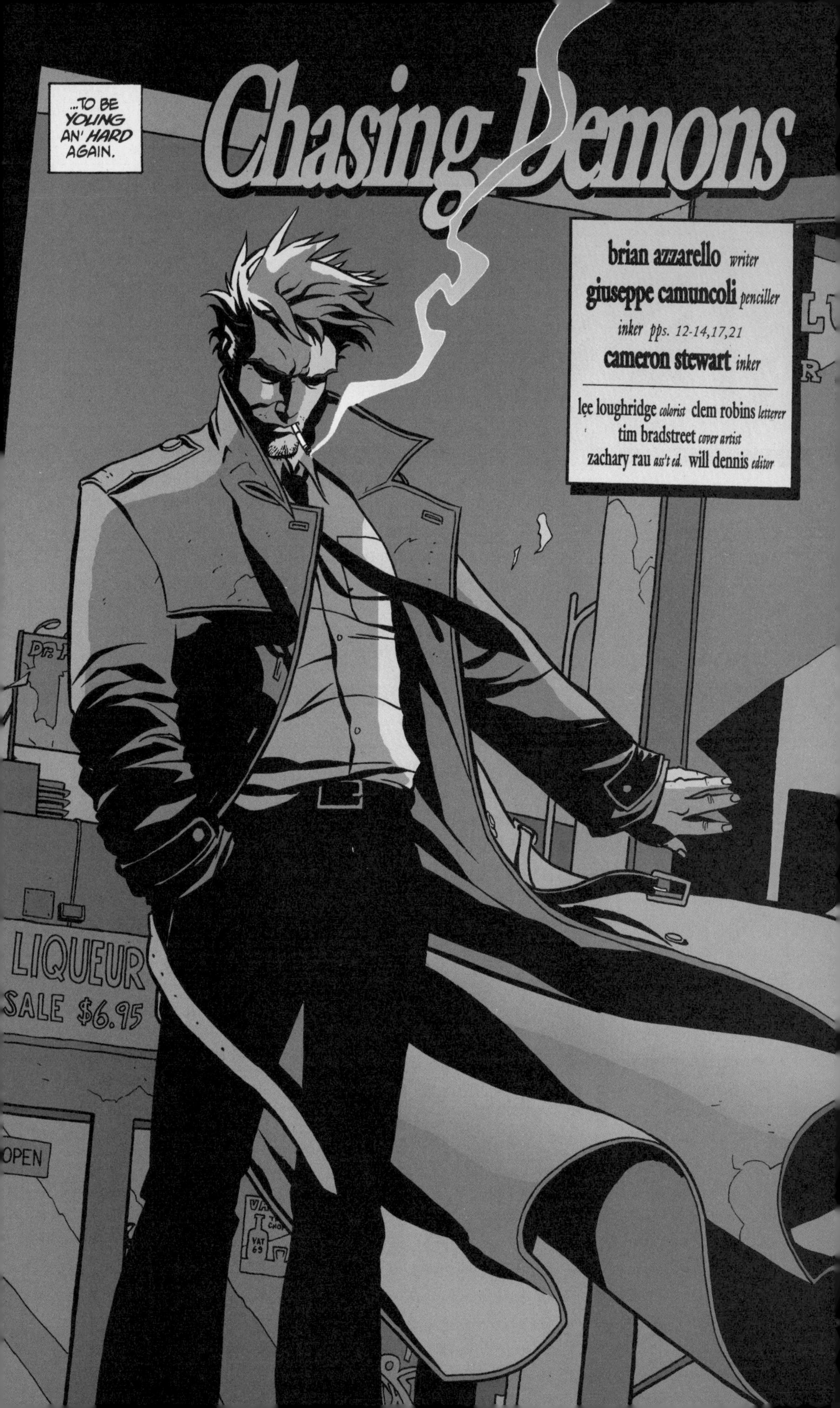

...TO BE YOUNG AN' HARD AGAIN.
Chasing Demons
brian azzarello writer
giuseppe camuncoli penciller
inker pps. 12-14,17,21
cameron stewart inker
lee loughridge colorist clem robins letterer
tim bradstreet cover artist
zachary rau ass't ed. will dennis editor
LIQUEUR
SALE $6.95
OPEN

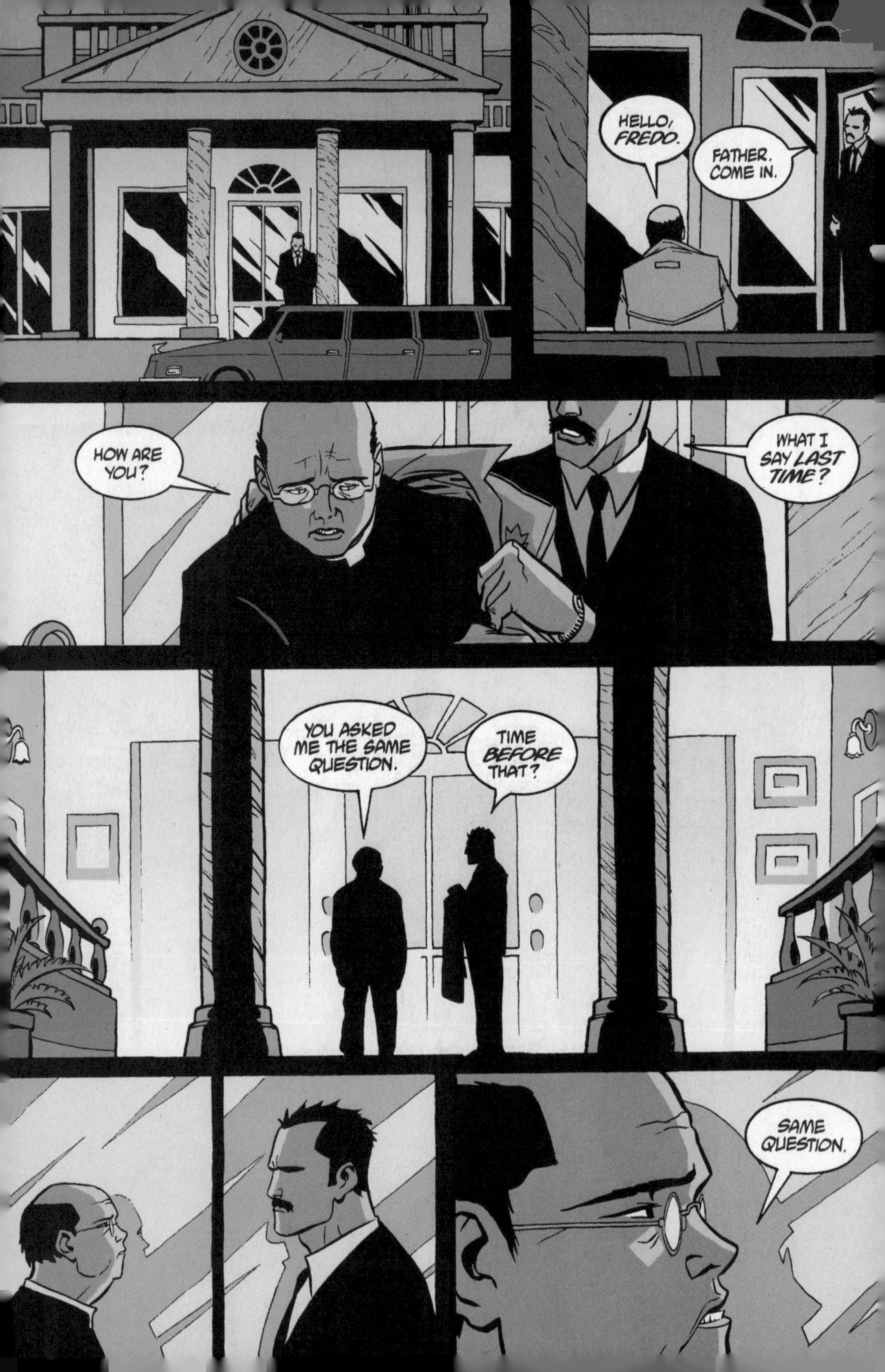
HELLO, FREDO.
FATHER. COME IN.
HOW ARE YOU?
WHAT I SAY LAST TIME?
YOU ASKED ME THE SAME QUESTION.
TIME BEFORE THAT?
SAME QUESTION.

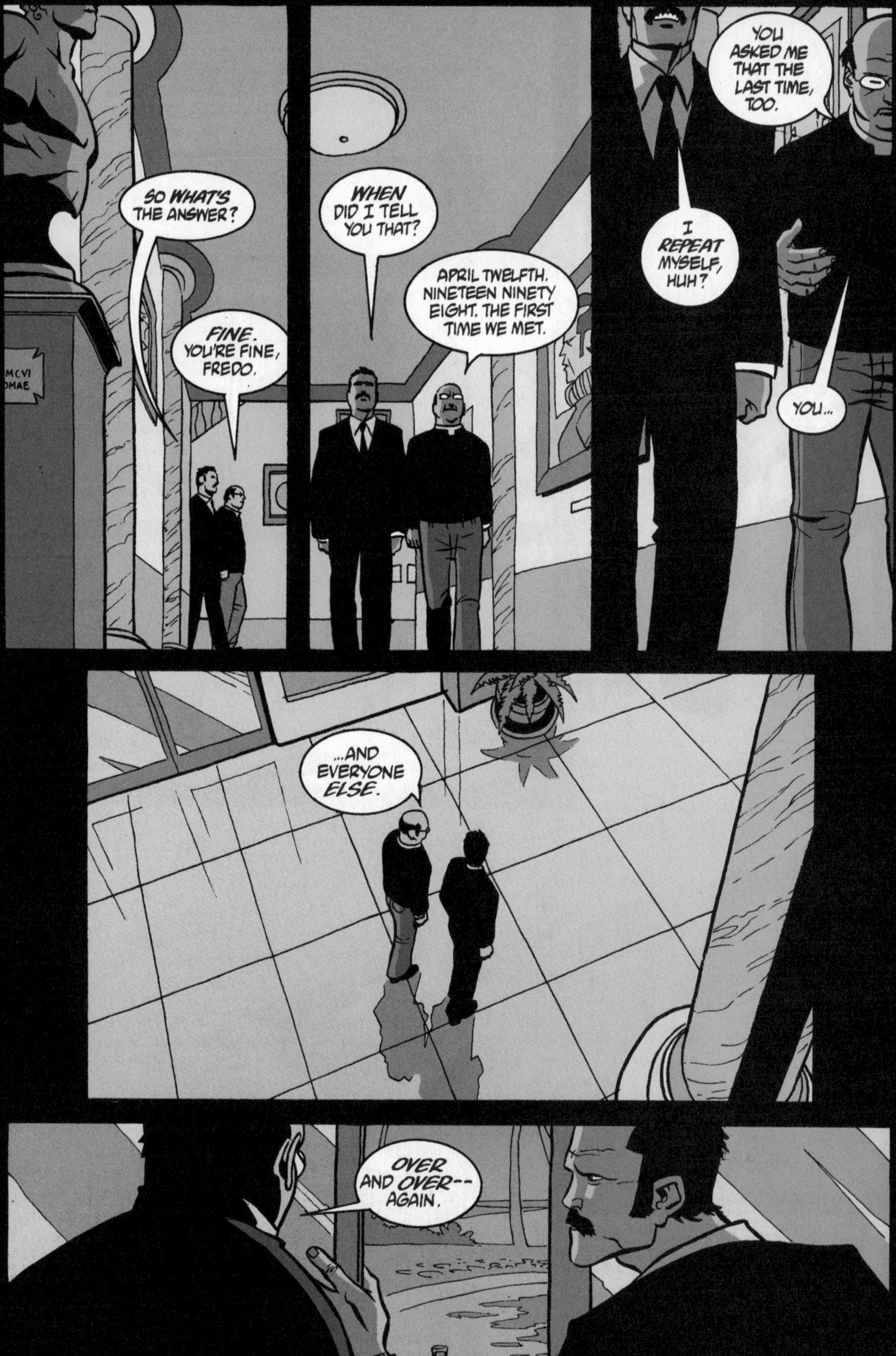
MCVI
DMAE
SO WHAT'S THE ANSWER?
FINE. YOU'RE FINE, FREDO.
WHEN DID I TELL YOU THAT?
APRIL TWELFTH. NINETEEN NINETY EIGHT. THE FIRST TIME WE MET.
YOU ASKED ME THAT THE LAST TIME, TOO.
I REPEAT MYSELF, HUH?
YOU...
...AND EVERYONE ELSE.
OVER AND OVER-- AGAIN.

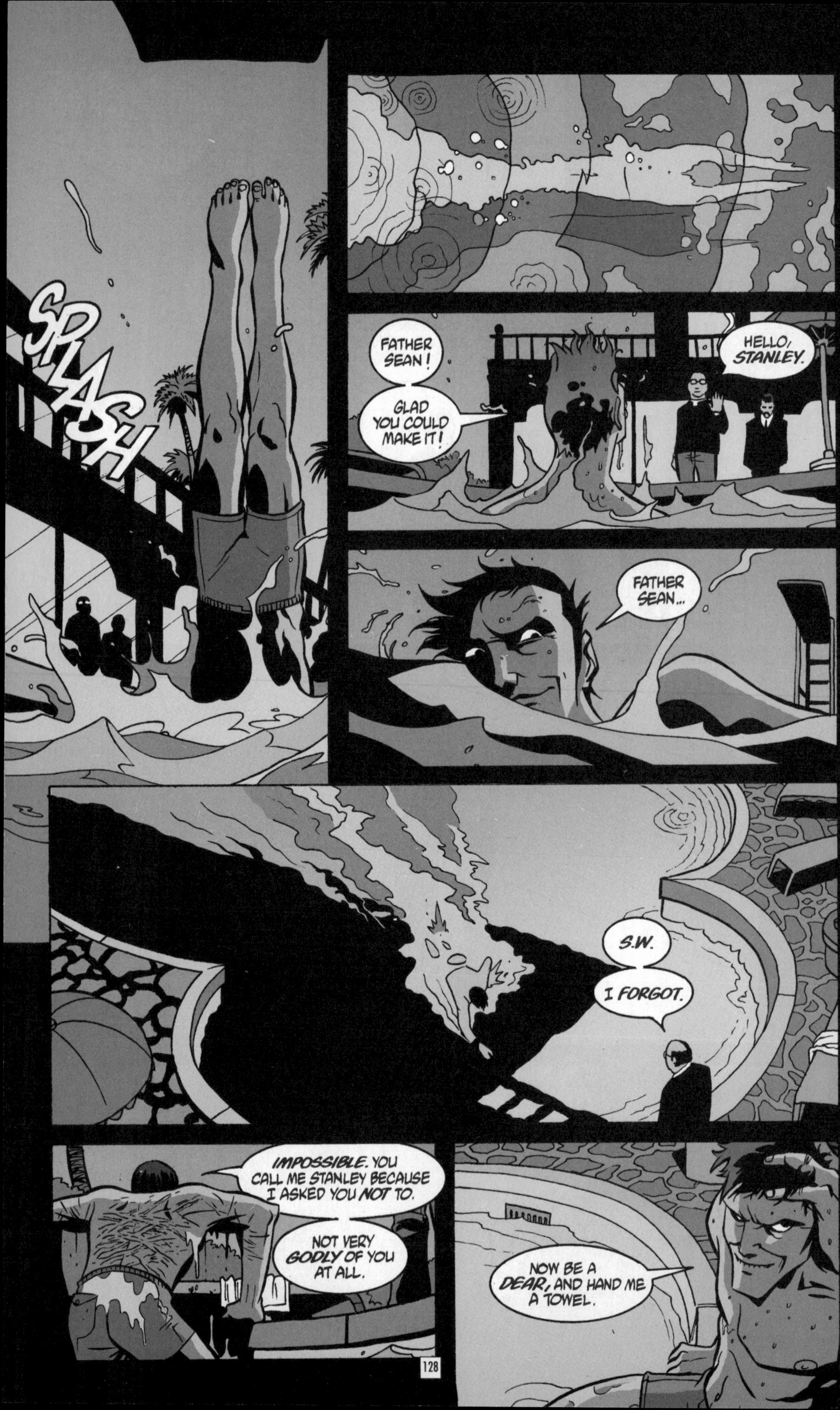
SPLASH
FATHER SEAN!
GLAD YOU COULD MAKE IT!
HELLO, STANLEY.
FATHER SEAN...
S.W.
I FORGOT.
IMPOSSIBLE. YOU CALL ME STANLEY BECAUSE I ASKED YOU NOT TO.
NOT VERY GODLY OF YOU AT ALL.
NOW BE A DEAR, AND HAND ME A TOWEL.

BLOODY *FUCKIN'* HELL...

ACHK!

SORRY 'BOUT THAT, BUDDY.

MY SINUSES-- THIS WEATHER'S *MURDERIN'* 'EM.

WON' BE *JUS'* THE WEATHER, YOU *GAK* ON ME AGAIN LIKE THAT.

TAKE IT *EASY.*

KILKENNY

MENU FISH AND CHIPS HAMB

LOS ÁNGELA

SEBA

TAKE IT *EASY?* I SHOULD BE TAKIN' ME *MEDICINE* AFTER ALL THE NASTY VIRAL BITS YA JUS' BLEW IN MY DIRECTION.

YOU NEED *MEDICINE?*

YOU A *DOCTOR?*

CLU IRI

GUINNESS

MY MOTHER *WANTED* ME TO BE ONE.

AN' WHAT WAS *SHE?*

DELUSIONAL. ALWAYS THINKIN' ABOUT *TOMORROW.* REALITY... WAS SOMETHIN' SHE NEVER QUITE GOT HER *MIND* AROUND.

WHISKEY?

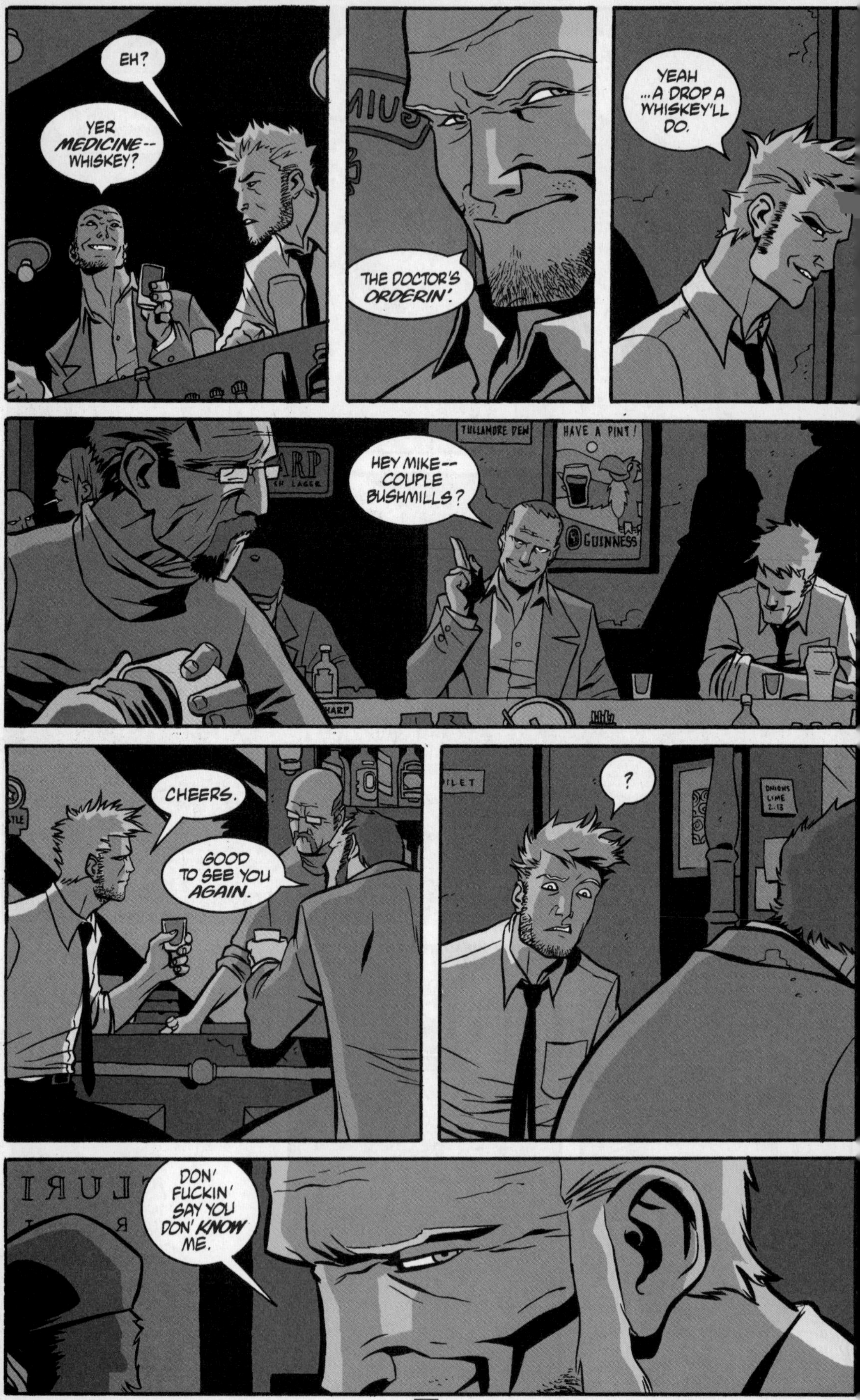
EH?
YER MEDICINE-- WHISKEY?
THE DOCTOR'S ORDERIN'.
YEAH ...A DROP A WHISKEY'LL DO.
TULLAMORE DEW
HAVE A PINT!
GUINNESS
HARP
HEY MIKE-- COUPLE BUSHMILLS?
CHEERS.
GOOD TO SEE YOU AGAIN.
?
DON' FUCKIN' SAY YOU DON' KNOW ME.

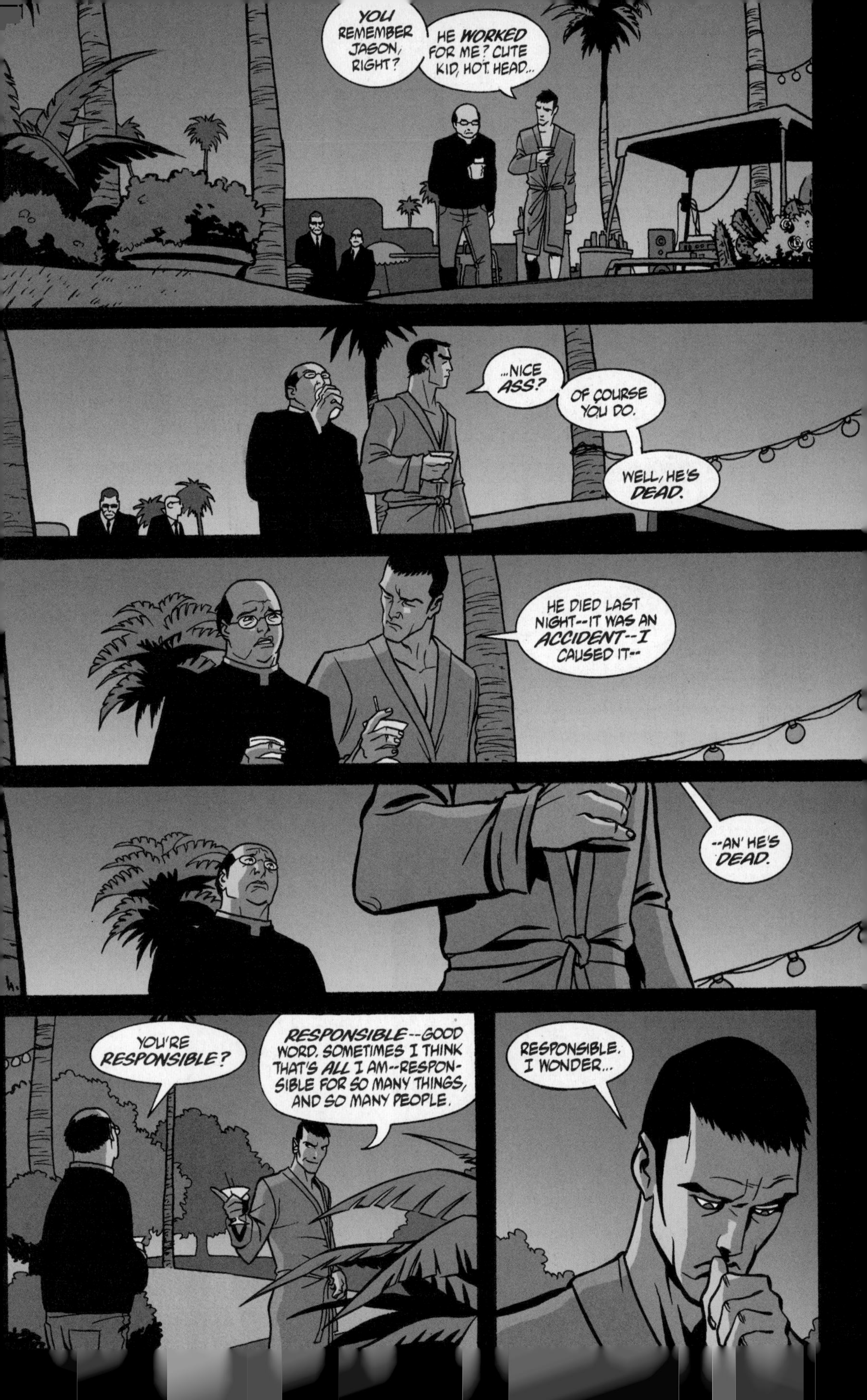
YOU REMEMBER JASON, RIGHT?
HE WORKED FOR ME? CUTE KID, HOT HEAD...
...NICE ASS?
OF COURSE YOU DO.
WELL, HE'S DEAD.
HE DIED LAST NIGHT--IT WAS AN ACCIDENT--I CAUSED IT--
--AN' HE'S DEAD.
YOU'RE RESPONSIBLE?
RESPONSIBLE--GOOD WORD. SOMETIMES I THINK THAT'S ALL I AM--RESPONSIBLE FOR SO MANY THINGS, AND SO MANY PEOPLE.
RESPONSIBLE. I WONDER...

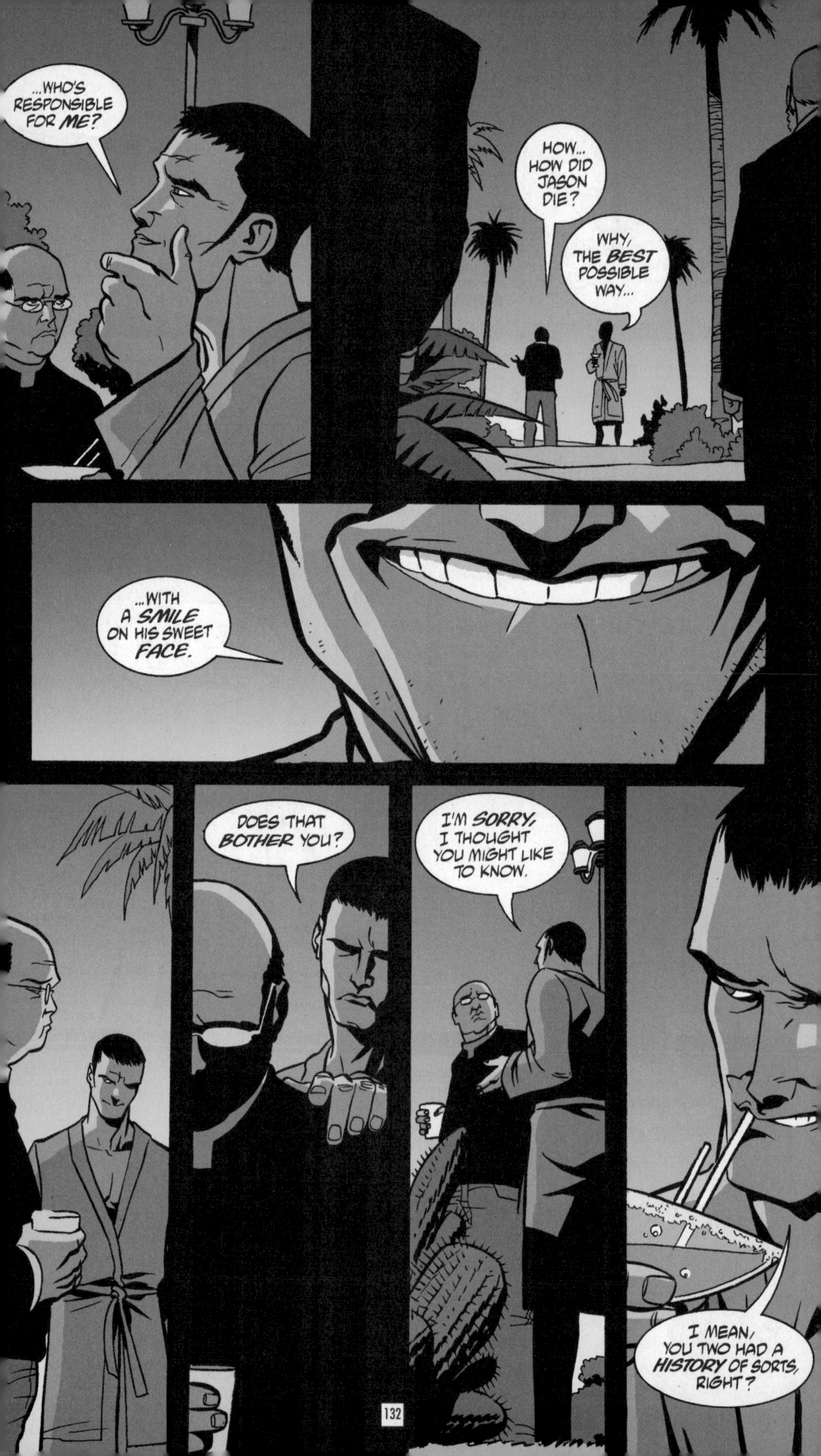
...WHO'S RESPONSIBLE FOR ME?
HOW... HOW DID JASON DIE?
WHY, THE BEST POSSIBLE WAY...
...WITH A SMILE ON HIS SWEET FACE.
DOES THAT BOTHER YOU?
I'M SORRY, I THOUGHT YOU MIGHT LIKE TO KNOW.
I MEAN, YOU TWO HAD A HISTORY OF SORTS, RIGHT?

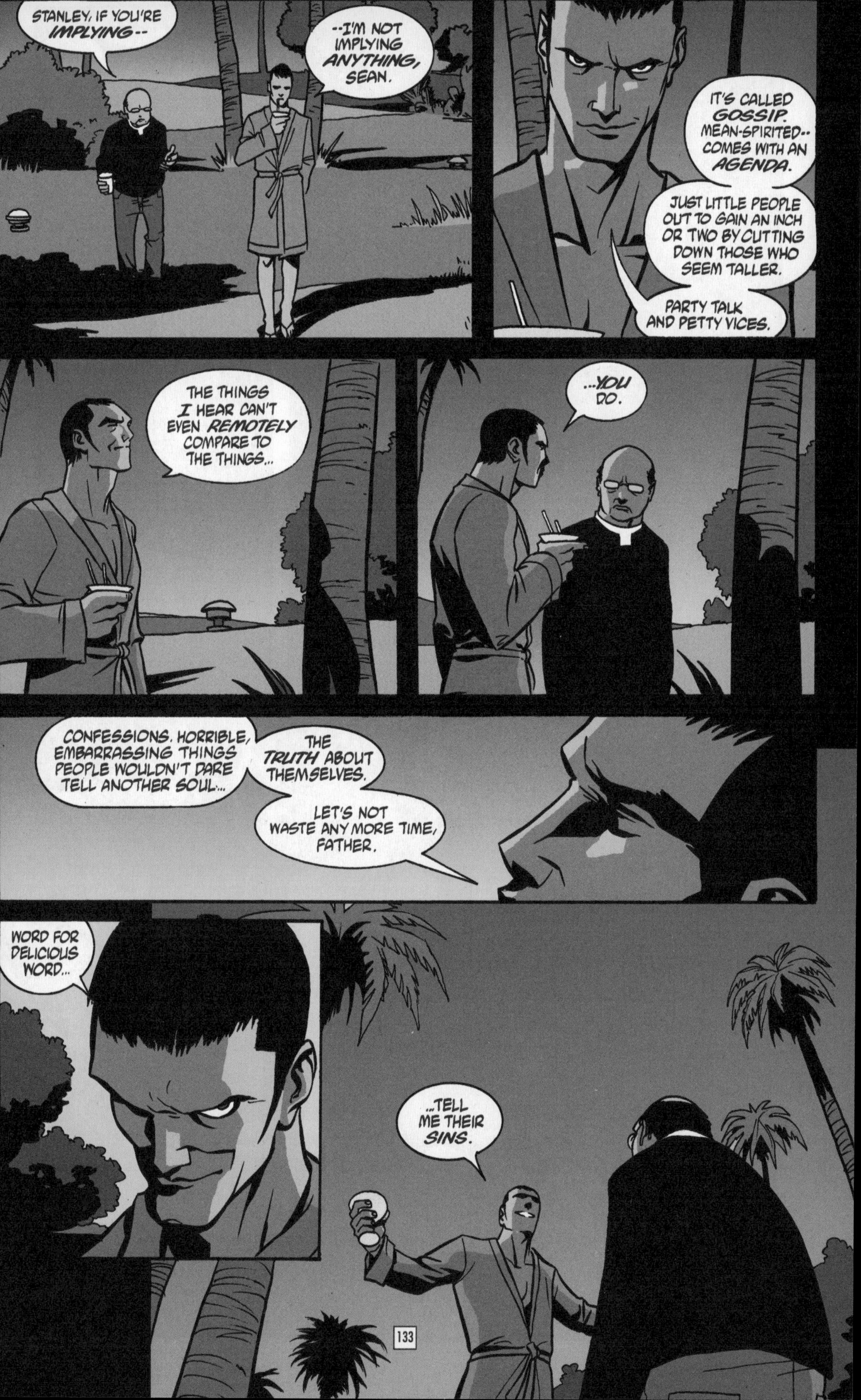

STANLEY, IF YOU'RE IMPLYING--
--I'M NOT IMPLYING ANYTHING, SEAN.
IT'S CALLED GOSSIP. MEAN-SPIRITED-- COMES WITH AN AGENDA.
JUST LITTLE PEOPLE OUT TO GAIN AN INCH OR TWO BY CUTTING DOWN THOSE WHO SEEM TALLER.
PARTY TALK AND PETTY VICES.
THE THINGS I HEAR CAN'T EVEN REMOTELY COMPARE TO THE THINGS...
...YOU DO.
CONFESSIONS. HORRIBLE, EMBARRASSING THINGS PEOPLE WOULDN'T DARE TELL ANOTHER SOUL...
THE TRUTH ABOUT THEMSELVES.
LET'S NOT WASTE ANY MORE TIME, FATHER.
WORD FOR DELICIOUS WORD...
...TELL ME THEIR SINS.

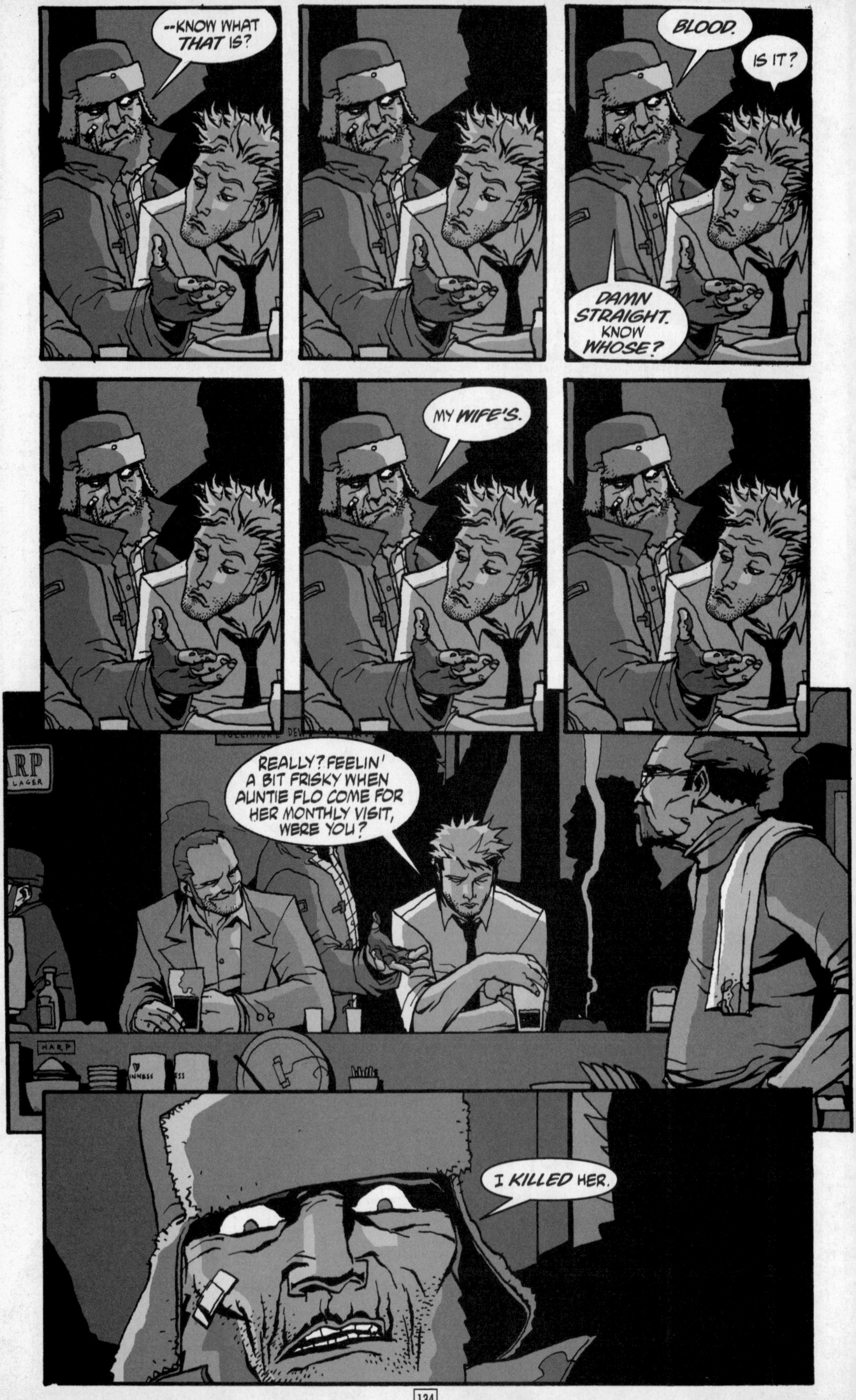
--KNOW WHAT THAT IS?
BLOOD.
IS IT?
DAMN STRAIGHT. KNOW WHOSE?
MY WIFE'S.
REALLY? FEELIN' A BIT FRISKY WHEN AUNTIE FLO COME FOR HER MONTHLY VISIT, WERE YOU?
I KILLED HER.

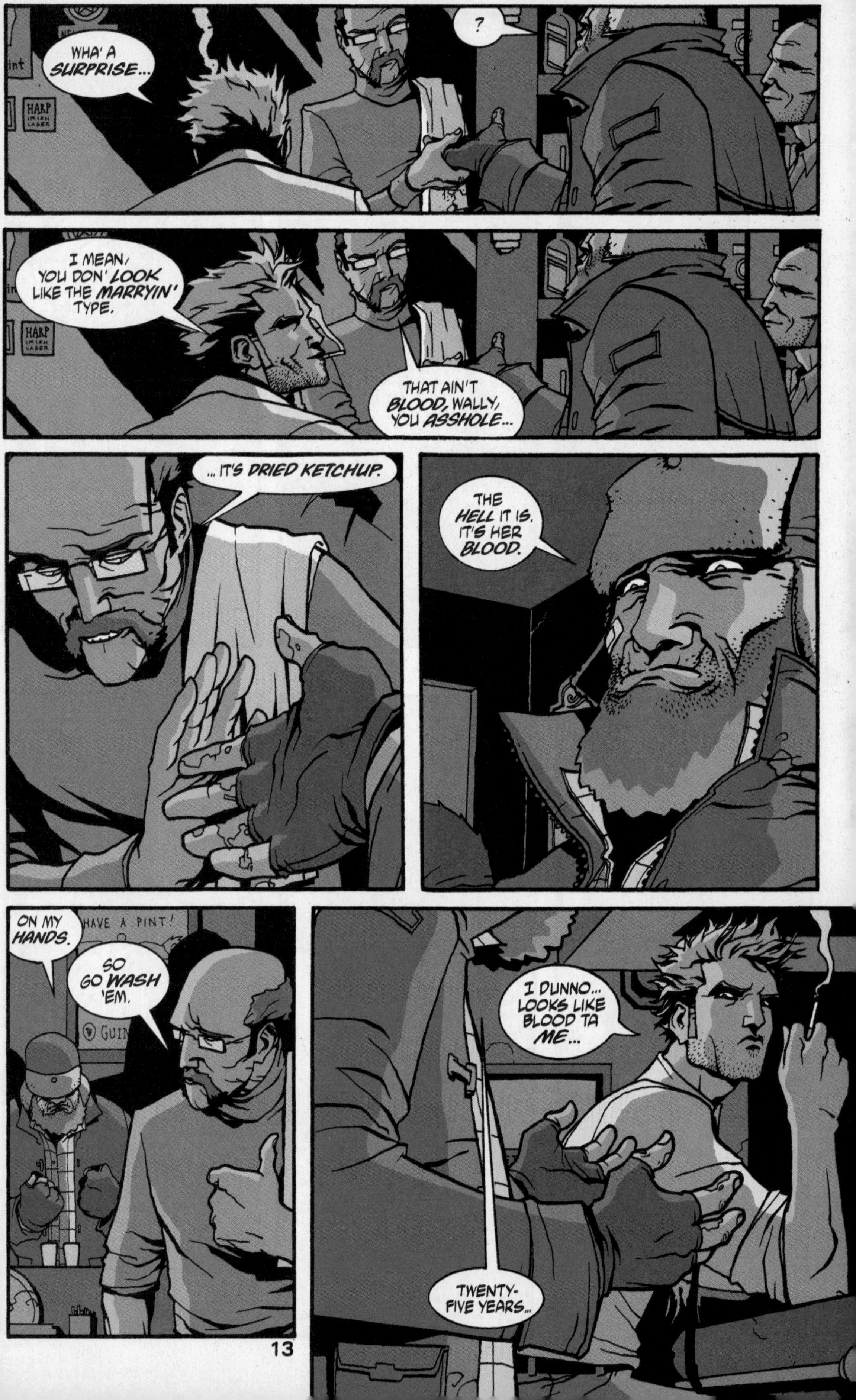
WHA' A SURPRISE...
?
I MEAN, YOU DON' LOOK LIKE THE MARRYIN' TYPE.
THAT AIN'T BLOOD, WALLY, YOU ASSHOLE...
... IT'S DRIED KETCHUP.
THE HELL IT IS. IT'S HER BLOOD.
ON MY HANDS.
SO GO WASH 'EM.
I DUNNO... LOOKS LIKE BLOOD TA ME...
TWENTY-FIVE YEARS...
HAVE A PINT!
HARP IRISH LAGER

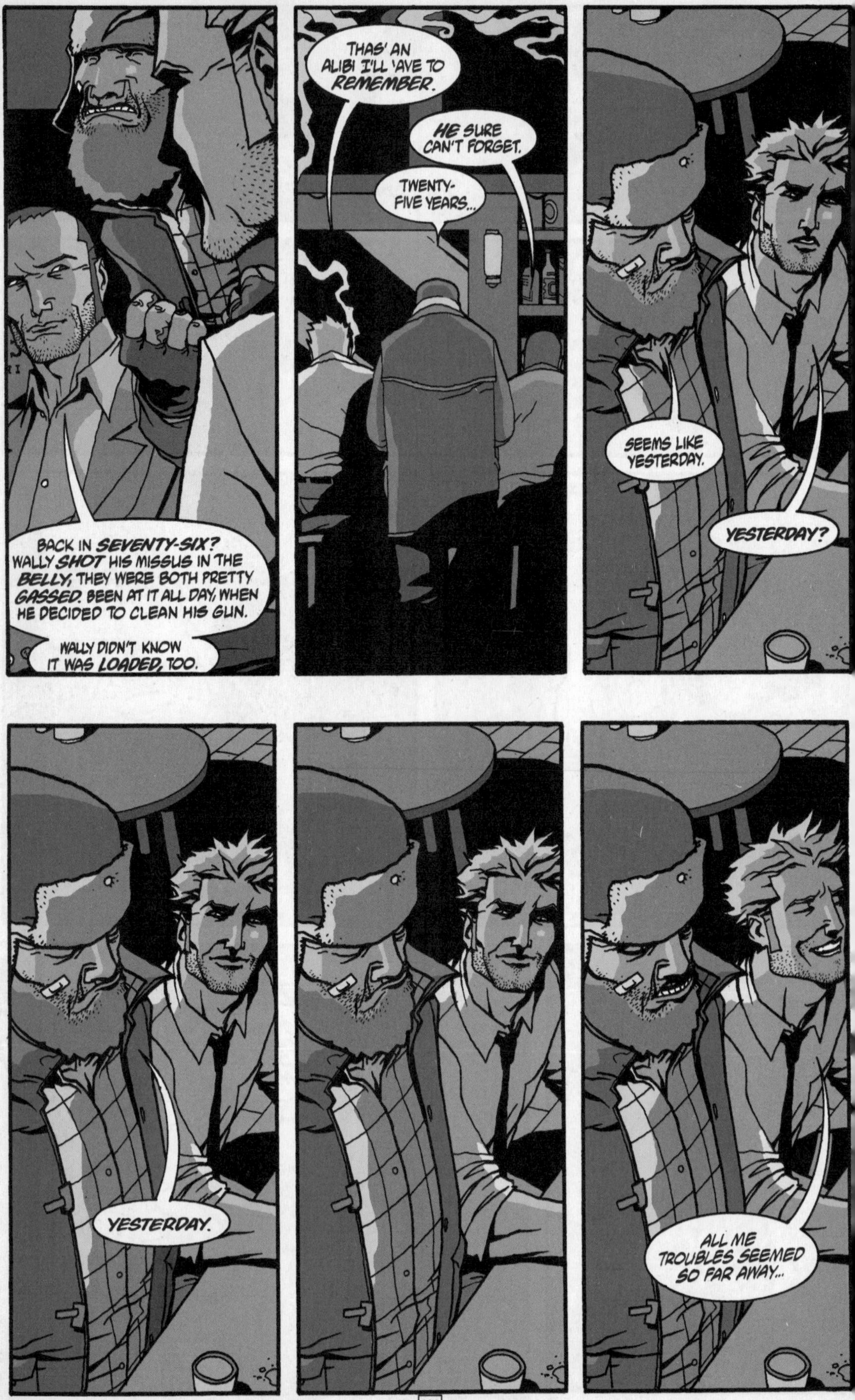
BACK IN SEVENTY-SIX? WALLY SHOT HIS MISSUS IN THE BELLY, THEY WERE BOTH PRETTY GASSED. BEEN AT IT ALL DAY, WHEN HE DECIDED TO CLEAN HIS GUN.
WALLY DIDN'T KNOW IT WAS LOADED, TOO.
THAS' AN ALIBI I'LL 'AVE TO REMEMBER.
HE SURE CAN'T FORGET.
TWENTY-FIVE YEARS...
SEEMS LIKE YESTERDAY.
YESTERDAY?
YESTERDAY.
ALL ME TROUBLES SEEMED SO FAR AWAY...

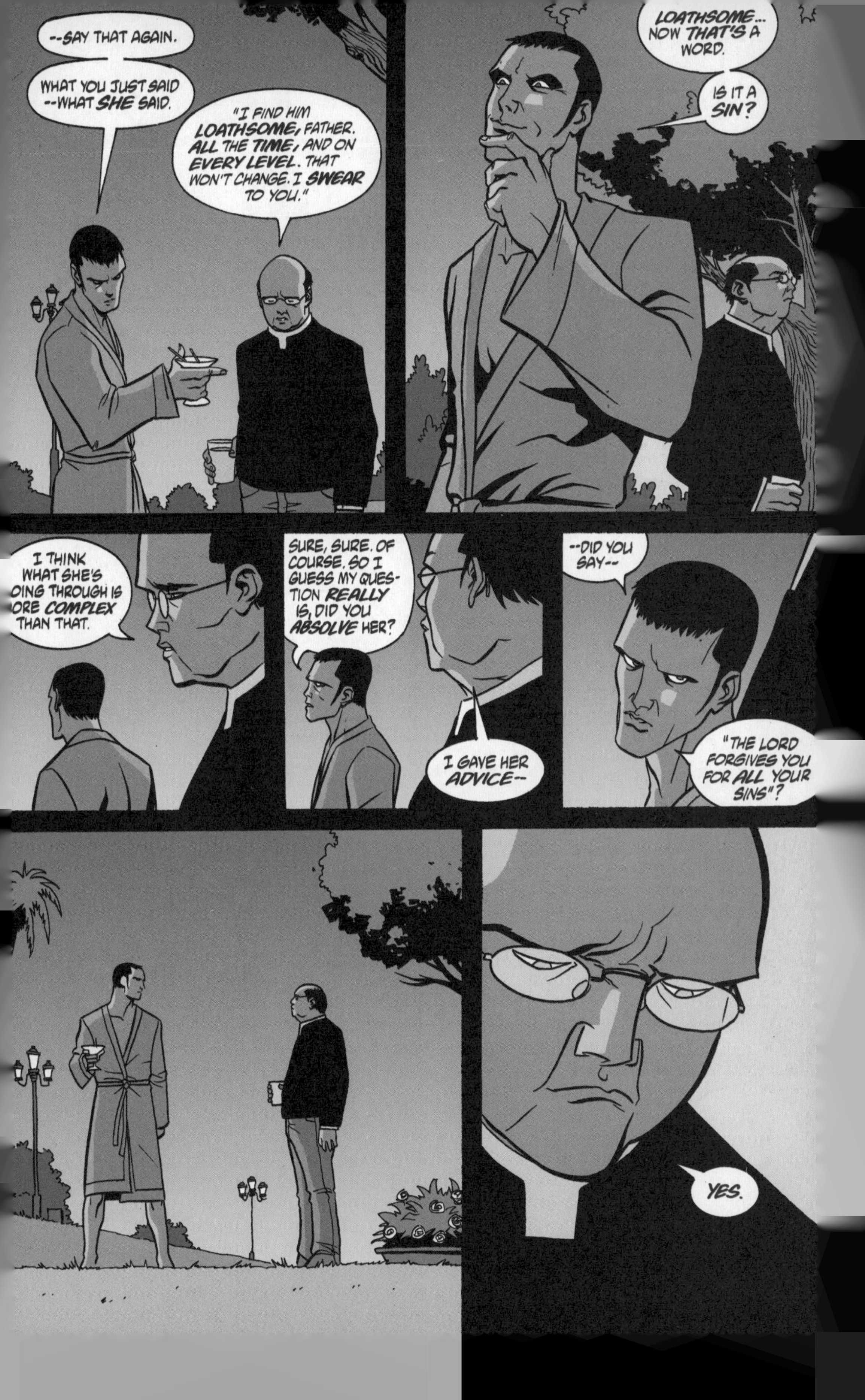
--SAY THAT AGAIN.
WHAT YOU JUST SAID --WHAT SHE SAID.
"I FIND HIM LOATHSOME, FATHER. ALL THE TIME, AND ON EVERY LEVEL. THAT WON'T CHANGE. I SWEAR TO YOU."
LOATHSOME... NOW THAT'S A WORD.
IS IT A SIN?
I THINK WHAT SHE'S OING THROUGH IS ORE COMPLEX THAN THAT.
SURE, SURE. OF COURSE. SO I GUESS MY QUESTION REALLY IS, DID YOU ABSOLVE HER?
I GAVE HER ADVICE--
--DID YOU SAY--
"THE LORD FORGIVES YOU FOR ALL YOUR SINS"?
YES.

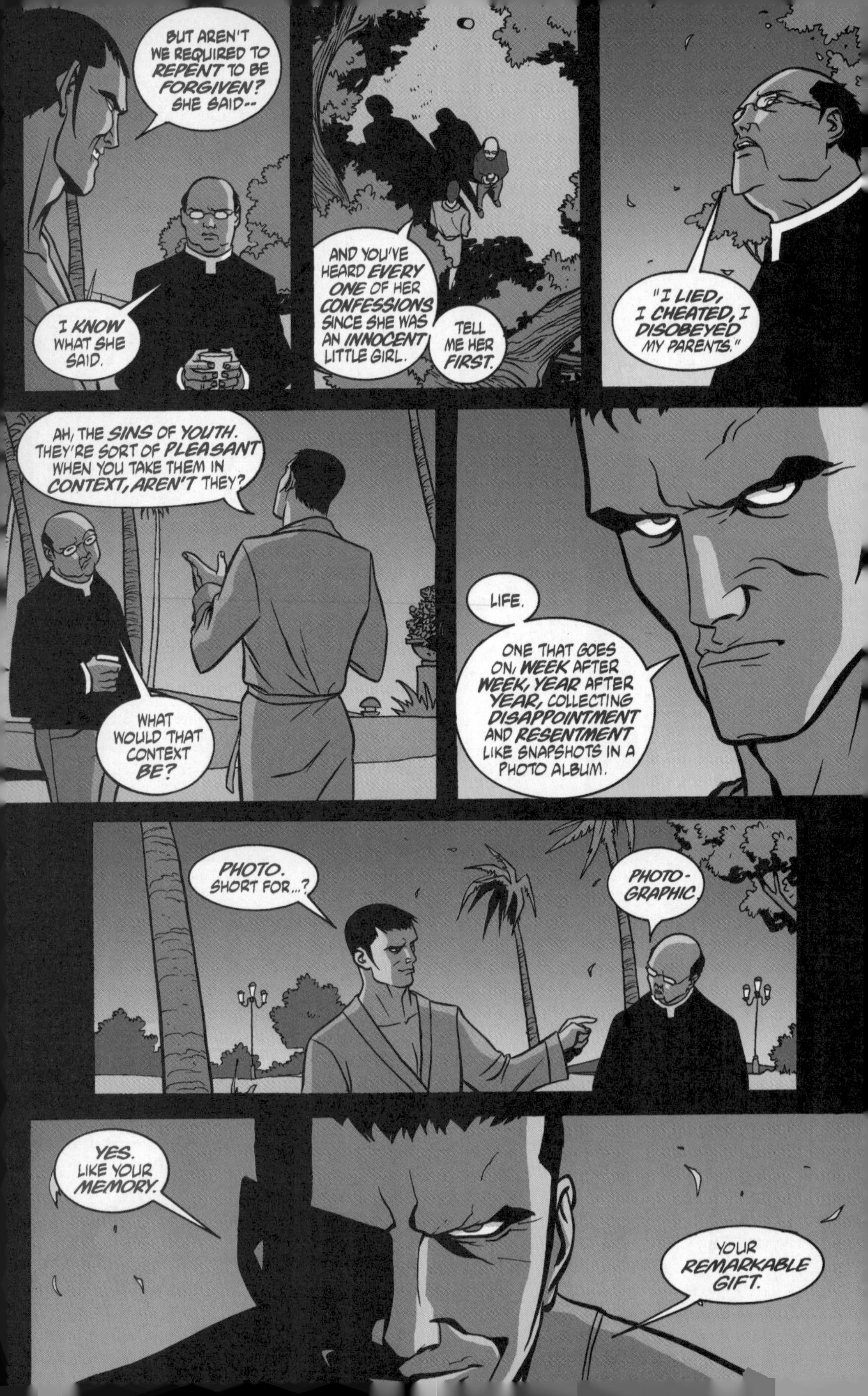

BUT AREN'T WE REQUIRED TO REPENT TO BE FORGIVEN? SHE SAID--
I KNOW WHAT SHE SAID.
AND YOU'VE HEARD EVERY ONE OF HER CONFESSIONS SINCE SHE WAS AN INNOCENT LITTLE GIRL.
TELL ME HER FIRST.
"I LIED, I CHEATED, I DISOBEYED MY PARENTS."
AH, THE SINS OF YOUTH. THEY'RE SORT OF PLEASANT WHEN YOU TAKE THEM IN CONTEXT, AREN'T THEY?
WHAT WOULD THAT CONTEXT BE?
LIFE.
ONE THAT GOES ON, WEEK AFTER WEEK, YEAR AFTER YEAR, COLLECTING DISAPPOINTMENT AND RESENTMENT LIKE SNAPSHOTS IN A PHOTO ALBUM.
PHOTO. SHORT FOR...?
PHOTO-GRAPHIC.
YES. LIKE YOUR MEMORY.
YOUR REMARKABLE GIFT.

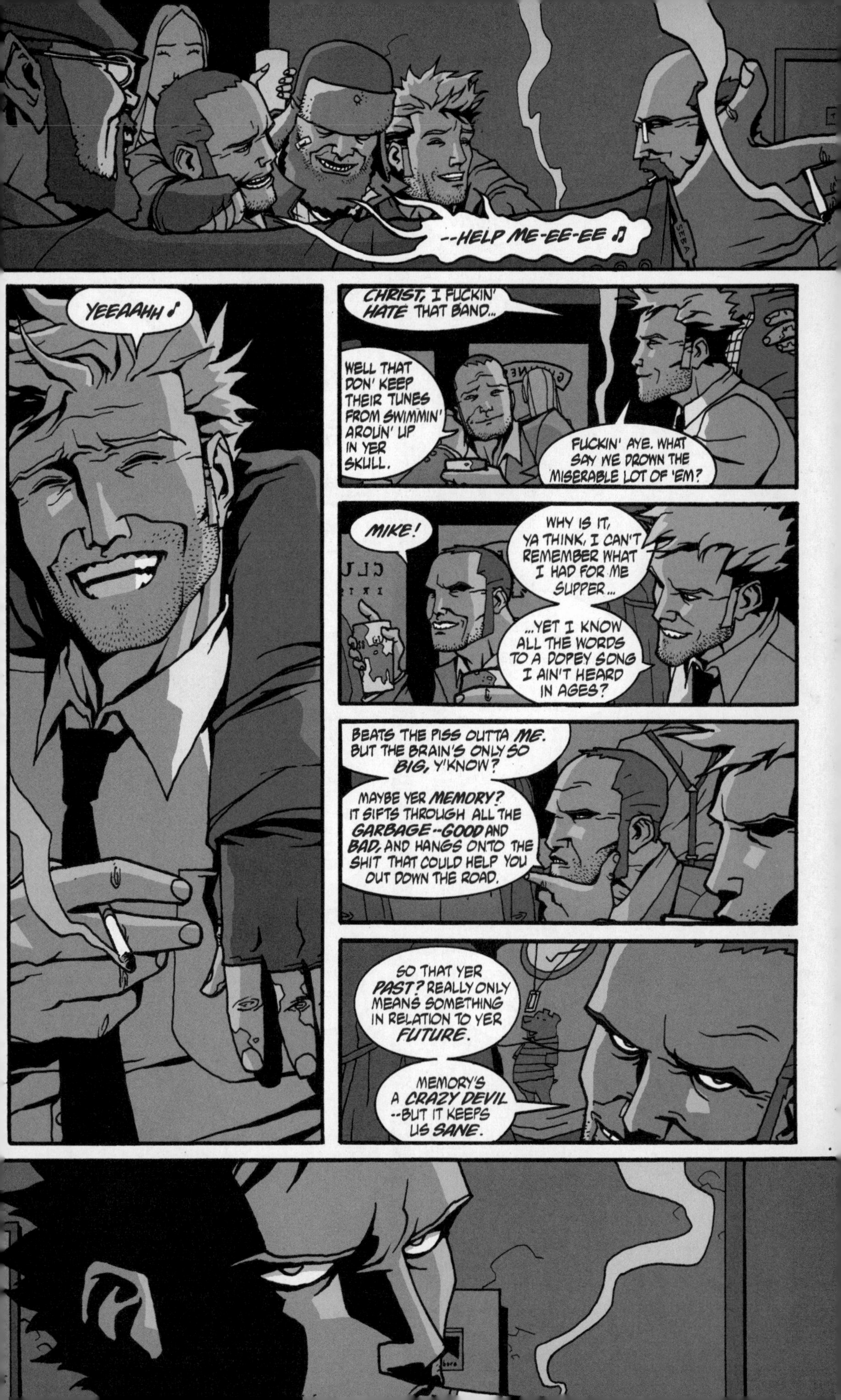
--HELP ME-EE-EE ♫
SEBA
YEEAAHH ♪
CHRIST, I FUCKIN' HATE THAT BAND...
WELL THAT DON' KEEP THEIR TUNES FROM SWIMMIN' AROUN' UP IN YER SKULL.
FUCKIN' AYE. WHAT SAY WE DROWN THE MISERABLE LOT OF 'EM?
MIKE!
WHY IS IT, YA THINK, I CAN'T REMEMBER WHAT I HAD FOR ME SUPPER...
...YET I KNOW ALL THE WORDS TO A DOPEY SONG I AIN'T HEARD IN AGES?
BEATS THE PISS OUTTA ME. BUT THE BRAIN'S ONLY SO BIG, Y'KNOW?
MAYBE YER MEMORY? IT SIFTS THROUGH ALL THE GARBAGE--GOOD AND BAD, AND HANGS ONTO THE SHIT THAT COULD HELP YOU OUT DOWN THE ROAD.
SO THAT YER PAST? REALLY ONLY MEANS SOMETHING IN RELATION TO YER FUTURE.
MEMORY'S A CRAZY DEVIL --BUT IT KEEPS US SANE.

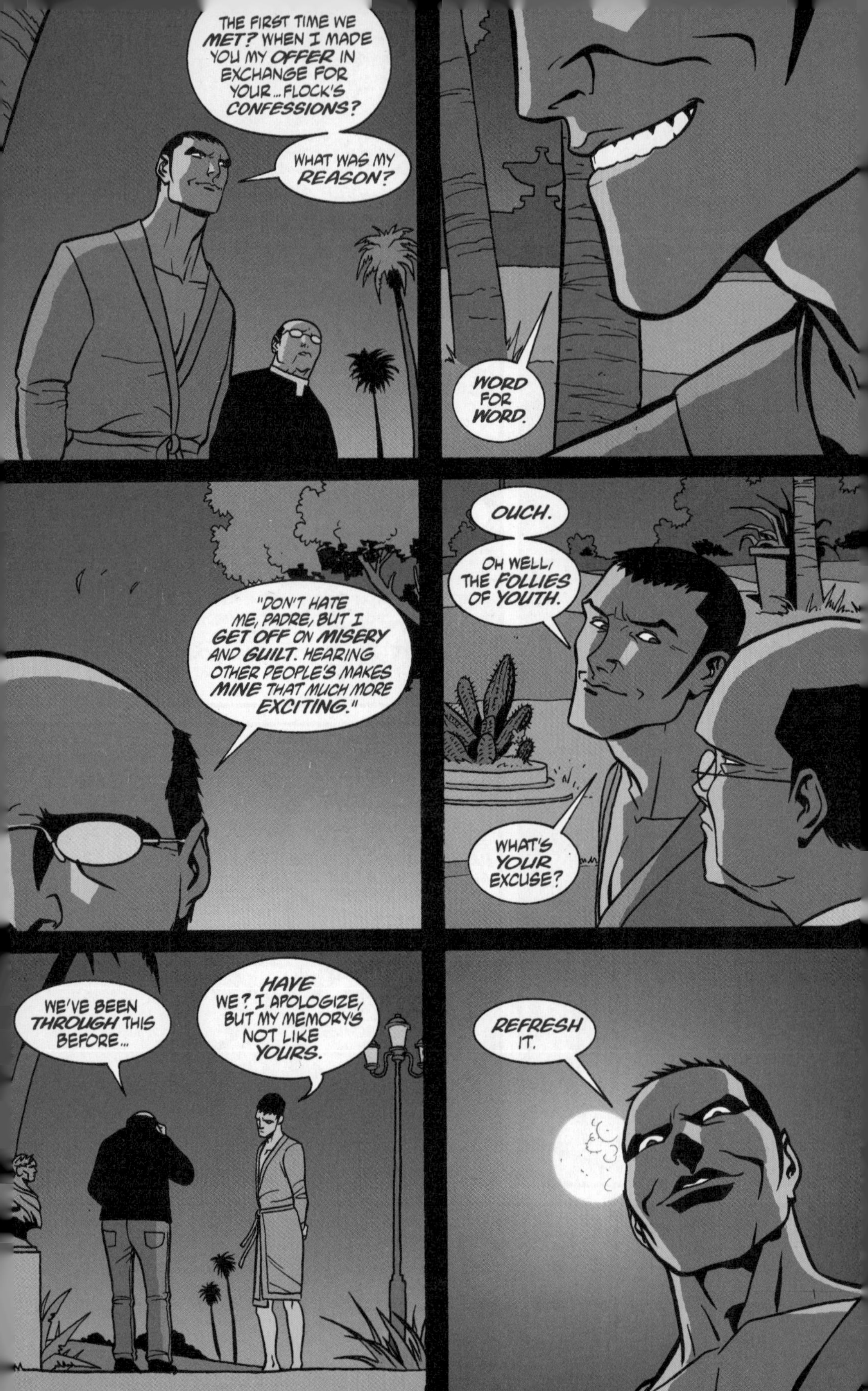
THE FIRST TIME WE MET? WHEN I MADE YOU MY OFFER IN EXCHANGE FOR YOUR...FLOCK'S CONFESSIONS?
WHAT WAS MY REASON?
WORD FOR WORD.
"DON'T HATE ME, PADRE, BUT I GET OFF ON MISERY AND GUILT. HEARING OTHER PEOPLE'S MAKES MINE THAT MUCH MORE EXCITING."
OUCH.
OH WELL, THE FOLLIES OF YOUTH.
WHAT'S YOUR EXCUSE?
WE'VE BEEN THROUGH THIS BEFORE...
HAVE WE? I APOLOGIZE, BUT MY MEMORY'S NOT LIKE YOURS.
REFRESH IT.

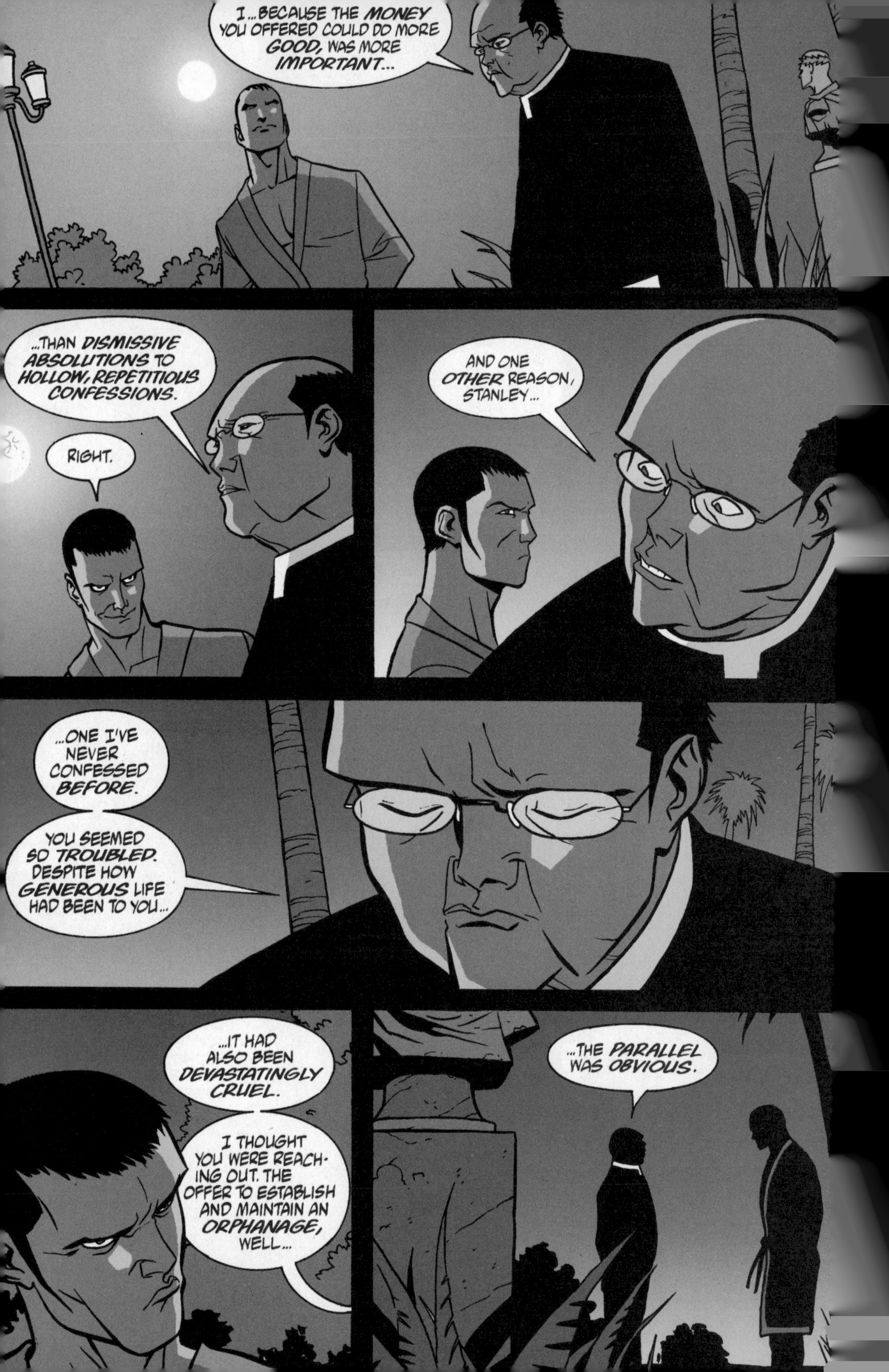
I...BECAUSE THE MONEY YOU OFFERED COULD DO MORE GOOD, WAS MORE IMPORTANT...
...THAN DISMISSIVE ABSOLUTIONS TO HOLLOW, REPETITIOUS CONFESSIONS.
RIGHT.
AND ONE OTHER REASON, STANLEY...
...ONE I'VE NEVER CONFESSED BEFORE.
YOU SEEMED SO TROUBLED. DESPITE HOW GENEROUS LIFE HAD BEEN TO YOU...
...IT HAD ALSO BEEN DEVASTATINGLY CRUEL.
I THOUGHT YOU WERE REACHING OUT. THE OFFER TO ESTABLISH AND MAINTAIN AN ORPHANAGE, WELL...
...THE PARALLEL WAS OBVIOUS.

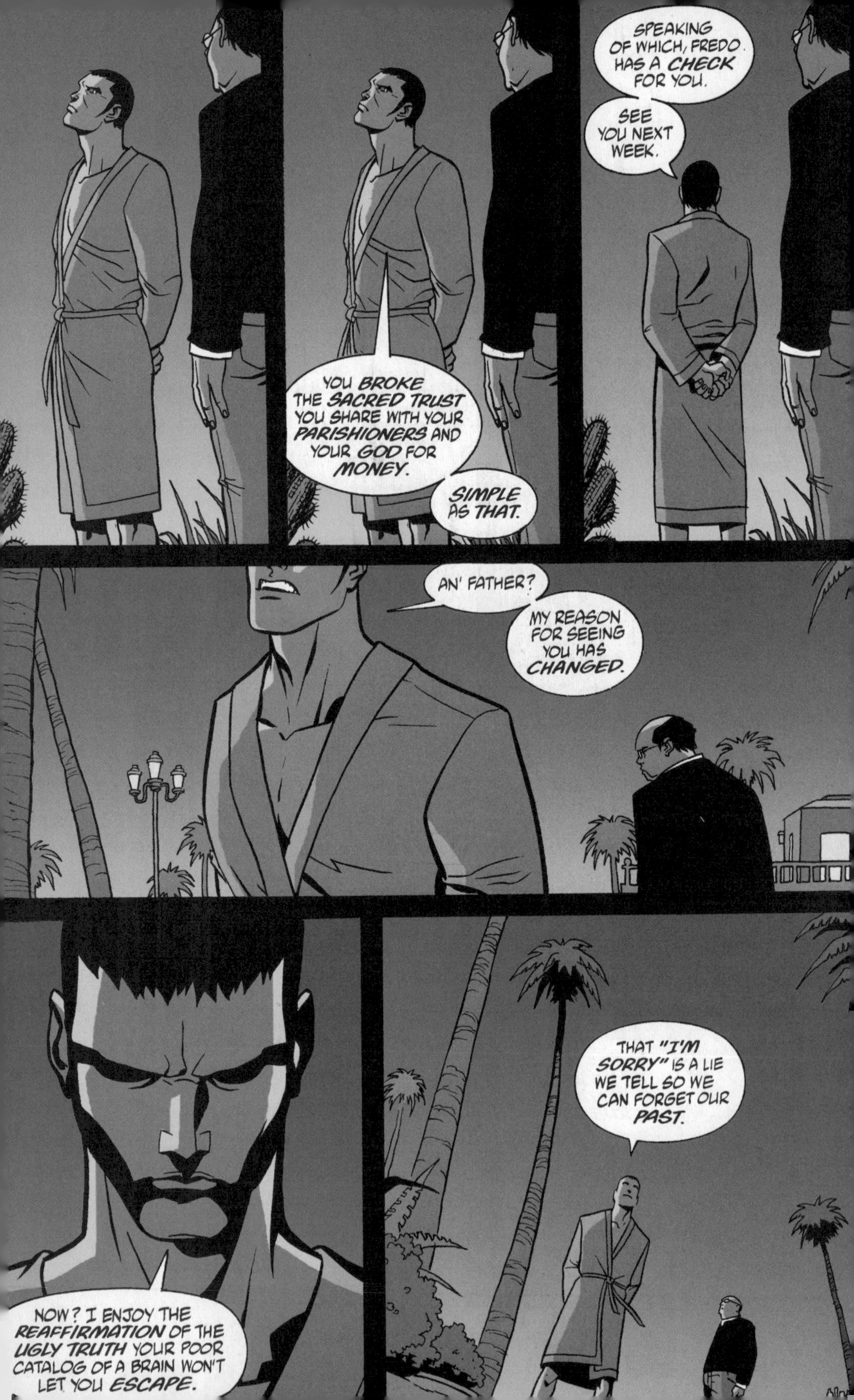
YOU BROKE THE SACRED TRUST YOU SHARE WITH YOUR PARISHIONERS AND YOUR GOD FOR MONEY.
SIMPLE AS THAT.
SPEAKING OF WHICH, FREDO HAS A CHECK FOR YOU.
SEE YOU NEXT WEEK.
AN' FATHER?
MY REASON FOR SEEING YOU HAS CHANGED.
NOW? I ENJOY THE REAFFIRMATION OF THE UGLY TRUTH YOUR POOR CATALOG OF A BRAIN WON'T LET YOU ESCAPE.
THAT "I'M SORRY" IS A LIE WE TELL SO WE CAN FORGET OUR PAST.

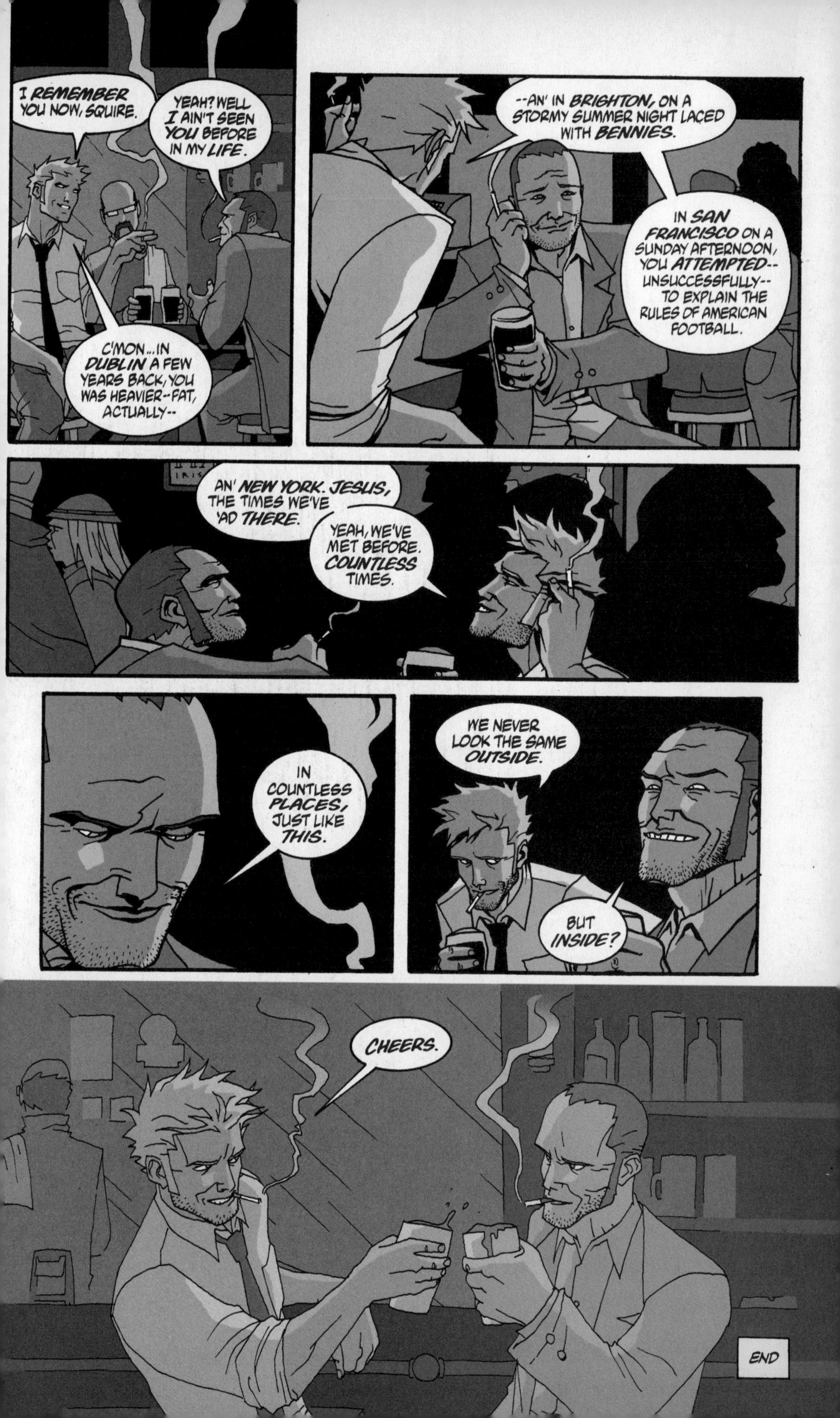

I REMEMBER YOU NOW, SQUIRE.
YEAH? WELL I AIN'T SEEN YOU BEFORE IN MY LIFE.
C'MON... IN DUBLIN A FEW YEARS BACK, YOU WAS HEAVIER--FAT, ACTUALLY--
--AN' IN BRIGHTON, ON A STORMY SUMMER NIGHT LACED WITH BENNIES.
IN SAN FRANCISCO ON A SUNDAY AFTERNOON, YOU ATTEMPTED--UNSUCCESSFULLY--TO EXPLAIN THE RULES OF AMERICAN FOOTBALL.
AN' NEW YORK. JESUS, THE TIMES WE'VE 'AD THERE.
YEAH, WE'VE MET BEFORE. COUNTLESS TIMES.
IN COUNTLESS PLACES, JUST LIKE THIS.
WE NEVER LOOK THE SAME OUTSIDE.
BUT INSIDE?
CHEERS.
END

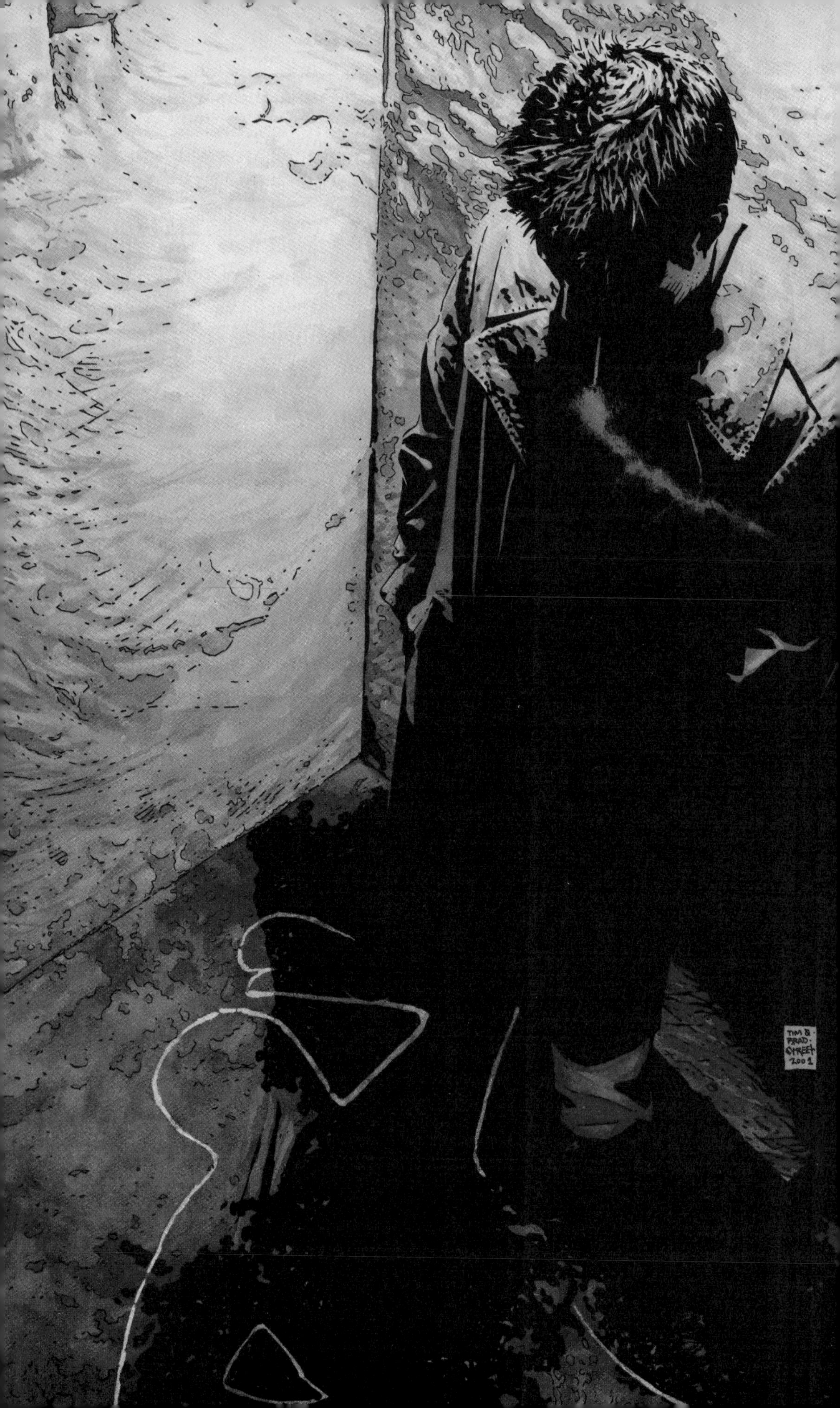
TIM B. BRAD-STREET 2001

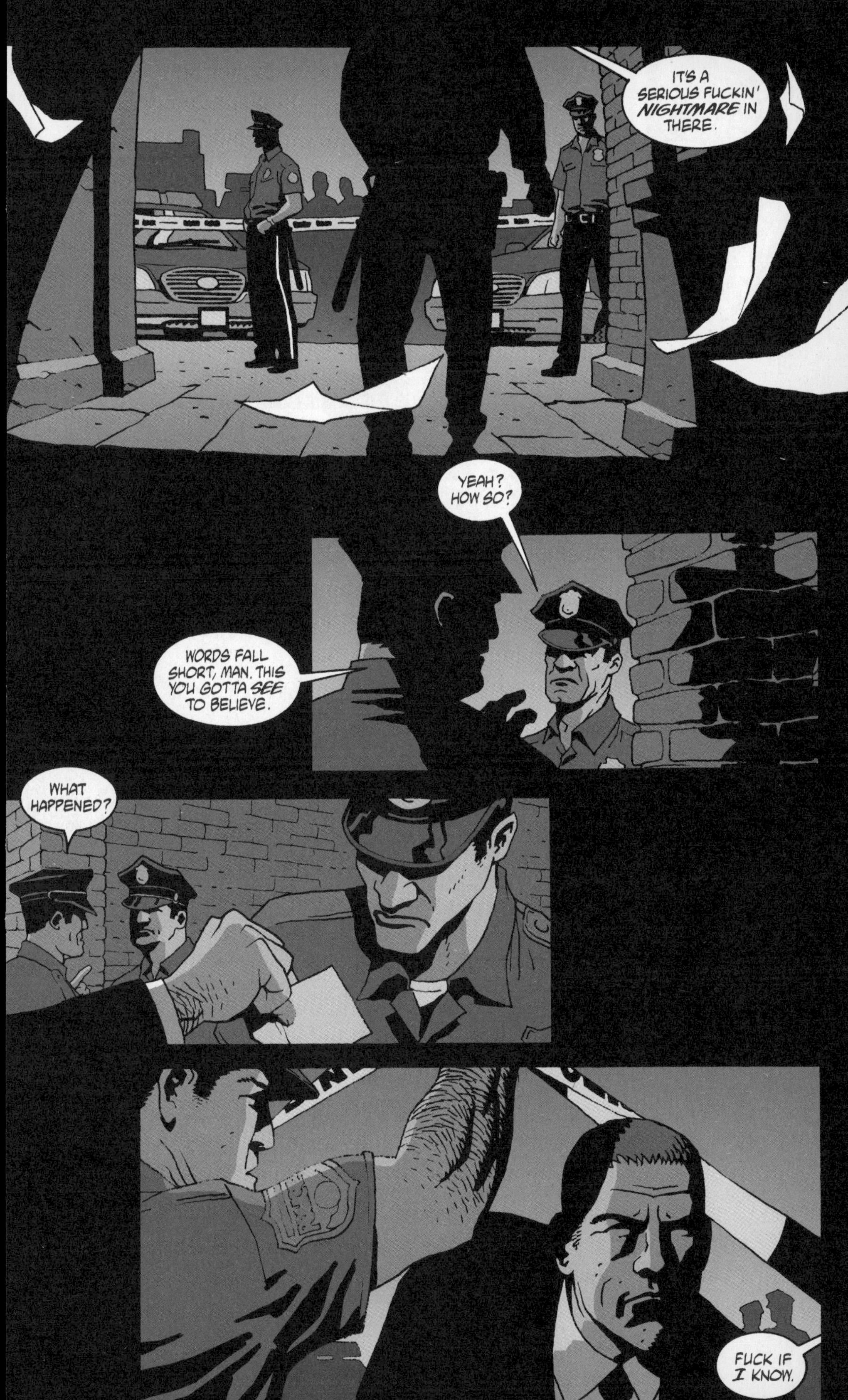
IT'S A SERIOUS FUCKIN' NIGHTMARE IN THERE.
YEAH? HOW SO?
WORDS FALL SHORT, MAN. THIS YOU GOTTA SEE TO BELIEVE.
WHAT HAPPENED?
FUCK IF I KNOW.

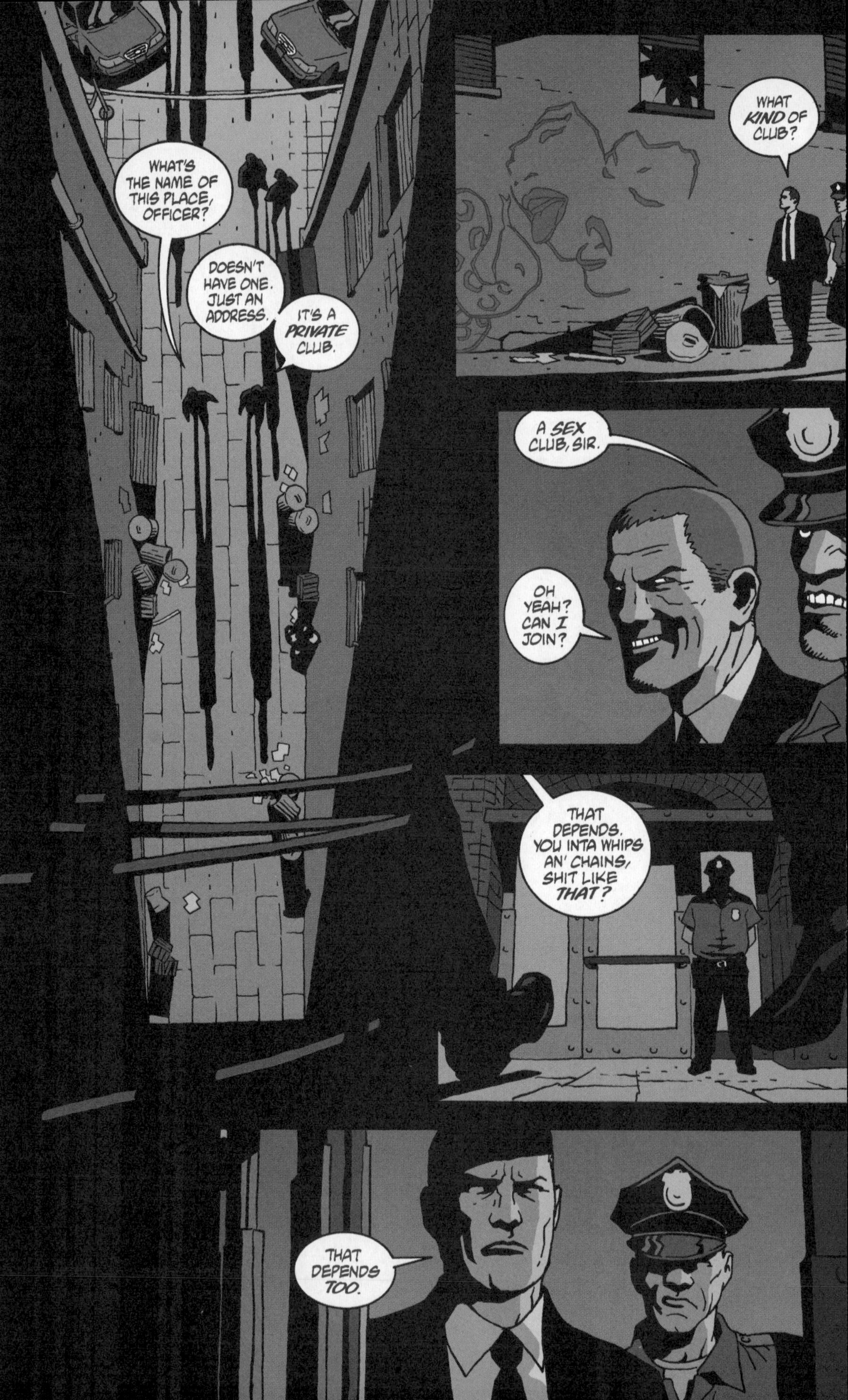
WHAT'S THE NAME OF THIS PLACE, OFFICER?
DOESN'T HAVE ONE. JUST AN ADDRESS.
IT'S A PRIVATE CLUB.
WHAT KIND OF CLUB?
A SEX CLUB, SIR.
OH YEAH? CAN I JOIN?
THAT DEPENDS. YOU INTA WHIPS AN' CHAINS, SHIT LIKE THAT?
THAT DEPENDS TOO.

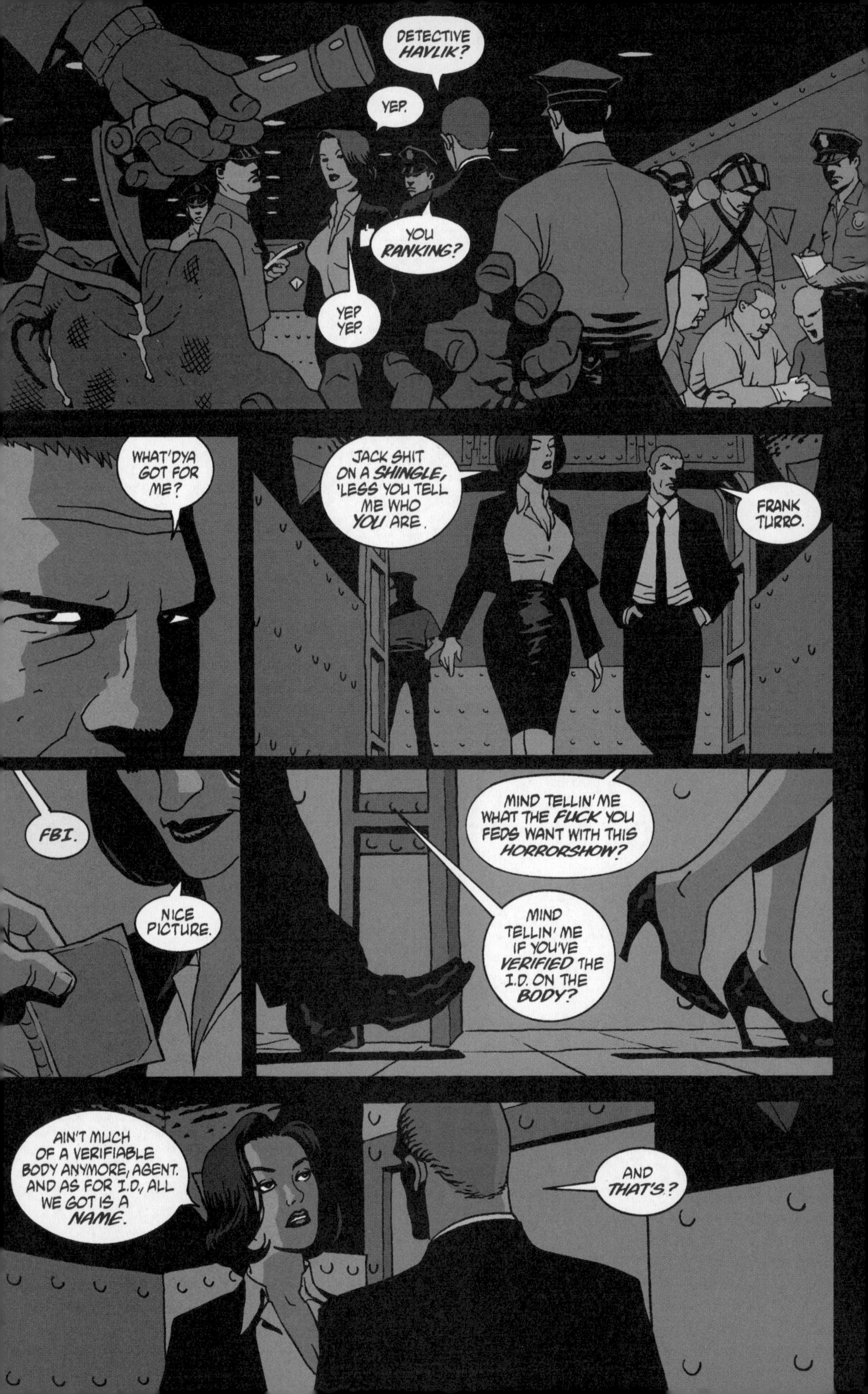
DETECTIVE HAVLIK?
YEP.
YOU RANKING?
YEP YEP.
WHAT'DYA GOT FOR ME?
JACK SHIT ON A SHINGLE, 'LESS YOU TELL ME WHO YOU ARE.
FRANK TURRO.
FBI.
NICE PICTURE.
MIND TELLIN' ME WHAT THE FUCK YOU FEDS WANT WITH THIS HORRORSHOW?
MIND TELLIN' ME IF YOU'VE VERIFIED THE I.D. ON THE BODY?
AIN'T MUCH OF A VERIFIABLE BODY ANYMORE, AGENT. AND AS FOR I.D., ALL WE GOT IS A NAME.
AND THAT'S?

CONSTANTINE.

JOHN CONSTANTINE.

Ashes & Dust in the City of Angels
part one

Brian Azzarello, WRITER   **Marcelo Frusin,** ARTIST

Lee Loughridge   Clem Robins   Tim Bradstreet   Zachary Rau   Will Denni

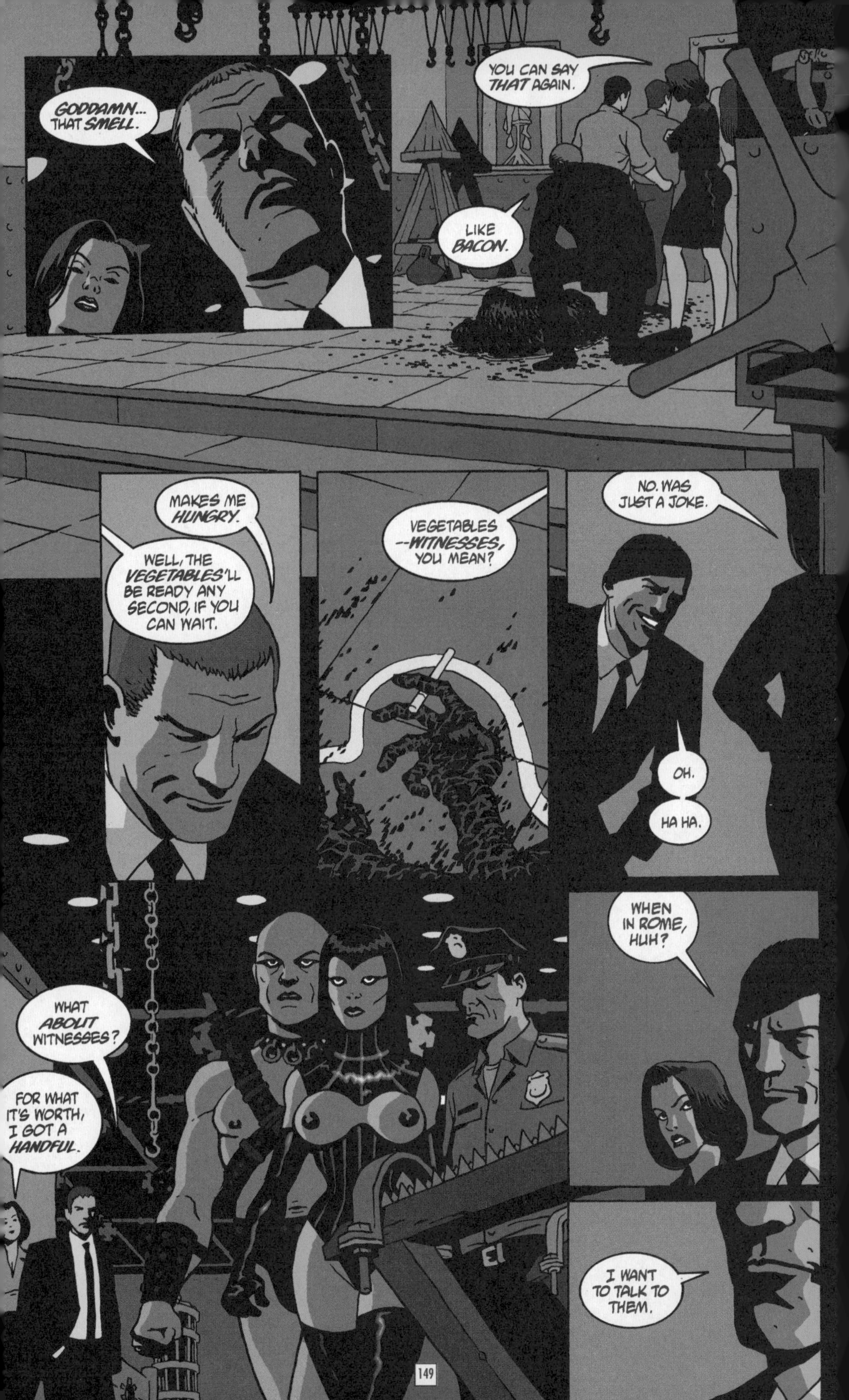
GODDAMN... THAT SMELL.
YOU CAN SAY THAT AGAIN.
LIKE BACON.
MAKES ME HUNGRY.
WELL, THE VEGETABLES'LL BE READY ANY SECOND, IF YOU CAN WAIT.
VEGETABLES --WITNESSES, YOU MEAN?
NO. WAS JUST A JOKE.
OH.
HA HA.
WHAT ABOUT WITNESSES?
FOR WHAT IT'S WORTH, I GOT A HANDFUL.
WHEN IN ROME, HUH?
I WANT TO TALK TO THEM.

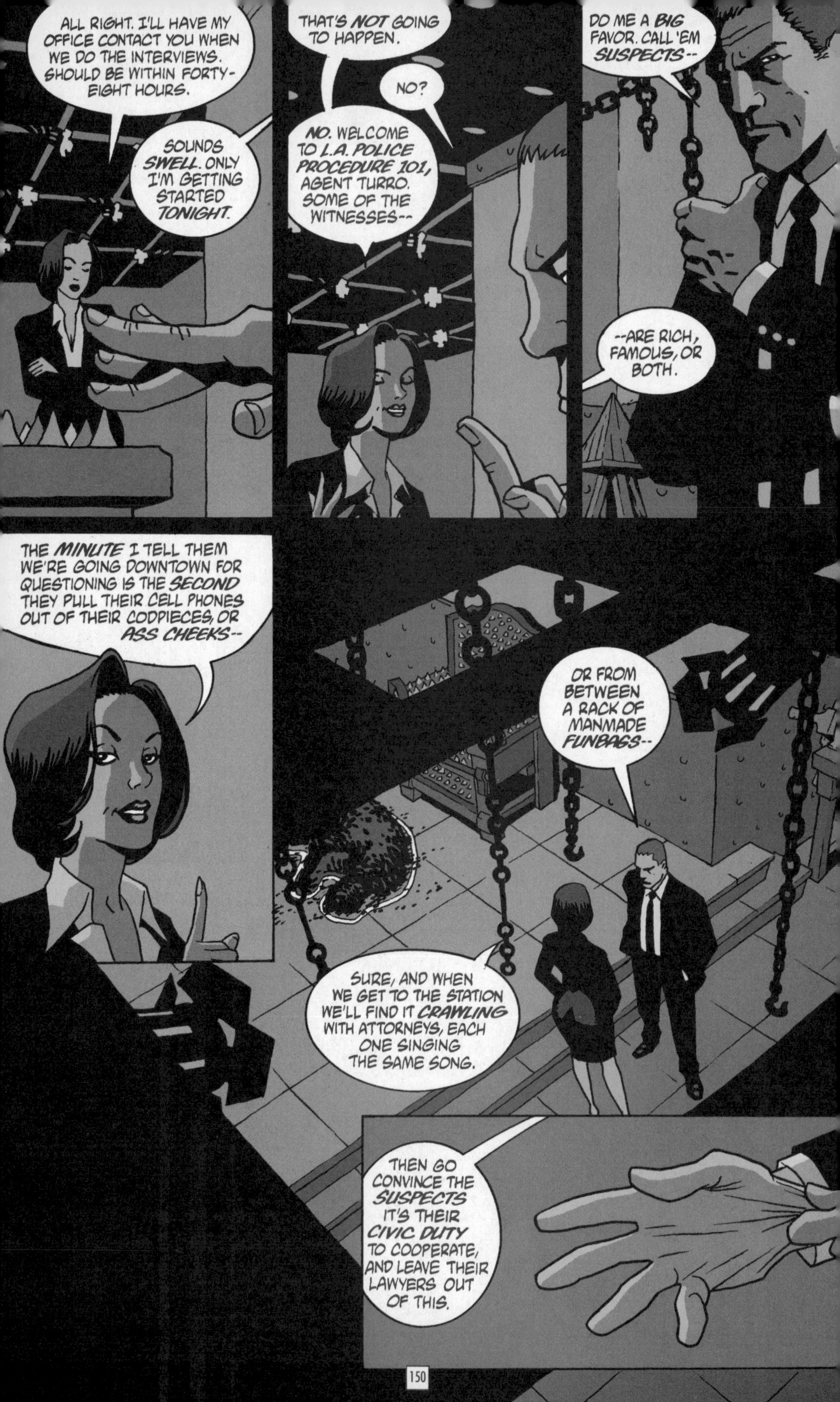
ALL RIGHT. I'LL HAVE MY OFFICE CONTACT YOU WHEN WE DO THE INTERVIEWS. SHOULD BE WITHIN FORTY-EIGHT HOURS.
SOUNDS SWELL. ONLY I'M GETTING STARTED TONIGHT.
THAT'S NOT GOING TO HAPPEN.
NO?
NO. WELCOME TO L.A. POLICE PROCEDURE 101, AGENT TURRO. SOME OF THE WITNESSES--
DO ME A BIG FAVOR. CALL 'EM SUSPECTS--
--ARE RICH, FAMOUS, OR BOTH.
THE MINUTE I TELL THEM WE'RE GOING DOWNTOWN FOR QUESTIONING IS THE SECOND THEY PULL THEIR CELL PHONES OUT OF THEIR CODPIECES, OR ASS CHEEKS--
OR FROM BETWEEN A RACK OF MANMADE FUNBAGS--
SURE, AND WHEN WE GET TO THE STATION WE'LL FIND IT CRAWLING WITH ATTORNEYS, EACH ONE SINGING THE SAME SONG.
THEN GO CONVINCE THE SUSPECTS IT'S THEIR CIVIC DUTY TO COOPERATE, AND LEAVE THEIR LAWYERS OUT OF THIS.

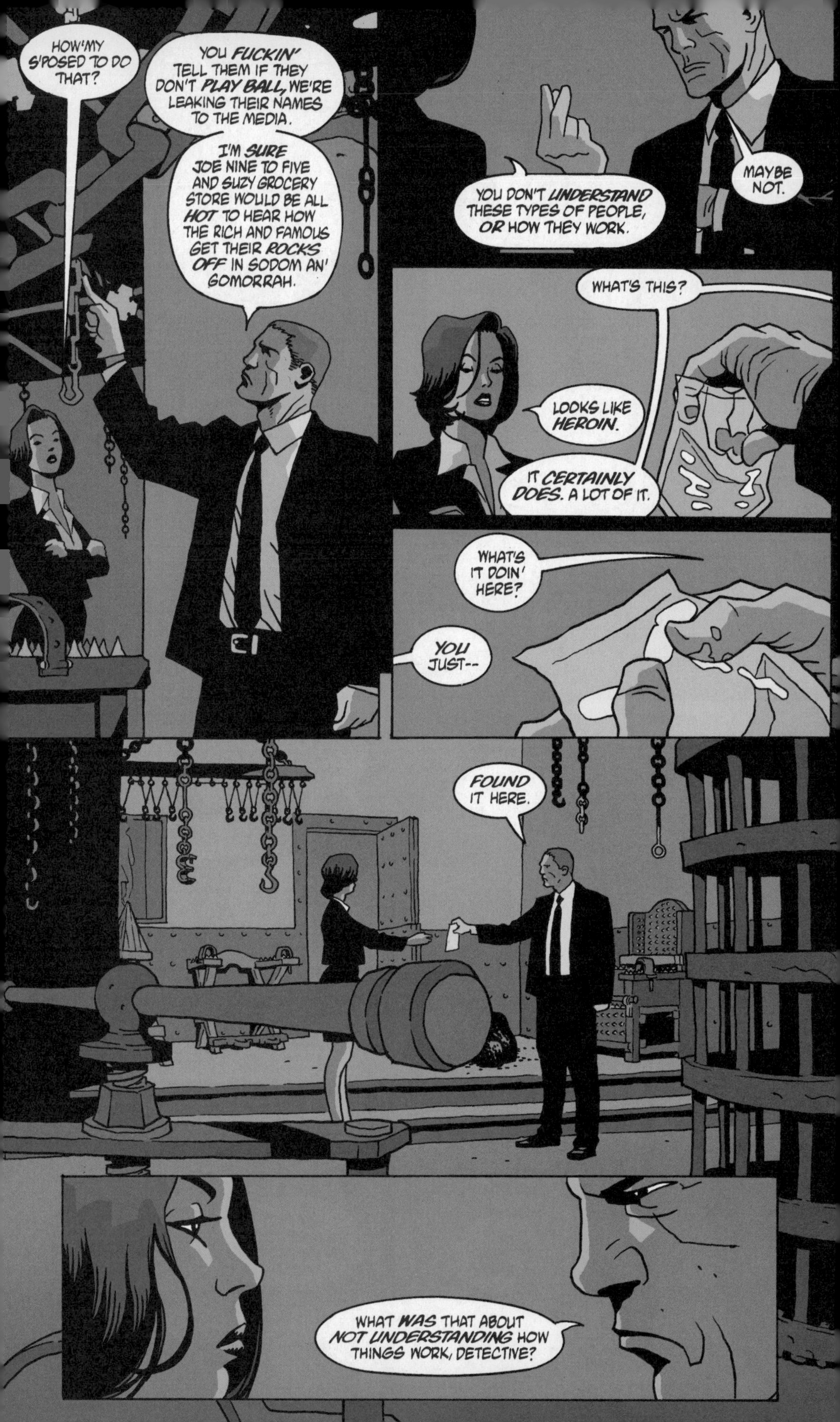
HOW'MY S'POSED TO DO THAT?
YOU *FUCKIN'* TELL THEM IF THEY DON'T *PLAY BALL,* WE'RE LEAKING THEIR NAMES TO THE MEDIA.
I'M *SURE* JOE NINE TO FIVE AND SUZY GROCERY STORE WOULD BE ALL *HOT* TO HEAR HOW THE RICH AND FAMOUS GET THEIR *ROCKS OFF* IN SODOM AN' GOMORRAH.
YOU DON'T *UNDERSTAND* THESE TYPES OF PEOPLE, *OR* HOW THEY WORK.
MAYBE NOT.
WHAT'S THIS?
LOOKS LIKE *HEROIN.*
IT *CERTAINLY DOES.* A LOT OF IT.
WHAT'S IT DOIN' HERE?
YOU JUST--
FOUND IT HERE.
WHAT *WAS* THAT ABOUT *NOT UNDERSTANDING* HOW THINGS WORK, DETECTIVE?

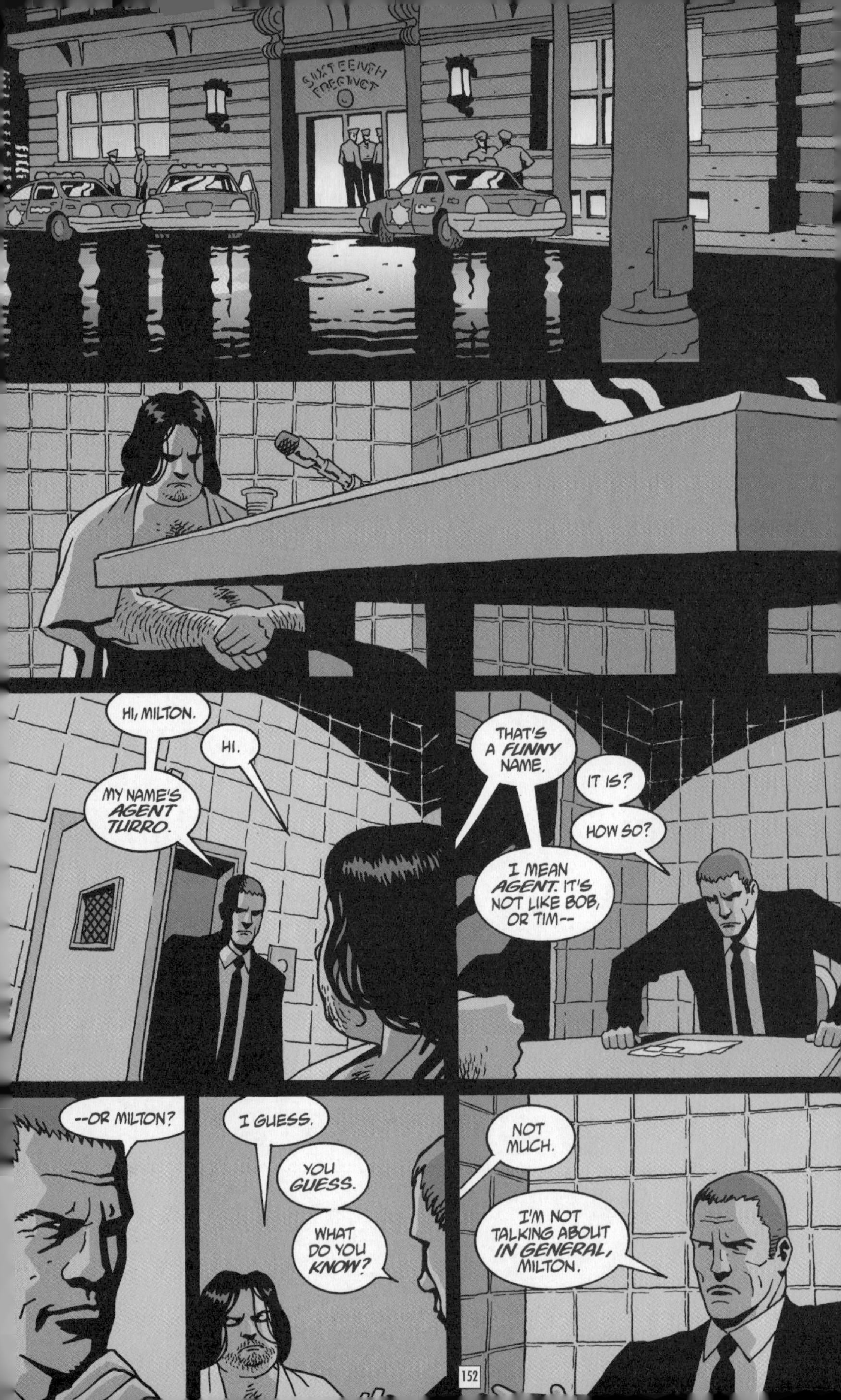
SIXTEENTH PRECINCT
HI, MILTON.
HI.
MY NAME'S *AGENT TURRO.*
THAT'S A *FUNNY* NAME.
IT IS?
HOW SO?
I MEAN *AGENT.* IT'S NOT LIKE BOB, OR TIM--
--OR MILTON?
I GUESS.
YOU *GUESS.*
WHAT DO YOU *KNOW?*
NOT MUCH.
I'M NOT TALKING ABOUT *IN GENERAL,* MILTON.

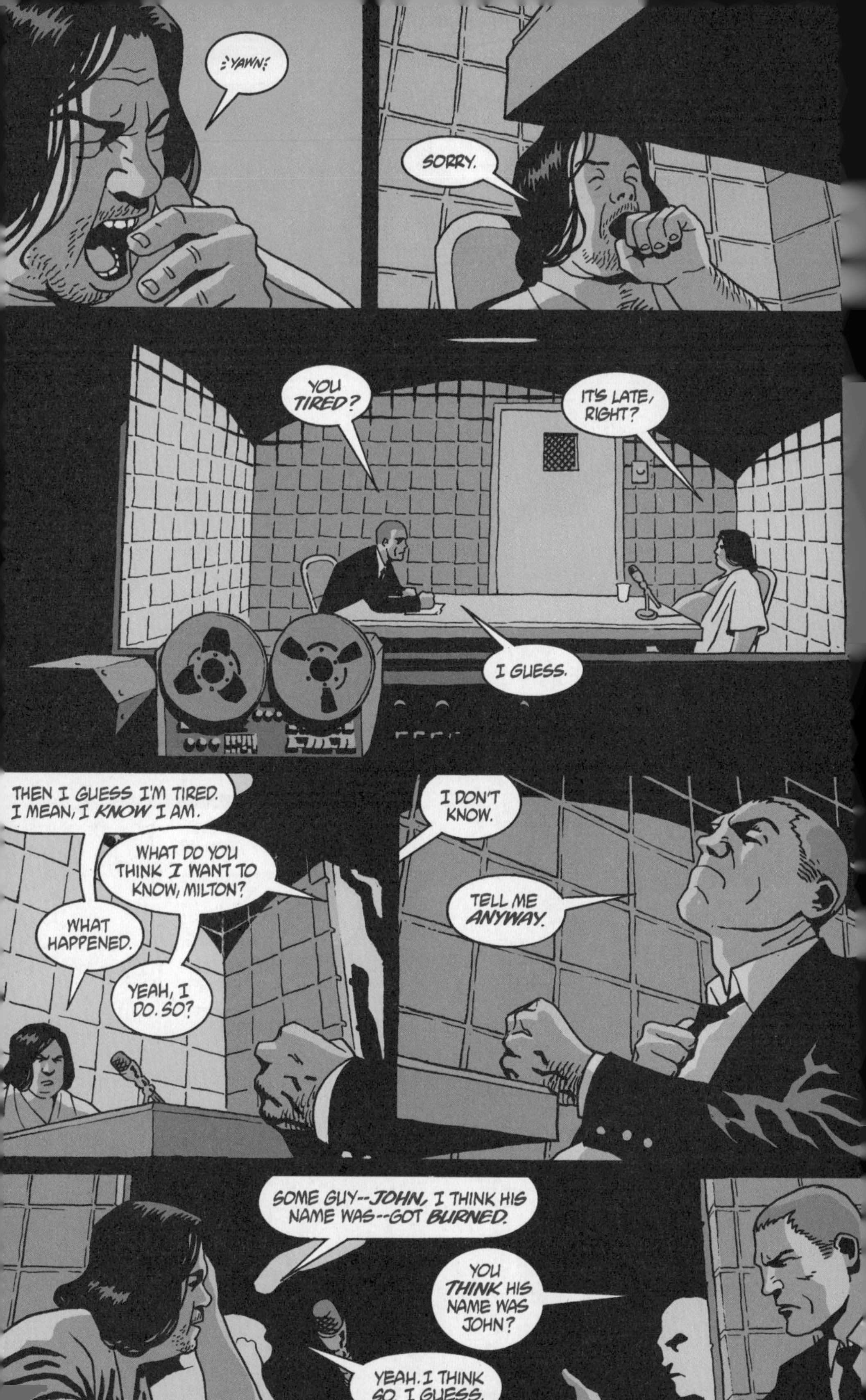

YAWN
SORRY.
YOU TIRED?
IT'S LATE, RIGHT?
I GUESS.
THEN I GUESS I'M TIRED. I MEAN, I KNOW I AM.
WHAT HAPPENED.
WHAT DO YOU THINK I WANT TO KNOW, MILTON?
YEAH, I DO. SO?
I DON'T KNOW.
TELL ME ANYWAY.
SOME GUY--JOHN, I THINK HIS NAME WAS--GOT BURNED.
YOU THINK HIS NAME WAS JOHN?
YEAH. I THINK SO. I GUESS.

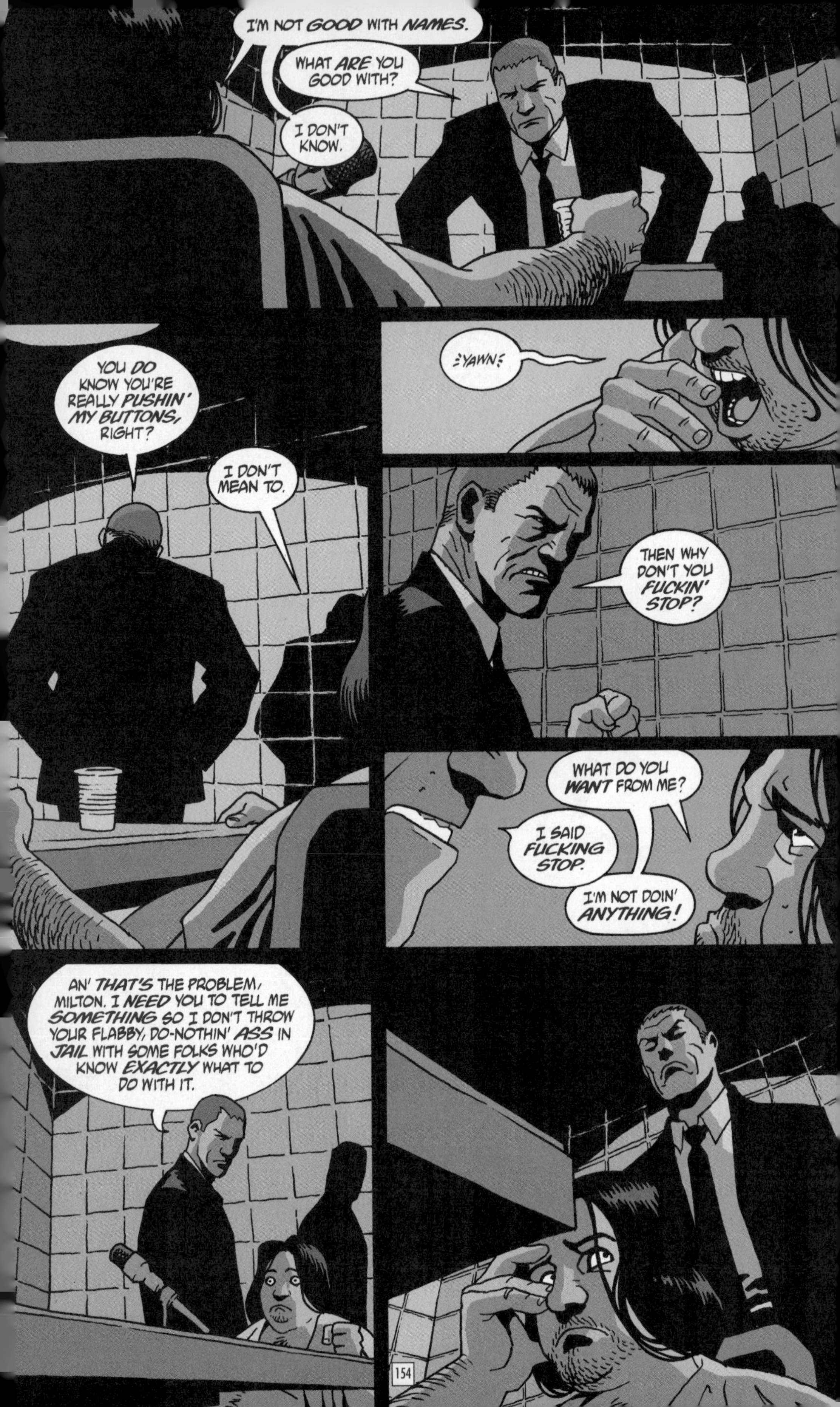
I'M NOT GOOD WITH NAMES.
WHAT ARE YOU GOOD WITH?
I DON'T KNOW.
YOU DO KNOW YOU'RE REALLY PUSHIN' MY BUTTONS, RIGHT?
I DON'T MEAN TO.
YAWN
THEN WHY DON'T YOU FUCKIN' STOP?
WHAT DO YOU WANT FROM ME?
I SAID FUCKING STOP.
I'M NOT DOIN' ANYTHING!
AN' THAT'S THE PROBLEM, MILTON. I NEED YOU TO TELL ME SOMETHING SO I DON'T THROW YOUR FLABBY, DO-NOTHIN' ASS IN JAIL WITH SOME FOLKS WHO'D KNOW EXACTLY WHAT TO DO WITH IT.

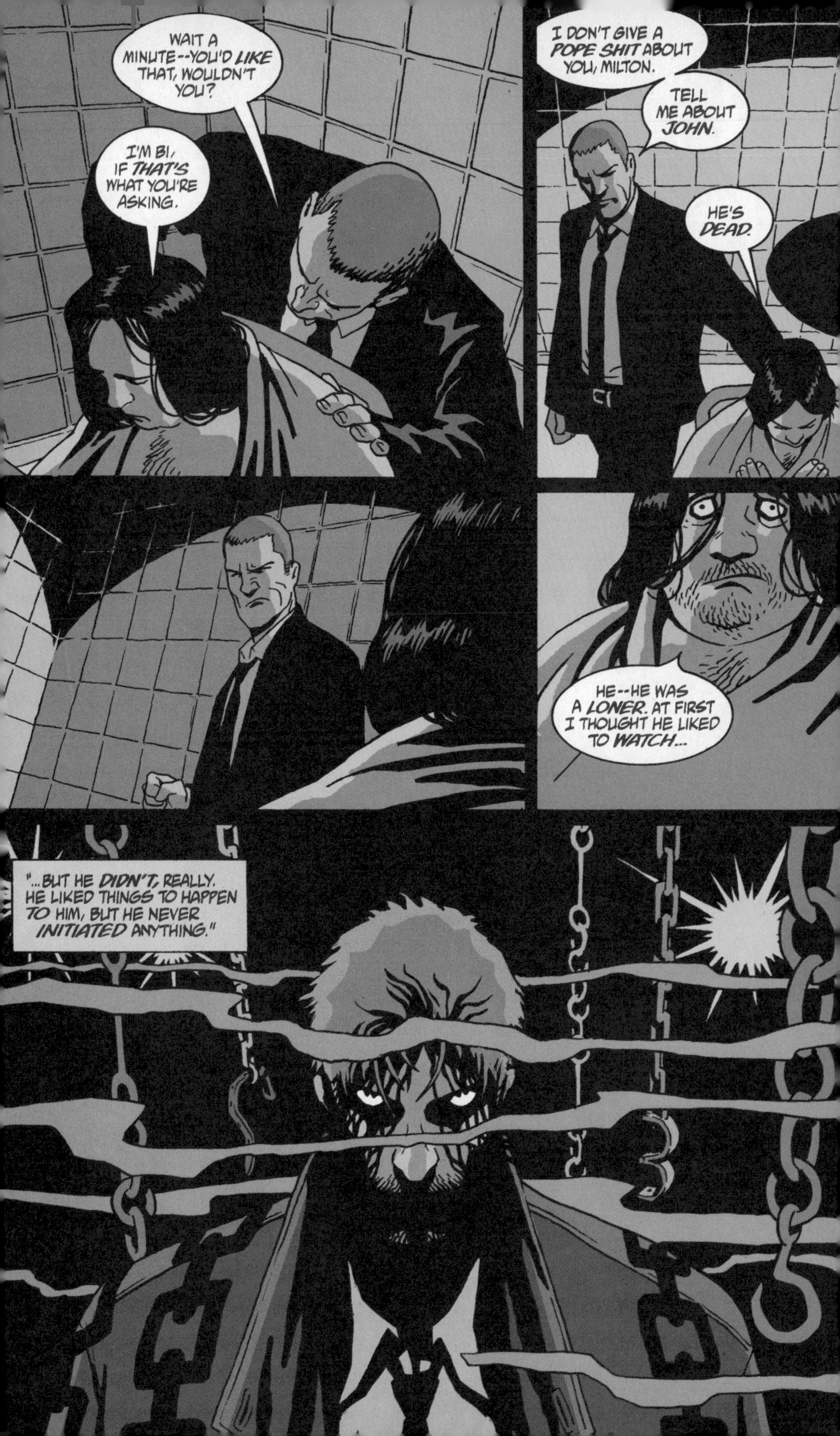
WAIT A MINUTE--YOU'D LIKE THAT, WOULDN'T YOU?
I'M BI, IF THAT'S WHAT YOU'RE ASKING.
I DON'T GIVE A POPE SHIT ABOUT YOU, MILTON.
TELL ME ABOUT JOHN.
HE'S DEAD.
HE--HE WAS A LONER. AT FIRST I THOUGHT HE LIKED TO WATCH...
"...BUT HE DIDN'T, REALLY. HE LIKED THINGS TO HAPPEN TO HIM, BUT HE NEVER INITIATED ANYTHING."

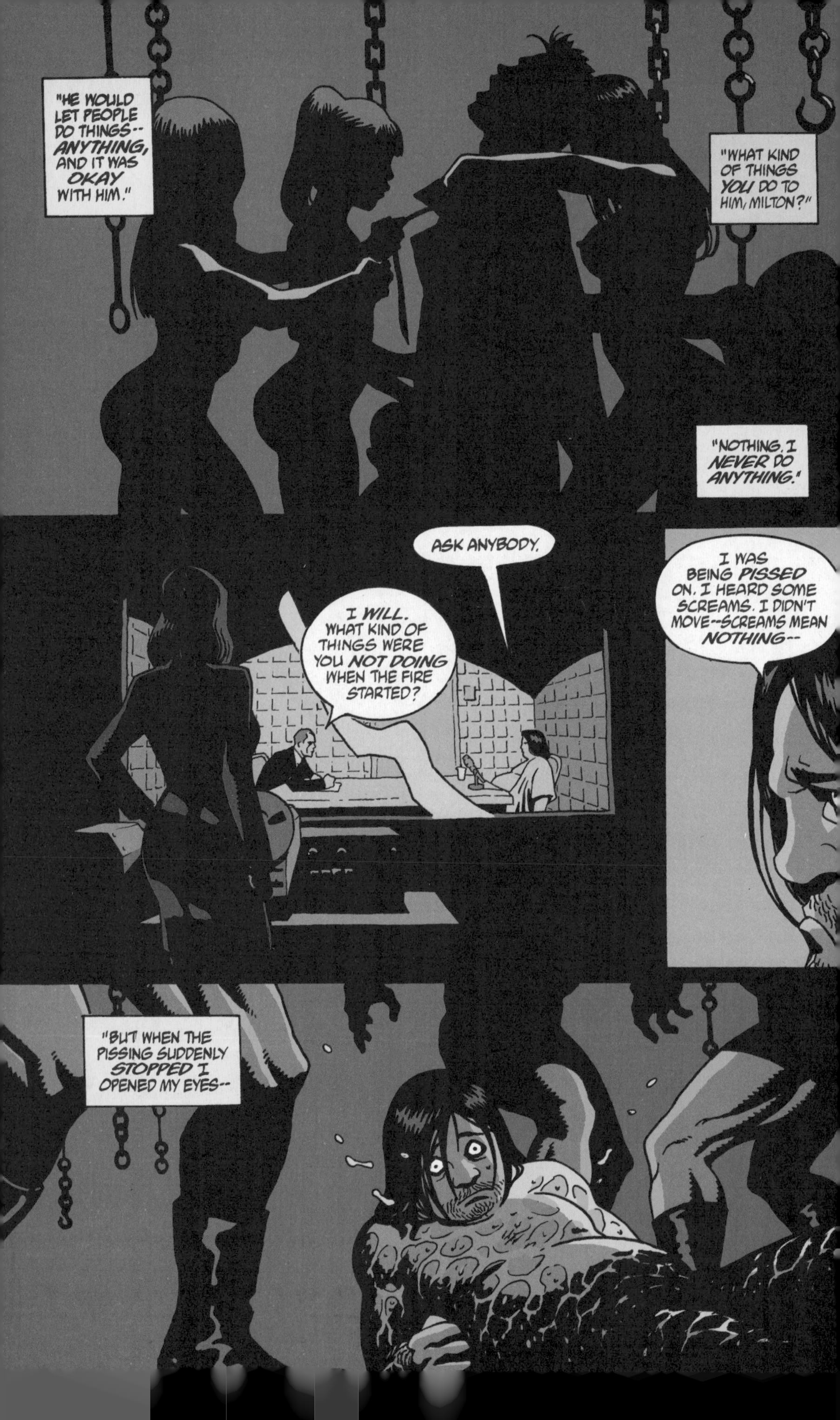
"HE WOULD LET PEOPLE DO THINGS-- ANYTHING, AND IT WAS OKAY WITH HIM."
"WHAT KIND OF THINGS YOU DO TO HIM, MILTON?"
"NOTHING. I NEVER DO ANYTHING."
ASK ANYBODY.
I WILL. WHAT KIND OF THINGS WERE YOU NOT DOING WHEN THE FIRE STARTED?
I WAS BEING PISSED ON. I HEARD SOME SCREAMS. I DIDN'T MOVE--SCREAMS MEAN NOTHING--
"BUT WHEN THE PISSING SUDDENLY STOPPED I OPENED MY EYES--

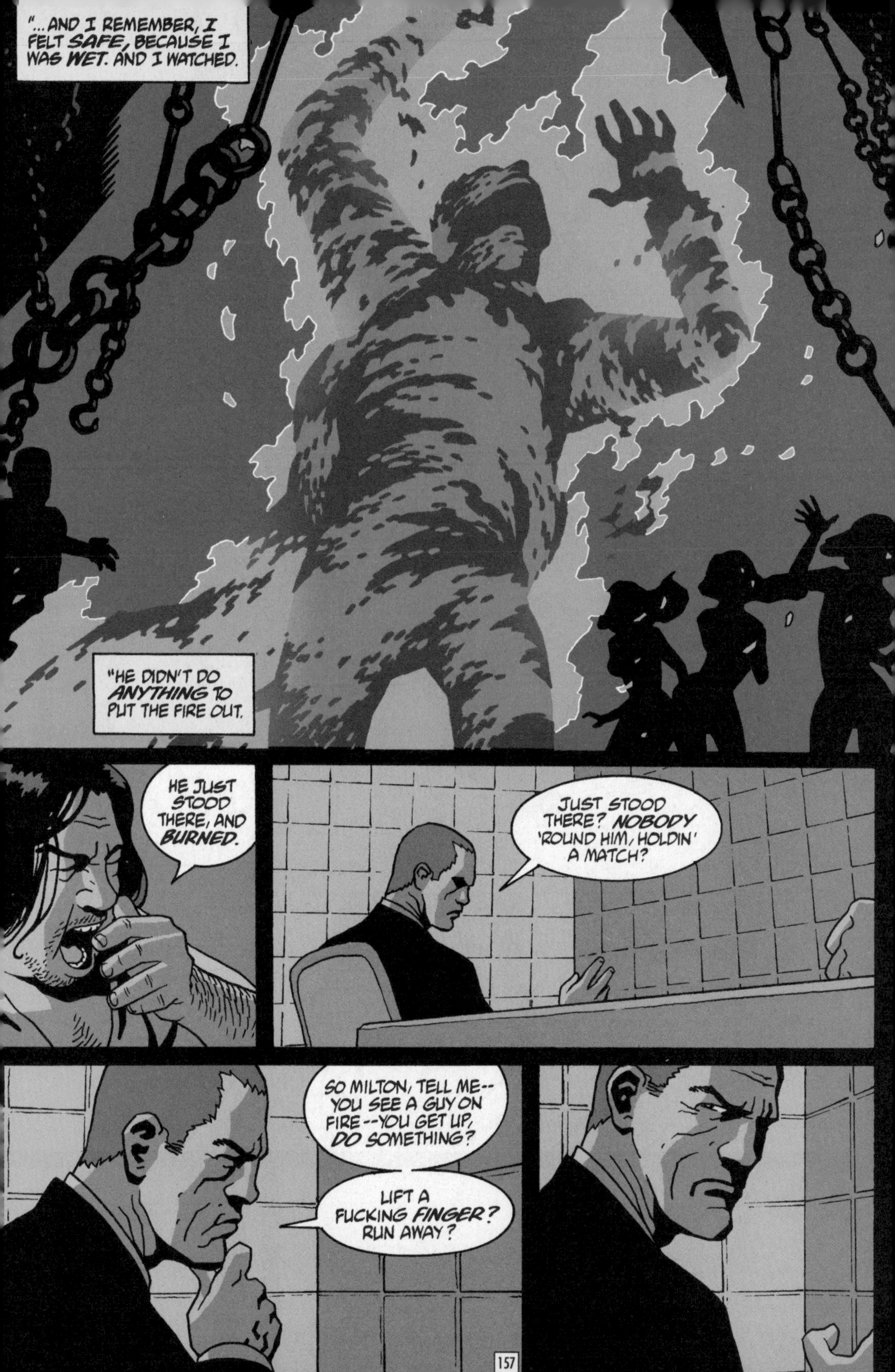
"...AND I REMEMBER, I FELT SAFE, BECAUSE I WAS WET. AND I WATCHED.
"HE DIDN'T DO ANYTHING TO PUT THE FIRE OUT.
HE JUST STOOD THERE, AND BURNED.
JUST STOOD THERE? NOBODY 'ROUND HIM, HOLDIN' A MATCH?
SO MILTON, TELL ME-- YOU SEE A GUY ON FIRE--YOU GET UP, DO SOMETHING?
LIFT A FUCKING FINGER? RUN AWAY?

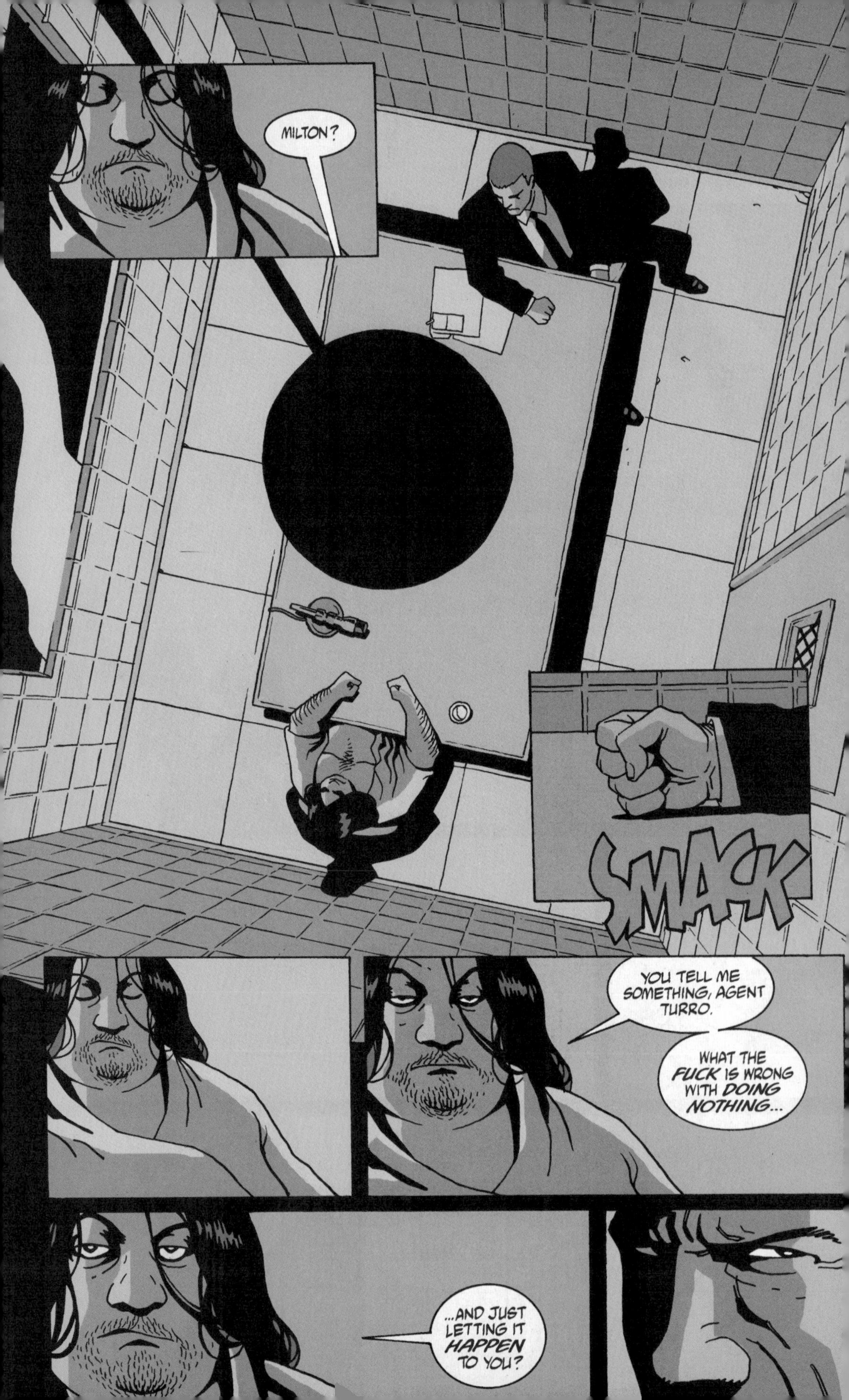
MILTON?
SMACK
YOU TELL ME SOMETHING, AGENT TURRO.
WHAT THE FUCK IS WRONG WITH DOING NOTHING...
...AND JUST LETTING IT HAPPEN TO YOU?

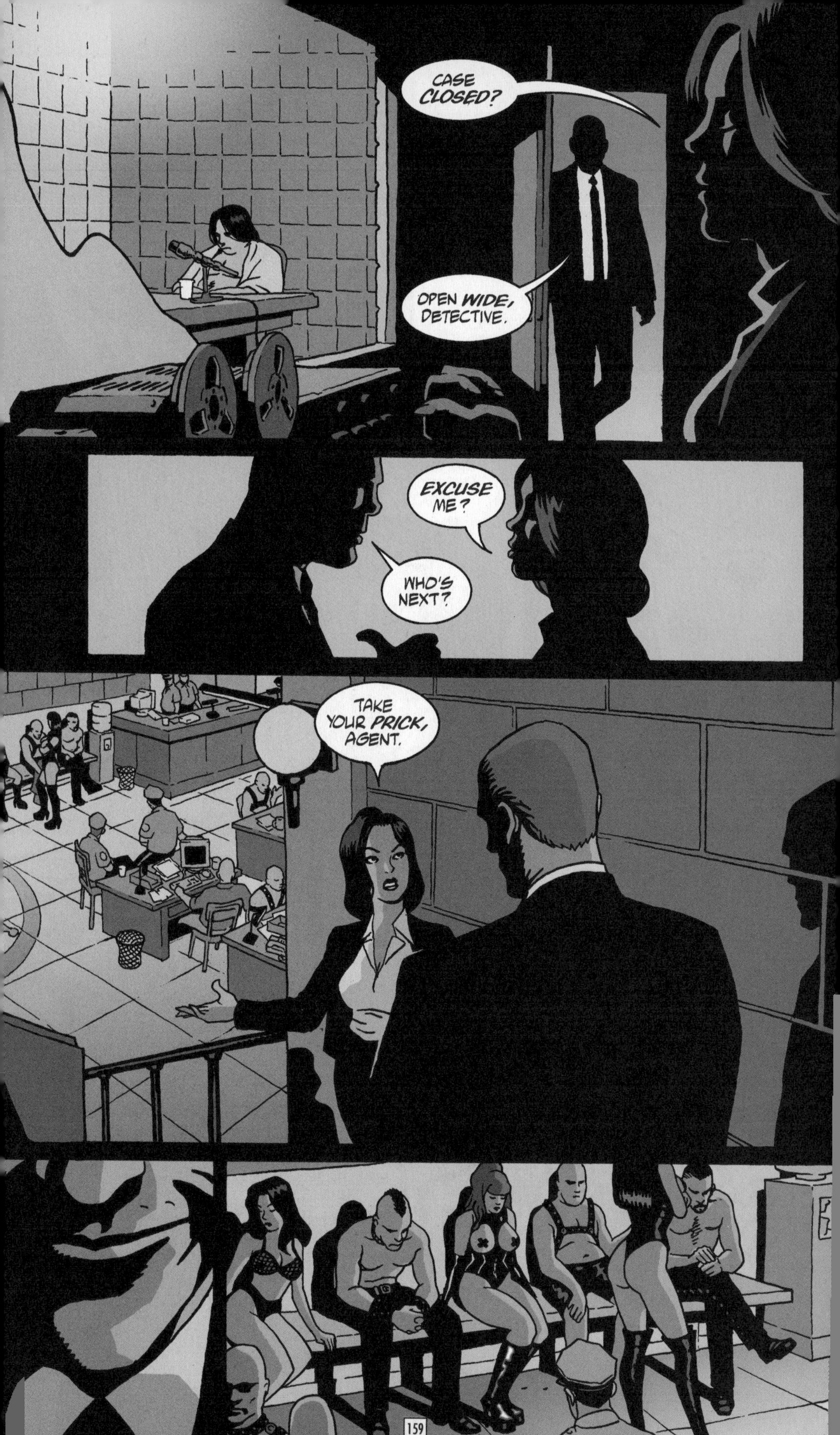
CASE CLOSED?
OPEN WIDE, DETECTIVE.
EXCUSE ME?
WHO'S NEXT?
TAKE YOUR PRICK, AGENT.

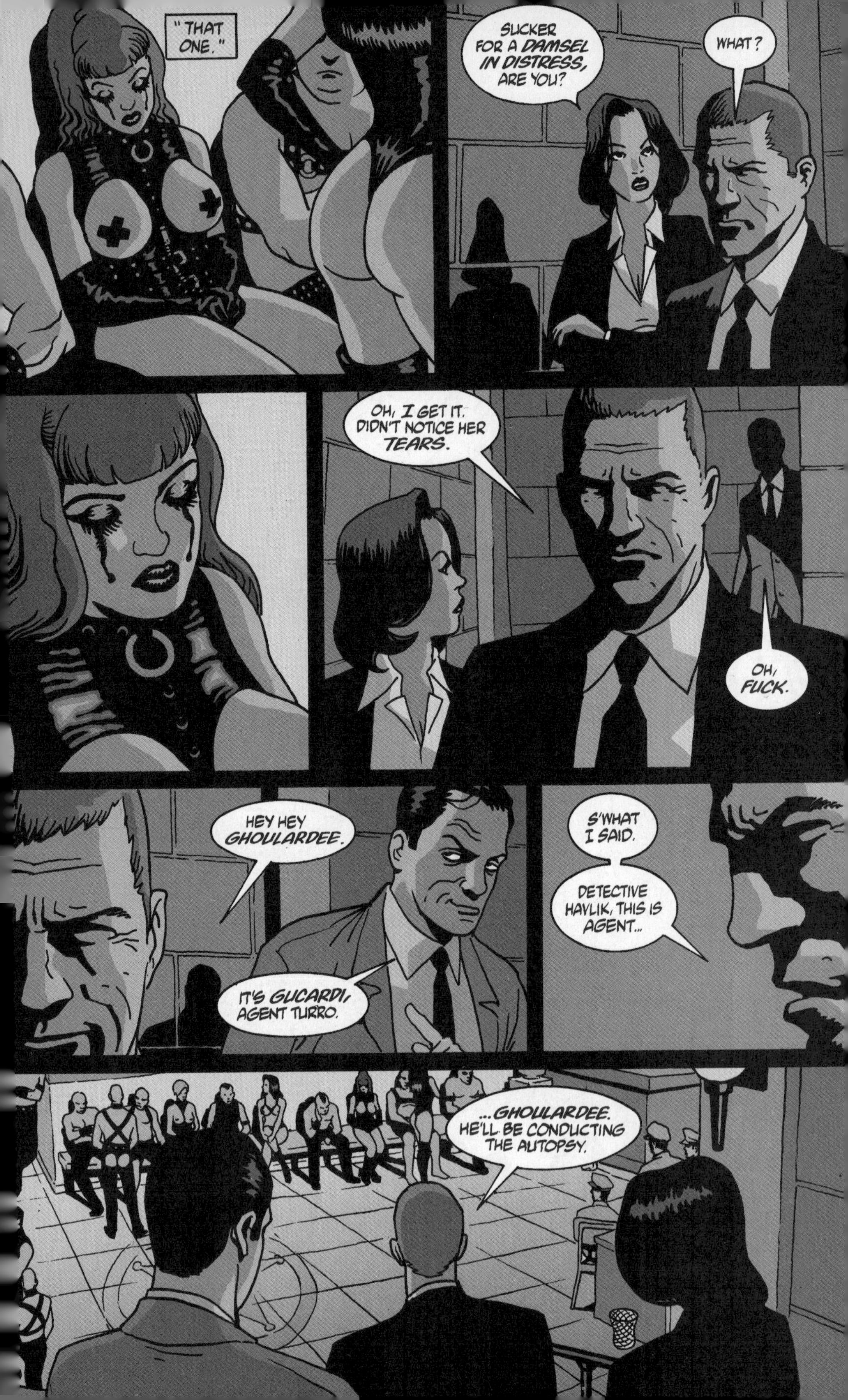
"THAT ONE."
SUCKER FOR A DAMSEL IN DISTRESS, ARE YOU?
WHAT?
OH, I GET IT. DIDN'T NOTICE HER TEARS.
OH, FUCK.
HEY HEY GHOULARDEE.
IT'S GUCARDI, AGENT TURRO.
S'WHAT I SAID.
DETECTIVE HAVLIK, THIS IS AGENT...
...GHOULARDEE. HE'LL BE CONDUCTING THE AUTOPSY.

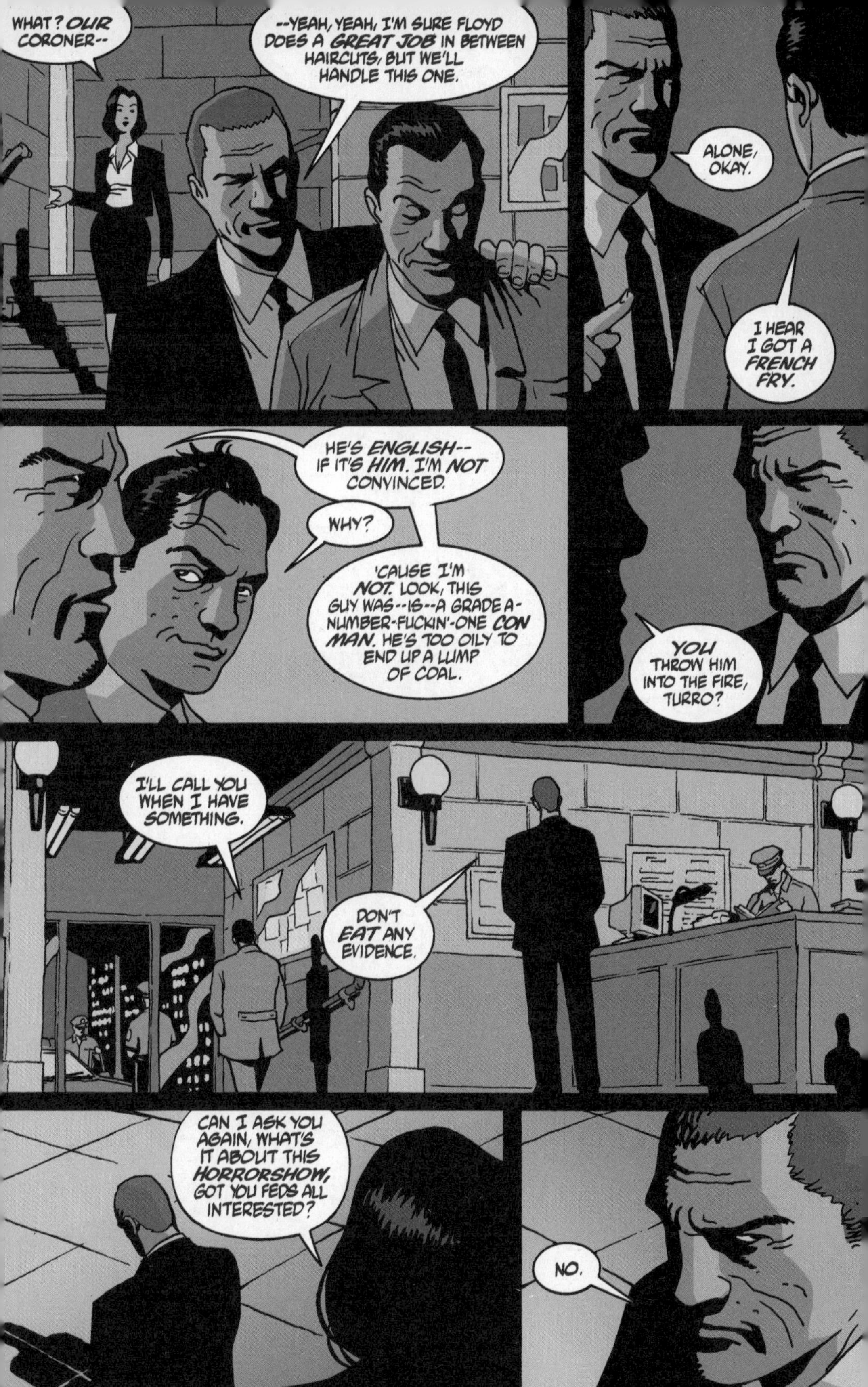
WHAT? OUR CORONER--
--YEAH, YEAH, I'M SURE FLOYD DOES A GREAT JOB IN BETWEEN HAIRCUTS, BUT WE'LL HANDLE THIS ONE.
ALONE, OKAY.
I HEAR I GOT A FRENCH FRY.
HE'S ENGLISH-- IF IT'S HIM. I'M NOT CONVINCED.
WHY?
'CAUSE I'M NOT. LOOK, THIS GUY WAS--IS--A GRADE A-NUMBER-FUCKIN'-ONE CON MAN. HE'S TOO OILY TO END UP A LUMP OF COAL.
YOU THROW HIM INTO THE FIRE, TURRO?
I'LL CALL YOU WHEN I HAVE SOMETHING.
DON'T EAT ANY EVIDENCE.
CAN I ASK YOU AGAIN, WHAT'S IT ABOUT THIS HORRORSHOW, GOT YOU FEDS ALL INTERESTED?
NO.

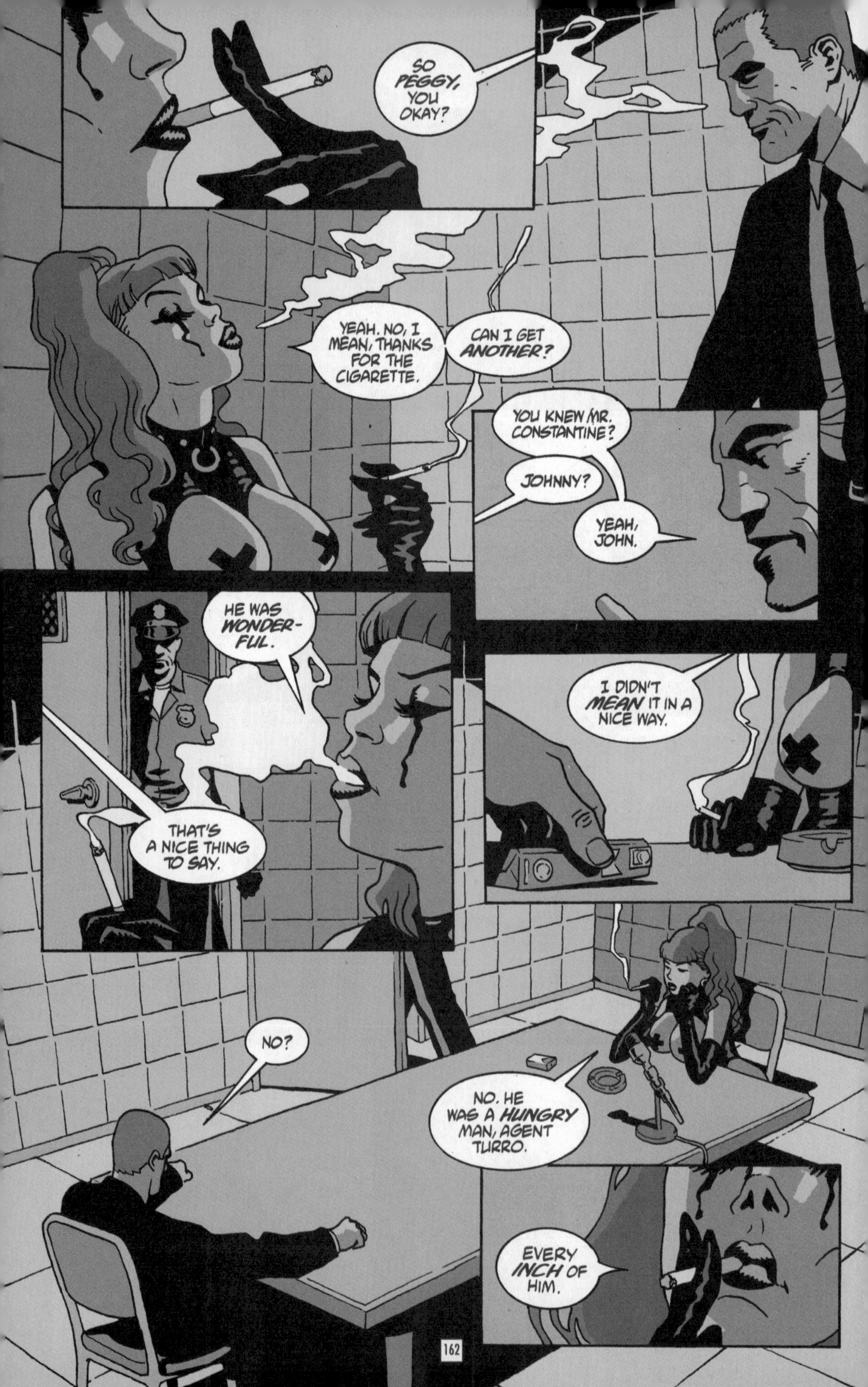
SO PEGGY, YOU OKAY?
YEAH. NO, I MEAN, THANKS FOR THE CIGARETTE.
CAN I GET ANOTHER?
YOU KNEW MR. CONSTANTINE?
JOHNNY?
YEAH, JOHN.
HE WAS WONDERFUL.
THAT'S A NICE THING TO SAY.
I DIDN'T MEAN IT IN A NICE WAY.
NO?
NO. HE WAS A HUNGRY MAN, AGENT TURRO.
EVERY INCH OF HIM.

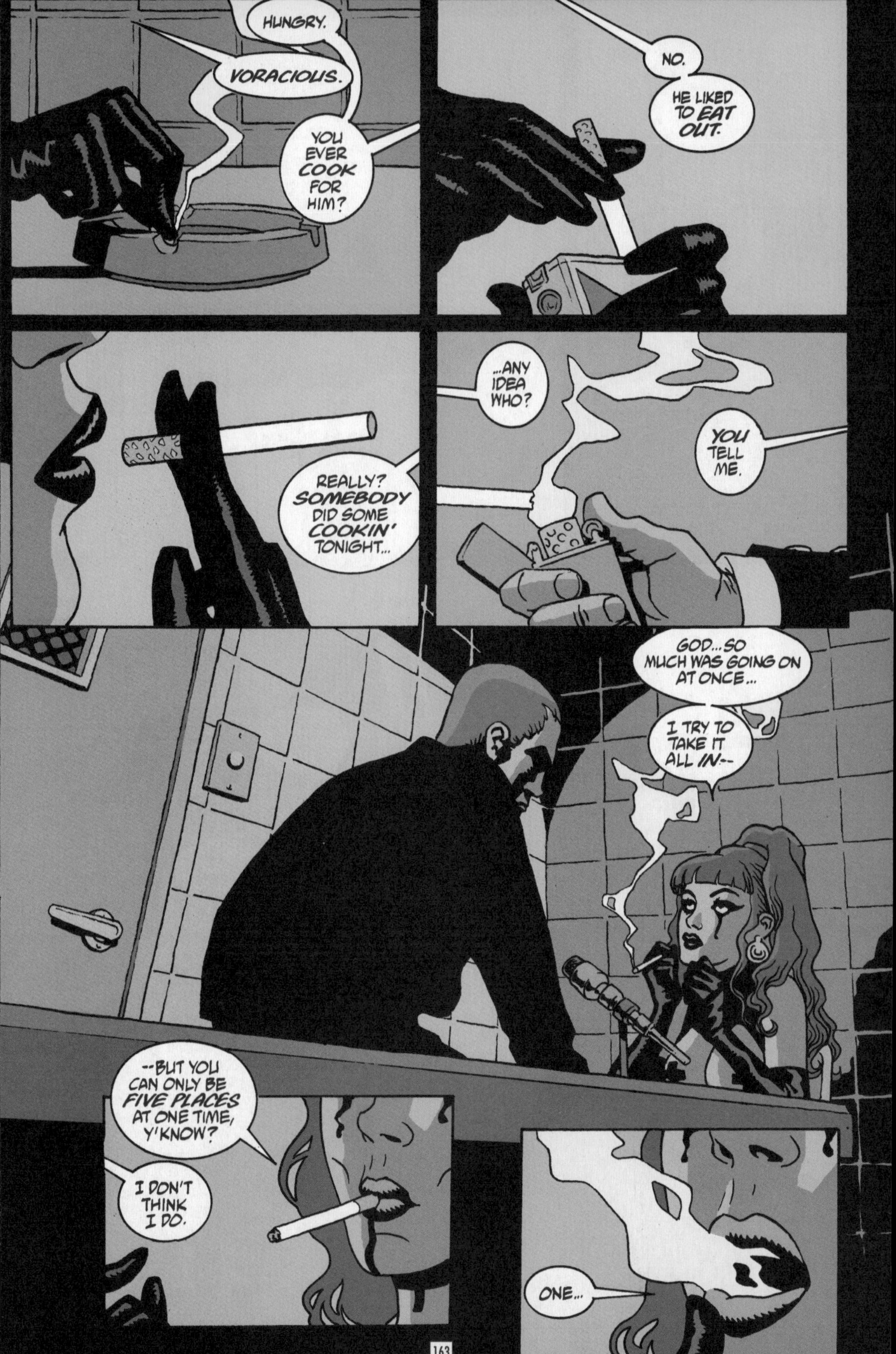
HUNGRY.
VORACIOUS.
YOU EVER COOK FOR HIM?
NO.
HE LIKED TO EAT OUT.
REALLY? SOMEBODY DID SOME COOKIN' TONIGHT...
...ANY IDEA WHO?
YOU TELL ME.
GOD...SO MUCH WAS GOING ON AT ONCE...
I TRY TO TAKE IT ALL IN--
--BUT YOU CAN ONLY BE FIVE PLACES AT ONE TIME, Y'KNOW?
I DON'T THINK I DO.
ONE...

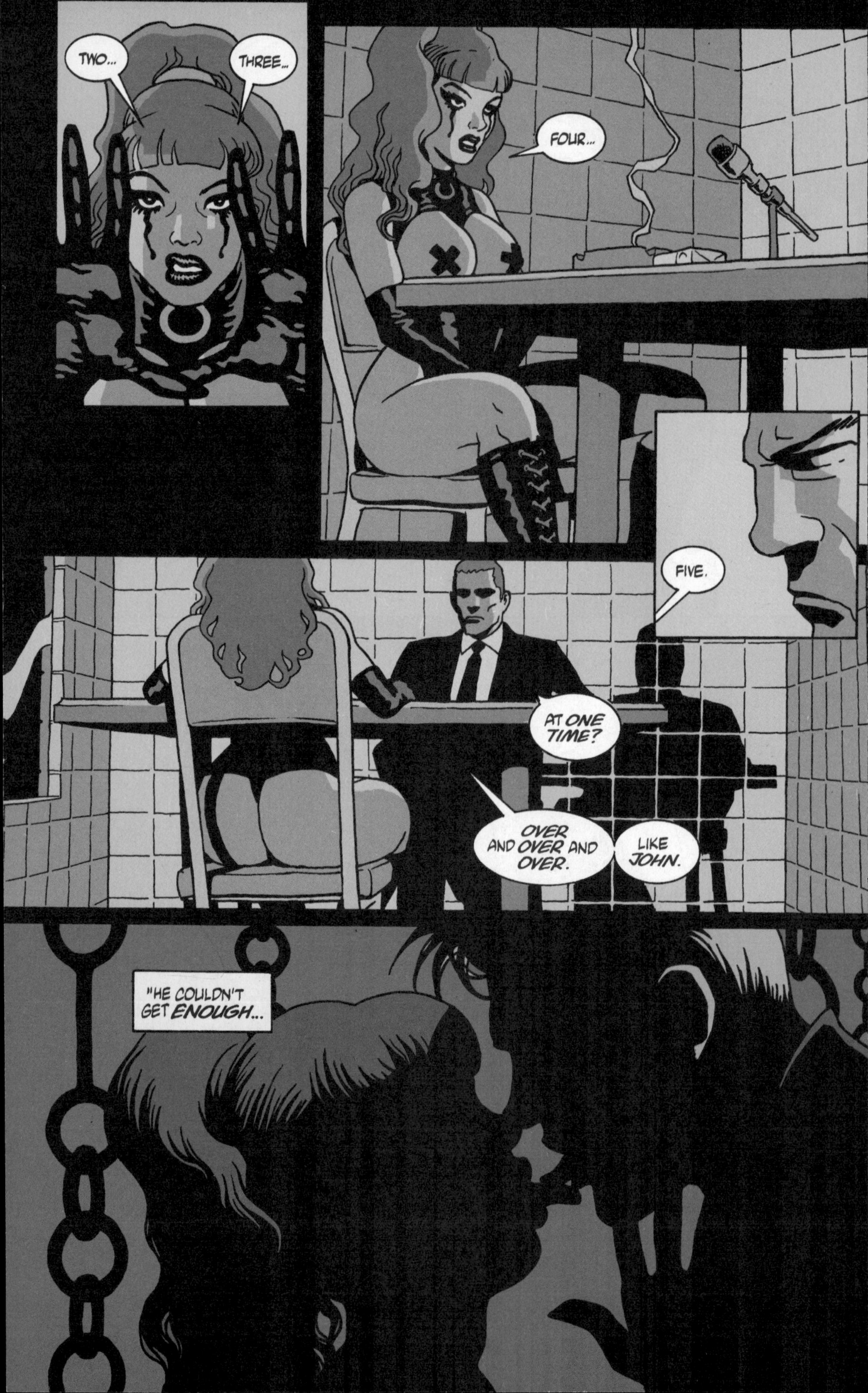
TWO...
THREE...
FOUR...
FIVE.
AT ONE TIME?
OVER AND OVER AND OVER.
LIKE JOHN.
"HE COULDN'T GET ENOUGH...

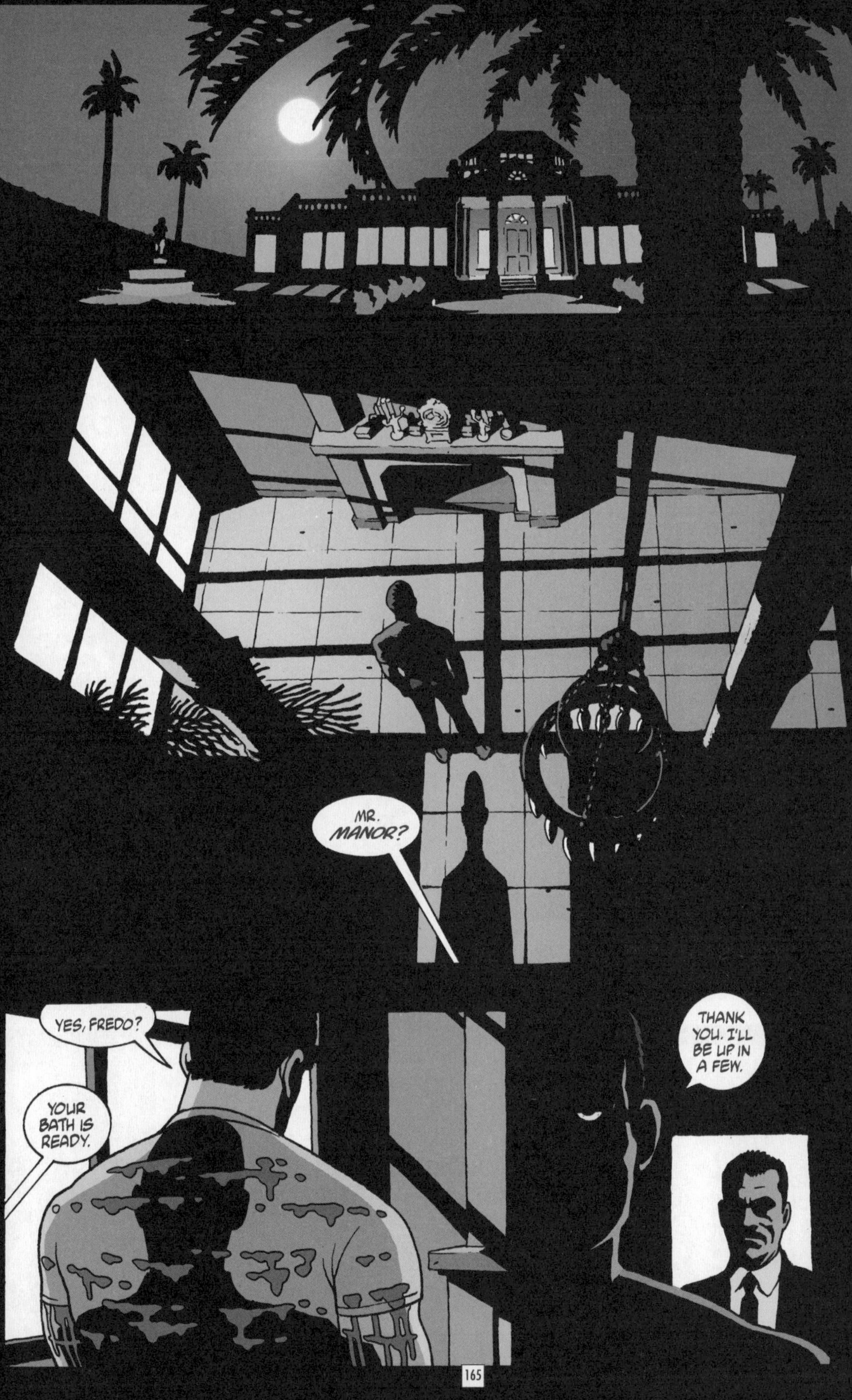
MR. MANOR?
YES, FREDO?
YOUR BATH IS READY.
THANK YOU. I'LL BE UP IN A FEW.

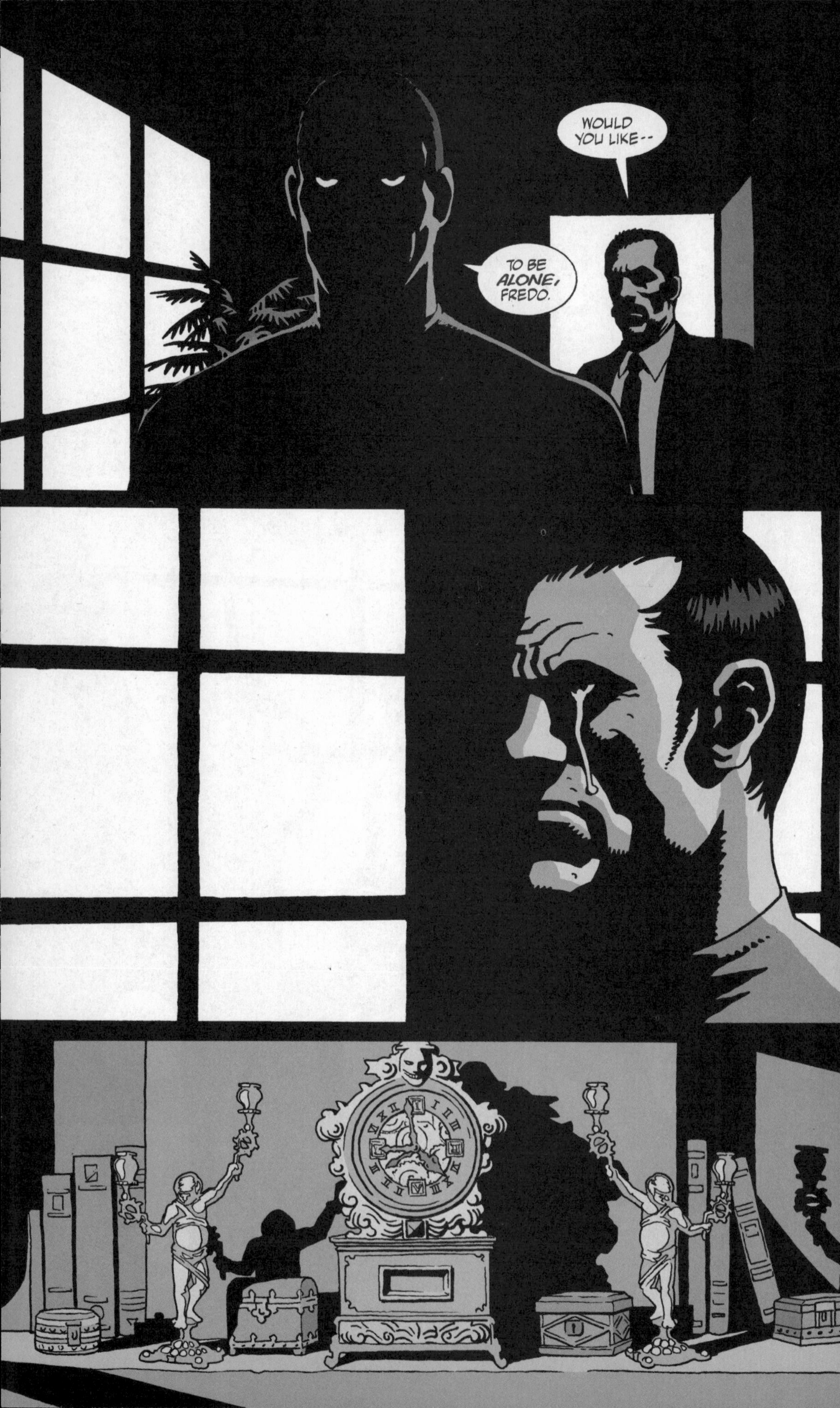
WOULD YOU LIKE--
TO BE ALONE, FREDO.

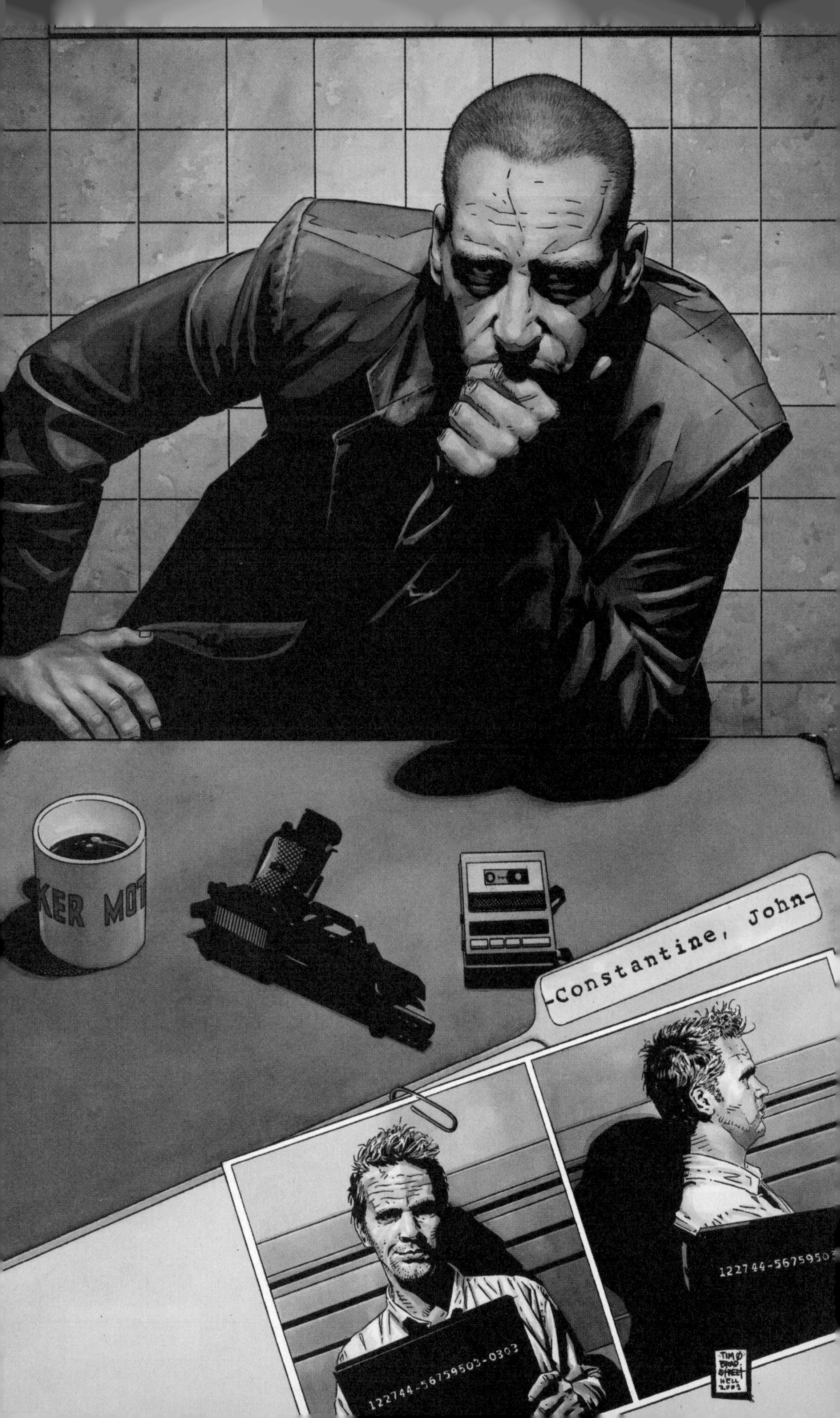
KER MOT
-Constantine, John-
122744-56759503-0303
122744-5675950

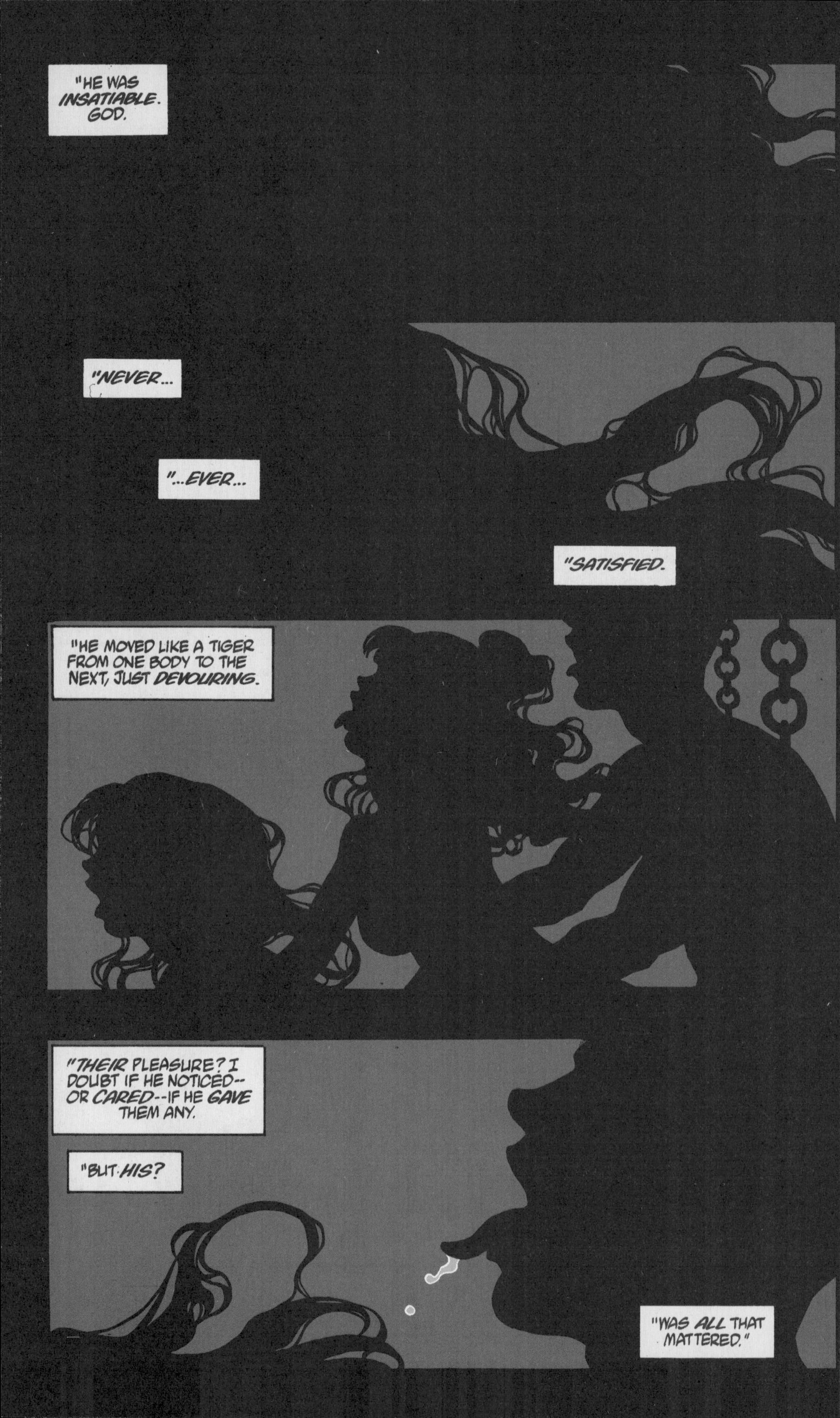
"HE WAS INSATIABLE. GOD.
"NEVER...
"...EVER...
"SATISFIED.
"HE MOVED LIKE A TIGER FROM ONE BODY TO THE NEXT, JUST DEVOURING.
"THEIR PLEASURE? I DOUBT IF HE NOTICED-- OR CARED--IF HE GAVE THEM ANY.
"BUT HIS?
"WAS ALL THAT MATTERED."

"IT WAS *BEAUTIFUL* TO BEHOLD.

Ashes & Dust
in the City of Angels
PART TWO

Brian Azzarello, WRITER   **Marcelo Frusin,** ARTIST

Lee Loughridge
COLORS

Clem Robins
LETTERS

Tim Bradstreet
COVER

Zachary Rau
ASSISTANT EDITOR

Will Dennis
EDITOR

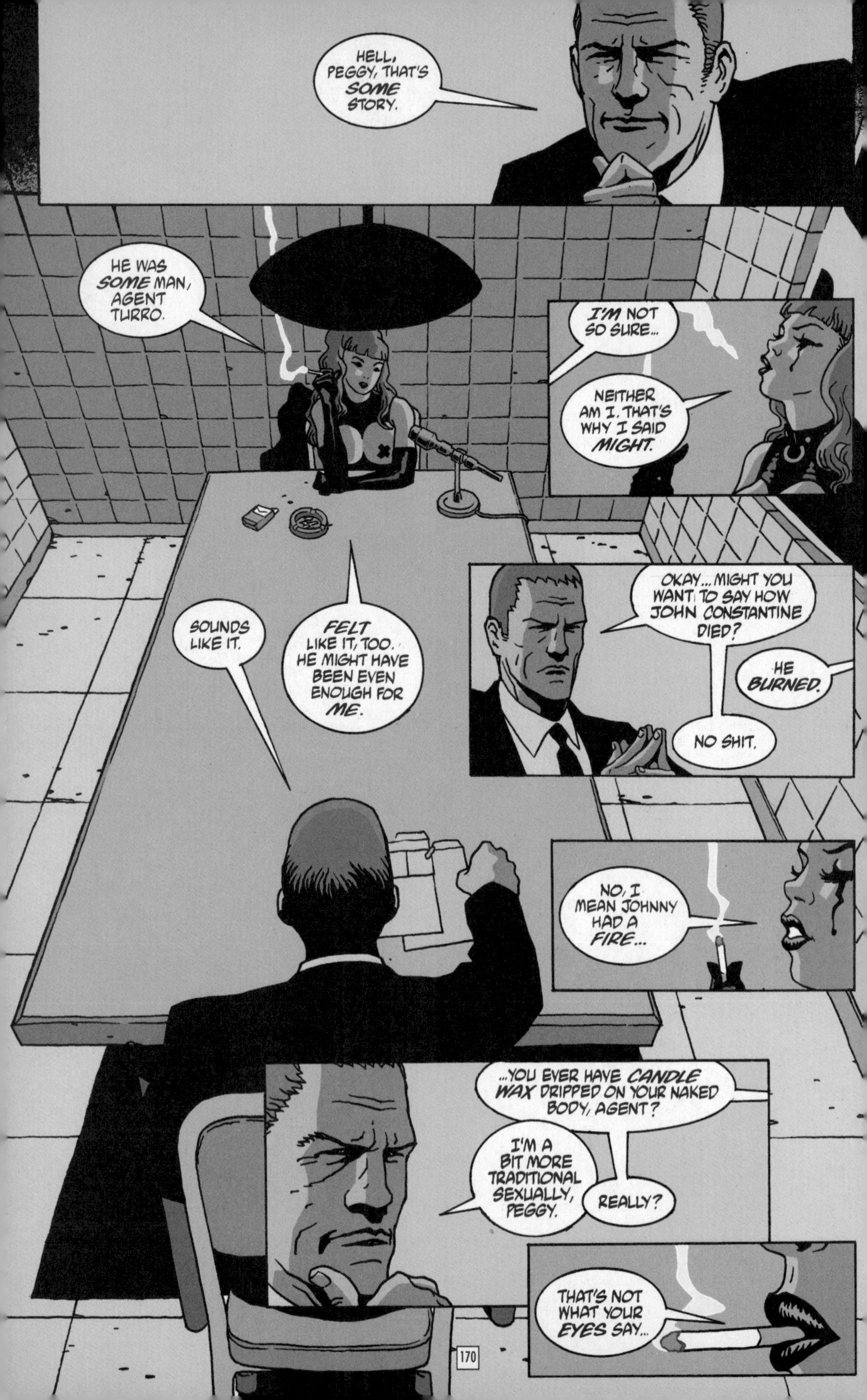
HELL, PEGGY, THAT'S SOME STORY.
HE WAS SOME MAN, AGENT TURRO.
I'M NOT SO SURE...
NEITHER AM I. THAT'S WHY I SAID MIGHT.
SOUNDS LIKE IT.
FELT LIKE IT, TOO. HE MIGHT HAVE BEEN EVEN ENOUGH FOR ME.
OKAY... MIGHT YOU WANT TO SAY HOW JOHN CONSTANTINE DIED?
HE BURNED.
NO SHIT.
NO, I MEAN JOHNNY HAD A FIRE...
...YOU EVER HAVE CANDLE WAX DRIPPED ON YOUR NAKED BODY, AGENT?
I'M A BIT MORE TRADITIONAL SEXUALLY, PEGGY.
REALLY?
THAT'S NOT WHAT YOUR EYES SAY...

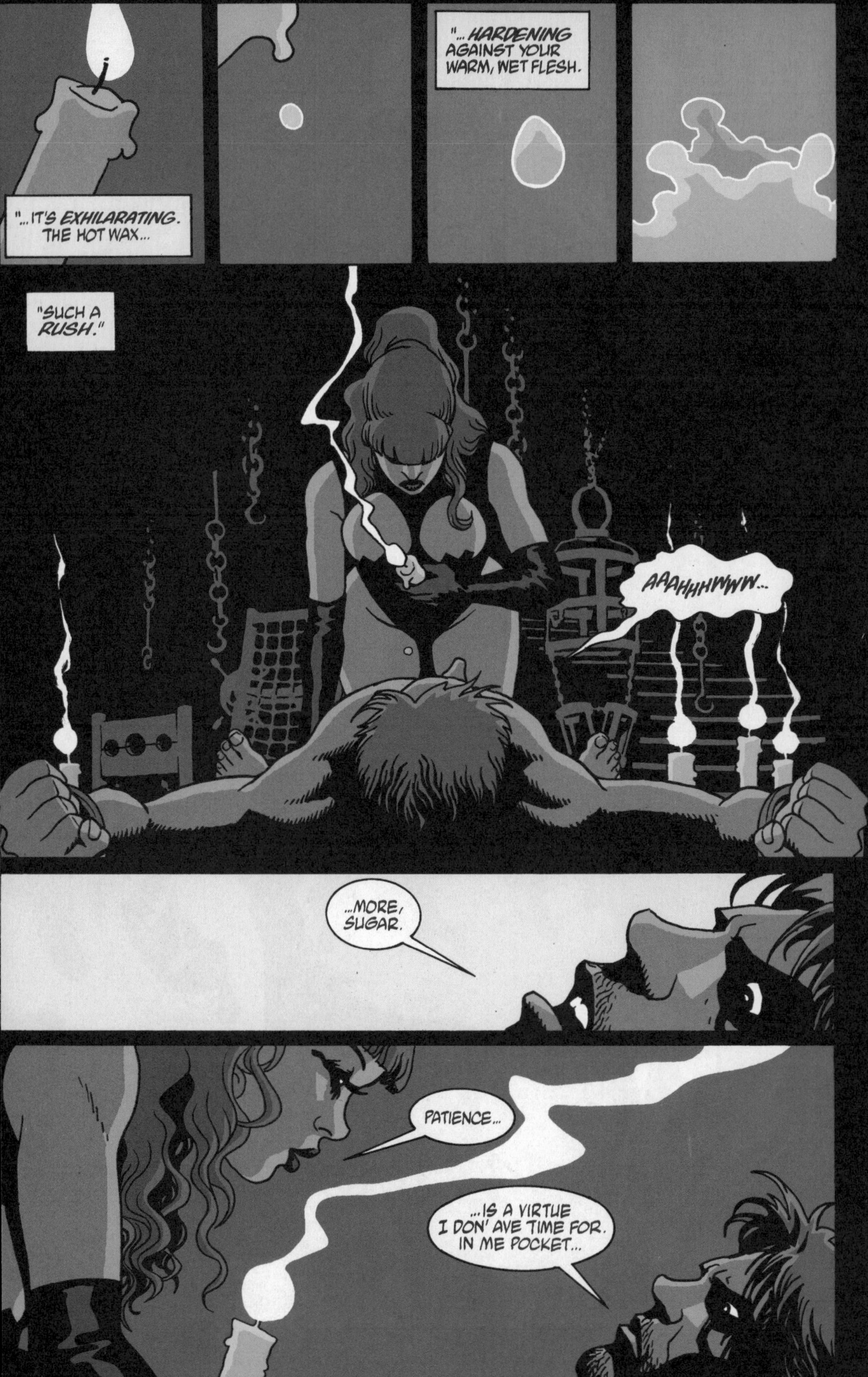
"...IT'S *EXHILARATING*. THE HOT WAX...
"...*HARDENING* AGAINST YOUR WARM, WET FLESH.
"SUCH A *RUSH*."
AAAHHHWWW...
...MORE, SUGAR.
PATIENCE...
...IS A VIRTUE I DON' AVE TIME FOR. IN ME POCKET...

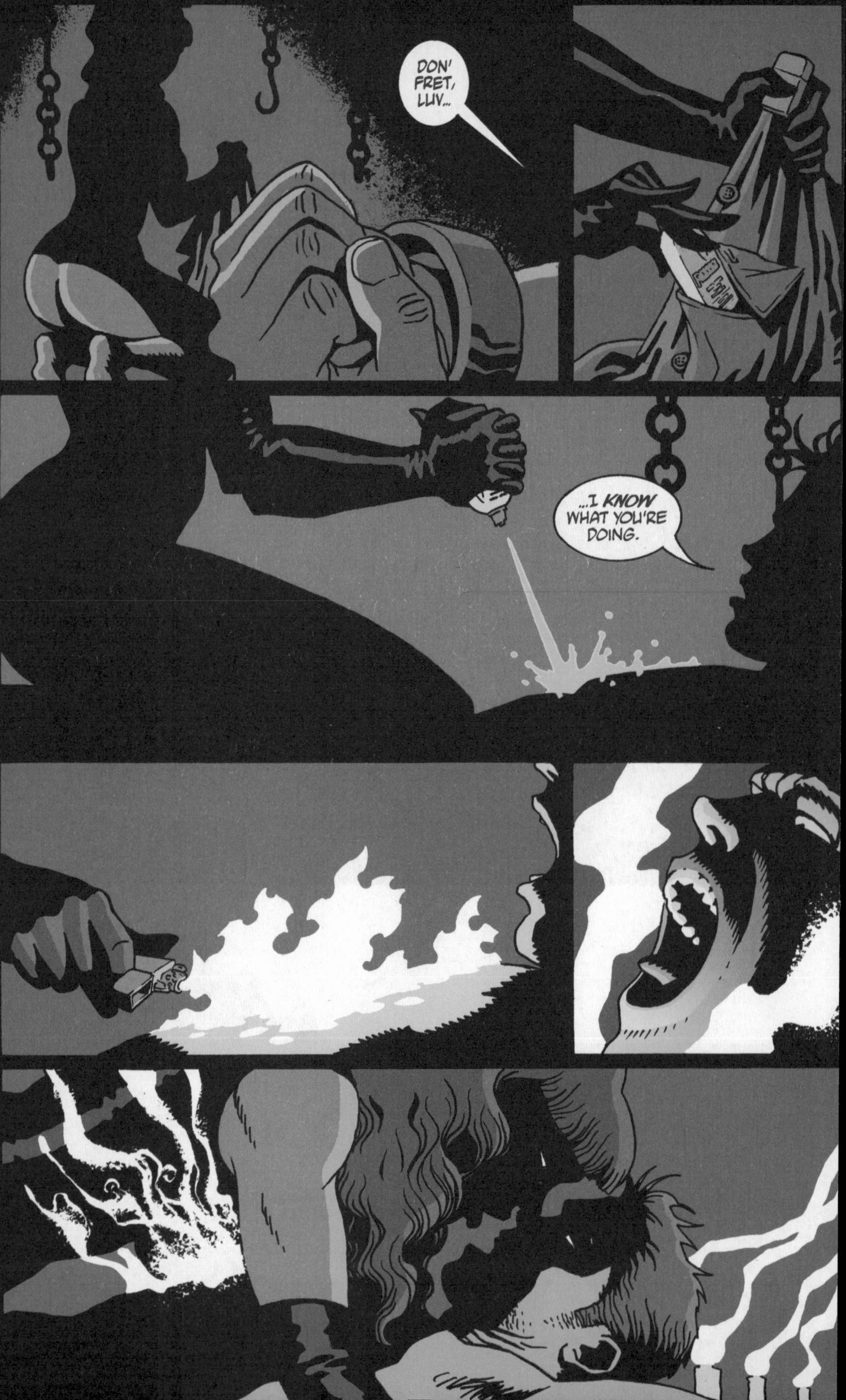

DON' FRET, LUV...
...I KNOW WHAT YOU'RE DOING.

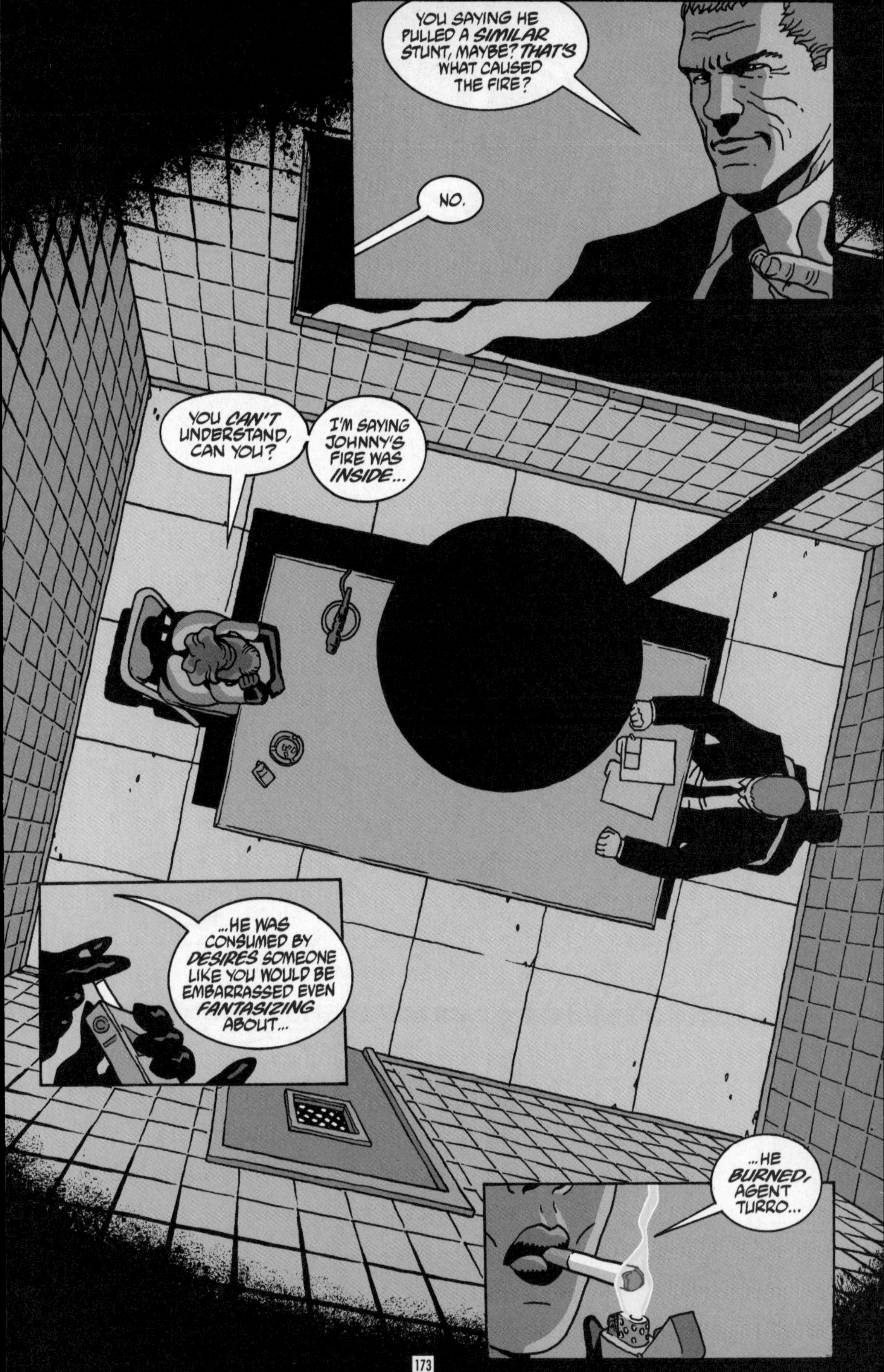
YOU SAYING HE PULLED A SIMILAR STUNT, MAYBE? THAT'S WHAT CAUSED THE FIRE?
NO.
YOU CAN'T UNDERSTAND, CAN YOU?
I'M SAYING JOHNNY'S FIRE WAS INSIDE...
...HE WAS CONSUMED BY DESIRES SOMEONE LIKE YOU WOULD BE EMBARRASSED EVEN FANTASIZING ABOUT...
...HE BURNED, AGENT TURRO...

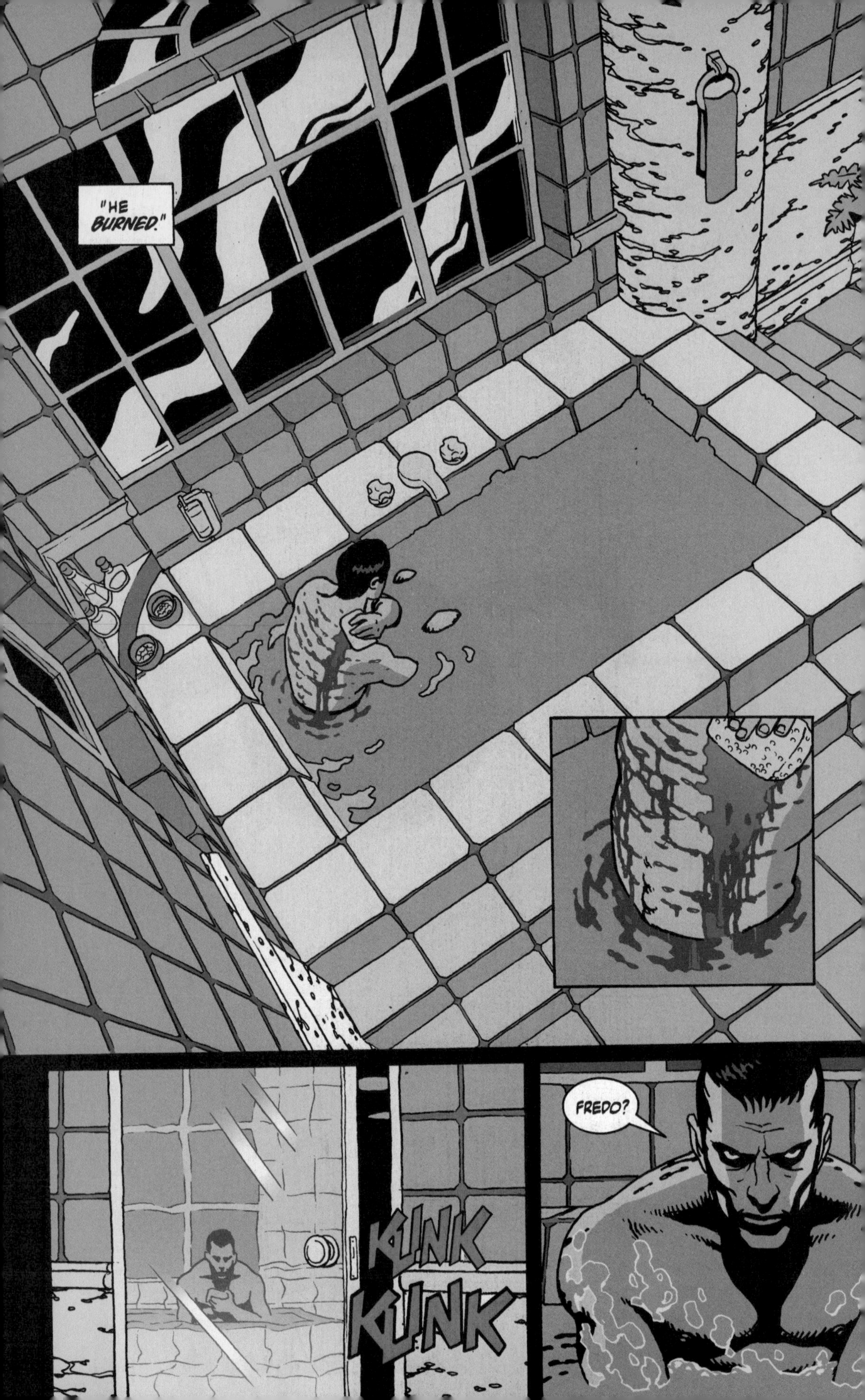
"HE BURNED."
KLINK KLINK
FREDO?

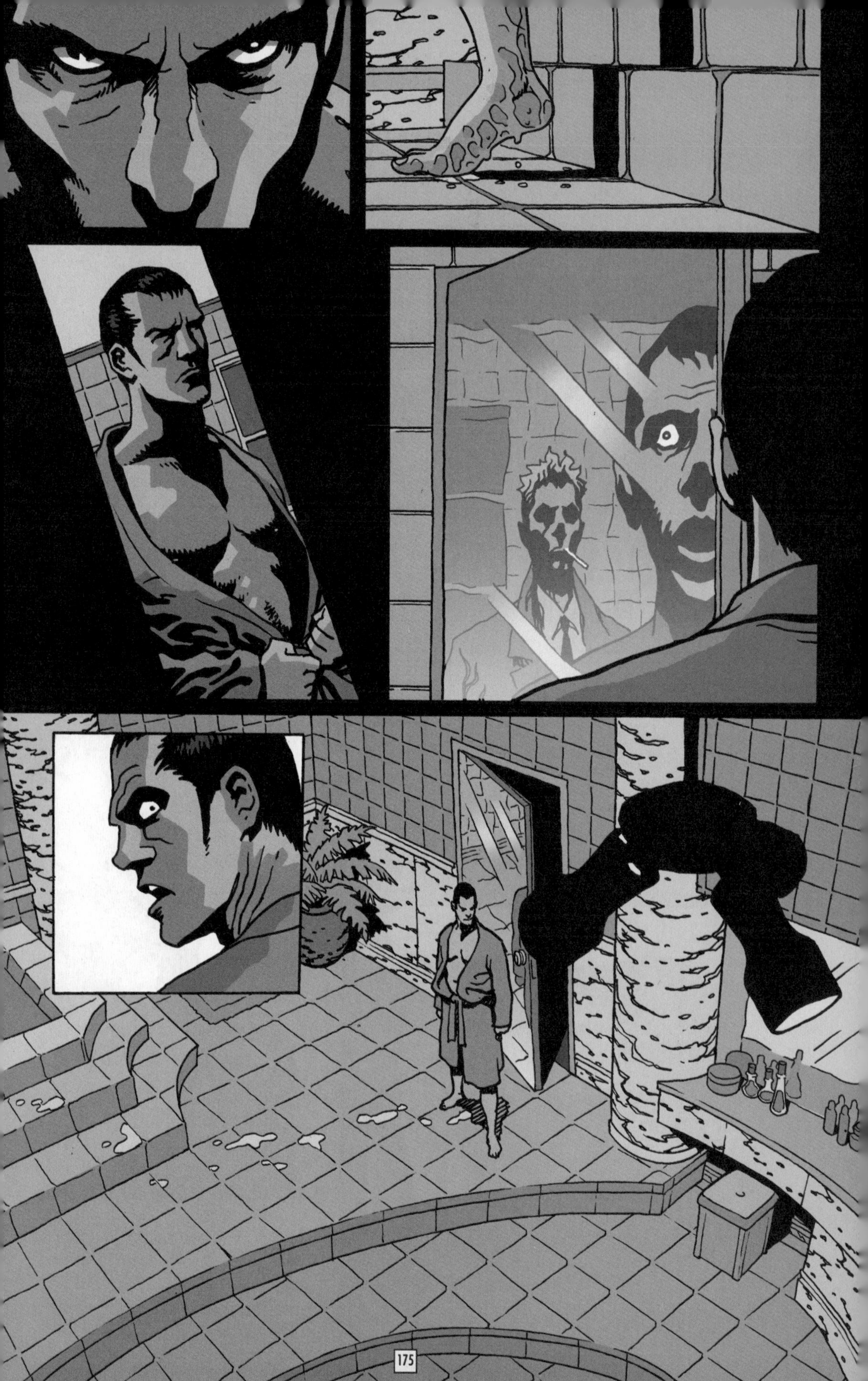

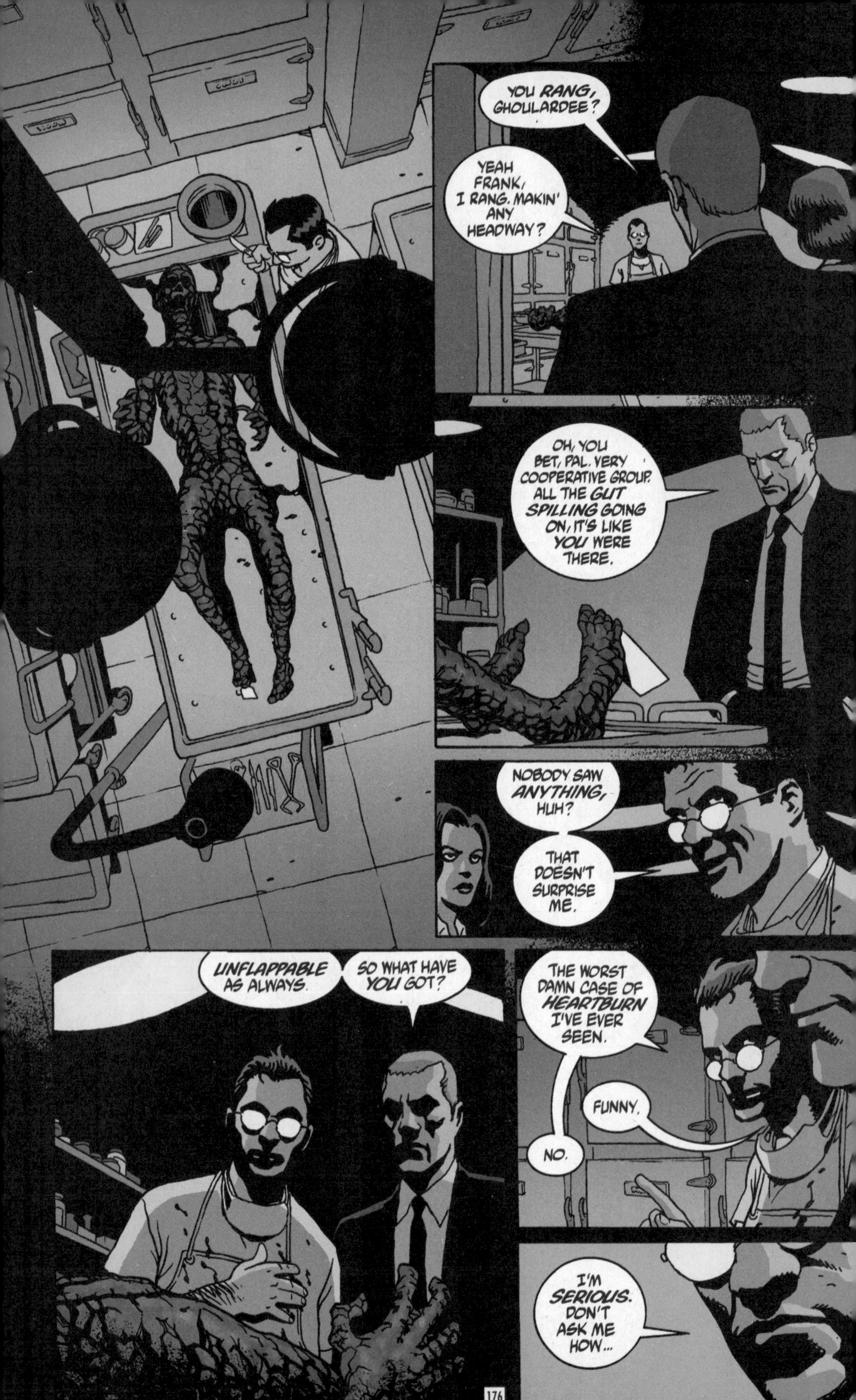
YOU RANG, GHOULARDEE?
YEAH FRANK, I RANG. MAKIN' ANY HEADWAY?
OH, YOU BET, PAL. VERY COOPERATIVE GROUP. ALL THE GUT SPILLING GOING ON, IT'S LIKE YOU WERE THERE.
NOBODY SAW ANYTHING, HUH?
THAT DOESN'T SURPRISE ME.
UNFLAPPABLE AS ALWAYS.
SO WHAT HAVE YOU GOT?
THE WORST DAMN CASE OF HEARTBURN I'VE EVER SEEN.
FUNNY.
NO.
I'M SERIOUS. DON'T ASK ME HOW...

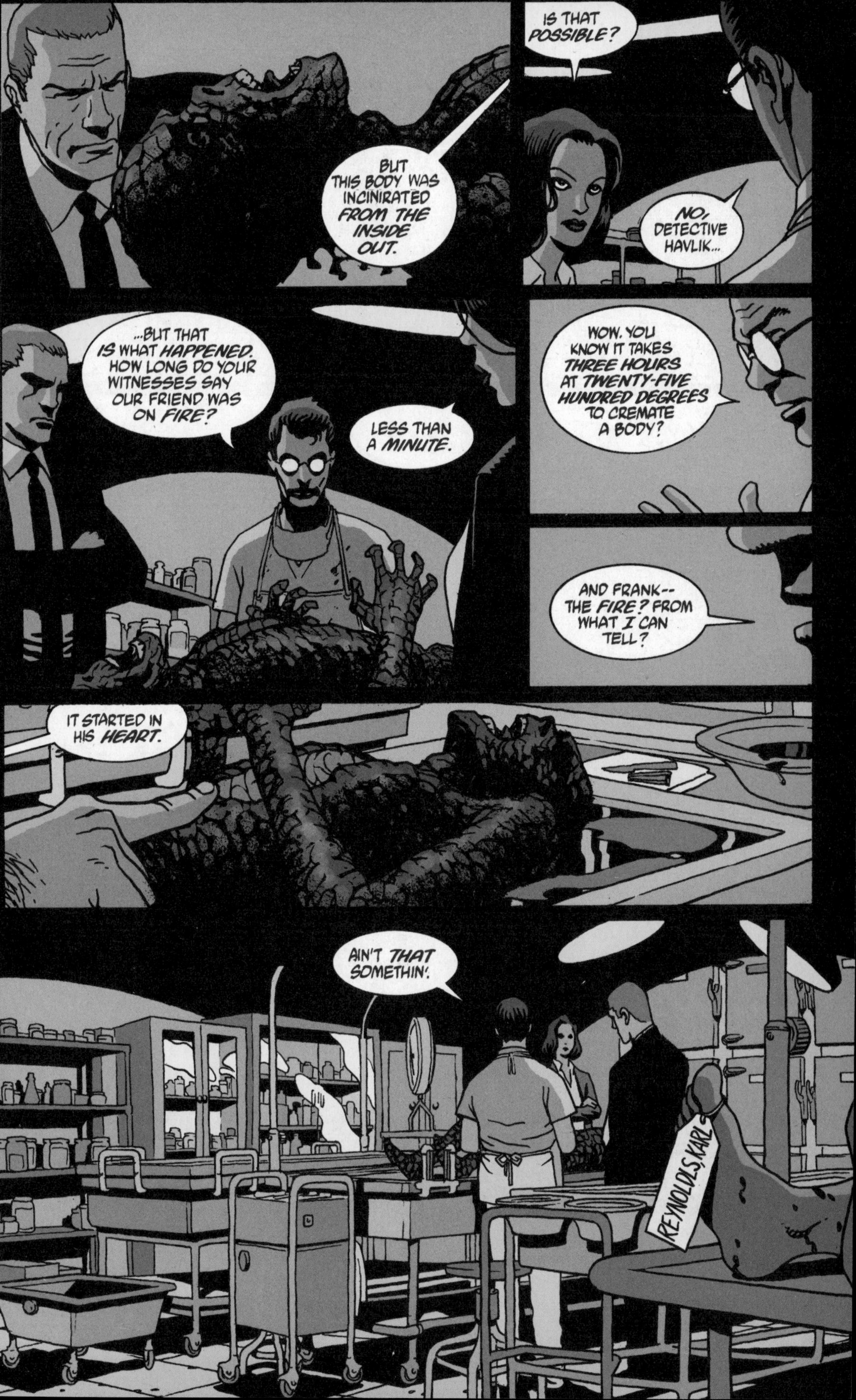
BUT THIS BODY WAS INCINIRATED FROM THE INSIDE OUT.
IS THAT POSSIBLE?
NO, DETECTIVE HAVLIK...
...BUT THAT IS WHAT HAPPENED. HOW LONG DO YOUR WITNESSES SAY OUR FRIEND WAS ON FIRE?
LESS THAN A MINUTE.
WOW. YOU KNOW IT TAKES THREE HOURS AT TWENTY-FIVE HUNDRED DEGREES TO CREMATE A BODY?
AND FRANK-- THE FIRE? FROM WHAT I CAN TELL?
IT STARTED IN HIS HEART.
AIN'T THAT SOMETHIN'.
REYNOLDLS, KARL

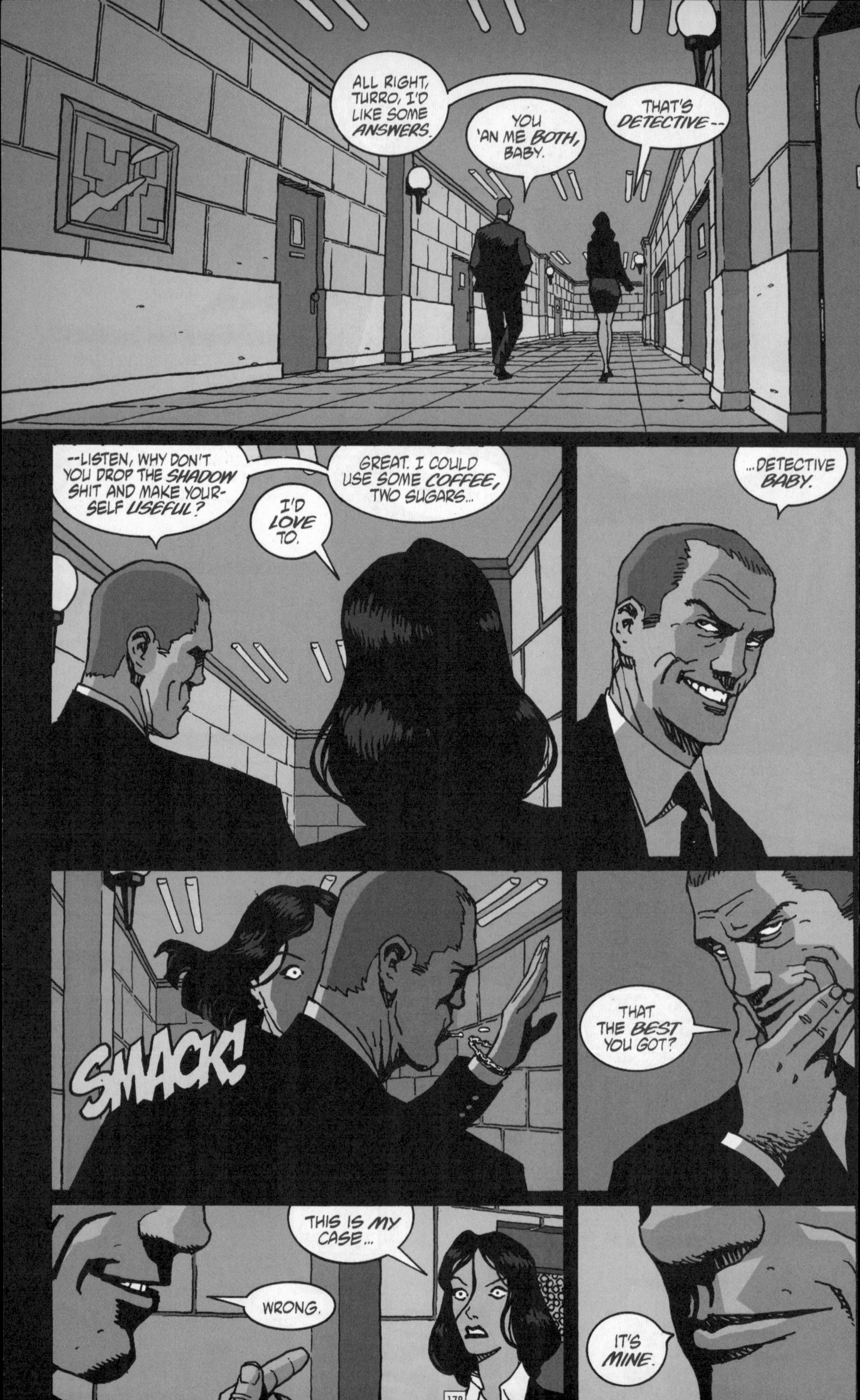
ALL RIGHT, TURRO, I'D LIKE SOME ANSWERS.
YOU 'AN ME BOTH, BABY.
THAT'S DETECTIVE--
--LISTEN, WHY DON'T YOU DROP THE SHADOW SHIT AND MAKE YOURSELF USEFUL?
I'D LOVE TO.
GREAT. I COULD USE SOME COFFEE, TWO SUGARS...
...DETECTIVE BABY.
SMACK!
THAT THE BEST YOU GOT?
THIS IS MY CASE...
WRONG.
IT'S MINE.

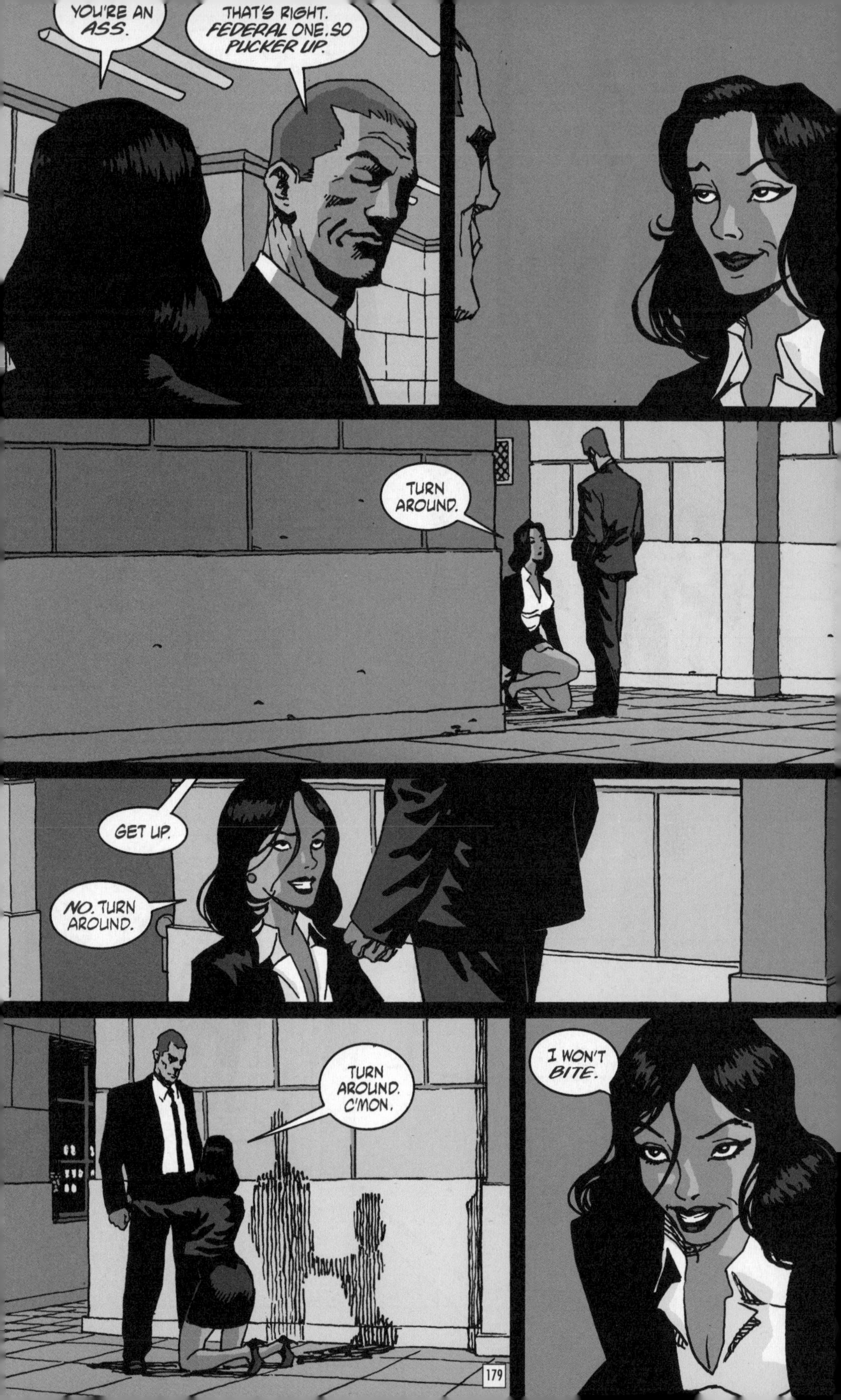

YOU'RE AN ASS.
THAT'S RIGHT. FEDERAL ONE. SO PUCKER UP.
TURN AROUND.
GET UP.
NO. TURN AROUND.
TURN AROUND. C'MON.
I WON'T BITE.

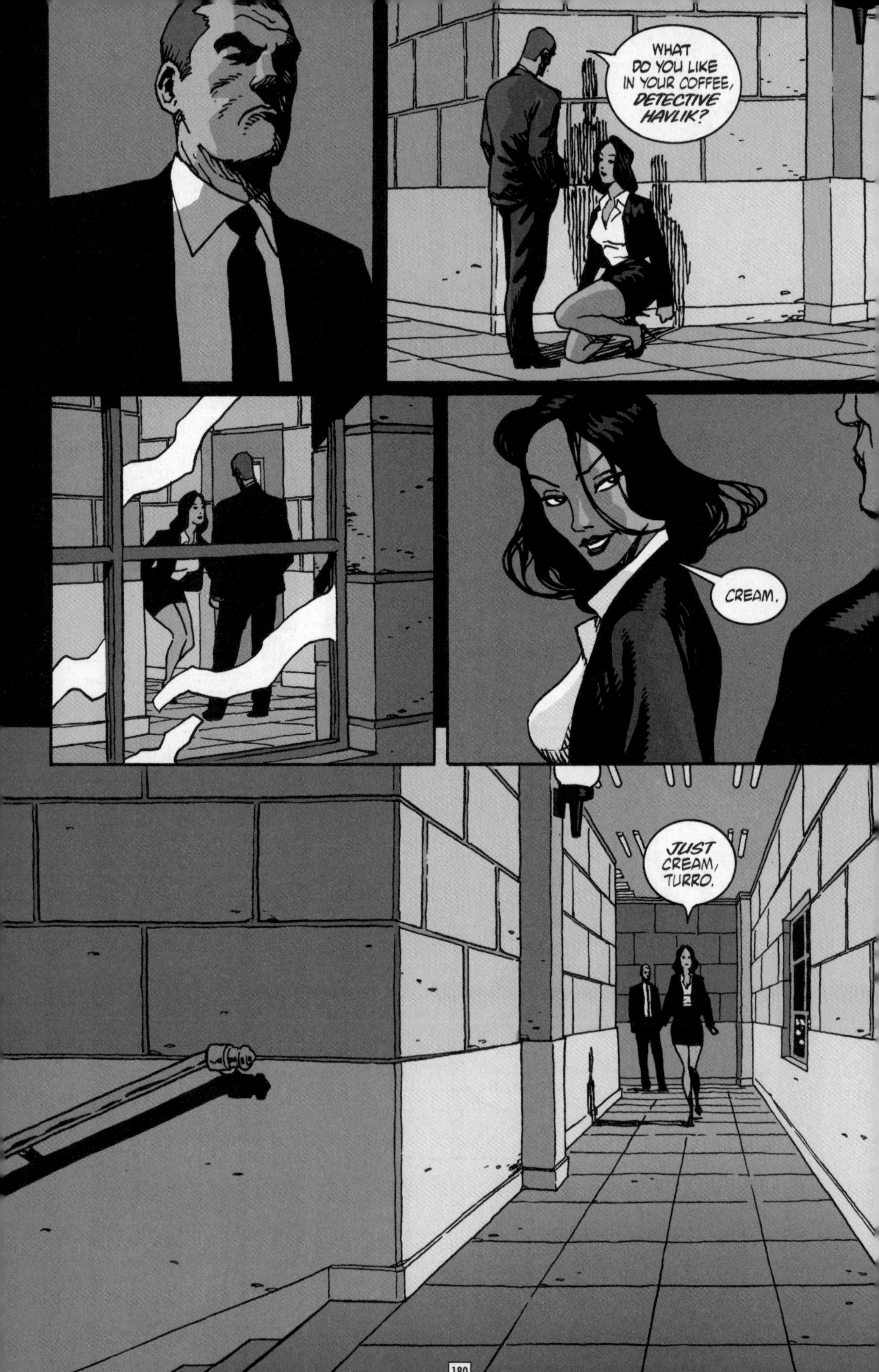
WHAT DO YOU LIKE IN YOUR COFFEE, DETECTIVE HAVLIK?
CREAM.
JUST CREAM, TURRO.

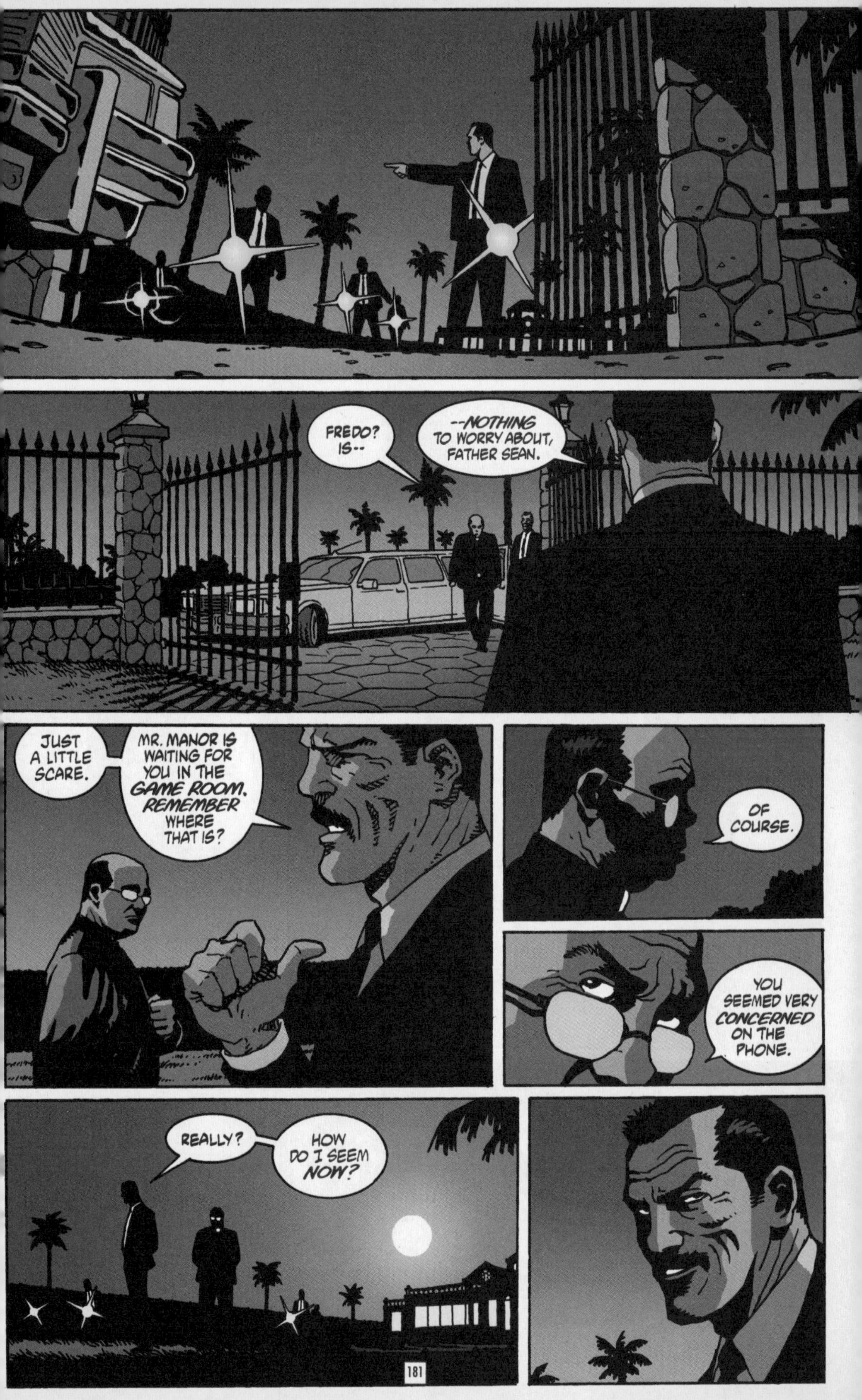
FREDO? IS--
--NOTHING TO WORRY ABOUT, FATHER SEAN.
JUST A LITTLE SCARE.
MR. MANOR IS WAITING FOR YOU IN THE GAME ROOM. REMEMBER WHERE THAT IS?
OF COURSE.
YOU SEEMED VERY CONCERNED ON THE PHONE.
REALLY?
HOW DO I SEEM NOW?

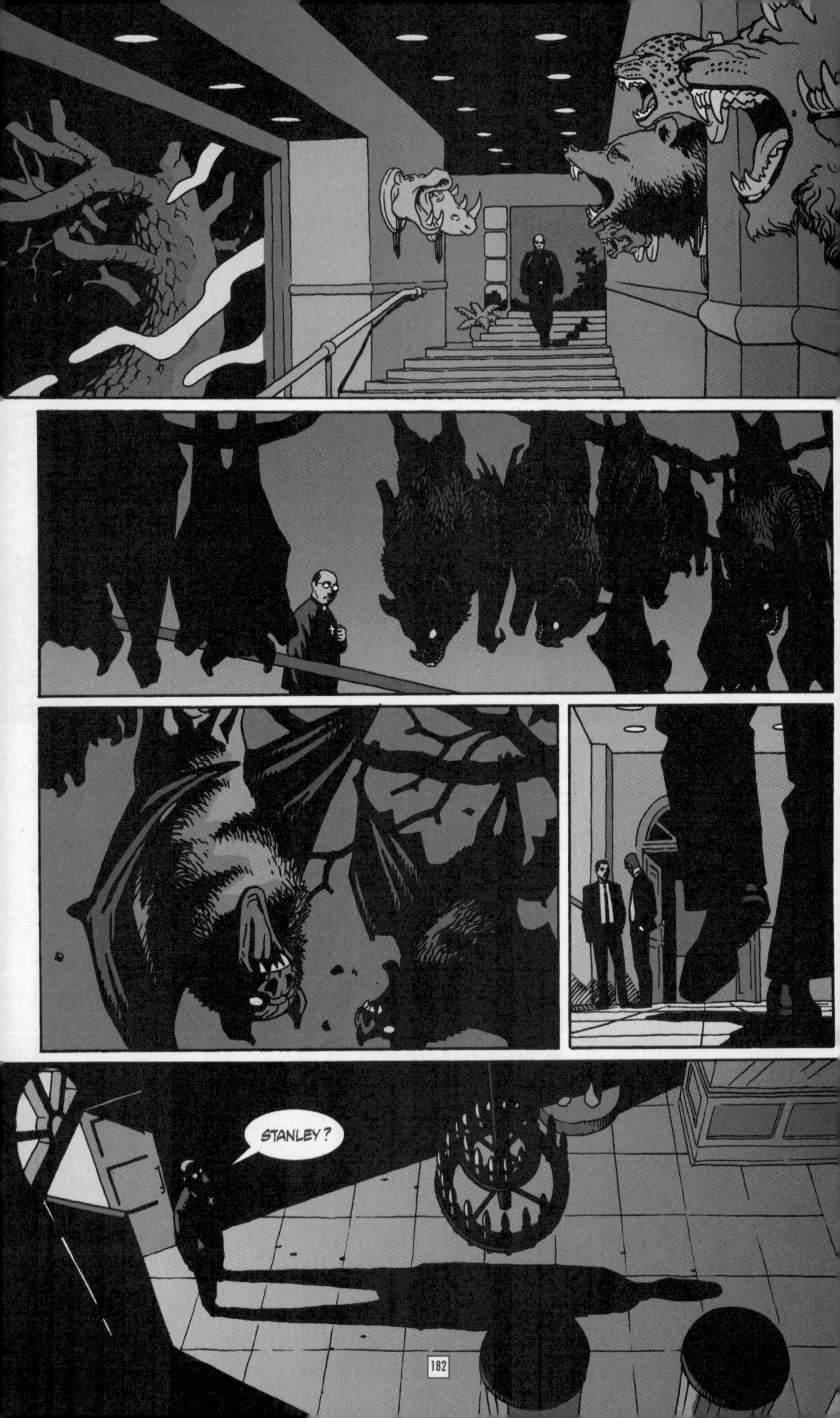
STANLEY?

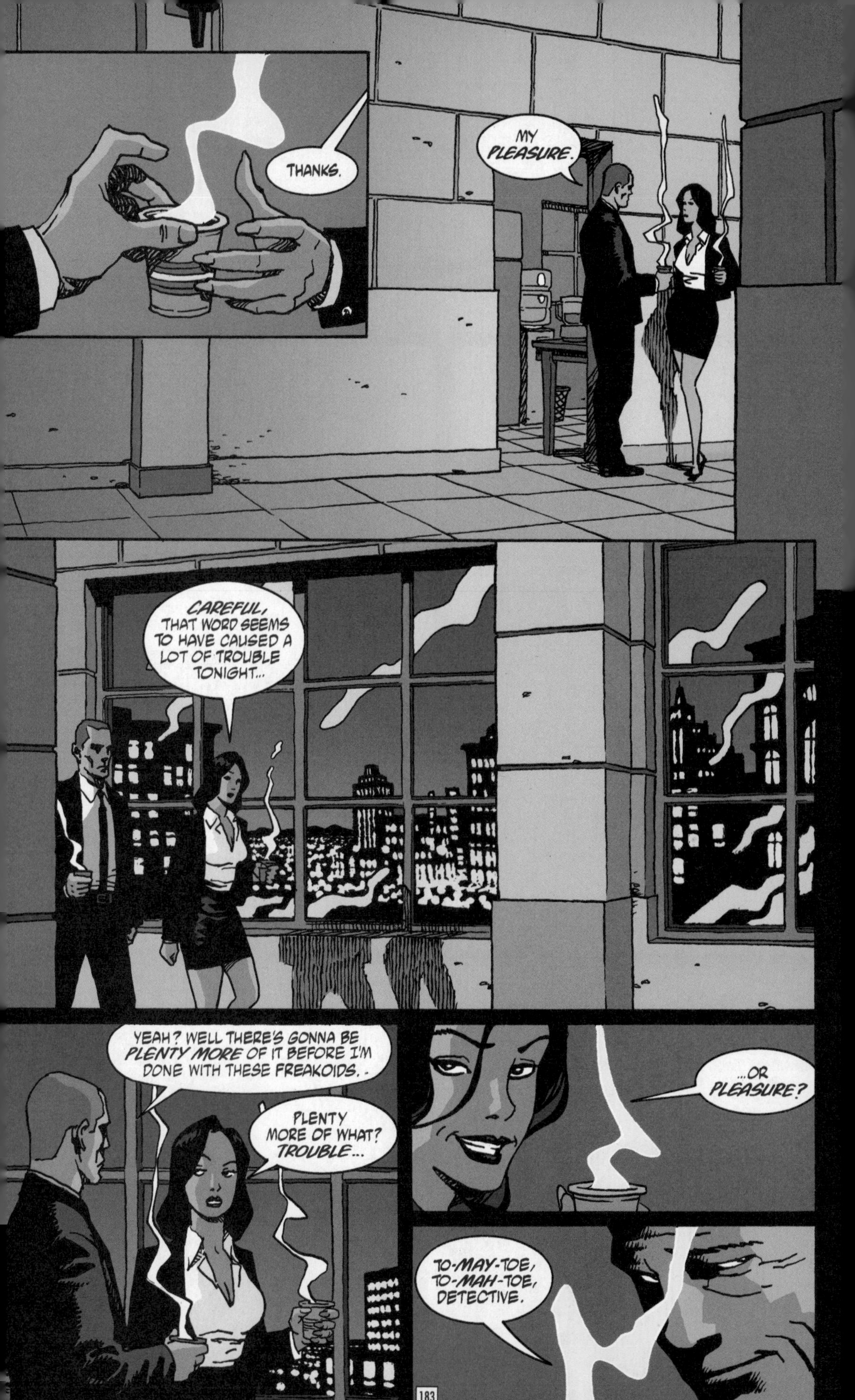
THANKS.
MY PLEASURE.
CAREFUL, THAT WORD SEEMS TO HAVE CAUSED A LOT OF TROUBLE TONIGHT...
YEAH? WELL THERE'S GONNA BE PLENTY MORE OF IT BEFORE I'M DONE WITH THESE FREAKOIDS. .
PLENTY MORE OF WHAT? TROUBLE...
...OR PLEASURE?
TO-MAY-TOE, TO-MAH-TOE, DETECTIVE.

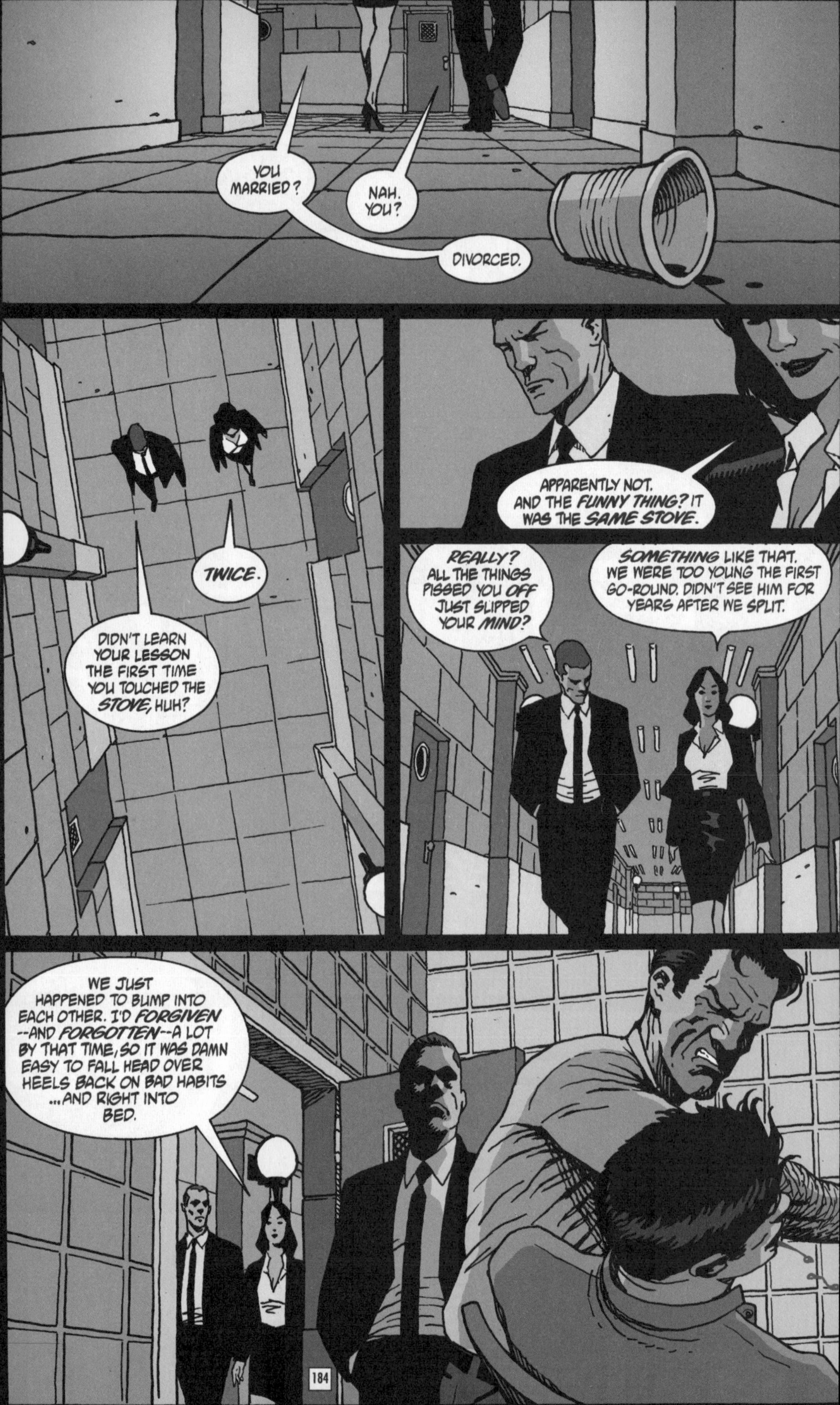
YOU MARRIED?
NAH. YOU?
DIVORCED.
TWICE.
DIDN'T LEARN YOUR LESSON THE FIRST TIME YOU TOUCHED THE STOVE, HUH?
APPARENTLY NOT. AND THE FUNNY THING? IT WAS THE SAME STOVE.
REALLY? ALL THE THINGS PISSED YOU OFF JUST SLIPPED YOUR MIND?
SOMETHING LIKE THAT. WE WERE TOO YOUNG THE FIRST GO-ROUND. DIDN'T SEE HIM FOR YEARS AFTER WE SPLIT.
WE JUST HAPPENED TO BUMP INTO EACH OTHER. I'D FORGIVEN --AND FORGOTTEN--A LOT BY THAT TIME, SO IT WAS DAMN EASY TO FALL HEAD OVER HEELS BACK ON BAD HABITS ...AND RIGHT INTO BED.

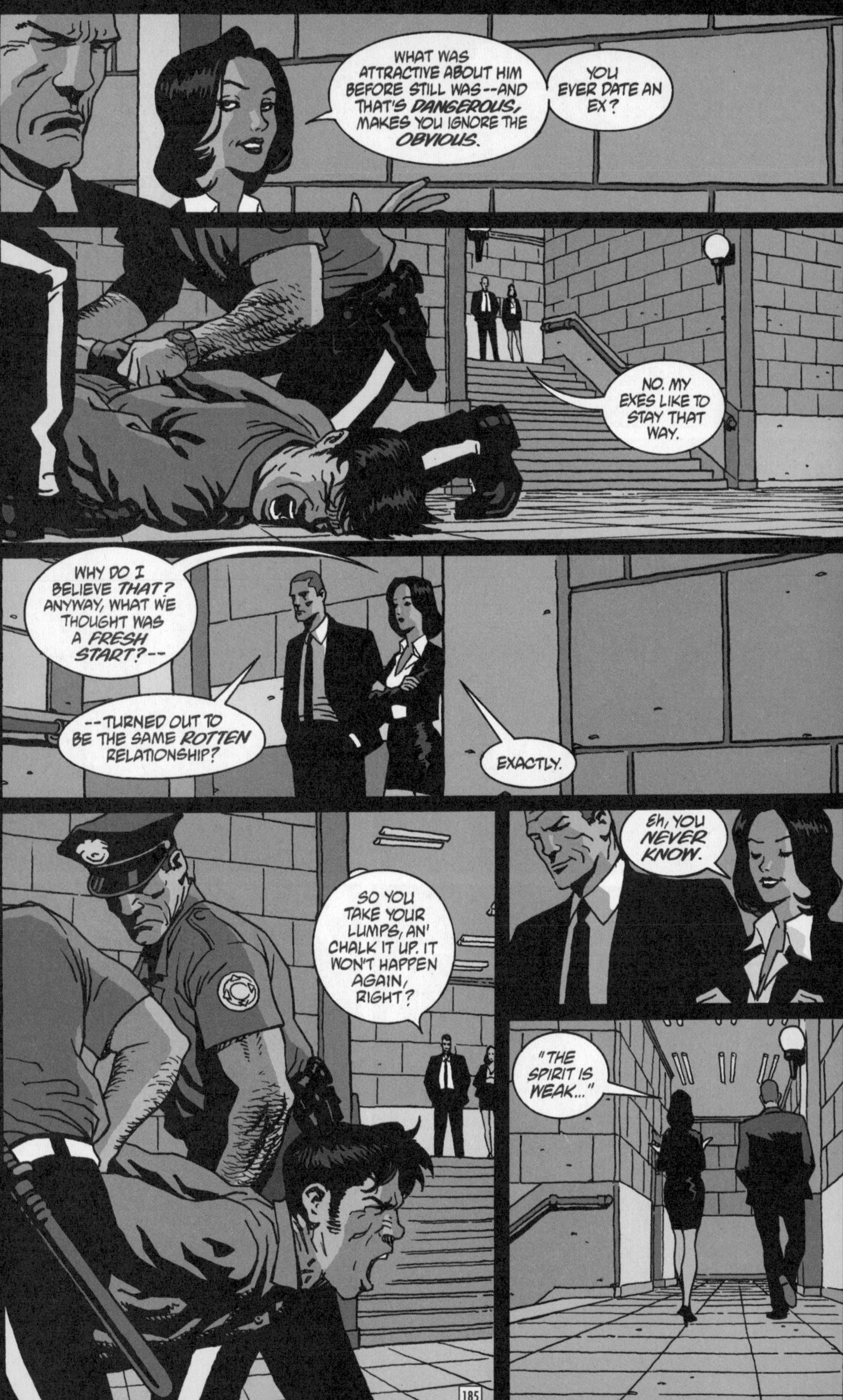
WHAT WAS ATTRACTIVE ABOUT HIM BEFORE STILL WAS--AND THAT'S DANGEROUS, MAKES YOU IGNORE THE OBVIOUS.
YOU EVER DATE AN EX?
NO. MY EXES LIKE TO STAY THAT WAY.
WHY DO I BELIEVE THAT? ANYWAY, WHAT WE THOUGHT WAS A FRESH START?--
--TURNED OUT TO BE THE SAME ROTTEN RELATIONSHIP?
EXACTLY.
SO YOU TAKE YOUR LUMPS, AN' CHALK IT UP. IT WON'T HAPPEN AGAIN, RIGHT?
Eh, YOU NEVER KNOW.
"THE SPIRIT IS WEAK..."

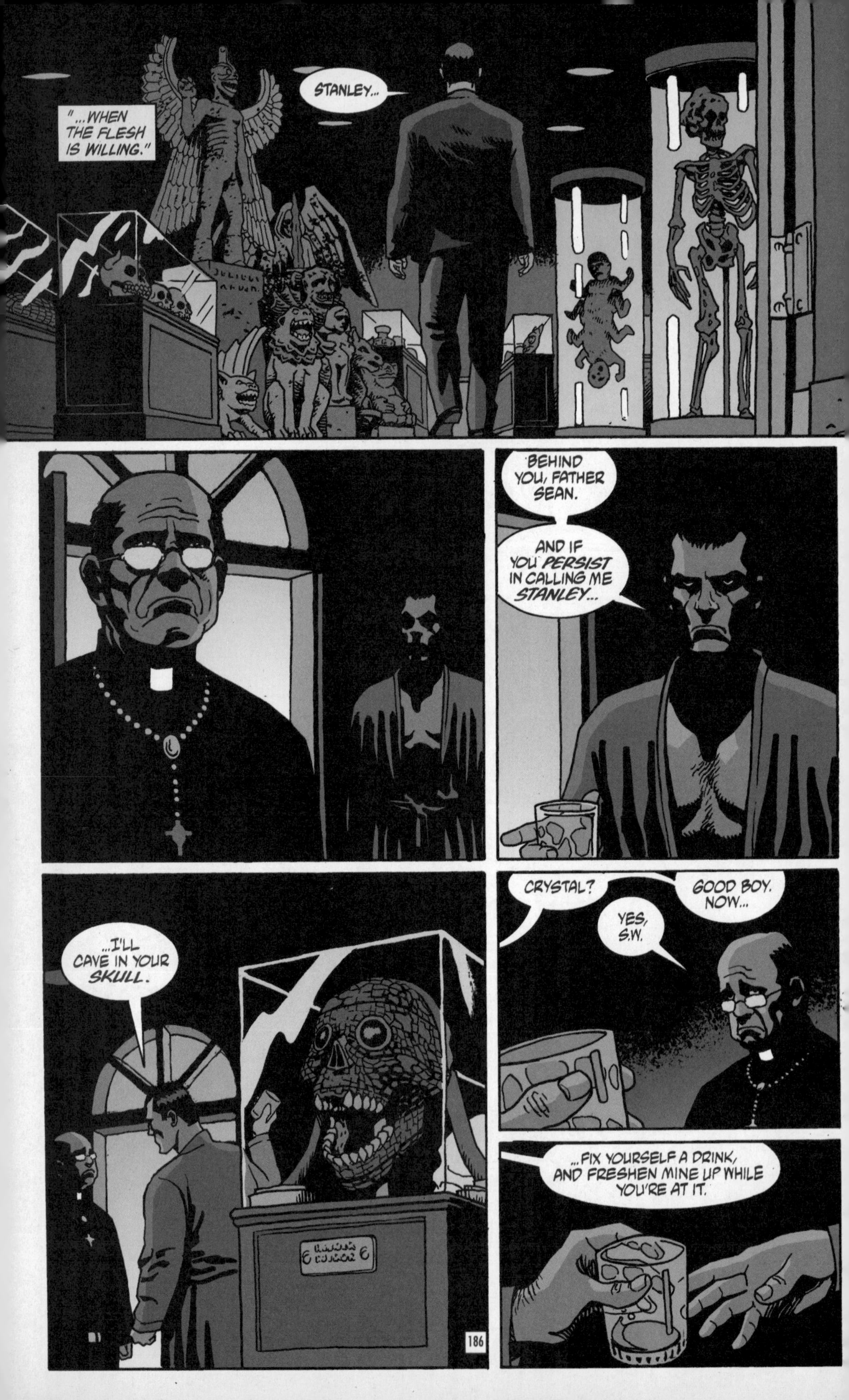
"...WHEN THE FLESH IS WILLING."
STANLEY...
BEHIND YOU, FATHER SEAN.
AND IF YOU PERSIST IN CALLING ME STANLEY...
...I'LL CAVE IN YOUR SKULL.
CRYSTAL?
GOOD BOY. NOW...
YES, S.W.
...FIX YOURSELF A DRINK, AND FRESHEN MINE UP WHILE YOU'RE AT IT.

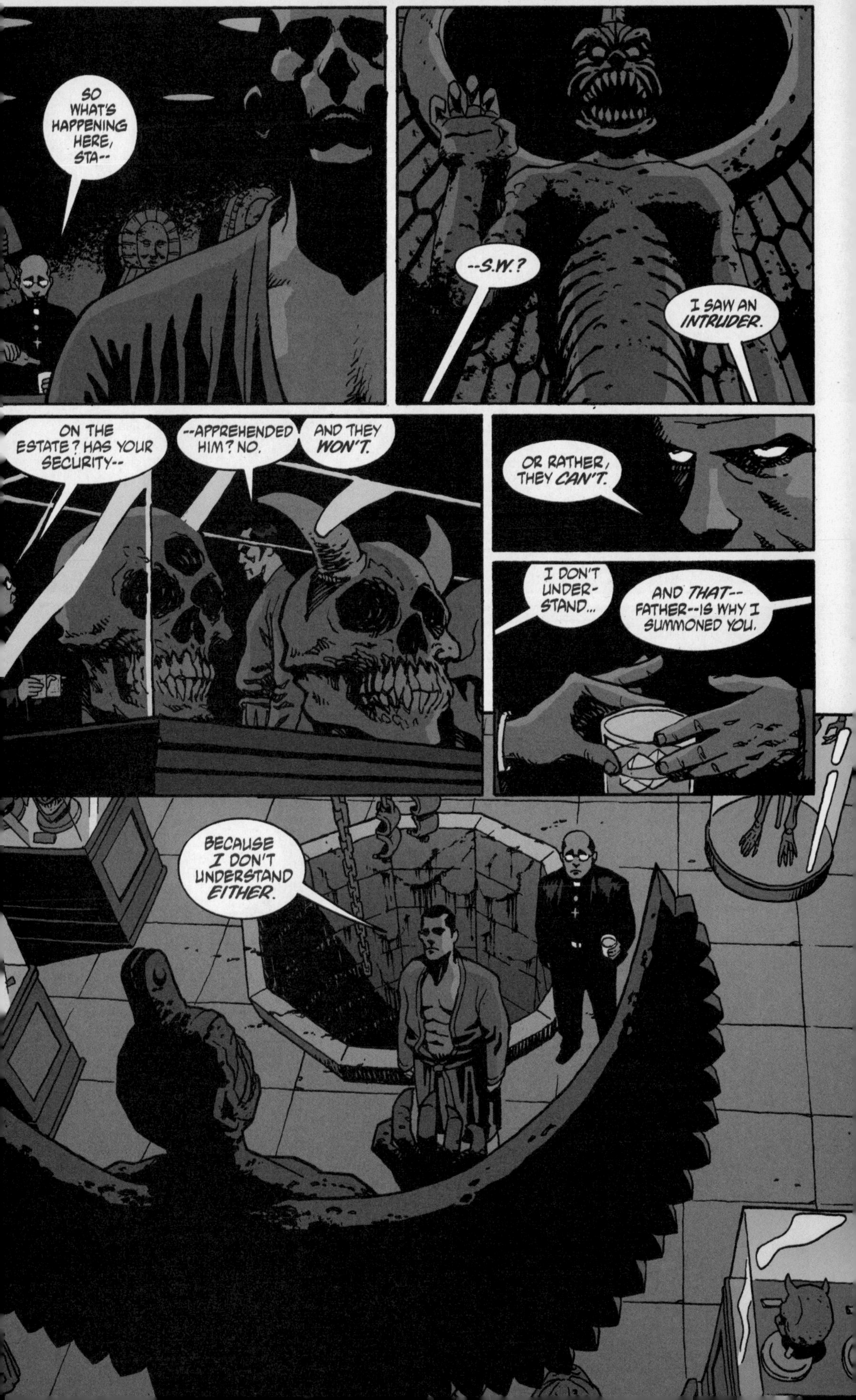
SO WHAT'S HAPPENING HERE, STA--
--S.W.?
I SAW AN INTRUDER.
ON THE ESTATE? HAS YOUR SECURITY--
--APPREHENDED HIM? NO.
AND THEY WON'T.
OR RATHER, THEY CAN'T.
I DON'T UNDER-STAND...
AND THAT--FATHER--IS WHY I SUMMONED YOU.
BECAUSE I DON'T UNDERSTAND EITHER.

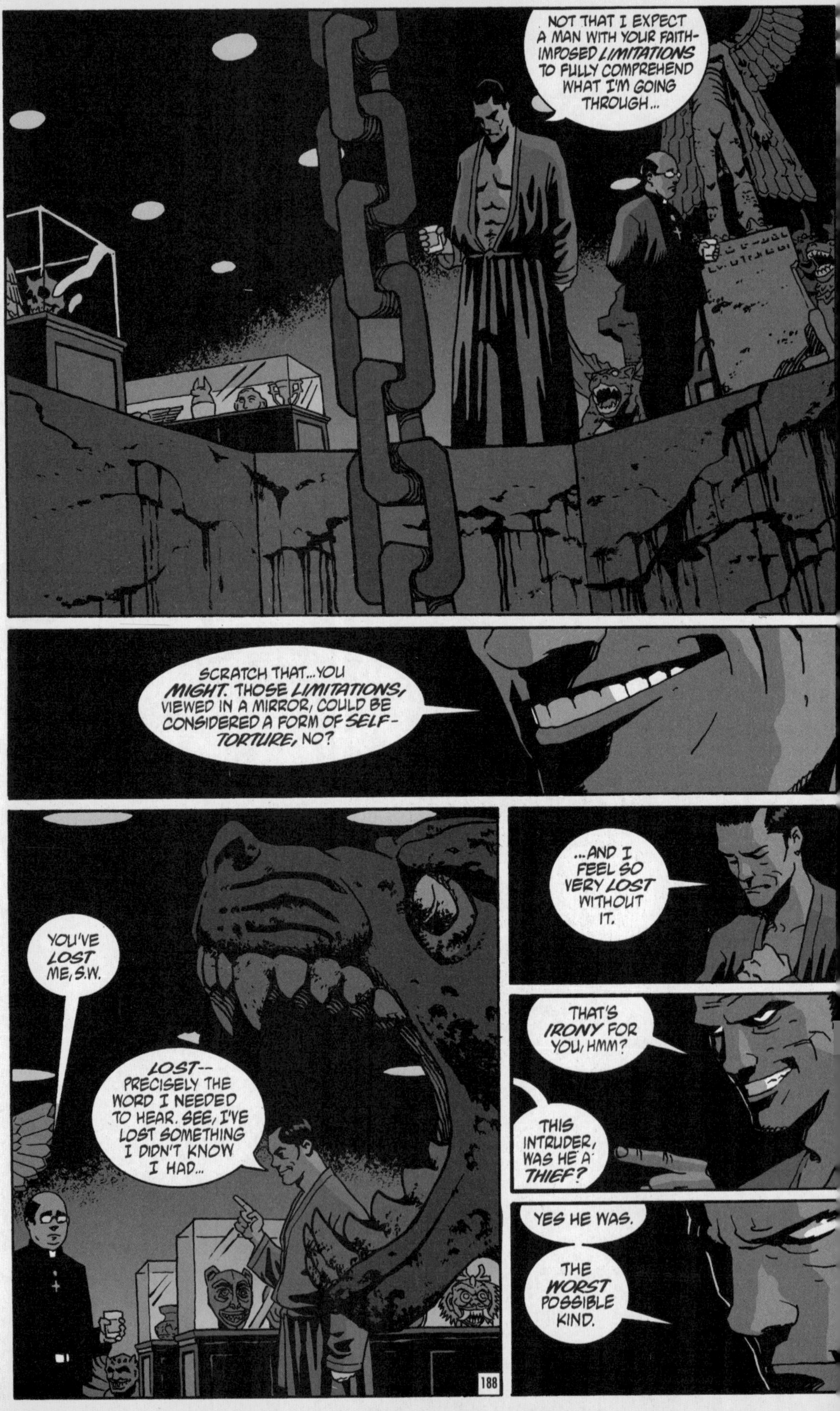
NOT THAT I EXPECT A MAN WITH YOUR FAITH-IMPOSED LIMITATIONS TO FULLY COMPREHEND WHAT I'M GOING THROUGH...
SCRATCH THAT...YOU MIGHT. THOSE LIMITATIONS, VIEWED IN A MIRROR, COULD BE CONSIDERED A FORM OF SELF-TORTURE, NO?
YOU'VE LOST ME, S.W.
LOST-- PRECISELY THE WORD I NEEDED TO HEAR. SEE, I'VE LOST SOMETHING I DIDN'T KNOW I HAD...
...AND I FEEL SO VERY LOST WITHOUT IT.
THAT'S IRONY FOR YOU, HMM?
THIS INTRUDER, WAS HE A THIEF?
YES HE WAS.
THE WORST POSSIBLE KIND.

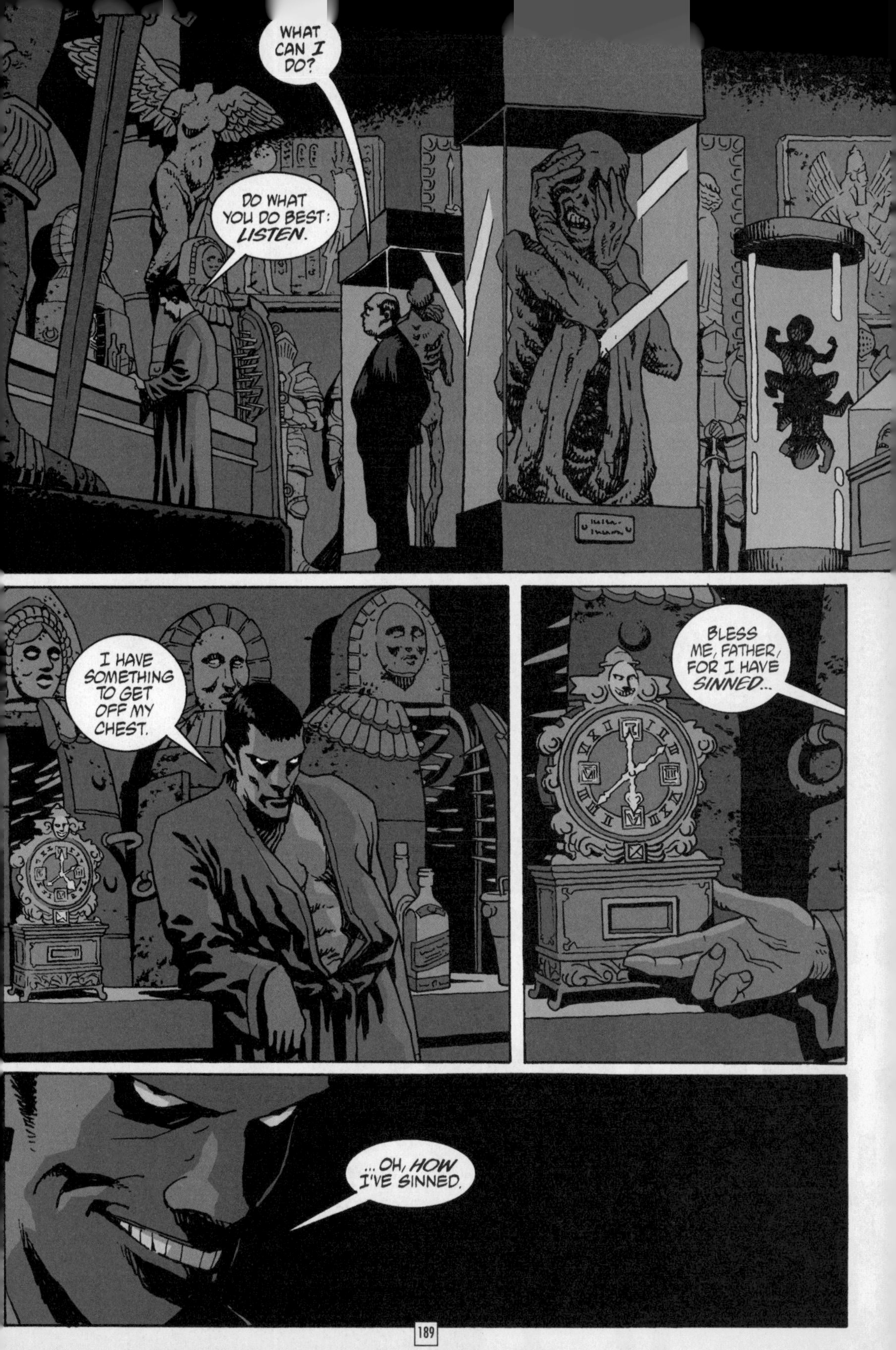
WHAT CAN *I* DO?
DO WHAT YOU DO BEST: *LISTEN.*
I HAVE SOMETHING TO GET OFF MY CHEST.
BLESS ME, FATHER, FOR I HAVE *SINNED...*
...OH, *HOW* I'VE SINNED.

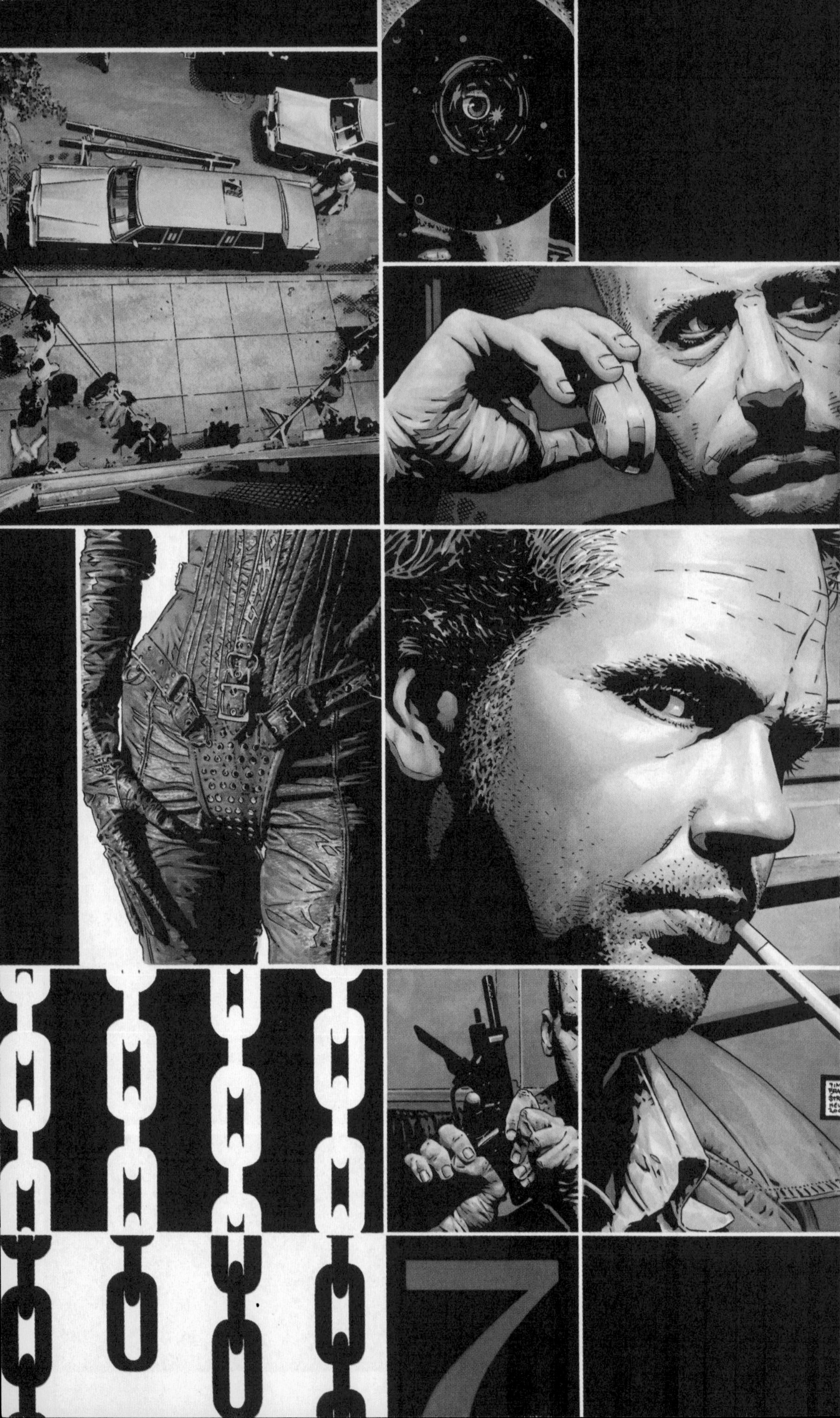
7

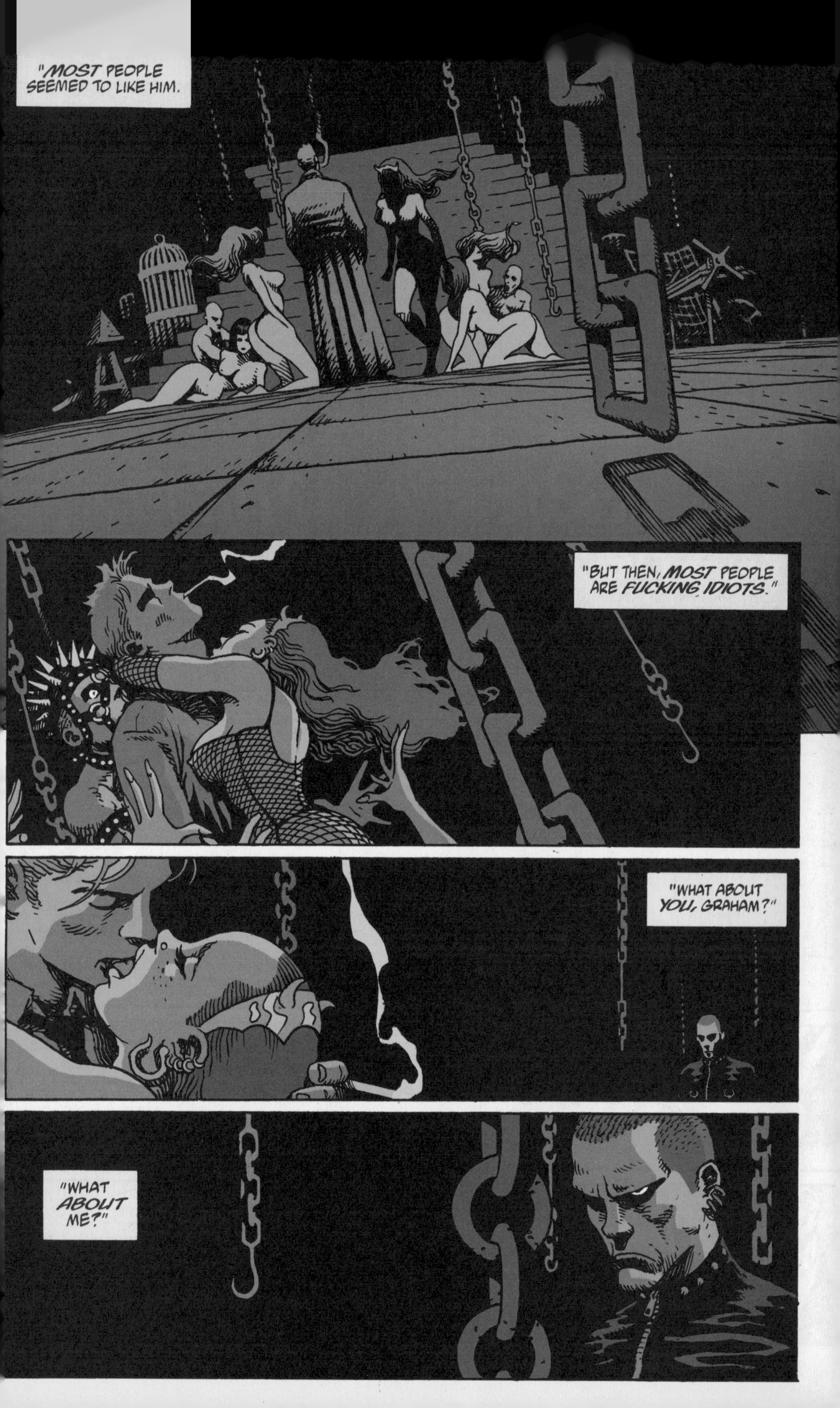
"MOST PEOPLE SEEMED TO LIKE HIM.
"BUT THEN, MOST PEOPLE ARE FUCKING IDIOTS."
"WHAT ABOUT YOU, GRAHAM?"
"WHAT ABOUT ME?"

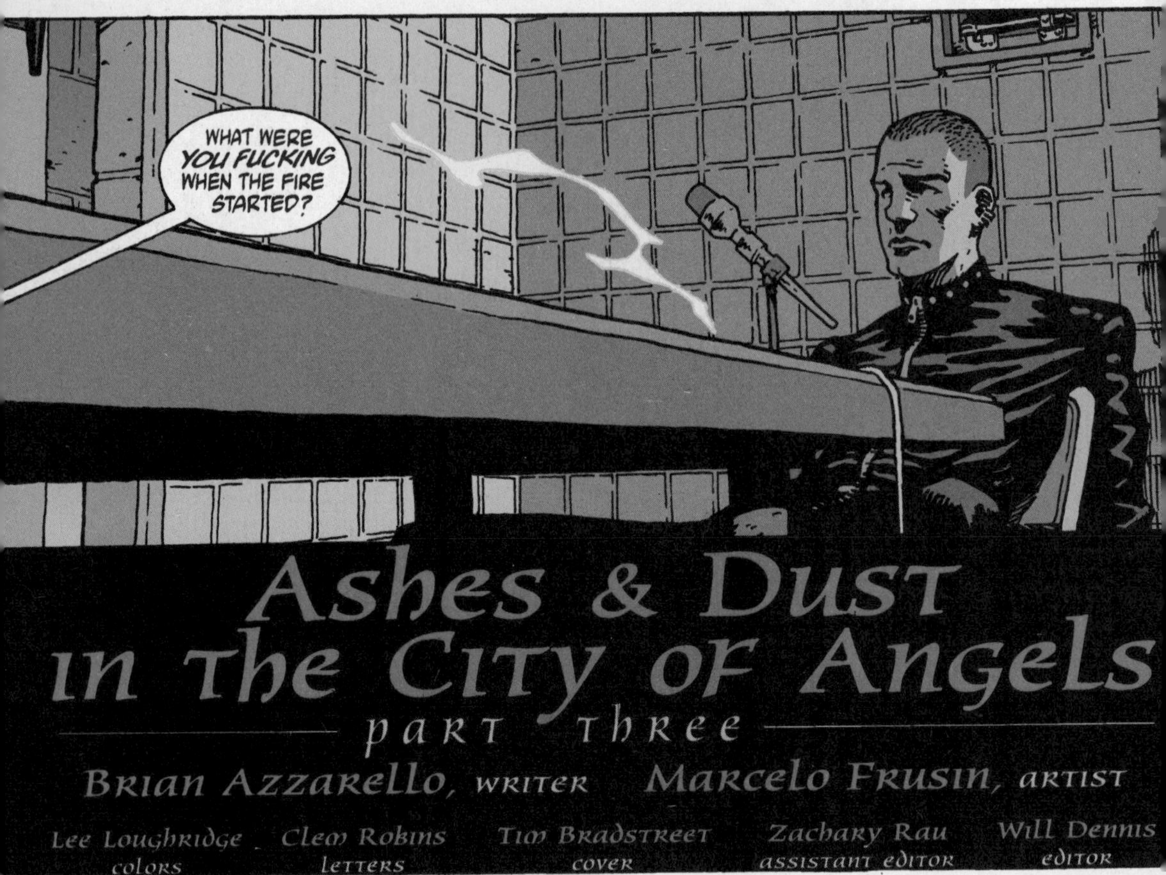
WHAT WERE YOU FUCKING WHEN THE FIRE STARTED?

Ashes & Dust in the City of Angels

part three

Brian Azzarello, writer Marcelo Frusin, artist

Lee Loughridge colors
Clem Robins letters
Tim Bradstreet cover
Zachary Rau assistant editor
Will Dennis editor

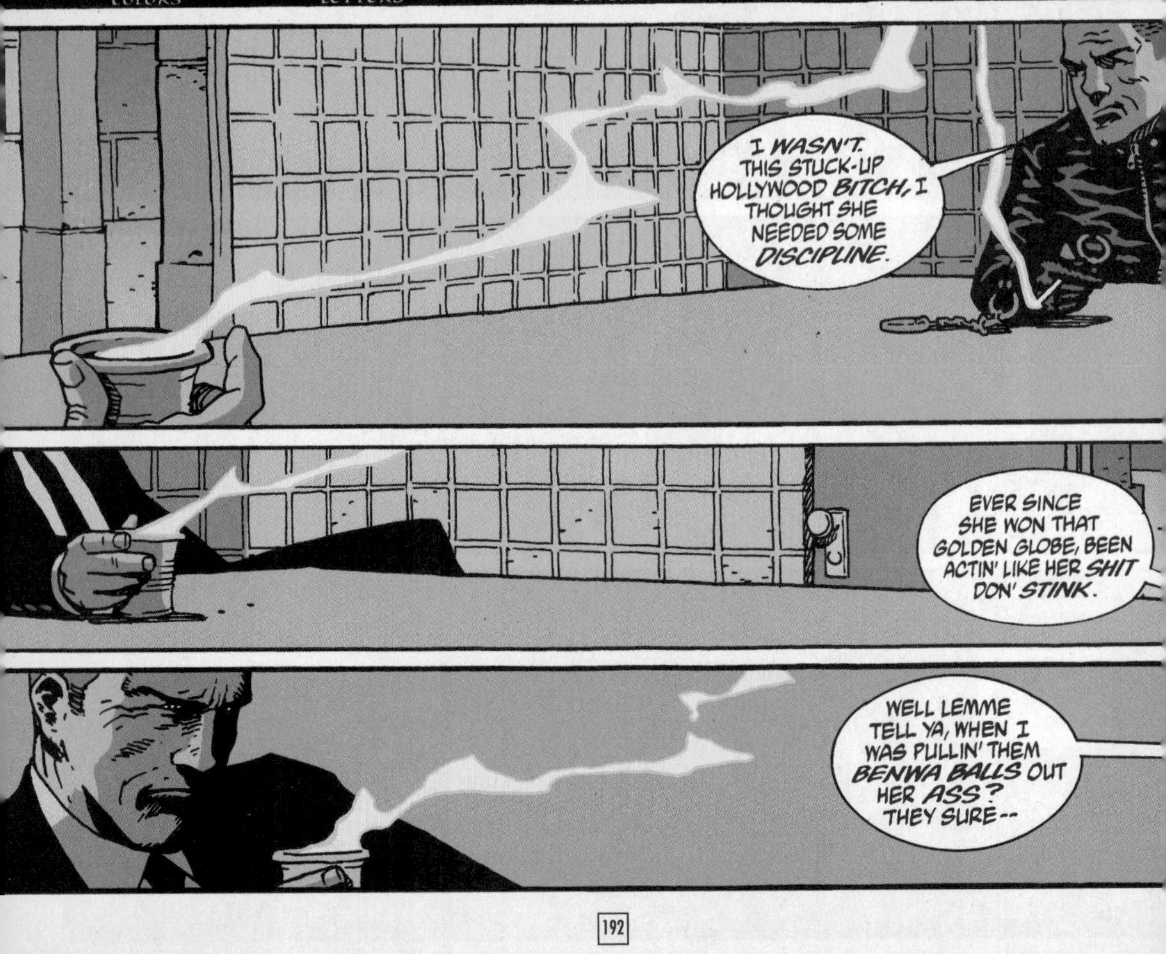
I WASN'T. THIS STUCK-UP HOLLYWOOD BITCH, I THOUGHT SHE NEEDED SOME DISCIPLINE.
EVER SINCE SHE WON THAT GOLDEN GLOBE, BEEN ACTIN' LIKE HER SHIT DON' STINK.
WELL LEMME TELL YA, WHEN I WAS PULLIN' THEM BENWA BALLS OUT HER ASS? THEY SURE--

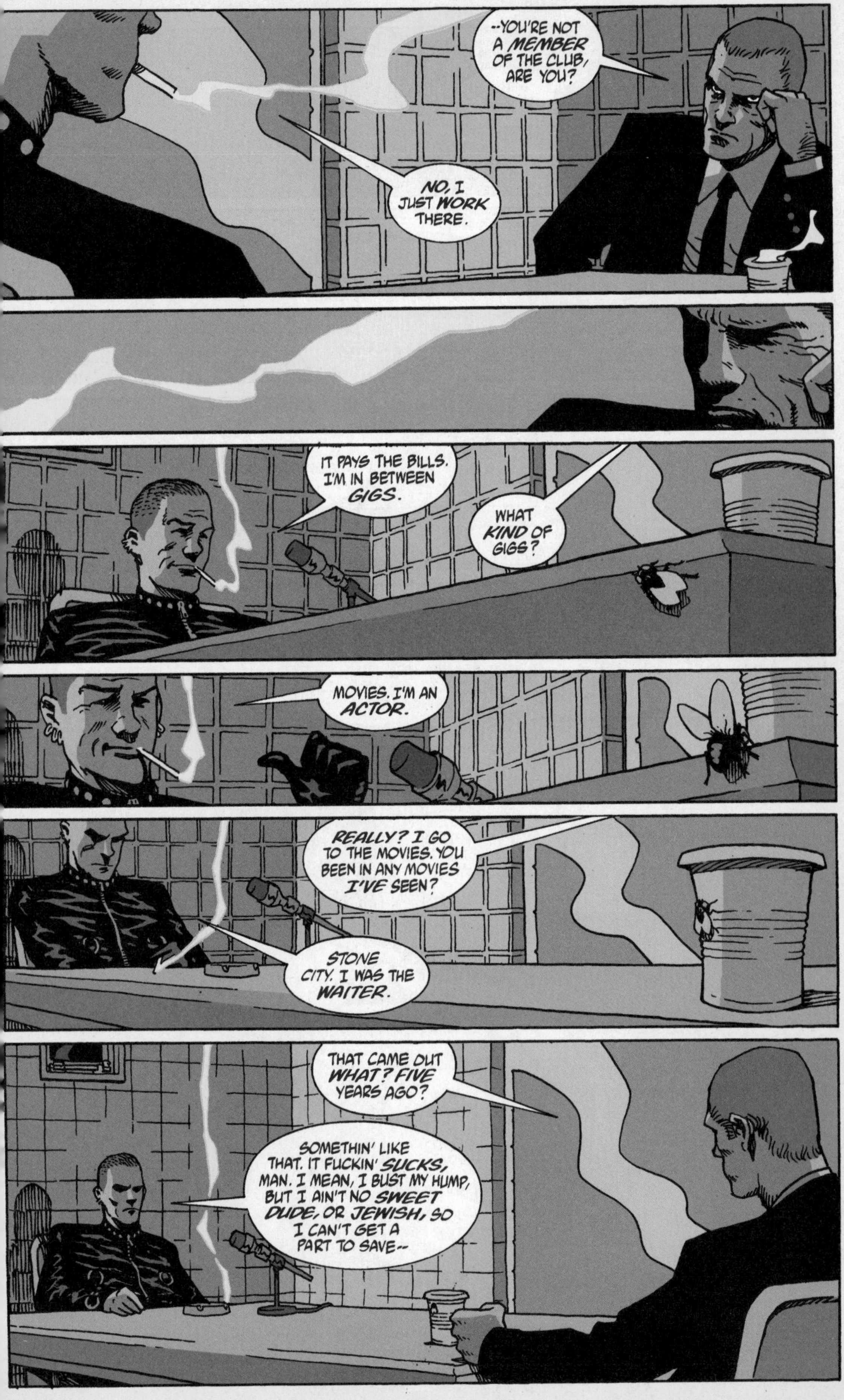
--YOU'RE NOT A MEMBER OF THE CLUB, ARE YOU?
NO, I JUST WORK THERE.
IT PAYS THE BILLS. I'M IN BETWEEN GIGS.
WHAT KIND OF GIGS?
MOVIES. I'M AN ACTOR.
REALLY? I GO TO THE MOVIES. YOU BEEN IN ANY MOVIES I'VE SEEN?
STONE CITY. I WAS THE WAITER.
THAT CAME OUT WHAT? FIVE YEARS AGO?
SOMETHIN' LIKE THAT. IT FUCKIN' SUCKS, MAN. I MEAN, I BUST MY HUMP, BUT I AIN'T NO SWEET DUDE, OR JEWISH, SO I CAN'T GET A PART TO SAVE--

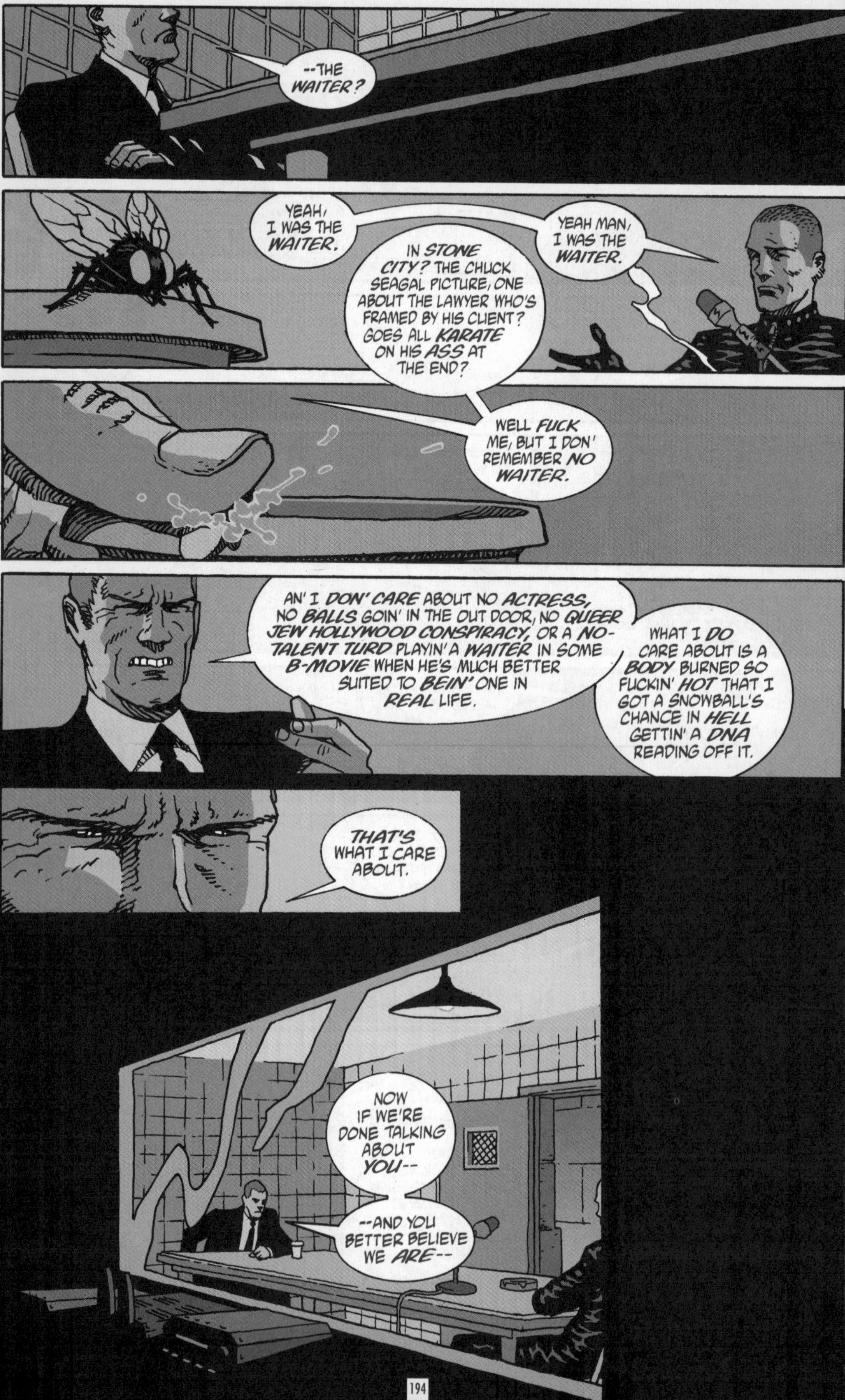
--THE WAITER?
YEAH, I WAS THE WAITER.
YEAH MAN, I WAS THE WAITER.
IN STONE CITY? THE CHUCK SEAGAL PICTURE, ONE ABOUT THE LAWYER WHO'S FRAMED BY HIS CLIENT? GOES ALL KARATE ON HIS ASS AT THE END?
WELL FUCK ME, BUT I DON' REMEMBER NO WAITER.
AN' I DON' CARE ABOUT NO ACTRESS, NO BALLS GOIN' IN THE OUT DOOR, NO QUEER JEW HOLLYWOOD CONSPIRACY, OR A NO-TALENT TURD PLAYIN' A WAITER IN SOME B-MOVIE WHEN HE'S MUCH BETTER SUITED TO BEIN' ONE IN REAL LIFE.
WHAT I DO CARE ABOUT IS A BODY BURNED SO FUCKIN' HOT THAT I GOT A SNOWBALL'S CHANCE IN HELL GETTIN' A DNA READING OFF IT.
THAT'S WHAT I CARE ABOUT.
NOW IF WE'RE DONE TALKING ABOUT YOU--
--AND YOU BETTER BELIEVE WE ARE--

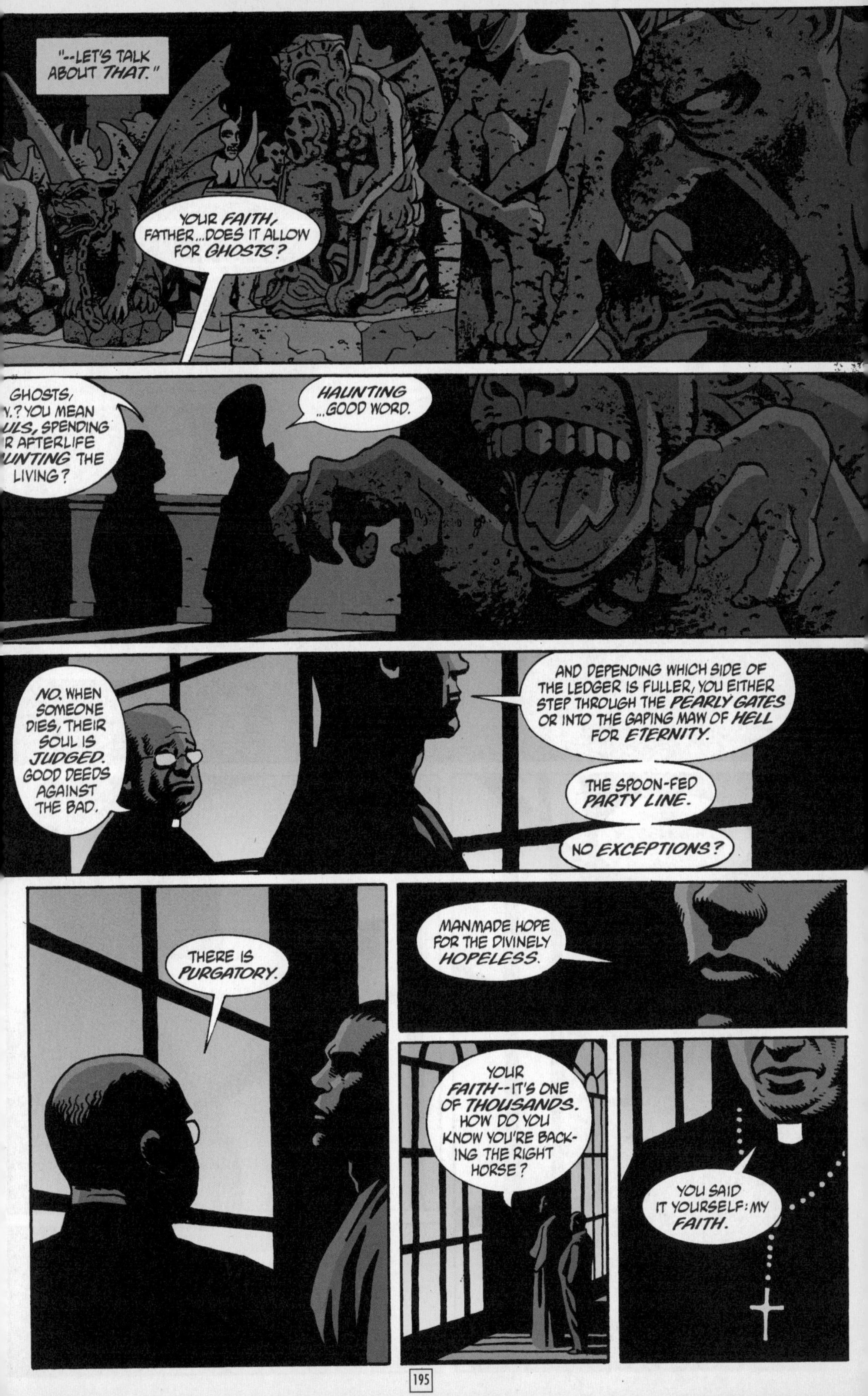
"--LET'S TALK ABOUT *THAT.*"
YOUR *FAITH,* FATHER...DOES IT ALLOW FOR *GHOSTS?*
GHOSTS, Y.? YOU MEAN ULS, SPENDING R AFTERLIFE UNTING THE LIVING?
HAUNTING ...GOOD WORD.
NO. WHEN SOMEONE DIES, THEIR SOUL IS *JUDGED.* GOOD DEEDS AGAINST THE BAD.
AND DEPENDING WHICH SIDE OF THE LEDGER IS FULLER, YOU EITHER STEP THROUGH THE *PEARLY GATES* OR INTO THE GAPING MAW OF *HELL* FOR *ETERNITY.*
THE SPOON-FED *PARTY LINE.*
NO *EXCEPTIONS?*
THERE IS *PURGATORY.*
MANMADE HOPE FOR THE DIVINELY *HOPELESS.*
YOUR *FAITH*--IT'S ONE OF *THOUSANDS.* HOW DO YOU KNOW YOU'RE BACK-ING THE RIGHT HORSE?
YOU SAID IT YOURSELF: MY *FAITH.*

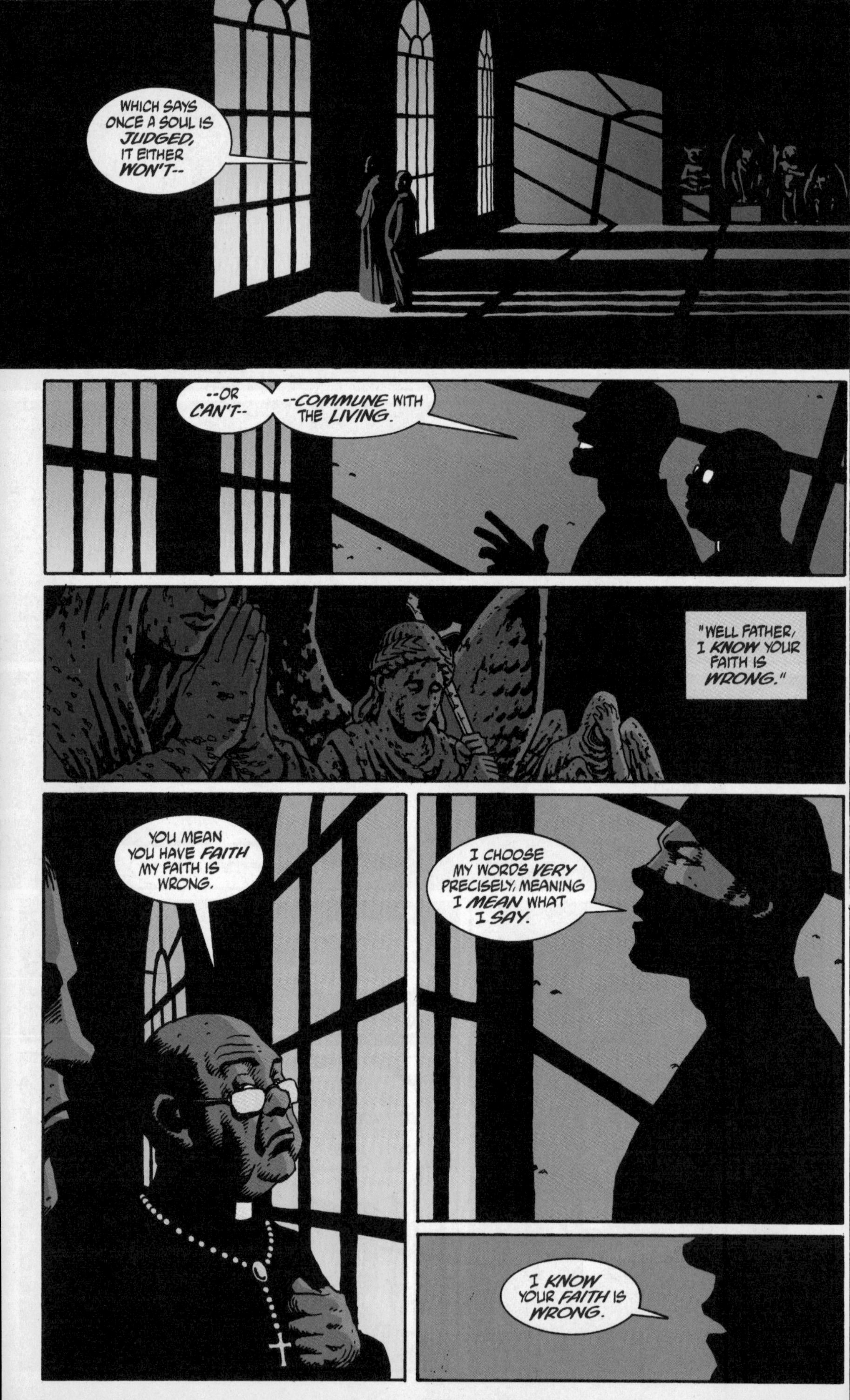
WHICH SAYS ONCE A SOUL IS JUDGED, IT EITHER WON'T--
--OR CAN'T--
--COMMUNE WITH THE LIVING.
"WELL FATHER, I KNOW YOUR FAITH IS WRONG."
YOU MEAN YOU HAVE FAITH MY FAITH IS WRONG.
I CHOOSE MY WORDS VERY PRECISELY, MEANING I MEAN WHAT I SAY.
I KNOW YOUR FAITH IS WRONG.

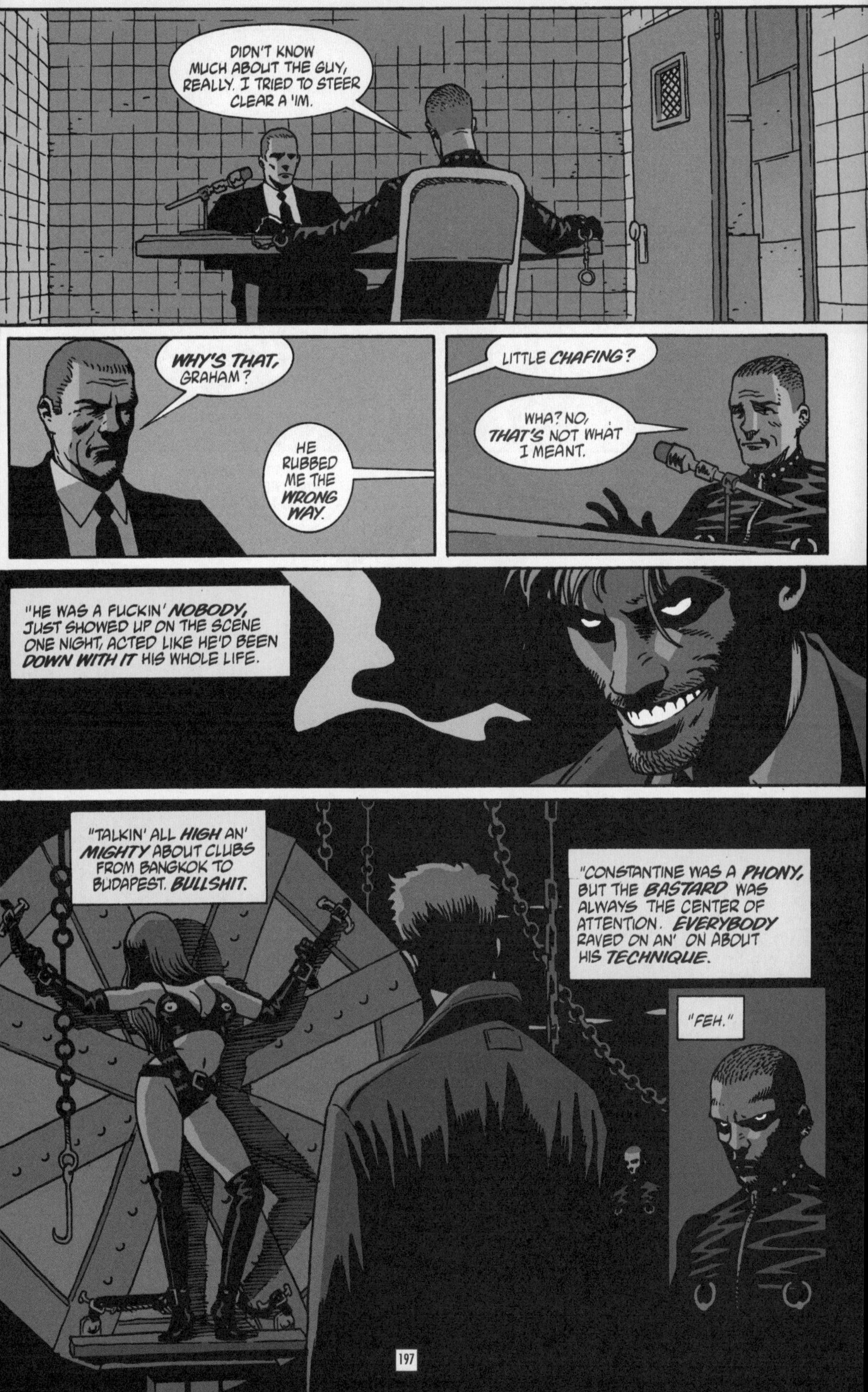

DIDN'T KNOW MUCH ABOUT THE GUY, REALLY. I TRIED TO STEER CLEAR A 'IM.
WHY'S THAT, GRAHAM?
HE RUBBED ME THE WRONG WAY.
LITTLE CHAFING?
WHA? NO, THAT'S NOT WHAT I MEANT.
"HE WAS A FUCKIN' NOBODY, JUST SHOWED UP ON THE SCENE ONE NIGHT, ACTED LIKE HE'D BEEN DOWN WITH IT HIS WHOLE LIFE.
"TALKIN' ALL HIGH AN' MIGHTY ABOUT CLUBS FROM BANGKOK TO BUDAPEST. BULLSHIT.
"CONSTANTINE WAS A PHONY, BUT THE BASTARD WAS ALWAYS THE CENTER OF ATTENTION. EVERYBODY RAVED ON AN' ON ABOUT HIS TECHNIQUE.
"FEH."

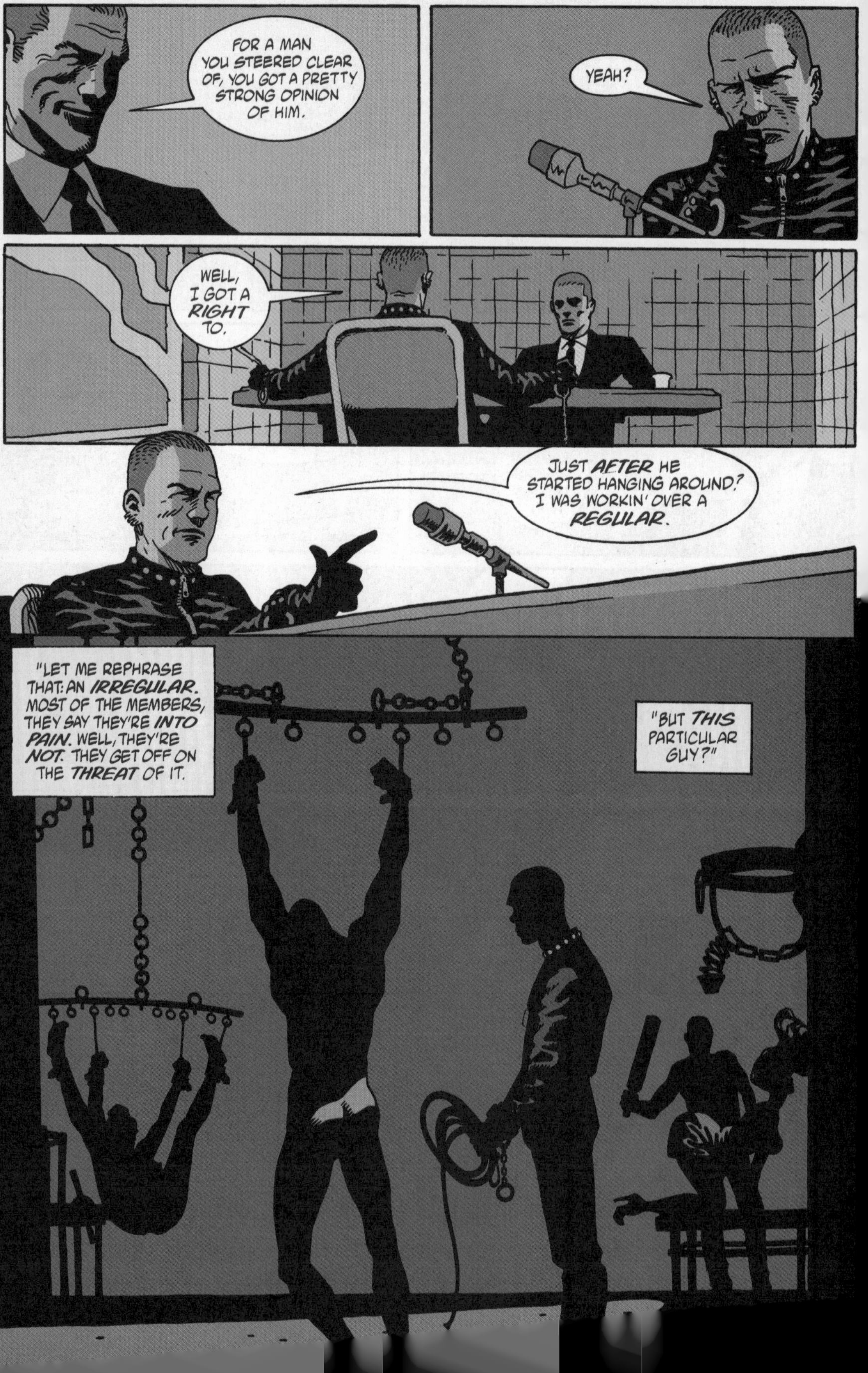
FOR A MAN YOU STEERED CLEAR OF, YOU GOT A PRETTY STRONG OPINION OF HIM.
YEAH?
WELL, I GOT A RIGHT TO.
JUST AFTER HE STARTED HANGING AROUND? I WAS WORKIN' OVER A REGULAR.
"LET ME REPHRASE THAT: AN IRREGULAR. MOST OF THE MEMBERS, THEY SAY THEY'RE INTO PAIN. WELL, THEY'RE NOT. THEY GET OFF ON THE THREAT OF IT.
"BUT THIS PARTICULAR GUY?"

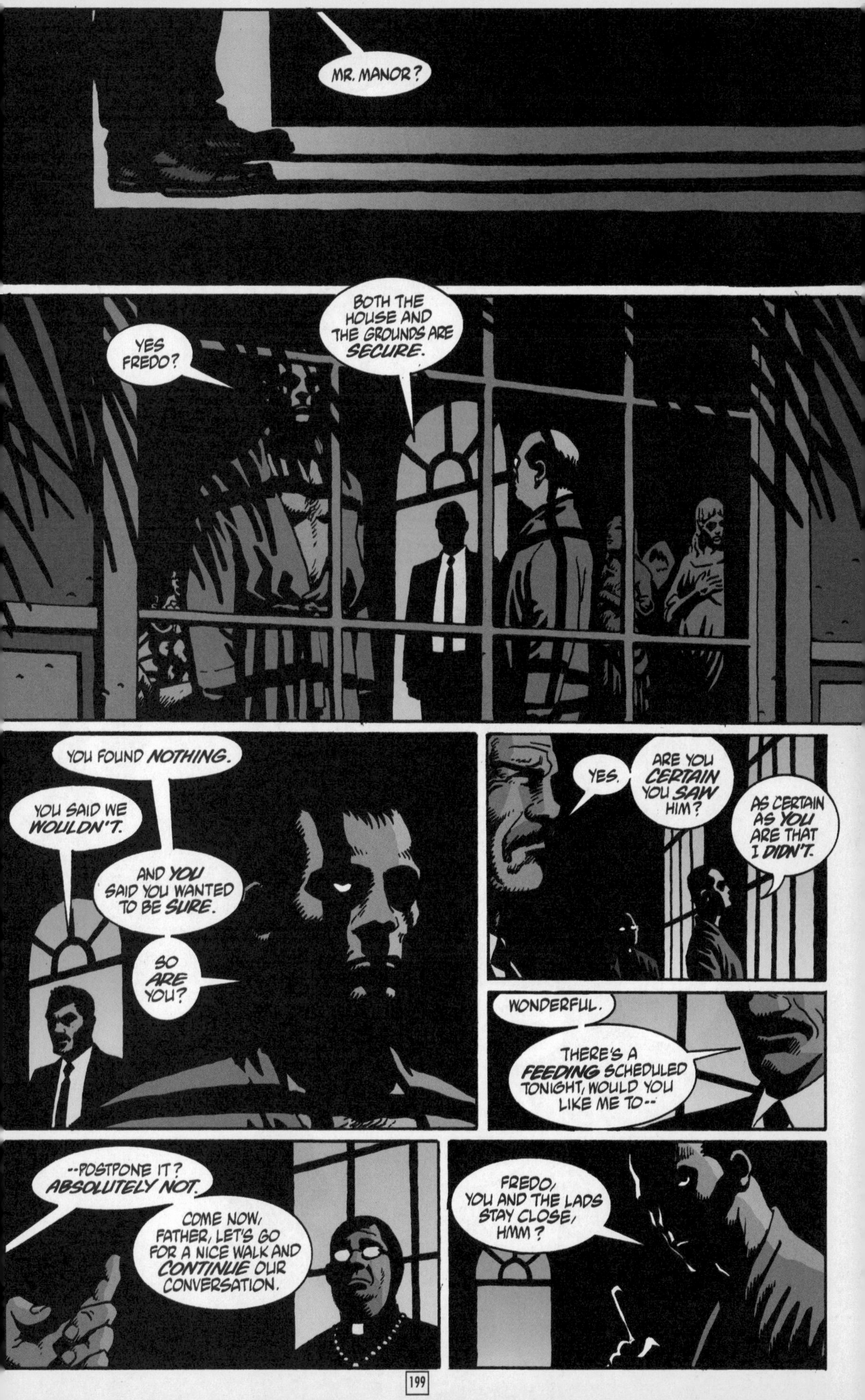
MR. MANOR?
YES FREDO?
BOTH THE HOUSE AND THE GROUNDS ARE SECURE.
YOU FOUND NOTHING.
YOU SAID WE WOULDN'T.
AND YOU SAID YOU WANTED TO BE SURE.
SO ARE YOU?
YES.
ARE YOU CERTAIN YOU SAW HIM?
AS CERTAIN AS YOU ARE THAT I DIDN'T.
WONDERFUL.
THERE'S A FEEDING SCHEDULED TONIGHT, WOULD YOU LIKE ME TO--
--POSTPONE IT? ABSOLUTELY NOT.
COME NOW, FATHER, LET'S GO FOR A NICE WALK AND CONTINUE OUR CONVERSATION.
FREDO, YOU AND THE LADS STAY CLOSE, HMM?

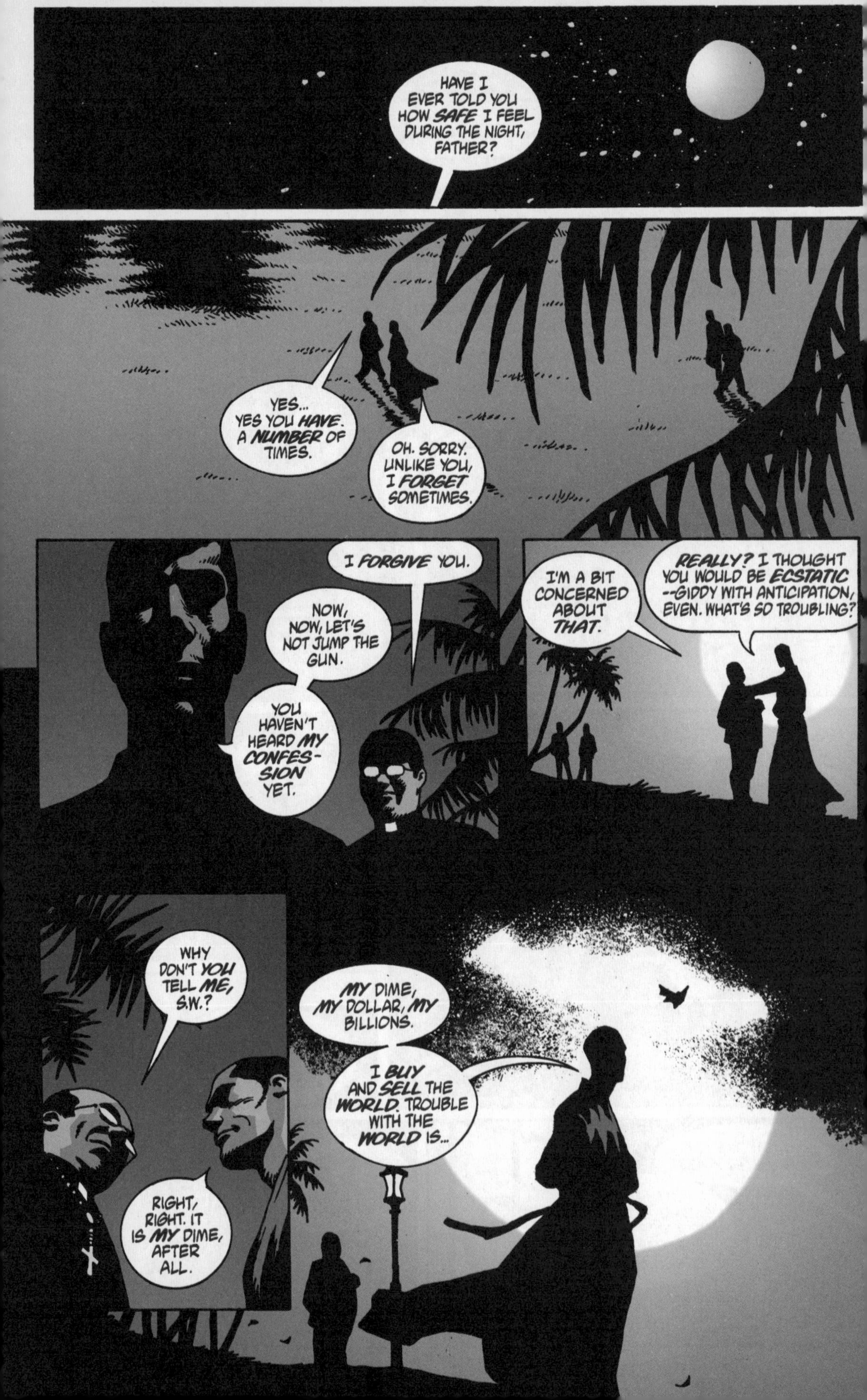
HAVE I EVER TOLD YOU HOW SAFE I FEEL DURING THE NIGHT, FATHER?
YES... YES YOU HAVE. A NUMBER OF TIMES.
OH. SORRY. UNLIKE YOU, I FORGET SOMETIMES.
I FORGIVE YOU.
NOW, NOW, LET'S NOT JUMP THE GUN.
YOU HAVEN'T HEARD MY CONFES-SION YET.
I'M A BIT CONCERNED ABOUT THAT.
REALLY? I THOUGHT YOU WOULD BE ECSTATIC --GIDDY WITH ANTICIPATION, EVEN. WHAT'S SO TROUBLING?
WHY DON'T YOU TELL ME, S.W.?
RIGHT, RIGHT. IT IS MY DIME, AFTER ALL.
MY DIME, MY DOLLAR, MY BILLIONS.
I BUY AND SELL THE WORLD. TROUBLE WITH THE WORLD IS...

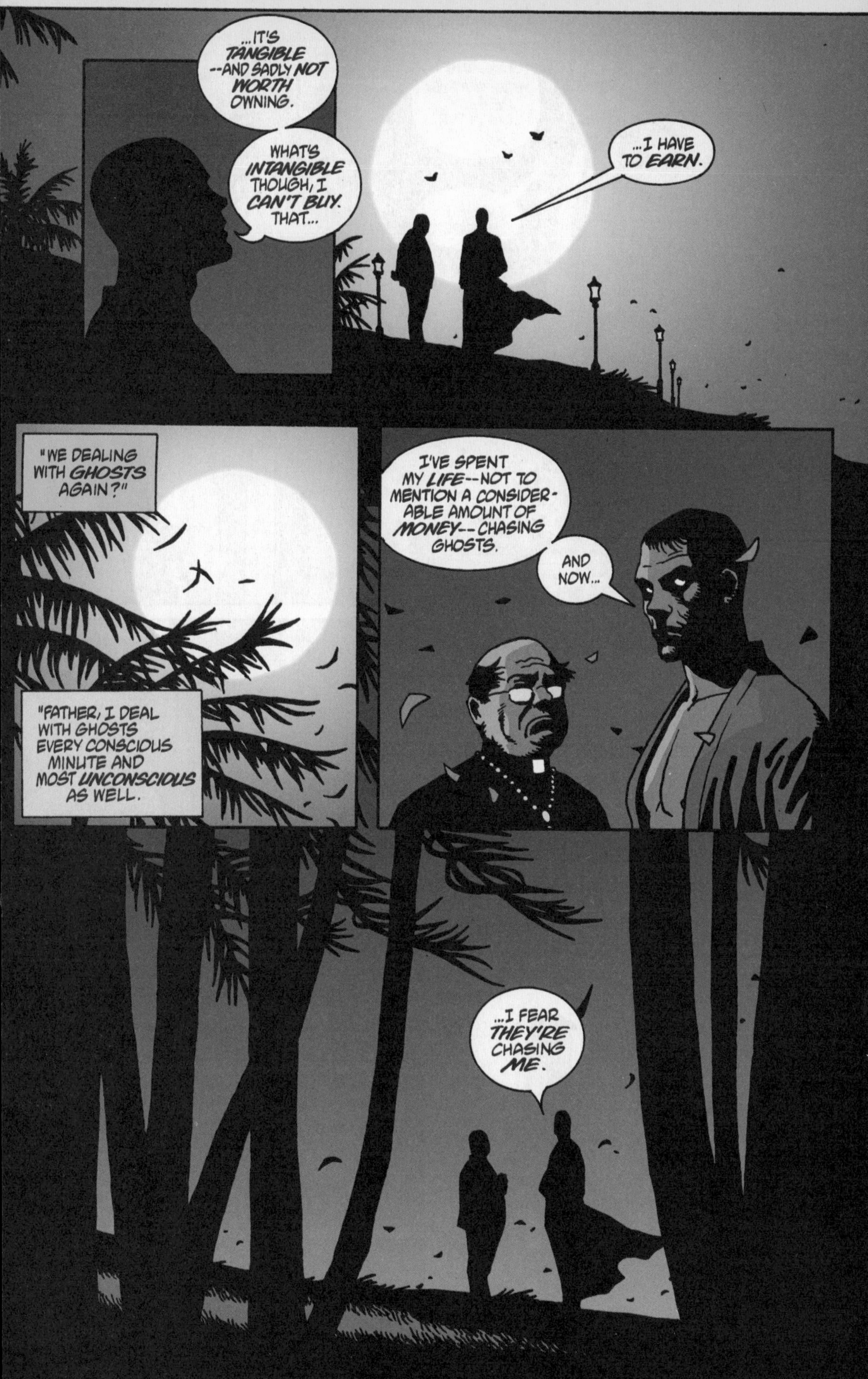
...IT'S TANGIBLE --AND SADLY NOT WORTH OWNING.
WHAT'S INTANGIBLE THOUGH, I CAN'T BUY. THAT...
...I HAVE TO EARN.
"WE DEALING WITH GHOSTS AGAIN?"
"FATHER, I DEAL WITH GHOSTS EVERY CONSCIOUS MINUTE AND MOST UNCONSCIOUS AS WELL.
I'VE SPENT MY LIFE--NOT TO MENTION A CONSIDERABLE AMOUNT OF MONEY-- CHASING GHOSTS.
AND NOW...
...I FEAR THEY'RE CHASING ME.

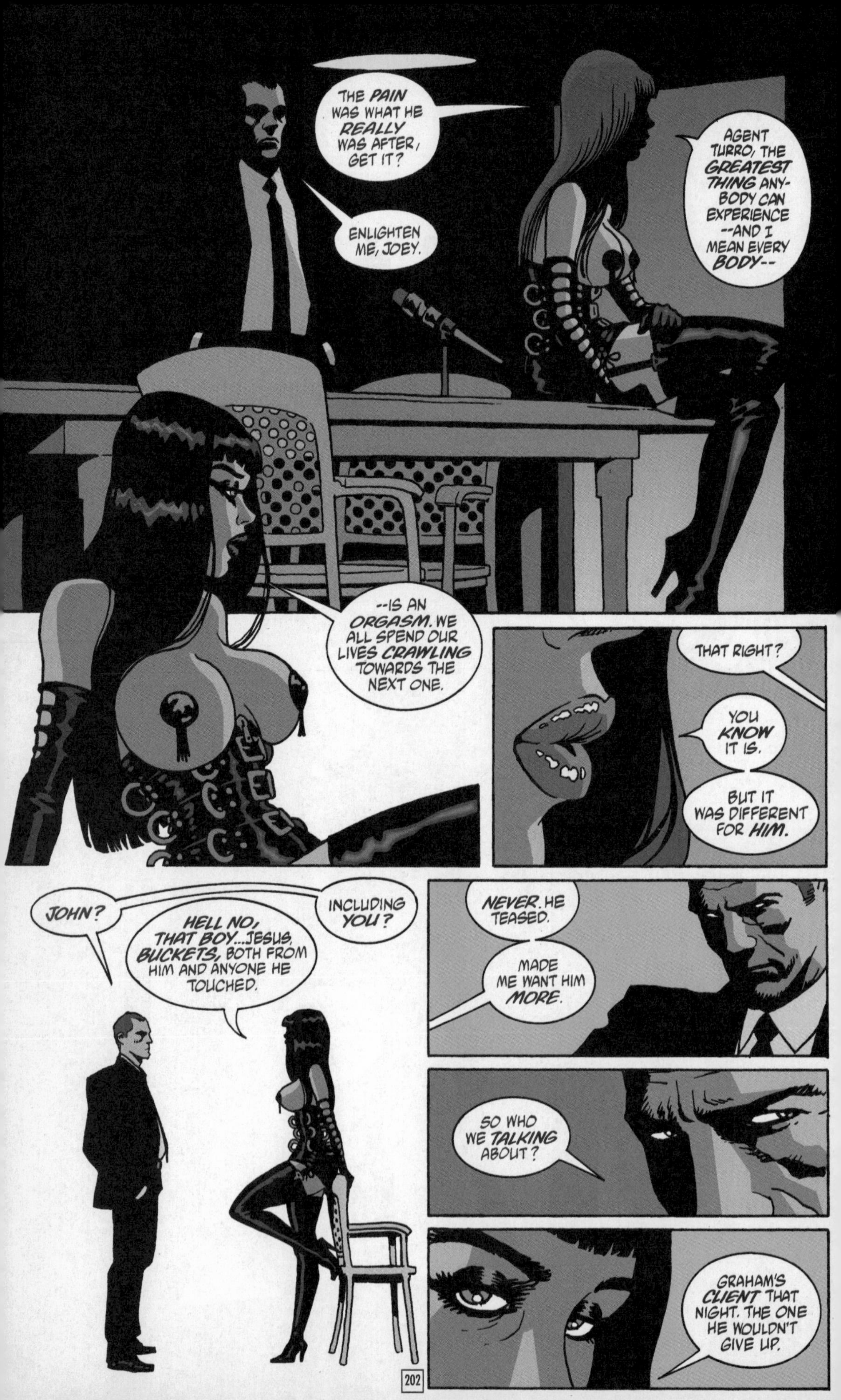
THE PAIN WAS WHAT HE REALLY WAS AFTER, GET IT?
AGENT TURRO, THE GREATEST THING ANYBODY CAN EXPERIENCE --AND I MEAN EVERY BODY--
ENLIGHTEN ME, JOEY.
--IS AN ORGASM. WE ALL SPEND OUR LIVES CRAWLING TOWARDS THE NEXT ONE.
THAT RIGHT?
YOU KNOW IT IS.
BUT IT WAS DIFFERENT FOR HIM.
JOHN?
INCLUDING YOU?
HELL NO, THAT BOY...JESUS, BUCKETS, BOTH FROM HIM AND ANYONE HE TOUCHED.
NEVER. HE TEASED.
MADE ME WANT HIM MORE.
SO WHO WE TALKING ABOUT?
GRAHAM'S CLIENT THAT NIGHT. THE ONE HE WOULDN'T GIVE UP.

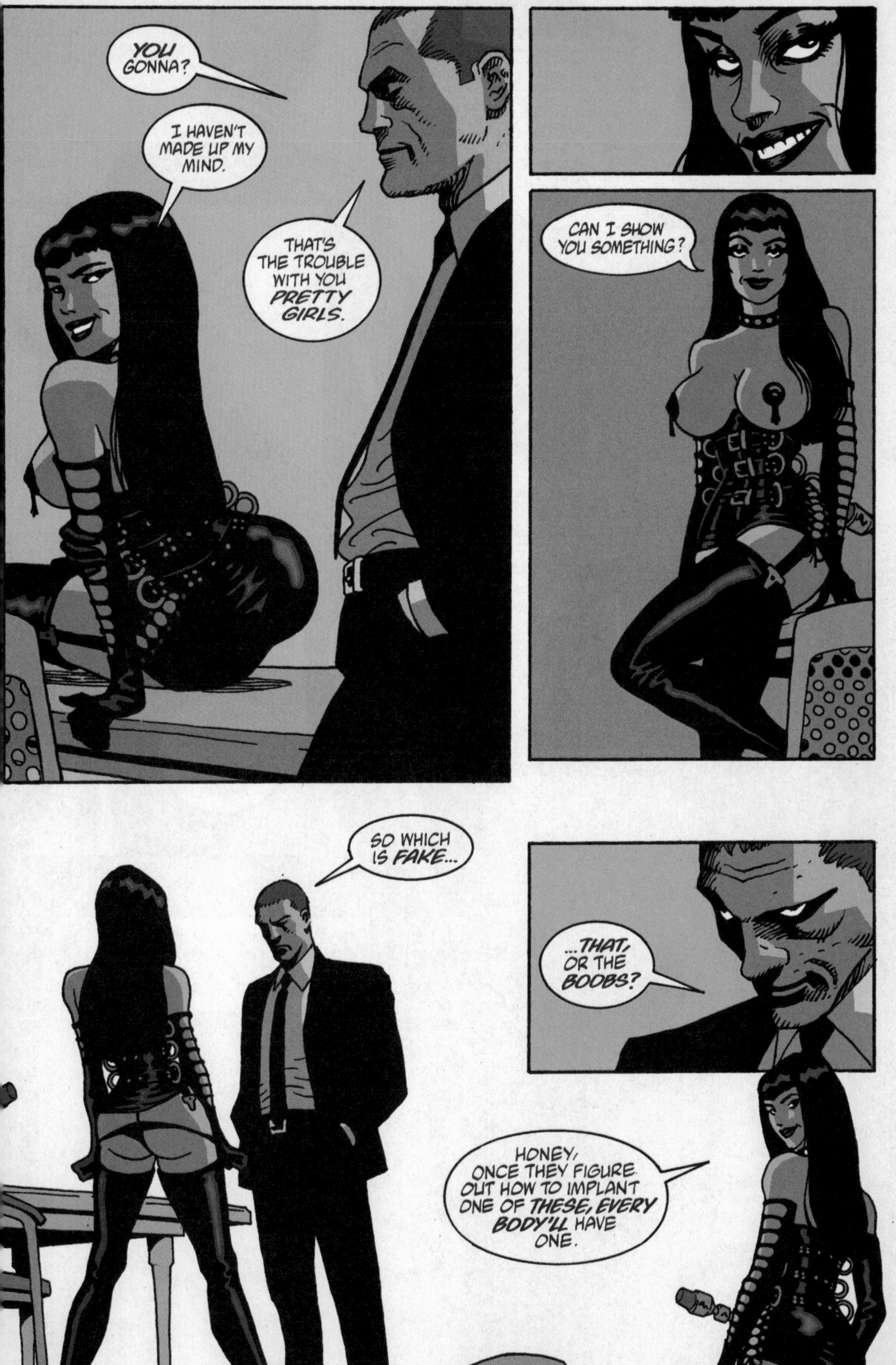
YOU GONNA?
I HAVEN'T MADE UP MY MIND.
THAT'S THE TROUBLE WITH YOU PRETTY GIRLS.
CAN I SHOW YOU SOMETHING?
SO WHICH IS FAKE...
...THAT, OR THE BOOBS?
HONEY, ONCE THEY FIGURE OUT HOW TO IMPLANT ONE OF THESE, EVERY BODY'LL HAVE ONE.

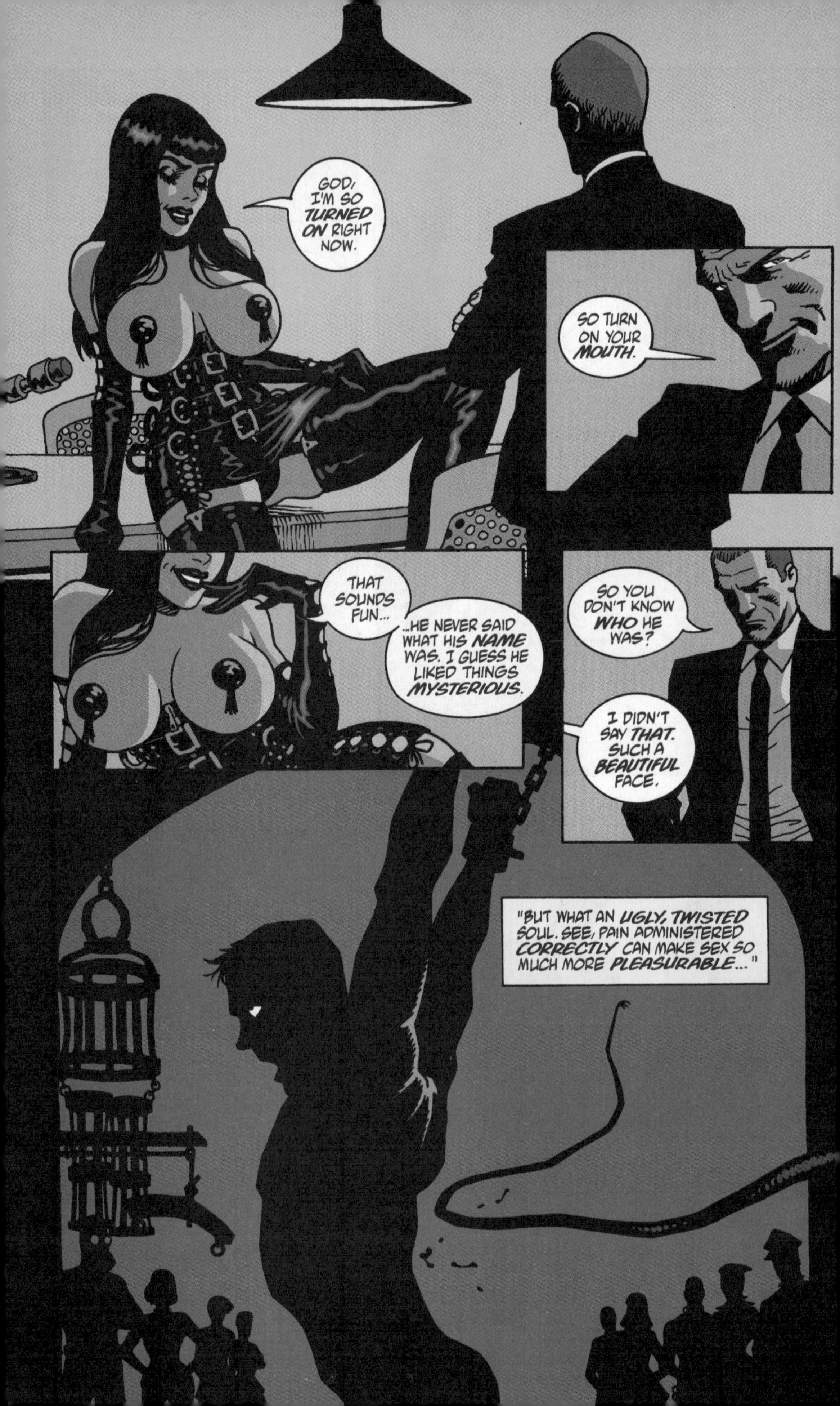
GOD, I'M SO TURNED ON RIGHT NOW.
SO TURN ON YOUR MOUTH.
THAT SOUNDS FUN...
...HE NEVER SAID WHAT HIS NAME WAS. I GUESS HE LIKED THINGS MYSTERIOUS.
SO YOU DON'T KNOW WHO HE WAS?
I DIDN'T SAY THAT. SUCH A BEAUTIFUL FACE.
"BUT WHAT AN UGLY, TWISTED SOUL. SEE, PAIN ADMINISTERED CORRECTLY CAN MAKE SEX SO MUCH MORE PLEASURABLE..."

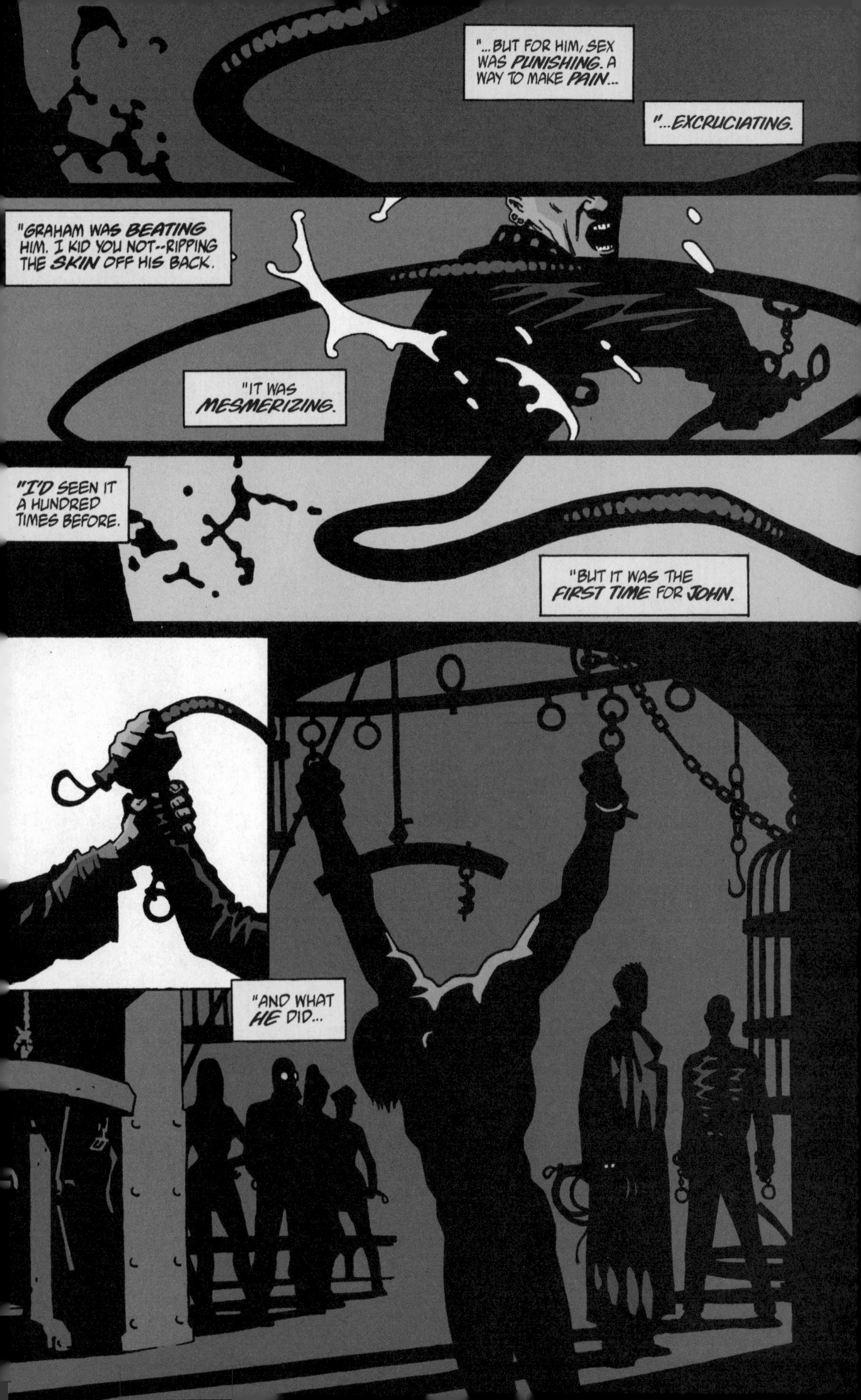
"...BUT FOR HIM, SEX WAS PUNISHING. A WAY TO MAKE PAIN...
"...EXCRUCIATING.
"GRAHAM WAS BEATING HIM. I KID YOU NOT--RIPPING THE SKIN OFF HIS BACK.
"IT WAS MESMERIZING.
"I'D SEEN IT A HUNDRED TIMES BEFORE.
"BUT IT WAS THE FIRST TIME FOR JOHN.
"AND WHAT HE DID...

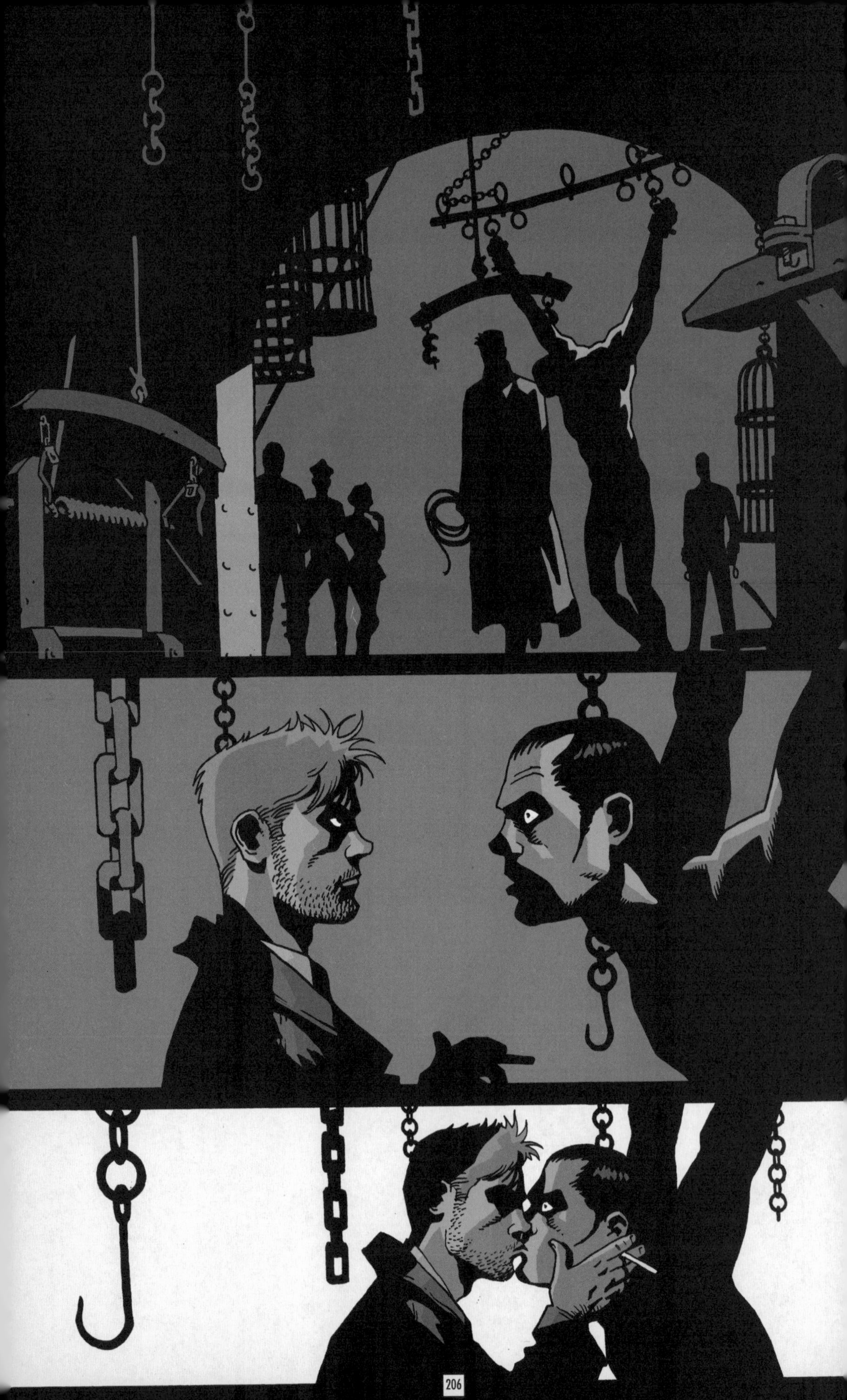

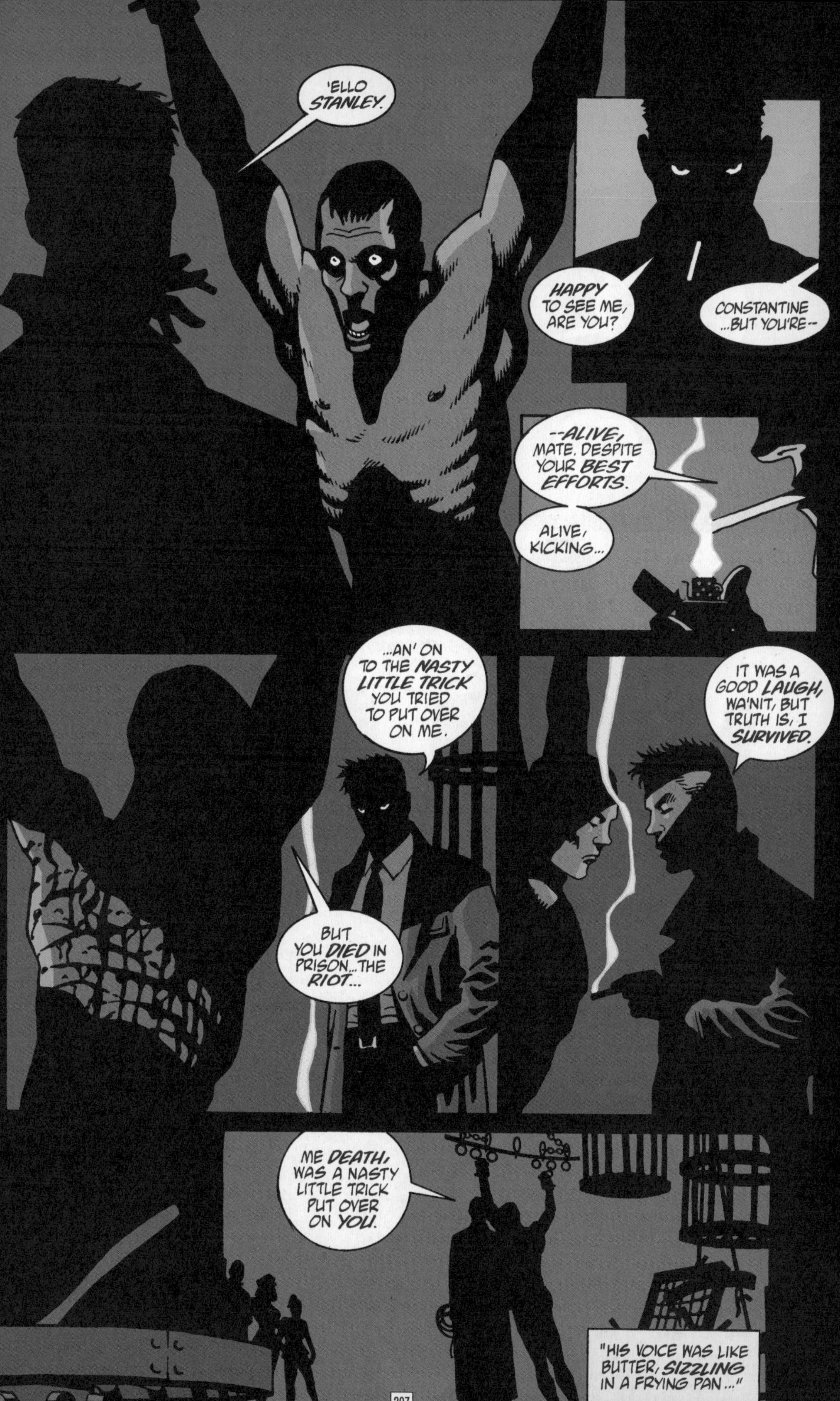
'ELLO STANLEY.
HAPPY TO SEE ME, ARE YOU?
CONSTANTINE ...BUT YOU'RE--
--ALIVE, MATE. DESPITE YOUR BEST EFFORTS.
ALIVE, KICKING...
...AN' ON TO THE NASTY LITTLE TRICK YOU TRIED TO PUT OVER ON ME.
BUT YOU DIED IN PRISON...THE RIOT...
IT WAS A GOOD LAUGH, WA'NIT, BUT TRUTH IS, I SURVIVED.
ME DEATH, WAS A NASTY LITTLE TRICK PUT OVER ON YOU.
"HIS VOICE WAS LIKE BUTTER, SIZZLING IN A FRYING PAN..."

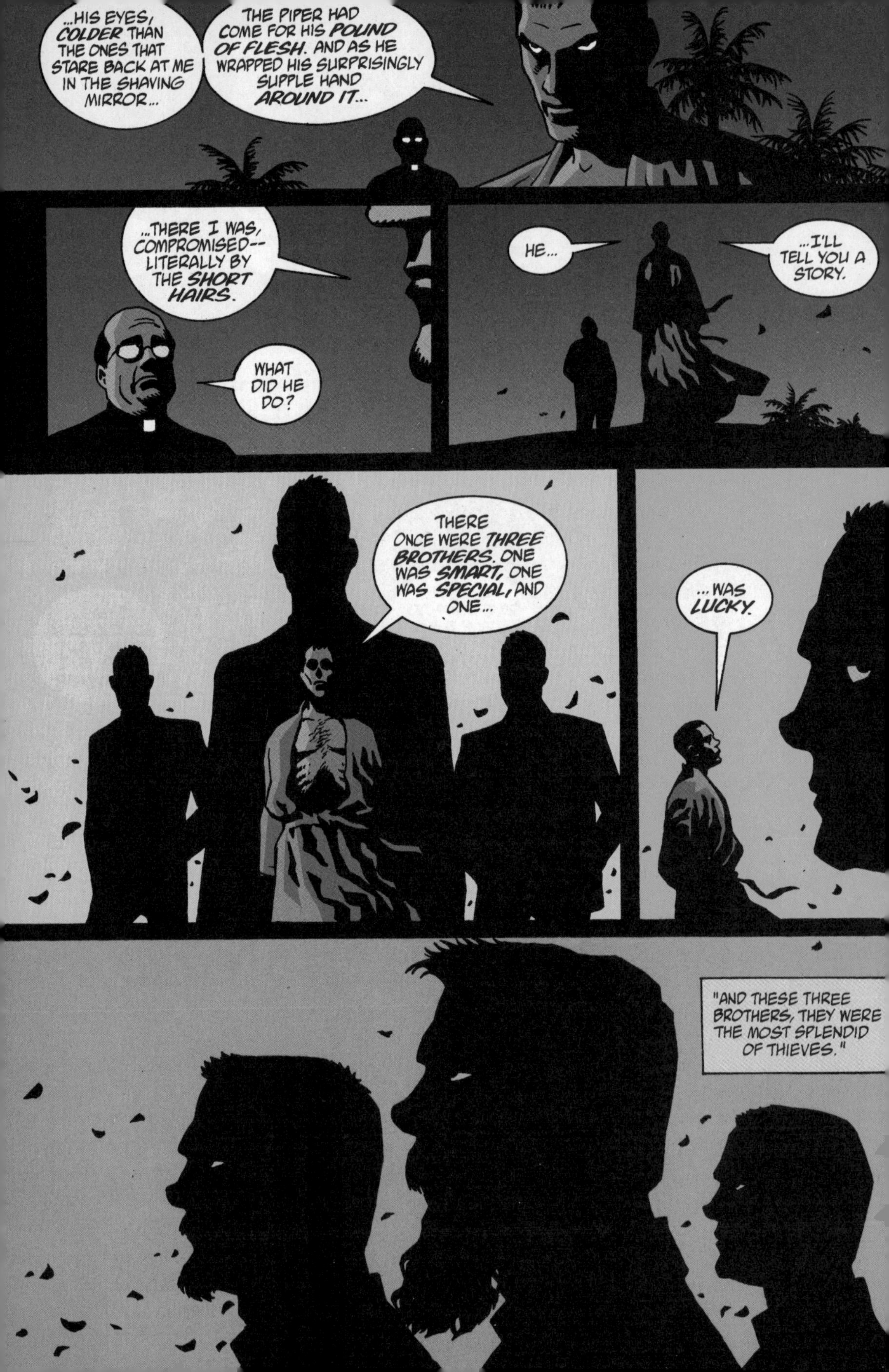
...HIS EYES, COLDER THAN THE ONES THAT STARE BACK AT ME IN THE SHAVING MIRROR...
THE PIPER HAD COME FOR HIS POUND OF FLESH. AND AS HE WRAPPED HIS SURPRISINGLY SUPPLE HAND AROUND IT...
...THERE I WAS, COMPROMISED--LITERALLY BY THE SHORT HAIRS.
WHAT DID HE DO?
HE...
...I'LL TELL YOU A STORY.
THERE ONCE WERE THREE BROTHERS. ONE WAS SMART, ONE WAS SPECIAL, AND ONE...
...WAS LUCKY.
"AND THESE THREE BROTHERS, THEY WERE THE MOST SPLENDID OF THIEVES."

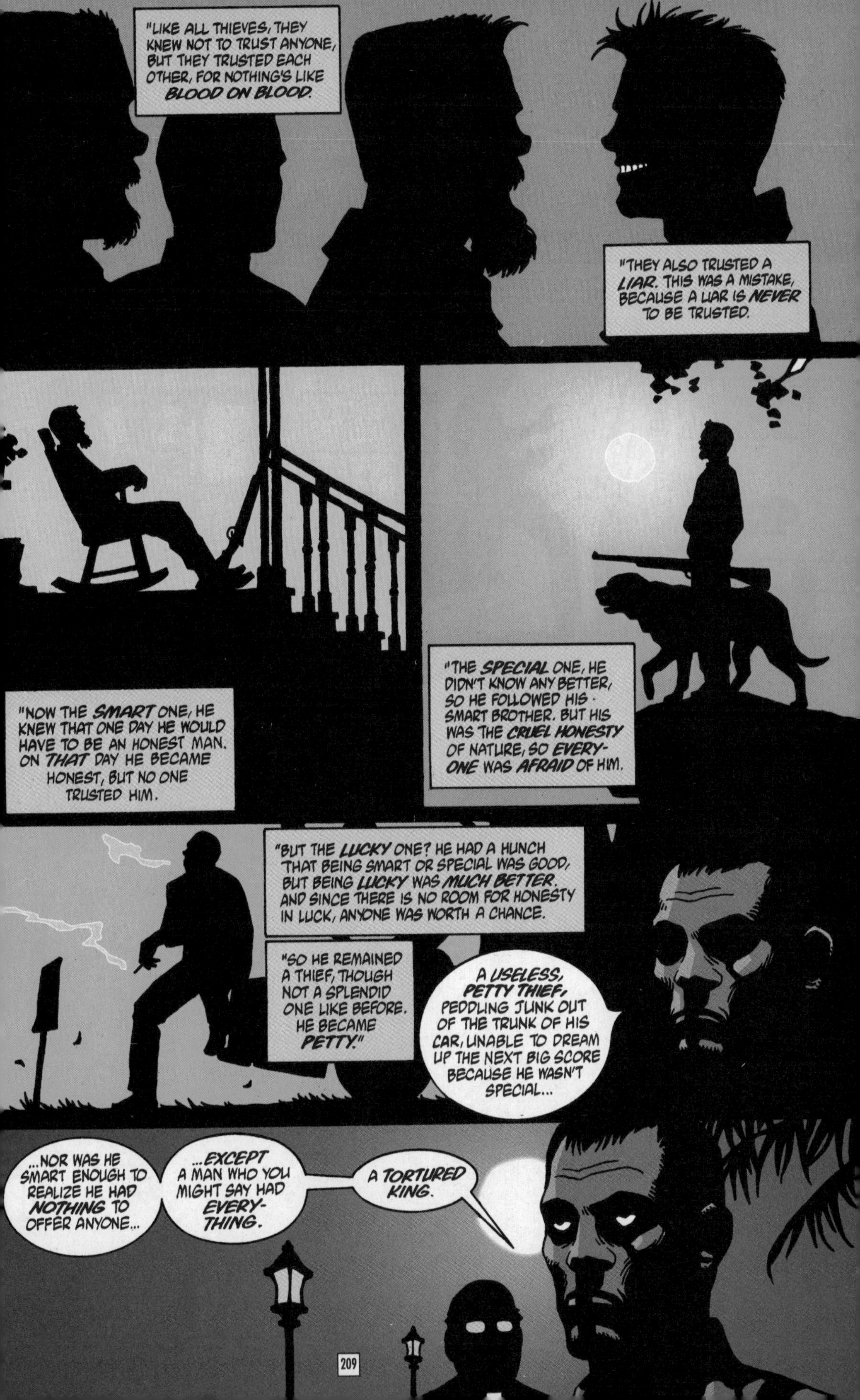
"LIKE ALL THIEVES, THEY KNEW NOT TO TRUST ANYONE, BUT THEY TRUSTED EACH OTHER, FOR NOTHING'S LIKE BLOOD ON BLOOD.
"THEY ALSO TRUSTED A LIAR. THIS WAS A MISTAKE, BECAUSE A LIAR IS NEVER TO BE TRUSTED.
"NOW THE SMART ONE, HE KNEW THAT ONE DAY HE WOULD HAVE TO BE AN HONEST MAN. ON THAT DAY HE BECAME HONEST, BUT NO ONE TRUSTED HIM.
"THE SPECIAL ONE, HE DIDN'T KNOW ANY BETTER, SO HE FOLLOWED HIS SMART BROTHER. BUT HIS WAS THE CRUEL HONESTY OF NATURE, SO EVERYONE WAS AFRAID OF HIM.
"BUT THE LUCKY ONE? HE HAD A HUNCH THAT BEING SMART OR SPECIAL WAS GOOD, BUT BEING LUCKY WAS MUCH BETTER. AND SINCE THERE IS NO ROOM FOR HONESTY IN LUCK, ANYONE WAS WORTH A CHANCE.
"SO HE REMAINED A THIEF, THOUGH NOT A SPLENDID ONE LIKE BEFORE. HE BECAME PETTY."
A USELESS, PETTY THIEF, PEDDLING JUNK OUT OF THE TRUNK OF HIS CAR, UNABLE TO DREAM UP THE NEXT BIG SCORE BECAUSE HE WASN'T SPECIAL...
...NOR WAS HE SMART ENOUGH TO REALIZE HE HAD NOTHING TO OFFER ANYONE...
...EXCEPT A MAN WHO YOU MIGHT SAY HAD EVERYTHING.
A TORTURED KING.

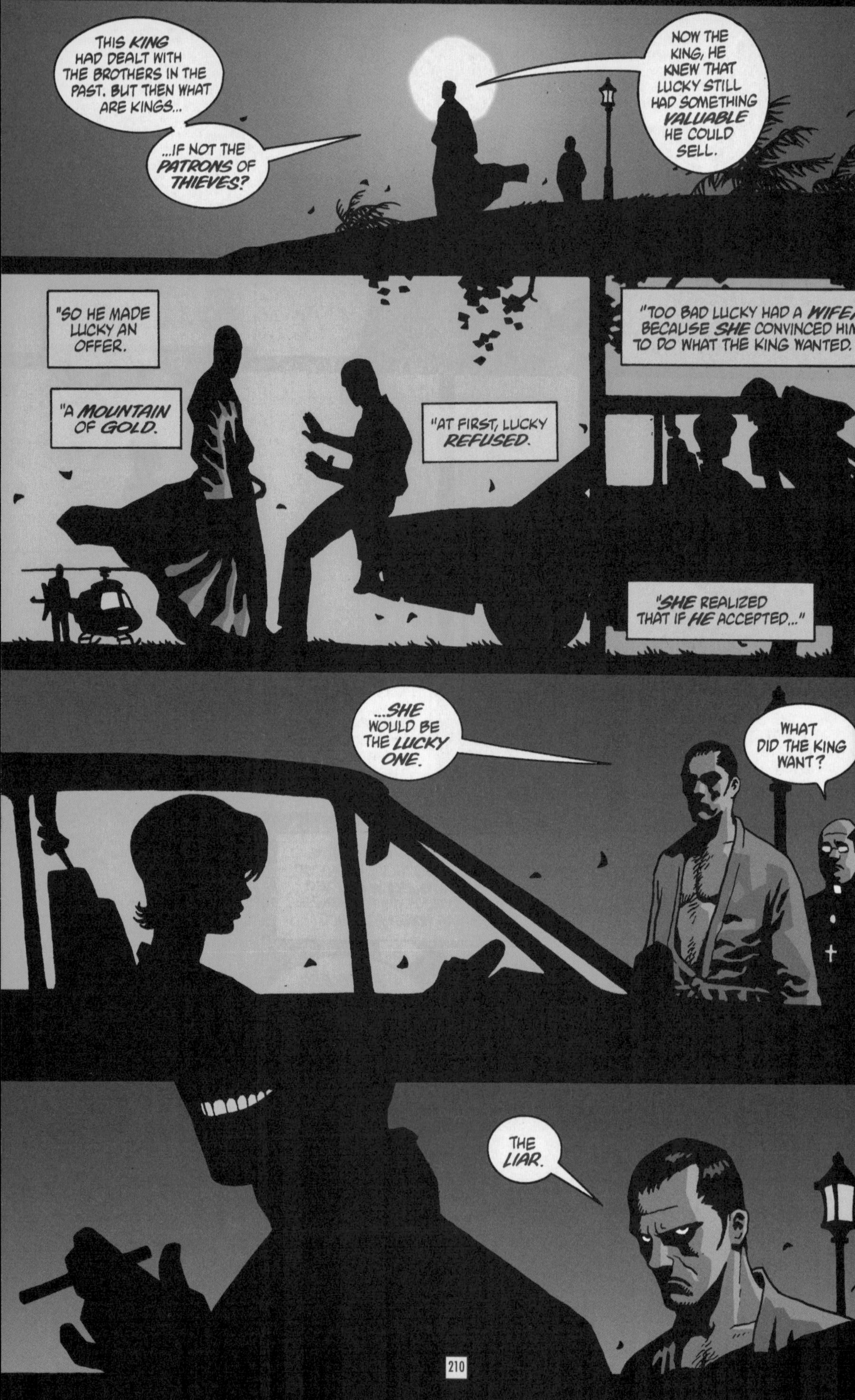
THIS KING HAD DEALT WITH THE BROTHERS IN THE PAST. BUT THEN WHAT ARE KINGS...
...IF NOT THE PATRONS OF THIEVES?
NOW THE KING, HE KNEW THAT LUCKY STILL HAD SOMETHING VALUABLE HE COULD SELL.
"SO HE MADE LUCKY AN OFFER.
"A MOUNTAIN OF GOLD.
"AT FIRST, LUCKY REFUSED.
"TOO BAD LUCKY HAD A WIFE, BECAUSE SHE CONVINCED HIM TO DO WHAT THE KING WANTED.
"SHE REALIZED THAT IF HE ACCEPTED..."
...SHE WOULD BE THE LUCKY ONE.
WHAT DID THE KING WANT?
THE LIAR.

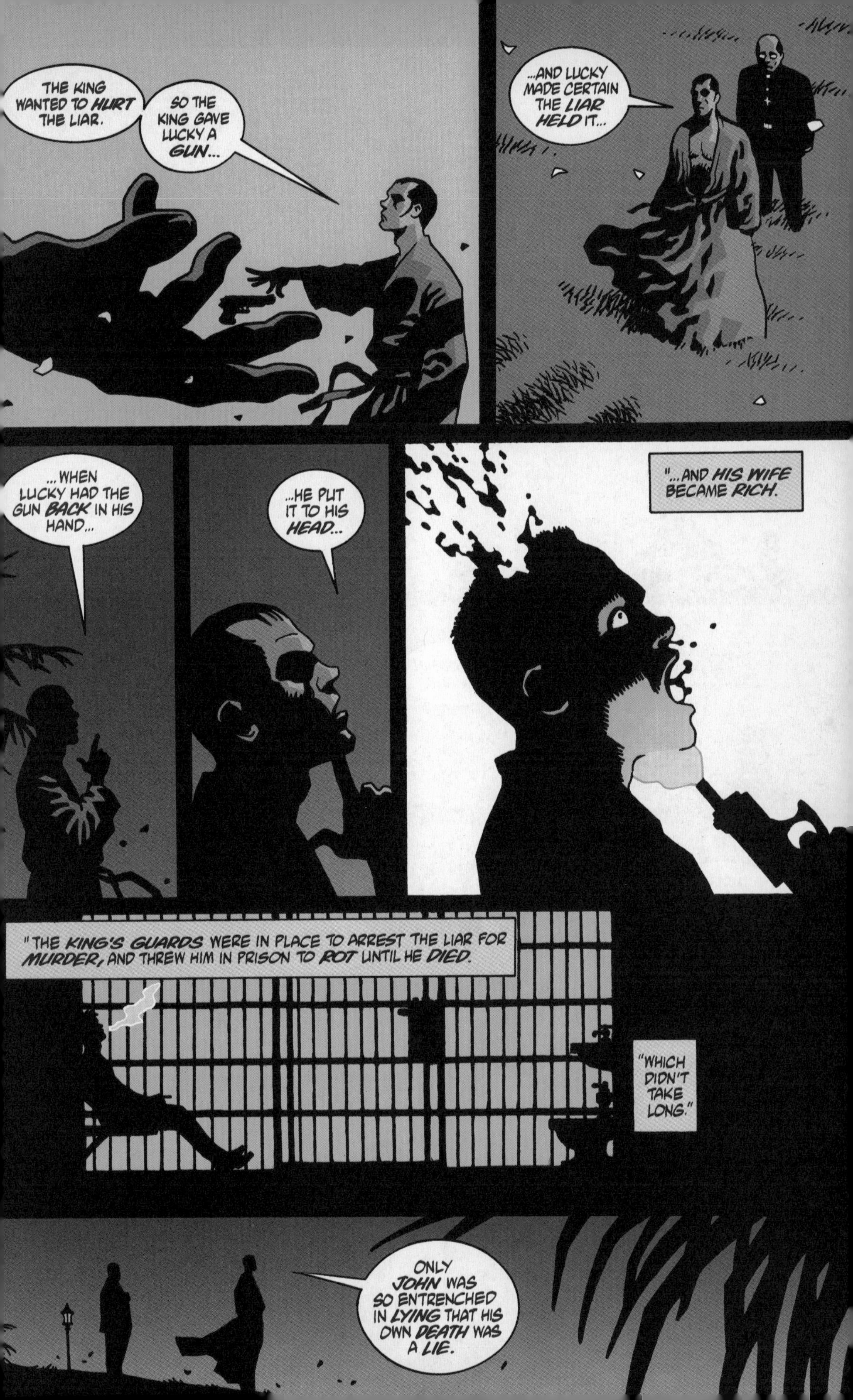
THE KING WANTED TO HURT THE LIAR.
SO THE KING GAVE LUCKY A GUN...
...AND LUCKY MADE CERTAIN THE LIAR HELD IT...
... WHEN LUCKY HAD THE GUN BACK IN HIS HAND...
...HE PUT IT TO HIS HEAD...
"...AND HIS WIFE BECAME RICH.
"THE KING'S GUARDS WERE IN PLACE TO ARREST THE LIAR FOR MURDER, AND THREW HIM IN PRISON TO ROT UNTIL HE DIED.
"WHICH DIDN'T TAKE LONG."
ONLY JOHN WAS SO ENTRENCHED IN LYING THAT HIS OWN DEATH WAS A LIE.

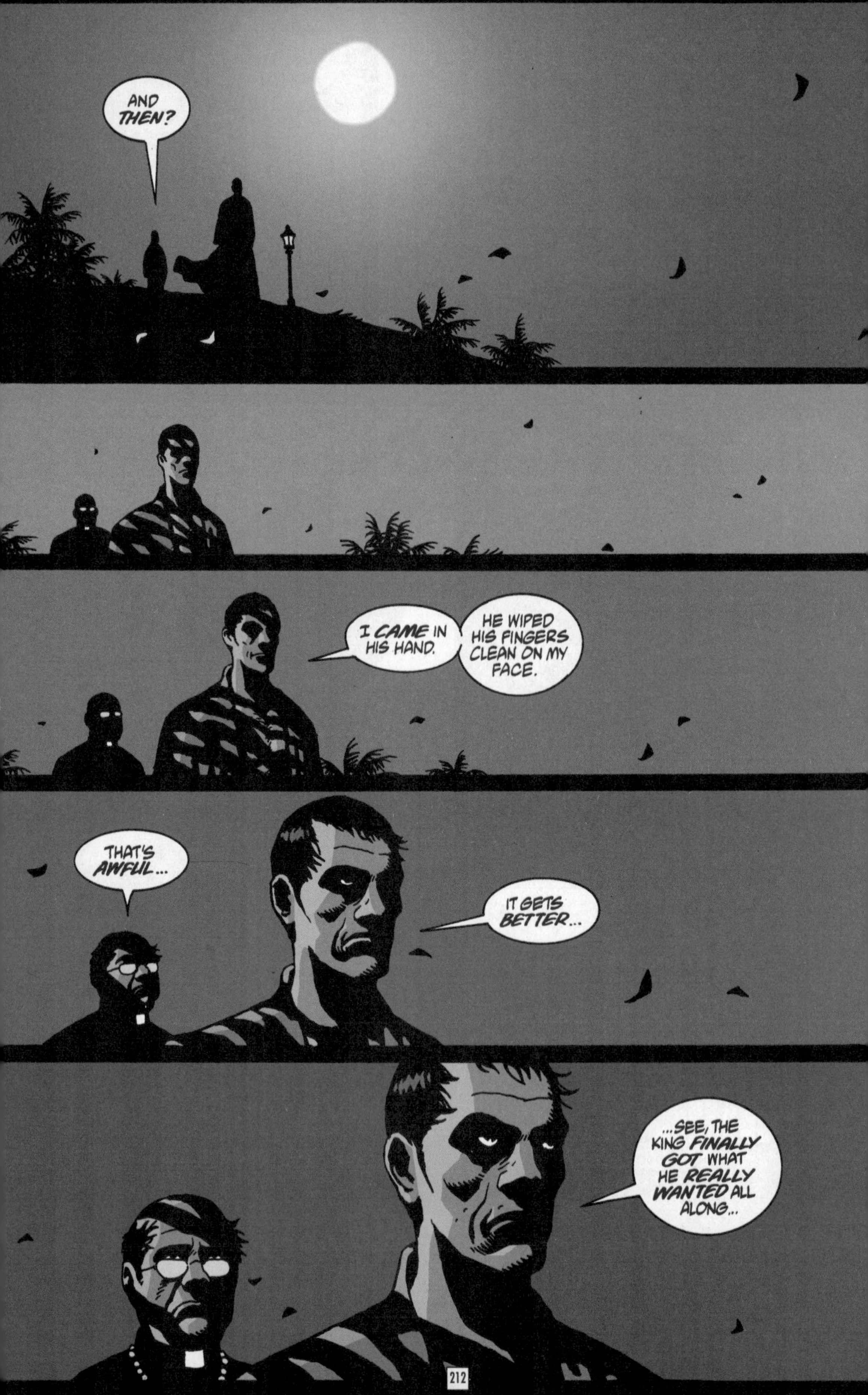
AND THEN?
I CAME IN HIS HAND.
HE WIPED HIS FINGERS CLEAN ON MY FACE.
THAT'S AWFUL...
IT GETS BETTER...
...SEE, THE KING FINALLY GOT WHAT HE REALLY WANTED ALL ALONG...

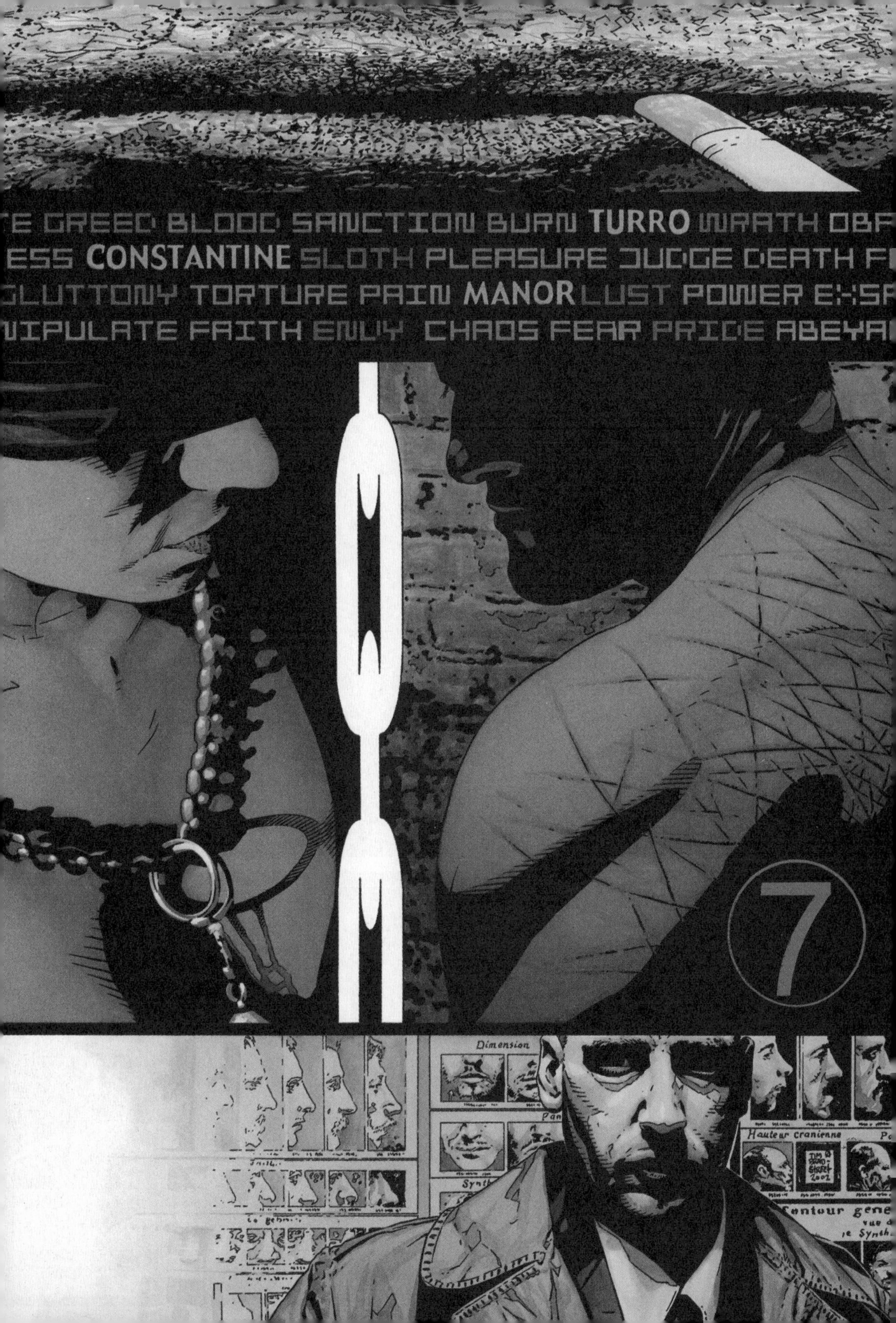
GREED BLOOD SANCTION BURN TURRO WRATH
CONSTANTINE SLOTH PLEASURE JUDGE DEATH
TORTURE PAIN MANOR LUST POWER
FAITH ENVY CHAOS FEAR PRIDE
7
Dimension
Hauteur cranienne

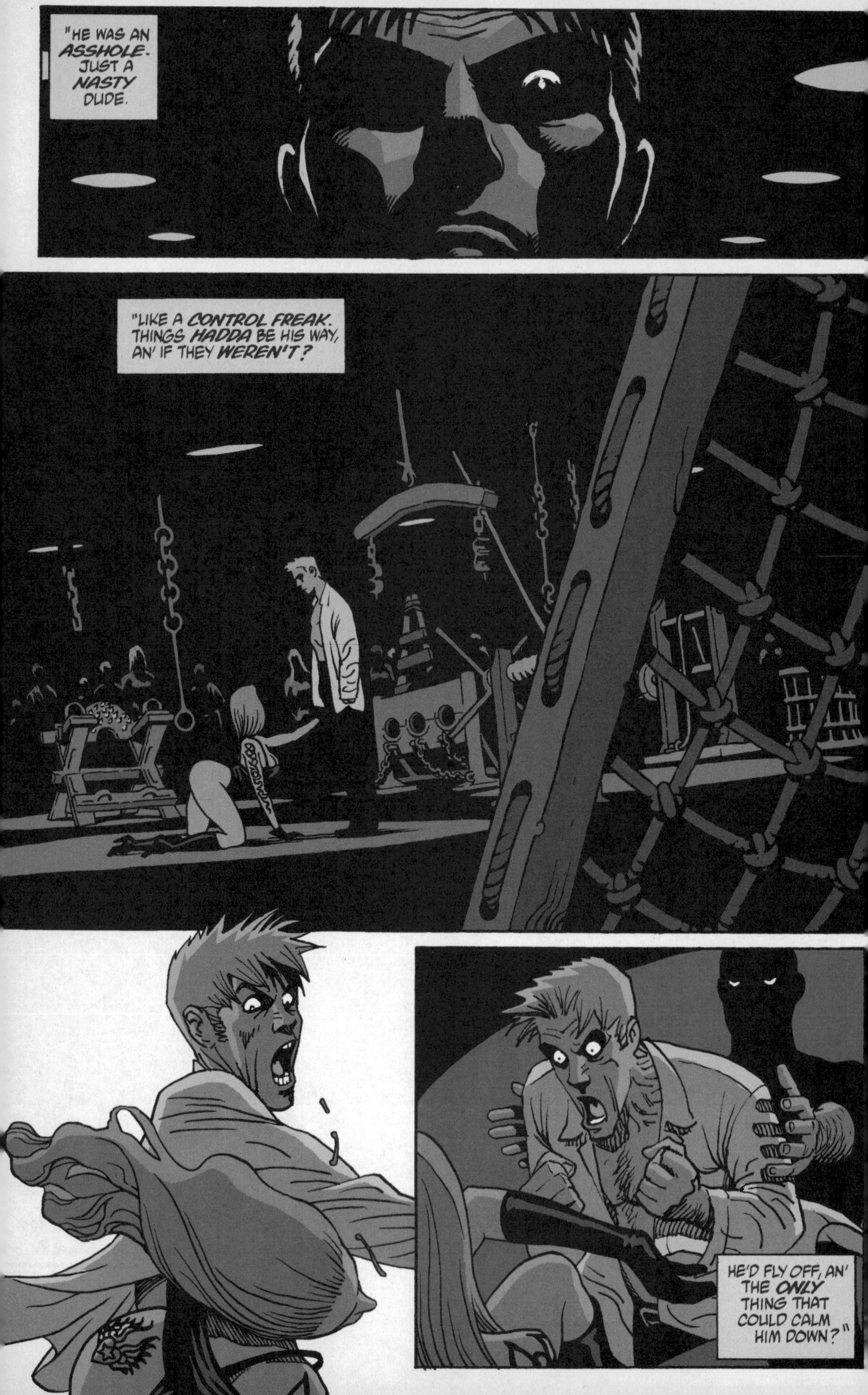
"HE WAS AN ASSHOLE. JUST A NASTY DUDE.
"LIKE A CONTROL FREAK. THINGS HADDA BE HIS WAY, AN' IF THEY WEREN'T?
HE'D FLY OFF, AN' THE ONLY THING THAT COULD CALM HIM DOWN?"

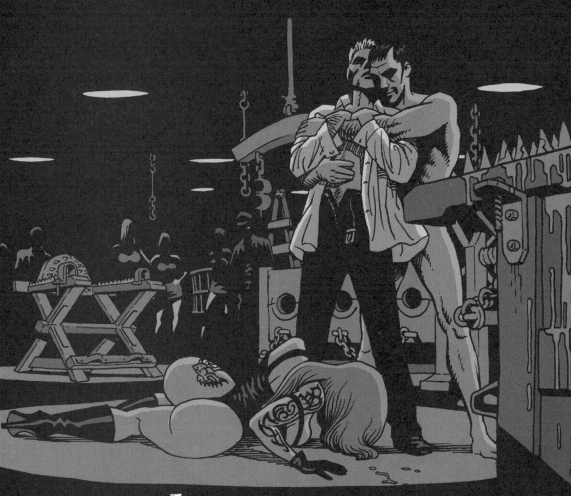

"WAS HIS **BOYFRIEND.**"

Ashes & Dust in the City of Angels

part four

Brian Azzarello, WRITER   **Marcelo Frusin,** ARTIST

Lee Loughridge
colors

Clem Robins
letters

Tim Bradstreet
cover

Zachary Rau
assistant editor

Will Dennis
editor

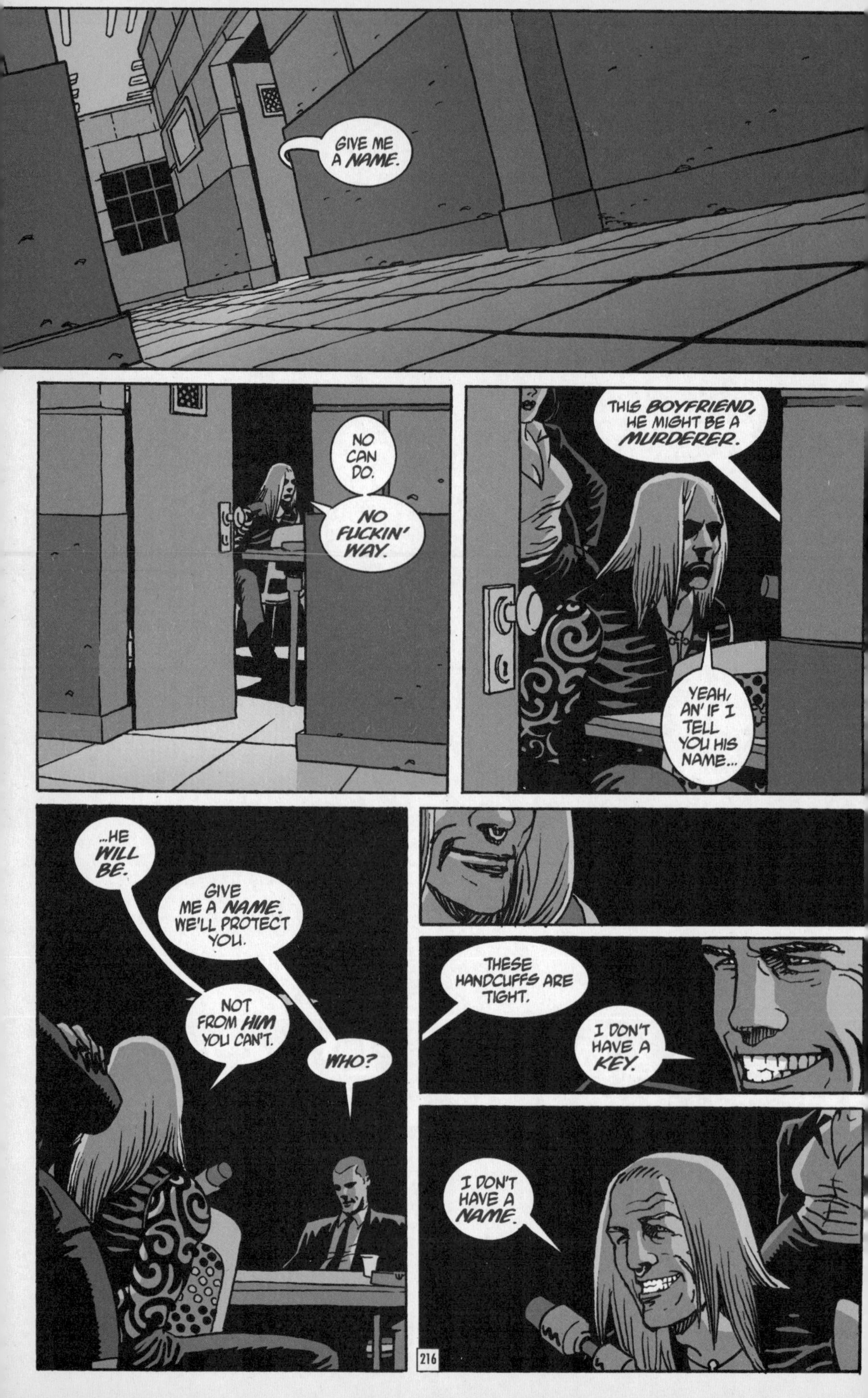
GIVE ME A NAME.
NO CAN DO.
NO FUCKIN' WAY.
THIS BOYFRIEND, HE MIGHT BE A MURDERER.
YEAH, AN' IF I TELL YOU HIS NAME...
...HE WILL BE.
GIVE ME A NAME. WE'LL PROTECT YOU.
NOT FROM HIM YOU CAN'T.
WHO?
THESE HANDCUFFS ARE TIGHT.
I DON'T HAVE A KEY.
I DON'T HAVE A NAME.

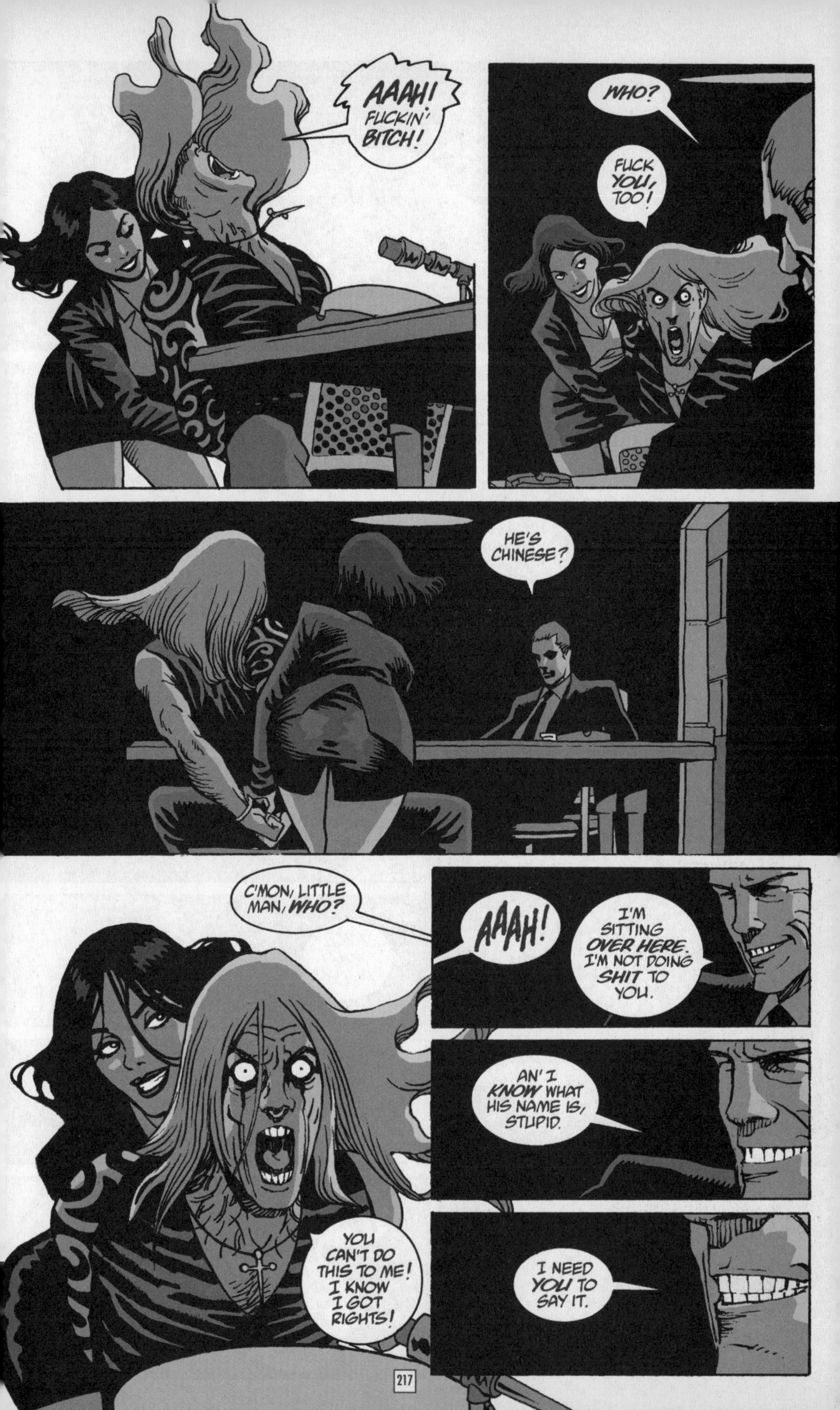
AAAH! FUCKIN' BITCH!
WHO?
FUCK YOU, TOO!
HE'S CHINESE?
C'MON, LITTLE MAN, WHO?
AAAH!
I'M SITTING OVER HERE. I'M NOT DOING SHIT TO YOU.
AN' I KNOW WHAT HIS NAME IS, STUPID.
YOU CAN'T DO THIS TO ME! I KNOW I GOT RIGHTS!
I NEED YOU TO SAY IT.

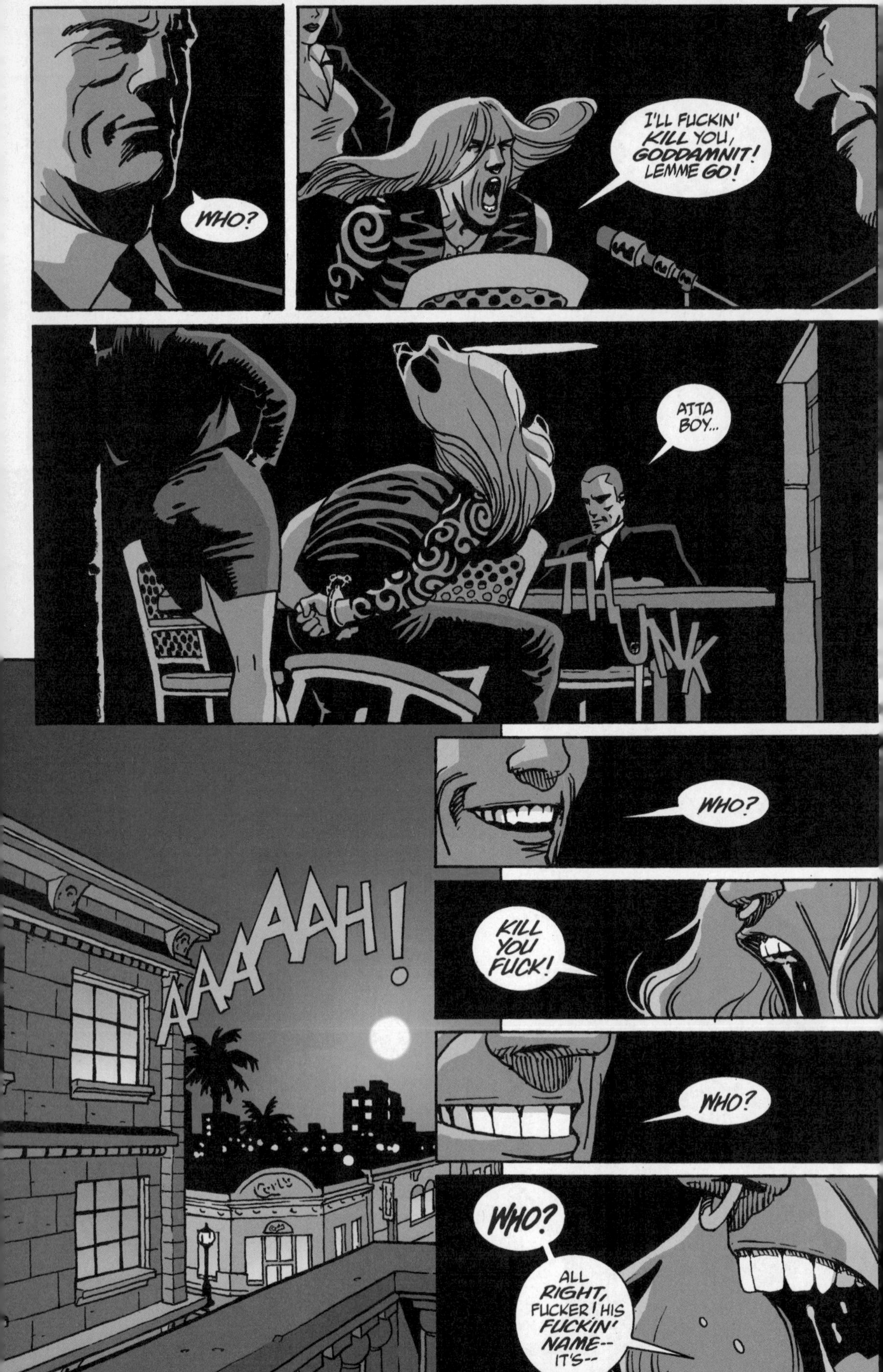
WHO?
I'LL FUCKIN' KILL YOU, GODDAMNIT! LEMME GO!
ATTA BOY...
THUNK
AAAAAH!
WHO?
KILL YOU FUCK!
WHO?
WHO?
ALL RIGHT, FUCKER! HIS FUCKIN' NAME-- IT'S--

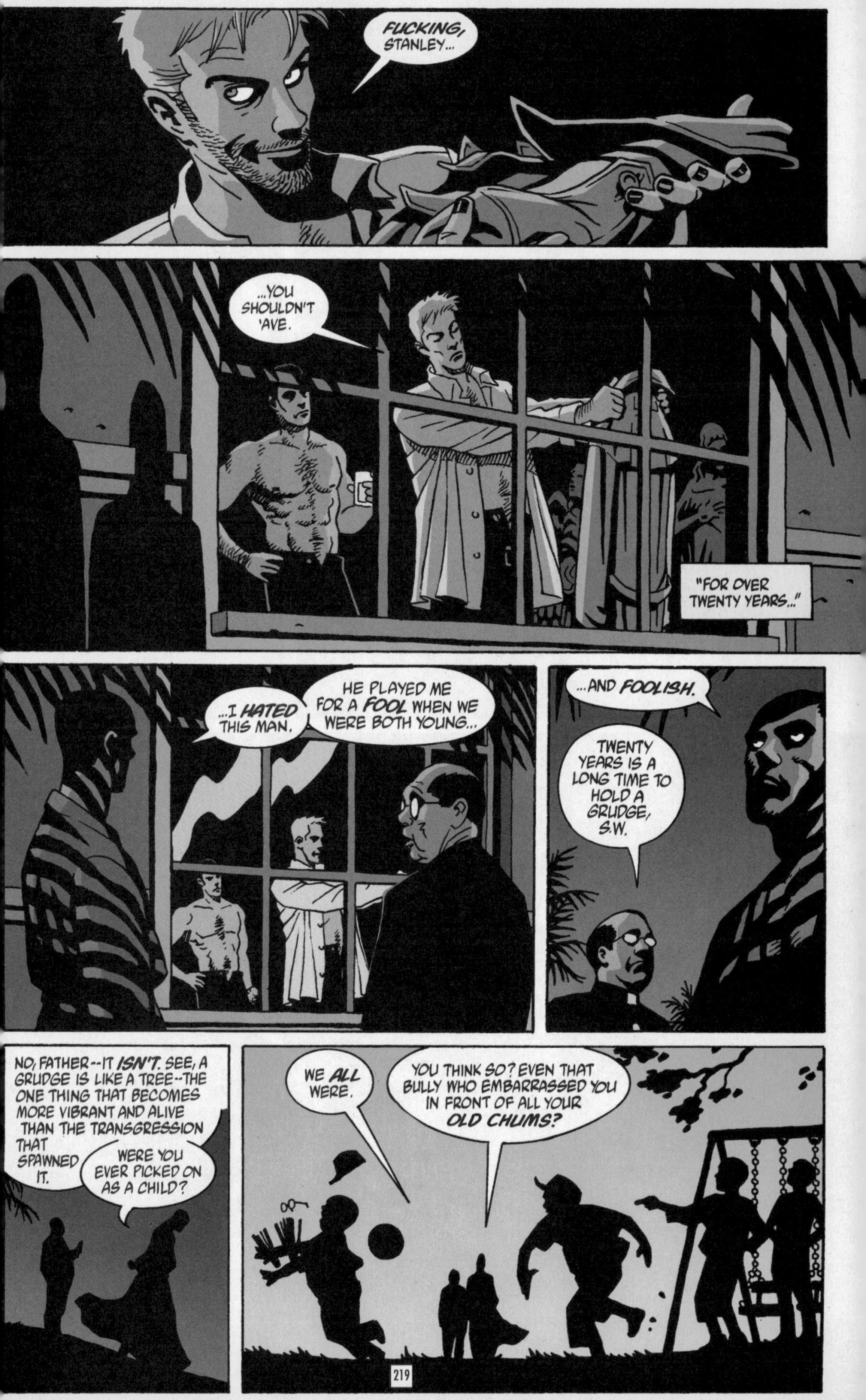

FUCKING, STANLEY...
...YOU SHOULDN'T 'AVE.
"FOR OVER TWENTY YEARS..."
...I HATED THIS MAN.
HE PLAYED ME FOR A FOOL WHEN WE WERE BOTH YOUNG...
...AND FOOLISH.
TWENTY YEARS IS A LONG TIME TO HOLD A GRUDGE, S.W.
NO, FATHER--IT ISN'T. SEE, A GRUDGE IS LIKE A TREE--THE ONE THING THAT BECOMES MORE VIBRANT AND ALIVE THAN THE TRANSGRESSION THAT SPAWNED IT.
WERE YOU EVER PICKED ON AS A CHILD?
WE ALL WERE.
YOU THINK SO? EVEN THAT BULLY WHO EMBARRASSED YOU IN FRONT OF ALL YOUR OLD CHUMS?

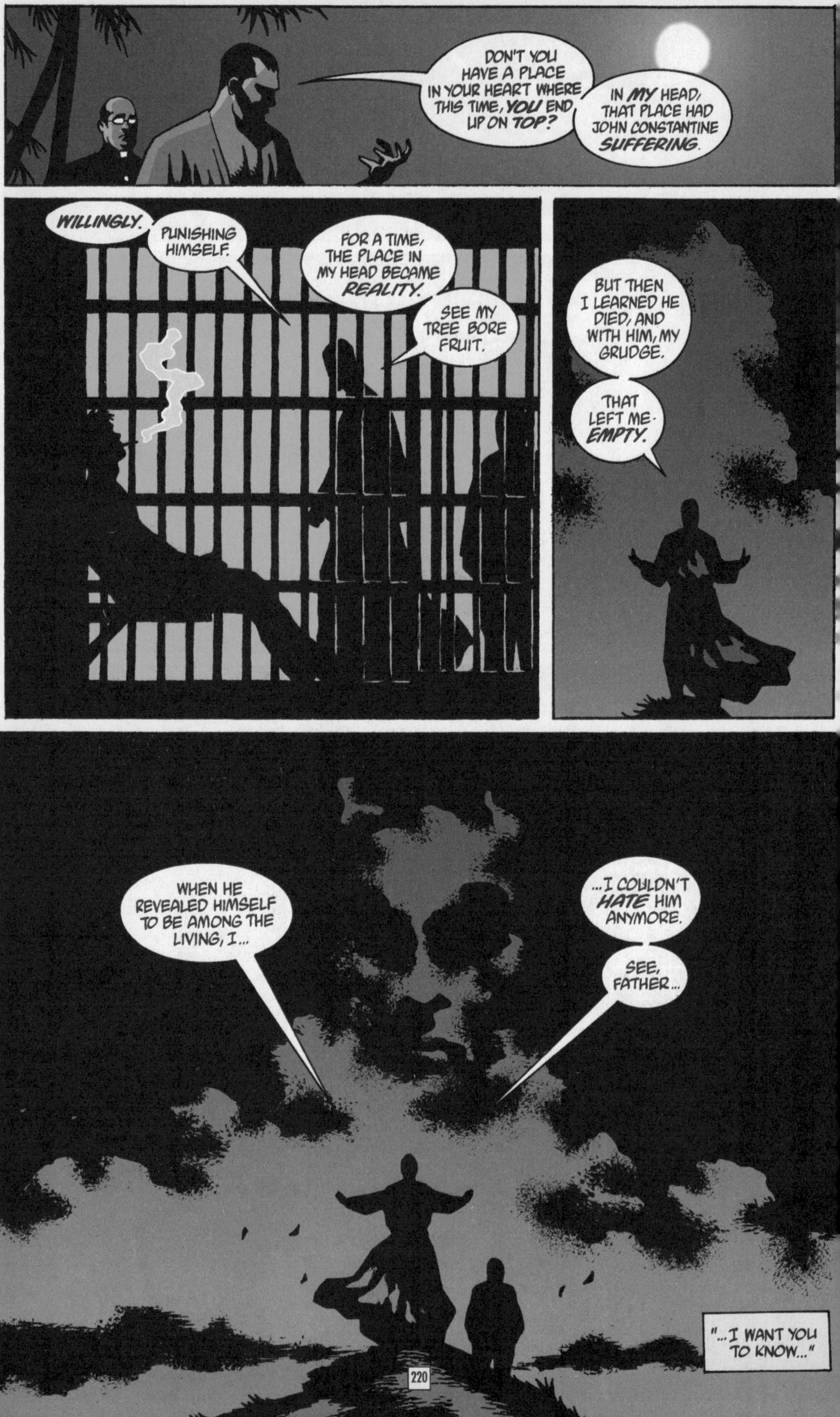
DON'T YOU HAVE A PLACE IN YOUR HEART WHERE THIS TIME, YOU END UP ON TOP?
IN MY HEAD, THAT PLACE HAD JOHN CONSTANTINE SUFFERING.
WILLINGLY.
PUNISHING HIMSELF.
FOR A TIME, THE PLACE IN MY HEAD BECAME REALITY.
SEE MY TREE BORE FRUIT.
BUT THEN I LEARNED HE DIED, AND WITH HIM, MY GRUDGE.
THAT LEFT ME EMPTY.
WHEN HE REVEALED HIMSELF TO BE AMONG THE LIVING, I...
...I COULDN'T HATE HIM ANYMORE.
SEE, FATHER...
"...I WANT YOU TO KNOW..."

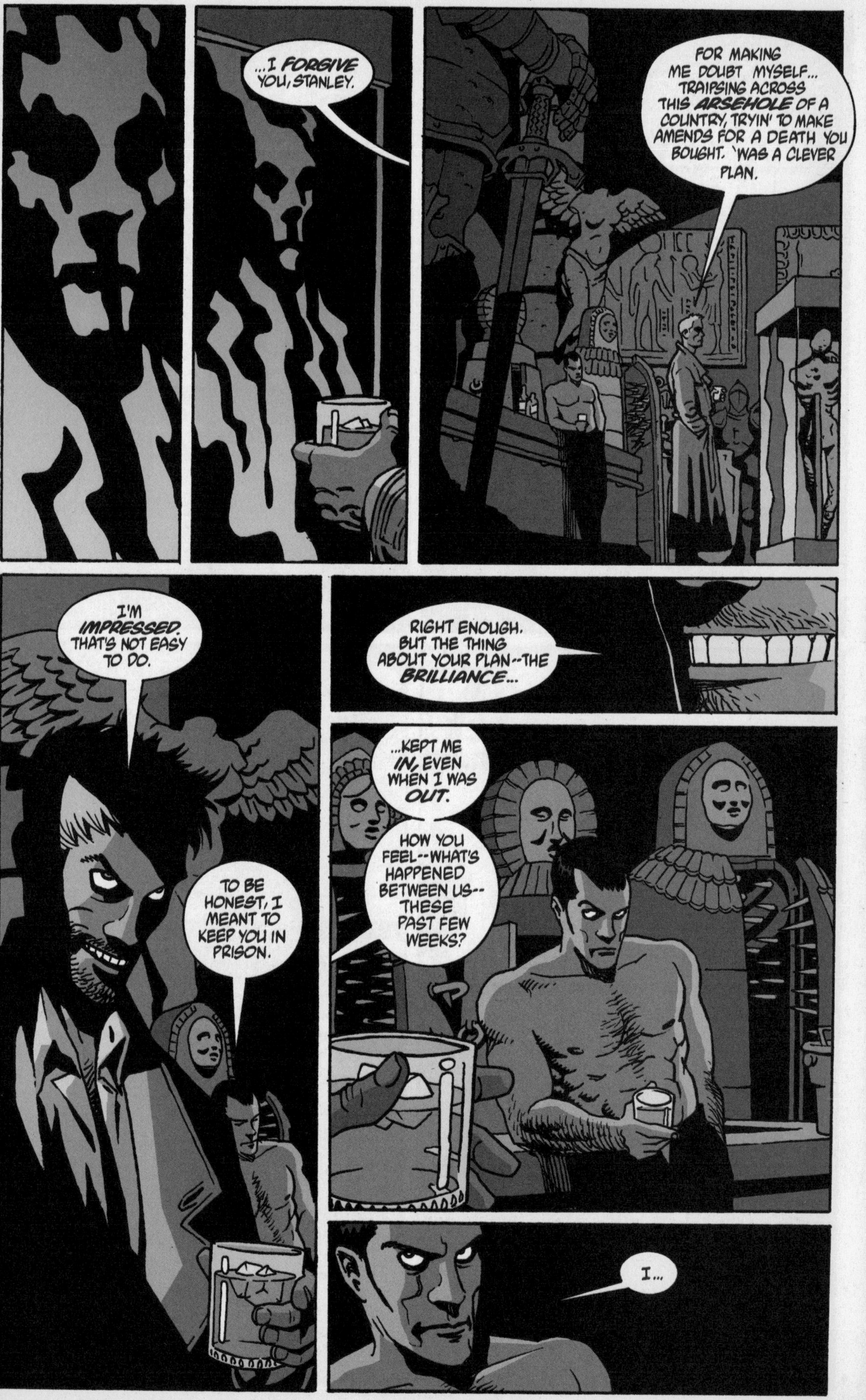
...I FORGIVE YOU, STANLEY.
FOR MAKING ME DOUBT MYSELF... TRAIPSING ACROSS THIS ARSEHOLE OF A COUNTRY, TRYIN' TO MAKE AMENDS FOR A DEATH YOU BOUGHT. 'WAS A CLEVER PLAN.
I'M IMPRESSED. THAT'S NOT EASY TO DO.
TO BE HONEST, I MEANT TO KEEP YOU IN PRISON.
RIGHT ENOUGH. BUT THE THING ABOUT YOUR PLAN--THE BRILLIANCE...
...KEPT ME IN, EVEN WHEN I WAS OUT.
HOW YOU FEEL--WHAT'S HAPPENED BETWEEN US--THESE PAST FEW WEEKS?
I...

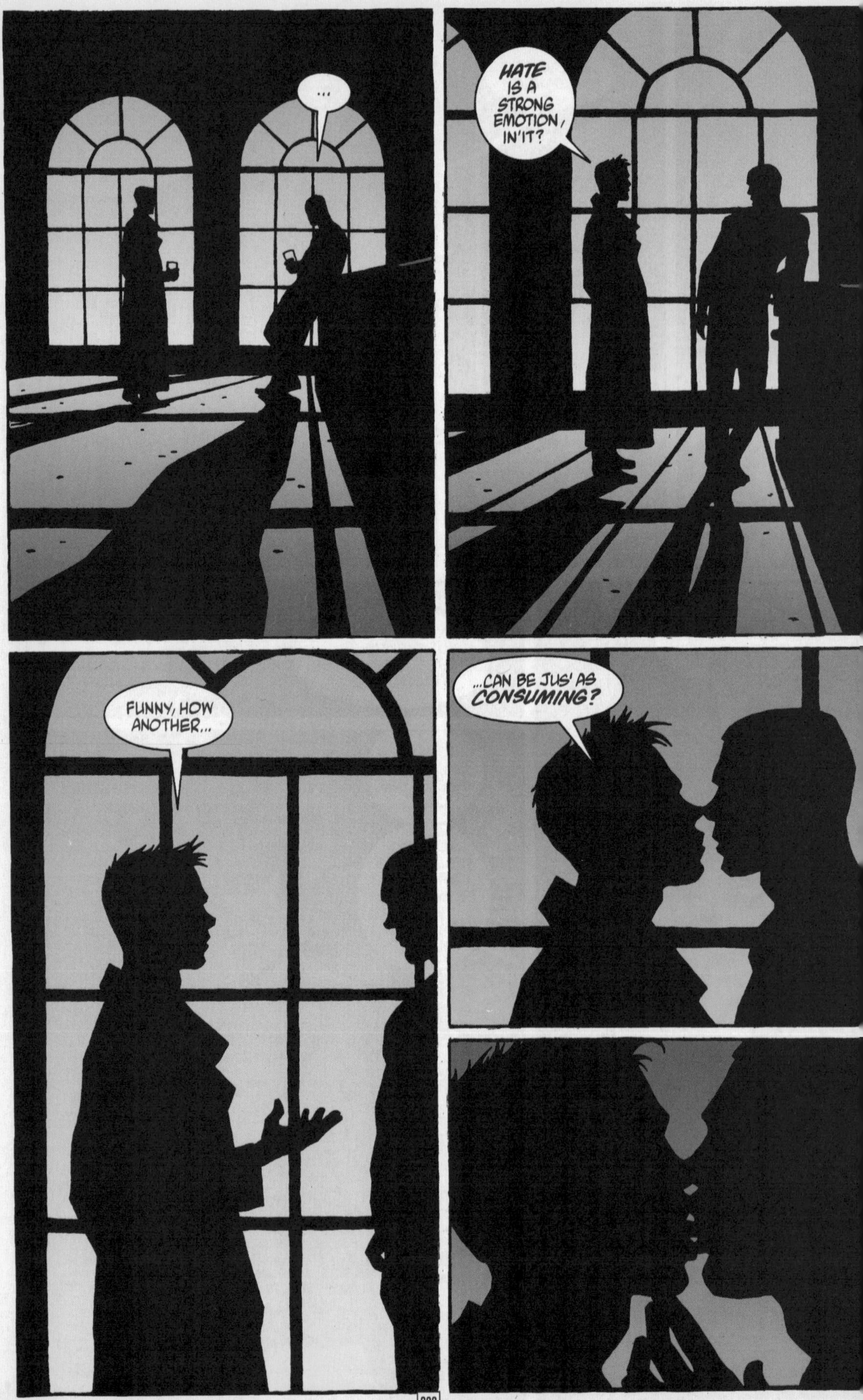
...
HATE IS A STRONG EMOTION, IN'IT?
FUNNY, HOW ANOTHER...
...CAN BE JUS' AS CONSUMING?

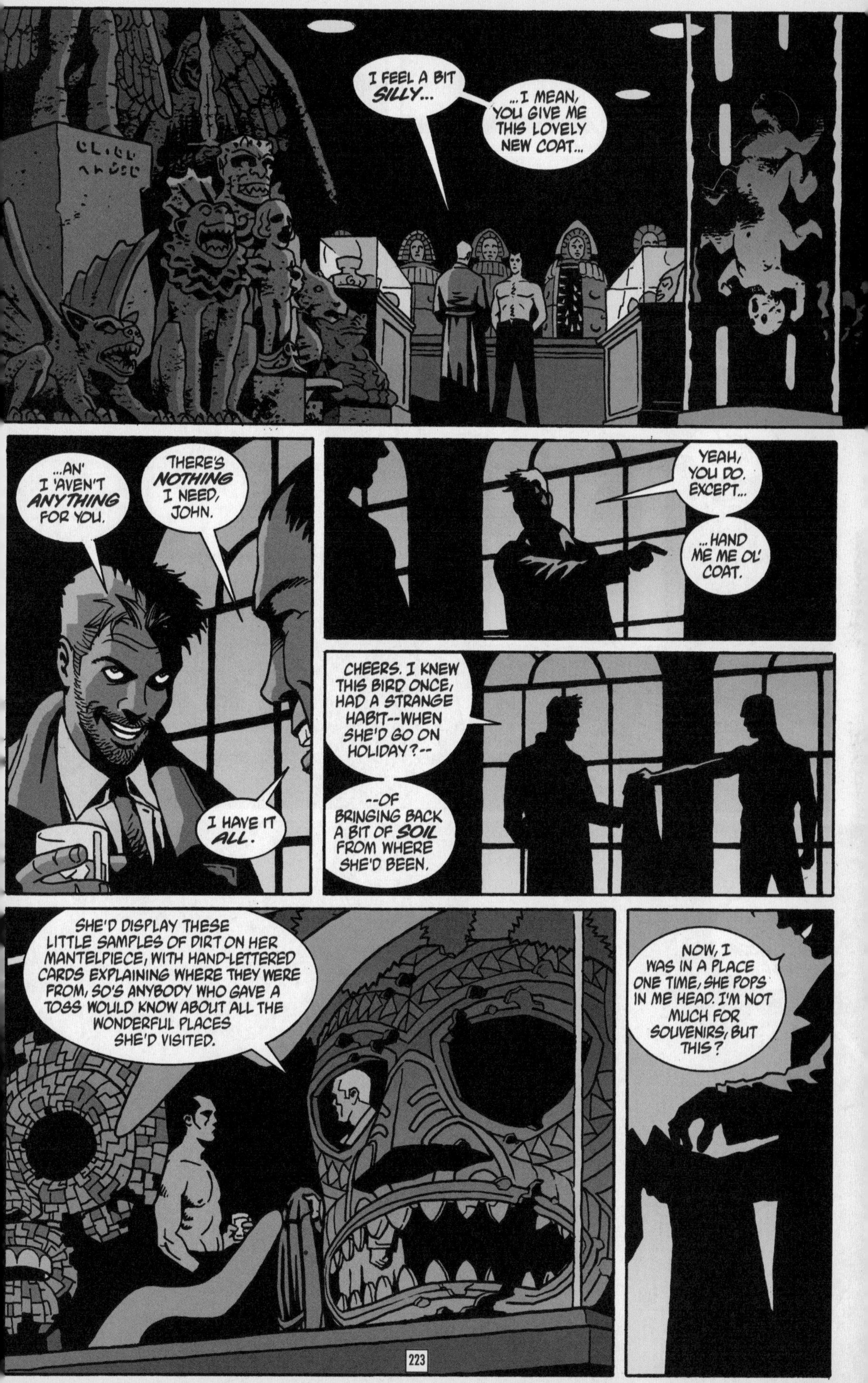
I FEEL A BIT SILLY...
...I MEAN, YOU GIVE ME THIS LOVELY NEW COAT...
...AN' I 'AVEN'T ANYTHING FOR YOU.
THERE'S NOTHING I NEED, JOHN.
I HAVE IT ALL.
YEAH, YOU DO. EXCEPT...
...HAND ME ME OL' COAT.
CHEERS. I KNEW THIS BIRD ONCE, HAD A STRANGE HABIT--WHEN SHE'D GO ON HOLIDAY?--
--OF BRINGING BACK A BIT OF SOIL FROM WHERE SHE'D BEEN.
SHE'D DISPLAY THESE LITTLE SAMPLES OF DIRT ON HER MANTELPIECE, WITH HAND-LETTERED CARDS EXPLAINING WHERE THEY WERE FROM, SO'S ANYBODY WHO GAVE A TOSS WOULD KNOW ABOUT ALL THE WONDERFUL PLACES SHE'D VISITED.
NOW, I WAS IN A PLACE ONE TIME, SHE POPS IN ME HEAD. I'M NOT MUCH FOR SOUVENIRS, BUT THIS?

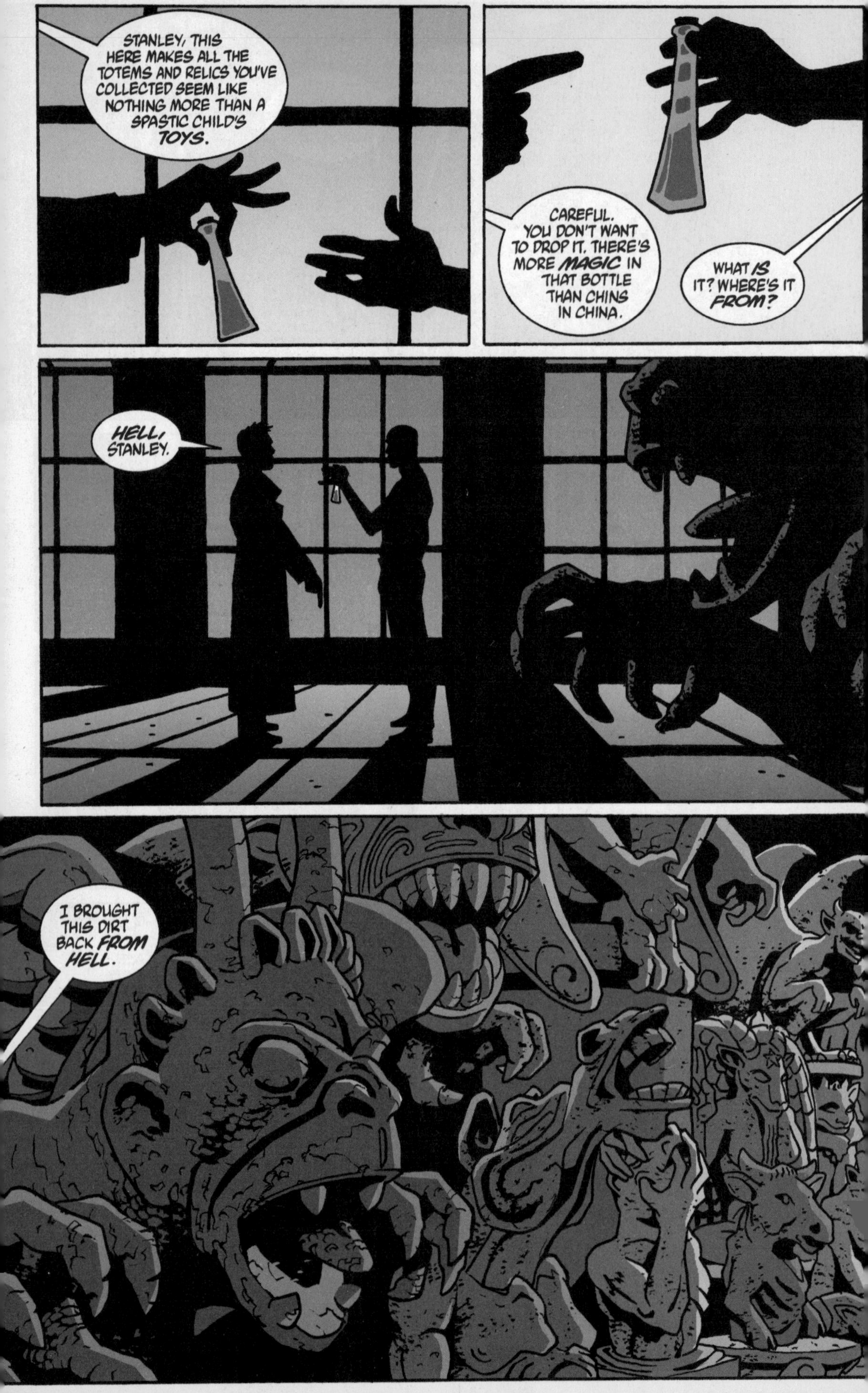
STANLEY, THIS HERE MAKES ALL THE TOTEMS AND RELICS YOU'VE COLLECTED SEEM LIKE NOTHING MORE THAN A SPASTIC CHILD'S TOYS.
CAREFUL. YOU DON'T WANT TO DROP IT. THERE'S MORE MAGIC IN THAT BOTTLE THAN CHINS IN CHINA.
WHAT IS IT? WHERE'S IT FROM?
HELL, STANLEY.
I BROUGHT THIS DIRT BACK FROM HELL.

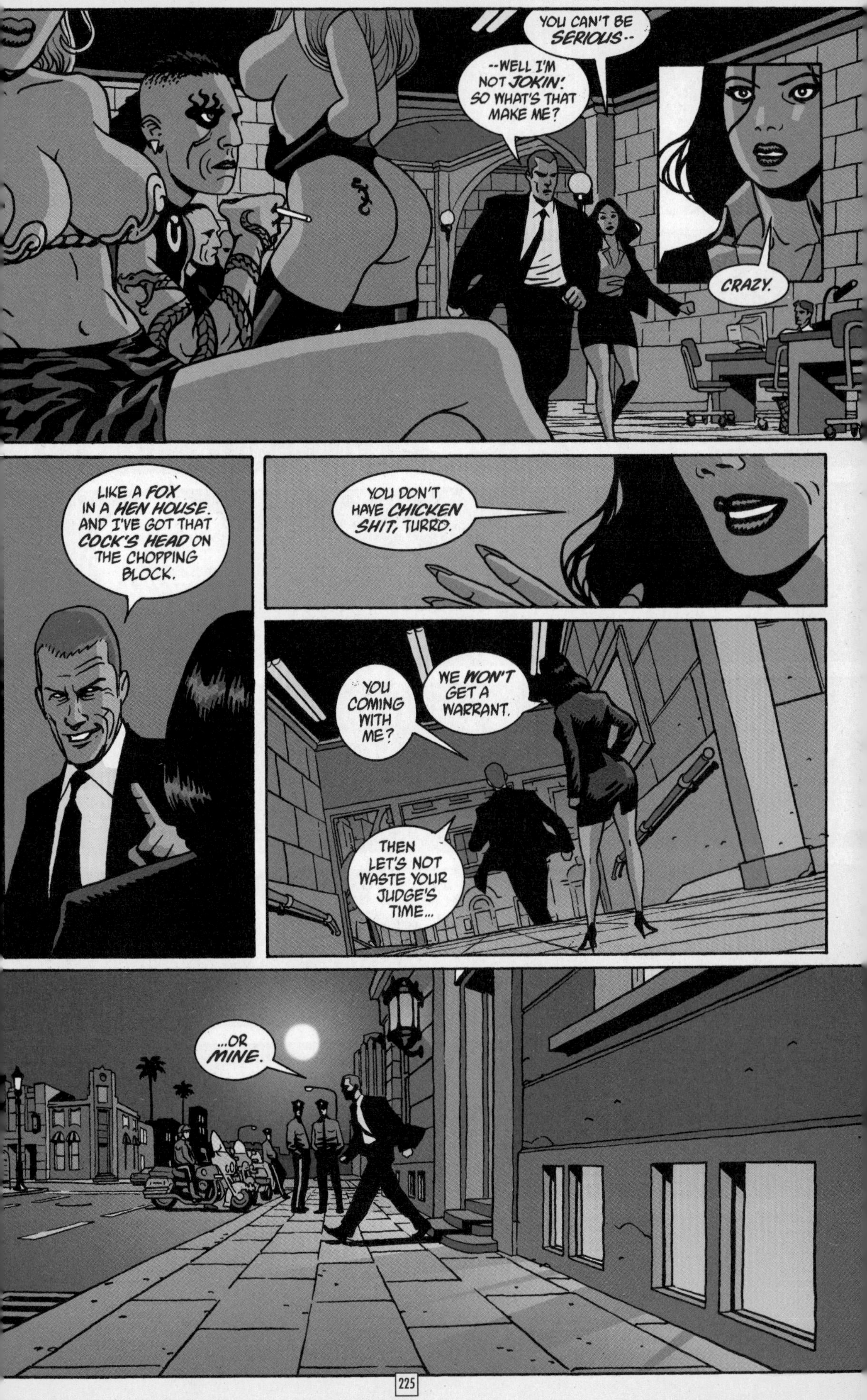

YOU CAN'T BE SERIOUS--
--WELL I'M NOT JOKIN'. SO WHAT'S THAT MAKE ME?
CRAZY.
LIKE A FOX IN A HEN HOUSE. AND I'VE GOT THAT COCK'S HEAD ON THE CHOPPING BLOCK.
YOU DON'T HAVE CHICKEN SHIT, TURRO.
YOU COMING WITH ME?
WE WON'T GET A WARRANT.
THEN LET'S NOT WASTE YOUR JUDGE'S TIME...
...OR MINE.

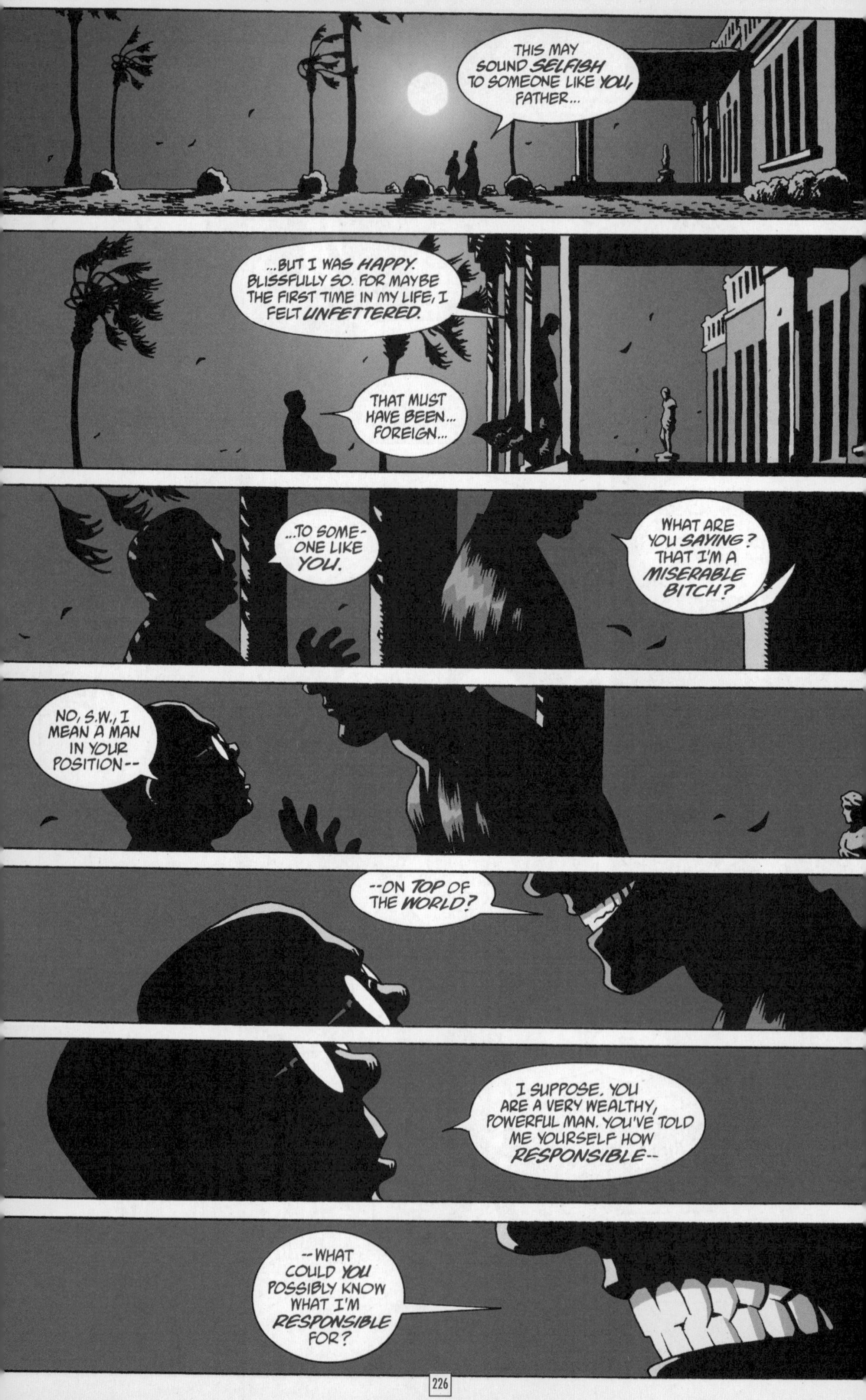

THIS MAY SOUND SELFISH TO SOMEONE LIKE YOU, FATHER...
...BUT I WAS HAPPY. BLISSFULLY SO. FOR MAYBE THE FIRST TIME IN MY LIFE, I FELT UNFETTERED.
THAT MUST HAVE BEEN... FOREIGN...
...TO SOME-ONE LIKE YOU.
WHAT ARE YOU SAYING? THAT I'M A MISERABLE BITCH?
NO, S.W., I MEAN A MAN IN YOUR POSITION--
--ON TOP OF THE WORLD?
I SUPPOSE. YOU ARE A VERY WEALTHY, POWERFUL MAN. YOU'VE TOLD ME YOURSELF HOW RESPONSIBLE--
--WHAT COULD YOU POSSIBLY KNOW WHAT I'M RESPONSIBLE FOR?

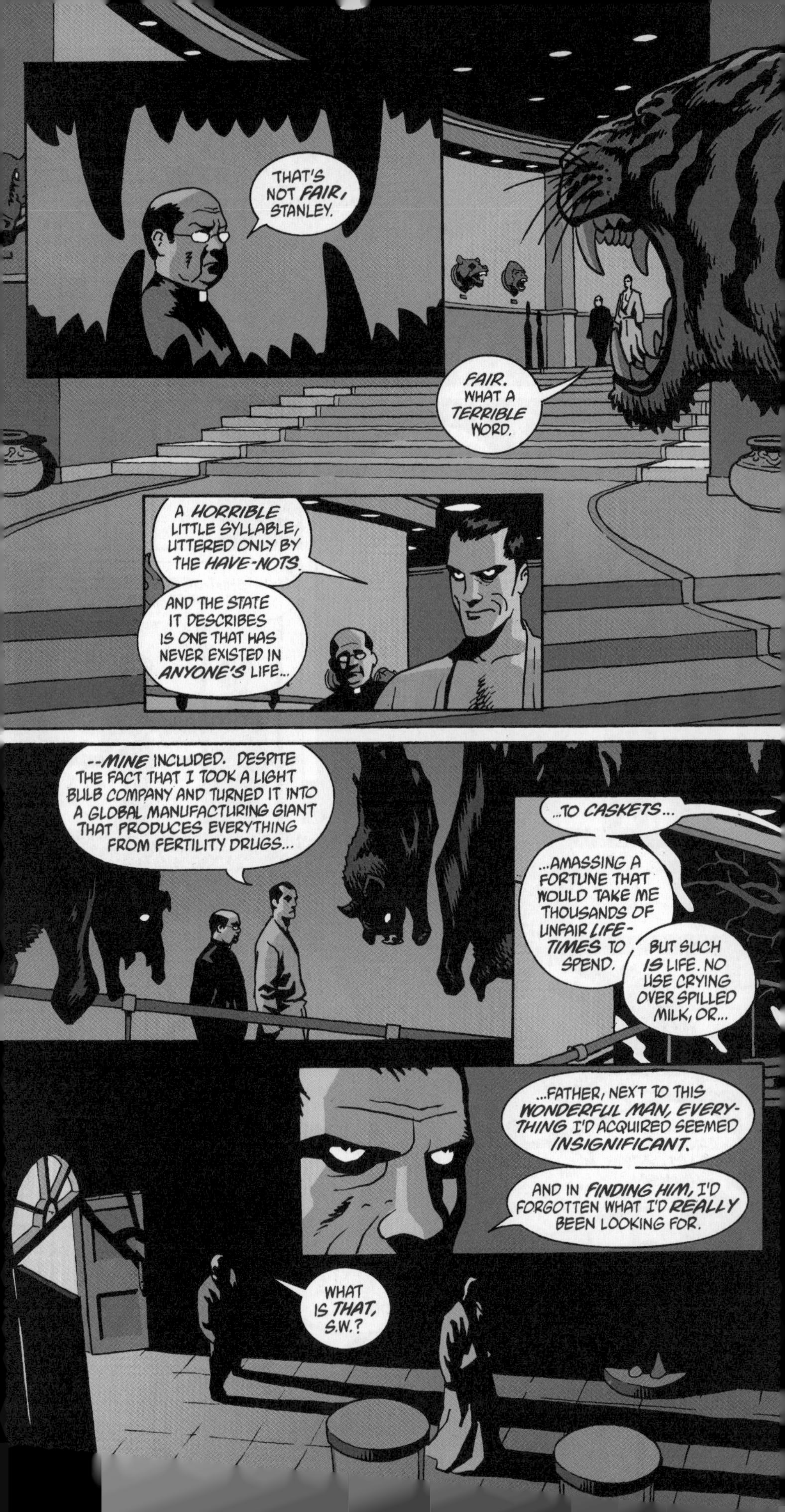
THAT'S NOT FAIR, STANLEY.
FAIR. WHAT A TERRIBLE WORD.
A HORRIBLE LITTLE SYLLABLE, UTTERED ONLY BY THE HAVE-NOTS.
AND THE STATE IT DESCRIBES IS ONE THAT HAS NEVER EXISTED IN ANYONE'S LIFE...
--MINE INCLUDED. DESPITE THE FACT THAT I TOOK A LIGHT BULB COMPANY AND TURNED IT INTO A GLOBAL MANUFACTURING GIANT THAT PRODUCES EVERYTHING FROM FERTILITY DRUGS...
...TO CASKETS...
...AMASSING A FORTUNE THAT WOULD TAKE ME THOUSANDS OF UNFAIR LIFE-TIMES TO SPEND.
BUT SUCH IS LIFE. NO USE CRYING OVER SPILLED MILK, OR...
...FATHER, NEXT TO THIS WONDERFUL MAN, EVERY-THING I'D ACQUIRED SEEMED INSIGNIFICANT.
AND IN FINDING HIM, I'D FORGOTTEN WHAT I'D REALLY BEEN LOOKING FOR.
WHAT IS THAT, S.W.?

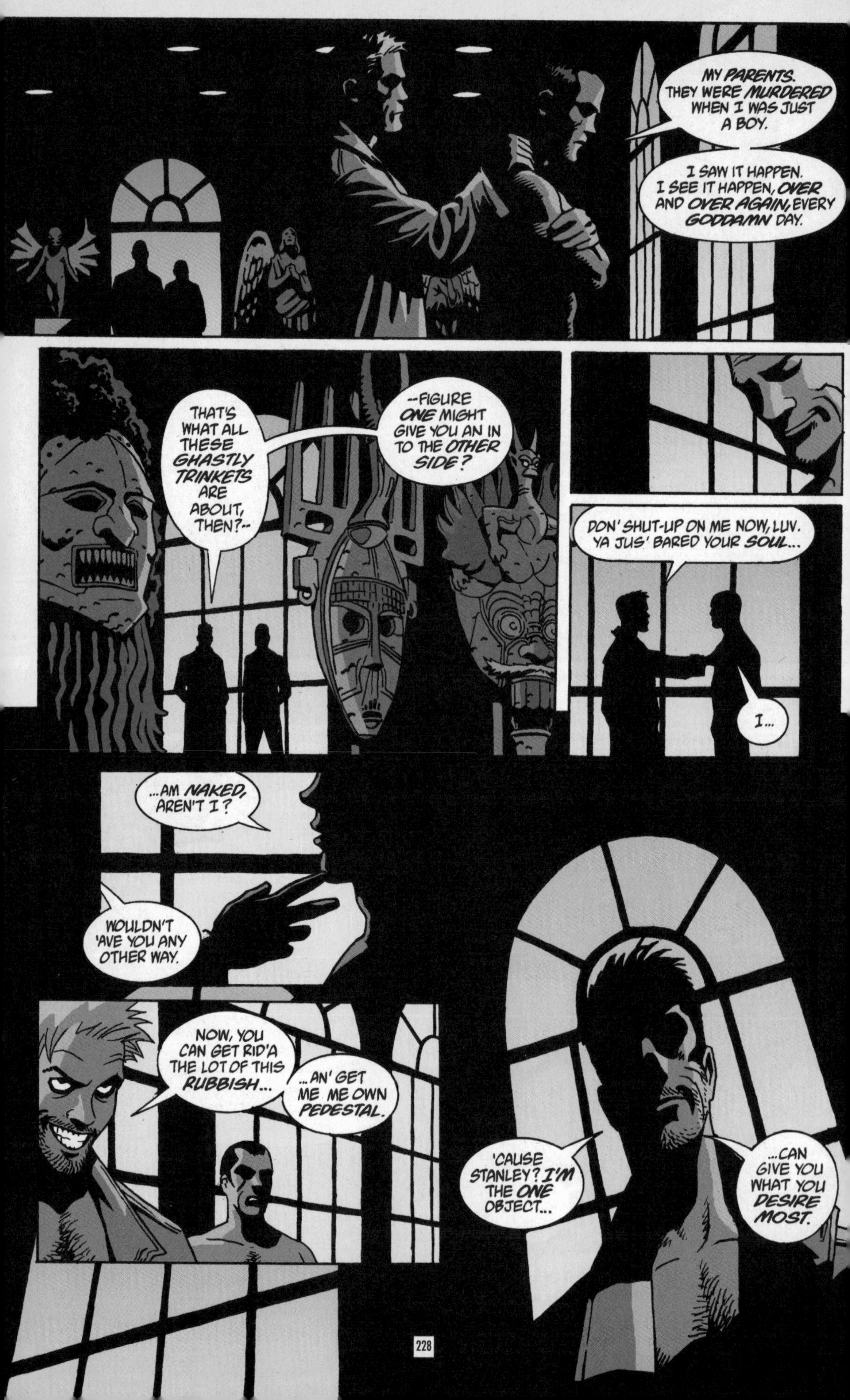
MY PARENTS. THEY WERE MURDERED WHEN I WAS JUST A BOY.
I SAW IT HAPPEN. I SEE IT HAPPEN, OVER AND OVER AGAIN, EVERY GODDAMN DAY.
THAT'S WHAT ALL THESE GHASTLY TRINKETS ARE ABOUT, THEN?--
--FIGURE ONE MIGHT GIVE YOU AN IN TO THE OTHER SIDE?
DON' SHUT-UP ON ME NOW, LUV. YA JUS' BARED YOUR SOUL...
I...
...AM NAKED, AREN'T I?
WOULDN'T 'AVE YOU ANY OTHER WAY.
NOW, YOU CAN GET RID'A THE LOT OF THIS RUBBISH...
...AN' GET ME ME OWN PEDESTAL.
'CAUSE STANLEY? I'M THE ONE OBJECT...
...CAN GIVE YOU WHAT YOU DESIRE MOST.

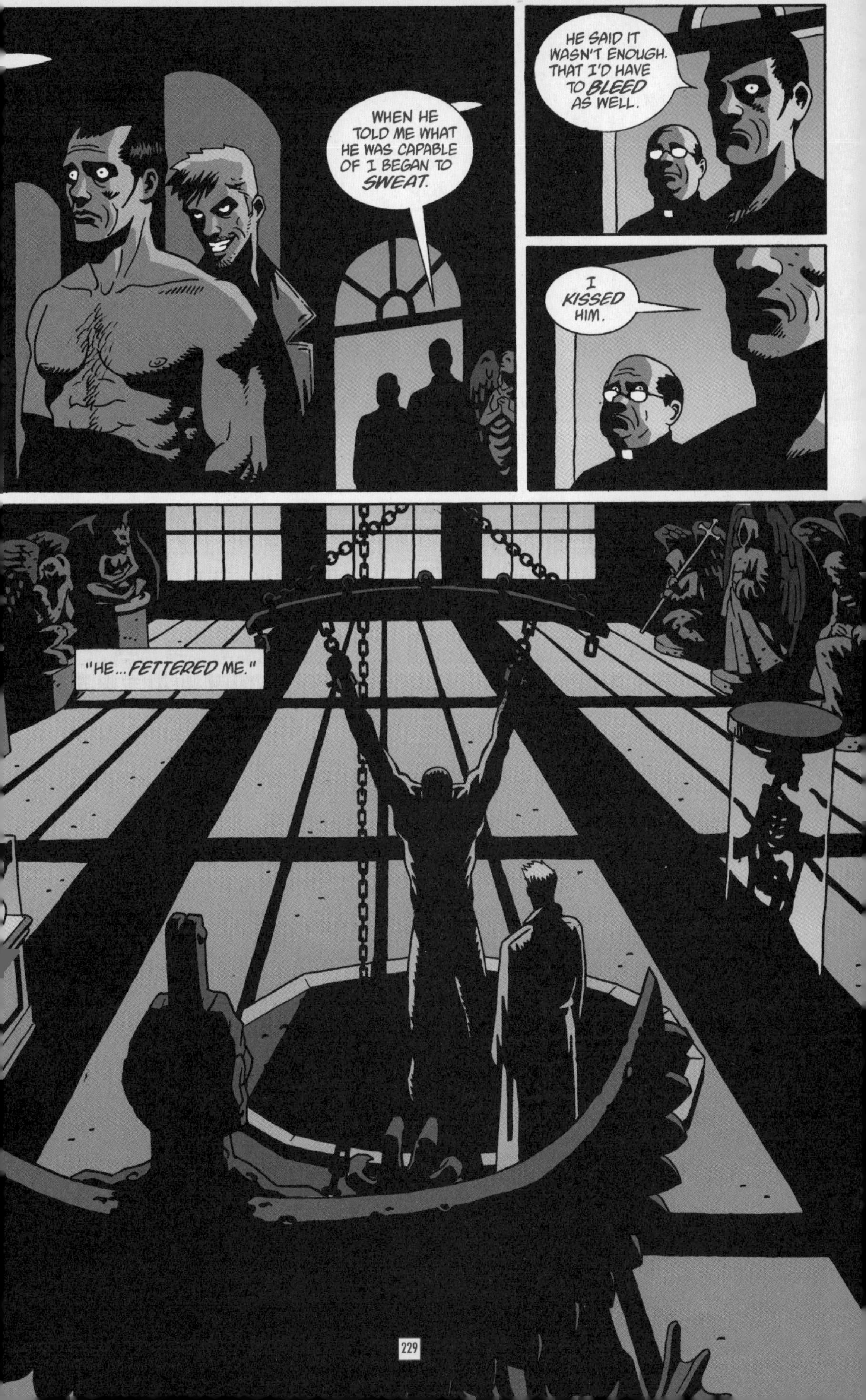
WHEN HE TOLD ME WHAT HE WAS CAPABLE OF I BEGAN TO SWEAT.
HE SAID IT WASN'T ENOUGH. THAT I'D HAVE TO BLEED AS WELL.
I KISSED HIM.
"HE... FETTERED ME."

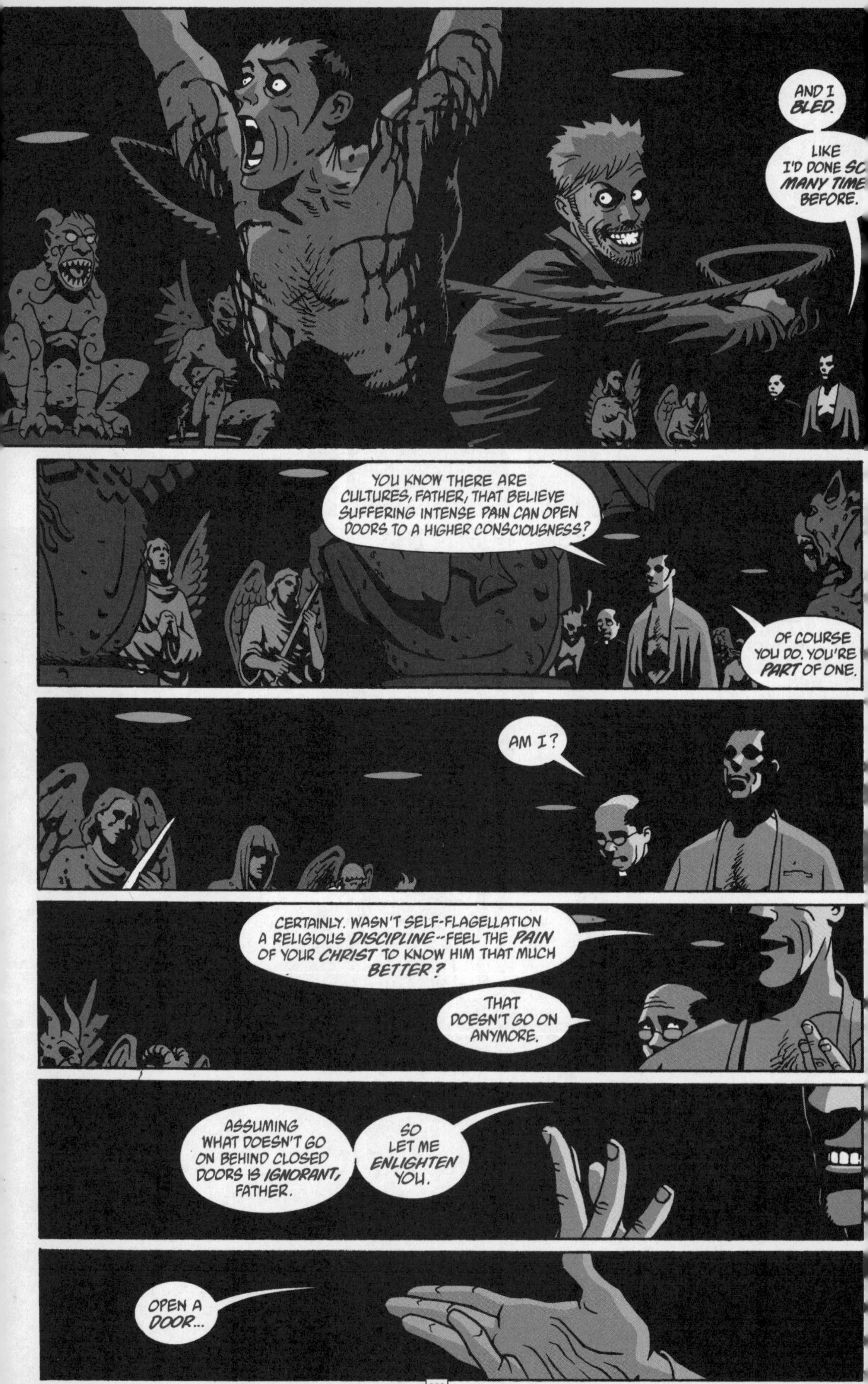
AND I BLED.
LIKE I'D DONE SO MANY TIMES BEFORE.
YOU KNOW THERE ARE CULTURES, FATHER, THAT BELIEVE SUFFERING INTENSE PAIN CAN OPEN DOORS TO A HIGHER CONSCIOUSNESS?
OF COURSE YOU DO. YOU'RE PART OF ONE.
AM I?
CERTAINLY. WASN'T SELF-FLAGELLATION A RELIGIOUS DISCIPLINE--FEEL THE PAIN OF YOUR CHRIST TO KNOW HIM THAT MUCH BETTER?
THAT DOESN'T GO ON ANYMORE.
ASSUMING WHAT DOESN'T GO ON BEHIND CLOSED DOORS IS IGNORANT, FATHER.
SO LET ME ENLIGHTEN YOU.
OPEN A DOOR...

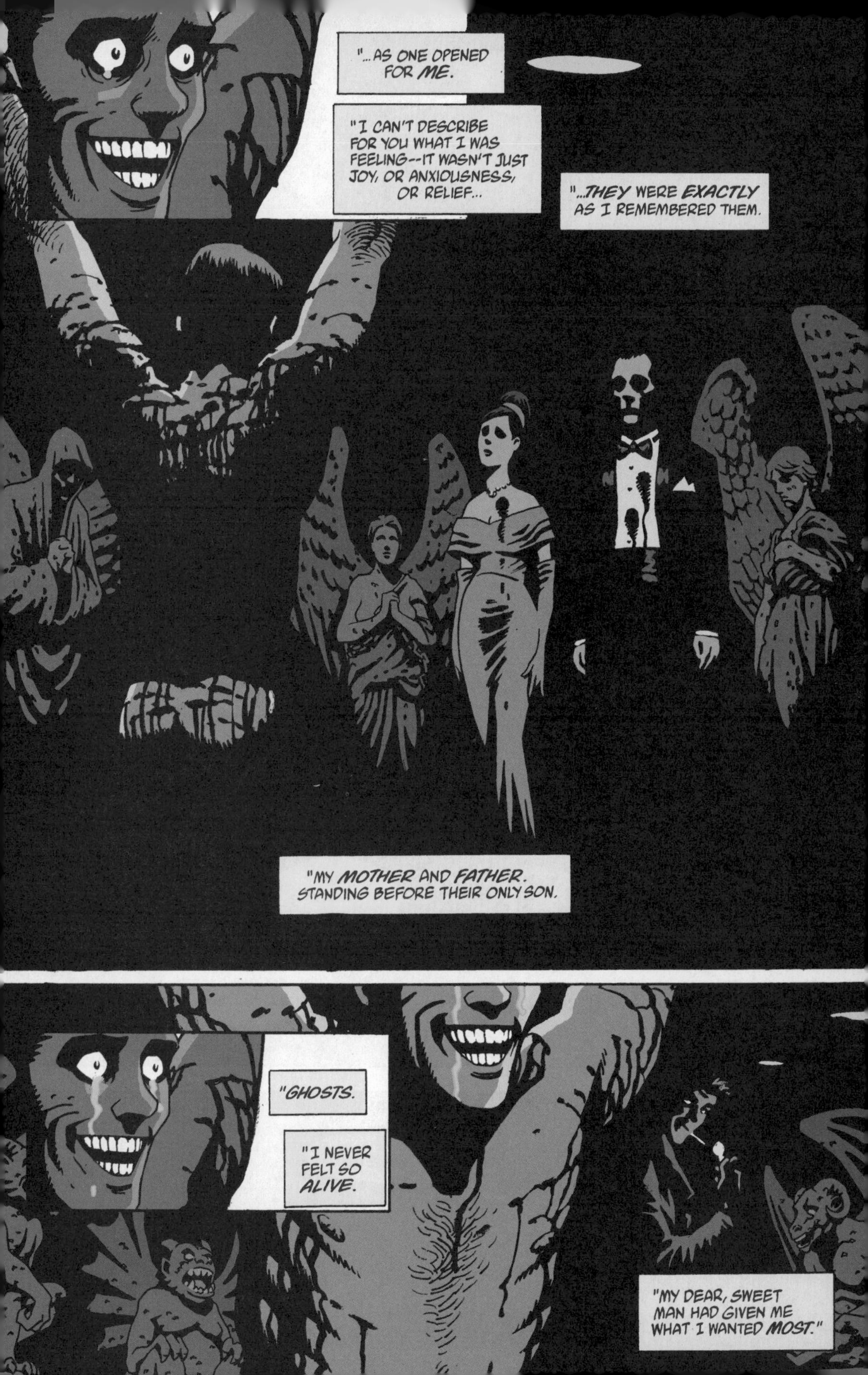
"...AS ONE OPENED FOR *ME*.
"I CAN'T DESCRIBE FOR YOU WHAT I WAS FEELING--IT WASN'T JUST JOY, OR ANXIOUSNESS, OR RELIEF...
"...*THEY* WERE *EXACTLY* AS I REMEMBERED THEM.
"MY *MOTHER* AND *FATHER*. STANDING BEFORE THEIR ONLY SON.
"*GHOSTS*.
"I NEVER FELT SO *ALIVE*.
"MY DEAR, SWEET MAN HAD GIVEN ME WHAT I WANTED *MOST*."

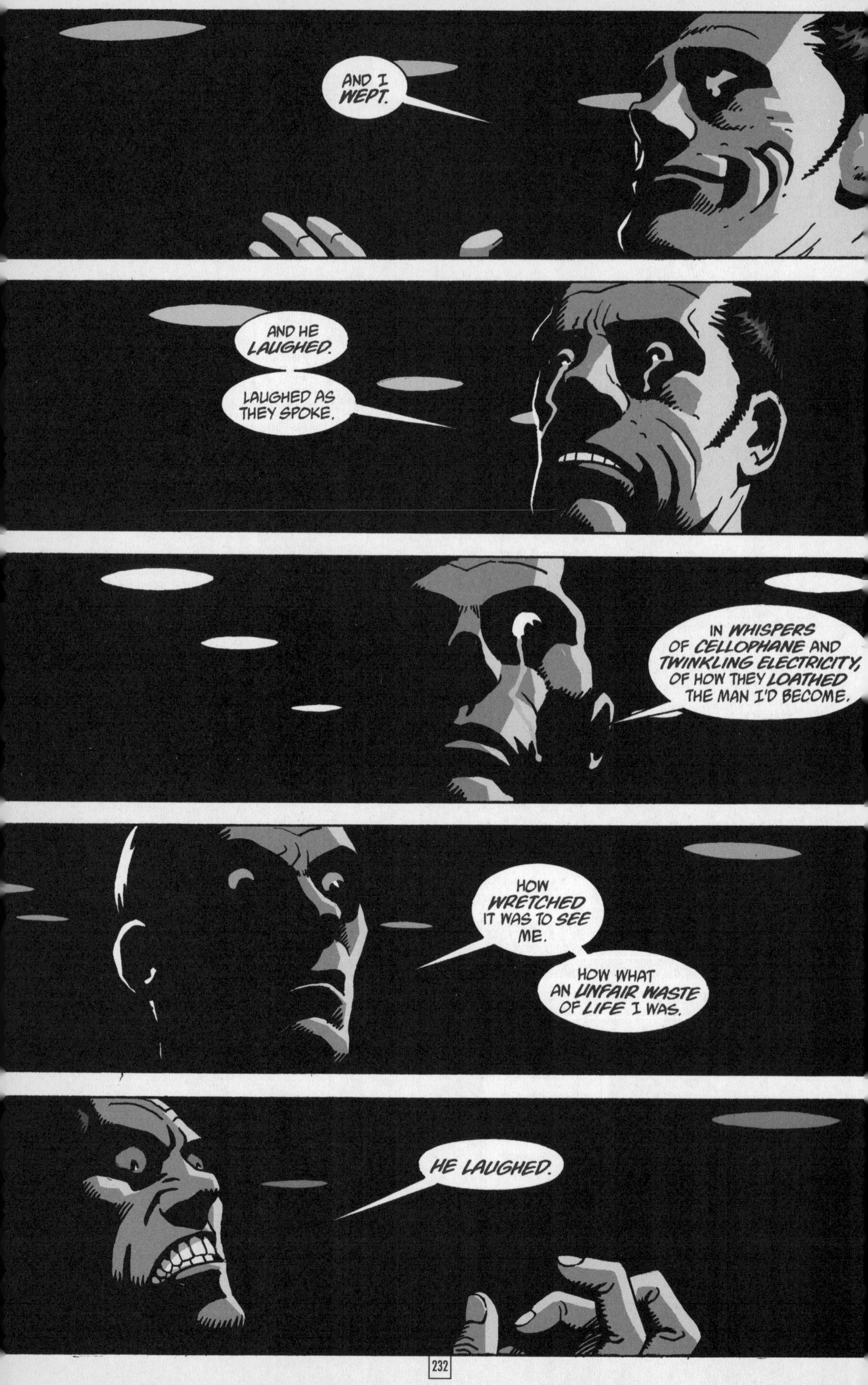

AND I WEPT.
AND HE LAUGHED.
LAUGHED AS THEY SPOKE.
IN WHISPERS OF CELLOPHANE AND TWINKLING ELECTRICITY, OF HOW THEY LOATHED THE MAN I'D BECOME.
HOW WRETCHED IT WAS TO SEE ME.
HOW WHAT AN UNFAIR WASTE OF LIFE I WAS.
HE LAUGHED.

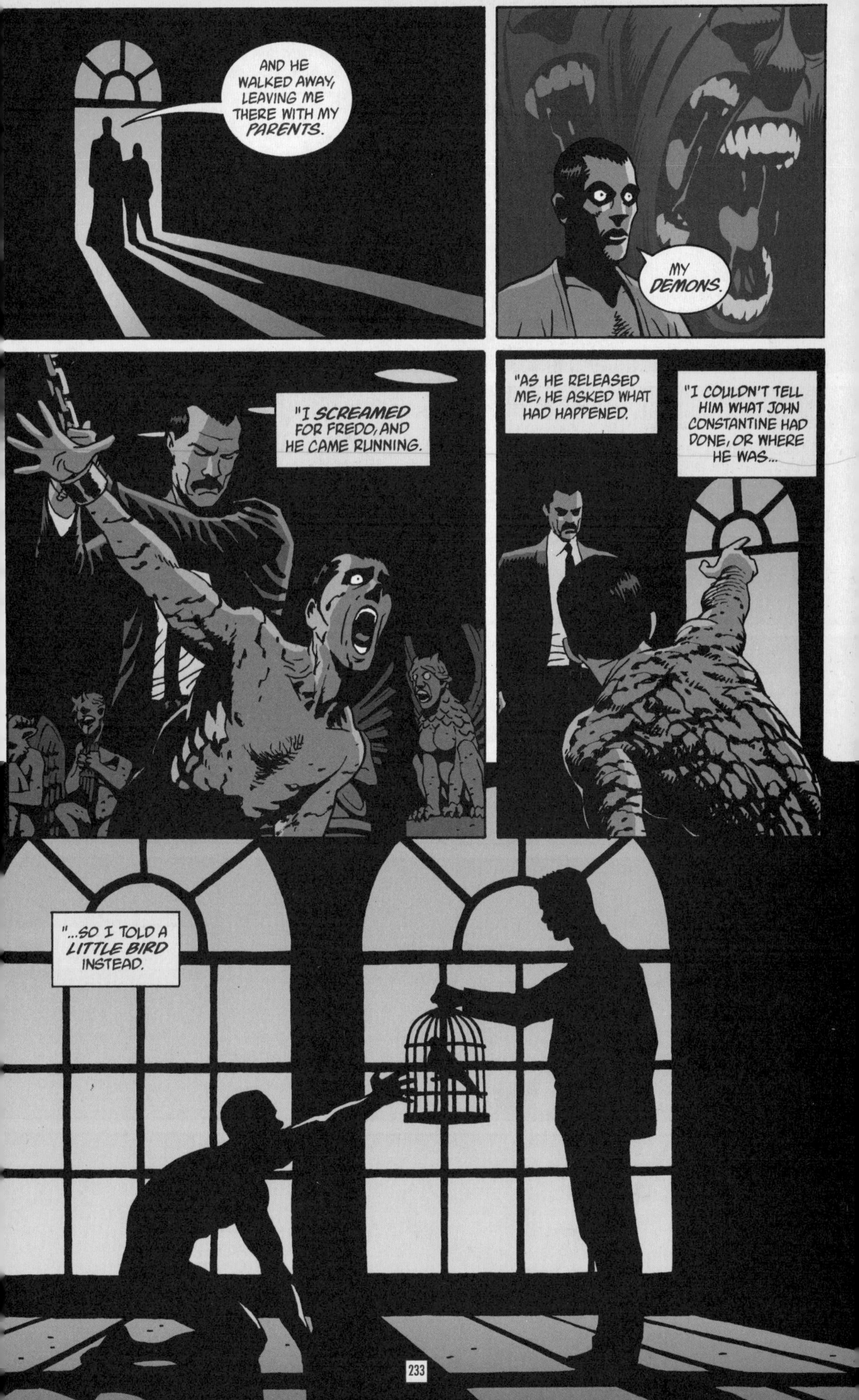
AND HE WALKED AWAY, LEAVING ME THERE WITH MY PARENTS.
MY DEMONS.
"I SCREAMED FOR FREDO, AND HE CAME RUNNING.
"AS HE RELEASED ME, HE ASKED WHAT HAD HAPPENED.
"I COULDN'T TELL HIM WHAT JOHN CONSTANTINE HAD DONE, OR WHERE HE WAS...
"...SO I TOLD A LITTLE BIRD INSTEAD.

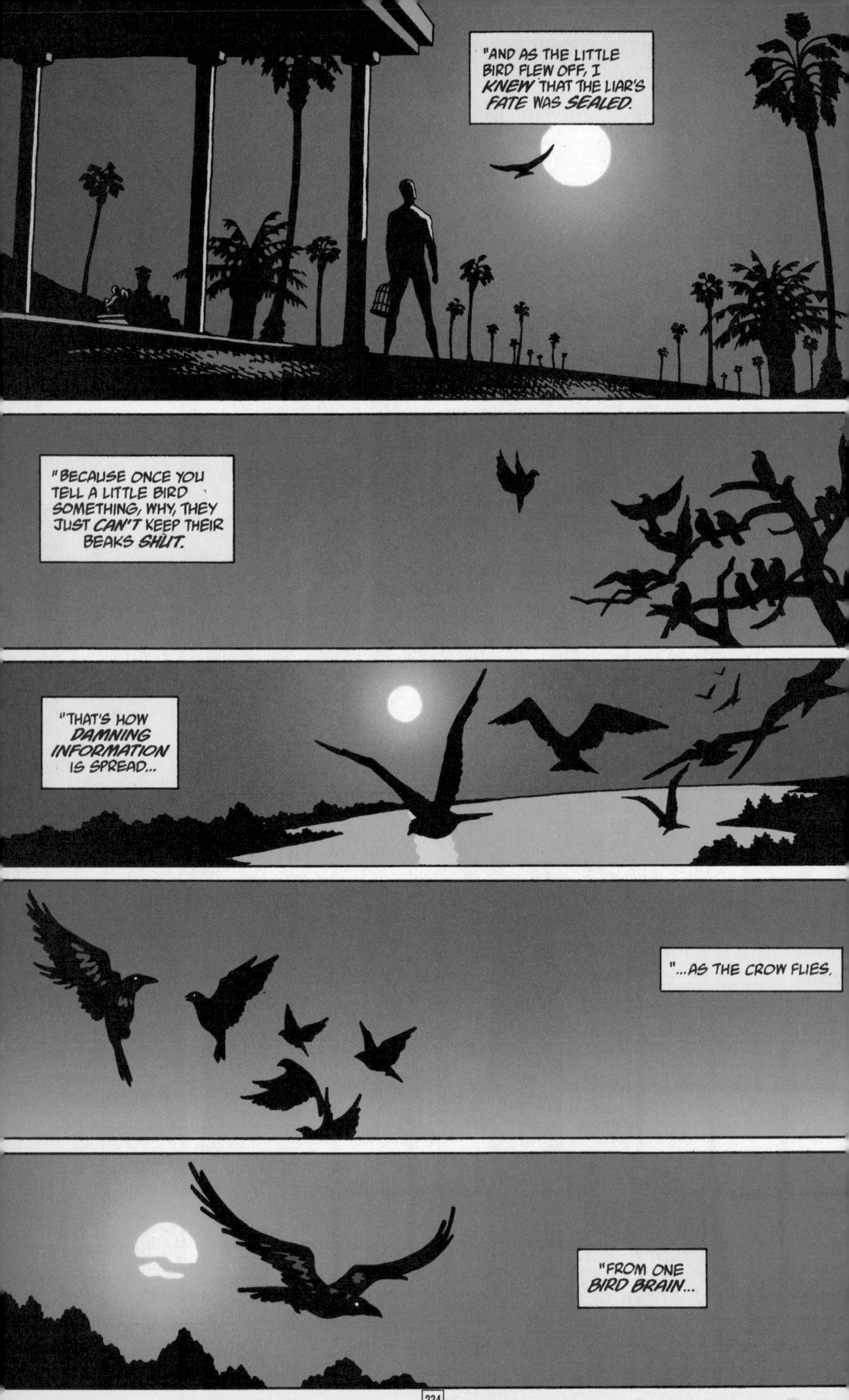
"AND AS THE LITTLE BIRD FLEW OFF, I KNEW THAT THE LIAR'S FATE WAS SEALED.
"BECAUSE ONCE YOU TELL A LITTLE BIRD SOMETHING, WHY, THEY JUST CAN'T KEEP THEIR BEAKS SHUT.
"THAT'S HOW DAMNING INFORMATION IS SPREAD...
"...AS THE CROW FLIES.
"FROM ONE BIRD BRAIN...

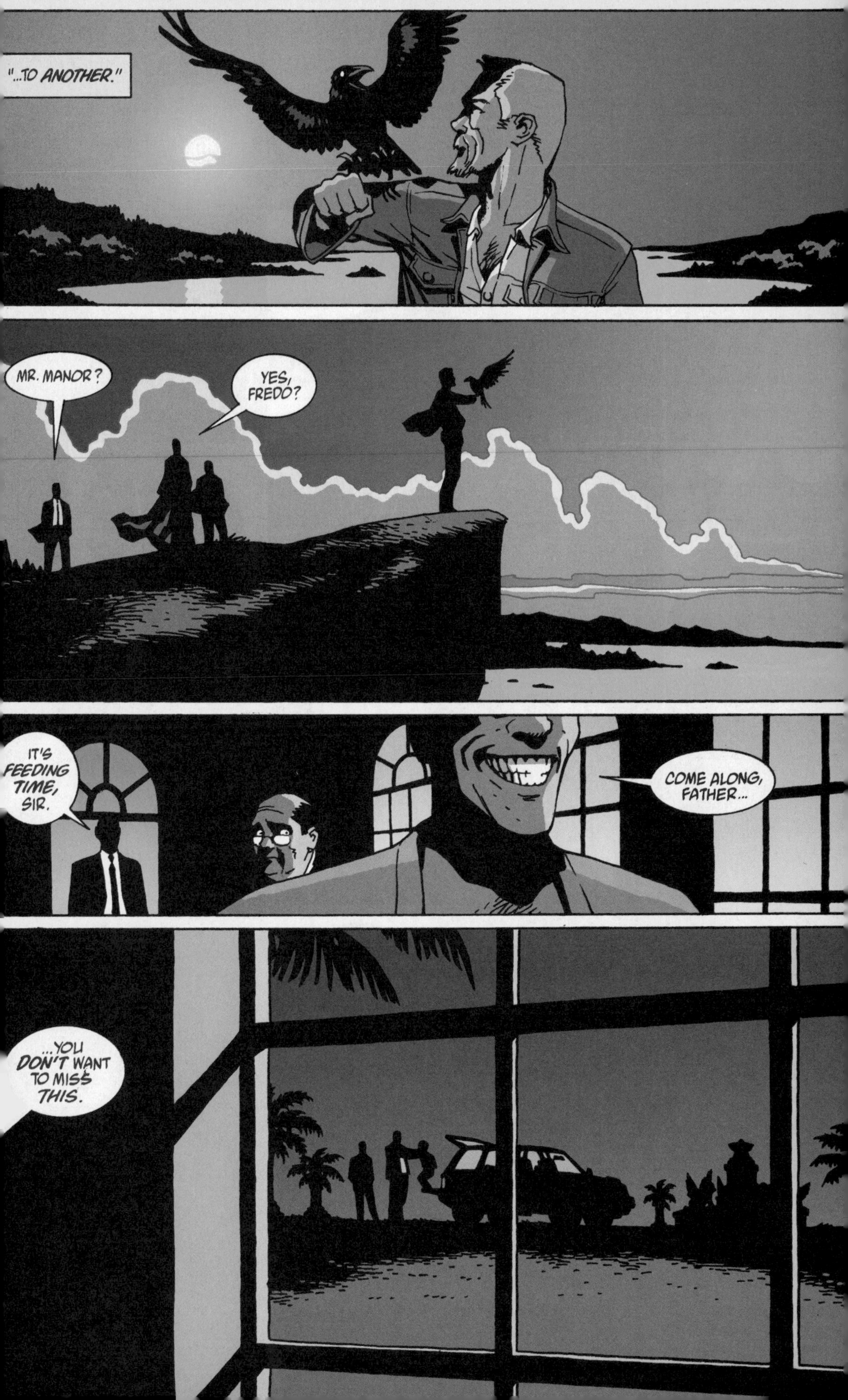
"...TO ANOTHER."
MR. MANOR?
YES, FREDO?
IT'S FEEDING TIME, SIR.
COME ALONG, FATHER...
...YOU DON'T WANT TO MISS THIS.

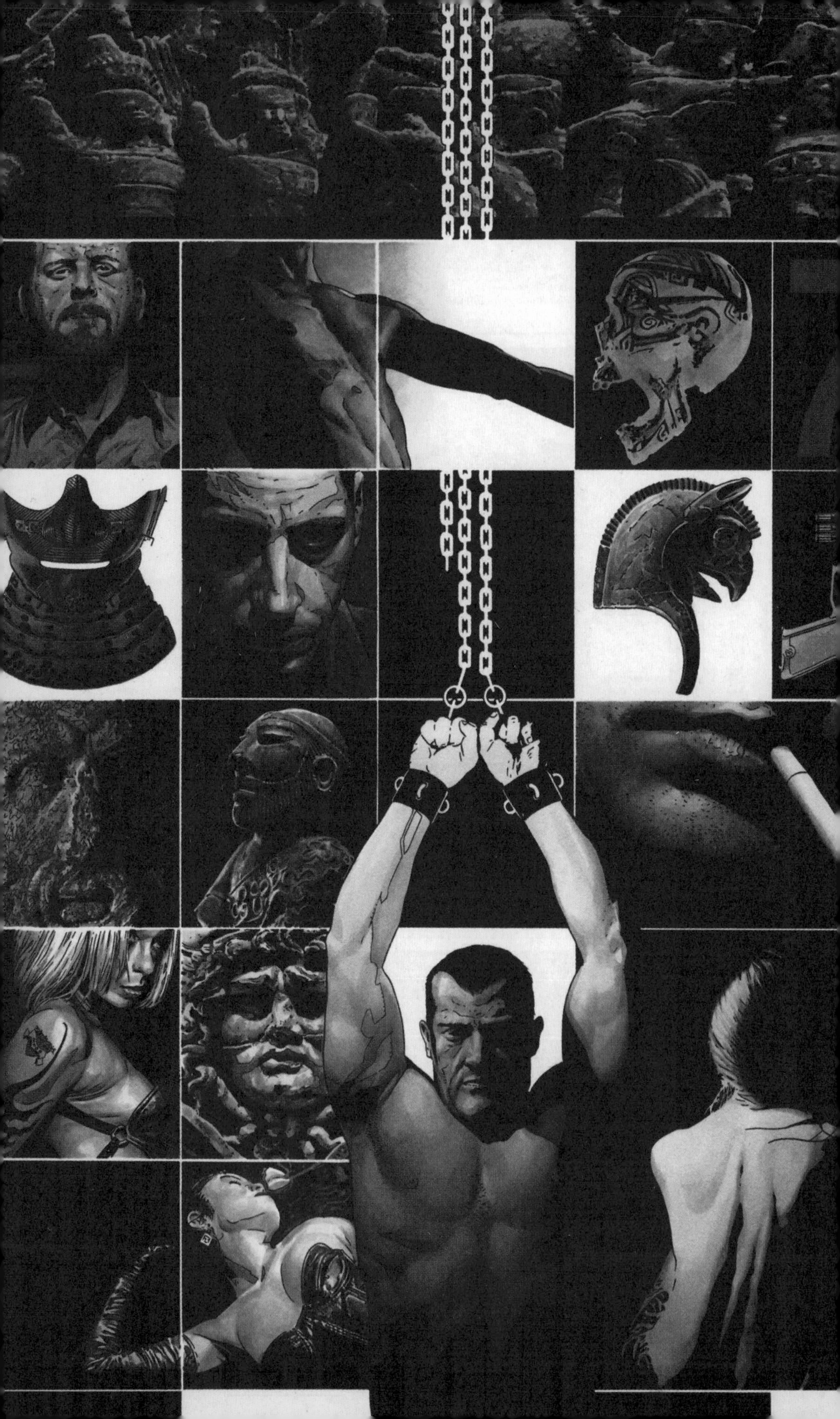

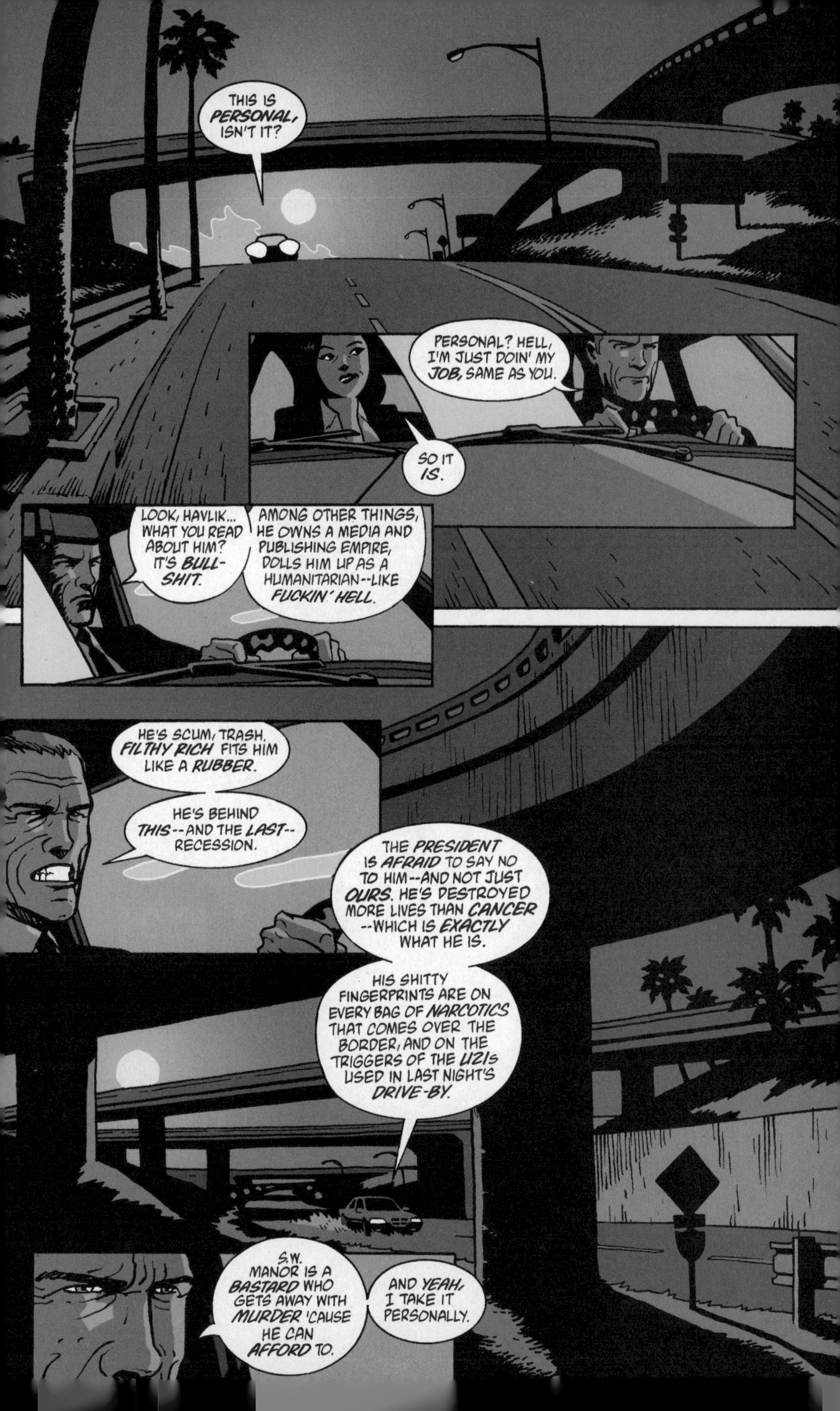
THIS IS PERSONAL, ISN'T IT?
PERSONAL? HELL, I'M JUST DOIN' MY JOB, SAME AS YOU.
SO IT IS.
LOOK, HAVLIK... WHAT YOU READ ABOUT HIM? IT'S BULL-SHIT.
AMONG OTHER THINGS, HE OWNS A MEDIA AND PUBLISHING EMPIRE, DOLLS HIM UP AS A HUMANITARIAN--LIKE FUCKIN' HELL.
HE'S SCUM, TRASH. FILTHY RICH FITS HIM LIKE A RUBBER.
HE'S BEHIND THIS--AND THE LAST--RECESSION.
THE PRESIDENT IS AFRAID TO SAY NO TO HIM--AND NOT JUST OURS. HE'S DESTROYED MORE LIVES THAN CANCER --WHICH IS EXACTLY WHAT HE IS.
HIS SHITTY FINGERPRINTS ARE ON EVERY BAG OF NARCOTICS THAT COMES OVER THE BORDER, AND ON THE TRIGGERS OF THE UZIs USED IN LAST NIGHT'S DRIVE-BY.
S.W. MANOR IS A BASTARD WHO GETS AWAY WITH MURDER 'CAUSE HE CAN AFFORD TO.
AND YEAH, I TAKE IT PERSONALLY.

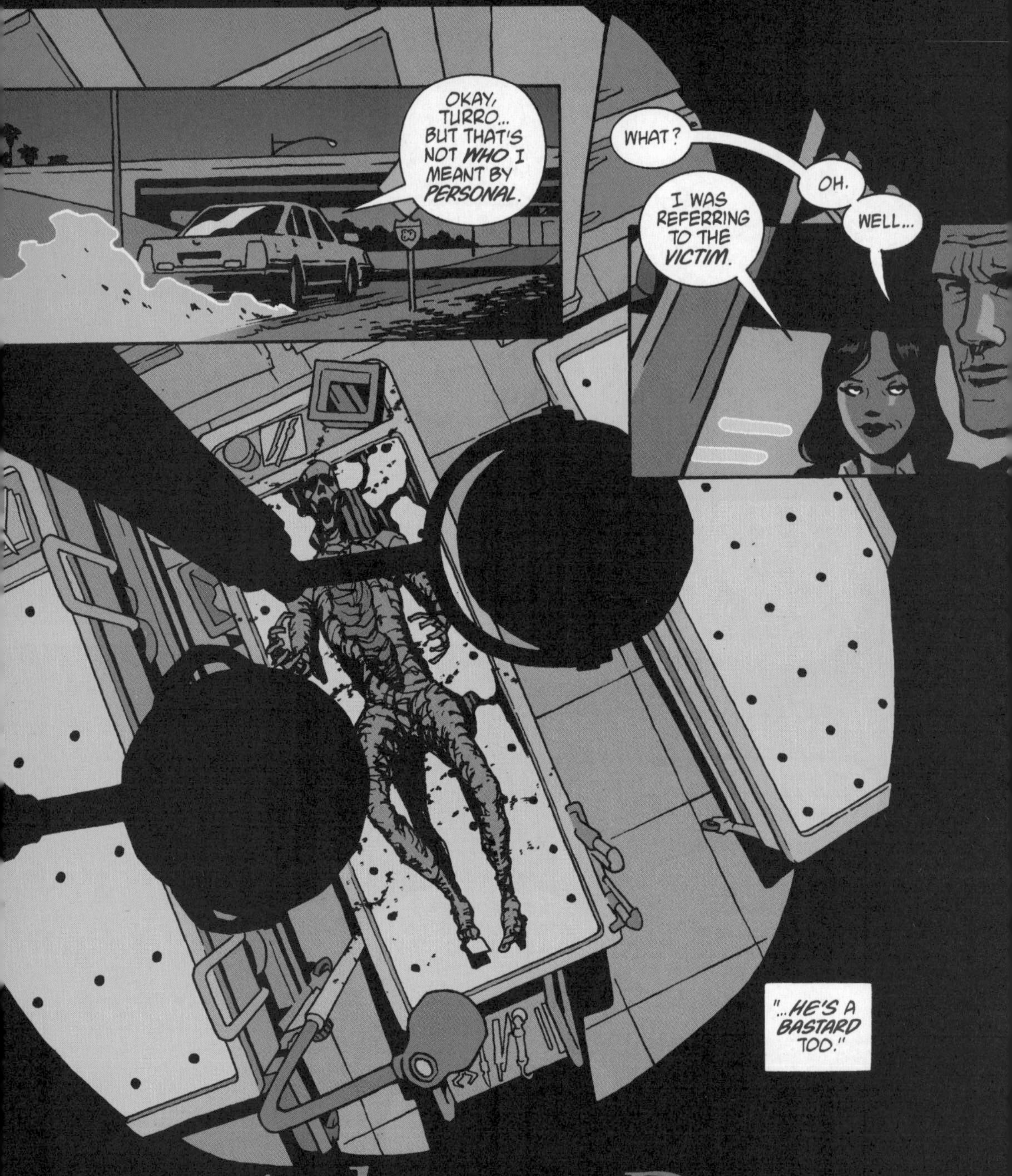
OKAY, TURRO... BUT THAT'S NOT *WHO* I MEANT BY *PERSONAL*.
WHAT?
I WAS REFERRING TO THE *VICTIM*.
OH.
WELL...
"...*HE'S* A BASTARD TOO."

Ashes & Dust in the City of Angels

conclusion

Brian Azzarello, writer Marcelo Frusin, artist

Lee Loughridge colors
Clem Robins letters
Tim Bradstreet cover
Zachary Rau assistant editor
Will Denni editor

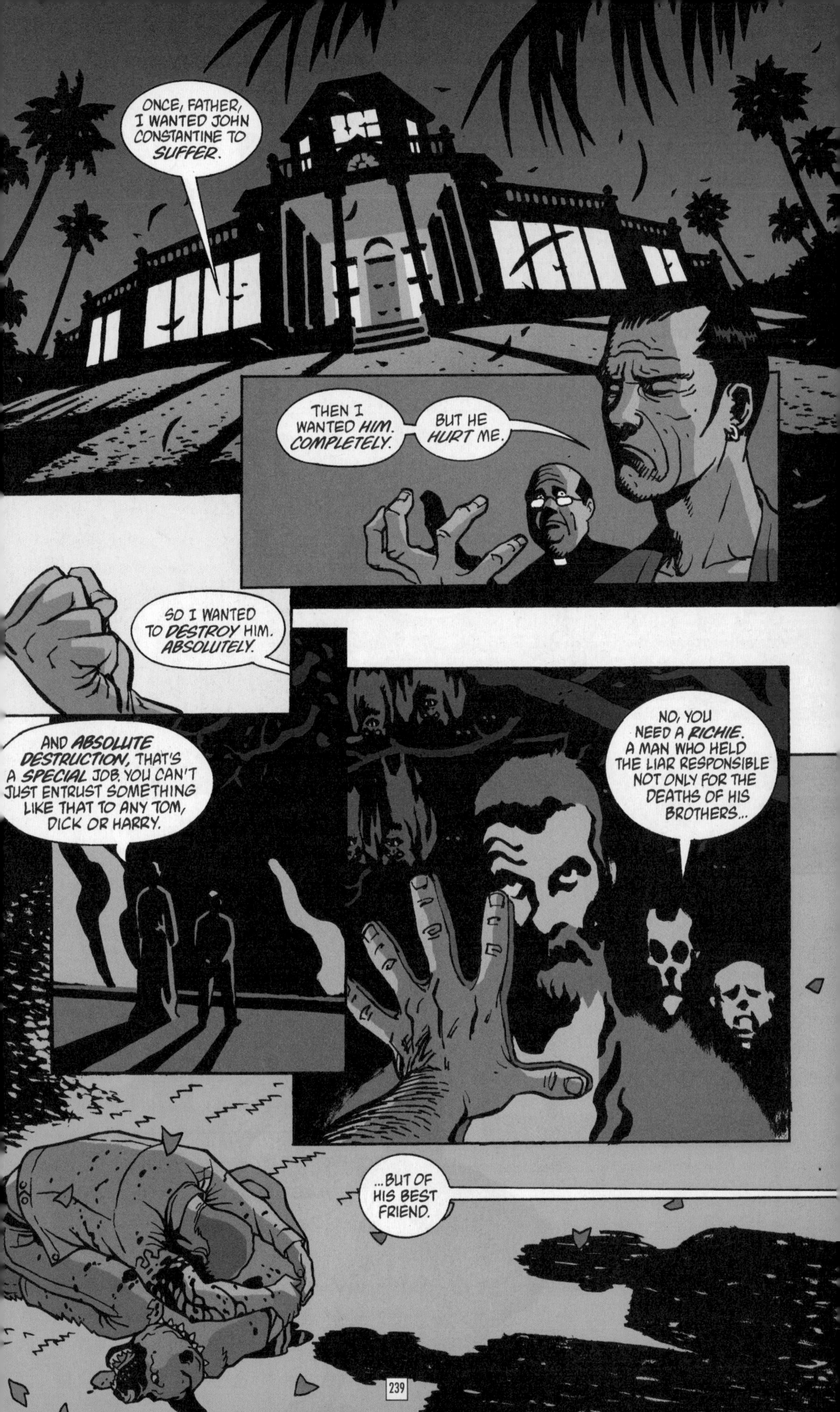
ONCE, FATHER, I WANTED JOHN CONSTANTINE TO SUFFER.
THEN I WANTED HIM. COMPLETELY.
BUT HE HURT ME.
SO I WANTED TO DESTROY HIM. ABSOLUTELY.
AND ABSOLUTE DESTRUCTION, THAT'S A SPECIAL JOB. YOU CAN'T JUST ENTRUST SOMETHING LIKE THAT TO ANY TOM, DICK OR HARRY.
NO, YOU NEED A RICHIE. A MAN WHO HELD THE LIAR RESPONSIBLE NOT ONLY FOR THE DEATHS OF HIS BROTHERS...
...BUT OF HIS BEST FRIEND.

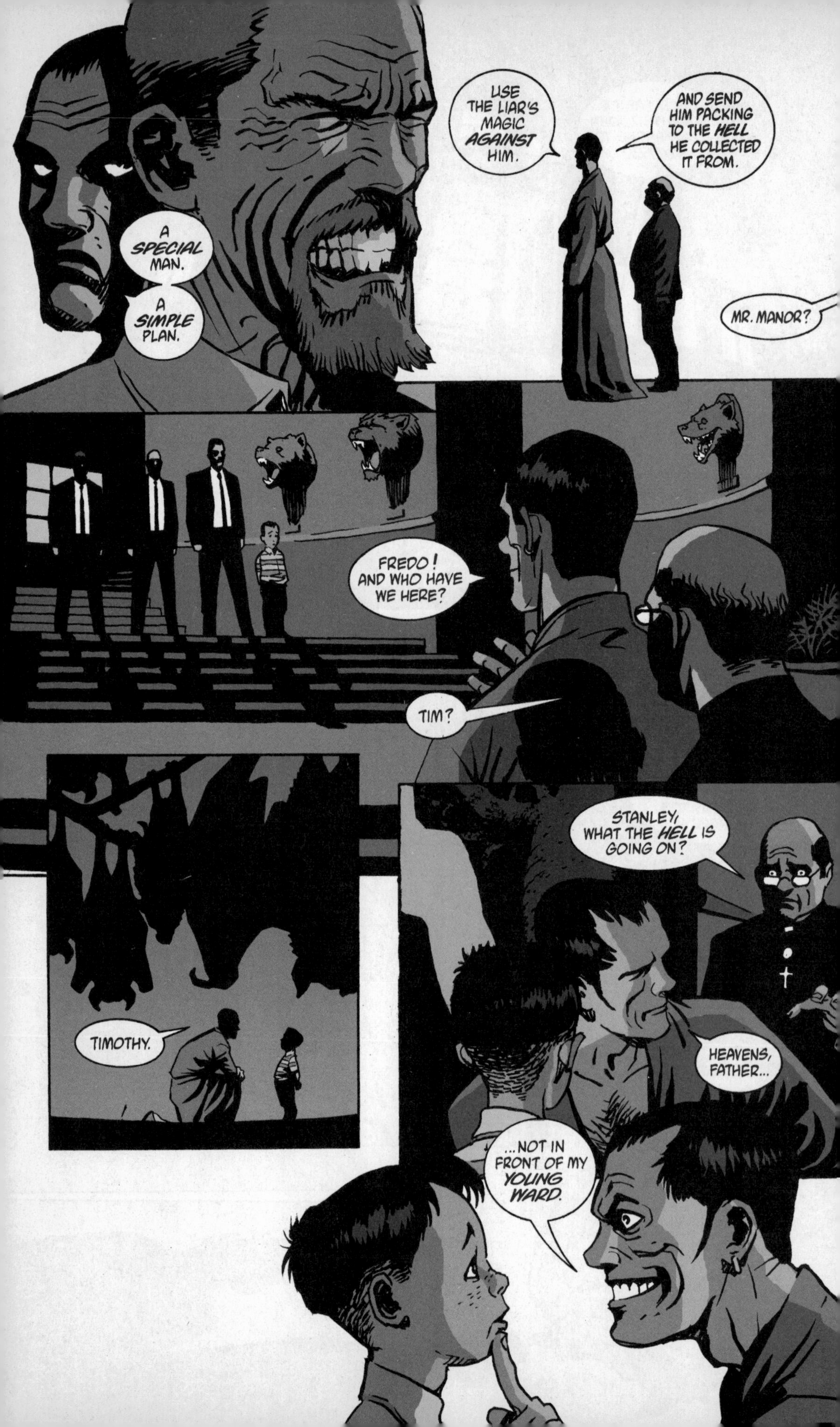
A SPECIAL MAN.
A SIMPLE PLAN.
USE THE LIAR'S MAGIC AGAINST HIM.
AND SEND HIM PACKING TO THE HELL HE COLLECTED IT FROM.
MR. MANOR?
FREDO! AND WHO HAVE WE HERE?
TIM?
TIMOTHY.
STANLEY, WHAT THE HELL IS GOING ON?
HEAVENS, FATHER...
...NOT IN FRONT OF MY YOUNG WARD.

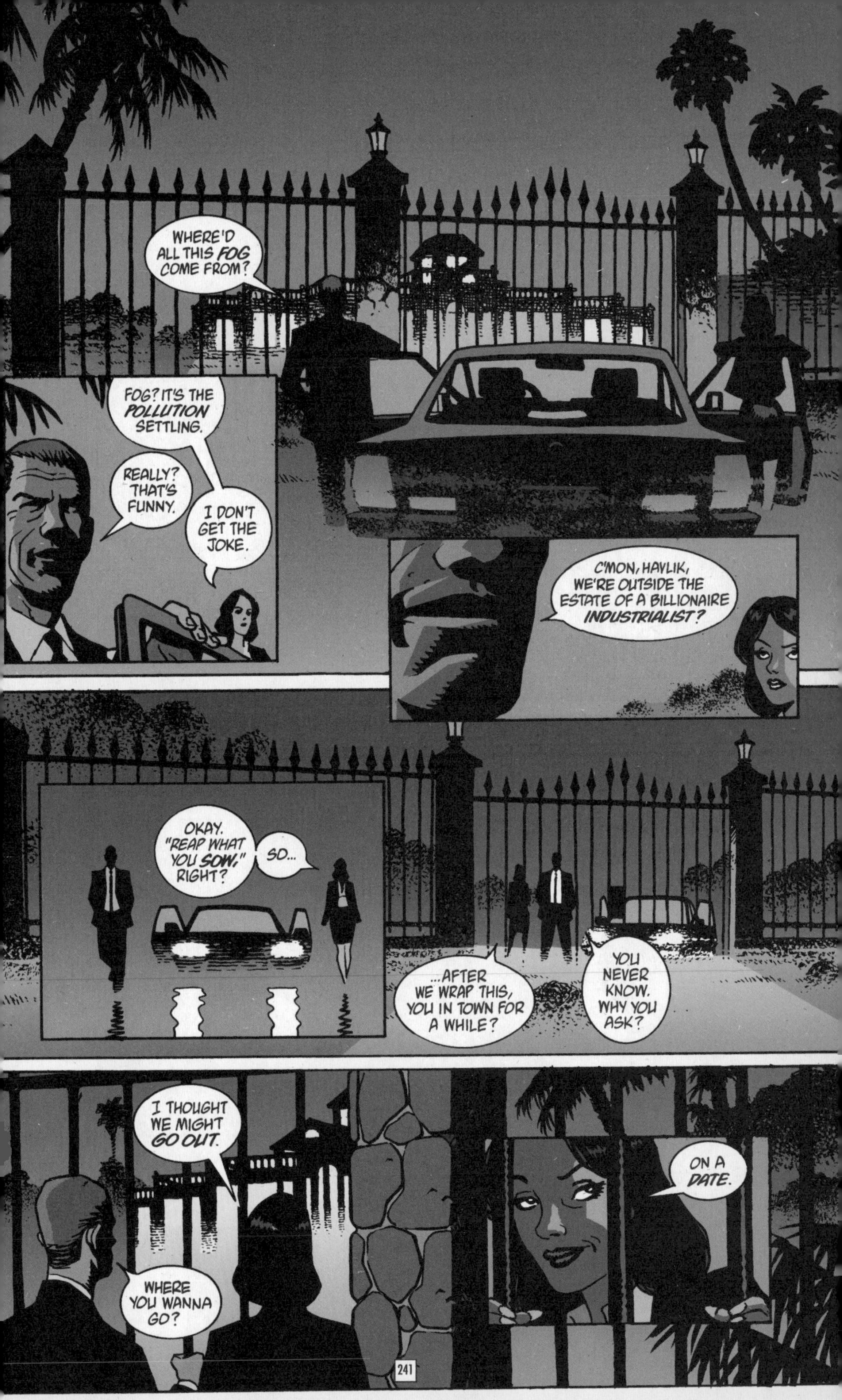
WHERE'D ALL THIS FOG COME FROM?
FOG? IT'S THE POLLUTION SETTLING.
REALLY? THAT'S FUNNY.
I DON'T GET THE JOKE.
C'MON, HAVLIK, WE'RE OUTSIDE THE ESTATE OF A BILLIONAIRE INDUSTRIALIST?
OKAY. "REAP WHAT YOU SOW," RIGHT?
SO...
...AFTER WE WRAP THIS, YOU IN TOWN FOR A WHILE?
YOU NEVER KNOW. WHY YOU ASK?
I THOUGHT WE MIGHT GO OUT.
ON A DATE.
WHERE YOU WANNA GO?

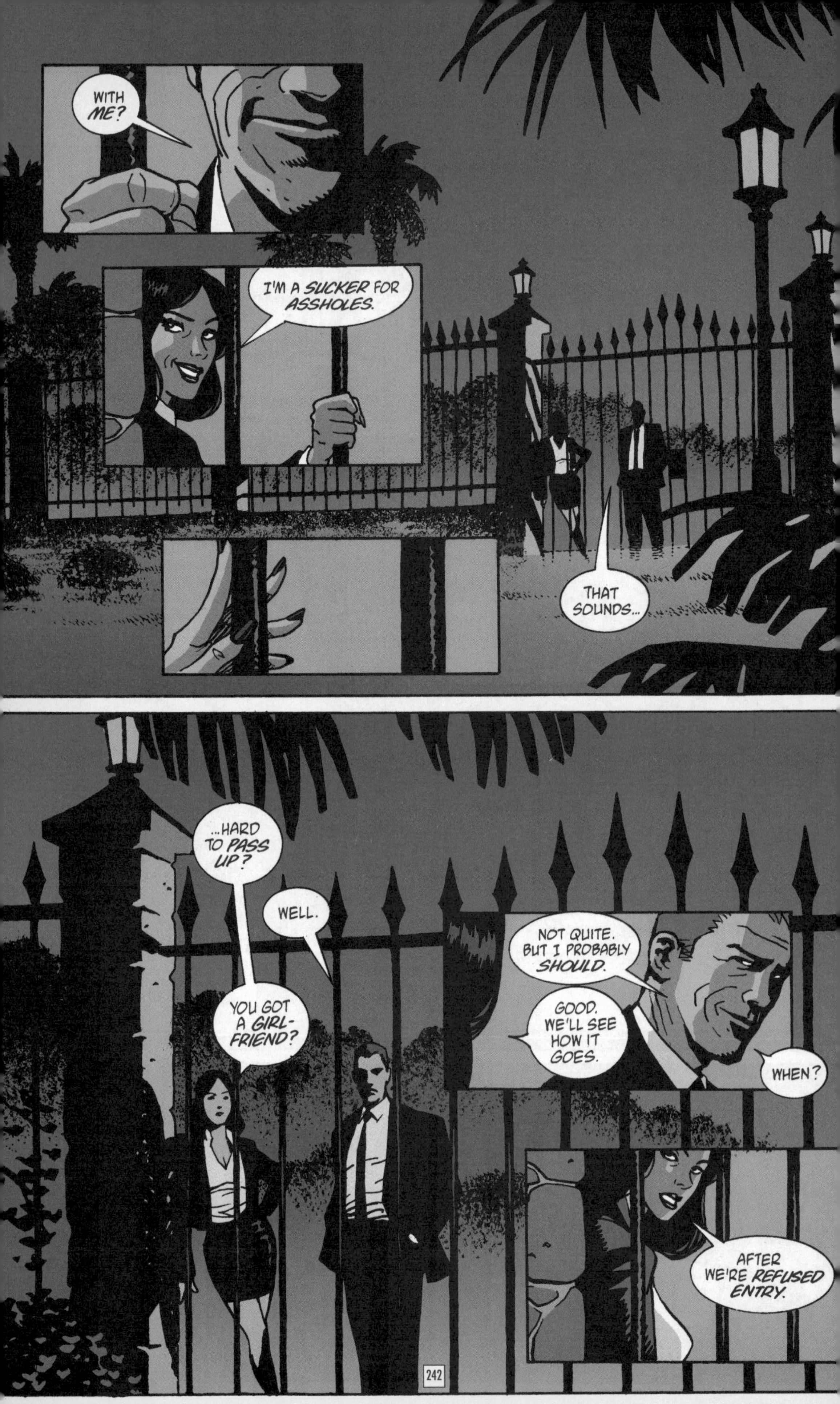
WITH ME?
I'M A SUCKER FOR ASSHOLES.
THAT SOUNDS...
...HARD TO PASS UP?
WELL.
YOU GOT A GIRL-FRIEND?
NOT QUITE. BUT I PROBABLY SHOULD.
GOOD. WE'LL SEE HOW IT GOES.
WHEN?
AFTER WE'RE REFUSED ENTRY.

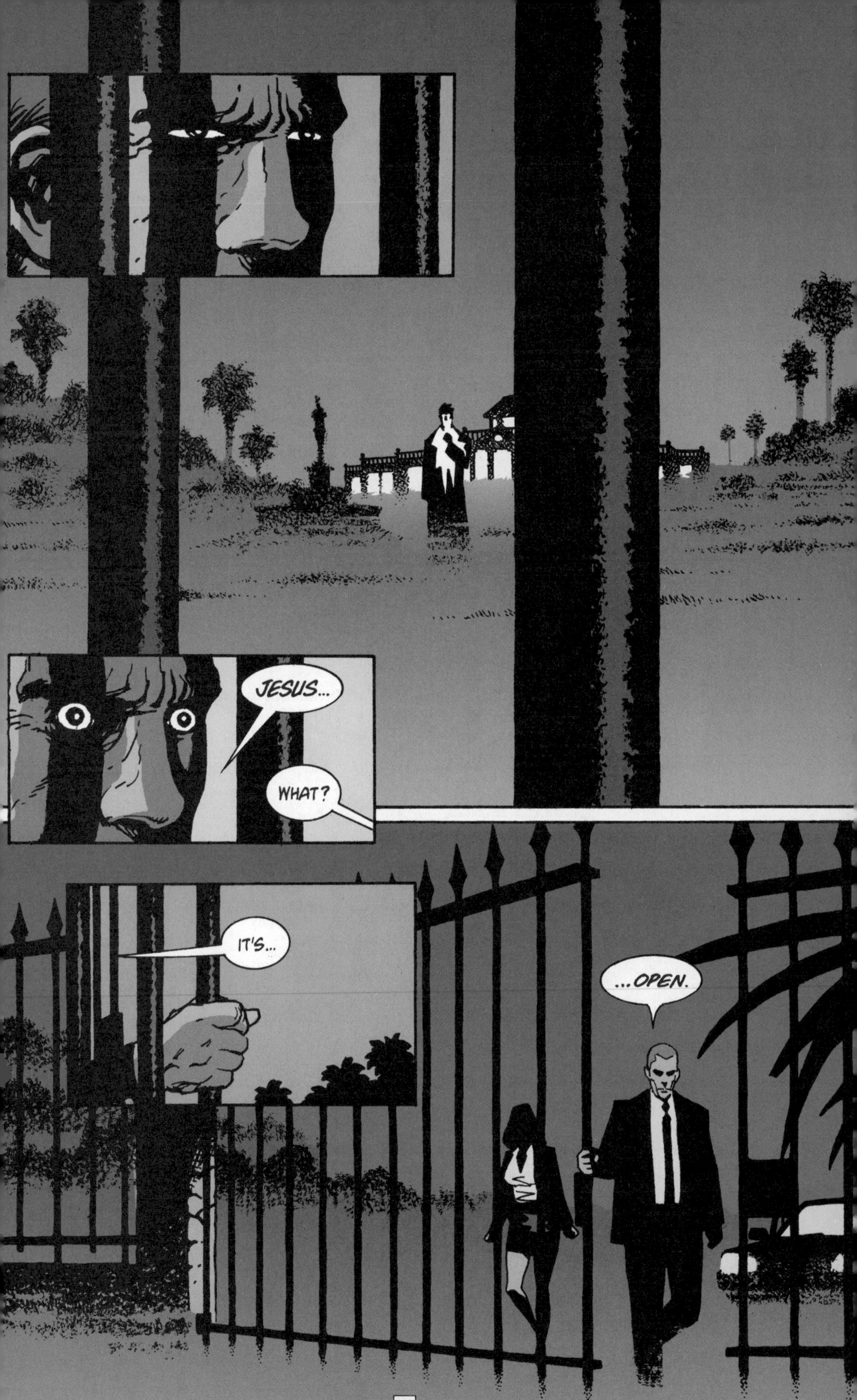
JESUS...
WHAT?
IT'S...
...OPEN.

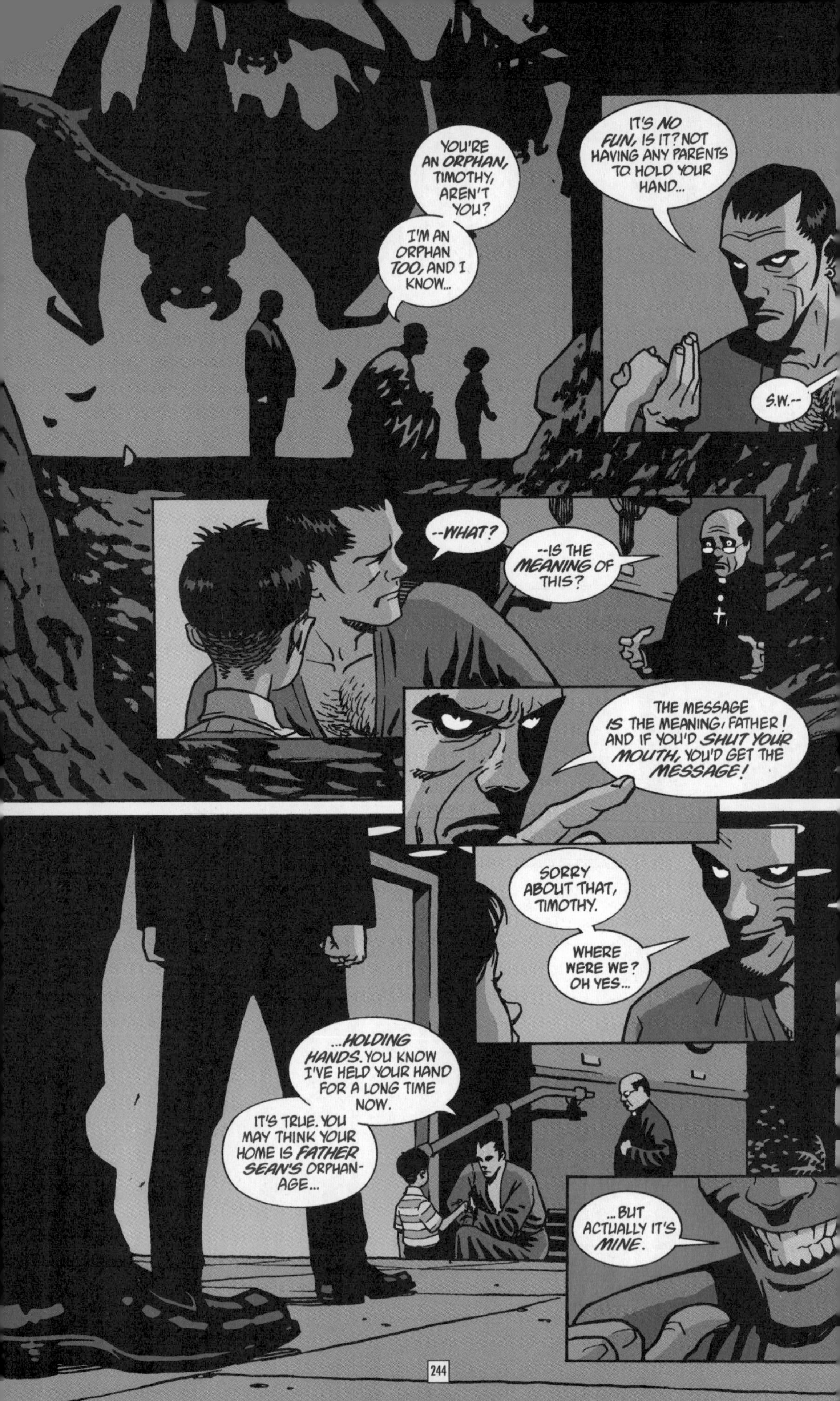
YOU'RE AN ORPHAN, TIMOTHY, AREN'T YOU?
I'M AN ORPHAN TOO, AND I KNOW...
IT'S NO FUN, IS IT? NOT HAVING ANY PARENTS TO HOLD YOUR HAND...
S.W.--
--WHAT?
--IS THE MEANING OF THIS?
THE MESSAGE IS THE MEANING, FATHER! AND IF YOU'D SHUT YOUR MOUTH, YOU'D GET THE MESSAGE!
SORRY ABOUT THAT, TIMOTHY.
WHERE WERE WE? OH YES...
...HOLDING HANDS. YOU KNOW I'VE HELD YOUR HAND FOR A LONG TIME NOW.
IT'S TRUE. YOU MAY THINK YOUR HOME IS FATHER SEAN'S ORPHAN-AGE...
...BUT ACTUALLY IT'S MINE.

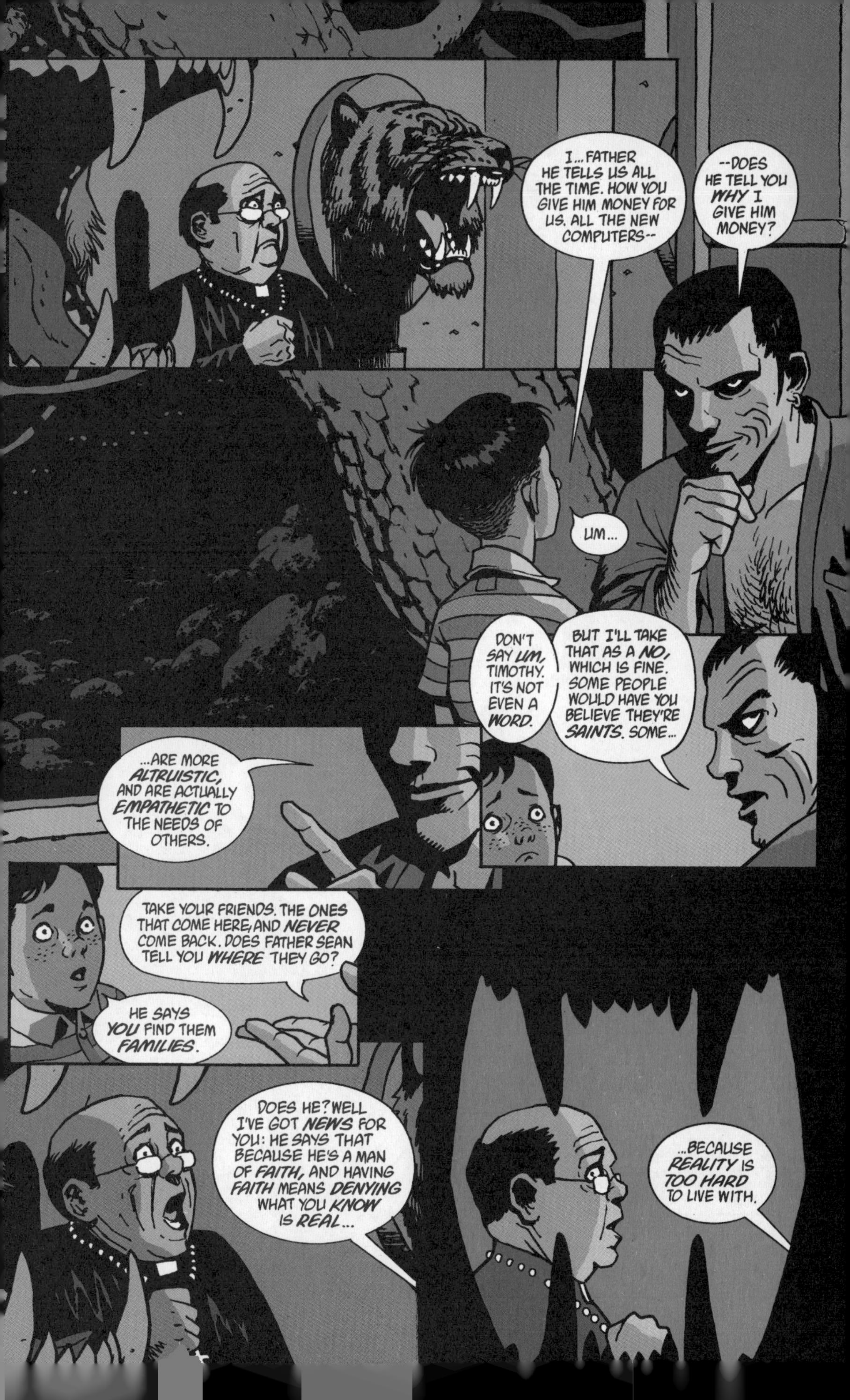

I... FATHER HE TELLS US ALL THE TIME. HOW YOU GIVE HIM MONEY FOR US. ALL THE NEW COMPUTERS--
--DOES HE TELL YOU WHY I GIVE HIM MONEY?
UM...
DON'T SAY UM, TIMOTHY. IT'S NOT EVEN A WORD.
BUT I'LL TAKE THAT AS A NO, WHICH IS FINE. SOME PEOPLE WOULD HAVE YOU BELIEVE THEY'RE SAINTS. SOME...
...ARE MORE ALTRUISTIC, AND ARE ACTUALLY EMPATHETIC TO THE NEEDS OF OTHERS.
TAKE YOUR FRIENDS. THE ONES THAT COME HERE, AND NEVER COME BACK. DOES FATHER SEAN TELL YOU WHERE THEY GO?
HE SAYS YOU FIND THEM FAMILIES.
DOES HE? WELL I'VE GOT NEWS FOR YOU: HE SAYS THAT BECAUSE HE'S A MAN OF FAITH, AND HAVING FAITH MEANS DENYING WHAT YOU KNOW IS REAL...
...BECAUSE REALITY IS TOO HARD TO LIVE WITH.

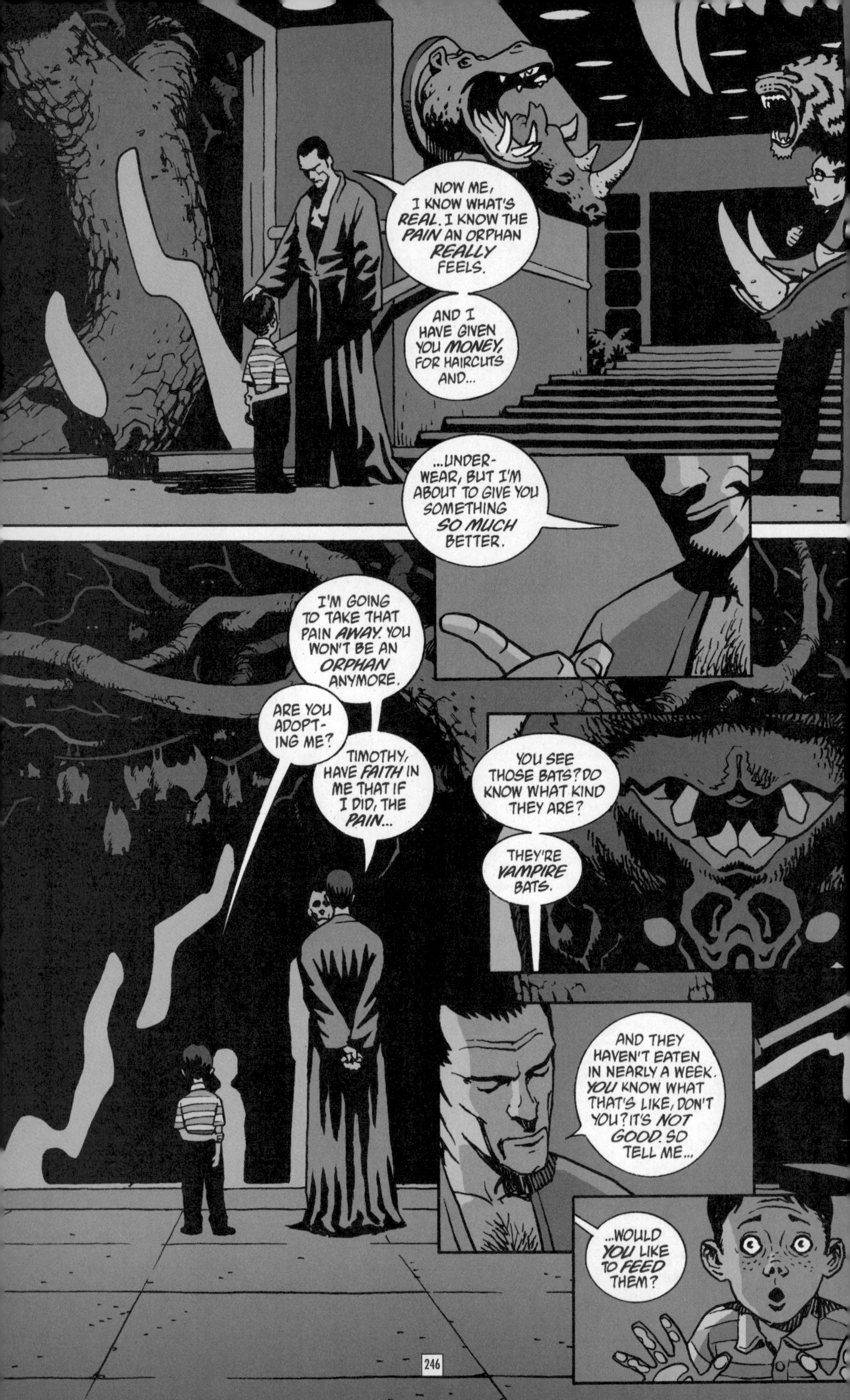

NOW ME, I KNOW WHAT'S REAL. I KNOW THE PAIN AN ORPHAN REALLY FEELS.
AND I HAVE GIVEN YOU MONEY, FOR HAIRCUTS AND...
...UNDER-WEAR, BUT I'M ABOUT TO GIVE YOU SOMETHING SO MUCH BETTER.
I'M GOING TO TAKE THAT PAIN AWAY. YOU WON'T BE AN ORPHAN ANYMORE.
ARE YOU ADOPT-ING ME?
TIMOTHY, HAVE FAITH IN ME THAT IF I DID, THE PAIN...
YOU SEE THOSE BATS? DO KNOW WHAT KIND THEY ARE?
THEY'RE VAMPIRE BATS.
AND THEY HAVEN'T EATEN IN NEARLY A WEEK. YOU KNOW WHAT THAT'S LIKE, DON'T YOU? IT'S NOT GOOD. SO TELL ME...
...WOULD YOU LIKE TO FEED THEM?

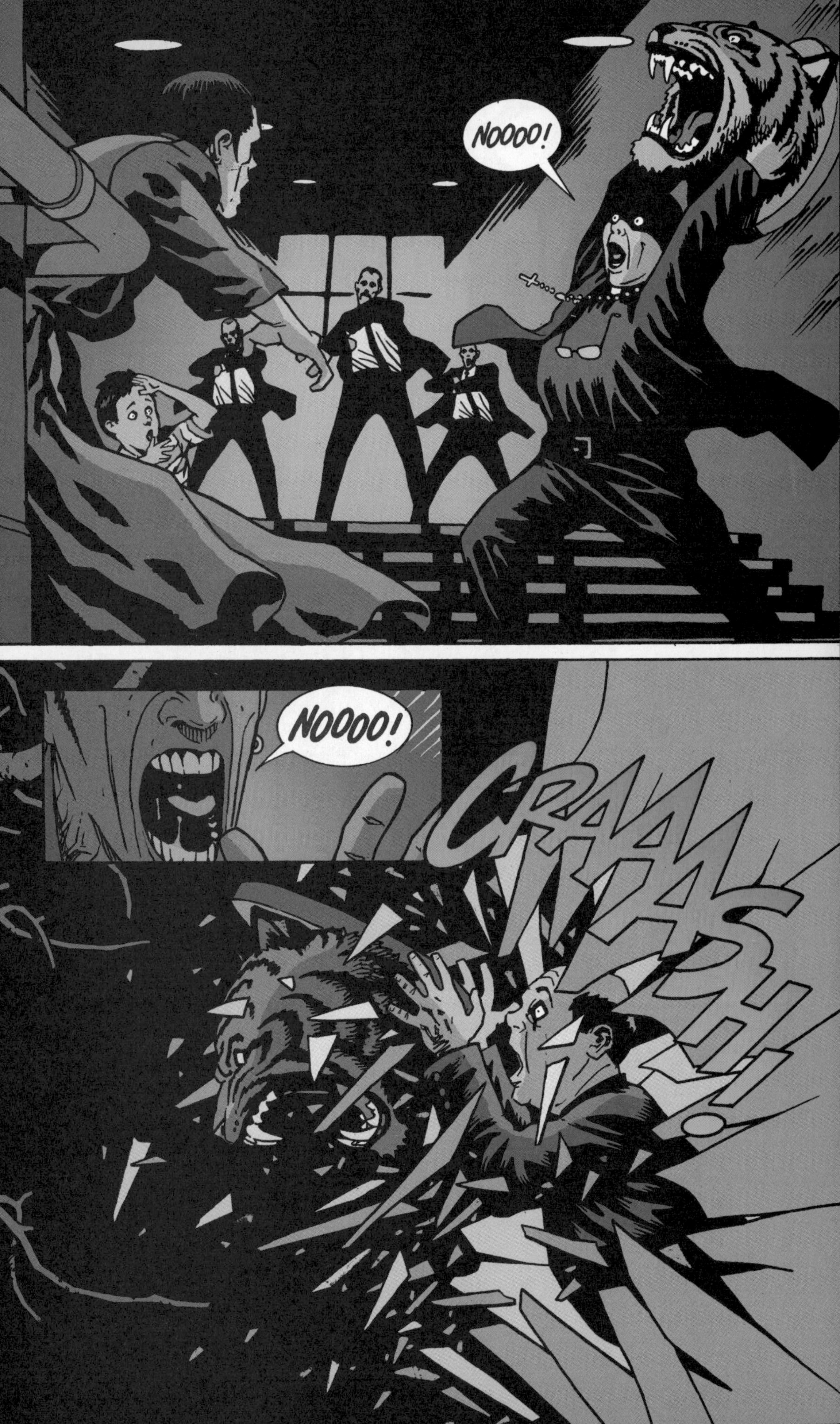
NOOOO!
NOOOO!
CRAAAASSHH!!

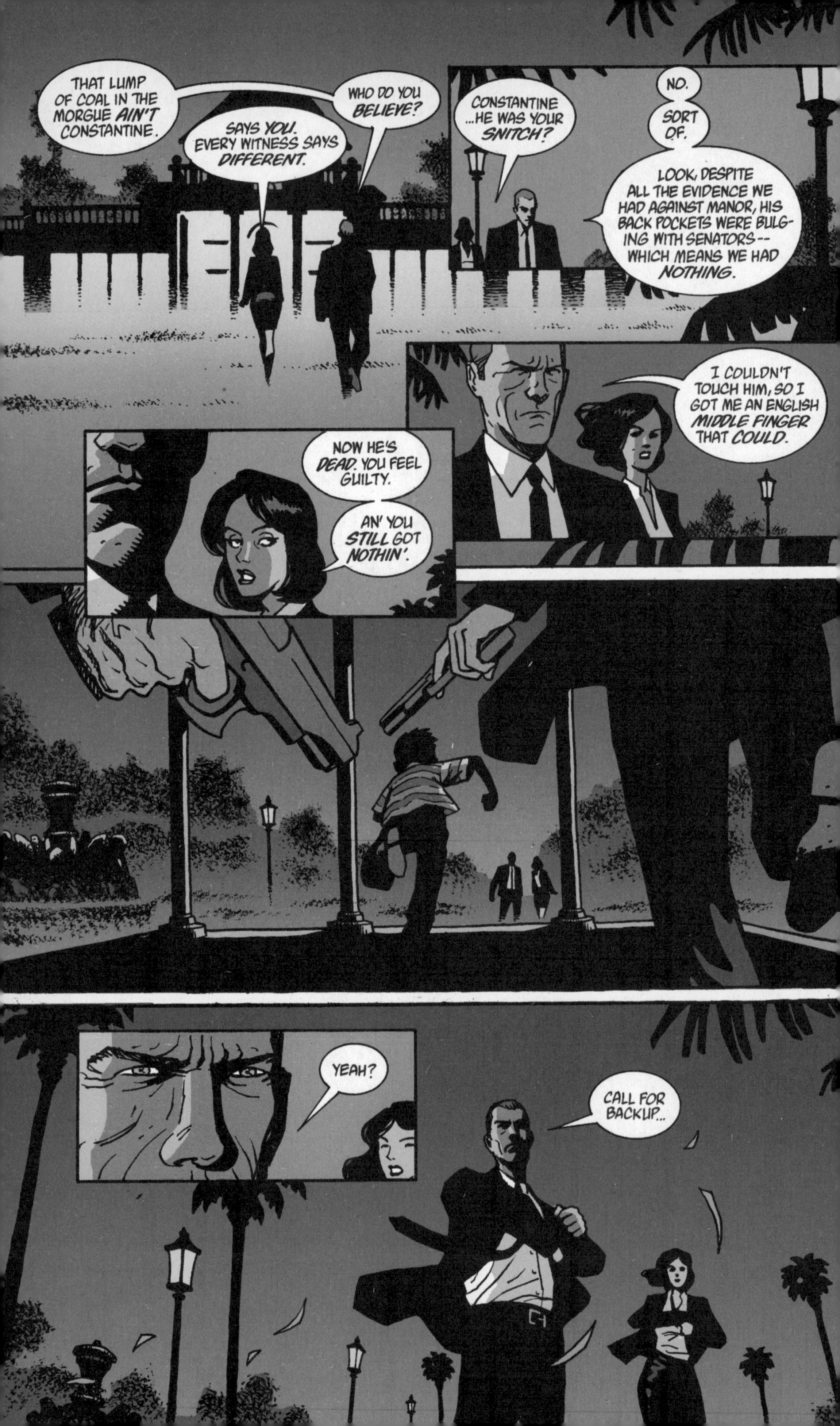
THAT LUMP OF COAL IN THE MORGUE AIN'T CONSTANTINE.
SAYS YOU. EVERY WITNESS SAYS DIFFERENT.
WHO DO YOU BELIEVE?
CONSTANTINE ...HE WAS YOUR SNITCH?
NO.
SORT OF.
LOOK, DESPITE ALL THE EVIDENCE WE HAD AGAINST MANOR, HIS BACK POCKETS WERE BULGING WITH SENATORS-- WHICH MEANS WE HAD NOTHING.
I COULDN'T TOUCH HIM, SO I GOT ME AN ENGLISH MIDDLE FINGER THAT COULD.
NOW HE'S DEAD. YOU FEEL GUILTY.
AN' YOU STILL GOT NOTHIN'.
YEAH?
CALL FOR BACKUP...

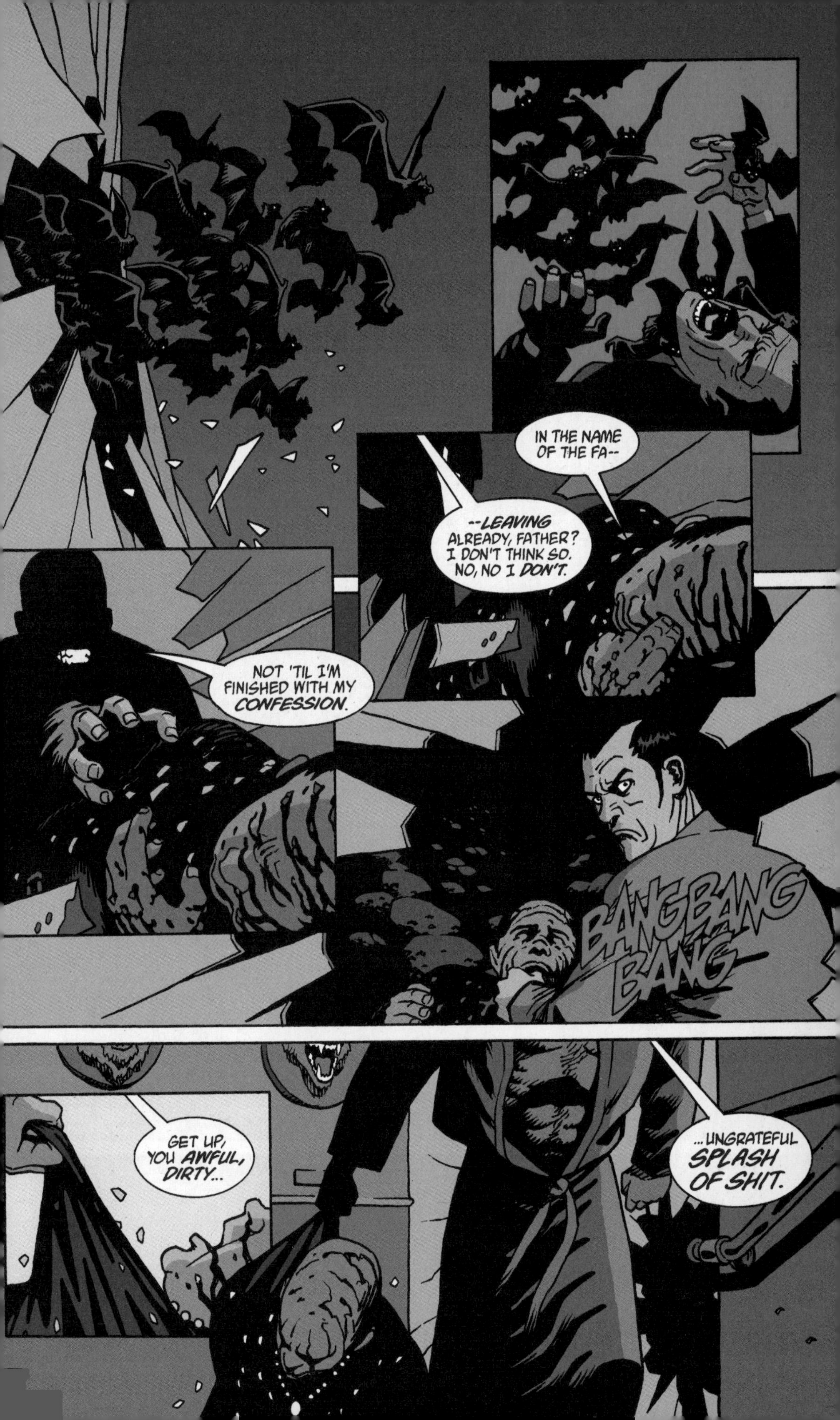
IN THE NAME OF THE FA--
--LEAVING ALREADY, FATHER? I DON'T THINK SO. NO, NO I DON'T.
NOT 'TIL I'M FINISHED WITH MY CONFESSION.
BANG BANG BANG
GET UP, YOU AWFUL, DIRTY...
...UNGRATEFUL SPLASH OF SHIT.

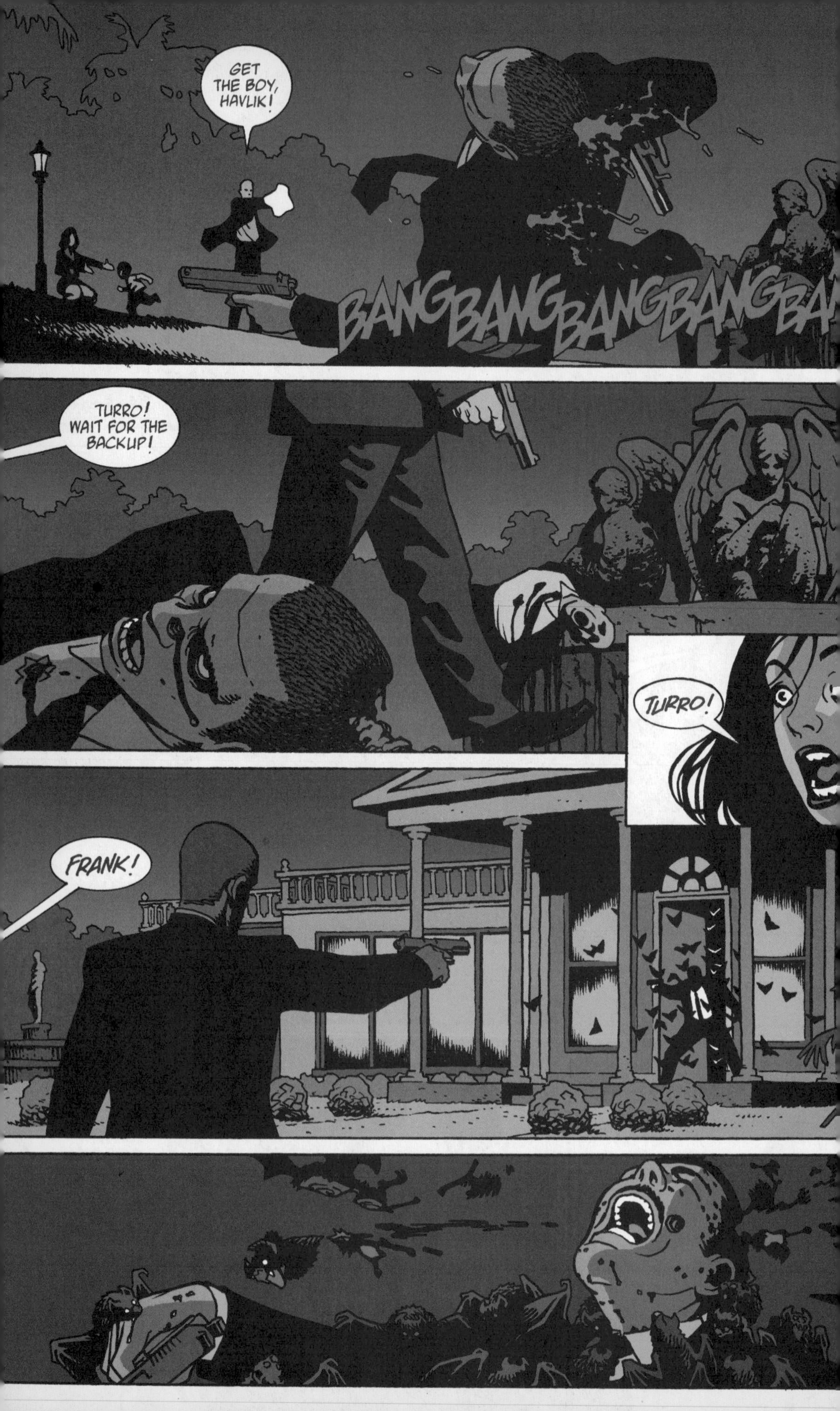
GET THE BOY, HAVLIK!
BANG BANG BANG BANG BA
TURRO! WAIT FOR THE BACKUP!
TURRO!
FRANK!

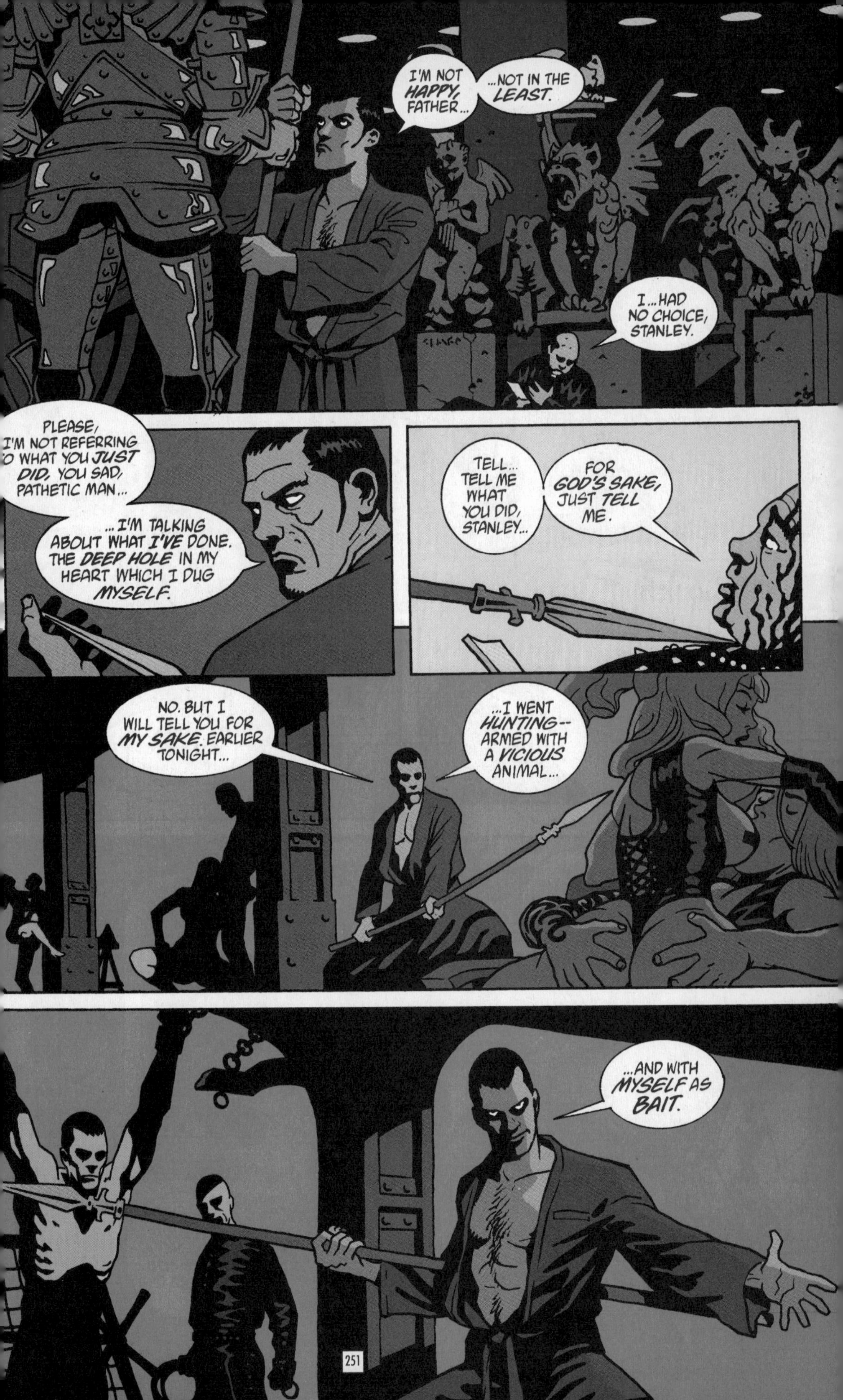
I'M NOT HAPPY, FATHER...
...NOT IN THE LEAST.
I...HAD NO CHOICE, STANLEY.
PLEASE, I'M NOT REFERRING TO WHAT YOU JUST DID, YOU SAD, PATHETIC MAN...
...I'M TALKING ABOUT WHAT I'VE DONE. THE DEEP HOLE IN MY HEART WHICH I DUG MYSELF.
TELL... TELL ME WHAT YOU DID, STANLEY...
FOR GOD'S SAKE, JUST TELL ME.
NO. BUT I WILL TELL YOU FOR MY SAKE. EARLIER TONIGHT...
...I WENT HUNTING-- ARMED WITH A VICIOUS ANIMAL...
...AND WITH MYSELF AS BAIT.

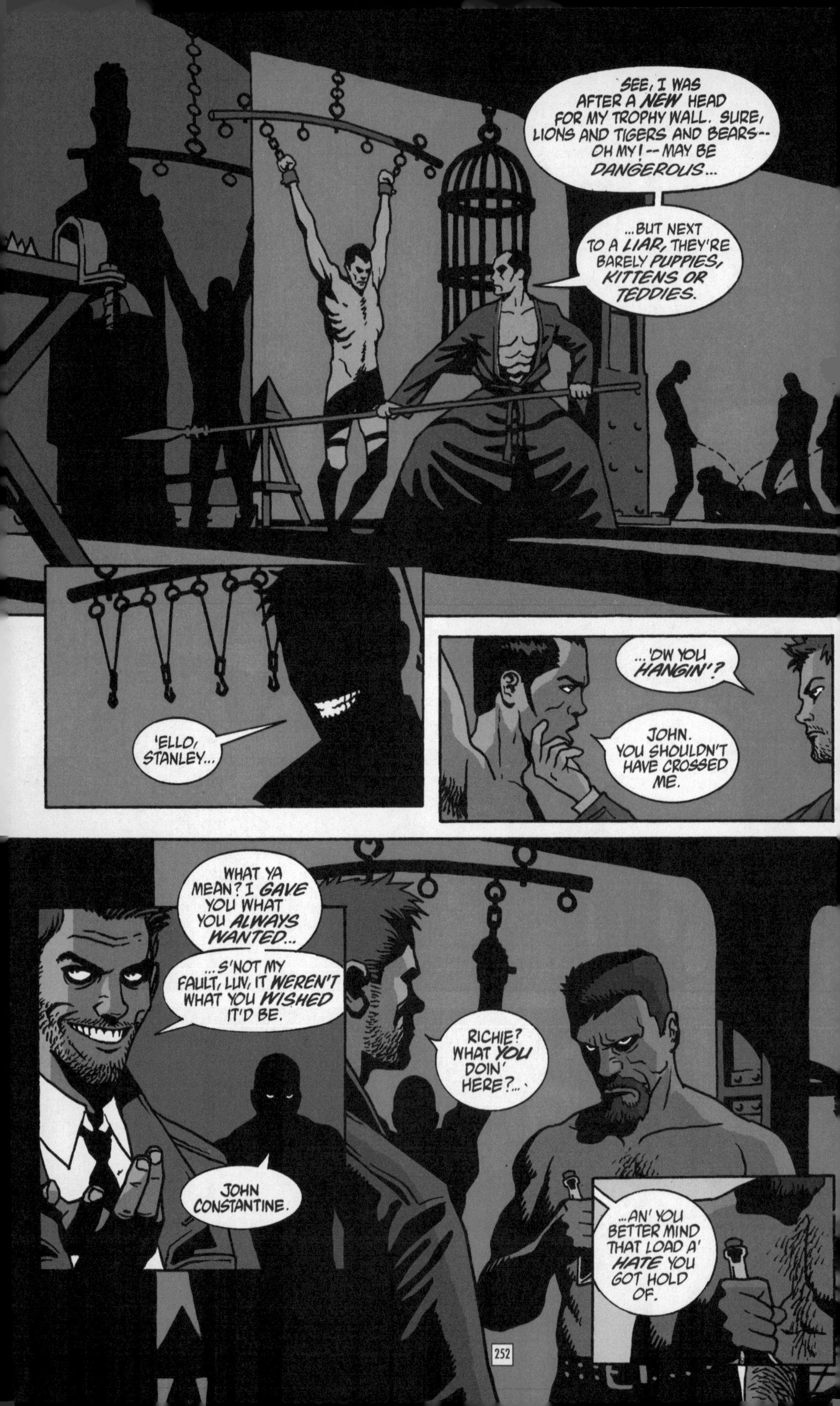
SEE, I WAS AFTER A NEW HEAD FOR MY TROPHY WALL. SURE, LIONS AND TIGERS AND BEARS-- OH MY! -- MAY BE DANGEROUS...
...BUT NEXT TO A LIAR, THEY'RE BARELY PUPPIES, KITTENS OR TEDDIES.
'ELLO, STANLEY...
...'OW YOU HANGIN'?
JOHN. YOU SHOULDN'T HAVE CROSSED ME.
WHAT YA MEAN? I GAVE YOU WHAT YOU ALWAYS WANTED...
...S'NOT MY FAULT, LUV, IT WEREN'T WHAT YOU WISHED IT'D BE.
JOHN CONSTANTINE.
RICHIE? WHAT YOU DOIN' HERE?...
...AN' YOU BETTER MIND THAT LOAD A' HATE YOU GOT HOLD OF.

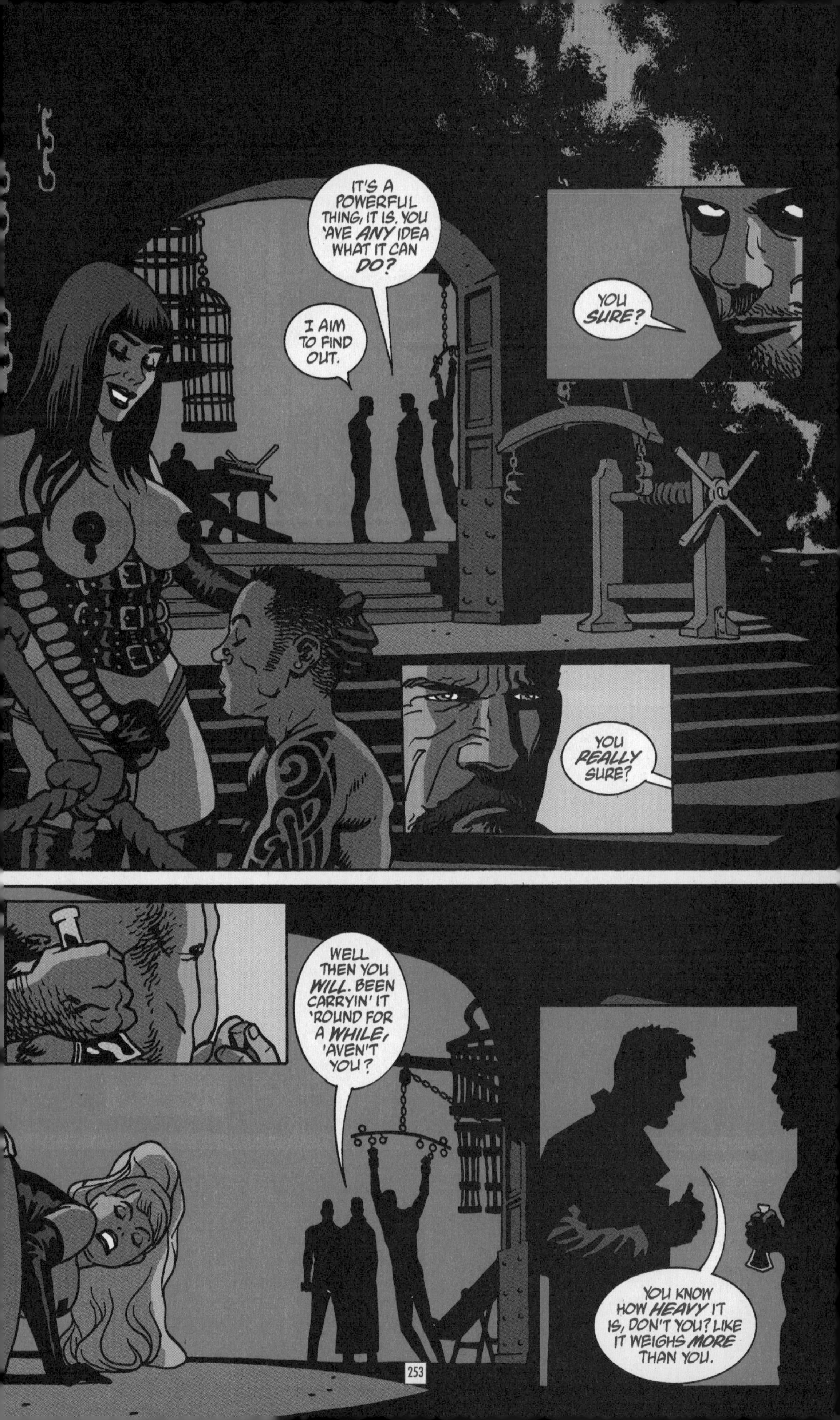
IT'S A POWERFUL THING, IT IS. YOU 'AVE *ANY* IDEA WHAT IT CAN *DO?*
I AIM TO FIND OUT.
YOU *SURE?*
YOU *REALLY* SURE?
WELL THEN YOU *WILL*. BEEN CARRYIN' IT 'ROUND FOR A *WHILE,* 'AVEN'T YOU?
YOU KNOW HOW *HEAVY* IT IS, DON'T YOU? LIKE IT WEIGHS *MORE* THAN YOU.

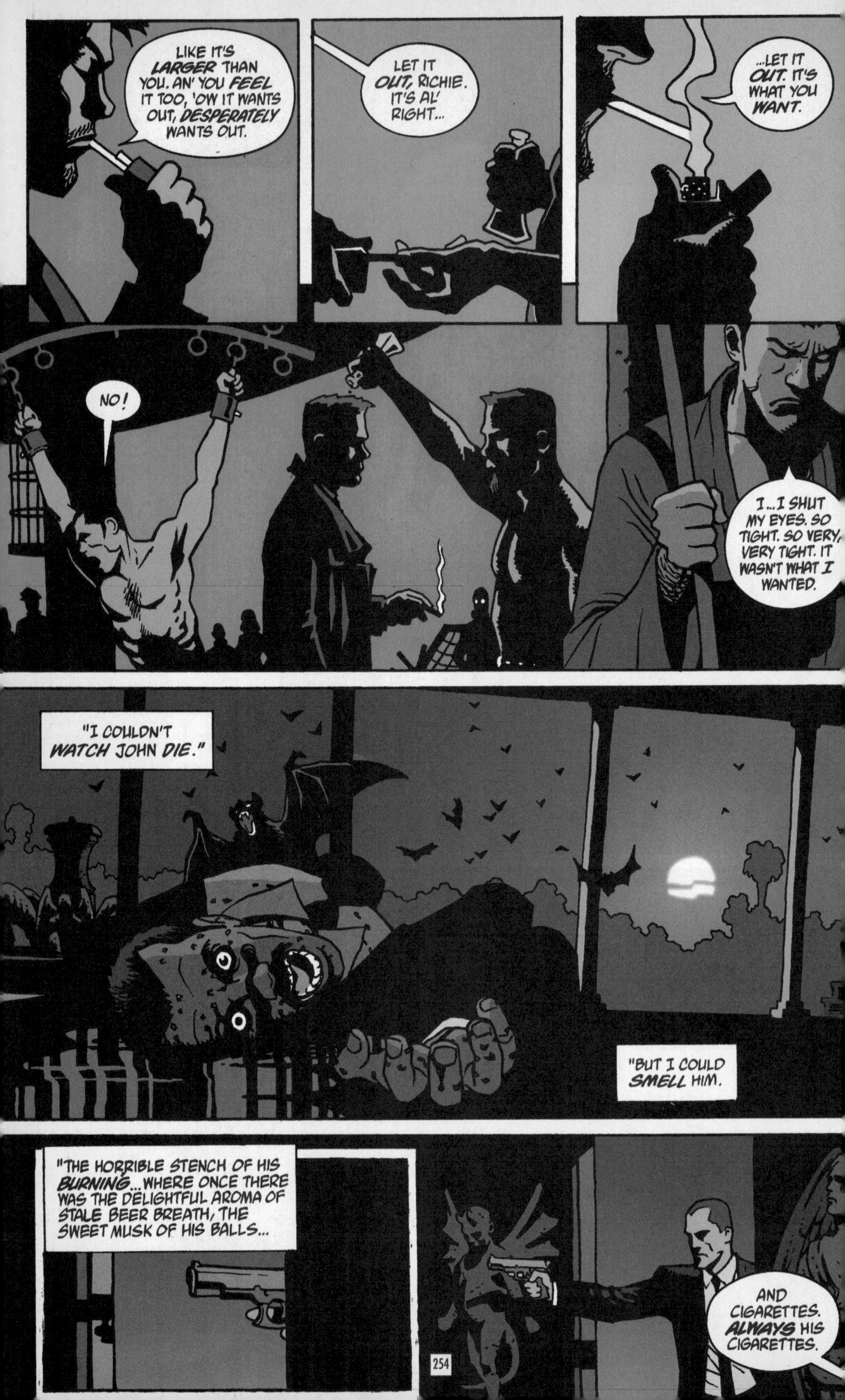
LIKE IT'S LARGER THAN YOU. AN' YOU FEEL IT TOO, 'OW IT WANTS OUT, DESPERATELY WANTS OUT.
LET IT OUT, RICHIE. IT'S AL' RIGHT...
...LET IT OUT. IT'S WHAT YOU WANT.
NO!
I...I SHUT MY EYES. SO TIGHT. SO VERY, VERY TIGHT. IT WASN'T WHAT I WANTED.
"I COULDN'T WATCH JOHN DIE."
"BUT I COULD SMELL HIM.
"THE HORRIBLE STENCH OF HIS BURNING... WHERE ONCE THERE WAS THE DELIGHTFUL AROMA OF STALE BEER BREATH, THE SWEET MUSK OF HIS BALLS...
AND CIGARETTES. ALWAYS HIS CIGARETTES.

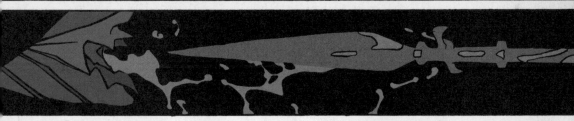

WHO ARE YOU?

JESUS FUCKIN' GOD...

REALLY? THOUGHT YOU WORE A *BEARD.* ANYWAY...

...WHERE WAS I? OH YES...

...ALONE.

CON...

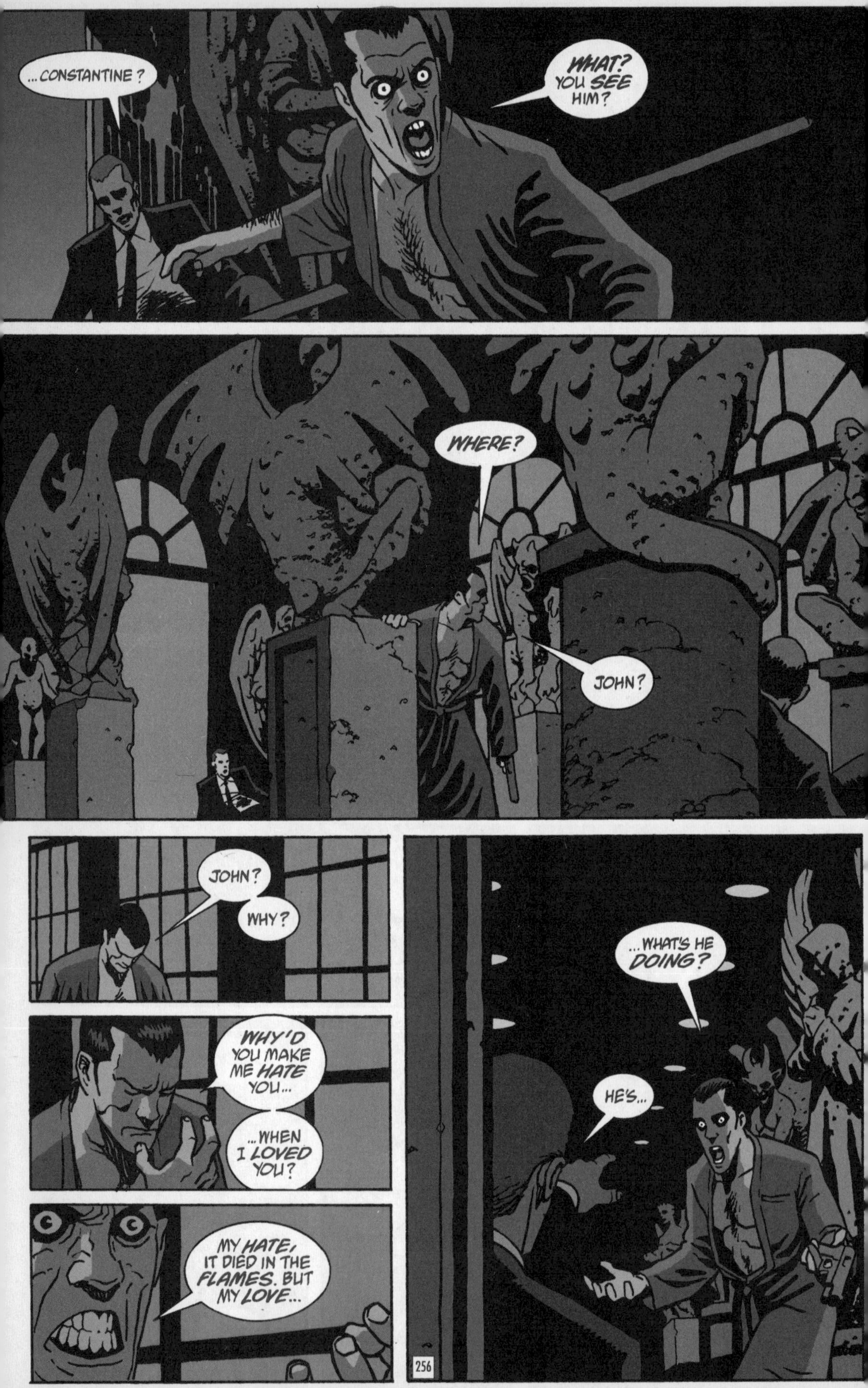

...CONSTANTINE?
WHAT? YOU SEE HIM?
WHERE?
JOHN?
JOHN?
WHY?
WHY'D YOU MAKE ME HATE YOU...
...WHEN I LOVED YOU?
MY HATE, IT DIED IN THE FLAMES. BUT MY LOVE...
...WHAT'S HE DOING?
HE'S...

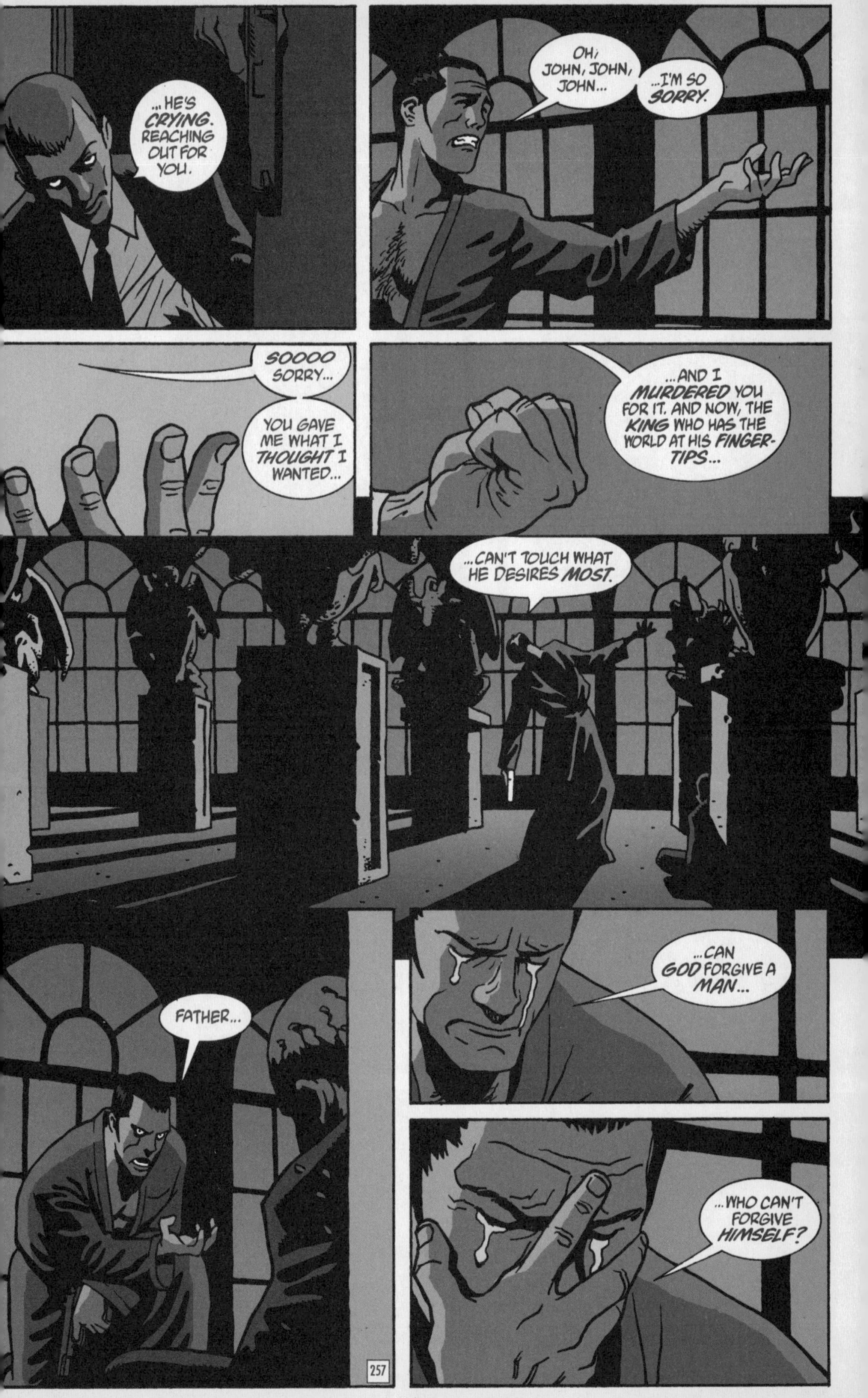

... HE'S CRYING. REACHING OUT FOR YOU.
OH, JOHN, JOHN, JOHN...
...I'M SO SORRY.
SOOOO SORRY...
YOU GAVE ME WHAT I THOUGHT I WANTED...
...AND I MURDERED YOU FOR IT. AND NOW, THE KING WHO HAS THE WORLD AT HIS FINGER-TIPS...
...CAN'T TOUCH WHAT HE DESIRES MOST.
FATHER...
...CAN GOD FORGIVE A MAN...
...WHO CAN'T FORGIVE HIMSELF?

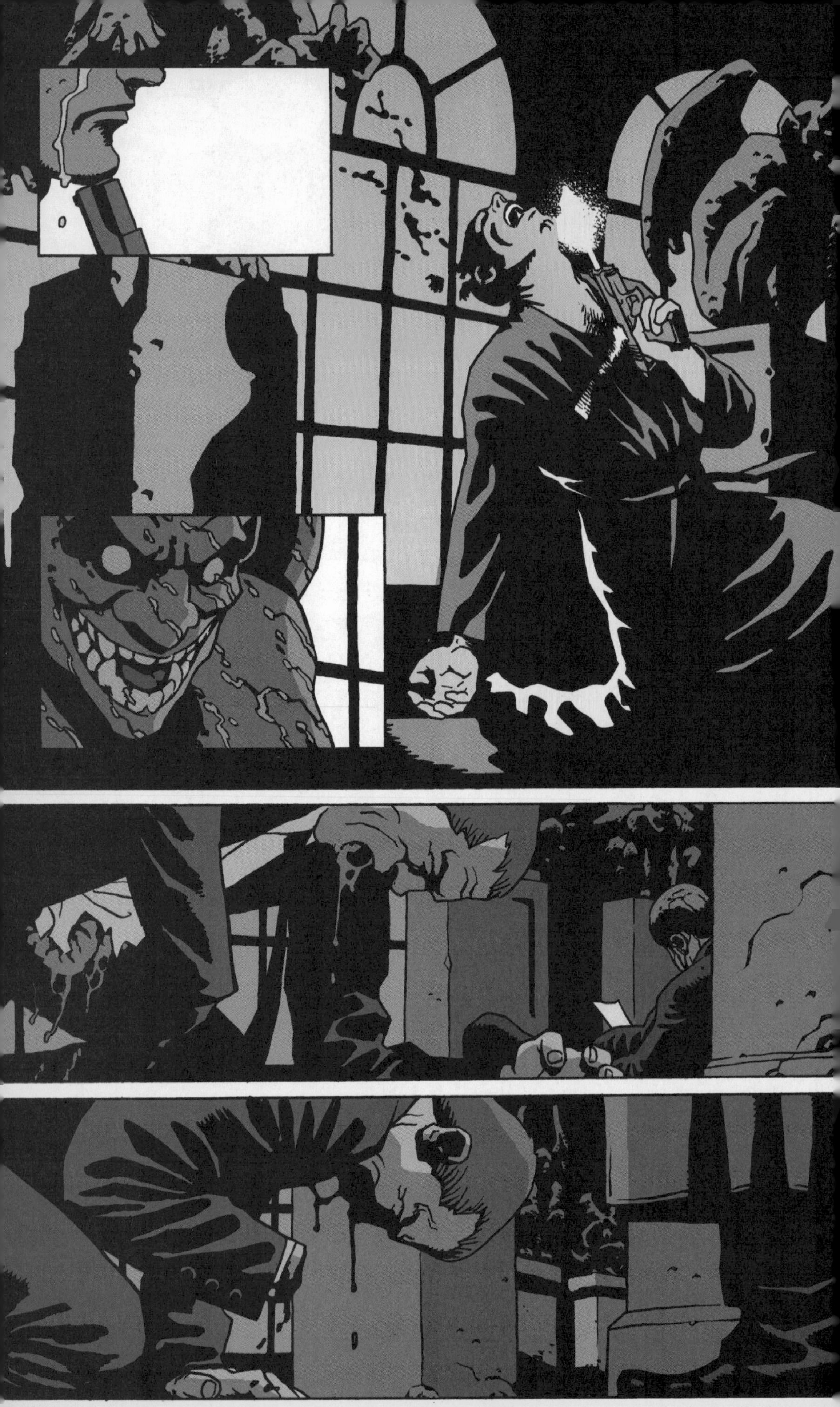

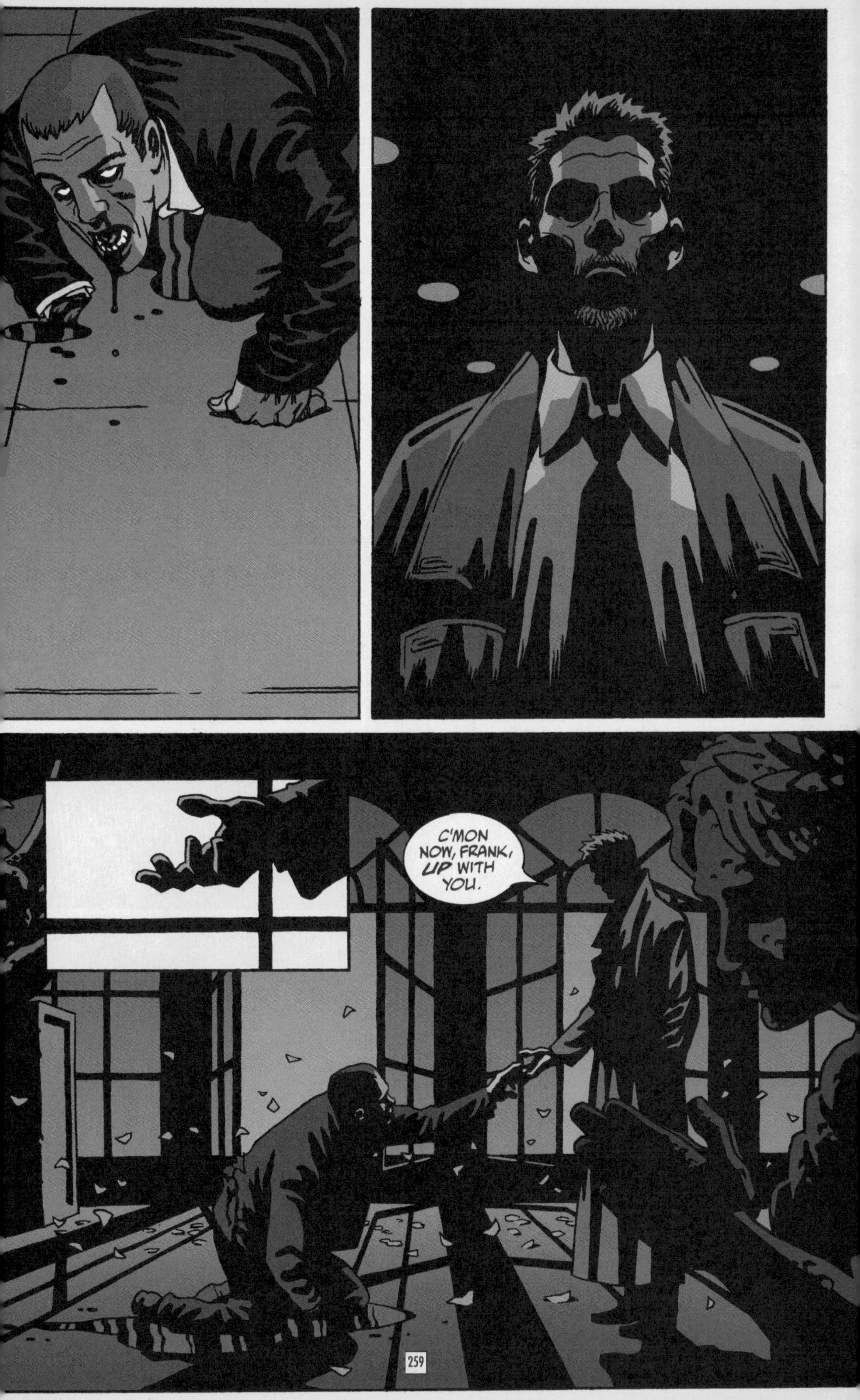
C'MON NOW, FRANK, *UP* WITH YOU.

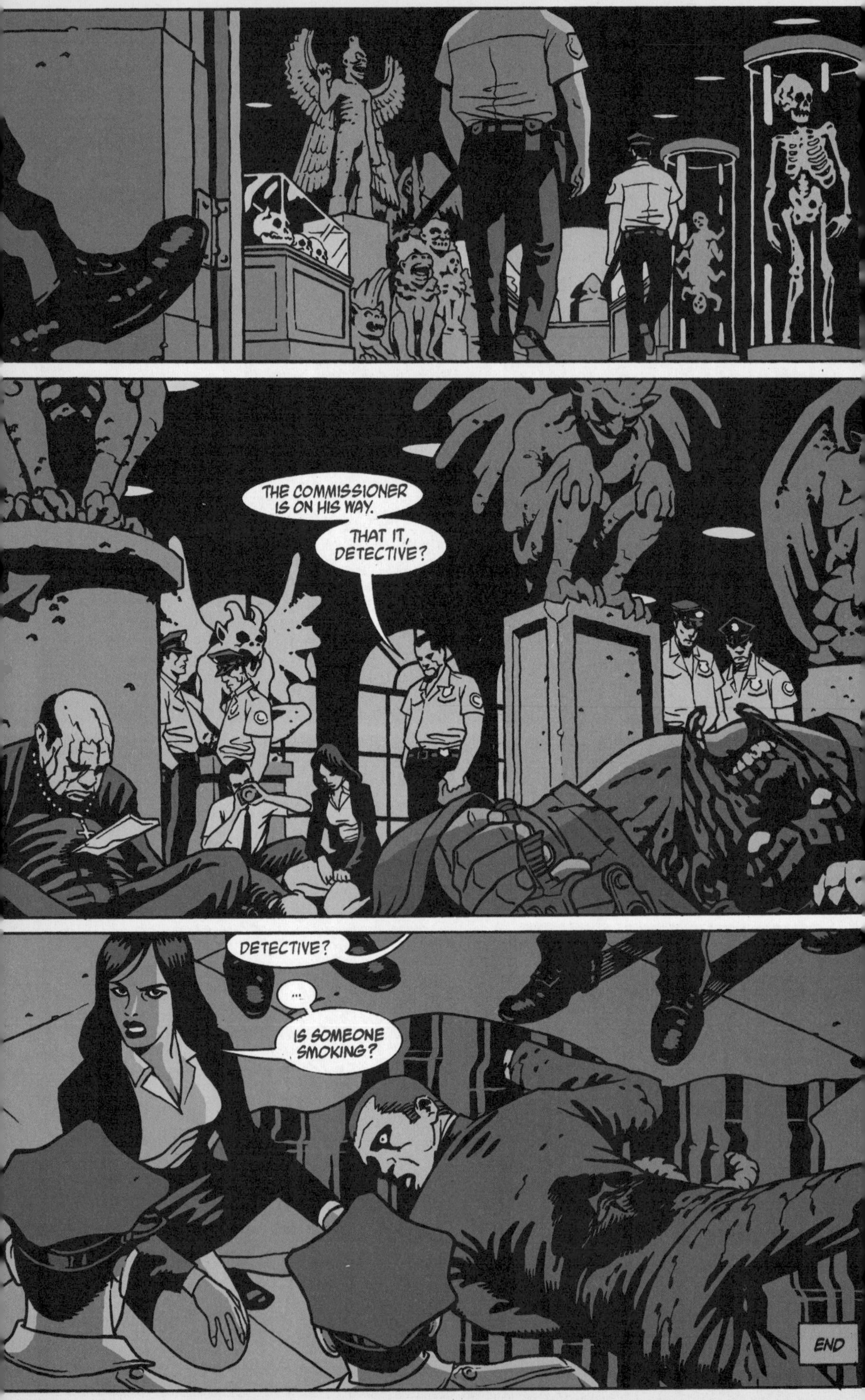
THE COMMISSIONER IS ON HIS WAY.
THAT IT, DETECTIVE?
DETECTIVE?
...
IS SOMEONE SMOKING?
END

E HELLBLAZER LIBRARY

ere horror, dark magic,
bad luck meet,
n Constantine is never far away.

ALL TITLES ARE SUGGESTED FOR MATURE READERS

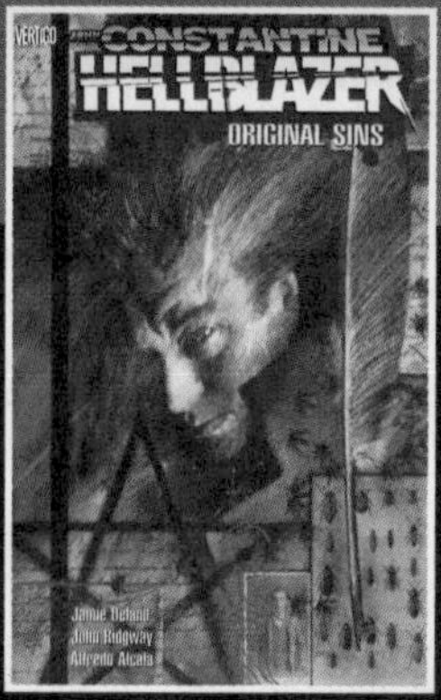
VERTIGO
CONSTANTINE
HELLBLAZER
ORIGINAL SINS
Jamie Delano
John Ridgway
Alfredo Alcala

ORIGINAL SINS
JAMIE DELANO/VARIOUS

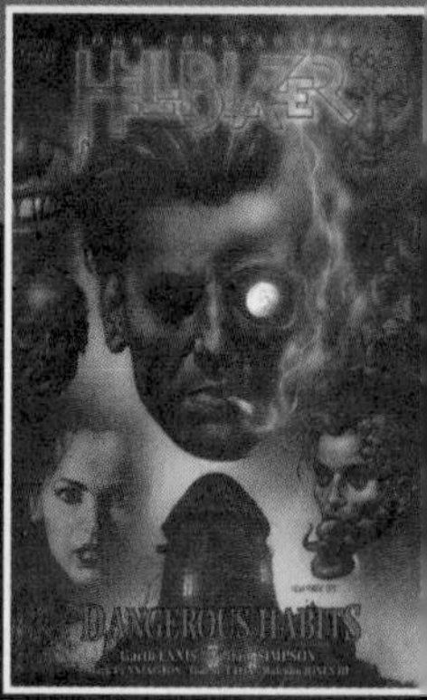
HELLBLAZER
DANGEROUS HABITS

DANGEROUS HABITS
GARTH ENNIS/VARIOUS

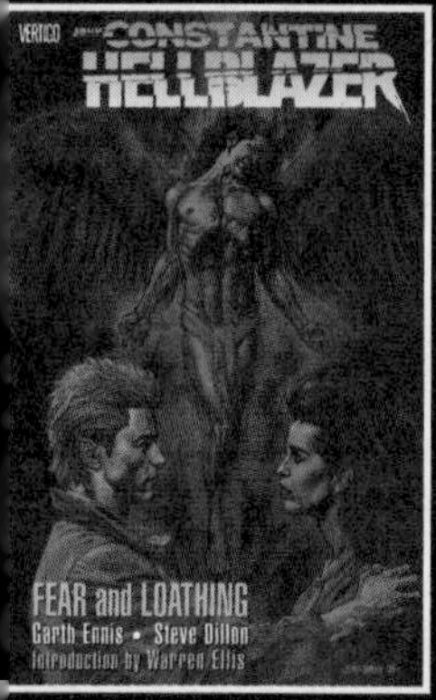
VERTIGO
CONSTANTINE
HELLBLAZER
FEAR and LOATHING
Garth Ennis • Steve Dillon
Introduction by Warren Ellis

FEAR AND LOATHING
GARTH ENNIS/STEVE DILLON

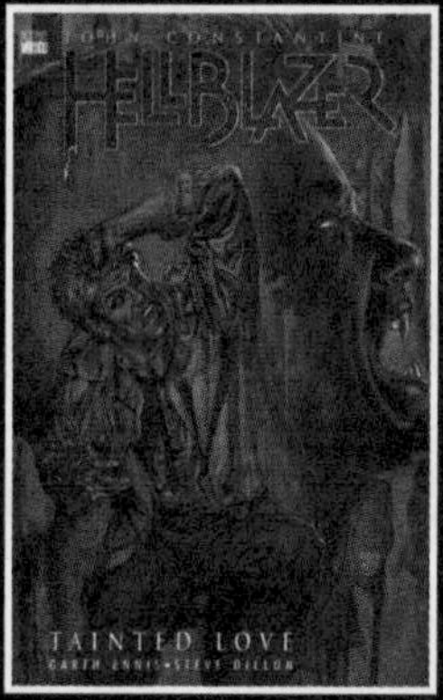
JOHN CONSTANTINE
HELLBLAZER
TAINTED LOVE

TAINTED LOVE
GARTH ENNIS/STEVE DILLON

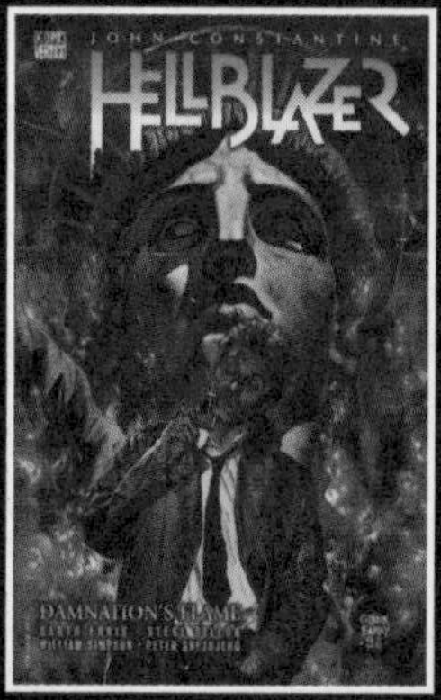
JOHN CONSTANTINE
HELLBLAZER
DAMNATION'S FLAME

DAMNATION'S FLAME
GARTH ENNIS/STEVE DILLON/
WILLIAM SIMPSON/PETER SNEJBJERG

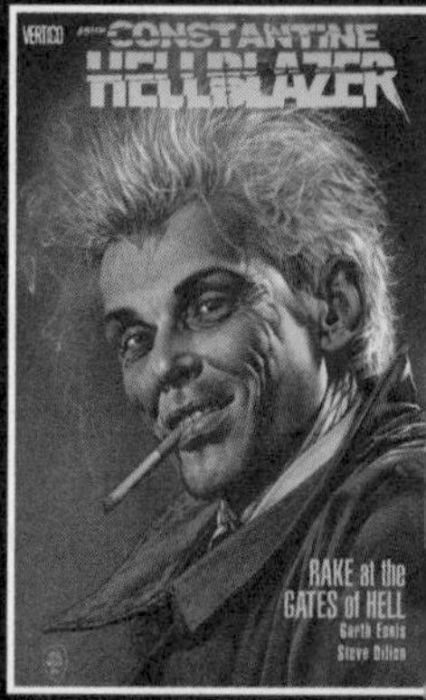
VERTIGO
CONSTANTINE
HELLBLAZER
RAKE at the
GATES of HELL
Garth Ennis
Steve Dillon

RAKE AT THE GATES OF HELL
GARTH ENNIS/STEVE DILLON

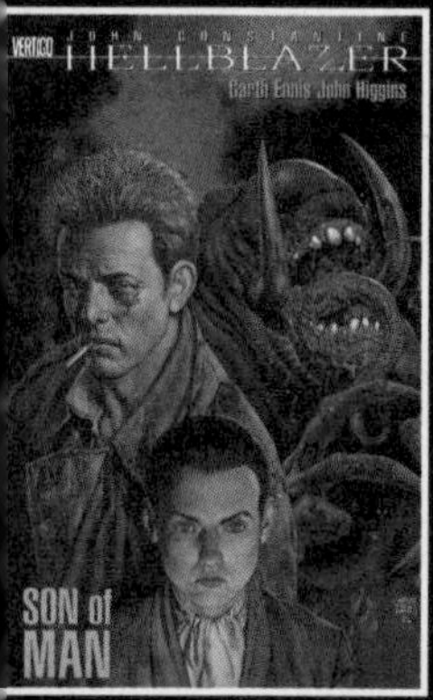
VERTIGO
JOHN CONSTANTINE
HELLBLAZER
Garth Ennis John Higgins
SON of
MAN

SON OF MAN
GARTH ENNIS/JOHN HIGGINS

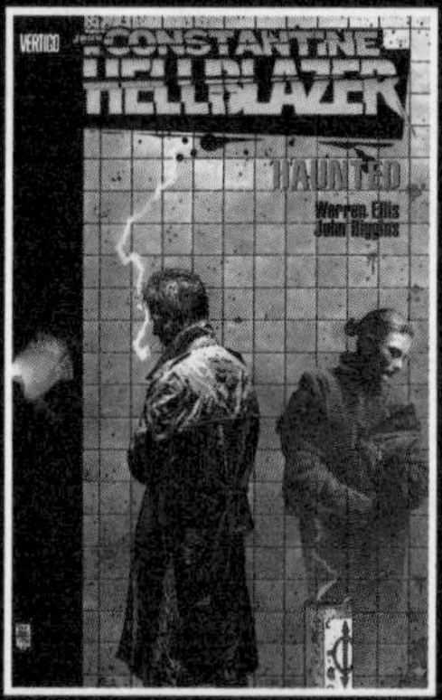
VERTIGO
CONSTANTINE
HELLBLAZER
HAUNTED
Warren Ellis
John Higgins

HAUNTED
WARREN ELLIS/JOHN HIGGINS

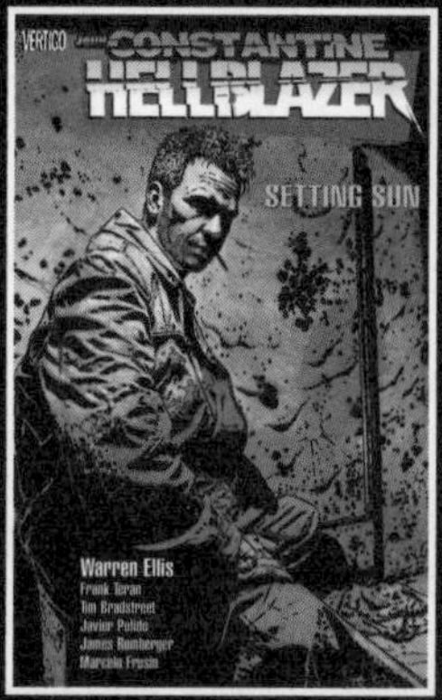
VERTIGO
CONSTANTINE
HELLBLAZER
SETTING SUN
Warren Ellis

SETTING SUN
WARREN ELLIS/VARIOUS

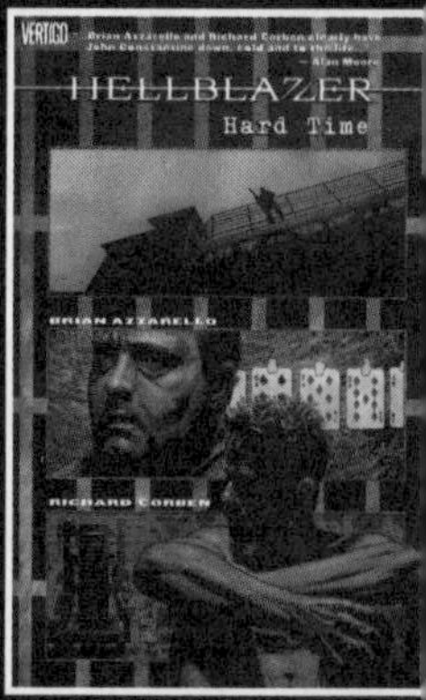
VERTIGO
HELLBLAZER
Hard Time
BRIAN AZZARELLO
RICHARD CORBEN

HARD TIME
BRIAN AZZARELLO/RICHARD CORBEN

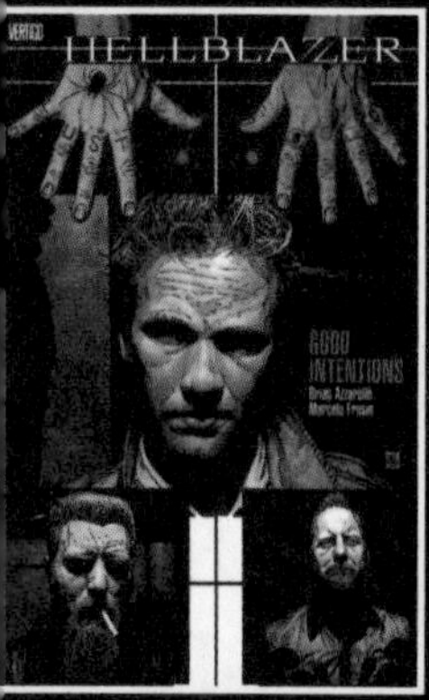
VERTIGO
HELLBLAZER
GOOD
INTENTIONS

GOOD INTENTIONS
BRIAN AZZARELLO/MARCELO FRUSIN

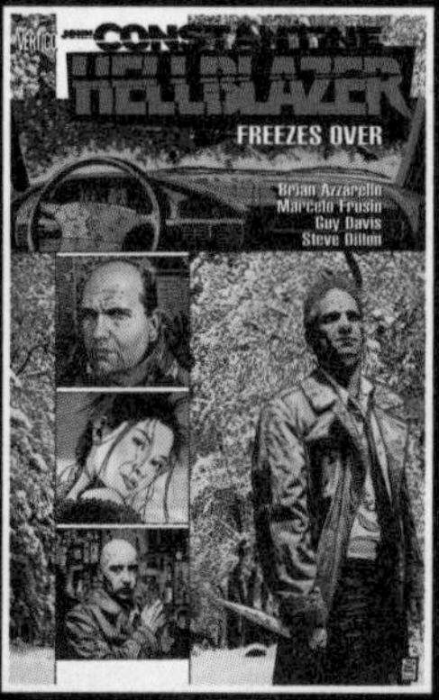
CONSTANTINE
HELLBLAZER
FREEZES OVER
Brian Azzarello
Marcelo Frusin
Guy Davis
Steve Dillon

FREEZES OVER
BRIAN AZZARELLO/MARCELO FRUSIN/

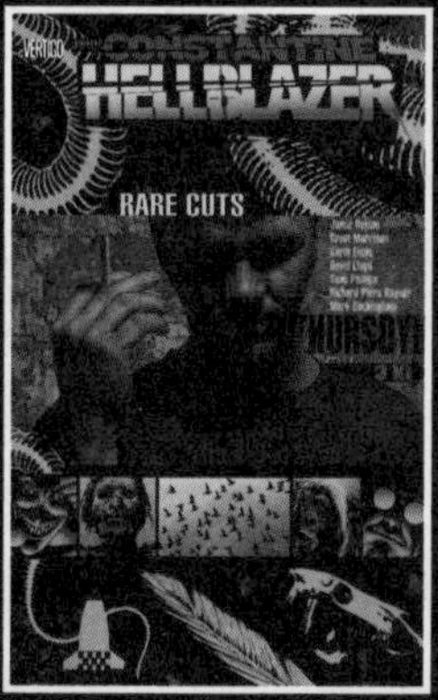
VERTIGO
CONSTANTINE
HELLBLAZER
RARE CUTS

RARE CUTS
GARTH ENNIS/GRANT MORRISON/

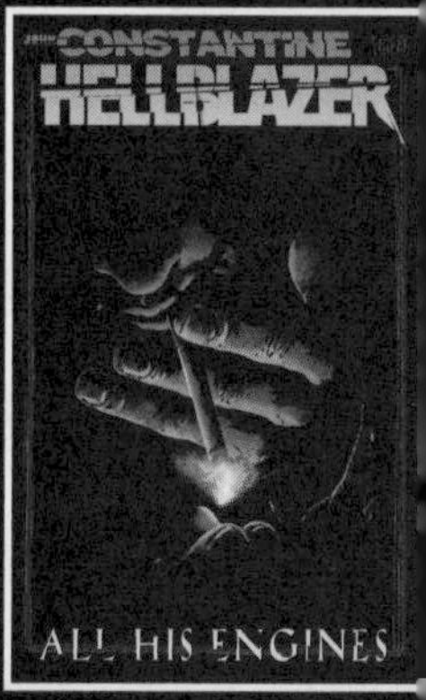
CONSTANTINE
HELLBLAZER
ALL HIS ENGINES

ALL HIS ENGINES
MIKE CAREY/LEONARDO MANCO

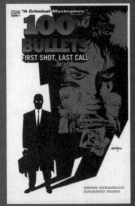

Look for these other VERTIGO books:

All VERTIGO titles are Suggested for Mature Readers

MERICAN CENTURY
oward Chaykin/David Tischman/
arc Laming/John Stokes
he 1950s were no picnic, but for a sharp operator ike Harry Kraft opportunity still knocked all over e world — and usually brought trouble right hrough the door with it.
ol 1: SCARS & STRIPES
ol 2: HOLLYWOOD BABYLON

NIMAL MAN
rant Morrison/Chas Truog/
oug Hazlewood/various
minor super-hero's consciousness is raised higher nd higher until he becomes aware of his own ictitious nature in this revolutionary and existenial series.
ol 1: ANIMAL MAN
ol 2: ORIGIN OF THE SPECIES
ol 3: DEUS EX MACHINA

HE BOOKS OF MAGIC
eil Gaiman/various
quartet of fallen mystics introduce the world of nagic to young Tim Hunter, who is destined to become e world's most powerful magician.

HE BOOKS OF MAGIC
ohn Ney Rieber/Peter Gross/various
he continuing trials and adventures of Tim Hunter, vhose magical talents bring extra trouble and onfusion to his adolescence.
ol 1: BINDINGS
ol 2: SUMMONINGS
ol 3: RECKONINGS
ol 4: TRANSFORMATIONS
ol 5: GIRL IN THE BOX
ol 6: THE BURNING GIRL
ol 7: DEATH AFTER DEATH

EATH: AT DEATH'S DOOR
ill Thompson
art fanciful *manga* retelling of the acclaimed THE ANDMAN: SEASON OF MISTS and part original tory of the party from Hell.

EATH: THE HIGH COST OF LIVING
eil Gaiman/Chris Bachalo/
lark Buckingham
ne day every century, Death assumes mortal form o learn more about the lives she must take.

EATH: THE TIME OF YOUR LIFE
eil Gaiman/Chris Bachalo/
lark Buckingham/Mark Pennington
young lesbian mother strikes a deal with Death for he life of her son in a story about fame, relationhips, and rock and roll.

OOM PATROL
rant Morrison/Richard Case/John Nyberg/
arious
he World's Strangest Heroes are re-imagined even tranger and more otherworldly in this groundbreaking eries exploring the mysteries of identity and madness.
ol 1: CRAWLING FROM THE WRECKAGE
ol 2: THE PAINTING THAT ATE PARIS

FABLES
Bill Willingham/Mark Buckingham/
Lan Medina/Steve Leialoha/Craig Hamilton
The immortal characters of popular fairy tales have been driven from their homelands and now live hidden among us, trying to cope with life in 21st-century Manhattan.
Vol 1: LEGENDS IN EXILE
Vol 2: ANIMAL FARM
Vol 3: STORYBOOK LOVE
Vol 4: MARCH OF THE WOODEN SOLDIERS
Vol 5: THE MEAN SEASONS

THE INVISIBLES
Grant Morrison/various
The saga of a terrifying conspiracy and the resistance movement combating it — a secret underground of ultra-cool guerrilla cells trained in ontological and physical anarchy.
Vol 1: SAY YOU WANT A REVOLUTION
Vol 2: APOCALIPSTICK
Vol 3: ENTROPY IN THE U.K.
Vol 4: BLOODY HELL IN AMERICA
Vol 5: COUNTING TO NONE
Vol 6: KISSING MR. QUIMPER
Vol 7: THE INVISIBLE KINGDOM

LUCIFER
Mike Carey/Peter Gross/Scott Hampton/
Chris Weston/Dean Ormston/various
Walking out of Hell (and out of the pages of THE SANDMAN), an ambitious Lucifer Morningstar creates a new cosmos modeled after his own image.
Vol 1: DEVIL IN THE GATEWAY
Vol 2: CHILDREN AND MONSTERS
Vol 3: A DALLIANCE WITH THE DAMNED
Vol 4: THE DIVINE COMEDY
Vol 5: INFERNO
Vol 6: MANSIONS OF THE SILENCE
Vol 7: EXODUS

PREACHER
Garth Ennis/Steve Dillon/various
A modern American epic of life, death, God, love, and redemption — filled with sex, booze, and blood.
Vol 1: GONE TO TEXAS
Vol 2: UNTIL THE END OF THE WORLD
Vol 3: PROUD AMERICANS
Vol 4: ANCIENT HISTORY
Vol 5: DIXIE FRIED
Vol 6: WAR IN THE SUN
Vol 7: SALVATION
Vol 8: ALL HELL'S A-COMING
Vol 9: ALAMO

THE SANDMAN
Neil Gaiman/various
One of the most acclaimed and celebrated comics titles ever published.
Vol 1: PRELUDES & NOCTURNES
Vol 2: THE DOLL'S HOUSE
Vol 3: DREAM COUNTRY
Vol 4: SEASON OF MISTS
Vol 5: A GAME OF YOU
Vol 6: FABLES & REFLECTIONS
Vol 7: BRIEF LIVES
Vol 8: WORLDS' END
Vol 9: THE KINDLY ONES
Vol 10: THE WAKE
Vol 11: ENDLESS NIGHTS

SWAMP THING: DARK GENESIS
Len Wein/Berni Wrightson
A gothic nightmare is brought to life with this horrifying yet poignant story of a man transformed into a monster.

SWAMP THING
Alan Moore/Stephen Bissette/John Totleben/
Rick Veitch/various
The writer and the series that revolutionized comics — a masterpiece of lyrical fantasy.
Vol 1: SAGA OF THE SWAMP THING
Vol 2: LOVE & DEATH
Vol 3: THE CURSE
Vol 4: A MURDER OF CROWS
Vol 5: EARTH TO EARTH
Vol 6: REUNION
Vol 7: REGENESIS

TRANSMETROPOLITAN
Warren Ellis/Darick Robertson/various
An exuberant trip into a frenetic future, where outlaw journalist Spider Jerusalem battles hypocrisy, corruption, and sobriety.
Vol 1: BACK ON THE STREET
Vol 2: LUST FOR LIFE
Vol 3: YEAR OF THE BASTARD
Vol 4: THE NEW SCUM
Vol 5: LONELY CITY
Vol 6: GOUGE AWAY
Vol 7: SPIDER'S THRASH
Vol 8: DIRGE
Vol 9: THE CURE
Vol 10: ONE MORE TIME
Vol 0: TALES OF HUMAN WASTE

Y: THE LAST MAN
Brian K. Vaughan/Pia Guerra/
José Marzán, Jr.
An unexplained plague kills every male mammal on Earth — all except Yorick Brown and his pet monkey. Will he survive this new, emasculated world to discover what killed his fellow men?
Vol 1: UNMANNED
Vol 2: CYCLES
Vol 3: ONE SMALL STEP
Vol 4: SAFEWORD
Vol 5: RING OF TRUTH